**Footprint**

# Colombia

DISCARD

CHRIS WALLACE

# This is
## Colombia

Once defined by 1980s stereotypes of moustachioed drug lords double-fisting Uzis, Colombia has finally reclaimed its identity. Boasting a variety of untouched natural landscapes, from arid deserts and vast savannahs to snow-capped volcanoes and white-sand beaches, Colombia offers inexhaustible opportunities for exploration and adventure. Adrenalin junkies can brave the raging rivers of San Gil, while nature-lovers can travel south deep into Amazonia, where the Great River yields an abundance of flora and fauna, including pink dolphins, caimans and the world's smallest primate. Visitors to the Zona Cafetera, Colombia's largest coffee-producing region, can stay at working coffee fincas and do a bit of birding — the country boasts nearly 2000 species — while learning the finer points of 'black gold' production. Seekers of urban culture will find satisfaction walking the ancient ramparts of Cartagena or visiting Bogotá's Gold Museum. And, when the sun goes down, Cali's famous salsa clubs and Medellín's upscale discos and downscale tango bars come into their own. Those eager to relax and recharge have their pick of either a Pacific coastline, where humpback whales cruise near the shore, or a Caribbean coast surrounded by crystalline waters and coral islands.

It was on the coasts that Afro-Caribbean rhythms first took hold in Colombia, leading to a musical diversity perhaps unsurpassed by any other country on the continent. *Vallenato*, *cumbia*, *salsa*: these sounds are ubiquitous, heard everywhere from village bars to big-city festivals. The vigorous musical pulse of the country is a testament to the mixed heritage of the population, the result of indigenous, European and African cultures co-mingling for centuries. But the Colombian experience is in the texture and the text as much as it is in the land and the music. Witness the exaggerated human figures sculpted by Fernando Botero or the dreamlike prose offered up by literary lion Gabriel García Márquez.

*Chris Wallace*

# Best of
# Colombia

## ❶ La Candelaria

Bogotá is a crowded, noisy, polluted chaotic city – like most capitals in Latin America. However, it is also an endearing cosmopolitan hub, rich in culture. La Candelaria, in the historical centre, is a well-preserved colonial neighbourhood notable for its churches and old houses, and the Museo del Oro (Gold Museum) possesses a dazzling collection of pre-Columbian art. Page 38.

## ❷ Zipaquirá

One of Colombia's most unusual attractions is an imposing cathedral carved inside an ancient salt mine. It makes for an unforgettable day trip from the capital. Page 76.

## ❸ San Gil

The town of San Gil has become the unofficial capital of the Colombian adventure sports scene. Three whitewater rivers flow through or near it, offering a range of rafting to satisfy everyone from timid beginners to big water veterans. There are also opportunities for abseiling, caving and paragliding, including a flight over the spectacular Chicamocha Canyon. Page 106.

## ❹ Cartagena

Cartagena is colonial Spain's finest legacy in the Americas, impressive in every respect. Spend several days exploring the fortified old centre, teeming with historical buildings, then laze on the city's beautiful beaches. It is the best base for visits to the Caribbean coast and the islands, and there are strange mud volcanoes nearby. Page 138.

## ❺ Ciudad Perdida

Located in the jungle in the far north of the country is the Lost City of the Tayrona people. The multi-day trek to this hidden archaeological site ranks alongside the Inca Trail in Peru and Roraima in Venezuela, as one of the classic South American adventures and is a truly memorable experience. Page 199.

## ❻ Guajira Peninsula

South America's northernmost point is an other-worldly landscape of arid desert and saltflats that is nonetheless home to vast flocks of flamingos and to the best-preserved indigenous culture in Colombia. Visit Cabo de la Vela, where the turquoise Caribbean laps against a desolate shore, and the Parque Nacional Natural Macuira, which provides a welcome splash of green in the desert. Page 213.

## ❼ Medellín

Medellín has shrugged off its notorious past and is now a modern, vibrant city with a spring-like climate. There is plenty of modern art to see and fascinating places to visit in the surrounding countryside. At night, take a turn in the city's tango bars or party till dawn in Parque Lleras. The best way to get an overview of the city is to ride a *teleférico* into the hillside suburbs. Page 233.

## ❽ La Zona Cafetera

Colombia's main coffee-producing region is characterized by rolling green hills, blanketed in plantations and forests. Stay on a coffee finca to learn about Colombia's 'black gold' and to appreciate the region's rich flora and fauna, particularly its prolific birdlife. Page 277.

## ❾ Los Nevados National Park

Easily accessible from Bogotá is a range of snow-covered volcanic peaks that rival any along the Andean chain. Three huge volcanos form the centre of the park, but there are also hot springs, volcanic lakes and vast tracts of *páramo* to explore. Page 291.

## ⑫ Tierradentro and San Agustín

Two unmissable pre-Columbian sites are located in beautiful scenery in the south of the country. The burial tombs of Tierradentro are spread across remote hillsides east of Popayán, while the mysterious statues at San Agustín are surrounded by subtropical vegetation, with the raging Río Magdalena nearby. Pages 341 and 349.

## ⑩ Cali

The 'capital' of the south, Cali has had an unhappy past but has now rediscovered its sensual side with a vibrant popular music scene and an unrivalled passion for salsa. The Farallones National Park lies a few kilometres to the west. Page 314.

## ⑪ Popayán

Popayán is one of the oldest Spanish towns in Colombia. Its whitewashed colonial houses have been beautifully restored and gleam in the southern sunshine. Visit at Easter to witness the famous Semana Santa parades, or at other times to soak up the cultured atmosphere and the fresh, mountain air. The sulphurous pools of Puracé National Park are a short trip to the east. Page 334.

Caribbean Sea

VENEZUELA

Puerto
Carreño

Río Orinoco

Puerto
Inírida

BRAZIL

# Route planner
## Colombia

A country as large and varied as Colombia has a great many sights worth visiting. A comprehensive tour will require a good deal of planning. If you have limited time and want to see as much as possible, you could consider air travel; cheap fares can be found through most local carriers. If you have more time, there are good long-distance bus services and minibuses.

## Two weeks

*the fast northern loop*

Most visitors to Colombia make a beeline for its sparkling Caribbean coast. Start by flying from **Bogotá** to **Santa Marta** and the beaches of **Tayrona National Park**. After a few days unwinding, it's a short hop along the coast to **Cartagena**. Spend a couple of days exploring the labyrinthine walled city before relaxing on Playa Blanca or the coral **Islas del Rosario** (depending on your budget). The colonial town of **Mompós** is a worthwhile (though travel-heavy and very, very hot) stopover en route to **Medellín**. After taking in the Antioquian capital's culture and nightlife, spend a few days sampling the department's beautiful traditional villages, such as **Santa Fe de Antioquia** or **Guatapé**, before catching a plane back to Bogotá.

## Three weeks

*the more leisurely northern loop*

An extra week allows for more bus travel and a chance to see Colombia's interior up close. Start by exploring Bogotá and its colonial sector, **La Candelaria**. A visit to the Gold Museum is a must. It's then a short bus ride to Villa de Leiva, with the magnificent **Zipaquirá** salt cathedral as a

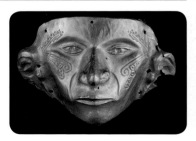

Right: Museo del Oro, Bogotá
Opposite page: Cartagena sign

convenient stopover. Soak up the colonial atmosphere in **Villa de Leiva** over a couple of days and explore its many surrounding attractions, such as the mountains and lakes outside Sogamoso, before heading up to **San Gil** for some rafting, kayaking and hiking. The neighbouring village of **Barichara** will provide more colonial architecture and sweeping views of Suárez Canyon. From San Gil, make your way up to **Santa Marta** and follow the same loop as above as far as **Medellín**, then travel overland to Bogotá, stopping off at the **Río Claro Nature Reserve** en route.

## Four weeks or more

the figure of eight

A month or more will give you the opportunity to see a good chunk of the country – though you will have to travel fast.

Start by following the second (leisurely) northern loop described above and then from Bogotá, take a bus due south, stopping off at the **Tatacoa Desert** for a night under the stars. From nearby **Neiva** it's a hard day's slog (but a worthwhile one) to **Tierradentro**. Spend a couple of days exploring the extraordinary tombs in the surrounding hills before heading down to **San Agustín** for more pre-Columbian archaeology and then a well-earned rest in one of the town's many comfortable

*hostales*. From San Agustín make the spectacular drive to the dazzling white city of **Popayán**, which has several attractions in its environs, including the market at Silvia and **Puracé National Park**. From here, head to the salsa-mad city of Cali for the weekend to hot-foot it with the locals. Next, venture into the 'coffee zone' for a stay on a finca. The villages of Salento and Salamina, the Cocora Valley and the snowy peaks of **Los Nevados National Park** are highlights of this region. From here it's a long bus journey or a short flight back to Bogotá.

Top: Salento
Left: Carnaval de los Blancos y Negros, southern Colombia
Opposite page: Tayrona National Park

# Best
## national
## parks

### El Cocuy

The Sierra Nevada del Cocuy is a premier climbing and hiking destination, with over 22 snow-capped peaks rising up to 5322 m and the largest expanse of glaciers in South America north of the equator. El Cocuy also offers plenty for nature lovers thanks to its biodiversity. Look out for *frailejón* shrubs and cardoon cactus, spectacled bear, wild boar, puma and several types of monkey. Page 103.

### Macuira

At the northeast tip of the remote La Guajira Peninsula, Macuira is an oasis of cloudforest in the middle of a semi-desert. The park is named after the Makui people, ancestors of the indigenous Wayúu who almost exclusively inhabit the peninsula. The park boasts over 140 species of bird, as well as insects, iguanas, toads and frogs. Page 214.

### Old Providence

The Caribbean island of Providencia has the third-longest barrier reef in the world and forms part of the UNESCO Seaflower Biosphere Reserve, along with neighbouring San Andrés. The archipelago is rich in marine life, including parrotfish, triggerfish, surgeonfish, the masked hamlet and several species of coral, plus on-shore mangroves and well-preserved tropical forest. Page 224.

## Los Nevados

The snow-capped peaks of Los Nevados rise sharply from the coffee heartland surrounded by cloudforest, glaciers, volcanic lakes and *páramo*. The highest of the three volcanoes is Nevado del Ruiz, which last erupted in 1985. Los Nevados is home to the Andean condor, golden eagle and various species of hummingbird. Page 291.

## Puracé

Most of this park lies more than 3000 m above sea level. It is home to the rare mountain tapir and Andean spectacled bear, plus many varieties of orchid, moss and lichen. Indigenous Páez and

Guambiano communities still live by traditional means within the park. Volcán Puracé (4760 m) is a popular climb, but there are also waterfalls, lakes, trails and sulphurous pools to visit. Page 344.

## Amacayacú

Amacayacú is surrounded by waterways that feed into the Amazon and Putumayo rivers. It is home to over 500 species of bird and around 150 species of mammal, including pink dolphin, danta and manatí, plus giant Victoria regia water lilies. Large sections of the park are flooded for part of the year and can only be explored in dug-out canoes. Page 378.

Top left: Los Nevados
Top right: Victoria regia water lilies, Amacayacú
Below: Guambiano women, Puracé
Opposite top: Laguna de la Plaza, El Cocuy
Opposite middle: Macuira
Opposite bottom: Old Providence marine life

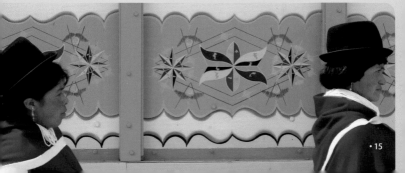

# When to go to
## Colombia

The climate varies little in Colombia, and, other than in the Chocó (northwest Colombia) where it rains almost daily, you will see plenty of sun year-round. There are no seasons to speak of and temperatures are dictated mainly by altitude. However, travellers should take note that March to September is the rainy season in the western departments, which can make travel difficult because of landslides and flooding. ▶ *See page 418 for more detailed information on climate.*

December to February are, on average, the driest months. It's worth remembering, though, that this is holiday season for many Colombians; prices rise significantly in the most popular places, and transport, including domestic flights, can be busy. During this period, a number of major annual fiestas are held, including the Días de los Blancos y Negros in January in Popayán and Pasto, and the Barranquilla Carnival in February. These events bring the locals out in force and it is a fun but crowded time to visit. Easter is also a local holiday time and almost every town has superb celebrations. In July and August, accommodation prices tend to rise because of school holidays.

## Weather Colombia

| January | February | March | April | May | June |
|---------|----------|-------|-------|-----|------|
| 24°C 17°C 81mm | 24°C 17°C 86mm | 24°C 18°C 110mm | 24°C 18°C 178mm | 24°C 18°C 193mm | 24°C 18°C 163mm |

| July | August | September | October | November | December |
|------|--------|-----------|---------|----------|----------|
| 24°C 17°C 133mm | 24°C 17°C 137mm | 24°C 17°C 159mm | 24°C 17°C 217mm | 24°C 17°C 195mm | 23°C 17°C 111mm |

## Festivals

García Márquez once said, "five Colombians in a room invariably turns into a party". It could also be said that a couple of hundred Colombians in a village invariably turns into a fiesta. Colombians will use almost anything as a pretext for a celebration; there are more festivals, parties and carnivals than days in the year. Every city, town and village has at least three or four annual events in which local products and traditions are celebrated with music, dancing and raucous revelry (these are listed throughout the book). Below are some of the most significant. ▸▸ See also Public holidays, page 440.

### January

**Early Jan** **Feria de Manizales**, www. feriademanizales.gov.co. Festivities in Manizales include horse parades, beauty pageants, bullfighting and general celebration of all things coffee.

**Early Jan** **Carnaval de los Blancos y Negros**, www.carnavaldepasto.org. The city of Pasto celebrates one of Latin America's oldest carnivals in which everyone daubs each other with black grease and white flour to commemorate the emancipation of black slaves. Celebrations begin late Dec with communal water fights and floats. There is dancing, parades and lots of costumes.

**2-12 Jan** **Carnaval del Diablo**. The town of Ríosucio in Caldas has celebrated this homage to the devil every 2 years since 1915. The whole town effectively becomes a masked ball as locals dress up as devils and other characters in a festival in which Hispanic, black and indigenous traditions collide.

**End Jan** **Hay Festival Cartagena**, www. hayfestival.com/cartagena. A branch of the UK's Hay Literary Festival turns Cartagena into a focus for all things bookish for 4 days.

### February

**2 Feb** **Fiesta de Nuestra Señora de la Candelaria**. Celebrated in several towns, including Cartagena and Medellín, this religious cult festival was inherited from the Canary Islands, where 2 goat herders witnessed the apparition of the Virgin Mary holding a green candle.

**Feb-Mar** **Barranquilla Carnival** (movable), www.carnavalde barranquilla.org. Beginning 4 days before Ash Wed, this is one of the best carnivals in South America and involve parades and plenty of dancing. 4 days of partying are compulsory by law.

### March-April

**Concurso Mundial de la Mujer Vaquera**, The women of the Llanos prove their cowboy skills during 3 days.

**Semana Santa** (Holy Week) (movable). Celebrated all over Colombia, but the processions in Popayán, Mompós and Pamplona are particularly revered.

**Late Apr** **Festival de la Leyenda Vallenata**, www.festivalvallenato.com. One of the most important music festivals in Colombia, 4 days of hard

## ON THE ROAD
### Best bizarre festivals

**Fiesta de las Aguas, Pasto, 5th February**
Following the grease- and talcum-coated fun of Carnaval (see page 18), the town of Pasto washes itself clean with a giant waterfight. Water is poured from balconies and everyone in town is fair game.

**Festival del Burro, San Antero, Córdoba, Easter**
The people of the Caribbean coastal town of San Antero love their donkeys so much that they have a festival dedicated to them. Each year around Easter the town's donkeys are paraded through the streets – in drag. Some wear lipstick and mascara, feather boas and pearl necklaces, while others sport jeans or bikinis, and the best get-up wins a prize. They have even built a Burrodome, a special stadium where man and beast can hang out drinking beer and listening to *vallenato*.

**Tomatina, Sutamarchán, Boyacá, June**
The premise of this festival is very simple: dump a bunch of tomatoes in a field and get several thousand people to throw them at each other. This festival took its cue from the Tomatína in Buñol, near Valencia in Spain, which claims to be the world s largest vegetable fight.

**Yipao, Armenia, Quindío, October**
Willys jeeps first arrived in Colombia in 1946 from the United States and they have become the most popular vehicles in the Zona Cafetera's hilly countryside thanks to their robust handling and capacity to carry loads far beyond their size. Colombians demonstrate their admiration for these Second World War army jeeps by holding *yipaos* – competitions in which Willys' owners must load as much produce as is physically possible onto their vehicles and parade down the street, often performing wheelies as they go. The most popular *yipao* is held in Armenia each October as part of the city's annual fiesta, but the largest is in Calaracá in June, with over 370 jeeps taking part.

partying in Valledupar culminate in the selection of the best *vallenato* musician.

### June-July
**Festival Folclórico y Reinado Nacional del Bambuco**. The city of Neiva hosts *Bambuco* dancing competitions and various parades in which bikini-clad beauty queens float downriver on boats while up to 5000 (often) drunken women ride horses through Neiva's streets. It culminates in the crowning of a *Bambuco* queen.

**Torneo Internacional del Joropo**, www.torneointernacionaldeljoropo. com. The city of Villavicencio gives itself over to a celebration of *llanero* culture, with more than 3000 couples dressed in traditional outfits dancing *joropo* in the streets, a large horse parade, a beauty contest and *coleo* (a type of rodeo).

## August

**1st 2 weeks  Feria de las Flores.**
Concerts, street parties, antique car parades, a *Paso Fino* horse parade and the *Desfile de Silleteros*, in which flower-growers file through the streets carrying their elaborate displays mounted on wooden 'chairs', have made this festival in Medellín a world-renowned event.
**Festival del Viento y de las Cometas** (windiest weekend in Aug). Villa de Leiva's enormous cobbled plaza fills with hundreds of kite-fliers displaying models of all shapes and sizes. Competition is fierce.

## September

**Jazz al Parque**, www.jazzalparque. gov.co. Bogotá's parks resonate to the sound of pianos, saxophones and trumpets during this festival that has grown exponentially since it began in 1996. Musicians from all over the world converge on Colombia's capital for a weekend.
**20 Sep-9 Oct  Fiestas de San Pacho.** For 20 days in late Sep/early Oct, the streets of Quibdó in Chocó convert themselves into a big party venue to commemorate the death of Saint Francis of Assisi. Religious processions, parades and *sancocho* cookouts all combine in this fusion of Catholicism and African customs.

## October

**Encuentro Mundial del Coleo**, www. mundialcoleo.com.co. More than 40,000 people descend on Villvicencio each year to watch mounted cowboys display their skills at *coleo*, a sport not dissimilar to rodeo that involves upending bulls by grabbing them by the tail and twisting until they fall over.

## November

**1st 2 weeks  Independencia and Concurso Nacional de la Belleza.** Cartagena celebrates being the first department to win Independence from the Spanish each 11 Nov with parades and traditional dancing in the streets. This has been somewhat supplanted by the National Beauty Pageant in which the winner will go on to represent Colombia at Miss Universe.
**Late Nov-early Dec  El Pirarucú de Oro.** This music festival in Leticia reflects the Colombian Amazon capital's position on the edge of 2 frontiers. With influences from Brazil and Peru, the festival celebrates music from the region.

## December

**7-9 Dec  Festival de Luces.** The skies above Villa de Leiva are lit by one of the best pyro-technic shows in Colombia while the streets are illuminated by hundreds of candles in this most picturesque of festivals.
**25-30 Dec  Feria de Cali**, www.feriade cali.com. What started as a bullfighting festival involving the best Spanish and South American matadors is now a city-wide party where Cali's self-imposed title of 'capital of salsa' is reaffirmed every year. The festival is opened by an impressive *Paso Fino* horse parade.

# What to do
# in Colombia

**overland, airborne and underwater adventures**

Colombia's disparate landscapes mean it really can offer something for everyone: tropical getaway, wildlife safari, metropolitan cultural tour, island hop, desert excursion, or all of the above. Adventurers have their pick of outdoor pursuits from hiking and climbing to rafting and parasailing, while others can eschew adrenaline for relaxation in the form of mud baths and white-sand beaches. ▸▸ *Operators are listed in the relevant places throughout the book.*

## Birdwatching

With almost 1900 confirmed bird species, Colombia is a hotspot for birders and wildlife enthusiasts. Top of the list of birding locales is Parque Ecológico Río Blanco, a 4343-ha protected cloudforest near Manizales, which is home to 335 species in its own right, including 33 species of hummingbird. There are also butterflies, orchids and rare mammals, such as spectacled bears, ocelots and white-tailed deer.

## Diving

Colombia's 2 extensive coastlines and numerous offshore islands offer myriad diving opportunities. Top of the list for aficionados must be the San Andrés and Providencia archipelago, which boasts the third-largest barrier reef in the world. There are several dive shops dotted around the two islands offering huge choice for exploring this underwater wonderland. Off the mainland, the Caribbean coast is

known for its large brain coral. There are coral islands off Cartagena and Tolú. The fishing village of Taganga has established itself as a dive centre, and Capurganá on the Darién coast also has some excellent dive sites. On the Pacific coast, Bahía Solano offers the chance to explore a scuttled navy vessel. Further south the ex-prison island of Gorgona has countless exotic fish and turtles, while the remote island of Malpelo is a mecca for hammerhead sharks.

## Hiking and walking

Colombia's varied topography offers a wealth of options for the hiking enthusiast. Everything from jungle treks and scampers over glacier fields to leisurely strolls through Arcadian landscapes can be enjoyed here. The most famous long-distance hike is the six-day return trek through the jungle to the Ciudad Perdida in the north. For high-altitude trekking the mountains of Los Nevados and El Cocuy national

## ON THE ROAD

### Visiting the national parks

Colombia has 41 Parques Nacional Natural (PNN), as well as numerous other sanctuaries and reserves (see Background, page 424), spread throughout the country and covering virtually every type of terrain. Although some are very remote and difficult to access, others offer visitors the best chance to get to know the country's diverse landscapes, flora and fauna.

Colombia's national parks are administered by Unidad Administrativa Especial del Sistema de Parques Nacionales Naturales (UAESPNN). If you intend to visit the parks, a good place to start is the main office at the Ministerio del Medio Ambiente, Vivienda y Desarrollo Territorial, Oficina de Ecoturismo, Carretera 10, No 20-30, piso 1, Bogotá, T1-353 2400 ext 138-139, www.parquesnacionales.gov.co, Monday-Friday 0800-1700. Staff can issue permits (see below), provide information about facilities and accommodation, and hand out maps. There is a library and research unit (Centro de Documentación) for more information. The *National Parks Guide* is attractive and informative, providing lavishly illustrated scientific information.

Permits (usually free) are required to visit the parks and are usually obtainable at offices near the parks themselves. Admission is charged at park entrances and may vary according to season, with higher prices at weekends, on public holidays, in June and July, December and January and Semana Santa. Accommodation in many of the more popular parks is run as a concession by Aviatur, www.concesionesparquesnaturales.com.

Volunteers can apply to work as park rangers for a minimum of 30 days at 20 or so national parks in Colombia; details are available from the UAESPNN office in Bogotá (see above). Corales del Rosario National Park has been particularly recommended. If you have a specific or professional scientific interest and would like to study in one of the parks, bring a letter from an educational or research institution in your home country indicating your specialism.

Other useful addresses include: Asociación Red Colombiana de Reservas Naturales de la Sociedad Civil, C 21N, No 8N-18, Santa Monica Residencial, Cali, T2-558 5046, www.resnatur.org.co, a network of privately owned nature reserves that work with local people to build a sustainable model of environmentally friendly tourism. Instituto Colombiano de Antropología e Historia, Calle 12, No 2-41, Bogotá, T1-444 0544, www.icanh.gov.co, Monday-Friday 0800-1700, also has useful information.

parks rival any along the Andean chain. Other national parks such as Puracé offer countless waterfalls, lakes and trails to explore. To get up close and personal with tropical wildlife the Colombian Amazon is the place to go. Reserva Natural Palmarí (actually in Brazil but best accessed from Leticia) offers guided jungle walks ranging from one to 72 hrs. Sal Si Puedes, T1-2833765, www.salsipuedes.org, and Corporación Clorofila Urbana, T1-6168711, www.clorofilaurbana.org, are 2 of several walking clubs that organize walks in the countryside just outside Bogotá and further afield.

## Parapenting and paragliding

Squeezed between the Andean mountain ranges of the Central and Eastern cordilleras, which create a very effective wind tunnel, the Mesa de Ruitoque near Bucaramanga is the perfect place for parapenting. There are 2 very professional schools, one of which has its own hostel. Nearby San Gil has two excellent locations for paragliding, one of which involves a flight over the spectacular Chicamocha Canyon.

## Rafting and kayaking

The town of San Gil has access to three whitewater rivers that offer various levels of rafting and kayaking. Several companies in the town offer professional and safety-conscious guidance and equipment, as well as new thrills such as hydrospeed, best described as whitewater boogie boarding. In southern Colombia, the village of San Agustín catches the Magdalena river at its wildest, while Cubarral on the Ariari River near Villavicencio is another popular rafting destination.

## Shopping tips

Colombia takes pride in its artisanal prowess, which can be seen in the handcrafted items on sale everywhere in the country, but with distinctive differences depending on the region. Ráquira in Boyacá Department is regarded as the centre of Columbian pottery, but the popular, brightly coloured folk art ceramics most associated with the country are made in Pitalito in the south and can be bought all over. Other good buys include hammocks in the north (especially around the Guajira Peninsula), leather goods in the south around Pasto, sisal-based textiles (known as *fique*), Panama hats, basketwork and gold (notably in Bogotá, Cartagena and Mompós). In most cases these items are very good value. A traditional *mochila* handbag, for example, which can cost hundreds of euros in Paris or Milan, can be bought for a song in Cartagena or Medellín. Bear this in mind when buying a handcrafted item in Colombia and do not haggle too much; your bargain may well be the only source of income for the vendor.

# Where to stay
## in Colombia

**from hammocks to hotels and everything in between**

In Colombia there are a number of quite exceptional hotels that are well worth seeking out. They are usually in colonial towns and not necessarily very expensive. There is also a small network of youth hostels of varying quality; they are used extensively by Colombian groups, but international members are welcome. Increasingly, more budget hotels and backpackers' hostels are opening up, as well as chic boutique hotels, often in restored colonial buildings.

### Hotels

Colombia has many names for hotels, including *posada, pensión, residencia, hostal, hostería, hospedaje, hospedería, mesón* and *hotelito*. Ignore them all and simply look at the price range as a guide to what to expect. *Motels* are almost always pay-by-the hour 'love hotels' (see box, opposite). Some *residencias* also double up as *acostaderos*, or love hotels, so it's best to avoid these.

**Prices** The Colombian hotel federation, COTELCO ⓘ *www.cotelco.org*, has lists of authorized prices for all member hotels, which can be consulted at tourist offices. In theory, new laws require all hotels to be registered, but to date many cheaper hotels remain unregistered. The more expensive hotels add 16% IVA (VAT) to bills. Strictly speaking foreigners should be exempt from this, but there seems to be some confusion about the application of this law; raise the matter with your hotel and you may well get a discount. Some hotels also add a small insurance charge.

## Price codes

| Where to stay | Restaurants |
|---|---|
| **$$$$** over US$150 | **$$$** over US$12 |
| **$$$** US$66-150 | **$$** US$7-12 |
| **$$** US$30-65 | **$** US$6 and under |
| **$** under US$30 | |

Price for a double room in high season, including taxes.

Price for a two-course meal for one person, excluding drinks or service charge.

## ON THE ROAD
## Love hotels

Every town has one but they are not what they seem. Colombia's motels are not cheap hotels for the weary motorist, but rather love hotels – convenient hideouts for lovers sneaking off for some alone-time that provide rates by the hour and the ultimate in discreet service.

You can recognize them by their suggestive nomenclature – names such as 'Hotel Seed' or 'Passion Hotel' – and by their lurid paintjobs, a mixture of electric blues or Pepto Bismol pinks, like sorry cast-offs from Miami's South Beach. Most have drive-in garages so that customers never have to show their faces at reception. Inside, a revolving dumb waiter allows the client to receive food, drinks, condoms and sex toys without ever having to meet the staff face-to-face. Some have jacuzzis, mirrored ceilings and pornography on TV, while others have special Saturday-night discounts.

Who goes there? Mainly teenagers and twenty-year-olds still living at home, but also adulterous couples and, of course, prostitutes with their clients. Colombia is a highly sexualized nation but also a predominantly Catholic country with strict moral codes. Motels are a convenient way of satisfying these conflicting desires and standards. You can measure how traditional a town is by the number of motels it has. For example, Armenia, in the heart of coffee country, has so many on its outskirts that the area has been nicknamed the Bermuda Triangle – no doubt because it's an easy place in which to lose yourself in passion.

Prices are normally displayed at reception, but in quiet periods it is always worth negotiating and ask to see the room before committing. From 15 December to mid- or late January, and 15 June to 31 August, some hotels in holiday centres may increase their prices by as much as 50%. Outside the main cities hotels may offer (very cheap) *en pensión* (full board) rates, but there will be no reduction if you choose to miss a meal. Most hotels in Colombia charge US$3 to US$10 for extra beds for children, up to a maximum (usually) of four beds per room.

**Safety and security** In cheaper hotels, beware of electric shower heaters, which can be dangerous through faulty wiring. Toilets may suffer from inadequate water supplies. In all cases, do not flush paper down the toilet bowl but use the receptacle provided. Carry toilet paper with you as cheaper establishments as well as restaurants, bars, etc, may not provide it, or make an additional charge for it.

Hotels are sometimes checked by the police for drugs. Make sure they do not remove any of your belongings. You do not need to show them any money. Cooperate but be firm about your rights. ▸▸ *For further information on drugs and the police, see Essentials A-Z, page 434 and page 440.*

## Camping

Local tourist authorities have lists of official campsites, but they are seldom signposted on main roads, so can be hard to find. Some hostels, particularly in rural areas, offer camping and often provide tents and other equipment at an additional cost that is still cheaper than a dorm bed. Permission to camp with tent, campervan or car may be granted by landowners in less populated areas; some haciendas have armed guards protecting their property, which will improve your safety. Never camp on private land without authorization. Those in vehicles can camp by the roadside, but it is not particularly safe and it can be difficult to find a secluded spot; the best option may be truck drivers' restaurants or sometimes at police or army posts. In all cases, check very carefully before deciding to camp: you may be exposing yourself to significant danger.

## Youth hostels

**La Federación Colombiana de Albergues Juveniles** ⓘ *Cra 7, No 6-10, Torre B, Oficina 201, Bogotá, T1-280 3232*, is affiliated to the International Youth Hostel Federation (IYHF) and has 12 hostels around the country, in Bogotá, Armenia, Cartagena, Medellín, Montenegro, Paipa, Santa Marta and Manizales. Hostels are often full in December and January and again from June to mid-July; it's best to telephone in advance at these times. Otherwise, it's usually possible to arrive without a reservation. Membership can be obtained in Colombia: Hostelling International Cards are recognized and qualify for discounts. An alternative is the **Colombian Hostel Association** ⓘ *www.colombianhostels. com*, which has hostels in Bogotá, Bucaramanga, Cartagena, Cali, Manizales, Medellín, Mompós, San Gil, Salento, San Agustín, Taganga, Valledupar and Villa de Leiva. **Hostel Trail Latin America** ⓘ *Cra 11, No 4-16, Popayán, T2-831 7871, www.hosteltrail.com*, is an online network of hostels and tour companies in South America providing information on locally run businesses for backpackers and independent travellers.

## Homestays

In many places, it is possible to stay with a local family; check with the local tourist office to see what is available. This is a good option for those interested in learning Spanish informally in a family environment. For a uniquely Colombian experience, you can also stay on a coffee finca; see box, page 283.

# Food & drink
## in Colombia

Colombia has yet to achieve international renown for its cuisine, but as tourism in the country grows, the word is getting out about the nation's culinary treats, which involve so much more than the hearty *sancocho* and the formidable *bandeja paisa*. There are gastronomy festivals in various cities and towns showcasing the best the country has to offer, but the foodie adventurer will need to travel far and wide to sample the many local specialities found in the different regions. ▸▸ *Standard menu items are listed on page 451.*

## Regional food

**Bogotá and Cundinamarca** *Ajiaco de pollo* (or *ajiaco santafereño*) is a delicious chicken stew with maize, manioc (yucca), three types of potato, herbs (including *guascas*) and other vegetables, served with cream, capers and pieces of avocado. It is a Bogotá speciality. *Chunchullo* (tripe) and *morcilla* (blood sausage) are also popular dishes. *Cuajada con melado (melao)* is a dessert of fresh cheese served with cane syrup, or *natas* (based on the skin of boiled milk).

**Boyacá** *Mazamorra* is a meat and vegetable soup with broad and black beans, peas, varieties of potato and cornflour. *Puchero* is a stew based on chicken with potatoes, yucca, cabbage, turnips, corn (on the cob) and herbs. *Cuchuco* is another soup with pork and sweet potato. *Masato* is a slightly fermented rice beverage. *Longaniza* (long pork sausage) is also very popular.

**Santander and Norte de Santander** *Hormigas culonas* (large black ants) are the most famous culinary delight of this area, served toasted and particularly popular in Bucaramanga and Barichara at Easter time. Locals claim they have aphrodisiac qualities. *Mute* is a traditional soup of various cereals including corn. Goat, often served with its *pepitoria* (tripe and intestines), and pigeon appear in several local dishes. *Rampuchada* is a north Santander stew based on the fish of the Zulia river, which flows into Venezuela. *Hallacas* are cornmeal turnovers, like oversized *tamales,* filled with different meats and whatever else is to hand; they're typical of neighbouring Venezuela. *Carne oreada* is salted dried meat marinated in a *panela* (unrefined sugarcane) and pineapple sauce; it has the consistency of beef jerky. Dishes featuring chickpeas and goat's milk are also popular. *Bocadillo veleño* is similar to quince jelly but made from guava. It takes its name from Vélez, but can be found elsewhere in Colombia.

**Caribbean Colombia**  Fish is naturally a speciality in the coastal regions. In *Arroz con coco*, rice is prepared with coconut. *Cazuela de mariscos*, a soup/stew of shellfish and white fish, sometimes including octopus and squid, is especially good. *Sancocho de pescado* is a fish stew with vegetables, usually simpler and cheaper than *cazuela*. *Chipichipi*, a small clam found along the coast in Barranquilla and Santa Marta, is a standard local dish served with rice. *Empanada* (or *arepa*) *de huevo*, is deep fried with eggs in the middle and is a good light meal. *Canasta de coco* is a local sweet pastry containing coconut custard flavoured with wine and topped with meringue.

**Northwest Colombia**  *Bandeja paisa* consists of various types of gut-busting pork cuts or other grilled meats, plus *chorizo* (sausage), *chicharrón* (pork crackling) and sometimes an egg, served with rice, beans, potato, manioc and a green salad; originally from Antioquia, this has now been adopted in other parts of the country. *Natilla*, a sponge cake made from cornflour, and *salpicón*, a tropical fruit salad, are popular desserts. *Lechona*, suckling pig with herbs, is a speciality of Ibagué (Tolima). *Viudo de pescado* is a dish based on small shellfish from the local Opía river. *Achira* is a kind of hot biscuit.

**Southern Colombia**  In contrast to most of Colombia, menus here tend not to include potato (in its many forms). Instead, emphasis is on corn, plantain, rice and avocado with the usual pork and chicken dishes. *Tamales* are a speciality of Cali, and *manjar blanco*, made from milk and sugar or molasses, served with biscuit, is a favourite dessert. *Cuy, curí* or *conejillo de Indias* (guinea pig) is typical of the southern department of Nariño. *Mazorcas* (baked corn-on-the-cob) can be found at roadside stalls throughout southern Colombia.

*Tinto* – the national small cup of black coffee rather than a glass of red wine – is taken at all hours; a *tinto doble* is a large cup. Colombian coffee tends to be mild, unless you're on a coffee finca, so if you want it strong, ask for *café cargado*. Coffee with milk is called *café perico*; *café con leche* is a mug of milk with coffee added. If you want a coffee with less milk, order *tinto y leche aparte* and they will bring the milk separately. For more on coffee in Colombia, see box, page 283.

Herbal tea, known as (*bebida*) *aromática*, is popular; flavours include *limonaria*, *orquídea* and *manzanilla*. *Té de menta* (mint tea) may only be available in an upmarket café or *casa de té* in one of the bigger cities. If you want Indian tea, *té Lipton en agua* should do the trick. Chocolate is also drunk: *chocolate Santafereño* is often taken during the afternoon in Bogotá with snacks and cheese. A milk and maize drink is widely available; it is known as *care* in Boyacá, *mazamorro* in Antioquia and elsewhere, and *peto* in Cundinamarca. *Agua de panela* (hot water with unrefined sugar) is another common beverage, also served with limes, milk or cheese.

Bottled soft drinks, commonly called *gaseosas*, are available throughout the country. If you want non-carbonated, ask for *sin gas*. You will find that many of the country's special fruits (see below) are used for bottled drinks. Water comes in bottles, cartons and small plastic packets, or even plastic bags: all safer than out of the tap, although tap water is generally of a reasonable quality.

Many acceptable brands of beer are available, although until recently they were almost all produced by the Bavaria group. Each region has a preference for different brands. The most popular are **Aguila**, the award-winning **Club Colombia**, **Costeño** and **Poker**. The **Bogotá Beer Company** (BBC) has its own small brewery in Chapinero and has several bars around the city serving delicious draught beer modelled on British and German ales. It has increased in popularity over the years, so much so that bottles are available at many supermarkets, bars and hostels throughout the country.

A traditional drink in Colombia is *chicha*. It is corn-based with sugar and/ or *panela* added. The boiled liquid is served as a non-alcoholic beverage, but becomes very potent if it is allowed to ferment over several days, and especially if it is kept in the fridge for a while.

> **Tip...**
> Take care when buying imported spirits in some bars and small shops, as bottles bearing well-known labels may have been 'recycled' and contain poor imitations of the original contents that can be dangerous. Also note that ice may not be made from drinking water.

The local rum (*ron*) is good and cheap; two of the best are **Ron Viejo de Caldas** and **Ron Medellín** (dark). Try *canelazo*: cold or hot rum with water, sugar, lime and cinnamon. As common as rum is *aguardiente* (literally 'fire water'), a white spirit distilled from sugar cane. There are two types, with *anís* (aniseed) or without. Wine is very expensive in Colombia: as much as US$15 in restaurants for an acceptable bottle of Chilean or Argentine wine, more for European and other wines. Local table wines include **Isabella**, but none of them is very good.

### Fruit and juices

Colombia has an exceptional range and quality of fruit – another result of the diversity of altitude and climate. Fruits familiar in northern and Mediterranean climates grow here, though with some differences, including: *manzanas* (apples); *bananos* (bananas); *uvas* (grapes); *limones* (limes; lemons are rarely seen); *mangos*; *melones* (melons); *naranjas* (oranges; usually green or yellow in Colombia); *duraznos* (peaches) and *peras* (pears).

Then there are the local fruits: *chirimoyas* (a green fruit, white inside with pips); *curuba* (banana passion fruit); *feijoa* (a green fruit with white flesh, high in vitamin C); *guayaba* (guava); *guanábana* (soursop); *lulo* (a small orange fruit); *maracuyá* (passion fruit); *mora* (literally 'blackberry' but actually more like a loganberry); papaya; the delicious *pitahaya* (taken either as an appetizer or dessert); *sandía* (watermelon); *tomate de árbol* (tree tomato, several varieties normally used as a fruit), and many more.

All of these fruits can be served as juices, or with milk (hopefully fresh) or water (hopefully bottled or sterilized). Watch the drinks being prepared on street stalls and experiment to find your favourite. There are few better ways to beat the coastal heat than with an icy cup of *mandarina* or *limonada* from a street vendor.

Fruit yoghurts are nourishing and cheap; **Alpina** brand is good, especially *crema* style. **Kumis** is a type of liquid yoghurt.

## Eating out

Restaurant food in Colombia is generally good and, occasionally, very good; this guide tries to list a tested choice at all available price levels. Note that more expensive restaurants may add a discretionary 16% IVA tax to the bill. In the main cities (Bogotá, Cartagena, Medellín and Cali) you will find a limitless choice of menu and price. The other departmental capitals have a decent range of specialist restaurants and all the usual national and international fast-

## SIX OF THE BEST
### Gastronomic experiences

Sample fresh juice from a roadside cart in Medellín, page 30.
Join the in-crowd for international dining in the **Zona Rosa**, Bogotá, page 60.
Eat roast goat in ant sauce at **Al Cuoco**, Barichara, page 115.
Dine on seafood at **Club de Pesca** in Cartagena, page 156.
Enjoy a high-octane cup of coffee at **Hacienda Venecia**, page 284.
Order banana leaf-wrapped *tamales* at the **Mercado Alameda** in Cali, page 321.

food outlets. Only in the smaller towns and villages, not catering for tourists, will you struggle to find a choice of places to eat. Most of the bigger cities have vegetarian restaurants, which are listed in the text; the **Govinda** chain is widely represented. In other towns and villages vegetarians will have to ask for special food to be prepared. Watch out for opening times in the evenings and at weekends, as some restaurants still close around 1800. On Sundays it can be particularly difficult to find an open restaurant and even hotel dining rooms may be closed.

Lunch (*almuerzo*) is the main Colombian meal of the day, when restaurants will serve a *menú ejecutivo/del día*, with soup, main course and fruit juice or *gaseosa* (soft drink) included; many restaurants will display the menu and cost in the window. If you are economizing, ask for the *plato del día*, *bandeja* or *plato corriente* (just the main dish).

The cheapest food can be found in markets (when they are open), on street stalls in most downtown areas and at transport terminals, but bear in mind that standards of hygiene and food safety may not be good. Watch what the locals are eating as a guide to the best choice and follow these general rules: keep away from uncooked food and salads; eat fruit you have peeled yourself; take it easy with unfamiliar dishes, especially if you have arrived from a different climate or altitude, and only drink from sealed bottles. Having said that, you may find that fresh fruit drinks are irresistible, in which case you will have to take your chances! ▸▸ *See also Health, page 434.*

# Bogotá & around

leave your preconceptions at the airport

Colombia's capital is a vast, sprawling, traffic-choked metropolis set high in a valley surrounded by the mountains of the Cordillera Oriental. Once known for drugs, crime and corruption, Bogotá has undergone a renaissance in the past 20 years to become one of the most exciting capitals in Latin America.

However, although its nightlife, dining, fashion and culture may now be equal to anything that Buenos Aires or Rio de Janeiro can offer, it's a city that still suffers from extremes of wealth and poverty. Air-conditioned, tinted-windowed cars stand bumper to bumper with rubbish-collecting horse and carts, and the conspicuous consumption on show in the enormous, flashy shopping centres and gated communities in the north of the city stand in stark contrast to the depressing shanty towns to the south and east.

**Best** for
Museums ▪ Churches ▪ Nightlife

# Footprint
## picks

★ **La Candelaria**, page 38

Stroll the cobbled streets of the historic centre.

★ **Emerald Trade Centre**, pages 50 and 65

Haggle over or just gawp at Colombia's most precious gemstones.

★ **Museo del Oro**, page 50

Discover the pre-Columbian treasures at the Gold Museum; it's one of the finest museums on the continent.

★ **Monserrate**, page 51

Climb to this hilltop sanctuary for unrivalled views over the city and beyond.

★ **Mercado de Paloquemao**, pages 54 and 65

Revel in the sights, sounds and smells of Bogotá's central market, especially its wonderful flower stalls.

★ **Jardín Botánico José Celestino Mutis**, page 54

See native species of orchid and other plants without leaving the city.

★ **Zipaquirá**, page 76

Head into the ancient salt mine to see its awe-inspiring cathedral.

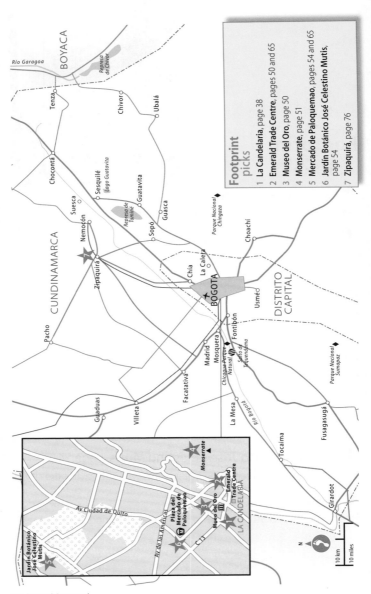

## Footprint picks

1. **La Candelaria**, page 38
2. **Emerald Trade Centre**, pages 50 and 65
3. **Museo del Oro**, page 50
4. **Monserrate**, page 51
5. **Mercado de Paloquemao**, pages 54 and 65
6. **Jardín Botánico José Celestino Mutis**, page 54
7. **Zipaquirá**, page 76

# Bogotá city

The old centre is La Candelaria, a rabbit warren of colonial buildings, narrow, cobbled streets, theatres, universities and countless cafés buzzing with intellectual debate. La Candelaria is home to one of Latin America's most impressive cultural attractions, the Gold Museum, a dazzling display of pre-Columbian treasures. Beyond the noisy, polluted Downtown area, the northern suburbs are effectively a new city, characterized by the opulent restaurants, bars and nightclubs of the Zona G, Zona T and Parque 93. Further afield there are numerous attractions and pretty towns to visit, perfect for day or weekend excursions; the most impressive of these is the extraordinary salt cathedral at Zipaquirá. *Colour map 2, C5.*

# Essential Bogotá

## Finding your feet

Bogotá is bounded to the east by the mountains of the Eastern Cordillera, a useful landmark for getting your bearings. Most of the interesting parts of the city follow the foot of the cordillera in a north–south line. La Candelaria, full of character, occupies the area bordered by Avenida Jiménez de Quesada, Calle 6, Carrera 3 and Carrera 10. There is some modern infill but many of the houses here are well preserved in colonial style, one or two storeys high with tiled roofs, projecting eaves, wrought ironwork and carved balconies. The main colonial churches, palaces and museums are concentrated around and above the Plaza Bolívar. Some hotels are also found in this area, especially along the margins. Downtown Bogotá runs in a band northeast along Carrera 7 from Avenida Jiménez de Quesada to Calle 26. It is a thorough mix of styles including modern towers and run-down colonial buildings. The streets are full of life, but can be paralysed by traffic at busy times. The bohemian area of La Macarena (also known as Zona M), along Carrera 4 between Calle 25 and Calle 27, was formerly inhabited by struggling artists but is now becoming increasingly fashionable with many good restaurants and bars.

From Calle 50 to Calle 68 is El Chapinero, once the outskirts of the city and now a commercial district with a sprinkling of old, large mansions. It also doubles up as the epicentre of Bogotá's thriving gay scene, known as 'Chapigay', with many bars and clubs. Beyond Calle 60, the main city continues north to a comparatively new district,

North Bogotá, which is split into various points of interest. Most of the best hotels, restaurants and embassies are in this area, which is regarded as the safest in Bogotá. Between Carrera 4 and Carrera 5 and Calle 68 and Calle 71 is what is known as the Zona G (for 'gourmet'), home to some of Bogotá best (and most expensive) restaurants. The T-shaped pedestrianized area made up by Calle 83 and Carrera 13 is Bogotá's Zona Rosa (also known as the Zona T) with many fashionable bars, clubs and restaurants. Further north the streets around Parque 93 have some of the most expensive bars and restaurants in the city, while at the very limits of the city, off Carrera 7 between Calle 117 and Calle 119, is Usaquen, formerly a satellite town of Bogotá and now a popular evening and weekend excursion for rolos (as bogotanos are sometimes called), looking to get a break from the metropolis.

## Best restaurants

La Paella, page 60
Sopas de Mamá, page 60
Archie's, page 61
Estrella de los Ríos, page 61
H Sasson, page 61

## Getting around

Walking is the best way to explore the downtown area and La Candelaria, as distances are short and the traffic is heavy. North Bogotá is more spacious, so buses and taxis are a more convenient option here. The TransMilenio bus service is good for crossing the city from north to south, but if you are short of time or have luggage or valuables, take a licensed taxi.

These are relatively cheap and plentiful,
and the service is generally good. At
night, always travel by licensed taxi.

**Addresses**

It is easy enough to find a place once
the Colombian address system is
understood. The *Calles* (abbreviated
as 'C', or 'Cll') run at right angles across
the *Carreras* ('Cra' or 'K'). The address
C 13, No 12-45 is the building on
Calle 13 between Carreras 12 and 13
at 45 paces from Carrera 12; however
*Transversales* (Tra) and *Diagonales* (Diag)
can complicate the system. *Avenidas*
(Av), broad and important streets, may
be either *Calles* or *Carreras* or both (19 is
Calle 19 in the centre and Carrera 19 in
the North). The *Calles* in the south of
the city are marked 'Sur' or 'S'; this is an
integral part of the address and must
be quoted.

**Safety**

As in any city of this size, take care not
to tempt thieves by careless displays
of money or valuables. Beware anyone
approaching you in the street, as they

may well be a thief or a con-artist. This
is a particular problem around Plaza
de Bolívar. Note that they may be
well-dressed and plausible, may pose as
plain-clothes officials and often work in
pairs. La Candelaria district is relatively
safe by day, but there have been several
reports of muggings and robberies by
night. Begging is also common in this
area as well as in the city centre. You are
strongly advised to take registered taxis,
preferably radio taxis, if travelling in the
city at night; keep the doors locked. If
you are the victim of theft or other crime,
contact a **Centro de Atención Inmediata**
(CAI) office or call T156. For further advice,
read the Safety section in Practicalities
carefully (see page 441) and take note of
safety comments throughout the text.

**When to go**

Bogotá is an all-year-round city thanks
to its temperate climate: cool to warm in
the middle of the day but normally much
cooler at night, when a light sweater
or even a coat may be required. There
can be showers at any time of year. The
surrounding countryside is noticeably
warmer. Holiday times such as Easter and
Christmas are quiet, but attractions are
often closed. You'll need three to four
days to explore the city, or a week if you
want to venture further afield.

**Weather** Bogotá

| Month | High | Low | Rainfall |
|-------|------|-----|----------|
| January | 18°C | 6°C | 40mm |
| February | 18°C | 7°C | 50mm |
| March | 19°C | 8°C | 80mm |
| April | 18°C | 8°C | 110mm |
| May | 18°C | 8°C | 100mm |
| June | 17°C | 8°C | 60mm |
| July | 17°C | 8°C | 40mm |
| August | 17°C | 7°C | 40mm |
| September | 18°C | 7°C | 50mm |
| October | 18°C | 8°C | 140mm |
| November | 18°C | 8°C | 110mm |
| December | 18°C | 7°C | 60mm |

★The Plaza de Bolívar, marked out by the city's founders as Plaza Mayor, is at the heart of the historic centre. Around the plaza are the narrow streets and mansions of the **Barrio La Candelaria**, occupying some 70 city blocks to the south of Avenida Jiménez de Quesada, north of Calle 6 and east of Carrera 10. The main commercial and residential focus of the city moved down the hill and to the north early in the city's history, so much of the original colonial town remains. It is one of the best-preserved major historical centres in Latin America and, as such, has attracted artists, writers and academics. The barrio is filled with theatres, libraries and universities, for which Colombia is renowned in the Spanish-speaking world. It is a delight to wander the cobbled streets, admiring the colonial houses with their barred windows, carved doorways, red-tiled roofs and sheltering eaves, many of which are being preserved and renovated by the local authorities. Many of the best of Bogotá's churches and colonial buildings are also in this district. Modern and boutique hotels can be found along the margins of La Candelaria, for example on Avenida Jiménez de Quesada. The streets are relatively uncrowded and safe, although care should be exercised after dark. West of Carrera 10 and south of Calle 6 the streets are seedier and not recommended for pedestrians.

## Plaza Bolívar and around

Plaza de Bolívar is the central square of Bogotá, with a statue of the Liberator at its centre. The **cathedral** ① *Tue-Sun 0900-1700*, stands on the northeast corner of the square. The first was completed in 1553 to replace a small chapel where Fray Domingo de las Casas said the first Mass in Bogotá. The present building was constructed between 1807 and 1823. It has a fine, spacious interior, decorated in cream and gold with high ceilings across three naves. There are lateral chapels in classical style, a notable choir loft of carved walnut, wrought silver on the altar of the Chapel of El Topo and elaborate candelabras. Treasures and relics include paintings attributed to Ribera and the banner brought by Jiménez de Quesada to Bogotá in the sacristy, which also houses portraits of past archbishops. There are monuments to Jiménez and to Antonio Nariño inside the cathedral. **Gregorio Vázquez de Arce y Ceballos** (1638-1711), the most notable painter in colonial Colombia, is buried in one of the chapels near the altar. A number of his paintings can be seen in the cathedral.

Next to the cathedral is the **Capilla del Sagrario** ① *Cra 7, No 10-40, T1-341 1954 (closed Sat), Mass Mon-Fri 1200, Sat 1200, 1700, Sun 1000, 1200, 1700*, built at the end of the 17th century. There are two aisles with wooden balconies above and a fine red and gilt ceiling and screen. The inside of the dome was painted by Ricardo Acevedo Bernal. There are several paintings by Gregorio Vázquez de Arce y Ceballos. Next door is the **Palacio Arzobispal** ① *Cra 7, No 10-20*, with splendid bronze doors, and opposite, at the bottom of Calle 10, is **Colegio de San Bartolomé** ① *Cra 7, No 9-96*, originally Bogotá's oldest university, founded in 1573, where many notable

The city of Santa Fe de Bogotá (also written Santafé and with or without accent) was founded by Gonzalo Jiménez de Quesada on 6 August 1538 in territory inhabited by the indigenous Muisca. The name of the king, Bacatá, was adopted for the new city. In 1575, Philip II of Spain confirmed the city's title as the "very noble and very loyal city of Santafé de Bogotá", adopting the name of Jiménez de Quesada's birthplace of Santa Fe in Andalucía. It was the capital of the Viceroyalty of Nueva Granada in 1740. After Independence in 1819, Bogotá became the capital of Gran Colombia, a confederation of what is today Venezuela, Ecuador, Panama and Colombia, and remained capital of Colombia as the other republics separated.

For much of the 19th century, Bogotá suffered from isolation in economic terms mainly due to distance and lack of good transport. The population in 1850 was no more than 50,000. By 1900, however, a tram system unified the city and railways connected it to the Río Magdalena. Migrants from the Colombian countryside flocked to the city; by 1950, the population was 500,000, and the move to develop the north of the city accelerated. Since then it has re-emphasized its position as the dominant city in Colombia.

The official name of the city is now simply Bogotá, the urban area of the metropolis is known as the Distrito Capital (DC), and it is also the capital of the surrounding Department of Cundinamarca.

Colombians of the past were educated, including Antonio Nariño, Antonio Ricaurte and General Santander. The imposing early 20th-century classical building, now an important secondary school, fits appropriately into the corner of Plaza Bolívar.

On the south side of the Plaza Bolívar is the **Capitolio Nacional**, originally the site of the Viceroy's Palace. In 1846, Thomas Reed, born in Tenerife and educated in England, was commissioned to build the Capitolio, but it was fraught with difficulties from the start. Construction was suspended in 1851, to be recommenced in 1880 by Pietro Cantini, who finished the façade to the original design in 1911. The rest was finally 'finished' in 1927 by Alberto Manrique Martín, although many other architects and engineers were involved at various times. The building is still being restored.

On the corner of Carrera 8/Calle 10 is the **Casa de Los Comuneros** ⓘ *Cra 8, No 9-83, T1-327 4850, Mon-Fri 0930-1900, www.culturarecreacionydeporte.gov.co.* The building dates from the 17th century, when it housed commercial premises with living quarters above, and it retains typical wrought-iron balconies. There are also examples of later modifications to the building from the 19th and 20th centuries. It now belongs to the **Instituto Distrital de Cultura y Turismo** and includes the main tourist office of the city (see page 57).

The **Alcaldía** ⓘ *Cra 8, No 10-65, www.bogota.gov.co,* Bogotá's city hall, is on the west side of the plaza. It is known as the Liévano Building and is in the French

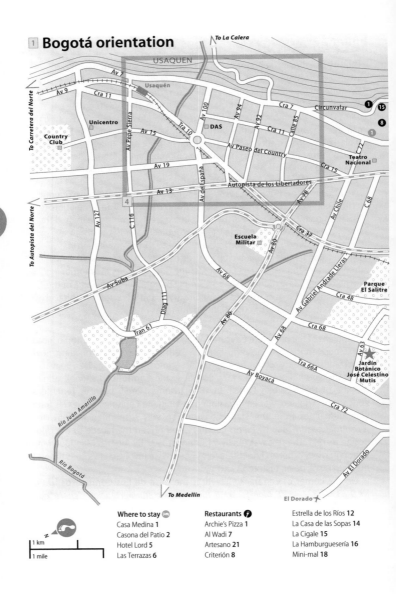

## 1 Bogotá orientation

**Where to stay** 🛏
Casa Medina **1**
Casona del Patio **2**
Hotel Lord **5**
Las Terrazas **6**

**Restaurants** 🍴
Archie's Pizza **1**
Al Wadi **7**
Artesano **21**
Criterión **8**

Estrella de los Ríos **12**
La Casa de las Sopas **14**
La Cigale **15**
La Hamburguesería **16**
Mini-mal **18**

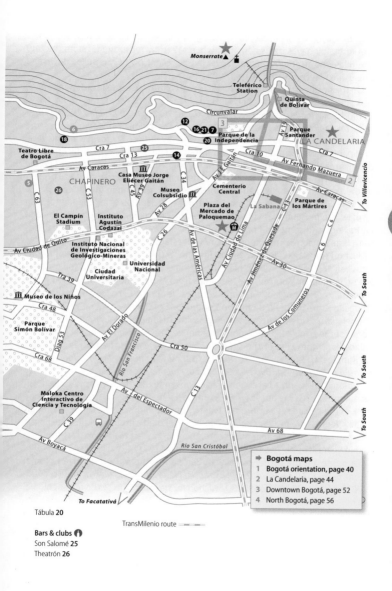

Monserrate ▲ ✝

Teleférico Station

Circunvalar

Quinta de Bolívar

3

Parque de la Independencia

Parque Santander

LA CANDELARIA

Cra 7

Cra 13

Cra 10

Av Fernando Mazuera

2

To Villavicencio

Teatro Libre de Bogotá

Av Caracas

CHAPINERO

Casa Museo Jorge Eliécer Gaitán

Museo Colsubsídio

Cementerio Central

La Sabana

Parque de los Mártires

Av Caracas

El Campín Stadium

Instituto Agustín Codazzi

Plaza del Mercado de Paloquemao

Av Ciudad de Quito

Instituto Nacional de Investigaciones Geológico-Mineras

Universidad Nacional

Av Jiménez de Quesada

Av 30

Ciudad Universitaria

To South

Museo de los Niños

Cra 48

Av de los Comuneros

Parque Simón Bolívar

Cra 68

Av El Dorado

Cra 50

To South

Río San Francisco

Maloka Centro Interactivo de Ciencia y Tecnología

Av del Espectador

C 13

Av 68

To South

Av Boyacá

Río San Cristóbal

To Facatativá

Tábula **20**

TransMilenio route ═══

**Bars & clubs** 🎵
Son Salomé **25**
Theatrón **26**

style of the early 20th century. Until 1960, the ground-floor galleries were business premises. On the north side of the plaza you will see the **Palacio de Justicia.** The former building was badly damaged when the Army recaptured it from the M19 guerrillas who attacked and took it over in 1985. Eventually it was pulled down and a new one was completed in April 1999.

On the northeast corner of Calle 11/Carrera 7 is the **Museo de la Independencia**, also known as the **Casa del Florero** ① *C 11, No 6-94, T1-336 6419, www. quintadebolivar.gov.co, Tue-Fri, 0900-1700, Sat and Sun 1000-1500, US$1.60, free entry for senior citizens and children under 5.* The colonial building houses the famous flower vase that featured in the 1810 revolution. The owner of the vase, the Spaniard José González Llorente, refused to lend the vase for the decoration of the main table at an event in honour of Antonio Villavicencio, a prominent Creole (person born in Latin America of Spanish descent). This snub was used as a pretext by the Creoles for rebellion against the Spaniards, resulting in the independence of Nueva Granada nine years later. A copy of the Declaration of Independence is on display. The museum has collections from the period, including documents and engravings and some fine portraits of Simón Bolívar. Nearby, on Calle 11 at Nos 6-42, is an attractive inner courtyard, now a restaurant, which is worth a look.

Just off the plaza is **Iglesia de San Ignacio** ① *C 10, No 6-35,* built by the Jesuits between 1605 and 1635 with plans from Rome. Over the choir and the galleries is a rich ceiling in Moorish style; emeralds from Muzo in Boyacá were used in the monstrance. Paintings by Gregorio Vázquez de Arce y Ceballos are in the nave. Opposite is the **Plazuela de Rufino Cuervo**, one of the few original squares in La Candelaria, a garden of trees and flowers with balconied buildings around and the dome of the Capilla del Sagrario visible above. The Palacio Arzobispal (Cardinal's Palace) is to the west of the square, while to the east is the **Museo de Trajes Regionales** ① *C 10, No 6-20, T1-282 6531, www.museodetrajesregionales.com, Mon-Fri 0900-1600, Sat 0900-1400, US$1,60, reduction for students,* with a display of regional dress and a collection of handwoven textiles showing pre-Columbian techniques. This is the house where Manuela Sáenz, Bolívar's mistress, lived. At the back of the square is **La Imprenta**, where Antonio Nariño's translation of Thomas Paine's 'Rights of Man' was published in 1794. This had a profound influence on the growing demand for Independence from Spain. You can read an extract from the text in Spanish on the wall of the building.

Opposite, on the corner of Calle 10/Carrera 6 is the **Museo de Arte Colonial** ① *Cra 6, No 9-77, T1-341 6017, www.museoiglesiasantaclara.gov.co, Tue-Fri 0900-1700, Sat-Sun 1000-1600, US$1.60, reduction for students,* one of the finest colonial buildings in Colombia. It belonged originally to the Society of Jesus and was once the seat of the oldest University in Colombia and of the National Library. It has a splendid collection of colonial art and paintings, including a whole room of works by Gregorio Vázquez de Arce y Ceballos, all kinds of silver, furniture, glassware and utensils of the time. Particularly impressive is the collection of portable writing cabinets with inlay marquetry in one of the upstairs rooms. It also has a private chapel and two charming patios.

## East of Carrera 6

Further up Calle 10, at No 5-51, is the **Palacio de San Carlos**, where Bolívar lived for a time. He is said to have planted the now huge walnut tree in the courtyard. On 25 September 1828, there was an attempt on his life; his mistress, Manuela Sáenz, thrust him out of the window (a plaque facing Calle 10 marks the event) and he was able to hide for two hours under the stone arches of the bridge across the Río San Agustín, now Calle 7. Santander, suspected of complicity, was arrested and banished. Later, the palace was the home of the presidents of Colombia at various times until 1980. At present it houses the Ministry of Foreign Affairs. Opposite is the **Teatro Colón** ⓘ *C 10, No 5-32*, which opened in 1892 on the 400th anniversary of Columbus' discovery of America. It presents operas, ballets, plays and concerts and is the home of the Colombian Symphony Orchestra which performs there regularly. The auditorium is late 19th century, lavishly decorated and seats 1200. There are plans to offer guided tours of the theatre in 2015. Next door is the **Fundación Rafael Pombo** ⓘ *C 10/Cra 5-22, www.fundacionrafaelpombo.org*, named after the writer of children's books who lived here. The foundation is dedicated to services to children, and has a library, workshops and a film studio.

Across Carrera 5 is the **Museo Militar** ⓘ *C 10, No 4-92, Tue-Sun 0830-1630, free*. The building was originally constructed as part of the National University but now houses a interesting collection of weapons. There is also a detailed presentation of the Independence campaign of 1819.

One block north is the **Casa de Moneda** (**The Mint**) ⓘ *C 11, No 4-93, www. banrepcultural.org, Mon-Sat 0900-1900, Sun and holidays 1000-1700, closed Tue, free*. The mint was established on this site in 1620, although the present building dates from 1753, constructed with traditional materials including stone and adobe. Note the courtyard and thick walled arcades. The exhibition traces the history of currency from the earliest trading in gold, salt and tumbago to the present day. There is good commentary (much also in English) with interactive exhibits. The hoard of 1630 coins, known as the *Tesoro del Mesuno*, which was found in 1936 on a small island in the Río Magdalena, is displayed. There is a coin and banknote exhibition upstairs and occasional art shows. Next door, there is a permanent display of Fernando Botero's work in the **Museo Botero** ⓘ *C 11, No 4-41, www. banrepcultural.org, Mon-Sat 0900-1900, Sun 1000-1700, closed Tue, free*, with three salons of his sculptures and paintings as well as an impressive collection of works by Picasso, Matisse, Lucian Freud, Henry Moore, Dalí and Giacometti, among others. Well worth a visit.

Opposite, and running the full block between Carrera 4 and Carrera 5, is the **Biblioteca Luis Angel Arango** ⓘ *C 11, No 4-14, T1-343 1224, www.banrepcultural. org, Mon-Sat 0800-2000, Sun 0800-1600, free*. A facility of the Banco de la República, this library has one of the best collections in Latin America. There are research rooms, art galleries, three reading rooms and internet services on the second and third floors. Public concerts are held in the splendid concert hall and are usually cheap or free. The cafeteria on the sixth floor has a good view and reasonable food. The library is very popular with students, who will be found queuing an hour before it opens at 0800 to secure a study place in the reading room.

100 metres
100 yards

**Sights** ○
Colegio de San Bartolomé
   1 C5
Colegio Mayor de Nuestra
   Señora del Rosario 2 C3
Colegio Salesiano
   León XIII 3 C5
La Imprenta 4 C5

**Where to stay** ⊜
Abadía Colonial 1 B4
Alegría's Hostel 13 B5
Ambala 2 C3
Casa Platypus 3 B2
The Cranky Croc 11 B3
Hostal Fátima 4 B3
Hostal Sue 5 B3
Hostal Sue Candelaria 6 B3
Hotel de la Opera 7 C5

San Sebastián 10 B3
Swiss Hostal Martinik 8 B4

**Restaurants** 🍴
Asociación Construimos
   Futuro 1 B3
La Cicuta 5 A5
La Paella 2 C4
La Totuma 3 B3
Moros y Cristianos 4 C6
Rosita 6 B3
Sopas de Mamá y Postres
   de la Abuela 7 D5

**Bars & clubs** 🍸
Escobar y Rosas 9 B3
Quiebra Canto 10 C2

TransMilenio 🚉

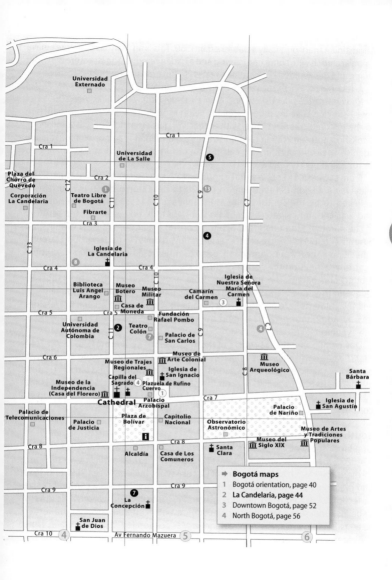

Universidad Externado

Cra 1

Cra 1

⑤

Universidad de La Salle

Cra 2

Plaza del Chorro de Quevedo

C 12

①

C 11

C 10

C 9

⑬

Corporación La Candelaria

Teatro Libre de Bogotá

Fibrarte

Cra 3

④

C 13

Iglesia de La Candelaria

⑧

Cra 4

Cra 4

Iglesia de Nuestra Señora María del Carmen

Biblioteca Luis Angel Arango

Museo Botero

Museo Militar

Camarín del Carmen

③

Casa de Moneda

Cra 5

Cra 5

Universidad Autónoma de Colombia

②

Teatro Colón

⑦

Fundación Rafael Pombo

Palacio de San Carlos

C 9

④

Cra 6

Museo de Arte Colonial

Museo de Trajes Regionales

Iglesia de San Ignacio

Museo Arqueológico

Capilla del Sagrado

④

Plazuela de Rufino Cuervo

Museo de la Independencia (Casa del Florero)

①

Santa Bárbara

Palacio Arzobispal

Cathedral

Cra 7

Iglesia de San Agustín

Palacio de Telecomunicaciones

Palacio de Justicia

Plaza de Bolívar

Palacio de Nariño

Capitolio Nacional

Observatorio Astronómico

ℹ

Cra 8

Cra 8

Museo de Artes y Tradiciones Populares

Alcaldía

Casa de Los Comuneros

Santa Clara

Museo del Siglo XIX

Cra 9

Cra 9

⑦

La Concepción

➡ **Bogotá maps**

1  Bogotá orientation, page 40
2  **La Candelaria, page 44**
3  Downtown Bogotá, page 52
4  North Bogotá, page 56

San Juan de Dios

Cra 10

④

Av Fernando Mazuera

⑤

⑥

On the corner of Calle 11/Carrera 4 is **Iglesia de La Candelaria**, part of an Augustinian friary originally established in 1560. This is an 18th-century three-nave colonial church with some fine carving and a gilded reredos. The structure is in poor shape and desperate steps have been taken to buttress the southwest corner.

A few blocks north of here is **Casa de Poesía Silva** ⓘ *C 12C, No 3-41, T1-286 5710, www.casadepoesiasilva.com, Mon-Fri 0900-1800, 1400-1800, free*. The poet José Asunción Silva lived here until his death in 1895. This is a good introduction to the restored colonial house, with a peaceful garden patio. There is a museum, bookshop and a fine audio and book library with taped readings of almost every Spanish-speaking author. CDs can be bought in the bookshop. There are also lectures and poetry readings.

From the Casa de Poesía to Calle 14/Carrera 2, turn right up a delightful narrow alleyway (Callejón del Embudo) to the **Plaza del Chorro de Quevedo**. This is believed to be the centre of the Muisca village of Teusaquillo (or Tibsaquillo) and was certainly where Jiménez de Quesada took possession of the territory in the name of King Charles of Spain to form the kingdom of New Granada on 6 August 1538. The centre of the city later moved down to flatter ground (around what is now the Parque Santander), but a commemorative chapel (now a cultural centre) was built on the corner of this plaza and many other houses were built around and below. The name dates from about 1800 when Father Francisco Quevedo provided a *chorro* (well) for the local people. Throughout the day you will see students here taking a break from their studies at the several universities nearby, adding to the activity (and the safety) of the area until around 2000 in the evening.

Down Calle 13 is the first home of the **Teatro Libre de Bogotá** ⓘ *C 12, No 2-44, T1-281 4834, www.teatrolibre.com*. It still houses a professional acting school with occasional public performances, although the main home of this company is now in Chapinero (see page 54). Also on this street is the **Corporación La Candelaria** ⓘ *C 13, No 2-58*, part of the government of the barrio and an information point. Look in at the attractive colonial patio with its trees and lawns.

## South of Plaza Bolívar

One block south of the plaza is the museum of **Santa Clara** ⓘ *Cra 8, No 8-91, T1-337 6762, Tue-Fri 0900-1700, Sat and Sun 1000-1600, US$1.60, reduction for students*, formerly the church of the convent of Clarissa nuns, built between 1619 and 1630 and preserved very much as it was in the 17th century. There is a comprehensive collection of religious art, including paintings by Gregorio Vázquez de Arce y Ceballos, and some fine interior decoration with coffered ceilings and lattice screens behind which the nuns attended Mass concealed from the public. Note the extensive remains of the original wall paintings. Though discreet signs on the walls tell you what to look for, a guide is a great help; ask at the entrance. Concerts are occasionally staged here.

Opposite is the **Observatorio Astronómico**, built in 1802, one of the first in Latin America, while further south, at Carrera 8/Calle 8 is the **Museo del Siglo XIX** ⓘ *Cra 8, No 7-93, T1-281 7362, Mon-Fri 0830-1300 and 1400-1700, Sat 0900-1300,*

*US$1.75*, formerly a private house, renovated in the Republican style around 1880. It was acquired by Bancafé in 1977 and now has a collection of 19th-century paintings, clothes and furniture. The *Botica de los pobres* is a fascinating recreation of a 'poor man's chemist' shop of the period. Note the decoration of the rooms on the second floor and the staircase woodwork. A 19th-century-style coffee shop on the site serves good coffee, mini sandwiches and snacks – not cheap, but very pleasant. There are newspapers and books to read.

The entrance to the **Palacio** (or **Casa**) **de Nariño**, the presidential palace, is on Calle 7. It has a spectacular interior with a fine collection of contemporary Colombian paintings. Enquire if there are guided tours. The changing of the guard ceremony normally takes place on Monday, Wednesday, Friday and Sunday at 1730.

Opposite is the **Iglesia de San Agustín** ⓘ *Cra 7, No 6-25, T1-246 4195, Mon-Fri 0700-1800, Sun 0800-1900, closed Sat, free*, built between 1637 and 1668, the tower being a later addition. It is richly ornamented with an interesting coffered ceiling in the crypt. Note the ceilings and chandeliers in the nave. There are several paintings by Gregorio Vázquez de Arce y Ceballos. The Image of Jesus was proclaimed Generalissimo of the army in 1812.

East of here is the **Museo Arqueológico** ⓘ *Cra 6, No 7-43, Tue-Fri 0830-1700, Sat 0900-1600, free*, which is sponsored by the Banco Popular. This is the restored mansion of the Marqués de San Jorge, which is itself a beautiful example of 17th-century Spanish colonial architecture. The museum is arranged in themes rather than periods and is not well labelled. However, it has an impressive and comprehensive collection of decorated ceramics from all the early cultures of Colombia. The restored murals of the original house are also interesting.

A block further east is the **Iglesia de Nuestra Señora María del Carmen** ⓘ *Cra 5, No 8-36, T1-342 0972*, the most striking church in Bogotá. The architecture is bright and interesting with a graceful western tower and fine cupola over the transept, all in red and white bricks and stones. It has been repainted to brighten up this corner of La Candelaria. Inside the red and white motif continues with elegant arches and an impressive altar. The stained-glass windows, unusually illustrating fruit and flowers, are slanted to give maximum light to the congregation, and the windows in the apse are particularly fine. The overall impression of freshness and light is emphasized by the detail in the rose windows of the clerestory and the intricate ornamentation inside and outside the building. Time your visit to see inside; Masses are normally held at 0700, 1200 and 1830. Next to the church along Carrera 5 is the **Colegio Salesiano Leon XIII**, a boys' college. Inside, a cobbled 'street' leads upwards, flanked on the left by three courtyards and the buildings of the former Carmelite community, all in the same style as the church. On the corner of Carrera 5/Calle 9 is the former Carmelite chapel with its bell tower above; a rounded balcony on Calle 9 houses the altar. This building, known as the **Camarín del Carmen** ⓘ *entrance at Calle 9, No 4-93*, was faithfully restored in 1957 and is now used as a theatre.

## ON THE ROAD
### Antanas Mockus

In the early 1990s, Bogotá had a reputation as a world capital of anarchic disorder: it was choked with traffic and pollution; kidnappings, murders and car bombings were rife, and much of the population suffered abject poverty.

Enter 'anti-politician' Antanas Mockus, the son of Lithuanian immigrants and a former mathematics professor at the Universidad Nacional de Colombia who served as Mayor of Bogotá for two terms (1995-1997 and 2001-2003) and oversaw the city's transformation into a place where citizens felt safe to walk the streets.

Mockus first came to public attention when he dropped his pants and mooned a class of students. His time in office would be full of equally imaginative stunts.

Many felt that it would take a superhero to restore a sense of moral fibre to a society apparently falling apart at the seams, and Mockus took them at their word, often dressing up in spandex and a cape, taking on the character of 'Supercitizen'.

To combat *bogotanos'* disregard for the highway code, he employed 420 mime artists to mock and shame motorists into heeding stoplights and pedestrian crossings, believing that Colombians were more afraid of ridicule than being fined. When there was a water shortage in the city, he starred in an ad on TV in which he was shown turning off the water while he soaped in the shower.

To tackle gun crime, he offered an amnesty on guns in exchange for food and had the melted metal from the weapons recast as spoons for babies. He also encouraged a 'Ladies' Night' in which men were asked to stay at home while their wives went out on the town.

While there were those who mocked Mockus, labelling him little more than a clown, many of his initiatives were effective. Homicide rates fell from 80 per 100,000 to 23 per 100,000 during his tenure, while traffic accidents decreased by 50% and water usage by 40%. His government managed to provide a sewage system that reached 100% of the population, up from 78%. He even managed to leave a US$700 million surplus to his successor, partly aided by his success in persuading 63,000 people to pay a voluntary extra 10% tax. Diagnosed with Parkinson's disease in 2010, he became the Partido Verde Colombiano (Colombian Green Party) candidate for president the same year, finishing second in the polling and only losing to current president Juan Manuel Santos in the run-off election. Today he maintains a strong social media presence.

### North of Plaza Bolívar

From Plaza Bolívar, Carrera 7 (La Séptima), which was the first important street in the city, runs four blocks to Avenida Jiménez de Quesada, which connects the administrative centre of the city with Parque Santander, the first residential area and now the commercial hub of the capital. This street is locally known as the Calle Real del Comercio.

On the corner of Carrera 7/Calle 12A, on the site of the colonial church of Santo Domingo, is the **Palacio de Telecomunicaciones**, the headquarters of the country's postal services. It houses the **Museo Postal** ① *Mon-Fri 0830-1630*. Up Calle 13 and left at Carrera 6 there are two universities: **La Gran Colombia** and **Colegio Mayor de Nuestra Señora del Rosario,** near the corner at Calle 14, No 6-25. The latter is the second oldest in Bogotá, founded by Father Cristóbal de Torres of the order of Santo Domingo in the 16th century, and is a typical cloistered school of the period. **José Celestino Mutis**, the botanist, taught natural sciences and medicine here. You can buy a good cheap lunch at the cafeteria and great crêpes. Alongside is the chapel of the Order – **La Bordalita**. Inside is an embroidered Virgin made by Queen Isabel de Borbón for Father Cristóbal on his appointment as Archbishop of Santa Fe de Bogotá. The elegant façade has some fine stone carvings above the entrance.

**Museo de Bogotá** ① *Cra 4, No 10-18, T1-352 1865, www.museodebogota.gov. co, Tue-Fri 0900-1700, Sat-Sun 1000-1600, free*, depicts the history of the city. It's housed inside Casa Sámano.

## Parque Santander

Although not strictly in the Barrio de La Candelaria, the cluster of interesting buildings around the Parque Santander are part of Old Bogotá and include three of the finest churches in Colombia.

After crossing Jiménez de Quesada, the **Iglesia de San Francisco** ① *www. templodesanfrancisco.com, Mon-Fri 0630-2000, Sat 0630-1240, 1600-2000 Sun 0630-1400, 1630-2000, holidays 0800-1300*, is immediately to your left. It is an interesting mid-16th-century church with paintings of famous Franciscans, choir stalls, an ornate, gold high altar (dated 1622) and a fine Lady Chapel with blue and gold ornamentation. The remarkable ceiling is in Spanish *mudéjar* (Moorish) style. Try to see this church when it's fully illuminated. Behind it along Avenida Jiménez de Quesada is the **Palacio de San Francisco** ① *Av Jiménez Nos 7-50*, built between 1918 and 1933 for the Gobernación de Cundinamarca, on the site of the Franciscan friary. Designed in the Republican style, it has a fine façade and competed to some degree with the Capitolio Nacional. It is now part of the Rosario University.

Next to the San Francisco church and overlooking Parque Santander is the **Iglesia de la Veracruz**, first built eight years after the founding of Bogotá, but rebuilt in 1731 and again in 1904. In 1910 it became the Panteón Nacional e Iglesia de la República. José de Caldas, the famous scientist, was buried under the church along with many other patriots, victims of the Spanish 'Reign of Terror' around 1815. It has a bright white-and-red interior and a fine decorated ceiling. Fashionable weddings are held here.

Across Calle 16 is the third major church, **La Tercera Orden**, a colonial church famous for its carved woodwork along the nave and a high balcony, massive wooden altar reredos and confessionals. It was built by the Third Franciscan Order in the 17th century.

## ★Emeralds

Thinking about buying a diamond? Think again. A fine emerald is a much rarer gemstone, and the finest emeralds in the world hail from Colombia. Like diamonds, emeralds are evaluated according to the four 'C's – Colour, Clarity, Cut and Carat weight – although colour, not clarity, is considered the most important attribute. A dark green emerald is considered the most precious variety, although they vary in colour. Unlike other gemstones, all emeralds have flaws or 'inclusions'. However, rather than detracting from their value, inclusions are said to give an emerald its personality.

If you are in the market for a stone, go to Avenida Jiménez in Bogotá, which is the heart of Colombia's unofficial emerald exchange, and visit the Emerald Trade Center, among other vendors. The emeralds sold in this area come from Colombia's three most prolific mines – Muzo, Coscuez and Chivor – all located in the cloudforests of Boyacá, just a few hours to the north. These mines have a long history that dates back to AD 1000, long before the Spanish invasion. To catch a glimpse of some exquisite examples of emerald jewellery from pre-Hispanic times, check out the Museo del Oro, see below.

## ★Museo del Oro

*C 16, No 5-41, T1-343 2222, www.banrepcultural.org/museo-del-oro. Tue-Sat 0900-1900 (last entry 1800), Sun and holidays 1000-1700 (last entry 1600). US$1.60, free on Sun.*

On the northeast corner of the Parque de Santander is the **Museo del Oro** (the Gold Museum) in the splendid premises of the Banco de la República. This collection is a 'must', as it is perhaps the finest museum in all of South America. There are more than 35,000 pieces of pre-Columbian goldwork in the total collection, most of which is held here, with the rest divided between other regional Museos de Oro throughout Colombia (all of which are worth a visit).

Two upper floors are devoted to the dozen or so pre-Spanish indigenous groups that have been identified in Colombian territory, and how they found and worked gold and other metals. It is a fascinating story, illustrated by many examples of their work. They used techniques that some might say are unsurpassed by goldsmiths of today. The first floor sets the scene: each culture is placed in its geographical and historical environment and the characteristics of their art are described. Illustrative models include one of Ciudad Perdida as it would have looked when inhabited. In each section there are helpful portable boards with explanatory notes in English. The second floor has many more examples of the extraordinary goldwork of these pre-Columbian peoples. The centrepiece of the exhibition is the Salón Dorado, a glittering display of 8000 pieces inside an inner vault – an unforgettable experience.

On the ground floor is a souvenir/bookshop and exhibition rooms. Audio guides can be hired at the ticket office. On the first floor, 20-minute films are shown throughout the day; times and languages are displayed.

# ★Monserrate

*T1-284 5700 (answer service also in English), www.cerromonserrate.com. Funicular every 30 mins, Mon-Sat 0745-1145, Sun and holidays 0530-1700; cable car every 20 mins Mon-Sat 1200-2300, Sun and holidays 0900-1700 (times change frequently). Fares: Mon-Sat before 1700, US$4.30 one way; Mon-Sat after 1700, US$8.90 return; Sun US$2.45 one way.*

There is a very good view of the city from the top of Monserrate (3152 m), the lower of the two peaks rising sharply to the east. It is reached by a funicular railway and a cable car. From the summit, the city's tiled roofs spread out below, with the plains beyond stretching to the rim of the Sabana. Sunrise and sunset can be spectacular. The convent at the top is a popular shrine and pilgrimage site. The **Calle del Candelero**, a reconstruction of a Bogotá street of 1887, has plenty of street stalls and snack bars. There are also two upmarket touristy restaurants at the top, both overpriced and closed Sunday. Behind the church are popular picnic grounds.

If you wish to walk up, possibly the safest time is at the weekend about 0500, before the crowds arrive but when there are people about. At this time you will catch the sunrise. The path is dressed stone and comfortably graded all the way up with refreshment stalls at weekends every few metres. It takes about one hour 15 minutes to walk up (if you don't stop).

**Safety**  There have been reports of tourists being mugged at both the summit and the foot of the hill, even during the day. Keep cameras, wallets and other valuables hidden. It is best not to walk to the top of Monserrate alone, and on no account walk down in the dark. You should also take a bus or taxi to/from the foot of the hill; there are usually taxis waiting by the footbridge across the road. The walk up to Guadalupe, the higher peak opposite Monserrate, is not recommended.

## Quinta de Bolívar

*C 20, No 2-91 Este, T1-336 6419, www.quintadebolivar.gov.co. Tue-Sat 0900-1700, Sun 1000-1600. US$1.60, reductions for students and children, free entry Sun; guided tours available.*

At the foot of Monserrate is the Quinta de Bolívar, a fine colonial mansion with splendid gardens and lawns. There are several cannons captured at the battle of Boyacá. The elegant house, once Bolívar's home, is now a museum showing some of his personal possessions and paintings of events in his career. Opposite the Quinta is the attractive campus of the prestigious private university, Los Andes.

Downtown Bogotá, the old commercial centre with shops, offices and banks, runs in a band northwards from Avenida Jiménez de Quesada. It is very patchy, with a thorough mix of architectural styles, including modern towers and colonial buildings in various states of repair. This commercial hub narrows to a thin band of secondary shops extending between Carrera 7 and Avenida Caracas to around Calle 60.

Despite the migration north of company headquarters and offices in recent years, this area seems busier than ever. The streets are full of life; they are also often paralysed by traffic and choked with fumes. The pavements can be very congested too, particularly Carrera 7 and Avenida (Calle) 19. However, the former is closed to traffic every Sunday 0700-1400, creating a totally different atmosphere. For the visitor, there are plenty of attractions and accommodation options. Safety remains an issue in this area, but conditions are improving. For the sights around Parque de Santander, see page 49.

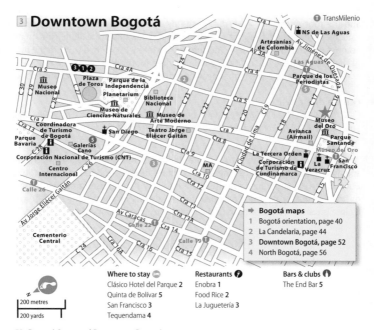

### 3 Downtown Bogotá

➡ **Bogotá maps**
1 Bogotá orientation, page 40
2 La Candelaria, page 44
3 Downtown Bogotá, page 52
4 North Bogotá, page 56

| Where to stay 🛏 | Restaurants 🍴 | Bars & clubs 🍸 |
|---|---|---|
| Clásico Hotel del Parque **2** | Enobra **1** | The End Bar **5** |
| Quinta de Bolívar **5** | Food Rice **2** | |
| San Francisco **3** | La Juguetería **3** | |
| Tequendama **4** | | |

200 metres
200 yards

## Avenida Jiménez de Quesada

One of Bogotá's best-known streets follows the curves and bends of a riverbed (which, incidentally, was opened up in 2000). **Iglesia de Nuestra Señora de las Aguas** ① *Cra 3, No 18-66*, is a charming 17th-century church overlooking a small park and Avenida Jiménez de Quesada. It has a wide façade with seven bells. The name refers to the San Francisco river, which now flows under the avenida. It has a single nave and a baroque altar, with a wood carving of tropical fruits at its base. The convent next door has been inhabited by Dominicans for over a century, serving as both a hospital and a school; it is now occupied by **Artesanías de Colombia** ① *Cra 2, No 18A-58, www.artesaniasdecolombia.com.co*, one of the best places to buy local crafts.

## Along Carrera 7

**Teatro Jorge Eliécer Gaitán** ① *Cra 7, No 22-47, T1-334 6800, www.teatrojorgeeliecer. gov.co*, built in art-deco style around 1945 as a movie house, is now one of the biggest theatres in the country, holding an audience of over 1500 for shows, concerts and theatre productions.

**Iglesia de San Diego** ① *Cra 7, No 26-37*, was built around 1606 by the Franciscans, with a chapel to the Virgin added in 1629. There is a fine statue of Our Lady in the chapel dedicated to the countryside (which surrounded it when it was built). The adjoining monastery was built about 1560, and its fine Moorish ceiling can still be seen. Local craft items are sold here.

**Museo de Arte Moderno** ① *C 24, No 6-00, T1-286 0466, www.mambogota.com, Tue-Sat 1000-1800, Sun 1200-1630, US$2.10, half price for students and seniors, photography only allowed by prior arrangement*, occupies an appropriately modern building, inaugurated in 1953. It has an interesting, well-displayed collection of modern Colombian art, with sculptures, graphic arts and other media represented. There's also a good café and bookshop.

On the east side of Carrera 7, the Parque de la Independencia is popular at weekends though not recommended for visits during the week. In the park is the **Planetarium** ① *C26, No 5-93, T1-281 4150, www.planetariodebogota.gov.co, Tue-Sun (and holidays) 1000-1700, free entrance, events US$6.25*, offering lectures, courses, seminars and a public astronomical show. There are occasional son et lumière shows, and there's also a good **internet café** ① *US$1 per hr*. Beside the park is the **Plaza de Toros** (**Bull Ring**) ① *9 Parque de los Mártires (Park of the Martyrs), Cra 6, No 26-50*, with a monument in memory of the many patriots shot by the Spanish during the struggle for Independence. The brick bull ring was built in 1927 and has a capacity of 16,000. Access to the bullfighting museum is through door No 6.

To the northeast is the **Museo Nacional** ① *Cra 7, No 28-66, T1-381 6470, www. museonacional.gov.co, Tue-Sat 1000-1800, Sun 1000-1700, free, various tours available*, founded by Santander in 1823 and later moved to this building, designed by Thomas Reed (see Capitolio Nacional) around 1900 as a prison. It houses a well-displayed archaeological collection, one of the best in the country. Even if you are short of time, try to see this display. There is a collection of gold items in the vault. The top floor has a fine art section, comprising 20th-century national paintings and sculptures. There's an expensive but good café serving salads and desserts named after the exhibits.

The centre of Bogotá comes to a natural end where Carreras 7 to 13 come together beyond the Centro Internacional, a large complex that includes the Tequendama Hotel. In the link between central and north Bogotá, there are a number of places of interest.

Along Calle 26 is the **Cementerio Central**, an oval-shaped construction full of large mausoleums and pine trees. This is Bogotá's principal cemetery, built between 1830 and 1929, and it is the resting place of many of Colombian history's most influential figures. Among them are Luis Carlos Galán, a liberal politician and journalist who was assassinated during the drug wars of the late 1980s, and the murdered leader of the M19 guerrilla group, Carlos Pizarro. Round the corner from the inner ellipse is the grave of Leo S Kopp, founder of Bavaria, Colombia's largest beer company. Presided by an impressive bronze statue, the site has something of a cult following (see box, opposite).

★Nearby is the **Plaza del Mercado de Paloquemao** ① *Av 19 with Cra 25, www.plazadepaloquemao.com*, an enormous covered market with over 1800 stalls selling fruit and vegetables, meats, herbs and flowers as well as some handicrafts. To catch the flower market in full flow, visit between 0500 and 1000; Friday and Sunday are the best days (see page 65).

**Casa Museo Jorge Eliécer Gaitán** ① *C 42, No 15-52, www.casamuseogaitan. blogspot.com Tue-Fri 0900-1700, Sat-Sun 1000-1400, free*, is the former residence of the populist leader whose assassination in April 1948 triggered the infamous 'Bogotazo', at the outset of La Violencia. The museum is dedicated to this period of Colombia's history.

The **Museo de Arte y Cultura Colsubsidio** ① *C 36, No 5A-19, T1-744 7667, www. colsubsidio.com*, has exhibitions of contemporary artists and other special events.

**Instituto Nacional de Investigaciones Geológico-Mineras** (INGEOMINAS) ① *Diagonal 53, No 34-53, T1-220 0200, www.ingeominas.gov.co*, has a library and pleasant museum. It is in the corner of the Universidad National campus, close to other Earth Science institutions including the Instituto Geográfico Agustín Codazzi.

The natural sciences are presented in a child-friendly way at the **Museo de los Niños** ① *Cra 60, No 63-27, T1-742 8981, www.museodelosninos.org.co, Mon-Fri 0900-1600, weekends and holidays 1000-1600, US$2.20 for 30-min tour, purchase tickets 20 mins in advance.*

There are two important theatres in this area. The **Teatro Nacional** ① *C 71, No 10-25, T1-256 1399, www.teatronacional.com.co*, hosts traditional performances by national and international artists and has important facilities for training young people. (It has other premises in North Bogotá at C 95, No 47-15.) The **Teatro Libre de Bogotá** ① *Cra 11, No 61-80, T1-217 1988, www.teatrolibre.com*, has frequent performances; it has another theatre in La Candelaria (see page 46).

★**Jardín Botánico José Celestino Mutis** ① *C 63, No 68-95, T1-437 7060, www. jbb.gov.co, Mon-Fri 0800-1700, Sat, Sun and hols 0900-1700, US$1.40 adult, US$0.75*

## Good Kopp

The tomb of Leo S Kopp in Bogotá's Cementerio Central has something of a cult following. Kopp, of German origin, founded Bavaria Beer, Colombia's largest brewery. Famously generous, he was known to find employment for anyone who came and asked him.

It appears that his capacity for giving continues after his death. On any given day it's not uncommon to see the poor and the unemployed laying flowers at his grave or kissing the magnificent bronze statue that guards it. Rumour has it that the statue retains its radiance thanks to a civil servant who, having prayed at the feet of Kopp's statute, was rewarded with a job and now shows his gratitude by secretly cleaning and shining the effigy.

*child*, is an interesting and well-organized botanical garden, with a collection of over 5000 native orchids, plus roses, gladioli and trees from all over the country. If you can't get to the national parks, you can at least see many of the local species here. It has a fine documentation centre with resident experts.

**Maloka Centro Interactivo de Ciencia y Tecnología** ⓘ *Cra 68D, No 24A-51, T1-427 2707, www.maloka.org, Mon-Fri 0800-1700, weekends and holidays 1000-1700, US$12.50 including cinema*, is a complex of science exhibits and instructive entertainment for all ages. There are over 200 exhibits in nine halls, a 135° large-screen cinema, internet rooms, restaurants and other facilities. A full visit takes about three hours.

## North of the centre

hotels, restaurants and shopping malls

Beyond Calle 60, the main city continues north to a comparatively new area, North Bogotá, where there has been great commercial expansion with the development of wealthy suburbs. Most of the best hotels and restaurants are in this area, which is regarded as the safest in Bogotá. The T-shaped area made up by Calle 83 and Carrera 13 is the **Zona Rosa**, also known as the Zona T, where many bars, clubs and restaurants can be found. Small towns, such as **Chapinero**, **Chicó** and **Usaquén** have been absorbed, and the city now extends north to around Calle 200. Many commercial and financial companies have moved here but most government offices and many businesses remain downtown.

North Bogotá is noted for its huge, lavish shopping malls, which have sprung up in the last few years. They are worth a visit even if the prices don't grab you. The **Hacienda Santa Bárbara** ⓘ *Cra 7 115-60, www.haciendasantabarbara.com.co*, has been constructed within a large country mansion, and parts of the colonial architecture, arches, and stone floors have been incorporated. Even some of the old gardens have been retained.

**Museo de 'El Chicó' Mercedes Sierra de Pérez** ⓘ *Cra 7, No 93-01, www.museo delchico.com, Mon-Fri 1000-1300, 1400-1700, guided tours US$3.75,* formerly the **Hacienda de El Chicó**, is a fine example of colonial architecture. It contains a worldwide collection of mostly 18th-century porcelain, furniture and paintings.

## Usaquén

Usaquén was once one of the more important towns, but has now been absorbed by the growing metropolis of Bogotá. The small plaza in the centre has become an attractive shopping and restaurant area, popular in the evenings. The railway station can be used for the tourist train to Zipaquirá at weekends (see Transport, page 71, for more details). **World Trade Center** ⓘ *C 100, No 8A-55, T657 8757, www. wtcbogota.com.co,* is a large convention and exhibition centre with all the usual services. The **Bogotá Royal Hotel** is alongside.

## 4 North Bogotá

**Bogotá maps**
1 Bogotá orientation, page 40
2 La Candelaria, page 44
3 Downtown Bogotá, page 52
4 North Bogotá, page 56

🚇 TransMilenio

| Where to stay 🛏 | Restaurants 🍴 | Salto del Angel 12 |
|---|---|---|
| Andino Royal 1 | 80 Sillas 5 | Wok 13 |
| H Sasson 5 | Camino del Café 8 | Yumi Yumi 1 |
| Morrison Hotel 2 | El Corral Gourmet 6 | |
| Viaggio Suites 3 | K-Listo 9 | **Bars & clubs** 🍸 |
| Windsor House 4 | La Hamburguesería 11 | Alma 14 |

500 metres
500 yards

## Tourist information

There are 10 tourist information kiosks dotted around the city, including in **La Candelaria** at Pl Bolívar, Cra 8, No 10-83, T1-283 7115, Mon-Sat 0700-1800, Sun 0800-1700, at the **Centro Internacional**, Cra 13, No 26-62, T1-286 2248, Mon-Sat 0900-1800, in the **Unicentro** shopping centre, Av 15 No 123-30, zona exterior, T1-637 4482, Mon-Sat 1100-1900, Sun 1000-1800, and at the airport and the bus station. The Candelaria office is friendly and helpful and can supply good local guidebooks and maps.

## Where to stay

Accommodation is plentiful in Bogotá. All 3 sections of the city have top-class and middle-range hotels but budget travellers will find more choice in the **Downtown** and **La Candelaria** areas. If possible, book hotels in advance, even if only from the airport or bus terminal. For hostel organizations, see page 26.

Taxi drivers at the airport or bus station occasionally say that the hotel you have chosen is 'closed', or that they've never heard of it, especially the cheaper ones listed in La Candelaria. Insist they take you to the right address.

**Note** In 2011 there were a spate of attacks targeting backpacker hostels in La Candelaria. CCTV cameras have since been added on many streets and safety has improved, but it's still best to exercise caution in La Candelaria at night.

### La Candelaria

**$$$ Hotel de la Opera**
*C 10, No 5-72, T1-336 2066,*
*www.hotelopera.com.co.*
This privately owned hotel was previously the residency of Simón Bolívar's personal guard. Spread out over 2 buildings, 1 colonial, 1 Republican, now joined together, this is Colombian opulence at its best, with period pieces adorning its exquisite rooms. It has 2 rooftop restaurants with superb views as well as a sauna, Turkish bath, jacuzzi, gym, bar and pool. The junior suites have original bathtubs.

**$$$-$$ Abadía Colonial**
*C 11, No 2-32, T1-341 1884,*
*www.abadiacolonial.com.*
Fine colonial building in the heart of La Candelaria, with comfortable but smallish rooms. Best to ask for a street-facing room as otherwise they have no windows. Rooms have Wi-Fi, cable TV and safe. The restaurant serves Italian food.

**$$$-$$ Casa Platypus**
*Cra 3, No 12f-28, T1-281 1801,*
*www.casaplatypusbogota.com.*
In a beautiful colonial building overlooking the Parque de los Periodistas. Excellent rooms, a kitchen and a fine roof terrace with views of Monserrate. Wi-Fi and good breakfasts. Highly recommended.

**$$ Ambalá**
*Cra 5, No 12b-46, T1-342 6384,*
*www.hotelambala.net.*
In a pretty colonial building, Ambalá's rooms are clean but a little small and with dated decor.

### $$ San Sebastián
*Av Jiménez, No 3-97, T1-243 8937.*
The lobby of this hotel has some amusing Picasso imitation murals. It was plainly a fashionable location in its time but those days are long gone. The rooms are a little dated but functional and have hot water, Wi-Fi and good writing desks as well as views of Monserrate.

### $$-$ Swiss Hostal Martinik
*Cra 4, No 11-88, T1-283 3180,*
*www.hostalmartinik.com.*
New Canadian management. Great location and good facilities. US$11 pp in dorm, also private rooms.

### $ Alegrías Hostel
*C 9, No 2-13, T1-282 3168,*
*www.alegriashostel.com.*
New hostel in the heart of La Candelaria, set around a pleasant patio. 10- and 7-bed dorms available.

### $ The Cranky Croc
*C 12d, No 3-46, T1-342 2438,*
*www.crankycroc.com.*
This Aussie-run hostel is located in a beautiful 300-year-old building, carefully restored to retain many of the original features. Excellent facilities include Wi-Fi, free luggage storage and a lounge with a fireplace. Has several private rooms with bathrooms and dorms with bunks. Restaurant with varied breakfast menus and good cocktails.

### $ Hostal Fátima
*C 12c, No 2-24, T1-281 6389,*
*www.hostalfatima.com.*
**Fátima** is a maze of brightly coloured rooms and sunny patios with lots of stained-glass windows and potted plants. It has lots of added bonuses such as a sauna and jacuzzi, a TV room and even a dance studio teaching contemporary and jazz dance, yoga and pilates. Has several private rooms with bathrooms as well as dorms with bunks. Nice bar, also open to the public. Offers IH and student discounts. Long-term stays available, ask at reception.

### $ Hostal Sue and Hostal Sue Candelaria
*C 12f, No 2; Cra 3, No 12c-18,*
*T1-334 8894 and T1-341 2647,*
*www.suecandelaria.com.*
Both have excellent facilities, including Wi-Fi, kitchen, free lockers, hot water, laundry service and hammocks for relaxing. The Candelaria one also has a ping-pong table. **Hostal Sue** is for a younger, party crowd, while **Hostal Sue Candelaria** is for those seeking a quieter atmosphere. Dorms with bunks available.

## Downtown Bogotá

The downtown area of Bogotá suffers from petty crime and muggings by night.

### $$$ Augusta
*Jimenez, No 4-77, T1-283 8300, www.hotelaugusta.com.co.*
Another traditional Bogotá hotel, **Augusta** has large rooms with minibar, cable TV and Wi-Fi, as well as a sauna, gym and restaurant.

### $$$ Tequendama
*Cra 10, No 26-21, T1-382 0300, www.sht.com.co.*
Colombia's largest hotel, the **Tequendama** has been witness to some of Colombia's most important political events since its inauguration in 1953. With 2 restaurants, a spa, pool, Wi-Fi throughout and large rooms and suites, it is well equipped for the conferences it invariably hosts.

### $$ Clásico Hotel del Parque
*C 24, No 4A-79 (esq Cra 5), T1-284 2200, www.hoteldelparqueclasico.inf.travel.*
In the heart of the Centro Internacional, this 1980s hotel has had little work done on it since it was built, but it does have a pool, sauna, Wi-Fi and breakfast included.

### $$ Quinta de Bolívar
*Cra 4, No 17-59, T1-337 6496.*
Located on the edge of La Candelaria, this Republican-era building has cosy rooms and breakfast is included. Wi-Fi, sauna and jacuzzi.

### $$ San Francisco
*Cra 10, No 23-63, T1-286 1677, www.sfcol.com.*
This modern hotel has good-sized rooms, a restaurant, Wi-Fi, free breakfasts and free transfer to and from the airport. Welcome drink upon arrival.

## Chapinero and around

### $$$ Casa Medina
*Cra 7, No 69A-22, T1-312 0299, www.hotelcharlestoncasamedina.com.*
Built in 1945 by Santiago Medina, with stone columns and carved wooden doors, this hotel is Bogotá at its most refined. It has a gym, Wi-Fi, iPod docks, a gym and a fine restaurant in a wood-panelled room. A new tower has been added with 34 additional rooms.

### $$ Casona del Patio
*Cra 8, No 69-24, T1-212 8805, www.lacasonadelpatio.net.*
With 24 immaculate rooms set around a sunny patio and well situated near the Zona G, this is one of the best mid-range options in Bogotá. Cable TV and Wi-Fi. Recommended.

### $$ Hotel Lord
*C 63, No 14-62.*
Popular with Colombian businessmen, some of the rooms are a little small with windows that face onto corridors but those with a street view are good value. Has an internet room and a restaurant.

### $$ Las Terrazas
*C 54A, No 3-12, T1-255 5777.*
Well placed in a quiet area of Chapinero Alto, this hotel is popular with foreigners. The building is an interesting shape, a kind of half pyramid, meaning that each room has a large balcony with excellent views of the city. Wi-Fi and cable TV. First 2 floors are student residences.

## North of the centre

### $$$ Andino Royal
*C 85, No 12-28, T1-651 3100, www.hotelesroyal.com.*
Well placed between Parque 93 and the Zona Rosa, this modern hotel has

all the conveniences you would expect, including a gym, Wi-Fi and cable TV. The rooms are light and airy with large windows.

### $$$ Morrison Hotel
*C 84 Bis, No 13-54, T1-266 3111, www.morrisonhotel.com.*
Conveniently located near the Zona T, this recently refurbished hotel, with a contemporary British design, has large rooms with Wi-Fi, LCD TVs and thermo-acoustic windows. It looks out onto the beautiful Parque León de Greiff. A bar and restaurant have recently been added to the premises.

### $$$ Windsor House
*C 95, No 9-97, T1-634 3630, www.hotelesestelar.com.*
English-style luxury hotel with restaurant and large bedrooms. Some have jacuzzis; all have Wi-Fi, a safe and a minibar. Use of a gym and Turkish bath is included.

### $$$-$$ Viaggio Suites
*Cra 18, No 86A-36, Edif Virrey, T1-744 9999, www.viaggio.com.co.*
Excellent value short-term and medium-let apartments. Spacious, modern and clean with fitted kitchens, daily house keeper and breakfast included. All apartments have Wi-Fi and laundry service. Prices drop for longer stays.

## Restaurants

Restaurants are spread throughout the city. The more exotic and fashionable places to eat are in **North Bogotá** but **La Candelaria** has its bistros and good-value Colombian eateries, as well as more upmarket restaurants. Take local advice if you want to eat really cheaply in markets or from street stalls. Increasingly, restaurants in La Candelaria are also open in the evenings.

## La Candelaria

### $$$ La Cicuta
*C 9A, No 1-95.*
The French chef cooks up a storm in this lovely restaurant, overlooking a beautiful garden. Good vegetarian options and also perfect steaks.

### $$ La Paella
*C 11, No 5-13.*
Opposite the Centro Cultural García Márquez, this restaurant serves Spanish food and specializes in paellas.

### $$ Rosita
*C 13A, No 1A-36.*
On the lovely Plazoleta Chorro de Quevedo, this is a great little breakfast and lunchtime spot. Sells cook-books and has a café with desserts next door.

### $ Asociación Construimos Futuro
*C 15A, No 2-21.*
Good breakfasts served up by a neighbourhood co-operative. Wi-Fi.

### $ La Totuma
*Cra 2, No 12B-90, T1-284 9462.*
On the hip Callejón del Embudo, this restaurant serves economic sushi and other Japanese dishes in colourful surroundings.

### $ Moros y Cristianos
*C 7, N0 5-30.*
Cuban food served in a sunny, glass-covered patio. Live music Fri-Sun nights.

### $ Sopas de Mamá y Postres de la Abuela
*Cra 9, No 10-59, www.sopasypostres.com.co.*
A real *rolo* institution, this restaurant serves traditional Colombian broths such as *ajiaco* and *sancocho* in a beautiful 2nd-floor gallery with stained-glass windows and large panelled wooden doors. Its other speciality is puddings.

## Downtown Bogotá

### $$ Enobra
*Cra 4A, No 26A-37.*
Fashionable, chic restaurant with sparse decor serving tapas and various cuts of steak.

### $$ La Juguetería
*C 27, No 4A-03, T1-300 0869, www. restaurantelajugueteria.com.co.*
A bit like **Andrés Carne de Res** (see page 62) but in town, **La Juguetería** cooks up excellent steaks in a slightly disturbing atmosphere: the restaurant's theme is toys and dolls which hang everywhere; some of the tables are even made out of dolls' heads.

### $ Food Rice
*Cra 4A, No 26C-13.*
This restaurant has a simple but effective formula: it only does rice, but rice dishes from around the world, everything from Chinese to Malaysian to Indian. There are some good vegetarian options. Takeaway delivery service.

## Chapinero and around
Bogotá has several gastronomic zones. The Zona 'G' ('G' stands for gourmet) is much talked about, but **La Macarena**, comprising several blocks along Cra 4, has several very good restaurants at more reasonable prices. Formerly an area frequented by artists, it is now becoming increasingly hip. All of Cra 4 and the side streets leading up to it are packed with a number of appealing restaurants.

### $$$ Criterión
*C 69A, No 5-75, T1-310 1377, www.criterion.com.co.*
This restaurant has minimalist decor and a French-influenced menu of dishes such as foie gras, goat's cheese salad, shellfish and various types of steak as well as a large wine list.

### $$$ Estrella de los Ríos
*C 26D, No 4-50, T1-337 4037, www.estrelladelosrios.com.*
Costeña Estrella calls her small place an 'anti-restaurant'. Her idea is that your dining experience should feel like she is cooking for you at home. Hence, you must book 24 hrs in advance and she reserves the right to turn you away if she doesn't like the look of you! Estrella, the author of several cookbooks, conjures up *costeño* and Cuban food in her intimate kitchen. Highly recommended.

### $$$ H Sasson
*C 9, No 75-70, www.harrysasson.com.*
Harry Sasson is one of Colombia's best known chefs and owns a number of Bogotá's most popular restaurants. **H Sasson** does contemporary Asian food, such as crispy duck and curries, in stylish surroundings.

### $$ Archie's
*C 82, 13-07, www.archies.co.*
A pizza chain that does some of the best gourmet pizzas in all of South America. Pricey, but worth it. Excellent range, outdoor seating, even has a breakfast pizza.

### $$ Artesano
*Cra 4A, No 27-12, www.artesano gourmet.com.*
**Artesano**, specializing in 'woodfire cuisine', does a wide range of pizzas, fish and chicken dishes, all cooked *'a la leña'*.

### $$ La Cigale
*C 69A, No 4-93, T1-249 6839, www.lacigale.com.co.*
This French restaurant does all the Gallic specialities you would expect, including terrines and *magret de canard*.

## $$ Mini-mal
*Cra 4A, No 57-52, T1-347 5464,*
*www.mini-mal.org.*
As the name suggests, the focus of this restaurant/bar/design shop is on minimalism. The menu is contemporary Colombian cuisine with alternative takes on Pacific, Caribbean, Andean and Amazonian recipes.

## $$ Tábula
*C 29 bis, No 5-90.*
Gourmet international menu in stylish surroundings a couple of blocks from La Macarena.

## $ Al Wadi
*C 27, No 4A-14.*
Healthy Lebanese food, including kebabs, falafel and various types of rice.

## $ La Casa de las Sopas
*C 34, No 13-20.*
Excellent lunchtime venue serving traditional Colombian soups and broths, including *ajiaco*, *mondongo* and *sancocho*.

## $ La Hamburguesería
*Cra 4A, No 27-27, www.*
*lahamburgueseria.com.*
This fast-food chain is becoming increasingly popular in Bogotá for the quality of its hamburgers and hotdogs. There are several more outlets spread around town. Home delivery.

### North of the centre
North of C 76 are 3 popular areas for eating and drinking. The **Zona T**, also known as the **Zona Rosa**, is a T-shaped pedestrianized area, comprising C 83 and Cra 13, and has some of Bogotá's best restaurants and bars. Further north is **Parque 93** (www.parque93.com), for many years the most exclusive address in Bogotá, although some of Colombia's

chain restaurants are now beginning to encroach upon its territory.

## $$$ Andrés DC
*C 82 interior centro commercial el retiro, No 12-21, www.andrescarnederes.com. Thu-Sun.*
This is a branch of **Andrés Carne de Res** in Chía (C 3, No 11-56), just beyond the northern limits of the city, an arty, rustic restaurant and bar that has become an institution. Serves great Colombian food in a highly original setting, with 'performers' to liven things up and free arts and crafts workshops for children.

## $$ El Corral Gourmet
*C 93A, No 12-57.*
This popular Colombian burger chain is a cut and some more above **McDonald's**. It serves mainly large hamburgers as well as onion rings and other side orders.

## $$ Salto del Angel
*Cra 13, No 93A-45, T1-654 5454, www.saltodelangel.com.co.*
This enormous restaurant on Parque 93 has a large varied menu of steaks, ceviches and picking food as well as some international options, which include fish and chips. At weekends, after dinner, the tables are cleared and it becomes a popular, upmarket disco.

## $$ Wok
*Cra 13, No 82-74, www.wok.com.co.*
Fashionable Asian restaurant.

## $ K-Listo
*C 93A, No 13-2, www.k-listo.com.*
Fast-food chain serving stuffed *arepas* and *empanadas*.

### Usaquén
Where C 117 joins Cra 6A and Cra 7 is Usaquén, formerly a town in its own right but now a part of the big

metropolis and a popular venue for evening and weekend dining. Cra 6A, in particular, has any number of new restaurants springing up.

## $$ 80 Sillas
*C 118, No 64-05, T1-644 7766, www.80sillas.com.*
All kinds of ceviches and other seafood served on wooden elevated patios with encroaching ferns.

## $$ Camino del Café
*Cra 6, No 117-26.*
Pleasant café with outdoor terrace and Wi-Fi. Good coffees, sandwiches, snacks, ice creams and cocktails.

## $ La Hamburguesería
*C 118, No 6A-40, T214 1943, www.lahamburgueseria.com.*
This hamburger diner, part of a popular Bogotá franchise, has very good burgers as well as salads, club sandwiches and soups. It often has live music at the weekends.

## $ Yumi Yumi
*C 119B, No 6A-97, www.yumiyumi.com.co.*
Restaurant serving sandwiches, crêpes and fruit juices. There is always a 2-for-1 offer on their cocktails. Also has a location in the Zona Rosa.

## Bars and clubs

Most bars and clubs are concentrated in the Cra 11-13, C 80-86 region, known as the **Zona Rosa** – a lively, upmarket area where many restaurants open late; some of these have live entertainment. Further south along Cra 7, from C 32 up to C 59, the bars draw an edgier crowd of filmmakers, artists and students. **La Candelaria** has little to offer in the way of nightlife, although Wed-Fri are the best nights.

### Alma Bar
*C 85, No 12-51, T1-622 8289. Wed-Sat 2130-0245. US$8.*
Bar/club playing jazz, house and funk; Wed night is salsa night.

### The End
*Centro Internacional Tequendama, piso 30, Cra 7 and C 29.*
The best place for late drinking.

### Escobar y Rosas
*Cra 4, No 15-01, La Candelaria.*
In a converted old chemist, packed on Fri and Sat nights with a student crowd.

### QuiebraCanto
*Cra 5, No 17-76, La Candelaria.*
A colonial house hosts world music, funk and salsa to a friendly crowd and is best on Wed and Thu nights.

### Son Salomé
*Cra 7, No 40-31, piso 2.*
No cover and cheap drinks at this popular salsa venue.

### Theatron
*C 58, No 10-32, www.portaltheatron.co.*
In an old cinema, this spectacular gay venue, spread out over 4 floors and with a capacity of 4000, has to be seen to be believed. It includes a rooftop garden and several different rooms playing everything from *vallenato* to electronic music. Straight couples are allowed in, but certain areas of the building are for men only.

## Entertainment

*Guía del Ocio* (known as *GO*, www.goguiadelocio.com.co) has listings on restaurants and clubs, as does *Plan B*, formerly a newspaper, now only online (www.planb.com.co) and *Vive.in* (www.vive.in).

## Cinema

Foreign films are shown in some commercial cinemas and at small screening rooms around the city (US$4.50-8). There is an international film festival in Oct (**Festival de Cine de Bogotá**, www.bogocine.com) and a **European film festival** (Eurocine, www.festivaleurocine.com). Consult *El Espectador*, *El Tiempo* or *PlanB* for weekly listings; there are frequent programme changes. For programme times call **CineColombia**, T1-404 2463, www.cinecolombia.com.

**Cine Bar Paraíso**, *Cra 6, No 120A-No 5-69, Usaquén, T1-755 9646, www.cinemaparaiso.com.co.*
**Cinemanía**, *Cra14, No 93A-85, T1-621 0122, www.cinemania.com.co.* Mainstream and foreign art films.
**Museo de Arte Moderno**, *see page 53.* Shows Colombian and foreign films all day, every day.

There are also cinema complexes in the principal shopping centres (see below). The best are **Centro Comercial Andino**, **Unicentro** and **Atlantis**.

## Festivals

There are many local religious festivals and parades at Easter and Christmas.

**Jan Fiesta de los Reyes Magos (Three Kings)**. The suburb of Egipto (up the hill to the east of Candelaria) has traditional processions.
**Mar Iberoamerican Theatre Festival**, www.festivaldeteatro.com.co. A biennial event hosted by Bogotá.
**May Feria Internacional del Libro** (book fair). Held in Corferias, Cra 37, No 24-67, www.feriadellibro.com.

**Apr, May, Jun Temporada de Opera y Zarzuela** is held in the Teatro Colón with international artists.
**Aug Rock al Parque**, the biggest annual rock festival in Latin America (www.rockalparque.gov.co).
**Aug-Sep Opera season**.
**Sep Festival Internacional de Jazz**.
**Dec Expoartesanía fair** (www.expoartesanias.com). An excellent selection of arts and crafts and regional food from across Colombia is on display at Corferias. Highly recommended.

## Shopping

There is a 16% VAT on all purchases. Heavy duty plastic for covering rucksacks is available at several shops around C 16 and Av Caracas; some have heat-sealing machines to make bags to size. In **Barrio Gaitán**, Cr 30 y C 65, are rows of leather shops. This is an excellent area to buy good-value made-to-measure leather jackets, but it's not safe at night, so go during the day. Designer labels are cheaper in Colombia than in Europe.

## Books

Books in Colombia are generally expensive.

**Forum**, *C 93A, No 13A-49, just off Parque 93*, www.forum.com.co. Foreign magazines, CDs, pleasant atmosphere.
**Librería Central**, *C 94, No 13-92*. Some English- and German-language books.
**Librería Lerner**, *Av Jiménez No 4-35*. Large bookshop with extensive selection in the heart of La Candelaria. Small English-language section downstairs. Also has location in Zona Rosa.
**Librería Nacional**, *www.librerianacional.com*. Has stores across town, including in the Unicentro and Santa Bárbara shopping centres. Good Colombian

history and current affairs section and some foreign press.

**Panamericana**, *Cra 7, No 12C-09, www. panamericana.com.co*. Disorganized, but has some guidebooks and maps. Other branches in the city.

**Taschen**, *Cra 40 No 20A-89*. Art books, small selection of English books and foreign magazines. Also at **Museum of Modern Art**.

**Villegas Editores**, *Av 82, No 11-50, int 3, www.villegaseditores.com*. Great coffee-table books on Colombia.

## Camping equipment

**Monodedo**, *Cra 16, No 82-22, T1-616 3467, www.monodedo.com*. Good selection of camping and climbing equipment. Enquire here for information about climbing in Colombia.

## Chemists

**Farmacity**, *T1-530 0000*. A chain of well-stocked chemists open 24 hrs across the city and offering home deliveries. There's a branch at C 93A, No-13-41, off Parque de la 93, Cra 13, No 63A-67.

## Computer repairs

**Technoloy Services**, *Cra 15 No 93-75 T1-634 8262*. Has other branches throughout the city. Also try **Unilago** shopping centre (see below).

## ★Gems and jewellery

The pavements and cafés along Av Jiménez, below Cra 7, and on Plazoleta del Rosario are frequented by emerald dealers Mon-Fri. There are also rows of jewellers and emerald shops along C 12 with Cra 6. Great expertise is needed in buying; there are bargains, but synthetics and forgeries abound. See box, page 50.

**Emerald Trade Centre**, *Av Jiménez, No 5-43, p 1*. German/English spoken.

**GMC Galería Minas de Colombia**, *C20, No 0-86, T1-281 6523, www.galeria minasdecolombia.com, at foot of Monserrate diagonal from Quinta de Bolívar*. Good selection of jewellery at reasonable prices.

## Handicrafts

**Artesanías de Colombia**, *Claustro de Las Aguas, next to the Iglesia de las Aguas, Cra 2, No 18A-58, www. artesaniasdecolombia.com.co*. Beautiful but expensive designer crafts.

**Tienda Fibrarte**, *Cra 3, No 11-24*. *Artesanías* from around Colombia and Latin America. Good *fique* products, coca tea. Credit cards accepted.

**Galería Cano**, *Ed Bavaria, Cra 13, No 27-98 (Torre B, Int 1-19), also at Unicentro, Loc 218 and at the airport, www.galeriacano. com.co*. Sells textiles, pottery and gold-plated replicas of some of the jewellery on display in the Gold Museum.

## Markets

**Mercado de Pulgas** *(flea market), Cra 7/ C 24, in car park beside Museo de Arte Moderno, Sun and holidays 0800-1700*. A better flea market can be found around the plaza in **Usaquén** on Sun; there's also a good arts and crafts market at the top of the hill in Usaquén.

**Pasaje Rivas**, *C10 y Cra 10*. Persian-style bazaar selling cheap hammocks and ceramics. A small arts and crafts market is open on most days opposite **Hotel Tequendama** in the centre.

**Plaza de Paloquemao**, *Cra 27, entre C19 y 22, www.plazadepaloquemao.com*. Bogotá's huge central market is good to visit just to see the sheer abundance of Colombia's tropical fruits and flowers. It's generally safe and has cheap stalls serving *menú del día*. Flower section is best between 0500 and 1000. See page 54. **San Andresito**, *Cra 38 y C12*. Popular contraband market, selling cheap alcohol, designer sports labels, electrical goods, football shirts. Relatively safe.

### Newspapers

US and European newspapers can be bought at **Librería Oma**, at Tacos de la 19, near the corner of Cra 7/C (Av) 19.

There are several excellent local English-language newspapers, eg *The City Paper*, www.thecitypaperbogota. com, for good travel stories on Colombia. It's available at many hotels, hostels, embassies and popular bars such as the **Bogota Beer Company**. There is also the *Bogotá Daily*, www.bogotadaily.com.

### Photography

**Poder Fotográfico**, *Cra 5, No 20-58 Ap 101, T1-342 9678*. For good developing in 2-3 hrs, used by professionals, also camera repairs. Other photo shops nearby.

### Shopping malls

**Exito**, **Pomona** and **Carulla** chains are probably Bogotá's best supermarket groups.

**Avenida Chile CC**, *Av Chile (C 72), No 10-34, www.avenidachilecentro comercial.com*.
**Bulevar Niza**, *Cra 52, No 125A-59*.
**Centro Comercial Andino**, *Cra 11, No 82-71, www.centroandino.com.co*.
**Centro Comercial Unilago**, *Cra 15, No 78-33, www.unilago.com*. Good for computers, gadgets and repairs.
**Hacienda Santa Bárbara**, *Cra 7 No 115-60, www.haciendasantabarbara.com.co*.
**Unicentro**, *Cra 15, No 124-30, www. unicentrobogota.com (take 'Unicentro' bus from centre, going north on Cra 10; takes about 1 hr)*.

### What to do

### Biking

**Bogotá Bike Tours**, *Cra 3, No 12-72, T1-281 9924, www.BogotaBikeTours.com*. Offers bilingual bike tours around Bogotá, as well as mountain-bike tours outside the city. You can also rent a bike and do your own thing, taking advantage of the *ciclovía* on Sun when major roads, especially La Séptima, are closed to traffic. Second-hand books for sale or exchange.

## Bullfighting

Bogota's mayor banned bullfighting after the 2012 season, but this ruling was overturned in 2014. Trying to predict the future legality of the sport is difficult. When bullfighting is allowed, there are *corridas* every Sat and Sun during the season (Jan-Feb), and occasionally during the rest of the year, at the municipally owned **Plaza de Santamaría**, near Parque Independencia.

## Football

Tickets for matches at El Campín stadium can be bought in advance at **Federación Colombiana de Fútbol**, Av 32, No 16-22, www.colfutbol.org. It is not normally necessary to book in advance, except for the local Santa Fe-Millonarios derby and, of course, for internationals.

## Hiking and walking

For details of other walking groups, consult *El Tiempo's 'Eskape'* section every Fri and the monthly *Go Guía del Ocio* guide, www.goguiadelocio.com.co.

Caminar por Colombia, *Cra 7, No 22-31, of 226 B, T1-286 7487, caminarcolombia@ hotmail.com.* A recommended operator offering walks around the capital and into Boyaca dept every Sat and Sun, US$40 includes transport and guide.
Corporación Clorofila Urbana, *Cra 49B, No 91-41, T1-616 8711, www.clorofila urbana.org.* Walking group with an emphasis on environmental awareness.
Sal Si Puedes, *Cra 7, No 17-01, office 640, T1-283 3765, www.salsipuedes.org. Office Mon-Fri 0800-1700.* Arranges walks in Cundinamarca every weekend and sometimes midweek, and further afield for national holidays such as Semana Santa. The group is very friendly and welcomes visitors. Hikes are graded

for every ability, from 6 km to 4-day excursions of 70 km and more with camping overnight. The groups are often big (30-60), but it is usually possible to stray from the main group. Reservations should be made and paid for a week or so in advance at the club's office. This is a very good way to see the national parks in the Cordillera Oriental near Bogotá.

## Horse riding

Riding Colombia, *www.ridingcolombia. com.* Small ecotourism company offering day-long and multi-day horse rides.

## Rafting and kayaking

Fundación Al Verde Vivo, *C 95, No 48-40, of 203, T1-218 3048, www.alverdevivo.org.* Organizes adventure water sports while trying to minimize environmental impact.

## Rock climbing

La Gran Pared, *Cra 7, No 50-02, T1-285 0903, www.granpared.com.* Artificial rock-climbing wall in the centre of Bogotá. US$14.50 including equipment.

## Skydiving

Club de Paracaidismo, *T1-476 4698, www.skydivecolombia.com.* 1 tandem jump costs US$275.

## Tour operators

Aventure Colombia, *Av Jiménez No 4-49, Of 204, T1-702 7069, www. aventurecolombia.com.* Specializes in classic (Caribbean coast, coffee region, the Andes) and alternative (Guajira, Sierra Nevada, Cocuy, Amazon) tours and expeditions across Colombia, focusing on trekking, eco and rural tourism. Their head office is in Cartagena (see page 159), but they have recently opened this branch in the capital. Highly recommended.

**De Una Colombia Tours**, *Cra 24, No 39b-25, of 501, La Soledad, T1-368 1915, www.deunacolombia.com*. Dutch-run tour agency with tailor-made trips throughout Colombia and an emphasis on introducing tourists to the country's people as well as landscapes. Particularly experienced in Los Nevados and Sierra Nevada del Cocuy.

**Ecoguías**, *T1-347 5736 or T1-212 1423 (for the US), www.ecoguias.com*. Colombian-British team specializing in ecotourism, trekking, adventure sports and stays on fincas. Efficient and well organized.

**See Colombia**, *T1800-553 8701 (US/Canada), T020-7101 9467 (UK), T1-874 6102 (international), www.seecolombia.travel*. Bogotá-based tour operator arranging tours across Colombia, including Sierra Nevada del Cocuy, La Zona Cafetera and the Tatacoa Desert. Also does an exclusive 3-hr Pablo Escobar tour of Medellín from US$50 per person. Some of the profits are donated to the Río Urbano Foundation, working to clean up the Bogotá River. Recommended.

### Travel agents

It is sometimes more economical to buy flights through local travel agents rather than dealing with the airlines direct.

**Vivir Volando**, *Cra 16, No 96-94, T321-205 9777, www.vivirvolando.co*. Flights and packages to Pacific, Amazon and Caribbean coast. Strong links with **Satena**.

## Transport

### Air

**Airport information** The international airport has 2 terminals: **El Dorado** and the **Puente Aéreo**. There is complimentary transport between the terminals.

**El Dorado** (T1-266 2000, www. bogairport.com) has comfortable departure areas with duty-free shops and restaurants. There's a post office in the main arrivals lounge, a Telecom office (for international calls) on the 1st floor and free Wi-Fi throughout, although connectivity can be erratic. There are tourist offices at the exits from international and domestic arrivals (Mon-Fri until 2100) and an **Aviatur** office on the 1st floor (daily 24 hrs). There is no baggage deposit. There are *casas de cambio* in the international terminal (daily 24 hrs) and the national terminal (daily 0600-2200). Note that exchange rates are marginally less favourable than in the city, and pesos cannot be exchanged back into dollars at the airport without receipts. Car hire counters are located opposite the *casa de cambio*.

**Puente Aéreo** has ATMs which accept international credit cards but no exchange services. There is a fast-food restaurant, international Telecom office and an internet café.

The average taxi fare from the airport to the city centre is US$13. Make sure you get a registered taxi, normally yellow, which can be found to your right as you leave the main terminal. Even better, go to domestic arrivals where there is a taxi ticket booth; the ticket will fix the price of your journey. You will be expected to tip if you are helped with any luggage, but use only uniformed porters. Unofficial taxis are not advisable. There are also *colectivos* (US$0.80-1.50 plus luggage per person) to the centre. Watch your belongings inside and outside the airport, especially at night.

**Flights** International and domestic flights use both terminals. There are a number of daily flights to most of Colombia's main cities, including **Medellín**, **Cartagena**, **Cali**,

Barranquilla, **Bucaramanga** and **Armenia,** with **Avianca, Aires, Easyfly, Satena** and **Copa Airlines**. Also flights to **Pereira, Popayán, Leticia, Pasto, Quibdó, San Andrés** and more obscure destinations. Most airlines have offices in both central and North Bogotá; note that many are closed on Sat and Sun.

**Local airline offices** **Copa Airlines,** Cra 10, No 27-51, Local 165, reservations T1-320 9292; **Avianca**, C 19, No 4-37, Local 2, T1-284 9060, airport T1-587 7700 ext. 1790; **Satena**, airport, T1-423 8530, former military airline, not always the best for comfort and schedules. **Easyfly**, T1-414 8111, www.easyfly.com.co.

**International airline offices** **Air Canada**, C 100, No 8A-49, Torre B piso 8, T1800-952 0337; **Air France**, Cra 9A, No 99-07, Torre 1 p 5, T1-650 6000; **American**, C 100, No 18A-30 in Hotel Bogota Plaza, T1-439 7777; **Continental**, Cra 7, No 71–52, Torre B, Oficina 1101, T1-376 5270; **Iberia**, Cra 19, No 85-11, T1-610 5066, also in airport T1-508 7515; **LAN**, Cra 11, No 84-09, T01-800 956 4509; **Lufthansa**, C 100, No 8A-49, Torre B, piso 8, T1-742 8525; **Mexicana**, Av 15, No 114-36, Oficina 108, T1-215 2626; **Qantas**, C 116, No 9-35, piso 1, T1800-752 2347; **TACA/LACSA**, C 113, No 7-21, Local 124, T01-800 951 8222 (toll free).

**Bus**
**TransMilenio** This is Bogotá's highly successful traffic-busting transport system, inaugurated in 2001, consisting of articulated buses on dedicated lanes. It can be a little baffling to work out at first but it's a quick, cheap way to get around once you get the hang of it. It runs north to south along Autopista Norte and Av Caracas with branches to various destinations in the west of the city. There is a branch along C 80 and

a link to La Candelaria (Parque de Los Periodistas on Av Jiménez de Quesada with a stop at the Gold Museum). *Corriente* services stop at all principal road intersections while *expresos* have limited stops. The journey from the centre to the north takes less than 30 mins, US$0.90. Using the TransMilenio is a good, quick way of getting around the city but it tends to be crowded. See www.transmilenio.gov.co for more details.

**Local** Bus fares start at US$0.65, but vary depending on length of route and time of day. Most buses have day/night tariff advertised in the window. Fares are a bit higher at night and on Sun and holidays. *Busetas* (small, green and often dirty) charge a little more. *Colectivos* (small, cramped vans) are faster, US$0.75. Buses stop (in theory) by 'Paradero' boards but there are very few left and normally passengers flag buses down near street corners. To go north, take a *colectivo* from C 19/Cra 3, or any bus marked 'Unicentro'; they follow Cra 7. The network can seem complicated and confusing, but most buses display the route on the front window, indicating the last Calle or Carrera they are passing. People waiting for the buses are also more than happy to help you to find the correct one. Urban buses are not good for sightseeing because you will most likely be standing.

**Long-distance** Buses to **Zipaquirá** (marked 'Zipa') depart from the C 174 terminus of the **TransMilenio** in North Bogotá opposite **Exito** supermarket; companies include Cra 30 (Av Ciudad de Quito) and **Flota Alianza**, US$2 each way, 1¼ hrs. The long-distance bus terminal, **Terminal de Transportes**, Diagonal 23, No 69-60, T1-423 3600, www.terminaldetransporte.gov.co, is located near Av Boyacá (Cra 72) between El Dorado (Av 26) and Av Centenario (C 13). There is also access from Cra 68. To get into town take buses marked 'Centro' or 'Germania' (which pass through the centre). Taxi fares from the terminal to the city are about US$5-6, depending on the destination, with a surcharge at night and on public holidays. Get a ticket from the taxi vending booth, which will show the exact fare to your destination. Do not take unofficial taxis, which are normally touting for particular hotels. To get to the terminal from the city take a bus marked 'Terminal terrestre' or a *buseta* on Cra 10. The terminal is divided into 'modules' serving the 4 points of the compass; each module has several bus companies serving similar destinations. If possible, buy tickets at the respective ticket office before travelling. It is possible to bargain to reduce the price of a ticket. Fares and journey times are given under destinations below. If you are travelling north, you can significantly cut down on the journey time by taking the **TransMilenio** to Portal del Norte, thus avoiding an arduous journey through Bogotá's traffic. **Velotax** *busetas* are slightly quicker and more expensive than ordinary buses, as are *colectivos*, which go to several long-distance destinations.

The terminal is well organized and comfortable, but, as usual, watch out for thieves who are well organized too – reports of baggage thefts are increasing. Free self-service luggage trolleys are provided. There are shops, restaurants, ATMs and showers (between Módulos 3 and 4). Tourist information is in Módulo 5, local 127, T1-295 4460, Mon-Sat 0700-2000, Sun 0800-1600. Módulo 4 also has a clinic giving free vaccinations, Mon-Fri 0800-1305, Sat 0800-1400.

To **Armenia**, frequent with **Bolivariano**, **Magdalena** and **Expreso Palmira**, from US$24, 8-10 hrs; to **Barranquilla**, frequent with **Brasilia**, 7 daily with **Copetran**, US$82, 20 hrs; to **Bucaramanga**, hourly from 0500, every 30 mins from 0600, US$35, 9 hrs; to **Buenaventura**, 1700, 1900 and 1930, US$43, 12 hrs; to **Cali**, hourly 0530-2330, US$25-30, 10 hrs; to **Cartagena**, only afternoon and evening departures, US$75, 18 hrs; to **Cocuy**, 0500, 1830, 1900, 2000 and 2030, from US$20, 10 hrs; to **Cúcuta**, hourly with **Berlinas**, US$47, 18 hrs; to **El Banco** (for connections to Mompos), **Copetran** and **Omega**, daily 1700, 14 hrs, US$70; to **Honda**, hourly 0400-2330 with **Rápido Tolima**, US$14, 4 hrs; to **Ibagué**, hourly with **Autofusa** until 1900, US$17, 4½ hrs; to **Ipiales**, 0945, 1230, 1430, 1730 and 2215 with **Bolivariano**, US$67, 24 hrs; to **Manizales**, frequent with **Expreso Palmira** and **Bolivariano**, US$25, 8 hrs; to **Medellín**, hourly, many companies, US$37, 10 hrs; to **Pasto**, 8 departures, US$60, 21 hrs; to **Pereira**, hourly, US$22, 8 hrs; to **Popayán**, 7 departures, US$50, 14 hrs; to **San Gil**, same times as Bucaramanga, US$26, 5 hrs; to **Santa Marta**, afternoon and evening departures only, US$75-80, 16 hrs; to **Tunja**, every 10 mins with **Rápido Duitama**, **Libertadores** (comfortable and recommended), **Transportes Alianza** or **Copetran**, 3-5 hrs, US$10.50; to **Valledupar**, US$71, 16 hrs; to **Villavicencio**, every 30 mins with **Bolivariano**, US$10, 2½ hrs.

**International** If going to **Venezuela**, it is best to make the journey to the border at Cúcuta in 2 stages to enjoy the scenery to the full; onward bus connections from San Antonio de Táchira (on the Venezuelan side of the border) to Caracas are good. A through ticket from Bogotá to Caracas with **Berlinas de Fonce** does not guarantee a seat and is only valid for 2 Venezuelan companies; moreover no refunds are given in Cúcuta.

## Car rental
Whilst not cheap, if you are in the city for several days this could be a good option. **Dollar Rent-a-Car**, C 90, No 11A-09, T1-691 4700 and at airport, is one of the cheapest. Alternatives include **Hertz**, at airport, T1-288 2636, and at Av 19, No 122-81, T1-327 6700, and **Colombian Rent a Car**, Autopista Norte 120-85, T1-214 5292, www.colombianrentacar.com.

## Taxi
Taxis are the best way to get between different sectors of the city and are recommended for all journeys at night. If you take a taxi on the street, try to pick one that looks in good condition. It should be yellow and have the driver's official ID card with photo displayed; non official taxis are not recommended. At busy times, empty taxis flagged down on the street may refuse to take you to less popular destinations. All official taxis have meters: insist that they are used. The *taxímetro* (meter) registers units starting at 25 then calculates the time and distance travelled. The driver converts the total into pesos using a green fare table. If the conversion card is not displayed, the driver should show it to you. Check if there are any additional charges for luggage or night journeys; a list should be posted in the taxi. The starting charge is US$1.90; an average fare from North Bogotá to the centre is US$6.

**Radio taxis** (T1-311 1111 or T1-411 1111) are recommended for safety and reliability. The dispatcher will give you a cab number, which you should write down and confirm when it arrives. There is a small charge but it is safer. Tipping is not customary, but is appreciated. If you are going to an address out of the city centre, it is helpful to know the area you are going to as well as the address, eg Chicó, Chapinero (ask at your hotel).

## Train
Long-distance services were suspended in 1992. There are no passenger services at present from **Bogotá La Sabana** station at C 13 No 18-24, except a tourist steam train, **Turistrén Ltda**, C 13, No 18-24, T1-375 0557, www.turistren. com.co, which runs on Sat, Sun and holidays, departing 0830 and calling at the following stations: **Usaquén** (C 110, Transversal 10) at 0930, **Zipaquirá** at 1130, and **Cajicá** at 1230. The service returns at 1515, reaching Usaquén at 1640 and La Sabana at 1740. Adult US$22.50, child 2-12, US$14.

# Around
## Bogotá

The buzz of Bogotá can sometimes be overshadowed by its chilly nights and frequent drizzle, but travel just a few hours away in most directions and it can be pleasingly sunny and hot. La Sabana de Bogotá, an area of savannah near the city, is dotted with white farms and groves of eucalyptus. Exiting northwest from the city, the road swiftly descends towards the valley of the Río Magdalena and a string of pretty towns, such as Guaduas and Honda. To the southwest, on the edge of the Sabana de Bogotá, lies the cloud-forested Chicaque Parque Natural, a private nature reserve popular with hikers and horse riders. Beyond is Girardot, a popular weekend retreat for *bogotanos*, nicknamed the 'swimming pool city'. Driving due north of Bogotá in the direction of Boyacá are two of the country's most impressive cultural trophies. The Laguna de Guatavita was a lake prized by the Muisca and believed to be the source of the legend of El Dorado. A few kilometres beyond is the salt cathedral at Zipaquirá, a truly awe-inspiring monument to religious devotion.

escape the city and head for the Río Magdalena

## Towards Girardot

The Simón Bolívar Highway runs southwest from Bogotá to Girardot, formerly the main port on the Río Bogotá and now a popular second-home destination, thanks to its climate. Only small boats can go upriver from here and it is known for the volume of swimming pools built by weekending *bogotanos*. The 132-km journey down the mountains from Bogotá is extremely picturesque. About 20 km from central Bogotá is **Soacha**, where the built-up area of the city finally ends. A right fork here leads along a poor road to the Indumil plant, 3 km after which there is a large sign for the **Parque Natural Chicaque**. The entrance is 300 m down a track.

## Parque Natural Chicaque

*T1-368 3114/368 3118, www.chicaque.com. Daily 0800-1700, US$7.25. Take a bus to Soacha and get onward transport from there.*

The park is a privately owned 300-ha estate on the edge of the Sabana de Bogotá, consisting principally of cloudforest between 2100 m and 2700 m. The estate has never been developed and has some 10 km of trails down and around its 500 m cliffs. It is a popular spot for walkers and riders at weekends with an 80 m waterfall and a new Swiss-style *refugio* at the bottom level, about one hour down the trail from the entrance. This provides meals, accommodation and facilities for day visitors. There is an abundance of birds, butterflies and a great natural diversity of forest cover. The owner also reports frequent sightings of UFOs.

## Towards Honda

The road to Honda passes through several small towns, including Madrid and **Facatativá**, 40 km from Bogotá. Some 3 km from Facatativá, on the road to the west, are the **Piedras de Tunja**, enormous stones set in a natural rock amphitheatre with numerous indigenous pictographs and an artificial lake. A further 71 km from Facatativá, **Villeta** is a popular weekend resort for *bogotanos*. It is a busy town at the centre of the *panela* (unrefined sugar cane) industry, in a cattle-raising area. Not far away are the waterfalls of **Quebrada Cune** ① *daily 0800-1200, 1400-1800*. The annual **National Panela Festival** is held during three days in January and there is a Band Festival in mid-August. Look out for *Piedra de Bolívar* (Bolívar's stone), on which is marked all the occasions when Bolívar passed through the town.

## Guaduas

Midway between Villeta and Honda is Guaduas. Of the towns in the *tierra caliente* northwest of the capital, Guaduas preserves its colonial charm more than the others. Founded three times between 1572 and 1644, it was a stopover on the Camino Real between Bogotá and the river at Honda. Policarpa Salavarrieta, heroine of the Independence movement, was born here on 26 January 1796 (see box, page 74). There is a statue of her in the plaza, and the **Casa de La Pola**, where she lived, is now an interesting museum. **Calle Real** is the best-preserved colonial

## ON THE ROAD

### La Pola

María Policarpa Salavarrieta Ríos, affectionately known as 'La Pola', managed to pack a lot into her short life, although perhaps not as much as the popular *telenovela* about the heroine of the Colombian Independence movement would have you believe. The fifth of seven children, Policarpa is believed to have been born in Guaduas, Cundinamarca in 1791, but even her given name is disputed, as her birth certificate has never been found. What is certain, however, is the date of her death. She was executed for high treason in Bogotá on 14 November 1817, after being caught by the Spanish Royalists. Working as a seamstress, she infiltrated royalist homes in Bogotá and supplied information to the revolutionary forces fighting to free the country from Spanish rule. La Pola and six others, including her lover Alejo Sabaraín, were executed by firing squad in Bolívar Square and La Pola is now buried in La Candelaria, thanks to the intervention of two of her brothers, both Augustinian friars. Legends about her abound, and in 2010 Colombian television created *La Pola – Amar La Hizo Libre* (La Pola – Love Set Her Free), based on her life in love and politics. It was a fresh but fictionalized look at one of the most intriguing figures of the Independence movement.

street. The oldest house in town is the **Alcaldía** on Avenida José Antonio Galán. Simón Bolívar slept in the room on the second floor before leaving by river for Santa Marta. About 10 km outside the town is the **Salto de Versalles**, a lovely 45-m waterfall, now a National Monument. There is a public swimming pool in Guaduas and a Sunday market. The best local dish is *quesillos*.

### Honda

Located at the junction of the Río Guali and the Río Magdalena, 32 km upstream from La Dorada, Honda is a pleasant old town, surrounded by hills. It was founded in 1539 and retains many colonial houses on its narrow, picturesque streets, including Colombia's oldest pharmacy. Many of the buildings are slowly and lovingly being restored to their former glory. Popular with visitors from much colder Bogotá, Honda, with an average temperature of 33°C, is now gradually being discovered by international travellers. A small group of expats has settled here, opening up new hotels and restaurants.

Honda is well known for its many bridges, some very old and rickety, spanning the Río Magdalena and Río Guali. **El Salto de Honda** (the rapids which separate the Lower from the Upper Magdalena) is just below the town. In February the Magdalena rises and people come from all over the region for the fishing, celebrated at the festival of the Subienda.

The town has an interesting covered market, selling mostly fruit and vegetables but some *artesanías* too in a grand old building next to the river. At the top of the town, up some steep cobbled streets, is the Parque Principal with a fine stone church,

**El Alto Rosario,** and a statue dedicated to David Hughes Williams, an Englishman who became a popular town mayor. A recommended walk is up to the Cerro Cacao en Pelota, one of the hills behind Honda. It takes 30 minutes and affords good views of the Magdalena. From Puente Navarro, walk up Calle las Trampas to Puente Quebrada Seca. Keep asking locals for directions; take lots of water and try to avoid the midday sun.

## Where to stay

### Honda
All accommodation is across the Gualí river in the newer part of Honda.

**$$ Casa Belle Epoque**
*C 12, No 12A-21, Cuesta de San Francisco, T310-481 4090,*
*www.casabelleepoque.com.*
A lovely old house with spacious, high-ceilinged rooms, all with bath and fan, beautiful roof terrace with jacuzzi, pool, free Wi-Fi, lots of antique, period touches. British/Colombian-run, excellent breakfasts, advance booking preferred. Also arranges horse riding, boat and fishing trips. Recommended.

**$$-$ Hotel Calle Real**
*Cra 11, No 14-40, T8-251 2260.*
The rooms are clean and there is a small swimming pool on the roof. Prices vary according to whether you want a/c or a fan. Parking available.

**$ Asturias Plaza**
*Cra 11, No 16-38.*
Large, rambling hotel near the bus terminal with swimming pool, private bathrooms and cable TV. The rooms are a little dusty but otherwise OK.

**$ Riviera Plaza**
*C 14, No 12-19, T312-745 1446.*
The French Riviera it is not, but nonetheless it has modern, clean rooms around a large swimming pool. If you get the rooms at the end there are good views over the Río Gualí and the colonial part of town.

## Restaurants

### Honda
There is a row of good cheap restaurants on the west bank of the Río Magdalena in **Puerto Bogotá**. There are also many economical fish restaurants by the river a short walk from town, serving fresh catch of the day, including **El Corralito de Tuky-Tuky**, Av Pacho María, Bahía 3.

## What to do

### Honda
Honda Travel, *C 9, No 21-30, T317-309 3633.* Offers boat trips up the Magdalena.

## Transport

### Honda
**Bus**
As a junction between Bogotá and Medellín, Honda is an ideal place to stop if you want to break up the long bus rides to these destinations. To **Bogotá**, with **Velotax** and **Rápido**. To **Lima**, US$11, 4 hrs. To **Manizales**, with **Bolivariano**, US$11, 4 hrs. **Rápido Tolima** run half-hourly buses to **La Dorada** (1 hr) and **Puerto Boyacá** (3 hrs). To **Medellín**, currently 5 hrs, US$15, although the Bogotá–Medellín highway which is currently being built will pass around the town.

### Guatavita

About 75 km northeast of Bogotá, overlooking the Embalse de Tominé, is the small, modern town of Guatavita Nueva, which was built in colonial style when the old town of Guatavita was submerged by the reservoir. The original inhabitants were unwilling to stay in the new town, so it is now a weekend haunt for *bogotanos* and tourists. There is a cathedral, artisan workshops and two small museums, one devoted to the indigenous Muisca and the other displaying relics of the old Guatavita church, including a delightful Debain harmonium. The Sunday market is best in the morning, before *bogotanos* arrive. To get there, catch a bus from Bogotá.

Two to three hours' walk or horse ride from Guatavita Nueva is the **Laguna de Guatavita** (also called **Lago de Amor** by locals), where the legend of El Dorado originated (see box, opposite). You can catch the bus from Guatavita towards Sesquilé and ask the bus driver to let you off where there is a sign 'via Lago Guatavita'. (There is a good campsite and places to eat nearby.) From the main road to the lakeside the route is paved as far as a school, about half way, and then becomes a decent track; follow the signs. A good car can travel to within 300 m of the lake, where there is a car park and good restaurant.

The lake is a quiet, beautiful place. You can walk right round it close to the water level in 1½ hours, or climb to the rim of the crater in several places. Opinions differ on whether the crater is volcanic or caused by a meteorite impact, but from the rim at 3100 m there are extensive views over the varied countryside. Access to the park is only allowed with a permit obtained in Bogotá from the **Corporación Autónoma Regional de Cundinamarca** (**CAR**) ① *Cra 7, No 36-45, T1-320 9000, www.car.gov.co.* A taxi tour from Bogotá costs around US$75 for a full day.

### ★Zipaquirá

*www.catedraldesal.gov.co/en/. Daily 0900-1730. Cathedral US$12, car park US$2.*

Zipaquirá (commonly called Zipa), 55 km from Guatavita, is the centre of a rich cattle-farming district, and famous for its rock salt mine which contains a fabulous **salt cathedral**. This should not be missed, as it is a truly awe-inspiring sight. Salt has been mined here since the 15th century, although it wasn't until 1606 that the town was established by the Spaniards. Many kilometres of tunnels have been excavated since then. A salt shrine had been carved in the tunnels by the miners many years before the original cathedral started to take shape in 1950. It was dedicated in 1954 to Nuestra Señora del Rosario (patron saint of miners). Continuing deterioration made the cave unsafe and it was closed in 1990. A new salt cathedral was begun in 1991, 500 m from the original cathedral in a lower cave. It was opened on 16 December 1995 by President Samper.

The entrance to the cave is in hills about 20 minutes' walk west of town. There is an information centre and a museum at the site; admission includes a 75-minute guided tour and a film on the history of salt mining. Beyond the

## ON THE ROAD
### The legend of El Dorado

The Spanish came to South America with an insatiable thirst for gold. Nowhere was this more evident than in their search for El Dorado, a fruitless quest that drove them to explore the furthest reaches of the continent and was responsible for the deaths of thousands of indigenous locals and Spaniards alike. The legend itself is based on an annual custom in which the Chibcha king was coated with gold dust and set adrift on a ceremonial raft. He would dive into the lake and emerge cleansed of the gold. It was said that the lake also had precious offerings thrown in.

The lake was eventually identified as Guatavita, just north of Bogotá, and the story was verified by the discovery of a miniature raft made from gold wire that now holds pride of place in Bogotá's Museo de Oro. Several attempts have been made to drain Lake Guatavita and many items have been recovered but never on the scale the Spanish imagined.

entrance passage are the 14 stations of the cross, each sculpted by a different artist; at their centre is a cross 4 m high, subtly lit and imaginatively executed. The next sections of the cave represent the choir, narthex, baptistry (with a natural water source) and sacristy. Finally, at the lowest point in the cave, 180 m below the surface, are the nave and the north and south aisles; huge pillars grow out of the salt dominated by the central cross, 16 m high. All is illuminated to provide a reverential atmosphere.

In the town, it's worth visiting the church in the attractive central plaza for its stonework (despite its external appearance, it has a modern interior). The market on Tuesday is good for fruit and vegetables.

### Nemocón → Colour map 2, C5.

Around 15 km northeast of Zipaquirá, at Nemocón, there are salt mines (closed to visitors), a church and a small but interesting **Museo de Sal** ① *on the plaza, Tue-Sun 0900-1700, US$1*, which has displays on local history and the beginnings of the salt industry at the time of the Muisca people. The main salt mine is four blocks above the museum, with some bizarre lamp posts on the approach road.

### Listings North of the city

### Where to stay

**Zipaquirá**

**$$ Cacique Real**
*Cra 6, No 2-36, T1-851 0209, www.hotelcaciquereal.com.*

Recently declared 'Patrimonio Cultural', this fine little hotel has a lovely courtyard with hanging baskets and good rooms with cable TV and hot water. There's Wi-Fi in the lobby and a car park.

## Casa Virrey
**$ Casa Virrey**
*C 3, No 6-21, T1-852 3720,*
*casavirreyorani@hotmail.com.*
New building with 36 clean, comfortable rooms and private bathrooms. Laundry service available.

**$ Torre Real**
*C 8, No 5-92, T1-851 1901.*
Light and airy rooms with large beds. Laundry service available.

## Restaurants

### Zipaquirá

**$$ La Cascada**
*Cra 10, No 3-50.*
Large restaurant and banquet hall specializing in regional dishes and grilled meats.

**$$ Parque Restaurante Funzipa**
*C 1A, No 9-99, www.restaurante funzipa.com.*
Enormous ranch with beautiful garden and original ovens for cooking salt. Serves *parrillas* and *bandejas*.

There are several cheaper options with lunch specials near the plaza.

## Transport

### Zipaquirá
**Bus**
The bus station is 15 mins' walk from the mines and cathedral. There are many buses to **Bogotá**, including **Cra 30** (Av Ciudad de Quito) and **Flota Alianza**, terminating at the C 174 terminus of the **TransMilenio** in North Bogotá opposite Exito supermarket, US$2 each way, 1¼ hrs. Note when arriving at the terminus from Zipaquirá you need to buy a **TransMilenio** bus ticket to leave the station; to avoid this, ask the driver to drop you off before the bus station.

**Train**
For details of the tourist steam train to Zipaquirá, see page 71.

# North of Bogotá

Heading north from Bogotá towards the border with Venezuela or the Caribbean coast, the road takes you on a historical journey through the heart of Colombia, passing picturesque valleys, canyons and spectacular high mountain passes.

Set on a high plateau is Tunja, capital of the Department of Boyacá and formerly the seat of power of the indigenous Muisca. The area also played its part in the liberation of Colombia from the Spanish, particularly at Puente de Boyacá where Simón Bolívar and his troops fought a decisive battle. Boyacá is dotted with dozens of colonial towns and villages, notably Villa de Leiva and Monguí.

From the Andean foothills of Boyacá, the road swoops down to the turbulent Río Fonce and the Department of Santander. Here too the Spanish colonial legacy is very much intact, particularly in Barichara, Guane and Girón. In recent years the area's countless tumbling rivers, caves and deep canyons have made it the capital of Colombia's burgeoning adventure sports scene, centred around the pretty town of San Gil. From the Department capital of Bucaramanga, a road climbs northeast over moorland for more lessons in Independence history around Pamplona and Cúcuta in Norte de Santander. Another road heads north towards the Sierra Nevada de Santa Marta and the Caribbean coast.

**Best** for
Adventure sports ■ Colonial heritage ■ Independence history

Bogotá

# Footprint picks

★ **Villa de Leiva and Barichara**, pages 90 and 112
Stroll around these beautiful and well-preserved colonial towns.

★ **Paipa and Iza hot springs**, page 99
Relax in the thermal waters and soak up the atmosphere.

★ **Lago de Tota**, page 100
Enjoy white sand and a picturesque setting at Playa Blanca.

★ **Sierra Nevada del Cocuy**, page 103
Trek among dazzling snow-capped peaks.

★ **San Gil**, page 106
Abseiling, caving, kayaking and rafting in the country's adventure capital.

★ **Chicamocha Canyon**, page 107
Marvel at the steep cliffs carved by the Río Chicamocha.

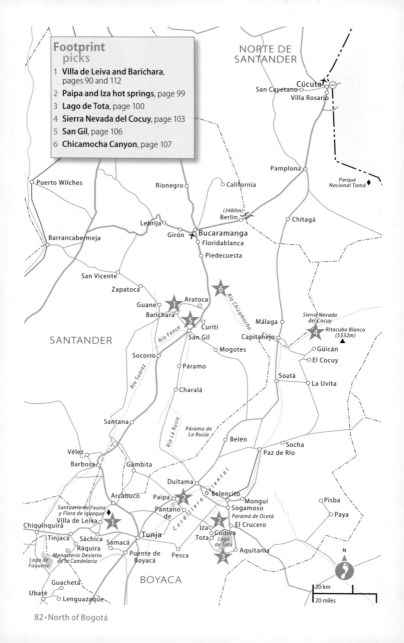

**Footprint**
picks

1 **Villa de Leiva and Barichara**,
pages 90 and 112
2 **Paipa and Iza hot springs**, page 99
3 **Lago de Tota**, page 100
4 **Sierra Nevada del Cocuy**, page 103
5 **San Gil**, page 106
6 **Chicamocha Canyon**, page 107

NORTE DE
SANTANDER

Cúcuta

San Cayetano
Villa Rosario

Puerto Wilches

Rionegro

California

Pamplona

*Parque
Nacional Tamá*

Lebrija

Berlin
*(3480m)*

Chitagá

Barrancabermeja

Girón

Floridablanca

**Bucaramanga**

Piedecuesta

San Vicente

Zapatoca

Aratoca

6

*Río Chicamocha*

Guane

Barichara

5

Curití

Málaga

*Sierra Nevada
del Cocuy*

Ritacubo Blanco
*(5332m)*

SANTANDER

*Río Fonce*

San Gil

Capitanejo

Güicán

Socorro

*Río Suárez*

Mogotes

El Cocuy

Páramo

Soatá

Charalá

La Uvita

Santana

*Río La Rusia*

*Páramo de
La Rusia*

Belén

Socha

Vélez

Barbosa

Gámbita

Paz de Río

Duitama

Pisba

Arcabuco

Paipa

2

Belencito

Monguí

Paya

*Santuario de Fauna
y Flora de Iguaque*

Chiquinquirá

Villa de Leiva

1

Pantano
de

Sogamoso

*Páramo de Ocetá*

El Crucero

Tinjacá

Sáchica

Ráquira

Sámacá

**Tunja**

Iza
Cuítiva
*Lago
de Tota*

Aquitania

*Monasterio Desierto
de la Candelaria*

Puente de
Boyacá

Pesca

3

*Lago de
Fúquene*

Guachetá

**BOYACA**

Ubaté

Lenguazaque

N

20 km

20 miles

# Essential North of Bogotá

## Finding your feet

The transport hubs are Tunja in Boyacá Department, Bucaramanga in Santander Department and Cúcuta on the border with Venezuela. All are served by regular buses to and from Bogotá. The main road north from Bogotá passes through Tunja and San Gil; at Bucaramanga it divides: north to the Caribbean coast and northeast to Cúcuta. There are regular flights from Bogotá to both Bucaramanga and Cúcuta.

## Getting around

Walking is the best way to explore colonial town centres, but you'll need buses, taxis and *colectivos* to explore outlying regions.

## When to go

The mountainous regions around Tunja and El Cocuy are cool and can be rainy or foggy even in the dry seasons (December to April and July to August). The weather becomes increasingly hot as you head north into Santander. Cúcuta is very warm year-round.

It is best to avoid Cocuy in the peak holiday times, as campsites can get very busy.

## Time required

Two weeks will allow you to explore some of the towns and villages; add another week for trekking.

## Weather North of Bogotá (Tunja)

| January | February | March | April | May | June |
|---|---|---|---|---|---|
| 19°C 7°C 16mm | 19°C 8°C 29mm | 19°C 9°C 55mm | 18°C 10°C 77mm | 17°C 10°C 84mm | 16°C 9°C 58mm |

| July | August | September | October | November | December |
|---|---|---|---|---|---|
| 16°C 8°C 46mm | 17°C 8°C 42mm | 17°C 8°C 54mm | 18°C 9°C 85mm | 18°C 9°C 69mm | 18°C 8°C 31mm |

# Boyacá
## Department

Boyacá is the cultural and historical heart of Colombia. This department of green valleys and colonial villages was the centre of the Muisca empire, whom the Spanish fought so vigorously to prize away their gold. The empire's capital was at Tunja, which at the time rivalled Bogotá in size and importance. Today, tourists mostly flock to nearby Villa de Leiva, with its whitewashed colonial mansions and cobbled streets, which is becoming a popular weekend retreat for affluent *bogotanos*. But there are many more undiscovered gems. Villages such as Iza and Paipa with their thermal springs, and Monguí with its rich history and fresh mountain air, are therapy for both body and soul. In the northeast of the department is the Sierra Nevada del Cocuy, a mountain range of jagged ice peaks and breathtaking lakes to rival any in South America.

Tunja, capital of Boyacá Department, is 137 km from Bogotá, in a cool dry mountainous area, on a platform that slopes down to the north and east to the valley of the Río Chulo. Ugly on the outside but with a pleasant centre and an interesting history, most travellers shun Tunja, probably as a result of impressions gained on arrival at its bus station. Tunja, however, is worth a peek, particularly to visit its impressive churches and museums. Moreover, it has very friendly people and good, cheap accommodation. The climate is cool, with an average temperature of 12°C, due to the altitude.

When the Spaniards arrived in what is now Boyacá, Tunja was already an indigenous city, the seat of the Zipa, one of the two Muisca kings. He ruled over the northern part of the Muisca territories, the most populous and well-developed indigenous area of what is modern-day Colombia. It was refounded as a Spanish city by Gonzalo Suárez Rendón in 1539. The city formed an independent Junta in 1811, and Bolívar fought under its aegis during the Magdalena campaign of 1812. Seven years later he fought the decisive battle of Boyacá nearby.

Note that most of Tunja's churches, except the San Lázaro chapel, are open to visitors during the day, or at least at Mass times.

## Plaza de Bolívar

The **cathedral**, on the Plaza de Bolívar, has a Romanesque façade and tower, with an unusual balustrade along the roof of the west front. It dates from the end of the 16th century. Inside, it is a mixture of Gothic and Moorish styles, with ornamented pillars and colonial paintings. There are several fine side chapels and a mausoleum honouring Gonzalo Suárez Rendón, founder of the city. The **Casa de la Cultura**, opposite the cathedral, also 16th century, is where Simón Bolívar stayed before the battle of Boyacá. Cultural events are held here from time to time. Next to the cathedral is the **Casa del Fundador Suárez Rendón** ① *daily 0800-1200, 1400-1800, US$1*, one of the few extant mansions of a Spanish conquistador in Colombia (1539-1543). See the attractive peaceful courtyard, which has a fine view of the countryside, and the unique series of plateresque paintings on the ceilings.

## East of the plaza

One block from the plaza, on Calle 20 with Carrera 9, is the house of the writer **Casa Don Juan de Vargas** ① *Tue-Fri 0900-1200, 1400-1700, Sat, Sun and holidays 0900-1200, 1400-1600, US$1.50 adults, US$1 children*, built in 1590. It has been restored as a museum of colonial Tunja, with many interesting exhibits

**Tip...**

The bus station is near the main highway on the east side of town. From the bus station to the main square is a steep walk uphill, but the centre of the town and main sights are readily accessible from the Plaza de Bolívar.

relating to the city. Note the murals, gold candlesticks and particularly the fine ceiling of the upper floor.

One block south, on Calle 19, the **Casa Juan de Castellanos** is another notable colonial building, much of it carefully restored and again contains some fine ceiling paintings, both religious and of flora and fauna. Juan de Castellanos was a chronicler and friend of Suárez Rendón. **Casa de Capitán Antonio Ruiz Mancipe** is now a bank, on Calle 18, but much of the original has been preserved or restored.

Two blocks east of the plaza is another fine building, the **Santa Clara La Real chapel** (1580), with some fine wood carving in Moorish style particularly in the ceiling of the single-nave chapel. There is fine ornamentation everywhere, interesting oil paintings and wall decorations revealed after restoration a few years back. This was the chapel of the Santa Clara convent, begun in 1574, probably the first to be established in Colombia. One of the nuns, Sister Josefa del Castillo y Guevara, lived in a cell near the choir for over 50 years and was buried here. Some of her writings are exhibited in the museum into which part of the former convent has been converted.

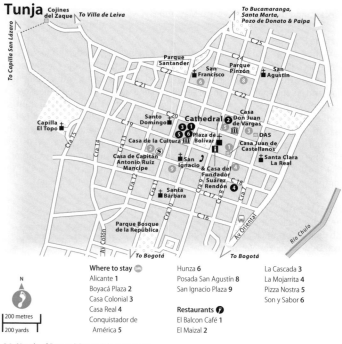

**Where to stay** 🛏
Alicante **1**
Boyacá Plaza **2**
Casa Colonial **3**
Casa Real **4**
Conquistador de
  América **5**
Hunza **6**
Posada San Agustín **8**
San Ignacio Plaza **9**

**Restaurants** 🍴
El Balcon Café **1**
El Maizal **2**
La Cascada **3**
La Mojarrita **4**
Pizza Nostra **5**
Son y Sabor **6**

## South of the plaza

The church of **San Ignacio** has an interesting embossed façade constructed by the Jesuits in the 17th century. It is now used for cultural presentations as well as offering Mass. Four blocks from the plaza, on Carrera 11, the church of **Santa Bárbara** dates from 1592 and has much fine ornamentation and a *mudéjar* ceiling. The treasury has many valuable items of gold and silver, part donated by the mother of Charles V of Spain. The chapel of La Epístola is the best of several. In the nearby parish house are some notable religious objects, including silk embroidery from the 18th century.

A short walk further south, in **Parque Bosque de la República**, is the adobe wall against which three martyrs of the Independence were shot in 1816. The wall and bullet holes are protected by a glass screen. Ask the tourist police guarding these buildings for information: they are helpful and knowledgeable.

## West of the plaza

Of the many colonial buildings, the most remarkable is the church of **Santo Domingo**, one block west of the plaza, a masterpiece begun in 1594, with its splendid interior covered with richly carved wood. There are several chapels in the side aisles; the Chapel of Our Lady of Rosario, the work of Fray Pedro Bedón, glistens with gold and glass ornamentation and is one of the finest examples of the period in Colombia.

## North of the plaza

The church and convent of **San Francisco** is another 16th-century construction notable for its white colonial façade, sculptures of San Francisco and Mary Magdalene, striated pillars and the gilded arch over the central retable. Also note the Altar de los Pelícanos, believed to have been brought from Quito, housed inside the chapel of the Virgin de las Angustias.

## Outskirts of Tunja

The small **San Lázaro** chapel, dating from 1587, restored during the 18th century, has four semi-circular arches supporting an ornamental ceiling. It overlooks the town from the west at 2940 m and is a fine viewpoint, but take advice before walking up there.

Nearby, is one of two pre-Columbian sites on the edge of the city. The **Cojines del Zaque** (literally the cushions of the Zaque, who was the principal chief of the Muisca government) is a ritual site around a large rock, which has pillow-like features carved into it. It is thought that sacrifices to the Sun God and ritualistic sun-worship were carried out here. The **Pozo de Donato (Pozo de Hunzahúa)**, a short distance northeast out of town on the road to Paipa, was a well or pond also used for Muisca rituals. Legend had it that this included gold offerings. In the early days of colonization, a Spaniard by the name of Jerónimo Donato drained the pool looking for gold – which he did not find. The Pozo de Donato is in the grounds of the Universidad Pedagógica, which has done considerable archaeological work in the region. There is now a small attractive park around the pond.

## Puente de Boyacá

*16 km south of Tunja, on the main road to Bogotá. Daily 0800-1800. Entry free, US$1.50 for presentation. Bus from Tunja, US$0.80; ask for 'El Puente'.*

The **Battle of Boyacá** was one of the most significant events in the history of Colombia. Bolívar took Tunja on 6 August 1819, and the next day his troops, fortified by a British Legion, the only professional soldiers among them, fought the Spaniards on the banks of the swollen Río Teatinos. With the loss of only 13 killed and 53 wounded, they captured 1600 Spanish soldiers and 39 officers. Only 50 Spaniards escaped back to Bogotá, and when these told their tale, the Viceroy Samano fled in such haste that he left behind him half a million pesos of the royal funds. There is a large monument to Bolívar overlooking the bridge at Boyacá, plus several other monuments, an exhibition hall and restaurant at the site.

## Listings Tunja and around *map p86*

### Tourist information

The tourist information office is in the **Casa del Fundado Suárez Rendón**, Pl de Bolívar, T8-742 3272, turismo@tunja.gov.co, next to the cathedral; the website www.tunja.gov.co also has good information (Spanish only).

### Where to stay

**$$$ Hunza**
*C 21A, No 10-66, T8-742 4111,*
*www.hotelhunza.com.*
Tunja's largest hotel, the Hunza has fine views of the Iglesia San Francisco from its lobby. Its modern rooms are spacious, with Wi-Fi throughout, a swimming pool and Turkish bath and a restaurant.

**$$$-$$ Boyacá Plaza**
*C 18, No 11-22, T8-740 1116/17,*
*www.hotelboyacaplaza.co.*
This smart, modern hotel has comfortable rooms and includes breakfast and Wi-Fi connection in the price.

**$$$-$$ San Ignacio Plaza**
*C 18, No 10-51, T8-743 7583,*
*www.hotelsanignacioplaza.com.*

This hotel has a pretty colonial façade, though it's modern on the inside with bright, airy rooms. Also has a restaurant, parking and Wi-Fi.

**$$ Alicante**
*Cra 8, No 19-15, T8-744 9967,*
*www.hotelalicantetunja.com.*
With its minimalist design and a sunny patio fringed by varieties of cacti, this hotel is a bargain. The rooms are full of light and have cable TV, while there is Wi-Fi in reception and some of the rooms. Sister hotel to the **Casa Real**.

**$$ Posada San Agustín**
*C 23, No 8-63, T8-742 2986,*
*www.posadadesanagustin.co.*
This beautiful colonial building on the Parque Pinzón is a bit of a gem, with comfortable rooms and a gorgeous balustraded courtyard painted olive green. The hotel is embellished with antiques and photographs of Tunja down the ages, while it also has Wi-Fi. Includes breakfast.

**$$ Casa Colonial**
*Av Colon, T8-742 2169.*
This hotel has a nice, sunny patio and rooms with cable TV and en suite

bathrooms – though they can be a bit dingy.

## $$ Casa Real
*C 19, No 7-65, T8-743 1764, www.hotelalicantetunja.com.*
Housed in a beautiful colonial building, this hotel is a real bargain and could easily charge 3 times the price. The rooms are comfortable and clean with private bathrooms and freshly varnished wooden floorboards. Some larger deluxe rooms. Sister hotel to **Alicante**. Friendly, welcoming service. Highly recommended.

## $$ Conquistador de América
*C 20, No 8-92, T8-742 3534.*
The **Conquistador** has a lovely foyer with a bright skylight, and while the rooms are small they are clean and comfortable with en suite bathrooms, hot water and cable TV.

## Restaurants

### $ El Balcón
*Pasaje Vargas C 19A, No 10-16, T8-743 3954.*
Expansive café overlooking the main plaza. Lovely wood interior, friendly service, free Wi-Fi, and a long list of excellent coffees.

### $ El Maizal
*Cra 9, No 20-30, T8-742 5876.*
This restaurant has a good varied menu of local specialities such as *mondongo* and trout.

### $ La Cascada
*Pasaje Vargas (C 19A), No 10-82, T8-744 5750.*
This large canteen is a popular lunchtime venue with *almuerzos* at US$3.25.

### $ La Mojarrita
*C 18, No 7-43, T8-743 8330.*
This seafood restaurant is famous in Tunja for its *mojarra* and *sancocho de pescado*.

### $ Pizza Nostra
*C 19, No 10-36, T8-740 2040.*
Pizzas and lasagnas on a pedestrianized street just off the main plaza.

### $ Son y Sabor
*Pasaje Vargas (C 19A), No 10-71, T8-740 2970.*
This typical restaurant has a good, varied menu serving rabbit and trout as well as steaks.

## Festivals

**Late May-1st Sun in Jun** The main local festival includes a special ceremony at the chapel of El Topo.
**17-24 Dec** A lively festival with local music, traditional dancing and fireworks.

## Shopping

The market is near the Plaza de Toros on the outskirts of town, open every day (good for *ruanas* and blankets). Fri is the main market day.

La Casa del Cuero, *Cra 9, No 20-09, T311-226 9950.* Artisanal shop selling a variety of leather goods from handbags to clothing. Makes jackets on premises starting at US$125.

## Transport

Four routes converge on Tunja, all busy and in good condition. The main road from Bogotá towards Bucaramanga bears northwest at the northern outskirts of the town. Heading northeast leads to Sogamoso, the Lago de Tota and the Sierras of Cocuy. West lies Villa de Leiva and Chiquinquirá. There are good bus services along all these roads. There are no air or passenger rail services to Tunja.

**Bus**
To Bogotá, with **Rápido Duitama**, **Libertadores** (comfortable and recommended), **Transportes Alianza** or **Copetran**, 3-3½ hrs Mon-Fri, 4½-5 hrs Sat, Sun and holidays, US$10.50. To **Bucaramanga**, frequent services, 7 hrs, US$25. To **Villa de Leiva**, frequent services in *colectivo* or mini bus, US$3.75, 45-60 mins. To **Zipaquirá**, catch a Bogotá-bound bus and change at La Caro, US$3.

## Villa de Leiva and around → *Colour map 2, B5.*
### perfectly preserved colonial town with historic and prehistoric sites nearby

★About 40 km west through the mountains is the colonial town of Villa de Leiva (also spelt Leyva). This is one of Colombia's very special places. It is not on any important through route and there are no significant natural resources nearby to be exploited, so it has been left alone and is now prized by Colombians and visitors alike. The town dates back, like Tunja, to the early days of Spanish rule, but unlike Tunja, it has been declared a National Monument, so will not be modernized. It was founded by Hernán Suárez de Villalobos in 1572 by order of the first president of Nueva Granada, Andrés Díaz Venero de Leiva.

Villa de Leiva and its surroundings are blessed with a bewildering mixture of topographies and climates. To the west the landscape is semi desert, typified by the reddish clay that is used to make bricks and terracotta tiles, and dotted with cacti. Fossils from the Jurassic and Cretaceous period are abundant. To the southeast, steep hills rise to *páramo* or moorland, sparse in vegetation. The nearby Iguaque Flora and Fauna Sanctuary is mainly high cloudforest.

### Towards Villa Leiva
To reach Villa Leiva from Bogotá, turn left at the Puente de Boyacá monument (see page 88) and go through the small attractive town of **Samacá**, which has a pretty plaza ornamented with bougainvillea arcades. The church has a bright white/yellow interior and a fine gilt retable. Alternatively, go via Tunja, heading northwest out of town. (This is the route taken by public buses.) On either route turn right at Sáchica for the final 6 km to Villa de Leiva. There is an alternative from Tunja: stay on the main road towards Bucaramanga, and after 34 km turn left at Arcabuco. This is an unsurfaced road and rough in places but you will see fine scenery as it goes alongside the Iguaque National Sanctuary.

**Tip...**
This is very much a place for walking around. Many of the streets are cobbled, and such traffic as there is travels at a snail's pace. Taxis will take you to outlying attractions.

### Sights
The town has an enormous, undulating plaza which appears to have buckled under the weight of the thousands of feet that have walked across it down the years. At 14,000 sq m it

is believed to be the largest cobbled square in South America. Almost the entire village is in pristine condition: whitewashed mansions have terracotta-tiled roofs and streets are paved with cobbles large and uneven enough to twist an ankle.

Two colonial houses are particularly worth a visit. One is the former home of **Antonio Nariño** ⓘ *Cra 9, No 10-25, free, Thu-Tue 0800-1200, 1400-1800,* who translated the *Rights of Man* into Spanish. The second is the building known as the **Casa del Primer Congreso** ⓘ *corner of the Plaza Mayor, Tue-Sat 0800-1200, 1400-1700, free,* in which the first Convention of the United Provinces of New Granada was held. This is the seat of the local authority and the building is closed to the public when they are in session.

Also worth a visit is the restored birthplace of the Independence hero **Antonio Ricaurte** ⓘ *Cra 8/C 15, Wed-Sun 0900-1200, 1400-1700, free.* Ricaurte was born in Villa de Leiva and died in 1814 at San Mateo, Venezuela, in a famous act of courageous

**Villa de Leiva**

To ②⑤, Museo Paleontológico, Arcabuco & Colombian Highlands

To Santa Sofía, Ecce Homo & El Fósil

To Bogotá, via Tunja or Chiquinquirá

N

| 200 metres |
| 200 yards |

| **Where to stay** 🛏 | Hostería del Molino | **Restaurants** 🍴 |
|---|---|---|
| Candelaria 1 | La Mesopotamia 6 | Carnes & Olivas 7 |
| Casa Viena 5 | Plaza Mayor 9 | Casa Blanca 1 |
| Colombian Highlands | Posada de los Angeles 7 | La Cocina de la Gata 3 |
| & Hostal Renacer 2 | Posada Don Blas 8 | Olivas & Especias 4 |
| Duruelo 3 | Posada de San Antonio 10 | Savia 5 |
| El Marqués de San Jorge 4 | | Zarina 6 |
| Hostal Sinduly 11 | | |

self-sacrifice while fighting in Bolívar's army. The house has an attractive courtyard and garden. There is also a statue of Richaurte on Plazuela San Agustín.

On the Plaza Mayor the **Casa-Museo Luis Alberto Acuña** ① *daily 0900-1800, US$12*, houses fascinating examples of Acuña's work and is well worth a visit.

The **Monasterio de las Carmelitas Descalzas** ① *C 14 and Cra 10, Sat-Sun and holidays 1030-1300, 1430-1700, US$1.50*, has one of the best museums of religious art in Colombia. The monastery also includes the **Convento** and the **Iglesia del Carmen** ① *open for Mass Mon-Fri 0700, 1800, Sat 0600, 1800, Sun 0600, 0700, 1100, 1800*, a simple, dignified church with a large fine Lady Chapel, all worth a visit. The **Iglesia de San Agustín** is now being converted into a museum.

An interesting and well-displayed **palaeontological museum** ① *Cra 9, No 11-42, Mon, Wed, Thu 0900-1200, Fri 1400-1700, Sat Sun 0800-1700, holidays 0800-1600, US$2*, has been opened 15 minutes' walk north of the town. It also has an old windmill, Molino de Losada, dating from the 16th century when Villa de Leyva was a leading wheat producer.

## Around Villa de Leiva

The wide valley to the west of Villa de Leiva is rich in fossils; 5 km along the road to Santa Sofía you will see the road signs for **El Fósil** ① *daily 0800-1800, US$3*. The skeleton displayed is a Plesiosaur group reptile, possibly a small Kronosaurus, found here in 1977, and the museum was built around it. The second exhibit is a baby of the same group, complete with tail, found in 2000 and placed alongside. These Plesiosaurs were similar to dolphins with flippers and a fine set of teeth. The museum contains a wide selection of other Mesozoic and Cretaceous exhibits.

About 2 km along the road to the village of Monquirá is **La Casa de Terracota** ① *www.casaterracota.com*, a house designed and belonging to Colombian architect Octavio Mendoza. This Gaudíesque construction, built entirely out of ceramic tiles extracted from the local area and worked directly onto the building, claims to be the largest such structure in the world. It's cheap, environmentally friendly and earthquake-proof. Almost everything is made from terracotta, including all the furniture, while there are fine examples of mosaics in the showers and clever use of light. Workshops and ceramics courses are held here.

About 1 km further along this road, 4 km from Villa de Leiva, is the well-endowed archaeological site of the **Parque Arqueológico de Monquirá** ① *Tue-Sun 0900-1200, 1400-1700, US$3 with guide*, otherwise known as El Infiernito, where there are several huge carved phalluses (which make for popular photo opportunities!). This is one of the most important Muisca religious sites in the country and features the only solar observatory in Colombia as well as a *dolmen* burial site. The site was discovered by the Spanish who baulked at the enormous stone penises and proclaimed that the Muisca would be banished to hell, hence the name 'El Infiernito' (Little Hell). Much of the site was destroyed and the stone used by local *campesinos* to build their homes. Some of it still remains, however, and was lovingly studied and maintained from the 1970s by archaeologist Eliecer Silva Célis, who passed away in 2007 at the age of 93. Close to Monquirá are the **Pozos Azules**, a series of aquamarine natural pools, US$2.50.

About 1 km beyond El Infiernito is the **Fibas Jardín de Desierto** ⓘ *Parque Ecológico, Espiritual y Educativo, T311-222 2399 (mob), Mon and Tue by appointment, Wed-Sun 0800-1730, free, meditation US$5 (with free plant),* run by former advertising executive Jaime Rodríguez Roldán. As well as selling many varieties of cactus and other desert plants, the nursery aims to educate visitors in environmentally friendly practices. No fertilizers, even organic ones, are used in nurturing the plants. The centre also features two mazes, based on ancient indigenous designs, in which Jaime holds meditation exercises.

**Tip...**
A good day trip is to take the Santa Sofía bus to Ecce Homo and then walk back to Villa de Leiva via El Fósil and El Infernito.

About 6 km beyond the Infiernito turning is a track on the left for the **Convento del Santo Ecce-Homo** ⓘ *0900-1800, US$2.50;* note the fossils in the floor at the entrance. The monastery has had a turbulent history. It was founded in 1620 and built in stone and adobe by the Dominicans between 1650 and 1695, but a century later it was taken over by the military and the friars were expelled. It was later abandoned until, in 1920, it was reclaimed by the Dominicans and some restoration was done. It has been repeatedly robbed since then, and some of the religious art is now in the Chiquinquirá museum for safe-keeping. What can be seen of the church, chapel and monastery is impressive, but the fabric and roof are in a poor state. To get to the monastery, catch a bus from Villa de Leiva (0800-1615) towards Santa Sofía, US$2, and ask to be dropped off; it is 30 minutes to the crossing, then a 1-km walk to the monastery.

## Towards Santa Sofía

Northwest of Villa de Leiva, on the way to Santa Sofía, is **Valle Escondido**, a verdant valley guarded by imposing mountains. Here there are various lodgings, including **El Arca Verde** ⓘ *www.arcaverde.blogspot.com*, an eco-friendly *maloka*. It is possible to abseil down some of the valley's many canyons. There are a number of expeditions to nearby waterfalls and bathing spots including **Paso del Angel**, near Santa Sofía, where the narrowest of natural bridges (less than a metre across) links two ridges with the 80-m **Guatoque waterfall** falling nearby.

## Santuario de Fauna y Flora de Iguaque

*3 km off the main Villa de Leiva–Arcabuco road, T8-341 3712. No entrance after 1000. US$16.50 for non-nationals. Bus from Villa de Leiva to the junction at 0645 (returns at 1230 and 1600), US$4; the best day for hitching a lift is Sat (market day).*

Some 14 km from Villa de Leiva on the road to Arcabuco is a right turn for the **Santuario de Fauna y Flora de Iguaque**, 3 km from the junction. About 40 minutes' walk up the valley from the entrance is a tourist centre with accommodation for 48 and a restaurant with good food at reasonable prices and a fine view of the surrounding countryside. There are guided paths and a marked trail to Lake Iguaque, a steep walk of three hours. The lake is central to Muisca mythology. The 6750-ha park is mainly high cloudforest of oak, fig and other temperate trees, much covered with epiphytes, lichens and bromeliads. There is also *páramo* (moorland) and a series of high-level lakes at over 3400 m, formed in the last Ice Age. The mountains rise to 3800 m and create clouds that cause frequent rain (about 1700 mm a year), giving the park a rich green quality. **Colombian Highlands** in Villa de Leiva (see page 98) is recommended for organized tours to the park.

## Ráquira

In the Chibcha language, Ráquira means 'city of pots'. There are over 100 *artesanía* shops selling earthenware pottery in this small village, which is rightly considered the capital of Colombian handicrafts, although in recent years there has been an influx of cheap products from Ecuador, somewhat diluting its appeal. The village itself has been painted in an array of primary colours and has a picturesque plaza embellished with terracotta statues, including one of a local version of Belgium's Manneken-Pis and another of Jorge Veloza, inventor of the musical genre *carranga*, who was born here.

## Monasterio Desierto de la Calendaria
*Daily 0900-1200, 1400-1600. US$2.50 includes Hermit's Cave.*

About 7 km from Ráquira is the beautiful 16th-century monastery of La Candelaria. In an otherwise dry area, the monastery is a small oasis, thanks to the water provided by the Río Guachaneco. It has a fine church, whose altar displays the painting of the Virgen de la Candelaria by Francisco del Pozo, dating from 1597. The painting was miraculously saved from burning and brought here by Augustinian monks, who founded the monastery in 1604 on the site of an indigenous altar. The anniversary of the painting is celebrated on 1 February and on 28 August, the saint's day.

The convent has two beautiful cloisters, one featuring a 170-year-old dwarf orange tree, the other virtually untouched since the 17th century. The monastery is an important location for novice Augustinian monks who come here on retreat for one year and are allowed no contact with their family during this time. A guided tour of the monastery includes a visit to the church, the cloisters, which are lined with anonymous 17th-century paintings of the life of San Agustín, and the catacomb-like Hermit's Cave, originally used by the local indigenous people but appropriated by the monks who built the monastery.

## Chiquinquirá

On the west side of the valley of the Río Suárez, 134 km from Bogotá and 80 km from Tunja, this is a busy market town for this large coffee and cattle region. In December thousands of pilgrims honour a painting of the Virgin whose fading colours were restored by the prayers of a woman, María Ramos. The picture is housed in the imposing **Basílica**, but the miracle took place in what is now the **Iglesia de la Renovación**. In 1816, when the town had enjoyed six years of Independence and was besieged by the Royalists, this painting was carried through the streets by Dominican priests from the famous monastery, to rally the people. The town fell, all the same. There are special celebrations at Easter and on 26 December, the anniversary of the miracle. The town is also known for making guitars.

## Tourist information

**Oficina Municipal de Turismo**, Cra 9, No 13-04, just off the plaza, Mon-Fri 0800-1200, 1400-1700, Sat-Sun 0800-1800, has some local maps and gives advice on cheaper accommodation. For information on environmental issues, contact the **Instituto von Humboldt**, Claustro de San Agustín, T8-7320 2767. The websites www.villadeleyva-boyaca.gov.co and www.villaleyvanos.com also have good information.

## Where to stay

**Villa de Leiva**
Villa de Leiva is usually quiet Mon-Thu but fills up at weekends.

**$$$$ Plaza Mayor**
*Cra 10, No 12-31, T8-732 0425, www.hotelplazamayor.com.co.*
28 rooms on 3 levels, right on the plaza, this worn brick building has a delightful octagonal courtyard with lemon trees and very comfortable rooms, plus Wi-Fi, parking and a good (expensive) restaurant.

**$$$$ Duruelo**
*Cra 3, No 12-88, T8-732 0222, www.duruelo.com.co.*
Villa de Leiva's most exclusive hotel, the building sits on a hill above the town, commanding views across the valley. The rooms are comfortable, though they perhaps could do with refurbishment but its biggest draw is the 4 swimming pools carved into the side of the hill and its spa and massage services.

**$$$$-$$$ Posada de San Antonio**
*Cra 8, No 11-80, T8-732 0538, www.hotellaposadadesanantonio.com.*

With its thick adobe walls, colourful decor, enormous antique beds and location on the beautiful Parque Nariño, this hotel is a popular choice with weekending *bogotanos*. The hotel also boasts a pool table, Wi-Fi in the lobby, and spa services for an additional charge.

**$$$ Candelaria**
*C del Silencio 18, No 8-12, T8-732 0534, www.hotelcandelariavilla deleyva.com.co.*
Located on the delightful cobbled Calle del Silencio, this refurbished colonial building has 9 rooms of monastic simplicity with thick, whitewashed walls and wooden beams. It also has a restaurant serving up international cuisine. Free tea, coffee, soft drinks, fruit basket and bottle of wine included.

**$$$ El Marqués de San Jorge**
*C 14, No 9-20, T8-732 0480, www.hospederiaelmarquesdesanjorge.com.*
This simple little place has rooms set around a courtyard and offers cable TV, Wi-Fi, parking and breakfast included.

**$$$ Hostería del Molino La Mesopotamia**
*C del Silencio, 15A-265, T8-732 0235.*
This former grain mill dates back to 1568, 4 years before Villa de Leiva was founded, and has retained much of its original lime and mud architecture in the house. It has delightful gardens with running rivulets of water fed by a spring, as well as a superb natural swimming pool. Recommended. Non-guests can use the pool for US$2.60.

**$$$-$$ Posada de los Angeles**
*Cra 10, No 13-94, T8-732 0562, www.villaleyvanos.com.*

This *posada* has basic, clean rooms in a fine building 2 blocks from the plaza and a restaurant serving American breakfasts and pastas. Be sure to ask for a room overlooking the beautiful Iglesia del Carmen.

### $$$-$$ Posada Don Blas
*C 12, No 10-61, T8-732 0406.*
This sweet and simple little place is just 1 block away from the plaza and has small, clean rooms with private bathrooms and cable TV.

### $$ Casa Viena
*Cra 10 No 19-114, T8-732 0711, www.casaviena.com.*
Owned by an Austrian who also owns **Casa Viena Cartagena**. 5 rooms, including 1 dorm, 3 private rooms and 1 larger private room with own bath and balcony overlooking the glorious mountain scenery. Internet access, herb garden, pizza oven and Wi-Fi.

### $$ Hostal Renacer
*Cra 10, No 21-finca Renacer, T8-732 1201/311-308 3739 (mob), www.colombianhighlands.com.*
A 15-min walk from town, this hostel, belonging to English-speaking biologist Oscar Gilède, has some of the most comfortable private rooms you are likely to find in any Colombian backpackers' hostel. This country finca has turned the grounds of a former mine into an extensive garden, complete with lovely lookout point, and there are excellent facilities, including a kitchen, a wood-fired pizza oven, hammocks, bike hire, internet and dorms with bunk beds. Oscar also runs a tour agency offering a variety of trips throughout Colombia (see page 98). Camping available, US$7 with own tent or US$10 for a tent and all equipment. Excellent for birdwatching, 75 species.

### $$-$ Hostal Sinduly
*Cra 11, No 11-77, T8-732 0345, www.hostalsinduly.com.*
Run by Austrian expat Manfred, this 10-bed hostel has 1 private room with bathroom and a couple of dorms in a colonial house 1 block from the plaza. There is use of kitchen and hot water, and Manfred also arranges trips to a finca he owns near the entrance to Iguaque National Sanctuary. English and German spoken.

## Iguaque National Sanctuary

### $ Furachiogua
*At the visitor centre.*
7 shared rooms (capacity 48) with bunk beds or single beds, US$19 per person. There is also a campsite with showers and toilets and cooking facilities, US$5.

## Ráquira and around

### $$ Hostería Nemqueteba
*T8-735 7016.*
This charming colonial house has a brightly painted patio brimming with bougainvillea as well as a swimming pool.

### $$ Suaya
*C del Comercio, T8-735 7029.*
1 block from the plaza, this colonial building has brightly painted rooms with en suite bathrooms and hot water.

## Monasterio Desierto de la Calendaria
Adjoining the monastery is a hotel often used for spiritual retreats.

### $$ Posada San Agustín
*www.agustinosrecoletos.com.co.*
A 16th-century building set around a colourful cloister with flower beds and a water feature, the rooms are simple but comfortable. There are 2 suites with jacuzzis as well as 2 saunas.

## Chiquinquirá

### $$$-$$ El Gran
*C 16 No 7A-55, T1-726 3700.*
This hotel is central, secure and comfortable and includes breakfast. It has a good restaurant, laundry service and parking.

### $$ Sarabita
*C 16, 8-13.*
This business hotel has a pool, sauna (when working) and restaurant, all housed in a building declared a National Monument.

### $$-$ Moyba
*Cra 9, on the plaza.*
This hotel is a bit dingy, cheaper without private bathroom.

## Restaurants

### Villa de Leiva
Villa de Leiva has dozens of good restaurants with varied international and local menus. Most, but not all, are concentrated in the town's upmarket foodcourts, **Casa Quintero** (on the plaza) and **La Guaca** (on C Caliente). Bear in mind that many are closed Mon-Wed or Mon-Thu.

### $$ La Cocina de la Gata
*Casa Quintero, Local 11, T8-732 1266.*
This pleasantly decorated fondue restaurant also serves chicken and steak.

### $$ Olivas & Especias
*Cra 10, No 11-99, T8-732 1261.*
On the corner of the plaza, this restaurant serves pizzas and pastas in homely surroundings. Also worth a try is **Carnes & Olivas ($$$)**, its prettier but pricier sister restaurant around the corner (also Cra 10).

### $$ Savia
*Casa Quintero, Local 20, T8-732 1778.*
Savia has an excellent range of organic dishes of all kinds, such as chicken in mango sauce.

### $$ Zarina
*Cra 9, No 11-75, Casa Quintero.*
This small restaurant serves up excellent Arabic and Oriental dishes as well as the usual chicken and steak.

### $ Casa Blanca
*C 13, No 7-16, T8-732 0821.*
This popular restaurant has been feeding locals for more than 20 years and serves up regional specialities such as *longaniza*.

### Ráquira and around

### $ La Raquireñita
*Cra 3, No 3-36.*
On the plaza, this lunchtime restaurant is brightly decorated with ceramic masks and other *artesanías* and serves up a mixture of fish, steak and chicken dishes.

### $ Nemqueteba
*Cra 3, No 3-04, T8-735 7016.*
This restaurant belonging to the hotel of the same name serves up local trout as well as chicken and steak in pleasant surroundings.

### Chiquinquirá
There are plenty of reasonable places to eat around and near Parque Julio Flores.

## Festivals

### Villa de Leiva
Jan-Feb **Astronomical festival**, during which telescopes are set up in the plaza principal for public use.
Apr **Encuentro de Musica Antigua** celebrates antique music from all over the world.

**13-17 Jul** **Virgen del Carmen** is celebrated each year.

**Aug** **International Kite Festival** is held in the Plaza Mayor.

**7 Dec** A **festival of light**, with impressive firework displays, is held every year from this date.

## Shopping

### Villa de Leiva

Shops in the plaza and the adjoining streets have an excellent selection of Colombian handicrafts and offer many bargains. **Ricardo Luna**, C 13, No 7-42, sells good leather products. Market day is Sat, held in the Plaza del Mercado (not the Plaza Mayor).

### Chiquinquirá

Many delightful toys are made locally. Along the south side of the Basilica are shops specializing in musical instruments.

## What to do

### Villa de Leiva
**Horse riding**

Raul Oswaldo, *T310-757 5327*. Offers horseback riding for US$20 for 1 hr, group discounts when booking with Colombian Highlands.

**Tour operators**

Colombian Highlands, *Cra 10, No 21 Hostel Renacer, T8-732 1862, T310-552 9079, www.colombianhighlands.com*. Biologist Oscar Gilède runs tours of the local area and throughout Colombia, as well as trips to local nature spots, such as Iguaque National Sanctuary and the Cascada La Periquera, specifically geared towards botanists, ornithologists and enthusiasts of adventure sports such as abseiling and caving. His office is located in the Hostel Renacer.

Zebra Trips, *C Caliente, T8-732 0487/311-870 1749 (mob), villadeleyva.net2011@gmail.com*. With its zebra-striped fleet of Land Rovers, this company provides a fun way to explore the desert area outside Villa de Leiva. 8 different tours starting at US$17, as well as bike hire and a gourmet outing.

## Transport

### Villa de Leiva
**Bus**

The bus station is on Cra 9 between C 11 and C 12. To **Tunja**, 45-60 mins, US$4.50 with **Flota Reina**, **Coomultrasvilla**, **Cootax**, **Libertadores** or **Trans Alianza**, or microbus every 15 mins 0530-1800. To **Bogotá**, via Tunja, 4 hrs, US$11, several companies; via Zipaquirá US$10. To **Santa Sofía**, 0800-1615, US$2. To **Chiquinquirá**, hourly minibus, 1 hr, US$3.75. To **Ráquira**, US$3.

**Taxi**

Taxi to outlying areas (including **Hostal Renacer**), US$2.50. To **Ráquira**, 30 mins, US$20. To **Iguaque National Sanctuary entrance**, round trip US$35.

### Ráquira and around
**Bus**

To **Villa de Leiva**, 30 mins, last bus 1600, US$3.

### Chiquinquirá
**Bus**

To **Villa de Leiva**, 1¾ hrs, US$3.75, several daily. To **Tunja**, 3 hrs, US$6. To **Zipaquirá**, US$7.50. To **Bogotá**, 2½ hrs, US$5.

**thermal springs, rural villages and a beautiful lake**

### ★Paipa

Along the road, 41 km northeast of Tunja is Paipa, noted for its Aguas Termales ⓘ *3 km southeast, daily 0900-1800, US$5, mud bath US$27.50, minibus US$2.50, taxi US$25*. The baths and the neighbouring **Lago Sochagota** (boat trips possible) are very popular with Colombians and increasingly with foreign tourists. There are innumerable hotels ($) and restaurants on the main street of Paipa and on the approach road to the Aguas Termales, though hotels at the springs are more expensive. Paipa is a good place to buy carpets, hammocks and handicrafts.

### Sogamoso

At Duitama, a town 15 km beyond Paipa known for basket weaving, turn right and follow the valley of the Río Chicamocha for Sogamoso, a large, mainly industrial town that is nevertheless a good base for trekking and exploring the outlying region (contact Finca San Pedro for information). This was an important Chibcha (Muisca) settlement, and the **Museo Arqueológico Suamox y Templo del Sol** ⓘ *Cra 7A, C Novena, Mon-Fri 0800-1200, 1400-1700, Sat 0800-1600, closed Sun US$2.50*, has been set up on the original site. A comprehensive museum describes the traditional techniques of mummification, statuary and crafts, including gold-working.

### ★Iza

South of Sogamoso the road winds its way through a grassy valley backed by imposing pine-clad hills. After 15 minutes, the road reaches the colonial village of Iza, founded in 1780. In Chibcha, Iza means 'place of healing', no doubt a reference to the thermal springs found outside the village. Not much happens in Iza but you could easily spend a week here soaking up its curative atmosphere.

It has what could classify as the most beautiful Parque Principal in Colombia, its four corners guarded by arched yew trees intertwined with bougainvillea bushes. On Sundays, the plaza is lined with stalls selling all types of sugary puddings. South of the village, lush water meadows shaded by the drooping fronds of willow trees run down to the Río Iza. A path runs over a picturesque covered wooden bridge and joins the road leading to the hot springs 1 km away.

There are several access points to the hot springs. The most popular is **Piscina Erika** ⓘ *US$4.50 with restaurant, changing rooms and showers*, which has a good-sized concrete pool and a children's paddling pool fed by piping hot sulphurous water from the spring just above. There are also two simple rooms for overnight stays (see Where to stay). Beyond Piscina Erika there is free access to natural pools, popular with locals at weekends. Unfortunately, these marshy pools are not well maintained and have been allowed to clog up with discarded rubbish.

There is good hiking around Iza, especially to **Cascada El Encanto del Amor**, a waterfall in the hills above the village. Ask at the Casa de la Cultura on the plaza or at Posada del Virrey Solis for directions.

## ON THE ROAD

### How Lago de Tota was formed

Many years ago an indigenous family was bequeathed a mysterious vessel of water by the gods. The gift was to be emptied to form a great lake. The husband and wife travelled over many lands looking for a suitable spot to create the lake. Their son and daughter did not understand their parents' obsession and decided to find out what was so special about this jar that they guarded so jealously. They accidentally spilt the water, causing a disaster. As soon as it hit the ground, the water swelled and flooded everything. The landscape changed. The boy, knowing he was the culprit, ran from his parents in fright. The girl ran to her mother and both were turned to stone, forming the two islands that today can be seen opposite Playa Blanca. The father tried to climb up to the moor above the lake but was overcome by the waters and turned into what is today known as the Potrero peninsula.

### ★Lago de Tota

Beyond Iza the road rises sharply through pastures rich in wild flowers, passing through Cuitiva and the indigenous village of Tota. Here, the landscape changes to *páramo* or moorland, tinged with traces of purple, pink and red, before the road drops down to the steely blue waters of Lago de Tota. At 15 km long and 10 km wide, this is the largest natural lake in Colombia. The indigenous *campesinos* who populate its edges cultivate tidy patches of onions right up to the shoreline. There are reeds and algae all along the banks and few beaches, the notable exception being **Playa Blanca**, on the southwest corner, which is a beach of white sand with shallow green water, backed by pine-clad hills. The beach would not look out of place in the Caribbean, but at 3015 m, the water is cold. There is camping and a restaurant serving trout. At weekends Playa Blanca fills up with Colombians but is generally quiet otherwise.

**Aquitania**, on the eastern shore, is the principal town on the lake. There are plenty of food shops and restaurants, including **Lucho** and **Pueblito Viejo** on the corner of the plaza, and a bright, restored church with modern stained-glass windows. Above the town, El Cumbre offers beautiful views. For more information about Lago de Tota and the outlying region, visit www.visitsugamuxi.com.

### Monguí → *Colour map 2, B6.*

About 12 km northeast of Sogamoso is Monguí, once voted 'the most beautiful village in Boyacá'. The department has many contenders for this title but it would be difficult to build a case against this village, set high in the hills with sweeping views down towards Sogamoso in the valley below. It has a large cobbled plaza and whitewashed houses with doors and windows in racing green and red. The magnificent **Basílica** ① *open only at weekends, free entry*, was constructed by the Franciscans in the 17th century and has many oil paintings, including the *Virgin de Monguí*, donated by Philip II of Spain. It has a very good museum, with exhibits that include the convent's original kitchen and dining room with 17th-century reliefs and a mummified cat found in the rafters of the building's ceiling.

Monguí is a very peaceful place to stroll around. It's not uncommon to see a horse or cow tethered outside the local bar while its owner chews the cud inside. Don't miss the walk down Carrera 3 to the **Calycanto Bridge**, built by the Spanish out of stone cemented with clay, lime and bull's blood in order to bring large stones across the river to the church. At the top of Calle 4, to the right of the church, is the **Plaza de Toros**. If you feel energetic, take any path beyond the bull ring to a rock on which stands a shrine to the Virgin and Child, illuminated at night. From here there are tremendous views in all directions. A recommended excursion is east to the **Páramo de Ocetá** with particularly fine *frailejones* and giant wild lupins, a three-hour walk from Monguí.

## Listings East of Tunja

### Where to stay

#### Paipa and around

**$$$$-$$$ Casona del Salitre**
*Vía Toca, Km 3, T317-362 5972,*
*www.haciendadelsalitre.com.*
*5 mins' drive from town.*
A National Monument and a memorable place to stay near the baths and lake in a well-preserved hacienda where Simón Bolívar slept before the Battle of Boyacá. Hot pools, spa, good restaurant, quiet, fireplace. Highly recommended.

#### Sogamoso

**$$$-$$ Bochica**
*C 11, No 14-33, T8-770 4140.*
Good value, with comfortable rooms, hot water, TV, tourist info, and a restaurant.

**$$ Finca San Pedro**
*Km 2 via Lago de Tota, T312-567 7102,*
*www.fincasanpedro.com.*
Newer hostel in a charming old colonial house in expansive, lush grounds. Juan runs the house and offers excursions and information about the area. Also yoga school (www.agamayoga

colombia.com), massage and activities. Highly recommended.

#### Iza

**$$ Piscina Erika**
*Vereda Agua Caliente, T310-881 0731.*
The complex has 2 simple but comfortable rooms with en suite bathrooms and access to the pool. Breakfast is included.

**$$ Posada del Virrey Solis**
*C 4A, No 4A-75, T312-567 7373.*
Just off the Parque Principal on a little *plazoleta* dominated by an enormous pine tree, this 180-year-old house, declared a National Monument, has baroque rooms full of religious paintings and iconography, old books and Egyptian statuettes.

#### Lago de Tota

**$$ Camino Real**
*Km 20 Vía Sogamoso a Aquitania,*
*T312-478 1116, on the lake.*
Pleasant public rooms, colourful gardens, boat slipway, boats for hire, restaurant, sauna, tourist information.

## $$ Refugio Pozo Azul
*3 km beyond Camino Real, in a*
*secluded bay on the lake, T1-620 6257*
*(Bogotá), T320-384 1000 (mob),*
*www.hotelrefugiopozoazul.com.*
With breakfast. Suitable for children,
comfortable, watersport facilities, good
food. Also has cabins for up to 6.

### Playa Blanca
Camping is free at Playa Blanca but there
are no facilities. Not recommended.

## Monguí

### $$ El Portón de Ocetá
*Neat the plaza.*
A beautiful, large converted
colonial house.

### $$ La Casona
*Cra 4, No 3-41, T8-782 498,*
*chopo11110@yahoo.es.*
This small hostel has clean comfortable
rooms with en suite bathrooms behind
a restaurant of the same name. It has
lovely views down into the valley.
Recommended.

### $ Hostal Calycanto
A pink house next to the bridge with a
lovely setting and a restaurant. Best to
book in advance.

### $ La Cabaña
*Chalet on road beyond river (cross bridge,*
*turn left).*
Basic but comfortable. Provides meals
if forewarned.

## Restaurants

### Sogamoso

#### $$ Gula y Lujuria
*C 13 No 10-27 T8-772 5252.*
One of the best restaurants in town, just
half a block from the plaza. Local and
international specialities include trout
and grilled meats.

### Iza
There are a couple of restaurants on the
Parque Principal.

## Shopping

### Monguí
There are good *artesanía* shops, selling
woollen *ruanas* and leather products.
Aside from traditional crafts, Monguí
is one of the leading manufacturers of
footballs, with many outlets in town
selling handmade balls.

## Transport

### Sogamoso
**Bus**
To **Bogotá**, 4-4½ hrs, US$11.50. To **Tunja**,
1-2 hrs, US$3.25. To **Iza**, with **Flota
Alianzana** or take a taxi to Puente de
Pesca, 5 or 6 blocks away, and catch the
bus from there. To **Lago de Tota**, US$2,
1½ hrs with **Flota Alianzana**; buses leave
every 1½ hrs, passing through Iza, Tota
and on to **Aquitania**.

### Monguí
**Bus**
Buses leave from the plaza. To
**Sogamoso**, every 20 mins by *buseta*,
US$2.50, 45 mins.

★The Sierra Nevada del Cocuy is a mecca for high-altitude hikers and climbers in Colombia. This breathtaking mountain area is located in three departments, Boyacá, Santander and Arauca, and consists of two parallel north—south ranges about 30 km long, offering peaks of rare beauty, lakes, cliffs, waterfalls and literally thousands of *frailejón* plants. There are more than 22 snowy peaks, which together form the biggest mass of snow and ice in South America north of the equator. The highest of the snow-clad peaks is the Ritacuba Blanco at 5330 m.

### Visiting the national park

*Entrance to the park is US$25 for non-Colombians, payable at the park office on the Plaza Mercado in El Cocuy, where you can also obtain a map with the main walking paths. For further information, see www.parquesnacionales.gov.co.*

The park is accessible in the south from the small town of **El Cocuy** or further north from **Güicán**. Both towns are perfect starting or ending points for any hiking or climbing activity in the park. A number of treks and hikes are available, but because the area around **La Laguna de La Plaza** is closed to visitors, it is no longer possible to make a circuit of the entire park; visitors should contact the park office for alternative routes. One of the most spectacular is walking from south to north (or vice versa), taking in a large part of what the park has to offer. Although the trail is clearly marked, it is highly recommend that you go with a guide as sudden changes in climate means visibility can unexpectedly drop to less than 10 m. You will need to know where to camp and where to get drinking water.

There is no accommodation in the park, so you will need to bring all equipment yourself. Basic food supplies can be bought in El Cocuy or Güicán, but otherwise you should bring your food from Bogotá. There is no need to bring ice axes or crampons, unless you are climbing Pan de Azúcar. Note that temperatures can drop below 0°C at night, as most campsites are located at 4000 m.

### Sights

**La Laguna de La Plaza** is probably the most beautiful lake of all those in the Sierra Nevada del Cocuy, surrounded by the snowy summits of **Pan de Azúcar** and **Toti** in the west and **Picos Negro** and **Blanco** in the east. Unfortunately it has been closed since 2013, but the indigenous people may reopen this area in the future; check with the national park office (Unidad de Parque Nacionales).

**Laguna Grande de la Sierra** is surrounded by the tops of Pan de Azúcar, Toti, Portales, Concavo and Concavito and is a perfect base camp for climbing to the summits of (one of) these peaks. **El Púlpito de Diablo** is an enormous, square rock in the shape of an altar at 5000 m. From El Púlpito you can continue to climb up to the top of **Pan de Azúcar** (5100 m) overlooking Laguna de la Plaza on one side and Laguna Grande de la Sierra on the other side. Just below Pan de Azúcar you can see **Cerro El Diamante**, a pointy rock that might remind you of a real *diamante*.

During sunrise, the colour of this rock can change from grey to yellow, gold, red and orange, if you are lucky with the weather.

**Valle de los Cojines** is an enormous valley surrounded by snow-capped peaks and filled with *cojines* (pillow plants), typical of the region. There are fabulous views of the valley and many other parts of the park from the summit of **Ritacuba Blanco**, the highest mountain of all (5322 m). An ascent with mountain guide is not too difficult and costs around US$75-100.

## Listings Sierra Nevada del Cocuy

### Where to stay

#### El Cocuy

**$ pp Cabañas Guaicany**
*At the entrance to Valle de Lagunillas.*
With shared bathroom. Great views of the Ritacuba Blanco, the peaks of San Pablín Sur and Norte and Concavo. Also possible to camp and to hire horses and/or guide.

**$ pp Cabañas Kanwarra**
*Located at the foot of Ritacuba Blanco.*
The perfect starting point to climb Ritacuba Blanco or to walk to Laguna Grande de los Verdes. With shared bathroom.

**$ pp Finca La Esperanza**
*At the entrance to Valle de Frailejones.*
Convenient for the walk to Laguna Grande de la Sierra. Simple rooms with shared bathroom.

**$ pp Hotel Casa Muñoz**
*On the main square.*
With private bathroom.

### What to do

**Aventure Colombia**, *based in Cartagena and Bogotá, www.aventurecolombia.com.* Runs a 7-day trek in Sierra Nevada de Cocuy, taking in the Valle de Lagunillas–Púlpito del Diablo–Pan de Azúcar–Laguna de la Plaza and costing US$950 per person. Price includes transport to/from Bogotá–El Cocuy/Güicán, park fees, accommodation, meals and a guide. A good level of physical fitness is required.

### Transport

**Bus**
El Cocuy and Güicán can be reached by direct bus (only late in the evening) from Bogota (10-12 hrs) with **Paz del Río**, **Libertadores** and **Concorde** (US$17-30). Milk trucks leave the main plaza of El Cocuy at around 0600, transporting visitors to the **Cabañas Guaicany** (southern entrance of the park), **Finca la Esperanza** (for Laguna Grande de la Sierra) or to **Hacienda Ritacuba** from where it is about 1 hr's walk to the **Cabañas Kanwarra**. An **Expreso** (private transport) costs around US$40 and can be arranged at the main plaza in El Cocuy.

# Santander
## Department

Tumbling rivers, green valleys and countless immaculately preserved colonial towns and villages – Santander has much to recommend it. Take away the tropical vegetation and you could almost imagine yourself in the mountains of southern Spain. With an established adventure-sports scene centred around the town of San Gil, this area of Colombia is becoming an increasingly popular destination for national and foreign visitors alike. What's more, it is also one of the cheapest parts of the country; you will get the chance to sample some of the regional culinary delicacies and stay in delightful colonial hotels without fear of breaking the bank. The village of Barichara was voted the most beautiful in Colombia and was declared a National Monument in 1975, while Girón, just a few kilometres from the industrial capital Bucaramanga, does not lag far behind. Bucaramanga itself is a modern city with a thriving nightlife and one of the best places for paragliding in the country.

★About 21 km northeast of Socorro, is San Gil, a colonial town with a good climate in the deep valley of the Río Fonce. San Gil is an important centre for adventure sports. The river systems of the Ríos Fonce and Chicamocha run through deep valleys and gorges in this part of Santander, providing the best rafting and canoeing in Colombia (see page 108). With a broad range of hotels, San Gil is also an excellent base from which to explore Santander's string of stunning colonial villages.

### Sights

Near the centre of the town by the river is the enchanting **Parque Gallineral** ① *T7-723 7305, daily, from US$2.50*, created in 1919 and covering 4 ha where the Quebrada Curití runs through a delta to the Río Fonce. It is named after the *chiminango* trees, which make up 80% of the trees in the park. These trees have a natural tendency to lean over and are therefore popular with roosting chickens (*gallinas*). There are streams everywhere which create a delightful botanical garden full of butterflies and birds. Notable are the heliconias and the moss-like *tillandsia*, a bromeliad that covers many of the trees. Note, too, the huge ceiba near the *playa* where the canoes end their trip down the Río Fonce. To find out more about the flora and fauna, ask one of the excellent guides, but tip generously as they are not paid by the park authorities. The park has a restaurant and a superb natural swimming pool, which uses water siphoned off from the Quebrada Curití.

In the centre of San Gil, the **Parque Principal** has a fountain surrounded by huge ceiba and heliconia trees, which is very attractive when illuminated in the evening.

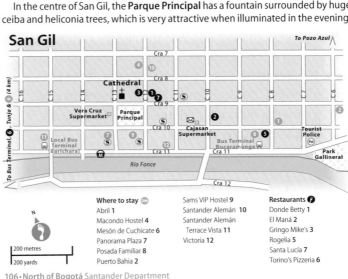

**Where to stay** 😑
Abril **1**
Macondo Hostel **4**
Mesón de Cuchicate **6**
Panorama Plaza **7**
Posada Familiar **8**
Puerto Bahia **2**

Sams VIP Hostel **9**
Santander Alemán **10**
Santander Alemán
Terrace Vista **11**
Victoria **12**

**Restaurants** 🍴
Donde Betty **1**
El Maná **2**
Gringo Mike's **3**
Rogelia **5**
Santa Lucía **7**
Torino's Pizzeria **6**

Overlooking it is the **church**, which has interesting octagonal towers. There is a good view of the town from **La Gruta**, a shrine to the north (look for the cross).

## South of San Gil

About 20 km south of San Gil on the road to Duitama is **Páramo,** another centre for adventure sport in this area. About 30 km further south is **Charalá**, which has a plaza with a statue of **José Antonio Galán**, leader of the 1781 Comunero revolt. It also has an interesting church and *casa de la cultura*.

## North of San Gil

On the main road to Bucaramanga is **Curití**, noted for handicrafts in *fique* (agave sisal). Mixed with cotton, it is used to make fabrics, shoes, bags and even building materials. You can see weaving at **Ecofibras** in the village. Near Curití are limestone caves that can be explored (see San Gil Activities, below). Transport to Curití costs US$1.50 by bus, or US$7.50 by taxi. About 28 km north of San Gil, a little off the road, is the picturesque village of **Aratoca**, which has a colonial church.

## ★ Cañón de Chicamocha

Near Aratoca you will notice a deep valley to the east of the road: this is the canyon of the **Río Chicamocha**. Look out for the place where the road takes to a narrow ridge with grandstand views on both sides as the river loops round to the southwest. The descent along the side of the steep cliff into the dry canyon with its spectacular rock colours is one of the most dramatic routes in Colombia, but note that, if driving, this is a demanding and dangerous stretch. The river at this point is a popular place for canoeing and whitewater rafting, especially between Cepitá and Pescadero (see page 108). After crossing the river, the road ascends again to the plateau for the remaining few kilometers to Bucaramanga.

Twelve kilometres north of Aratoca is the entrance to the **Parque Nacional Chicamocha** ⓘ *C 31, No 22-45, Canaveral, T7-656 9006, www.parquenacionaldel chicamocha.com, Wed-Fri 1000-1800, Sat-Sun and holidays 0900-1900, US$21 including cable car, children under 2 free*. It is more of a theme park than an actual national park, with an aqua complex, children's activities and sports, but the views are splendid, especially from the 6.3-km cable car across the canyon.

## Activities

San Gil is increasingly recognized as the centre of Colombia's burgeoning adventure-sports industry. There are a number of activities available in the surrounding countryside and numerous adventure companies in San Gil itself, some better equipped than others. See What to do, page 111, for recommendations, or speak to the staff at the **Macondo Guesthouse** for advice. For most activities wear good footwear, bring a hat and sunscreen.

**Abseiling** Known as *'rappelling'* in Colombia, abseiling down Juan Curi, a spectacular three-tier, 180-m waterfall, is a popular activity. A descent down one of the waterfall's 60-m cascades costs US$22.50 per person. The trip is best done in the mornings and should be pre-booked. It's also possible to cycle (two hours) or hike to the waterfalls from San Gil. There's a lovely swimming spot at the base of one of the falls and you can climb to the second of the three tiers using a number of ladders and ropes. From San Gil, take a bus (US$4 return) towards Charalá and ask to be dropped off at the waterfall. There are two approaches, passing through private fincas. You may have to pay a small fee for access, about US$3-5 (this entrance fee is included in the price if abseiling). A return taxi fare is US$25.

**Caving** On the road to Barichara is a series of caves known as La Antigua with saloons full of spiders and bats. A guided crawl through small tunnels of mud and water to underground waterfalls costs US$12.50. South of San Gil, near Páramo, is Cueva del Indio, a cave full of stalactites, stalagmites and bats. You have to slide down a zip line into the dark mouth of the cave before wading through waist-level water, US$14. To get there, take a bus (US$2) from bus station in San Gil or taxi (US$17 return). Another exciting cave to explore is Cueva Vaca near Curití; two-hour tours cost US$12.50. Pre-book all caving in San Gil.

**Hiking** The surrounding countryside has several old indigenous trails, known as the *lenguake* or Camino Real, linking many of its beautiful villages (see under Barichara, below, for more details).

**Kayaking** Three-day beginners' courses on the Río Fonce, including eskimo roll training in a local swimming pool, cost US$190. More experienced kayakers can make runs on different rivers with experienced guides.

**Paragliding** San Gil has two excellent locations for paragliding (known as *parapente*). The most spectacular location is over the Chicamocha Canyon and costs US$85, lasting between 30 minutes and one hour. The second is near Curití and lasts 15 to 20 minutes, costing US$30.

**Rafting** Blessed with three rivers in proximity to each other, San Gil can provide excellent rafting for people of all levels of experience.

The Río Fonce is the main river running through San Gil and is the best one for beginners with Grade II-III rapids. The trip begins 11 km from town and winds up in the centre of San Gil, opposite the Parque Gallineral. A trip costs US$15 with transport and safety equipment. It is best to wear sandals.

For a more extreme experience, the Río Suárez has Class IV+ rapids. The 20-km trip lasts one to two hours and costs US$65 per person.

**Swimming** There are lots of good swimming holes on San Gil's rivers. A local favourite is the Pozo Azul, just outside town, popular on Sundays. The most spectacular option is Pescaderito, just outside Curití, which has a number of beautiful, clear pools. From the main square in Curití, walk past the church four blocks and take the road leading out of town. Alternatively, Parque Gallineral in San Gil has a spectacular swimming pool.

## Where to stay

### San Gil

**$$$ Hotel Puerto Bahia**
*C 6 No 9-112, T316-727 3185,*
*www.hotelpuertobahiasangil.com.*
Probably the most upscale hotel in town,
this is a good option for travellers who
want to splurge on amenities such as
pool, sauna and in-room jacuzzis.

**$$ Abril**
*C 8, No 9-63 esq, T7-724 8795,*
*hotelabrilsangilss@yahoo.es.*
Strangely laid out with the reception
area essentially in the car park but it
has clean rooms with antique beds
(comfortable), hot water, Wi-Fi, fan,
TV and a minibar.

**$$ Mesón de Cuchicute**
*Km 1 Vía San Gil–Socorro, T7-724 2041.*
On the western outskirts of town,
**Mesón de Cuchicute** offers either
*cabañas* or 2 up, 2 down rooms with
balconies looking out over one of the
hotel's 2 enormous pools. With very
comfortable beds, all the mod cons
(TV, a/c, minibar, room service), jacuzzi,
gym, restaurant and some nice details
such as wash basins carved out of local
Barichara stone, it represents good value
for money.

**$$ Panorama Plaza Hotel**
*Cra 10, No 13-17, T7-724 2170,*
*panoramaplazahoteles@yahoo.es.*
Fine old building off the Parque Principal.
Has a restaurant serving breakfasts and
the occasional weekend lunch as well as
Wi-Fi, though the double rooms have no
windows. Prices tend to double during
high season.

**$$ Posada Familiar**
*Cra 10, No 8-55, T7-724 8136.*
Small place with 6 rooms set around a
sunny courtyard with a water feature
and hanging plants. Rooms are clean
and have TV, fan, Wi-Fi and private baths.
Recommended.

**$$ Victoria**
*Cra 11, No 10-40, T7-724 5955.*
Eccentrically decorated in garish colours
which somehow seem to work, the
Victoria has some bizarre ornaments,
including fake knitted sunflowers in one
room. Rooms open onto a long corridor-
courtyard with a fountain. Some rooms
with a/c or fan and even a DVD player
but no hot water.

**$$-$ Macondo Hostel**
*Cra 8 10-35, T7-724 8001,*
*www.macondohostel.com.*
Australian Shaun Clohesy has run this
hostel since 2003. There are private
rooms, 2 dorms, TV room, nice garden
jacuzzi and a place for barbecues.
**Macondo**'s biggest asset is the wealth of
information available on local activities
and the chance to swap tales with the
many backpackers who pass through.
Recommended.

**$$-$ Sam's VIP Hostel**
*Cra 10 12-33, T7-724 2746,*
*www.samshostel.com.*
The poshest backpackers' hangout in
San Gil, this hostel overlooking the main
plaza has everything from rooms with
private balconies to an outdoor rooftop
pool and a bar that stays open until
midnight. Recommended.

## $ San Carlos
*Cra 11, No 11-25, T7-724 2542.*
Sweet little place set round an atrium.
Has TV and private bath but some of the
rooms have no windows.

## $ Santander Alemán and Santander Alemán Terrace Vista
*C 10, No 15-07, T7-724 0329, www.
hostelsantanderalemantv.co.*
Large hostel with a beautiful roof
terrace for meals and beers. Several nice
common areas, hammocks, internet
access and book exchange. Emphasizes
that it's Catholic and family-oriented,
so not for the party crowd.

## Restaurants

### San Gil
San Gil has a number of good eating
options, but it is difficult to find places
open in the evening. The market on
Cra 11 between C 13 and 14 is a great
breakfast and lunch spot with lots of stalls
selling fruit salads and juices. If you don't
have a sweet tooth be sure to ask them
to lay off the condensed milk and cheese
on your salad. Can get a bit chaotic at
weekends, so watch your pockets.

### $$-$ Gringo Mike's
*C 12 No 8-35, T7-724 1695,
www.gringomikes.net.*
US/British-run restaurant and bar
specializing in West Coast cuisine with
some lovely Mexican influences. Great
burgers, salads, baked goods and maybe
the best sandwiches in Colombia.
Open daily for breakfast, lunch and
dinner. Friendly staff and good nosh.
Recommended.

## $ Donde Betty
*Cra 9, C 12 esq.*
Great little breakfast spot selling *arepas*,
scrambled eggs and fruit juices. On the
corner of the Parque Principal, hence
an excellent place for people-watching,
unless they bring the sun blinds right
down to street level, which they
frequently do in the afternoons.

## $ Elementales
*C 12, No 8-39.*
Located 2 doors down from **Gringo
Mike's**, this veggie option serves veggie
burgers, salads and juices.

## $ El Maná
*C 10, No 9-12, www.elmanasangil.
inf.travel.*
It would be difficult to leave this
restaurant without feeling a little
bloated what with the many set menu
courses you get for less than US$5.
Try the chicken stuffed with ham and
cheese. Open at lunchtime and evenings
except Mon.

## $ Rogelia
*Cra 9, No 8-09.*
Great little lunchtime place in a colonial
building with large wooden beams.
Serves local specialities such as *cabrito
con pepitorio* and *carne oreada* (a bit like
beef jerky). *Menú ejecutivo,* US$4.50.

## $ Torino's Pizzeria
*Centro Commercial Camino Real,
Cra 9 11-68.*
The shopping centre has several nice
bars and eateries, including this popular
pizzeria with brick oven. It serves pizzas,
pastas and calzones, is open in the
evenings and does home delivery. Other
recommendations are **Santa Lucía** on
the ground floor and **Habana** upstairs.

## Festivals

### San Gil

**Nov** **Festival San Gil**. During the 1st week of the month the city celebrates with dancers, music, horse parades and bullfighting.

## Shopping

### San Gil

Armando Palitos, *Cra 11, No 9-44, T7-724 3345*. Excellent selection of *artesanías*, ranging from furniture and plates to *bolsos de fique* (woven bags).

## What to do

For details of the most popular activities, see page 107; others include bungee jumping, hydrospeed and mountain biking.

### San Gil
**Adventure sports**
Colombia Rafting Expeditions, *Cra 10, No 7-83, T311-283 8647, www.colombiarafting.com*. The best for rafting, with International Rafting Federation-qualified guides. Also does hydrospeed, US$25.
Exploración Aventura Total, *C 7, esq Cra 11, T7-723 8888*. Biggest tour company in town, specializes in paragliding.

## Cycling
Hire bikes for US$12 per day from **El Ring**, C 7, No 10-14, or try at the **Macondo Guesthouse** (see Where to stay).
Colombia Bike Junkies, *www.colombian bikejunkies.com*. Downhill mountain-bike tours in the San Gil area, including Chicamocha Canyon and Barichara.

### South of San Gil

Páramo Santander Extremo, *Parque Principal, Cra 4 No 4-57, Páramo, T7-725 8944, www.paramosantanderextremo. com*. This company is best for abseiling and canyoning but also does caving, rafting and horse riding.

## Transport

### San Gil
**Bus**
The main bus station is 5 mins out of town by taxi on road to Tunja; the bus terminal for local destinations is on Cra 11 with C 15. To **Bogotá**, US$20. To **Barichara** from C 12, US$2.20, 45 mins, every 30 mins, taxi US$12.50. To **Bucaramanga**, **Cotransangil** has regular buses throughout the day, 2½ hrs, US$7.50; sit on the right, or in front next to the driver for beautiful views of the Chicamocha Canyon. For **Villa de Leiva** leave for Tunja by 1400 to catch the last onward minibus. To **Charalá**, US$2.50.

★From San Gil a direct paved road leads to Barichara, 22 km away. Often touted as the most beautiful small town in Colombia, Barichara is a lovely colonial settlement founded in 1741 and designated as a National Monument in 1975. There are several interpretations of its indigenous Guane name; the best is 'the place of rest with flowering trees'. It has a wonderfully peaceful, bohemian atmosphere. Many of the buildings are made from *tapia pisada*, which uses compacted mud mixed with water. The walls are whitewashed, and the doors and *zócalos* (the lower half of the building) are painted green, blue or turquoise. The finely carved churches are constructed from the brown stone found all over Santander, which is also used to pave the streets. Fortune has been kind to Barichara: it is a prosperous little town, with boutique-style *artesanía* and clothes shops. Artists and city-dwellers from Bucaramanga and Bogotá flock here at the weekends to relax, but it is quieter during the week.

**Baricharā**

To Guane  Camino Real to Guane

Santa Bárbara

Piedra de Bolívar

Jesús Resucitado

Cathedral

Tierrarte

Casa de Cultura

Parque Central

San Antonio

Casa de Aquileo Parra Gómez

To Salto de Mico

To Guane & San Gil

To Villanueva

N

200 metres
200 yards

**Where to stay**
Color de Hormiga Finca **3**
Coratá **2**
Hicasua **6**

Hostel Color de Hormiga **7**
La Mansión de Virginia **4**
La Posada de Pablo **5**
Tinto Hostel **8**

**Restaurants**
Al Cuoco **1**
El Compá **2**
Las Cruces **3**

## Sights

The **Catedral de la Inmaculada Concepción** is a fine colonial building, which sets the tone for the town. The façade and twin towers are strikingly illuminated at night. The interior is all in finished sandstone, with fluted columns, a carved wooden ceiling, gallery, cupola and a bright, gold-leaf *reredos*. There are three other interesting churches: **San Antonio** ① *Cra 4/C 5*, with a house for the elderly alongside; **Santa Bárbara** ① *C 6/Cra 11*, at the top of the town, and **Jesús Resucitado** ① *C 3/Cra 7*, with the cemetery next to it – all have simple, even stark, interiors. Among Barichara's other places of historical interest is the house of the former president, **Casa de Aquileo Parra Gómez** ① *Cra 2/ C 6, daily 0900-1700, free.* The **Casa de Cultura**, on the Parque Principal, has a small exhibition of local historical and archeological finds. At the corner of Carrera 10 and Calle 4, there is a **Piedra de Bolívar**, which shows the number of times the Liberator passed through the village.

There is a superb wide-ranging view from the mirador at the top of Carrera 10 across the Río Suárez to the Cordillera de los Cobardes, the last section of the Cordillera Oriental before the Magdalena valley.

## Walks around Barichara

You can walk from Barichara to Guane (see below), or vice versa, along the delightful Camino Real, originally used by the indigenous Guane and later appropriated by the Spanish. The path still retains much of the original paving and has been restored. You walk past lush green pastures, full of grazing cows and goats, and through orchards. It takes about two hours. It is best to leave in the early morning and to carry plenty of water and head protection as the sun can be punishingly hot at midday. There are a couple of fincas selling refreshments along the way. From Barichara, walk to the top of the town along Carrera 10 and continue downhill along the stone trail. From Guane, exit the plaza to the left of the church, walk uphill for two blocks and take a left; continue walking and you will eventually hit the path.

There is a more extensive, three-day walk taking in the villages of Barichara, Guane, Villanueva and Los Santos, and the ghost town of Jerico, involving a spectacular descent of the Chicamocha Canyon. There are various *hostales* to stay in on the way and places to sample local food and drink. Speak to the staff at the Macondo Guesthouse in San Gil for more details (see page 109).

## Guane → *Colour map 2, B6.*

Much like Barichara, the tiny village of Guane, 9 km away by road, is a place seemingly lost in time. That the surrounding valley abounds in fossils only adds to this impression. Former capital of the pre-Columbian Guane culture, it has a beautiful plaza dominated by a **church** of simple but imposing design, with an interesting beamed and ornamented roof, fine wooden doors, a balcony at the west end and an elegant chapel to Santa Lucía to the left of the altar. Also on the plaza is a monument, studded with fossils, dedicated to the last Guane chief, Guaneta, and several brilliant-orange acacia trees. An excellent and surprisingly large paleontological and archaeological **museum** ① *daily 0800-1200, 1300-1800 (times can be erratic), US$1,* is housed in the Parroquia San Isidro on the plaza. It has an enormous collection of fossils found in the local area (which is constantly being augmented by new finds), as well as woven Guane textiles and a mummified woman. If the museum is closed, ask someone at the local artisan shop on the plaza to take you on an informative if rather whirlwind tour.

## Listings Barichara and around *map p112*

### Tourist information

There is a new tourist office on Cra 5 at the corner of C 9, daily 0900-1700.

### Where to stay

**Barichara**

**$$$ Hotel Hicasua**
*Cra 7, No 3-85 T7-726 7700,*
*www.hicasua.com.*
If you have the cash to splash, this is the place to stay. Located at the edge of town, Hicasua offers tastefully decorated rooms with fans and flatscreen TVs. There is a restaurant and a stunning swimming pool in the courtyard, as well as a spa and sauna.

**$$$-$$ Coratá**
*Cra 7, No 4-08, T7-726 7110.*
This delightful colonial building has a beautiful balustraded terrace looking down onto a courtyard with an impressive *saucellaron* tree. TV in the rooms and hot water in private bathrooms. No fans or a/c but the high ceilings keep you cool.

**$$$-$$ Hostel Color de Hormiga**
*C 6, No 5-35, T7-726 7156/312-558 1256,*
*www.colordehormiga.com.*
Good budget option in a charming colonial building just off the plaza. Offers dorms and privates with en suite bath, but no hot water or fan. What it lacks in amenities it makes up for with friendly staff and a beautiful hammock-filled,

grapevine-covered courtyard. There's Wi-Fi and plans to offer breakfast and lunch in the future.

**$$ Finca Color de Hormiga**
*T315-297 1621/314-455 8268,*
*www.colordehormiga.com.*
This finca is run by Jorge, the same man who owns Hostel Color de Hormiga. This finca is located just 1 km outside town and sits on 29 ha of land. The immense rooms have the highest ceilings of any accommodation in town, and Jorge himself often cooks dinner for guests in the large, open-air kitchen. Tours of the grounds include visiting ant colonies, turtles and natural fish farms. Other amenities include open-air showers and Wi-Fi.

**$$ La Mansión de Virginia**
*C 8, No 7-26, T7-726 7170,*
*www.lamansiondevirginia.com.*
Impeccable colonial house with rooms set around a lovely courtyard. Fine, comfortable beds and private baths with hot water. Breakfast included. Recommended.

**$$ La Posada de Pablo 2**
*C 3, No 7-30, T7-726 7719.*
One of several places belonging to 'Pablo' in town. This one is next to the Iglesia de Jesús Resucitado and a gorgeous park. Has TV and good beds. Try for rooms 10 or 11, which have exquisite views across the rooftops to the cathedral. Another **Pablo** is at Cra 7, 3-50.

**$$-$ Tinto Hostel**
*Cra 4 No 5-39, T7-726 7725,*
*hosteltintobarichara.com.*
Probably the best hostel in town. It sits on
a hill with nice views of the surrounding
countryside. There are 4- and 6-bed
dorms, as well as large privates.

## Camping
Try **Baralomas** campsites, T311-828
0062 (ask for Rodrigo), or **La Chorrera**,
a natural swimming pool on the
road to San Gil, T318-832 7327, which
charges US$2 to camp, with meals by
arrangement; it's clean and attractive.

## Guane
Guane has 2 delightful and
economical hostels to stay in,
both highly recommended.

**$$-$ Hotel Santa Lucia**
*Cra 5, corner of C 7.*
1 block off the plaza, this option offers
rooms at affordable rates.

**$ Posada Mi Tierra Guane**
*Parque Principal, opposite museum.*
Run by a nice lady (the same woman
with the artisan shop on the plaza),
this small 6-room hostel is comfortable
and charming with a pleasant courtyard
and private bathrooms. Some rooms
have bunk beds.

## Restaurants

### Barichara

**$$ Al Cuoco**
*Cra 6, No 2-54, T312-527 3628.*
Located across from the Parque
Cemetario, owner Maximo serves up
handmade pastas in a cosy dining room
and large patio. The recipes have been
passed down through generations in
Rome and the quality shows in each bite.

**$$ Las Cruces**
*T7-726 7577, www.tallerdeoficios
barichara.com.*
Located in the Escuela Taller, situated
around a lush plant- and tree-filled
courtyard, this property offers cooking
and ceramics classes as well as an upscale
restaurant. Those who want to splurge
on a local speciality should go right for
the roast goat in ant sauce (yes, ants.)

**$ El Compá**
*C 5, No 4-48.*
Family-run restaurant serving typical
regional food, including *sobrebarriga*
and *arepa santandereana*.

### Guane
There are 3 good restaurants on the
plaza all serving typical regional food.

**$ Guayubi**
*To the left of the museum as you face it.*
Goat is the speciality, washed down
with *chicha de maíz*, a mild alcoholic
drink made from corn masticated by
the local women.

## Shopping

### Barichara
**Artesenias Samary**, *C 6, No 7-37.* Lots
of locally made handicrafts, including
*sandalias de fique* (woven sandals).
**Tierrarte**, *C 5, No 6-62.* Fine leather
products such as belts and bags,
as well as beautiful jewellery. Credit
cards accepted. Also has shops in
San Gil and Bucaramanga.

## Transport

### Barichara
To **San Gil**, every 30 mins from
early morning until 1830, with
**Cotransangil**, 45 mins, US$2.
To **Guane**, frequent, US$0.90.

Bucaramanga, 420 km from Bogotá, is the capital of Santander Department. A modern, industrial city with little remaining of its colonial past, it is nonetheless not without charm. It still has a small colonial area, some lovely parks and squares and fine dining and nightlife. It is also an important transport hub, connecting Bogotá with Cúcuta, the main border crossing to Venezuela, and with the Caribbean coast. If you are heading to any of these destinations it is more than likely that you will have to make a stop in Bucaramanga. It stands on an uneven plateau sharply delimited by eroded slopes to the north and west, hills to the east and a ravine to the south. The city's great problem is space for expansion. The metropolitan area has grown rapidly because of the success of coffee, tobacco and staple crops.

The city was founded in 1622 by Páez de Sotomayor but was little more than a village until the 19th century. Simón Bolívar established his campaign headquarters here in 1813 and lived here for some time in the **Casa de Bolívar**. Perú de la Croix, a French officer in Bolívar's army, wrote his *Bucaramanga Diary* here, an interesting study of his leader. Gold was found in the hills and rivers nearby, hence the Río Oro to the southwest, which was worked until the end of the 19th century.

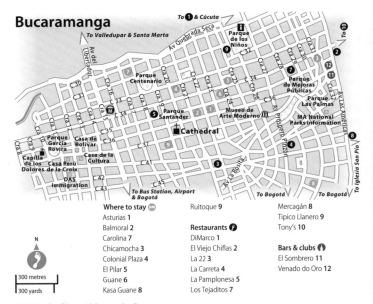

# Bucaramanga

| Where to stay | Ruitoque 9 | Mercagán 8 |
|---|---|---|
| Asturias 1 | | Tipico Llanero 9 |
| Balmoral 2 | **Restaurants** | Tony's 10 |
| Carolina 7 | DiMarco 1 | |
| Chicamocha 3 | El Viejo Chiflas 2 | **Bars & clubs** |
| Colonial Plaza 4 | La 22 3 | El Sombrero 11 |
| El Pilar 5 | La Carreta 4 | Venado do Oro 12 |
| Guane 6 | La Pamplonesa 5 | |
| Kasa Guane 8 | Los Tejaditos 7 | |

## Sights

The city can be divided into three sections, running west to east. The **Parque García Rovira** is the centre of the colonial area where you will find most of the museums and cultural centres. The **Parque Santander** is the heart of the modern city and this is where most of the budget hotels can be found. Further east is the Zona Rosa, centred around Calle 33 and Carrera 33, where many of the city's better restaurants, bars and clubs are located.

Bucaramanga is notable for its green spaces. There are a number of fine parks, including **Parque de Mejoras Públicas** ⓘ *C 36/Cras 29-32*, with an open-air *concha acústica* (concert shell) for public performances; **Parque de los Niños** ⓘ *C 30/Cra 26*, and **Parque Centenario**, from which buses used to leave before the new terminal was built. Other parks worth visiting are **Parque San Pío** ⓘ *C 45, No 33*, with its many trees, and **Parque Las Palmas** ⓘ *C 41, No 30*. Note that not all of these are safe; muggings have been reported even in daylight in and around Parque Centenario and the small park at C 33/Cra 22.

There are several churches of interest. The **Catedral de la Sagrada Familia** overlooks the Parque Santander, a clean white Romanesque building with twin towers and statues of the Virgin and San José in between. The church of **San Pío** ⓘ *C 45/Cra 36*, has several paintings by Oscar Rodríguez Naranjo, and the **Capilla de los Dolores** ⓘ *C 35/Cra 10*, was the first chapel to be built in the town and is where the poet Aurelio Martínez Mutis is buried.

The **Museo de Arte Moderno** ⓘ *C 37/Cra 26, free*, is a centre for art and culture with occasional film festivals. Just off Parque García Rovira, is **Casa de Bolívar** ⓘ *C 37, No 12-15, T7-630 4258, Mon-Fri 0800-1200, 1400-1800, US$1*, an interesting ethnographic and historical museum and a centre of research on Bolívar and his period. Across the street is the **Casa de la Cultura** ⓘ *C 37, No 12-46, T7-642 0163, Mon-Sat 0800-1200, 1400-1800*, in a fine colonial building with exhibitions, film showings and a local *artesanía* display. Also worth a visit is the **Museo Arqueológico Regional Guane** ⓘ *in the Casa de Cultura 'Piedra del Sol', Cra 7, No 4-35, Floridablanca, T7-619 8181*, which has a good collection of Guane artefacts and textiles.

Away from the centre, the **Club Campestre** is one of the most beautifully situated in Latin America. On the way out of the city northeast (towards Pamplona) is the **Parque Morrorico**, well maintained with a fine view. There is a sculpture of the Saviour overlooking the park, which is a point of pilgrimage on Good Friday.

**Parque El Lago** is an amusement park in the suburb of Lagos, southwest of the city. Continuing southwest, the suburb of **Floridablanca**, 8 km from the centre, has the famous **Jardín Botánico Eloy Valenzuela** ⓘ *daily 0800-1200 and 1400-1600, US$2* (also known as **El Paragüitas** gardens), belonging to the national tobacco agency. The Río Frío runs through the gardens, which have been recently restored. To get there, take a bus (US$1) from Carrera 33 in Bucaramanga, either 'Florida Villabel' which goes past the botanical gardens, or 'Florida Autopista' (continuation of Carrera 33) which goes direct to the square in Florida, from where you have to walk about 1 km; a taxi from the centre costs US$5.

**Girón**, a tobacco centre 9 km southwest of Bucaramanga on the Río de Oro, is a little gem of a colonial town. Far from the bustle of industrial Bucaramanga, at weekends it is filled with *bumangueses*, many of whom come for Mass at its beautiful church. In 1963 Girón was declared a National Monument: the buildings are well preserved and the town unspoilt by modernization. By the river are *tejo* courts and popular open-air restaurants with *cumbia* and *salsa* bands. In the square at weekends, sweets and *raspados* (crushed ice, rather like slush puppies) are sold, while children buy balloons and are wheeled about in miniature cars. Take the bus from Carrera 15 or 22 in Bucaramanga, US$1. A taxi costs US$5.

**Rionegro** is a coffee town 20 km north of Bucaramanga, with the Laguna de Gálago and waterfalls close by. One fine waterfall can be reached by taking the bus for 30 minutes from Rionegro to Los Llanos de Palma and then continuing on foot for two hours through citrus groves towards Bocas. Complete the walk along an old railway to the Bucaramanga–Rionegro road.

**Piedecuesta**, 18 km southeast of Bucaramanga, is where you can see cigars being made by hand, as well as furniture carving and jute weaving. Cheap, hand-decorated *fique* rugs can be bought. There are frequent buses from Carrera 22 in Bucaramanga (45 minutes), or a taxi costs US$10. Visit in June for the Corpus Christi processions.

## Berlín

A road (paved but narrow) runs east from the city to Berlín, and then northeast, making a very scenic ascent through cloudforest to the summit of the Eastern Cordillera and eventually on to Pamplona, about 130 km from Bucaramanga. Berlín is an ideal place to appreciate the grandeur of the Eastern Cordillera and the hardiness of the people who live on the *páramo*. The landscape is stark, barren and dramatic, much like the Scottish highlands. The village lies in a valley at 3100 m, surrounded by peaks of up to 4350 m; the temperature is constantly around 10°C, although on the infrequent sunny days it may seem much warmer. There is a tourist complex with cabins in the village and several basic eating places. Camping (challenging but rewarding) is possible with permission. At the highest point on the road between Bucaramanga and Berlín (3400 m) is a café where you can camp on the covered porch.

## Tourist information

The tourist office is on Parque de los Niños, underneath the library; information and maps are also provided by the **Oficina Asesora de Turismo**, Instituto Municipal de Cultura, C 30, No 26-117, T7-683 4141, Mon-Fri 0800-1200, 1400-1900.

## Where to stay

**Bucaramanga**
Since Bucaramanga has numerous national conventions, it is sometimes hard to find a room in more expensive hotels, especially mid-week.

**$$$$-$$$ Chicamocha**
*C 34, No 31-24, T7-634 3000,*
*www.hotelchicamocha.com.*
Large hotel near the Zona Rosa. Has a pool, sauna, gym, spa and Wi-Fi throughout, as well as 2 restaurants and 2 bars.

**$$$ Asturias**
*Cra 22, No 35-01, T7-635 1914,*
*www.hotelasturias.com.co.*
Rooms are set around a sunny atrium and vary in quality. Includes American breakfast in the price and has a pizza restaurant attached. Guests can use swimming pool at **La Ciudad Bonita** for free.

**$$$ El Pilar**
*C 34, No 24-09, T7-634 7207,*
*www.hotelpilar.com.*
Good rooms and lots of extras: private parking, Wi-Fi, restaurant and accident insurance. Cheaper with fan.

**$$$ Guane**
*C 34, No 22-72, T7-634 7014,*
*www.hotelguane.com.*
Smart hotel with large rooms that include reception areas. Has a pool, gym and solarium. Breakfast included.

**$$$ Ruitoque**
*Cra 19, No 37-26, T7-633 4567,*
*www.hotelruitoque.com.*
From the outside it may not be much to look at, but it's been recently refurbished, has good-sized, clean rooms with tiled bathrooms, a restaurant, Wi-Fi and is just a block from Parque Santander.

**$$ Balmoral**
*Cra 21, No 34-75.*
A good budget option with clean rooms, cable TV, internet, hot water, bar and jacuzzi. Also conveniently situated a block from Parque Santander. Its downside is that street-facing rooms are noisy while back rooms have no windows and can be stuffy.

**$$ Colonial Plaza**
*C 33, No 20-46.*
It's certainly not colonial, but the rooms are clean, it has hot water and Wi-Fi throughout. Slightly cheaper with fan. Friendly place, but take care in the nearby park even during the day. Ask for a room at the back, away from the street, as these are much quieter.

**$$ Kasa Guane**
*C 49, No 28-21, T7-657 6960,*
*www.kasaguane.com.*
This backpackers' hostel is the best budget option in town. Owned by Richie of Colombia Paragliding and British expats Milo and Tim, it's decorated with Guane artefacts and has several private

rooms as well as dorms with bunks. Additional services include a kitchen, table games, a pool table, lively bar with great mojitos, good information on the local area and Wi-Fi. Also runs volunteer programme **Goals for Peace**, www. goalsforpeace.com.

### $ Hotel Carolina
*Cra 18, No 30-56.*
Good value for the price. Rooms are simple but clean and there's a laundry service. The area, nicknamed the Zona Roja, can be dangerous, so be careful at night.

## Girón

### $$$-$$ Girón Chill Out
*Cra 25, No 32-06, T7-646 1119/315-475 3001, www.gironchillout.com.*
This Italian-owned hostel has 7 private rooms in a colonial house with high ceilings. As well as Wi-Fi, cable TV and use of a washing machine, there is also a kitchen for use by guests, though you might be tempted by the excellent restaurant serving Italian food with ingredients imported from the mother country, also owned by the hostel, on the corner of the same street.

### $$ Hotel Las Nieves
*C 30, No 25-71, T7-646 8968, www.hotellasnievesgiron.com.*
Colonial buidling on the main plaza, large rooms, TV and hot water. Street-facing rooms have balconies, Wi-Fi, good value restaurant. Much cheaper with fan.

## Restaurants

Try the *hormigas culonas* (large-bottomed black ants), a local delicacy mainly eaten during Holy Week (mostly sold in shops, but occasionally in restaurants and also sold on main highways in Santander at that time).

## Bucaramanga

### $$$ La Carreta
*Cra 27, No 42-27.*
Established by local football legend Roberto Pablo Janiot nearly 50 years ago, this very swish colonial building has been tastefully restored. *Parrillas* and seafood can be enjoyed around a courtyard of sculpted gardens and water features.

### $$$ Mercagán
*C 45, at Cra 33.*
The large photograph of a cow on the menu immediately tells you that this place is not for vegetarians. Steaks and hamburgers are the order of the day. Fine setting opposite the beautiful Parque San Pío.

### $$ DiMarco
*C 28, No 54-21.*
Top-notch steaks in pleasant surroundings.

### $$ El Viejo Chiflas
*Cra 33, No 34 esq.*
Good restaurant in the heart of the Zona Rosa. Try the *cabrito* (goat), a local speciality.

### $$ La 22
*Cra 22, No 45-18, www. restaurantela22.com.*
So popular is this local canteen that at weekends you will struggle to be seated. Paella and *sancocho* are some of their specialities. Also does a roaring trade in takeaways and home deliveries – very busy.

### $$ Los Tejaditos
*C 34 27-82.*
Popular with locals, with a varied menu of meats, seafood, pastas and salads.

## $$ Tony's
*Cra 33A, No 33-67.*
Not satisfied with their enormous breakfasts and lunches, *bumangueses* like to fit in an extra meal in between known as *onces* (elevenses). **Tony's** caters for them all. Good *tamales* and *arepas*. Popular with families.

## $ Alba
*Cra 10, No 41-01.*
For local sweets and delicacies, try this family-run *dulcería* that's more than 100 years old. It's so sweet you have to battle with a hive of bees that swarm around the shop.

## $ La Pamplonesa
*C 35, No 18-29.*
Just off Parque Santander, this *panadería* does good breakfasts as well as sandwiches, cakes and fruit juices.

## $ Típico Llanero
*C 31, No 25-07.*
Located just off Parque Los Niños, this corner restaurant serves up great regional food hot off a coal-fired grill. It's popular with locals and offers set-price *almuerzos* and refreshing iced juices for US$4.

## Bars and clubs

### Bucaramanga
When they want to party, most *bumangueses* head for the Zona Rosa in the eastern end of town, where many bars and clubs will jostle for your attention. **El Venado de Oro**, **Garibaldi** and **El Sombrero**, on Cra 33, all have live mariachi bands. In fact Cra 33 between C 37 and 39 is known as **Calle de los Marachis**, but there are also plenty of other bars and music to be enjoyed. **Moe's Bar**, **Saxo** and **Joy's Gourmet** are all in the same street.

## Festivals

### Bucaramanga
**Sep** **Feria Bucaramanga**. 2 weeks of music, dancing, food, theatre and every type of vendor under the sun.

## Shopping

### Bucaramanga
**Camping equipment**
**Centro Commercial Casique**, *Transversal 93 N 34-99, T7-691 7722.* Gigantic mall in El Tejar, in the south of the city.

**Handicrafts**
Try **Bosque**, near the Parque García Rovira, C 36, No 12-58, www.bosque decoracion.com, or opposite the market in Barrio Guarín, C 33A, No 33-23. There's typical clothing upstairs in the food market, C 34 y Cras 15-16.

## What to do

### Bucaramanga
There are opportunities for parapenting at the nearby Mesa del Ruitoque and over the Cañón de Chicamocha to the south of the city. Good schools are **Las Aguilas**, Km 2 vía Mesa de Ruitoque, Floridablanca, T7-678 6257, www.voladerolasaguilas.com.co, and **Colombia Paragliding**, T312-432 6266, www.colombiaparagliding.com, which also has a hostel where you can stay while you take lessons.

## Transport

### Bucaramanga
**Air**
The airport is at Palonegro, on 3 flattened hilltops on the other side of the ravine, south of the city. There are spectacular views on take-off and

landing. Taxi from town US$15; *colectivo*, US$5; buses to/from the airport are scarce. To **Bogotá**, several flights a day with **Avianca** and **VivaColombia**. To **Cúcuta,** 3 daily with **Lan** and **Avianca**. To **Medellín,** 6 flights a week with **Avianca**.

**Airlines offices** **Avianca**, C 52 No 35A-10, T7-657 3888/632 3938. **Satena**, C 36, No 15-56, T7-670 7087.

## Bus

The **bus terminal** is on the Girón road, with cafés, shops, a bank and showers. Taxi to centre, US$3.50; bus US$1. You can book tickets to all destinations here; call T7-637 1000, www.terminalbucaramanga.com, and you will be connected to all relevant bus companies. To **Bogotá**, 420 km, 8-11 hrs, US$30 (Pullman) with **Berlinas del Fonce** (C 53, No 20-40, T7-630 4468, www.berlinasdelfonce.com, or at bus terminal), at 0845, 1400, 1530, 1830, 2010, 2105, 2210 and 2245; with **Copetran**, www.copetran.com.co, US$25, frequent services day and night; this journey is uncomfortable, there are no relief stops, and it starts off hot and ends cold in the mountains; be prepared. To **Barranquilla**, 13 hrs, 1 departure daily 2100, US$55 with **Berlinas**. To **Cartagena**, US$42.50, 14 hrs, with **Copetran**, frequent services from 0800 until midnight, or 1 with **Berlinas** 2100, US$56, 12 hrs. To **Santa Marta**, 550 km, 11 hrs, US$32.50, 0930, 2030 and 2200 with **Copetran** or **Berlinas** 2230. To **Valledupar**, 10 hrs, US$30 with **Copetran**, 9 a day. To **El Banco** on the Río Magdalena, US$28, 7 hrs, several companies, direct or change at Aguachica; this journey should be made in daylight. To **Barrancabermeja**, 115 km, 2 hrs, US$9, a scenic ride with 1 rest stop; this road is paved. Hourly buses to **San Gil**, 2½ hrs, US$10. To **Tunja**, 7½ hrs, US$40. To **Berlín**, US$6. To **Pamplona**, 3 a day, US$5 (Pullman), US$11.50 (**Berlinas**, 4 daily). To **Cúcuta**, 198 km, 6 hrs, US$20.50 with **Berlinas**, 4 daily; *colectivo* US$22. The trip to Cúcuta is spectacular.

Other companies have local services to nearby villages on back roads; try the colourful folk art buses of **Flota Cáchira** (C 32, Cra 33-34), which go north and east.

## Taxi

Most taxis have meters; when you get in, make sure the driver switches the meter to '42', which is the code for the minimum fare (US$2.30) and should get you to most places within the city centre. Beware of overcharging. For longer journeys, taxis usually charge about US$10-15 per hr.

# Norte de Santander
## Department

The border between Santander and Norte de Santander departments is at the high pass near Berlín. From there the Cordillera Oriental slowly reduces in height to become a ridge along the border with Venezuela, ending at the peninsula of La Guajira and the Caribbean Sea. A spur, however, turns northeast, crosses the border at the Tamá National Park to become the Sierra Nevada de Mérida, the highest mountains in Venezuela. The northeast of the department is down in the Maracaibo basin, the hottest place in South America. This border country with Venezuela was intimately linked with the Wars of Independence and with Bolívar and Santander. Parts of Norte de Santander still have some guerrilla activity. Pamplona and Cúcuta are mostly safe, but travellers should take advice before venturing into other areas, particularly along the Venezuelan border.

Pamplona, set in a green valley and surrounded by mountains, is a more than worthwhile stopover between Bucaramanga and Cúcuta. It was founded in 1549 by Pedro de Orsúa and Ortún Velasco. During the colonial era it was as important as Bogotá. The Independence movement was started here in 1810 by Agueda Gallardo. It became significant as a mining town but is now better known for its university – students make up almost 40% of the population. Although an 1875 earthquake destroyed large sections of the town, it still manages to retain a certain colonial atmosphere. At 2200 m, it can get cold, especially at night when a jumper or even a coat is required. Pamplona is surrounded by a number of rivers and lakes, including Laguna de Cácota and Laguna Camagueta, both within an hour's drive. Trips to the villages of Pamplonita, famous for flower cultivation, and Mutiscua, renowned for its trout farms, are also easily organized from Pamplona.

### Sights

The severe earthquake of 1875 played havoc with Pamplona's monasteries and churches. There is now a hotel on the site of the former San Agustín monastery, but it is still possible to visit the remains of the ex-monasteries of **San Francisco** and **Santo Domingo**. The **cathedral** is in the spacious **Plaza Central** (Parque Agueda Gallardo) and is a massive building with five naves. It dates from the 17th century but has been damaged by earthquakes and rebuilt over the years. Also on the plaza is the **Museo de Arte Moderno** ⓘ *C 5 on the Plaza Central, Tue-Sun 0900-1200, 1400-1700, US$0.50*, which principally exhibits the paintings and sculptures of Eduardo Ramírez Villamizar of Pamplona, who died in 2004. The colonial building is a notable local example and was declared a National Monument in 1975. Nearby, the fine **Casa Colonial** ⓘ *C 6, No 2-56, Mon-Sat 0900-1200, 1800, US$1*, is now an archaeological museum. It's a little gem, with artefacts from the Motilones and other indigenous communities still living in the north of the department.

Just north of the plaza, the **Museo de Arte Religioso** ⓘ *C 4/Cra 5, Mon-Sat 1000-1200, 1500-1700, US$1*, has paintings by many Colombians including Vázquez de Arce y Ceballos. To the northeast, the **Ermita del Señor del Humilladero**, adjoining the cemetery, dates from the 17th century and is very picturesque, with a fine view of the city. Its sculpture, *Cristo del Humilladero*, came from Spain and is celebrated every year in September. Next to the church is the **Museo de Fotografía Antigua de Toto** ⓘ *Cra 7, No 2-36, open 'whenever possible', free*. Toto was the local undertaker and a prolific artist. The exhibition consists of hundreds of photographs sent in by the citizens of Pamplona, some dating back to the early 20th century, and makes for a fascinating archive of local history. Sadly, Toto passed away but the space is maintained by some of his 10 sons.

South of the Plaza Central, **Casa Anzoátegui** ⓘ *Cra 6, No 7-48, www.museo anzoategui.blogspot.com, Mon-Sat 0900-1200, 1400-1730, Sat US$0.50*, is where

Aside from Columbus, no single man has had a greater influence on South American history than Simón Bolívar. This Venezuelan aristocrat galvanized the many factions of the continent into a united army that succeeded in expelling the Spanish from present-day Colombia, Venezuela, Panama, Ecuador, Peru and Bolivia.

His campaign through the Departments of Norte de Santander, Santander and Boyacá remains one of his greatest achievements.

In May 1819, Bolívar marched into Colombia from Venezuela with a force of 2000 men, meeting with General Francisco de Paula Santander's forces at Tame. He proposed to cross the Andes by the rarely used route across the Páramo de Pisba, a barren, windswept section of the Cordillera Oriental, the lowest pass of which was over 3200 m. There were many deaths and few of his 800 horses survived, but the audacious manoeuvre outwitted the Spanish. The armies met near Paipa and Bolívar's troops inflicted a surprise defeat.

On 6 August, Bolívar marched into Tunja, but his route to the capital was blocked by the royalists at a bridge crossing the Río Boyacá, 16 km to the south. Despite the strength of their position, the Spanish were routed at the first attack and disintegrated. Over 1600 prisoners were taken, and, four days later, Bolívar entered Bogotá as the liberator of Colombia.

Two years later, on 6 May 1821, the First Congress of Gran Colombia met at Cúcuta. It was at this meeting that the plan to unite Venezuela, Colombia and Ecuador was ratified, the pinnacle of Bolívar's career.

one of Bolívar's generals, José Antonio Anzoátegui, died in 1819 at the age of 30, after the Battle of Boyacá. A state in northeast Venezuela is named after him. The restored colonial house is now a museum covering the Independence period.

### Parque Nacional Natural Tamá

Tamá National Park covers 48,000 ha of the Cordillera Oriental on the Venezuelan border. It is a high-altitude park, rising to the Páramo de Santa Isabel, with several sections above 3400 m. Access to the park is from Pamplona or Cúcuta; park administration is at Orocué.

There is comparatively heavy rainfall (over 3000 mm per year on the lower slopes) which, combined with a wide range of altitudes, produces a full set of forest habitats from jungle to high temperate woodland and *páramo* (moorland). The flora and fauna are richly varied and include anteaters, deer and spectacled bears. It is reported that a waterfall has recently been discovered in the park that is about 820 m high. If this proves to be true, the falls would be the third or fourth highest in the world.

## Tourist information

Next to the Alcaldía, off Plaza Central, is the **Oficina de Turismo Pamplona**, C 5, No 6-45, T7-568 2880. The staff are very helpful and friendly; they can organize tours into the surrounding area and guides for hiking in the hills.

## Where to stay

Hotel accommodation may be hard to find at weekends, when Venezuelans visit the town.

### $$$ 1549 Hostal
*C 8B, No 5-84, T317-699 6578, www.1549hostal.com.*
Another lovingly restored colonial building. Rooms are light and airy and decorated with great taste by owners Ricardo and Kokis. Wi-Fi throughout. There is also a coffee bar and *panadería* in a large courtyard out back. Highly recommended.

### $$$ Cariongo
*Cra 5/C 9, Plazuela Almeyda, T7-568 1515, www.cariongoplazahotel.com.*
A 1960s building that has seen better days, this was the best option in town until the opening of **El Solar** and **1549 Hostel**. A newer annex out back has comfortable rooms and a garden with playground but lacks character. Wi-Fi in lobby.

### $$$ El Solar
*C 5, No 8-10, T7-568 2010, www.elsolarhotel.com.*
Beautifully restored colonial building dating from 1776. Rooms upstairs are enormous and have their own kitchen and balconies looking onto the street. Rooms downstairs, without kitchen, are cheaper. Also has by far the best restaurant in town (see below).

### $$-$ Orsúa
*C 5, No 5-67.*
Probably the best budget option in town. Crumbling but characterful building on the east side of the Plaza Central. Friendly owner and good restaurant. Rooms are cheaper if they don't look onto plaza.

### $ Imperial
*Cra 5, No 5-36, T7-568 2571.*
Large modern building on the Plaza Central with a youth hostel vibe. Rooms are a little grubby but staff are friendly. Cable TV and hot water.

### $ Santa Clara
*Cra 6, No 7-21, T975-682 880.*
Rambling building in need of some tender loving care but easy on the eye in a dilapidated sort of way and has hot water and a restaurant.

## Restaurants

Pamplona is famous for its bread: there's a *panadería* on practically every corner. Particularly well known are **Panadería Chávez**, Cra 6, No 7-30 and **Panadería Araque**. Try *pastel de horno, queso de hoja, pan de agua* or *cuca*, a kind of black ginger biscuit often topped with cheese.

### $$ Delicias del Mar
*C 6, No 7-60, T7-568 4558.*
Popular lunchtime venue specializing in fish, particularly *robalo* and trout.

### $$ El Portón Pamplonés
*C 5, No 7-83.*
Specializes in locally caught trout and other fish.

## $$ El Solar
*C 5, No 8-10 (see Where to stay).*
By far the best in town. High-quality fare served in the peaceful courtyard of this colonial hotel. Try the side of pork in honey. Highly recommended.

## $$ La Casona
*C 6, No 7-58, T7-568 3555.*
Another local favourite serving meats and seafood. Try the *paella valenciana.*

## $$ Piero's Pizza
*Cra 5, No 5B-67.*
Pizzas cooked by an Italian family. Authentic.

## $ El Arriero
*C 6, No 7-14.*
Quirky little place serving basic fare.

## Festivals

**Easter** The town's Easter celebrations are famous throughout Colombia, with processions and cultural presentations.
**4 Jul** Pamplona was the first town in Colombia to declare Independence from the Spanish, a fact that is celebrated with bullfights, music concerts and art exhibitions.
**14 Sep** **Día del Señor del Humilladero.** Celebrated by *pamploneses.*

**Oct** **Festival de la Cuca**. Local bakers compete to produce the tastiest ginger biscuit.
**1 Nov** Concerts and exhibitions are held to celebrate the foundation of the town.

## Shopping

Pamplona is a great place to buy *ruanas*. There is a good indoor market 1 block west of the Plaza Central on C 6 (C del Mercado).

## Transport

**Bus**
To **Bogotá**, US$32.50, 13 hrs, daily with **Berlinas** and **Copetran**. To **Cúcuta**, frequent, US$5-7, 2 hrs. To **Bucaramanga**, frequent, US$10.50, 3-4 hrs, great views. To **Málaga** from Plaza Central, 3 hrs, US$10. To **Berlín**, US$5. Buy tickets only at the official counter upstairs; do not accept help from 'intermediaries'.

You can also take *colectivos* to **Bucaramanga** (US$15-20) and **Cúcuta** (US$6.50), which usually cuts the journey by 1 hr and includes door-to-door pickup and delivery. Try **Cooptmotilon** on Cra 9, No 2-127, T7-568 0291.

Cúcuta, capital of the Department of Norte de Santander, is only 16 km from the Venezuelan frontier. For a border town, it is a surprisingly pleasant place to visit, with plenty of green spaces and a bustling but non-threatening centre. It was founded in 1733 by Juana Rangel, severely damaged by the earthquake in 1875 and then elegantly rebuilt with tree-lined streets. Anyone spending more than five minutes here will appreciate the shade these afford, for Cúcuta is one hot place, with a mean temperature of 29°C. It also lays claim to being one of the few cities in the world with a street grid system that begins at 0. Note that despite its pleasant atmosphere, Cúcuta is a centre for smuggling. Be careful.

## Sights

The **Catedral de San José** ① *Av 5 between C 10/11*, is worth a visit. Note the oil paintings by Salvador Moreno. The **Casa de la Cultura** ① *C 13, No 3-67*, incorporates

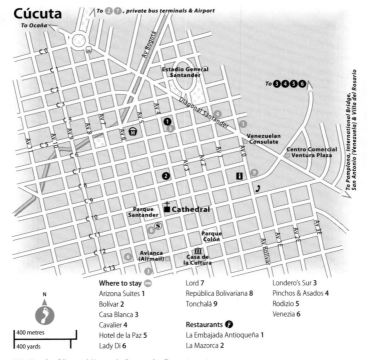

**Cúcuta**

To ② ⑦ , private bus terminals & Airport

To Ocaña →

To Pamplona, International Bridge, San Antonio (Venezuela) & Villa del Rosario

To ③④⑤⑥

Estadio General Santander

Av Bogotá

Diagonal Santander

Venezuelan Consulate

Centro Comercial Ventura Plaza

Parque Santander

✝ **Cathedral**

Parque Colón

Avianca (Airmail)

Casa de la Cultura

N

400 metres

400 yards

| **Where to stay** | Lord **7** | Londero's Sur **3** |
|---|---|---|
| Arizona Suites **1** | República Bolivariana **8** | Pinchos & Asados **4** |
| Bolívar **2** | Tonchalá **9** | Rodizio **5** |
| Casa Blanca **3** | | Venezia **6** |
| Cavalier **4** | **Restaurants** | |
| Hotel de la Paz **5** | La Embajada Antioqueña **1** | |
| Lady Di **6** | La Mazorca **2** | |

## ON THE ROAD

### Money matters

You can get a good rate of exchange for pesos in Cúcuta, at the airport, or on the border. As well as several banks and *casas de cambio* in town, there are money changers on the street all round the main plaza and many shops advertise the purchase and sale of bolivares. Change pesos into bolivares in Cúcuta or San Antonio as it is difficult to change them further into Venezuela. Similarly, if you're arriving from Venezuela, do not take bolivares further into Colombia; change them here.

the **Museo del la Ciudad**, which covers the history of a city very much involved with the Independence movement.

The **international bridge** between Colombia and Venezuela is southeast of the city (see box, page 131). Just beyond it is San Antonio del Táchira, the first Venezuelan town, and 55 km on is San Cristóbal. Just short of the border is the small town of **Villa del Rosario**, where the Congress met to agree the constitution of Gran Colombia in the autumn of 1821. This was one of the high points of Simón Bolívar's career. The actual spot where the documents were signed is now a park beside which is the **Templo del Congreso**, where the preliminary meetings took place. Formerly a church, it was severely damaged in the 1875 earthquake and only the dome has been reconstructed. Nearby is the **Casa de Santander** ⓘ *Tue-Sun 0800-1130, 1400-1730*, where General Francisco de Paula Santander was born in 1792 and spent his childhood. Bolívar entrusted the administration of the new Gran Colombia to Santander in 1821. The house became a National Monument in 1959 and a museum in 1971, dedicated to the Independence campaigns and the contribution made by General Santander.

### Listings Cúcuta *map p128*

#### Tourist information

The **Corporación Mixta de Promoción de Norte de Santander**, C 10, No 0-30, T7-571 8981, is helpful and has maps and brochures. Other maps are obtainable from the **Instituto Geográfico**, Banco de la República building, in the main plaza.

#### Where to stay

**$$$$-$$ Tonchalá**
*C 10/Av 0, T7-575 6444,*
*www.hoteltonchala.com.*

A bit of an eyesore from the outside, the Tonchalá nevertheless has friendly, professional staff and lots of added extras including a large pool, a spa and beauty parlour and Wi-Fi throughout. Breakfast included in price.

**$$$ Arizona Suites**
*Av 0, No 7-62, T7-573 1884,*
*www.hotelarizonasuites.com.*
Centrally placed, the **Arizona** has all the mod cons including Wi-Fi, safety boxes and a restaurant serving Italian food.

### $$$ Bolívar
*Av Demetrio Mendoza, Barrio San Luis,
T7-582 8666, www.hotel-bolivar.com.*
On the outskirts of town on the airport
road, the Bolívar is an old colonial
building with rooms in a series of
modern bungalows set around peaceful
gardens and 2 swimming pools. With a
paddling pool and playground, it's ideal
for children.

### $$$ Casa Blanca
*Av 6, No 14-55, T7-582 2160,
www.hotelcasablanca.com.co.*
The reception area of the **Casa Blanca**
looks kind of grand with lots of glass and
freshly painted white walls. The back,
where the rooms are, has also had a
recent facelift. The rooms are clean and
there is a large pool and a restaurant
serving regional and international food.
Hot water is only available in the suites,
which are more expensive.

### $$$-$$ Lord
*Av 7, No 8N-58, T7-529 7309.*
On a busy street and opposite a
shopping centre, the rooms are light
and airy and it offers parking and
laundry service. Cheaper with fan.

### $$ Cavalier
*Diagonal Santander C 6, No 1-28,
T7-583 0134.*
Basic but clean. Has a/c and offers
laundry service.

### $$ Hotel de la Paz
*C 6, No 3-48, T7-571 8002.*
Rooms are basic but at this price this
hotel is recommended for having a
pool and the delicious **La Embajada
Antioqueña** restaurant next door
(same address).

### $$-$ Lady Di
*Av 7, No 13-80, T7-583 1922.*
With an enormous photo of Princess
Diana above the doorway, you know
this hotel will be kitsch but kind of fun.
More photos feature throughout. The
rooms are clean but basic.

### $$-$ República Bolivariana
*Av 6, No 11-77, T7-571 8099.*
Well placed near Parque Santander, this
hotel is dedicated to Simón Bolívar and
features lots of murals of the Liberator.
Rooms are cheaper with fan.

## Restaurants

There are lots of fast-food outlets
on the 3rd level of the Centro
Comercial Ventura Plaza, C 10 y 11
Diagonal Santander.

### $$$-$$ Rodizio
*Av Libertadores, No 10-121, Malecon II
Etapa, T7-575 0095.*
Boasts 13 different types of meat as well
as seafood. Sometimes has live music.

### $$ La Embajada Antioqueña
*C 6, No 3-48, T7-5731874.*
Local and Antioquian food in a fine
open-air setting.

### $$ Londero's Sur
*Av Libertadores, No 0E-60, T7-583 3335.*
Argentine grill serving *parrillas,
empanadas,* ceviche and much more.

### $ La Mazorca
*Av 4, No 9-23, T7-571 2833,
www.restaurantelamazorca.com.*
More *comida criolla* served in a pleasant
courtyard decorated with hanging
baskets and Antioquian paraphernalia.
*Menú ejecutivo* US$3.50.

## BORDER CROSSING
### Colombia–Venezuela

**Cúcuta–San Antonio**
With all the right papers, the border crossing is easy and traffic normally flows smoothly, although there can be long queues at the Migración Colombia office, where exit and entry formalities are handled. (It's the white house before the international border bridge.) There are also immigration offices at the airport and in town (Avenida 1, No 28-57, T7-572 0033, daily 0800-1130, 1400-1700).
**Entering Colombia** You must obtain both a Venezuelan exit stamp and then a Colombian entry stamp at the Migración Colombia office. Without the former you will be sent back; without the latter you will have problems with police checks, banks and leaving the country. You can also be fined. Shared taxi from border, US$3, will wait for formalities, then charge US$1 to bus station. The Colombian Aduana (customs office) is on the road to the airport (small sign).
**Entering Venezuela** A taxi from Cucuta airport to the border costs US$10 and takes 15 minutes. There are buses to the border from Avenida 3 in town and also services to San Antonio and San Cristóbal (see Transport). Passports must be stamped with an exit stamp at the white Migración Colombia building before the border crossing. If you do not obtain an exit stamp, you will be turned back by Venezuelan officials to complete formalities and the next time you enter Colombia, you will be fined. For visas or other immigration matters, there is a Venezuelan consulate in Cúcuta (Avenida Camilo Daza, C 7, T7-579 1954, www.cucuta.consulado.gob.ve, Monday-Friday 0800-1000, 1400-1500). Car papers must be stamped at the SENIAT office in San Cristóbal.
**Note** There is a 30-minute time difference between Colombia and Venezuela.

**$ Pinchos & Asados**
*Av Libertadores, No 10-121, next to Rodizio.*
Delightful setting on a terrace overlooking landscaped wooded gardens, delicious *brochettes*.

**$ Venezia**
*Edif La Riviera, Local 5, T7-575 0006.*
Oven-fired pizzas.

### Shopping

**Centro Comercial Ventura Plaza**, C 10 y 11 Diagonal Santander. Has plenty of international brand shops, as well as *artesanías*. Also try C 10, Av 8 for leather boots and shoes; **Aquí Colombia**, C 10,

No 1-59, or **Artesanías Franco**, Cra 7, No 5-10, Villa del Rosario.

### Transport

**Air**
The **airport** is 5 km north of the centre, 15 mins by taxi from both the town, US$3, and the border, US$10. There are only domestic flights from Cúcuta airport. For flights to Venezuelan destinations you must cross the border and fly from San Antonio airport. Do not be conned into buying airline tickets from Cúcuta to Venezuelan destinations; all flights go from San Antonio.

To **Bogotá**, **Avianca** (Av 0, No 13-84, T7-571 6151 and at airport, T7-587

4884, www.avianca.com) has several daily; **LAN** (C 15 No 2E-138, T01800-094 9490, www.lan.com) has 3 a day. To **Barranquilla**, 4 daily, all via Bogotá with **Avianca** and **LAN**. To **Bucaramanga**, 3 a day. To **Medellín**, 5 flights per week with **Avianca**.

## Bus

The notorious **bus station** is on Av 7 and C 0 (a really rough area); a taxi from the bus station to the town centre costs US$2.50. There are also 2 private bus stations belonging to **Copetran** (Av Camilo Daza) and **Berlinas del Fonce** (2 km beyond the main terminal along Diagonal Santander); these are much safer than the main terminal. To **Bogotá**, hourly, 12-17 hrs, US$40-50, daily with **Berlinas del Fonce** and **Copetran**, making 2 stops, 1 of which is **Bucaramanga**. There are frequent buses, even during the night (if the bus you take arrives in the dark, sit in the bus station café until it is light). To **Cartagena**, daily with **Copetran** and **Berlinas**, 16-19 hrs, US$50-70. To **Bucaramanga**, US$15-20, 5-6 hrs, with **Copetrán** and **Berlinas del Fonce** Pullman, hourly. There are good roads to **Caracas** (933 km direct or 1046 km via Mérida), and to **Maracaibo** (571 km). Bus to Caracas, 15 hrs, US$30, **Expreso Occidente**, or taxi *colectivo*.

**To Venezuela** From Cúcuta, it is best to travel to San Antonio or (better) San Cristóbal and then change. To **San Cristóbal**, US$1.50 with **Bolivariano**, or US$3 by *colectivo*; to **San Antonio**, bus and *colectivo* from C 7, Av 4/5, or taxi US$10. On any form of transport crossing the border, make sure that the driver knows that you need to stop to obtain exit/entry stamps (see box, page 131).

# Caribbean Colombia

Reaching Colombia's Caribbean coast is like entering another world. Steamy, colourful and lively, the entire area pulses to the seductive rhythms of *vallenato*, heard at festivals throughout the region.

*Costeños* may be looked down on by their more sombre countrymen, but they certainly know how to enjoy themselves. The Barranquilla Carnival is second only to Rio for colour and size, and is much less commercial. There is fine architecture and an impressive literary legacy here too, particularly in Cartagena, the emerald in the crown of Colombia. This stunning colonial city is positively bursting with colour and history, and offers fine food, a lively nightlife and various sparkling coral islands within easy reach.

South from Cartagena is Mompós, a colonial town with one of the best Easter festivals in the world. Around the Gulf of Urabá, on the way to Panama, is a wild shoreline of coral reefs backed by the virgin jungles of the Darién. Travel east and you'll reach Santa Marta, Colombia's oldest city and gateway to the spectacular Tayrona National Park. The Sierra Nevada de Santa Marta is the highest coastal mountain range in the world, with tropical beaches and snow-capped mountains within 20 miles of each other. It also conceals the Ciudad Perdida, the culmination of an unforgettable trek. Further east is the arid landscape of the Guajira Peninsula, home to the indigenous Wayúu and enormous flocks of flamingos, where turquoise waters lap against a desert shoreline.

**Best** for
Beaches ▪ Fiestas ▪ Trekking

Cartagena
Bogotá

# Footprint picks

★ **Cartagena's ramparts**, page 139
Walk the perimeter of the colonial city and then watch the sun set over the bay.

★ **Islas de Rosario and San Bernardo**, pages 162 and 169
Soak up the sun, sea and sand on these quintessential Caribbean islands.

★ **Mompós**, page 165
Come to this beautifully preserved riverside town for its extraordinary Easter celebrations.

★ **Arboletes**, page 169
Wallow in the area's best mud volcano.

★ **Ciudad Perdida**, page 199
Trek through rainforest to the lost city of the Tayrona.

★ **La Guajira**, page 213
Learn about the Wayúu culture on this remote desert peninsula.

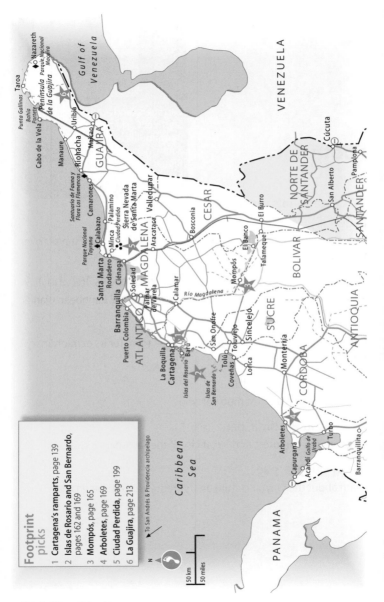

N

50 km
50 miles

To San Andrés & Providencia archipelago

*Caribbean Sea*

PANAMA

Capurganá
Acandí
Golfo de Urabá
Barranquillita
Turbo
Arboletes

Montería
CÓRDOBA
ANTIOQUIA

Lorica
Coveñas
Toluviejo
Sincelejo
San Onofre
SUCRE
Tolú

*Islas de San Bernardo*
*Islas del Rosario*
Barú
Cartagena
La Boquilla
Puerto Colombia
ATLÁNTICO
Barranquilla
Soledad
Palmar de Varela
Calamar

*Río Magdalena*

Mompós
El Banco
Talameque
BOLÍVAR

Ciénaga
Santa Marta
*Parque Nacional Tayrona*
Rodadero
Minca
Ciudad Perdida
Sierra Nevada de Santa Marta
Palomino
MAGDALENA
Aracataca
Fundación
Bosconia
Valledupar
CESAR
El Banco
El Burro

Camarones
*Santuario de Fauna y Flora Los Flamencos*
Calabazo
Riohacha
Manaure
GUAJIRA
Uribía
Maicao
Cabo de la Vela
Bahía Portete
Punta Gallinas
Taroa
Nazareth
*Parque Nacional Macuira*
Península de la Guajira

*Gulf of Venezuela*

VENEZUELA

Cúcuta
NORTE DE SANTANDER
Pamplona
San Alberto
SANTANDER

*Caribbean Colombia*

# Essential Caribbean Colombia

## Finding your feet

Cartagena's Rafael Núñez Airport is served by direct daily flights to/from major Colombian cities and other smaller places in the north of the country, as well as by direct international flights to/from Lauderdale, Miami, New York and Panama City. From December to March flights can be overbooked, so turn up at the airport early. Santa Marta's Simón Bolívar Airport also gets very crowded in tourist season, when you will need to book flights well in advance. Barranquilla's Ernesto Cortissoz Airport is a cheaper and less busy alternative. There are also regional airports at Corozal (near Sincelejo), at Valledupar and Riohacha in the northeast and at Acandí in Darién. Daily buses run from Bogotá to Cartagena, Barranquilla and Santa Marta, and there are also very frequent services to/from Medellín.

## Getting around

Boats are available all along the coast for trips to local beaches and offshore islands. A boat is also required for part of the journey to Mompós on the Río Magdalena. Most other destinations can be reached by bus or colectívo, although services are limited southwest of Monterría and are non-existent in the Darién and parts of the Península de la Guajira.

## When to go

The climate on the Caribbean coast varies little during the year. Temperatures rise marginally between August and November when there is more frequent rain and there can be flooding. This area is relatively humid, but trade winds between December and February provide relief from the heat. Fiestas are taken seriously in this region, and if you want a quiet time you might want to avoid certain periods, especially between Christmas and Easter. If you want to join in, be sure to plan in advance or be prepared to struggle for accommodation and expect higher prices.

## Time required

You'll need two to three weeks to visit Cartagena and Santa Marta, relax on the coast and explore the rainforest.

## Weather Caribbean Colombia (Cartagena)

| Month | High | Low | Rain |
|---|---|---|---|
| January | 29°C | 23°C | 4mm |
| February | 29°C | 24°C | 3mm |
| March | 30°C | 25°C | 2mm |
| April | 30°C | 25°C | 22mm |
| May | 30°C | 26°C | 90mm |
| June | 30°C | 26°C | 100mm |
| July | 30°C | 26°C | 80mm |
| August | 30°C | 26°C | 110mm |
| September | 30°C | 25°C | 130mm |
| October | 30°C | 25°C | 220mm |
| November | 30°C | 25°C | 130mm |
| December | 30°C | 24°C | 30mm |

# Cartagena
## & around

Besides being Colombia's top tourist destination and a World Heritage Site, Cartagena is one of the hottest, most vibrant and beautiful cities in South America. It combines superb weather and a sparkling stretch of coastline with an eclectic mix of Caribbean, African and Spanish tastes and sounds. Nuggets of history can be found around every corner and in every palm-shaded courtyard of this most romantic of places. With exquisitely preserved architecture, excellent museums and fine dining, it's a place to be savoured.

The walled city is a labyrinth of colourful squares, churches, mansions and pastel-coloured houses along narrow cobbled streets. The San Diego quarter and Plaza Santo Domingo perhaps best capture the lure of Cartagena; don't miss a drink at night in the cafés here.

Cartagena is also a popular beach resort: modern high-rise hotels line the seafront at Bocagrande and the road to Barranquilla, while, in the bay, sandy islands are lapped by the turquoise sea. *Colour map 1, B2.*

The old city streets are narrow. Each block has a different name, which can cause confusion, but don't worry: the thing to do is to wander aimlessly, savouring the street scenes, and allow the great sights to catch you by surprise. However, if you do want to know what you are looking at, places of outstanding interest are numbered on the map (see page 140). Most of the 'great houses' can be visited and some churches are open to the public for most of the day; others only at 1800. Weekends and holidays are the best times for photography as traffic is minimal.

### ★ The ramparts

In addition to being a spectacular feature of Cartagena, the city walls make a great walk and are an excellent way to visit many of the attractions inside the old city (see www.fortificacionesdecartagena.com). A good place to start is the **Baluarte San Francisco Javier (10)** from where, with a few ups and downs, the circuit is continuous to **La India Catalina (28)**. From this point, there are two further sections along the lagoons to the **Puente Román (1)**. The final section of the circuit along the Calle del Arsenal can be completed through the **Playa de Barahona**, a bayside park, which is busy at weekends. The entire walk takes about 1½ hours, although if you bring a camera it can take considerably longer. It is a spectacular walk in the morning around 0600 and equally at sunset. At many points you can drop down to see the sights detailed in the tour of the old city, below.

### Outer city

The **Puente Román (1)** is the bridge that leads from Manga Island, with its shipping terminals, into Getsemaní, characterized by its *casas bajas* (low houses), in which the artisan classes lived. Today, many of these one-storey houses are being restored and there is a concentration of hotels and restaurants here. The chapel of **San Roque (2)**, early 17th century, is at the eastern end of Calle Media Luna, near the hospital of Espíritu Santo. Just across the **Playa Pedregal (3)** from here is the Laguna de San Lázaro and the **Puente Heredia**, which leads to the Castillo San Felipe de Barajas (see below). North of Calle Media Luna is the modern downtown sector, known as **La Matuna**, where vendors crowd the pavements and alleys between modern commercial buildings. Several middle-range hotels are in this district, between Avenidas Venezuela and Lemaitre.

In an interesting plaza, is the church of **La Trinidad (4)**, built 1643 but not consecrated until 1839. Near the church, at No 10 Calle Guerrero, lived Pedro Romero, who set the revolution of 1811 going by coming out into the street shouting 'Long Live Liberty'. His statue can be seen outside La Trinidad. Along Calle Larga **(5)**, Calle 25, is the monastery of **San Francisco**. The church was built in 1590 after the pirate Martin Côte had destroyed an earlier church built in 1559. The first Inquisitors lodged at the monastery. From its courtyard a crowd surged into the streets claiming Independence from Spain on 11 November 1811. The

# Cartagena historical centre

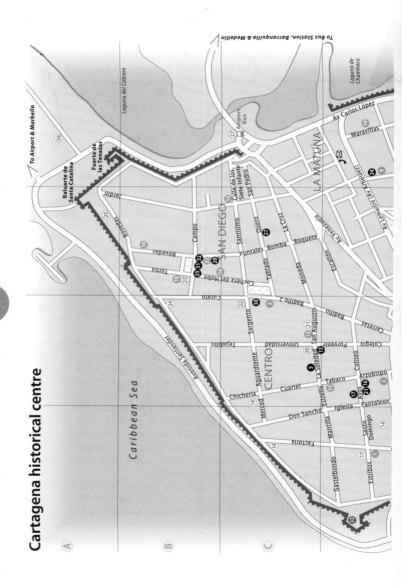

Caribbean Sea

Laguna de Cabrero

Laguna de Chambacú

To Bus Station, Barranquilla & Medellín

To Airport & Marbello

Baluarte de Santa Catalina

Fuerte de las Tenazas

Airport Bus

SAN DIEGO

CENTRO

LA MATUNA

Maravillas

Av Carlos López

Av Venezuela

Av Lemaitre (Av Arbeláez)

Avenida Santander

Bóveda

Jardín

Campo

Bóvedas

Torno

Cochera del Hobo

Curato

Santísimo

Quero

La Cruz

Puntales

Bomba

Boquete

Tablado

Badillo 2

Moneda

Escallón

Badillo

Carretas

Colegio

Coliseo

Arzobispo

Pantaleon

Iglesia

Santo Domingo

Don Sancho

Mantilla

Estribos

Gastelbondo

Factoría

Merced

Cuartel

Chichería

Aguardiente

Sargento

Tejadillo

Universidad

San Augustín

Porvenir

La Soledad

Estrella

Tabaco

Tumbamuertos

Calle de los Siete Infantes

San Pedro

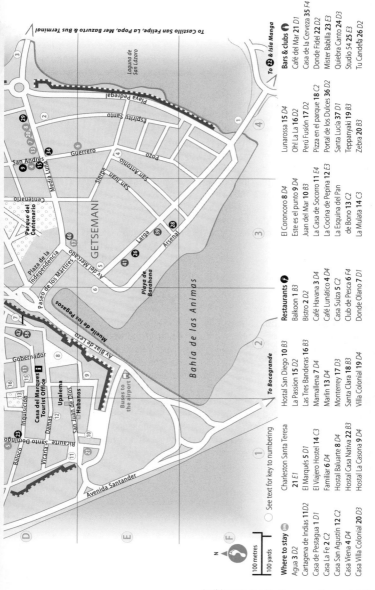

To Castillo San Felipe, La Popa, Mer Bazurto & Bus Terminal

Laguna de San Lázaro

To 21 & Isla Manga

**Bars & clubs**
Café del Mar **21** D1
Casa de la Cerveza **35** F4
Donde Fidel **22** D2
Mister Babilla **23** E3
Quiebra Canto **24** D3
Studio 54 **25** E3
Tu Candela **26** D2

GETSEMANÍ

Playa Pedregal

Espíritu Santo

Guerrero

San Andrés

Pozo

San Antonio

Sierpe

San Juan

Centenario

Parque del Centenario

Laiga

Arsenal

Plaza de la Independencia

Paseo de los Mártires

Av del Mercado

Playa de Bardhona

**Restaurants**
Balkoon **1** B3
Bistro **2** D2
Café Havana **3** D4
Café Lunático **4** D4
Casa Suiza **5** C2
Club de Pesca **6** F4
Donde Olano **7** D1
El Coroncoro **8** D4
Este es el punto **9** D4
Juan del Mar **10** B3
La Casa de Socorro **11** E4
La Cocina de Pepina **12** E3
La Esquina del Pan
   de Bono **13** C2
La Mulata **14** C3
Lunarossa **15** D4
Oh! La La **16** D2
Perú Fusión **17** D2
Pizza en el parque **18** C2
Portal de los Dulces **36** D2
Santa Lucía **37** D1
Teppanyaki **19** B3
Zebra **20** B3

Bahía de las Ánimas

To Bocagrande

Buses to
the airport

Muelle de los Pegasos

Av Blas de Lezo

Gobernador

Inquisición

Casa del Marqués
Tourist Office

Upalema
Habanos

San Juan de Dios

Ricaurte Santo Domingo

Damas

Vícaria

Baloco

Avenida Santander

N

100 metres
100 yards

**Where to stay**
Agua **3** D2
Cartagena de Indias **11** D2
Casa de Pestagua **1** D1
Casa La Fe **2** C2
Casa San Agustín **12** C2
Casa Viena **4** D4
Casa Villa Colonial **20** D3
Charleston Santa Teresa
   **21** E1
El Marqués **5** D1
El Viajero Hostel **14** C3
Familiar **6** D4
Hostal Baluarte **8** D4
Hostal Casa Nativa **22** B3
Hostal La Casona **9** D4
Hostal San Diego **10** B3
La Passion **15** D2
Las Tres Banderas **16** B3
Mamallena **7** D4
Marlin **13** D4
Monterrey **17** D3
Santa Clara **18** B3
Villa Colonial **19** D4

○ See text for key to numbering

# Essential Cartagena

## Finding your feet

The colonial heart of Cartagena, El Centro, lies within 12 km of ramparts at the northern end of the Bahía de Cartagena. Most of the upmarket hotels and restaurants are found here. Less touristy is the Getsemaní neighbourhood, where the colonial buildings house many budget hotels. Immediately adjoining Getsemaní is the downtown sector known as La Matuna. Beyond this central area the city sprawls for 10 km to the north, south and east. In the bay are several low, sandy islands, while further south, the Islas del Rosario are glistening examples of what tropical islands should look like.

## Best city beaches

## Getting around

Within the city green and white Metrocar buses are a recommended way to get to all areas, US$0.90; taxis are also quite cheap and may be more convenient. The walled city should, however, be explored on foot; take your time and don't fret about getting lost in the narrow streets. A stroll along the ramparts will give you an excellent overview. Boats from the Muelle Turístico go to outlying beaches and islands.

## Security

Carry your passport, or a photocopy, at all times. Failure to present it on police request can result in imprisonment and fines. Generally, the central areas are safe and friendly (although Getsemaní is less secure), but should you require the police, there is a station in Barrio Manga. Beware of drug pushers on the beaches, pickpockets in crowded areas and bag/camera snatchers on quiet Sunday mornings. At the bus station, do not be pressurized into a hotel recommendation different from your own choice.

## When to go

The weather is warm year-round; the hottest and wettest months are between August and November. Cartagena can become very crowded around Christmas and Easter and for its numerous festivals.

## Time required

Allow a couple of days to explore the city and a few more to relax on the beaches.

main part of the monastery has now been turned into business premises – take a look at the cloister garden as you pass by. Good-value fixed-price handicrafts are sold in the grounds of the monastery and, at the back, is the Centro Comercial Getsemaní, a busy shopping centre. On the corner of Calle Larga, formerly part of the Franciscan complex, is the **Iglesia de la Tercera Orden**, a busy church with a fine wooden roof of unusual design and some brightly painted niche figures. The church and monastery front on to the Avenida del Mercado on the other side of which is the **Centro Internacional de Convenciones (6)**. It holds gatherings of up to 4000 people and is frequently used for local and international conventions. It was built in 1972 on the site of the old colourful market, now banished to the interior part of the city. Although the severe fort-like structure is more or less in keeping with the surrounding historic walls and bastions, not everyone believes this is an improvement. When not in use, ask for a guide to show you around.

Immediately to the north is **Plaza de la Independencia**, with the landscaped **Parque del Centenario** next to it. The **Paseo de los Mártires** runs alongside the plaza, by the water, flanked by the busts of nine patriots executed in the square on 24 February 1816 by the royalist Pablo Morillo after he had retaken the city. At the western end of the Paseo is a tall clock tower, **Torre del Reloj**, often used as the symbol of Cartagena. To the left is the **Muelle de los Pegasos** (Muelle Turístico) from where the tourist boats leave. Under the clock tower is the **Puerta del Reloj**: these three arches are the principal entrance to the inner walled city.

### Inner city

Inside the Puerta del Reloj is the **Plaza de los Coches (7)**. As in almost all the plazas of Cartagena, its arcades offer refuge from the tropical sun. At one time this plaza was the slave market, and later it was the departure point for carriages (*coches*), which could be hired for local journeys. On the west side of this plaza is the **Portal de los Dulces**, a favourite meeting place where you can still buy all manner of local sweets and delicacies. It also has a number of good bars, often quite buzzing even during the day.

**Plaza de la Aduana (8)** has a statue of Columbus in the centre and the **Casa de la Aduana** along the wall, originally the tax office and now part of the city administration as the **Palacio Municipal**. Opposite is the **Casa del Marqués del Premio Real**, which was the residence of the representative of the Spanish king. In the corner of the wall is the **Museo de Arte Moderno** ⓘ *Mon-Fri 0900-1200, 1500-1800, Sat 1000-1300, US$2.50*, a collection of the work of modern Colombian artists. There is a museum shop.

Past the museum is the **Convento de San Pedro Claver (9)** ⓘ *daily 0900-1700, US$4.50*, and the church and monastery of the same name, built by Jesuits in 1603 and later dedicated to San Pedro Claver, a monk in the monastery, who died in 1654 and was canonized 235 years later. He was called *El Esclavo de los Esclavos*, or *El Apóstol de los Negros*: he used to beg from door to door for money to give to the black slaves brought to the city. His body is in an illuminated glass coffin set in the high marble altar, and his cell and the balcony from which he kept watch for slave ships are shown to visitors. There are brightly coloured birds in the small

## Fortifying Cartagena

The full name of Cartagena is Cartagena de Indias, a reminder that the early Spanish navigators believed they had reached the Far East. The city was founded by Pedro de Heredia on 13 January 1533 and was built by the Spaniards on an island separated from the mainland by marshes and lagoons, close to a prominent hill. It was near to the mouth of the Río Magdalena, the route to the interior of the continent, and thus became one of the most important depots for merchandise arriving from Spain and for treasure collected from the Americas to be sent back. The Bahía de Cartagena, which is 15 km long and 5 km wide, was protected by several low, sandy islands, which formed natural sea defences. There were originally just two approaches to the bay – Bocagrande, at the northern end of Tierrabomba island, and Bocachica, a narrow channel to the south – thus making it a perfect place for a harbour and, more importantly at the time, easy to defend against attack. The city's wealth made it a prize target for French and English privateers operating in the Caribbean, including Sir Francis Drake who took the city in 1586. In response, a series of forts were built to protect Cartagena from raids from the sea, and formidable walls were constructed around the city, making it almost impregnable.

The harbour was protected by fortifications on Tierrabomba, Barú, Bocagrande and on the mainland, while the Puente Román, which connected the old city with Manga island to the southeast, was defended by three forts:

monastery garden. Several upstairs rooms form a museum, with many interesting items linked or unrelated to Pedro Claver. In the pottery room, for example, is the chair used by the Pope on his visit to Cartagena in 1986. In another room there are several old maps, one of which shows the Caribbean maritime boundaries of Colombia, topical in that disputes with Nicaragua over San Andrés still persist today, despite an international court ruling in favour of Colombia.

Even if you're not walking the ramparts (see above), it is well worthwhile climbing up the **Baluarte San Francisco Javier** (10) for a good view of the city and the Caribbean. There is a **Museo Naval del Caribe** ① *C San Juan de Dios No3-62, T5-664 2440, www.museonavaldelcaribe.com, daily 1000-1730, US$3.50, US$2 for children*, with maps, models and displays of armaments, near the Baluarte.

On the corner of Calle Ricaurte is the convent of **Santa Teresa** (11), founded in 1609 by a rich benefactor as a convent for Carmelite nuns. It had various uses subsequently, as a prison, a military barracks, a school and in the 1970s, was occupied by the police. It was purchased by the Banco Central as a heritage investment and has been converted into a hotel, the **Charleston Santa Teresa** ① *Cra 3, No 31-23, www.hotelcharlestonsantateresa.com*. It is possible to visit the public areas of the hotel and admire the tasteful work of restoration. There is a great view from the roof.

San Sebastián del Pastelillo, built between 1558 and 1567 (now occupied by the Club de Pesca), San Lorenzo and the very powerful Castillo San Felipe de Barajas inland to the east. Yet another fort, La Tenaza, protected the northern point of the walled city from a direct attack from the open sea. In 1650, the Spaniards built the 145-km-long Canal del Dique connecting the city to the Río Magdalena and allowing free access for ships from the upriver ports. The city suffered a devastating raid by the French, led by Baron de Pointis and Jean Baptiste Ducasse, in 1697, but returned to prosperity during the 18th century as one of the most important cities in the newly formed Viceroyalty of New Granada. Following an unsuccessful but sustained attack by Admiral Edward Vernon in 1741, Bocagrande was blocked by an underwater wall, thus leaving only one entrance to the harbour.

The huge walls that encircle the old city were started early in the 17th century and finished by 1735. They were on average 12 m high and 17 m thick, with six gates. Besides barracks, they contained a water reservoir. The old city was in two sections, outer and inner, divided by a wall. The artisan classes lived in one-storey houses in the outer city, in an area known as Getsemaní where many colonial buildings survive. The inner city, or El Centro, was originally occupied by the high officials and nobility, with the clerks, merchants, priests and military living in San Diego at the northern end.

Cartagena declared its Independence from Spain in 1811. A year later Bolívar used the city as a jumping-off point for his Magdalena campaign. After heroic resistance, Cartagena was retaken by the royalists under General Pablo Morillo in 1815. It was finally freed by the patriots in 1821.

El Bodegón de la Candelaria (12) ⓘ *C Las Damas No 3-64*, was an elegant colonial residence. It has been faithfully restored and has some fine panelling and period furniture. A small shrine in one of the rooms marks the place where the Virgin appeared to a priest who was living there at the time.

One block away is Plaza de Bolívar (13) with an equestrian statue of the Liberator in the centre and attractive gardens. Formerly it was the Plaza de la Inquisición, with the Palacio de la Inquisición (14) ⓘ *Mon-Sat 0900-1900, Sun 1000-1600, US$5.50*, on its west side. First established in 1610, the jurisdiction of this tribunal extended to Venezuela and Panama, and at least 800 were sentenced to death here. The present building dates from 1706 and has a small window overlooking the plaza where the public were informed of the sentences. The stone entrance with its coats of arms and ornate wooden door is well preserved, and the whole building, with its balconies, cloisters and patios, is a fine example of colonial baroque. The small museum contains photos of Cartagena from the 20th century, paintings of historical figures and a torture chamber (with reproductions of actual instruments). Of special interest are the model of Cartagena in 1808, copies of Alexander Von Humboldt's maps showing the link he discovered between the Orinoco and Amazon rivers (*Canal de Casiquiare*) and of the Maypures rapids on the Orinoco – note that the longitude lines on the maps are west of Paris not Greenwich.

On the opposite side of the Plaza de Bolívar is the **Museo del Oro Zenú (15)** ⓘ *www.banrepcultural.org/gold-museum/regional-museums*, *Tue-Sat 0900-1700, Sun 1000-1500, free*, which focuses on the gold and pottery of the Zenú area to the south of Cartagena in the marshlands of the Sinú, San Jorge and Magdalena rivers. This area was densely populated between the second and 10th centuries during which time the gold working skills of the people were developed to a high level. Early drainage systems are featured, as is the advanced level of weaving techniques using the *cañafleche* and other fresh water reeds. Goldworking can still be seen today at Mompós at the northern edge of the Zenú region (see page 166).

The **cathedral (16)**, in the northeast corner of Plaza de Bolívar, begun in 1575, was partially destroyed by Francis Drake. Reconstruction was finished by 1612, but significant alterations were made between 1912 and 1923. It has a severe exterior, with a fine doorway, and a simply decorated interior. See the gilded 18th-century altar, the Carrara marble pulpit and the elegant arcades which sustain the central nave.

Across the street is the **Palacio de la Proclamación** named for the declaration of Independence of the State of Cartagena in November 1811. Before that it was the local governor's residence, and was also where Simón Bolívar stayed in 1826. The building was restored in 1950. The adjacent plaza has interesting local art and sculpture on display daily in high season.

The church and monastery of **Santo Domingo (17)**, built 1570 to 1579 is now a seminary. The old monastery was replaced by the present one in the 17th century. Inside, a miracle-making image of Christ, carved towards the end of the 16th century, is set on a baroque 19th-century altar. This is a very interesting neighbourhood, where very little has changed since the 16th century. In Calle Santo Domingo, No 33-29, is one of the great patrician houses of Cartagena, the **Casa de los Condes de Pestagua**, which was once the Colegio del Sagrado Corazón de Jesús and is now a boutique hotel (see page 152). It has a fine colonnaded courtyard, marble floors and magnificent palm trees in the centre garden. Beside the church is the **Plaza de Santo Domingo**, one of the most popular corners of Cartagena, with restaurants, bars and cafés. A sculpture by Fernando Botero, *Gertrudis*, or *La Gorda*, is in the plaza and creates an interesting juxtaposition between the colonial and the modern.

North of Santo Domingo at Calle de la Factoría 36-57 is the magnificent **Casa del Marqués de Valdehoyos (18)**, originally owned by the Marqués, who had the lucrative licences to import slaves and flour. The woodcarving is some of the best in Cartagena: the ceilings, chandeliers, wooden arches and balustrading are unique. The views of the city from the fine upper floor balconies are also recommended. It is used for cultural events and conferences.

A short walk northeast is the plaza, church and convent of **La Merced (19)**, founded 1618. The convent was a prison during Morillo's reign of terror. Its church is now the **Teatro Heredia**, which has been beautifully restored.

Two blocks east is Calle de la Universidad, at the end of which is the monastery of **San Agustín (20)**, built in 1580, currently the Universidad de Cartagena. From its chapel, the pirate Baron de Pointis stole a 500-pound silver sepulchre. It was returned by the King of France, but the citizens melted it down to pay their troops during the siege by Morillo in 1815. There is a luxury hotel here, Casa San Agustín ⓘ *C de la Universidad No 36-44, www.hotelcasasanagustin.com.*

One block along Calle de San Agustín is **La Casa Museo de Simón Bolívar (21)**, which houses a collection of memorabilia in the first Cartagena house he stayed in; it's now part of the **Biblioteca Bartolomé Calvo** owned by the Banco de la República.

One block along Badillo (Carrera 7) is the church of **Santo Toribio de Mogrovejo (22)** ⓘ *Mass Mon-Fri 0630, 1200, 1815, Sat 1800 and Sun 0800, 1000, 1800, 1900, closed at other times.* Building began in 1729. In 1741, during Admiral Vernon's siege, a cannon ball fell into the church during Mass and lodged in one of the central columns; the ball is now in a recess in the west wall. The font of Carrara marble in the Sacristy is a masterpiece. There is a beautiful carved ceiling in *mudéjar* style above the main altar with a rear-lighted figure of Christ.

The church and monastery of **Santa Clara de Assisi (23)** is close by. It was built 1617-1621 and has been spectacularly restored. It is now the **Santa Clara Hotel** ⓘ *C del Torno, No 39-29, www.sofitel.com,* but this is one you must see. Behind the hotel is the orange **Casa de Gabriel García Márquez (24)**, the former Cartagena home of Colombia's most famous author, on the corner of Calle del Curato.

Beyond the Santa Clara is the **Plaza de Las Bóvedas (25)**, whose walls, built in 1799, are 12 m high and 15-18 m thick. At the base of the wall are 23 dungeons, now containing tourist shops. An illuminated underground passage and a drawbridge lead from Las Bóvedas to the fortress of **La Tenaza**, which guarded the approach to the city from the coast to the northeast. Next to La Tenaza is the Baluarte de Santa Catalina, which houses the **Museo Fortificación de Santa Catalina** ⓘ *www.fortificacionesdecartagena.com, daily 0800-1800, US$3.50, children US$2,* inside the walls themselves. Towards the sea is a bank (*espiga*) leading to a jetty used in colonial times when the water came up to the walls, as shown on the 1808 map displayed in the **Palacio de la Inquisición**. All the land below the walls has since been reclaimed, with sports fields, recreational areas and the Avenida Santander/Paseo de la Muralla, a busy bypass to the city.

**Casa de Núñez (26)** ⓘ *Tue-Fri 0900-1700, Sat-Sun 1000-1600, free,* just outside the walls of La Tenaza in El Cabrero district, was the home of Rafael Núñez, four-time president of Colombia. He wrote the national anthem and established the constitution of 1886, to which there is a monument in the small park beside the lagoon. Núñez' grandiose marble tomb is in the delightful small **Ermita El Cabrero** church opposite.

Closer to the centre, where a major road leads into the city, is a roundabout, in the centre of which is the monument to **La India Catalina (27)**, Pedro de Heredia's indigenous interpreter in the early days of the Spanish conquest. A miniature of this statue is given to the winner of the annual Cartagena film festival – a Colombian 'Oscar'.

**a formidable fortress, a ruined convent and great views**

**Castillo San Felipe de Barajas** ① *daily 0800-1730, US$8, guides available*, is located 41 m above sea level on San Lázaro hill across the **Puente Heredia (3)** from the old city. It is the largest Spanish fort built in the Americas. Under the huge structure is a network of tunnels cut into the rock, lined with living rooms and offices. Visitors pass through these and on to the top of the fortress. Good footwear is advisable in the damp sloping tunnels, and although some are open and illuminated, a flashlight is handy in the others. In the **Almacén de Pólvora** (Gunpowder store), there is a reproduction of Admiral Vernon's map, dating from his abortive attempt to take the city in 1741. A statue of Don Blas de Lezo below the fortress has a plaque displaying the medal prematurely struck celebrating Vernon's 'victory'.

Further east on the Cerro de la Popa, nearly 150 m high, is the **Convento La Popa** ① *daily 0830-1730, US$2.25, children and students US$1.25, guides available*. There is a fine view of the harbour and the city from here, but it is not recommended to walk up on your own; either take a guided tour or take a public bus to Teatro Miramar at the foot of the hill (US$0.90), then bargain for a taxi up. The complex includes the Augustinian church and monastery of Santa Cruz (Convento La Popa) and the restored ruins of the convent dating from 1608. In the church is a beautiful image of the Virgin of La Candelaria, with a golden crown, reputed to be a deliverer from plague and a protector against pirates. The statue was blessed by the Pope on his visit in 1986. The Virgin's day is 2 February and for nine days before the feast thousands of people go up the hill by car, on foot, or on horseback, carrying lighted candles on the feast day itself. There is an attractive bougainvillea-covered cloister with a well in the centre, and a museum with illuminated manuscripts, old maps, music books, relics and an image of the *Cabro de Oro* (golden goat) found by the Augustinians on the site, presumed to be an object of veneration of the indigenous people who previously inhabited the area. The name was bestowed on the hill because of its imagined likeness to a ship's poop deck.

## Beaches and islands

**an unmissable part of the Cartagena experience**

Cartagena is surrounded on almost all sides by water and travellers will be drawn to the city's sparkling Caribbean beaches.

### Bocagrande
*To get to Bocagrande, take a bus south from the Puerta del Reloj, taxi US$3, or walk.*

Just under a kilometre from the old city, along a seafront boulevard, Bocagrande is a spit of land crowded with hotel and apartment towers. Thousands of visitors flock to the beach with its accompanying resort atmosphere, fast-food outlets, shops – and dirty seawater. The water quality improves if you go as far as the **Hilton** ① *www.cartagena.hilton.com*, an excellent hotel at the end of the peninsula. **Fuerte Castillo Grande** on the tip of Bocagrande was built to protect the inner harbour of Cartagena, along with **Fuerte San José de Manzanillo** on the mainland. Access to Castillo Grande itself is restricted, but there is a very good view of the harbour, cruise boats and port activity from the end of Calle 6/Carrera 14, Bocagrande: in the centre of the harbour is a statue of the Virgin, with the port installations of Manga Island visible on the other side of the bay.

## Marbella and the northern beaches
**Marbella beach** is just north of Las Bóvedas. This is the locals' beach and therefore quieter than Bocagrande during the week and good for swimming, though subject at times to dangerous currents. Beyond Marbella and the airport, the promontory is built up with high rises, including many well-known hotels which have their own access to the beach. City buses run to Los Morros and Las Américas conference centre, carrying on towards La Boquilla. Further north still, **Playa Manzanillo** is a sparsely populated stretch of beach, great for those looking to get away from the crowds but still stay close to the city.

## Isla de Tierrabomba
The island of Tierrabomba lies between Bocagrande and Barú Island, forming a natural barrier between the Bahía de Cartagena and the Caribbean. The passage into the bay, known as Bocachica, is overlooked by the fortress of **San Fernando** at the southern tip of Tierrabomba and by **Fuerte San José**, opposite on Barú. The two forts were once linked by heavy chains to prevent surprise attacks by pirates. Like Bocagrande, **Bocachica beach** on Tierrabomba isn't very clean and you may be hassled here too.

Boats leave for Tierrabomba from a two-storey glass building halfway along the Muelle Turístico, which also has some tourist information. The round trip can take up to two hours each way and costs about US$4 with the regular service, more with private boats. Boats taking in Bocachica and the San Fernando fortress include *Alcatraz*, which runs a daily trip. Alternatively, you can cross from Bocagrande; *lanchas* leave from near the Hilton hotel and go to **Punta Arena** beach on Tierrabomba.

## Isla de Barú
Barú is a long thin island, with mostly fine white-sand beaches, separated from the mainland only by the **Canal del Dique**. The stopping place for tourist boats from Cartagena is **Playa Blanca**, which is crowded in the mornings but peaceful after the tour boats have left at around 1400. There are several fish restaurants on the beach, a growing number of upmarket places to stay and a few hammock and camping places. Take repellent against sandflies if sleeping in a tent or *cabaña*, and bring food and water since these are expensive on Barú. There have been reports of people drinking alcohol and then renting jetskis at Playa Blanca; keep your wits about you when swimming or snorkelling, as safety measures aren't always complied with.

There are different ways of getting to **Playa Blanca**. The most common is to take a bus from the centre to **Pasacaballo**, US$0.90 and then cross over the Canal del Dique via a five-minute ferry, US$0.50. There is also a bridge which allows for direct trips via taxi, or visitors can take a motortaxi via **Santa Ana** (45 minutes), US$4.50-5.50. Alternatively, fast boats to Playa Blanca leave **Bazurto** market, near La Popa, 0700-0930 daily, US$14 one way; public boats cost US$5.50-8.50. Neither the area nor the boats are particularly safe and boatmen can be persistent; be sure to pay the captain and not his 'helpers' and arrange a return pick-up time. There are also boats from the tourist dock which may stop at Playa Blanca as part of a tour to the Islas del Rosario (see below). When taking boat trips be certain that you and the operator understand what you are paying for. You can arrange to be left and collected later, or you can try to catch an earlier boat on to Islas del Rosario or back to Cartagena after passengers have been dropped off at the beach.

## Listings Cartagena *map p140*

### Tourist information

The main tourist office, **Turismo Cartagena de Indias**, is in the Casa del Marqués del Premio Real, Pl de la Aduana, T5-660 1583, daily 0900-1700, and has very helpful and knowledgeable staff. There are also kiosks in Pl de los Coches and Pl de San Pedro Claver, Mon-Sat 0900-1300, 1500-1900; the latter also Sun 0900-1700. The **Instituto de Patrimonio y Cultura de Cartagena**, C Larga No 9A-47, T5-664 9443, www.ipcc.gov.co, may also provide information. For maps, contact **Instituto Agustín Codazzi**, C 34, No 3A-31, T5-664 4171, Edif Inurbe, www.igac.gov.co, Mon-Fri 0730-1545. Useful websites include www.ticartagena.com and www.cartagenacaribe.com.

### Where to stay

Hotel prices rise for the high seasons, Nov-Mar and Jun-Jul. From 15 Dec to 31 Jan they can increase by as much as 50% (dates are not fixed and vary at each hotel). Hotels tend to be heavily booked right through to Mar.

**Outer city: Getsemaní and La Matuna**
This area is very popular with travellers and has been smartened up, with many places to stay, eat and drink (lots of happy hour offers). Do not, however, walk alone late at night.

**$$$ Monterrey**
*Paseo de los Mártires, Cra 8B, No 25-103, T5-650 3030, www.hotelmonterrey.com.co.*
Just outside the old city walls and with a view onto the Puerta del Reloj, this hotel has rooms in simple colours with balconies, TV, hot water and internet. It also has a sunroof with pool and jacuzzi.

**$$$-$$ Hostal Casa Baluarte**
*Media Luna, No 10-81, T5-664 2208, www.hostalcasabaluarte.com.*
A family-run, converted colonial house with a fine courtyard shaded by a mango tree and wrought-iron furniture, rocking chairs and hammocks in which to relax. Also offers massage. Can arrange tours to the Islas del Rosario and has laundry service. Rooms a little small.

**$$ Marlin**
*C de la Media Luna, No 10-35, T5-664 3507, www.hotelmarlincartagena.com.*

Aquatic-themed hostel run by a friendly Colombian. Has a fine balcony looking onto the busy C de la Media Luna. Laundry service, free coffee, internet access, lockers, tours and bus tickets organized. Breakfast included. Recommended.

### $$-$ Hostal La Casona
*C Tripita y Media, Cra 10, No 31-32, T5-664 1301.*
Has a breezy central courtyard and rooms for 1-6 people, some with private bath, with a/c or fan. Laundry service provided.

### $$-$ Mamallena
*C de la Media Luna, No 10-47, T5-670 0499, www.hostelmamallenacartagena.com.*
Rooms and dorms (some with a/c) in what was the **Holiday**. It's in same group as the **Mamallena** hostels in Panama, www.mamallena.com. Thorough information on boat travel to Panama and on local activities, offers day tours. There's a small kitchen, café, Wi-Fi, breakfast, tea and coffee included.

### $$-$ Villa Colonial
*C de las Maravillas, No 30-60, Getsemaní, T5-664 4996, www.hotelvillacolonial.com.*
A safe, well-kept hostel run by a friendly family, English spoken, rooms are

cheaper with fan. Arranges tours to Islas del Rosario. Its sister hotel, **Casa Villa Colonial**, C de la Media Luna, No 10-89, T5-664 5421, www.casavillacolonial.com, is more upmarket ($$$) and is also recommended.

### $ Casa Viena
*C San Andrés, No 30-53, T5-668 5048, T320-538 3619, www.casaviena.com.*
Popular traveller hostel with very helpful staff who provide lots of information and sell tours and Brasilia bus tickets. Washing machine, TV room, book exchange, range of rooms from dorms to a few with private bath ($$), good value, security conscious. Enquire here for information about boats to Panama.

### $ Hotel Familiar
*C del Guerrero, No 29-66, off Media Luna, T5-664 2464.*
Fresh and bright, family-run hotel with rooms set around a colonnaded patio. Has a good noticeboard full of information, a laundry service and use of a kitchen. Friendly and recommended.

**Inner city: El Centro and San Diego**

### $$$$ Agua
*C de Ayos, No 4-29, T5-664 9479, www.hotelagua.com.co.*

Exclusive, expensive, small boutique hotel in colonial surroundings, quiet, with a very pleasant patio.

#### $$$$ Cartagena de Indias
*C Vélez Daníes 33, No 4-39, T5-660 0133, www.movichhotels.com.*
A small hotel in a colonial building, comfortable, luxury accommodation, good service, has a pool and a rooftop terrace with great view of the city.

#### $$$$ Casa de Pestagua
*C Santo Domingo, No 33-63, T5-664 9510, www.casapestagua.com.*
Formerly home to the Conde de Pestagua, this historic house has been restored by architect Alvaro Barrera Herrera with great care. From the street it opens up into a magnificent colonnaded courtyard lined with enormous palm trees. Beyond is a swimming pool and spa, and on the top floor a sun terrace with jacuzzi and sea views.

#### $$$$ Casa San Agustín
*C de la Universidad No 36-44, T5-681 0000, www.hotelcasasanagustin.com.*
A luxury boutique hotel in 3 historic buildings, combining colonial architectural style with all modern facilities. Some rooms and suites have plunge pools and jacuzzis, all are spacious and elegant. It has the **Alma** restaurant and bar. Arranges trips to Islas del Rosario for guests.

#### $$$$ Charleston Santa Teresa
*Cra 3, No 31-23, T5-664 9494, www.hotelcharlestonsantateresa.com.*
Formerly a convent, beautifully converted into a luxury hotel. Suites and standard rooms are in 2 wings, Colonial and Republican. 4 choices of restaurant, spa, stylish pool on the roof with great views of the colonial district and sea.

#### $$$$ El Marqués
*C Nuestra Señora del Carmen, No 33-41, T5-664 4438, www.elmarqueshotelboutique.com.*
Another house belonging to the Pestagua family. The central courtyard, dominated by a large crumbling wall of draping ivy, features giant birdcages, hanging bells and large palm trees. The rooms are crisp, white and have Wi-Fi. It has a Peruvian restaurant, a wine cellar and spa. Exquisite.

#### $$$$ La Passion
*C Estanco del Tabaco, No 35-81, T5-664 8605, www.lapassionhotel.com.*
In the heart of the old city, this grand building brings the concept of the Marrakech boutique hotel to Latin America. Its French owners have trawled the globe in search of exquisite furnishings. A mixture of colonial and Republican-era architecture, **La Passion** has cathedral-like rooms that provide modern, elegant and discreet comfort in the shape of plasma TVs, Wi-Fi and MP3 players. Breakfast is included in the price and served on the sublime roof terrace, next to the swimming pool. Also offers spa treatments including different massage and boat trips to nearby Islas del Rosario. Highly recommended.

#### $$$$ Santa Clara
*C del Torno, No 39-29, T5-650 4700, www.sofitel.com.*
The French Sofitel group own this magnificently restored early 17th-century convent on the enchanting Plaza de San Diego. Rooms, however, are in a modern annex and most have a balcony looking onto a large swimming pool, invariably with views of the sea. Has 2 restaurants, a bar and a spa.

#### $$$$-$$$ Casa La Fe
*Parque Fernández de Madrid, C 2a de Badillo, No 36-125, T5-664 0306, www.casalafe.com.*
A Republican-era house (c1930) on the delightful Parque Fernández de Madrid, the 14 en suite bedrooms of **Casa La Fe** have been restored by a British-Colombian team. It has a pool-jacuzzi on the roof and other services such as Wi-Fi and free breakfast served in a leafy patio. Organizes tours.

#### $$$ Hostal San Diego
*C de las Bóvedas, No 39-120, T5-660 1433, www.hostalsandiego.com.*
Near the delightful Plaza San Diego, this colonial building with its salmon pink exterior has modern rooms which open out onto a tiled courtyard. A/c and Wi-Fi.

#### $$$ Las Tres Banderas
*C Cochera de Hobo, No 38-66, T5-660 0160, www.hotel3banderas.com.*
Another hotel in the bohemian district of San Diego, this old building is split over 2 breezy courtyards with water features. Popular, helpful owner, very pleasant, safe, quiet, good beds, spacious rooms, massage treatments, small patio. Price depends on standard of room and season. Free ferry transport to sister hotel on Isla de la Bomba; has another hotel at Manzanillo.

#### $$ El Viajero Hostel
*C de los Siete Infantes 9-45, T5-660 2598, www.hostelcartagena.com.*
Member of the South American El Viajero chain of hostels, great location in the centre of the walled city. Spacious, with various dorms (US$14.50-17.50) private rooms with en suite bath. A/c in all rooms and dorms as well as safe boxes. Tourist office in the lobby, breakfast included, free Wi-Fi throughout,

activities everyday including free dance lessons, and a bar. Falls into the younger, party hostel category.

#### $$ Hostal Casa Nativa
*C Tumbamuertos No 38-68, T5-645 6064, www.casanativahostal.com.*
No frills *hostal* ideally located in the centre. Dorms (US$17) and no privates. Decent budget alternative when the **El Viajero** is fully booked.

### Bocagrande

#### $$$$ Capilla del Mar
*Cra 1 No 8-12, T5-650 1501, www.capilladelmar.com.*
Resort hotel across the road from the beach, with swimming pool on the top floor and 2 restaurants featuring regional cuisine.

#### $$$$ Hotel Caribe
*Cra 1, No 2-87, T5-650 1160, www.hotelcaribe.com.*
Enormous Caribbean-style hotel, the first to be built in Cartagena, retaining some splendour of bygone years, with 2 newer annexes, a/c, beautiful grounds and a swimming pool. Expensive restaurant, has several bars overlooking the sea, various tour agencies and a dive shop.

#### $$$$ Playa Club
*Av San Martín, No 4-87, T5-665 0552, www.hotelplayaclubcartagena.com.*
Some of the rooms are painted in lurid colours but are otherwise fine and it has an inviting pool and direct access to the beach. TV, a/c and breakfast included.

#### $$$$-$$$ Cartagena Millennium
*Av San Martín, No 7-135, T5-642 4747 ext 2, www.hotelcartagenamillennium.com.*
A range of different suites and spacious rooms at various prices. Chic and trendy, with minimalist decor, a small

pool, restaurant serving typical and international food, a terrace bar and a lobby bar, good service.

### $$$ Bahía
*Cra 4 with C 4, T5-665 0316,*
*www.hotelbahiacartagena.com.*
Retains the feel of a 1950s hotel – it was opened in 1958 – but with mod cons such as Wi-Fi and safes in rooms. Discreet and quiet, with a fine pool and restaurant.

### $$$ Charlotte
*Av San Martín, No 7-126, T5-642 4744 ext 2, www.hotelescharlotte.com.*
Comfortable rooms stylishly designed in cool whites. Has a small pool, and Wi-Fi in the lobby. Smart restaurant serving regional food. Recommended.

### $$ Mary
*Cra 3, No 6-53.*
Basic rooms but pleasant and friendly. A/c or fan.

### Marbella and the northern beaches

### $$$-$$ Hotel Kohsamui
*Trans 2 No 3-51, Playa Manzanillo, T317-648 9303, www.kohsamuicartagena.com.*
Situated 20 km north of Cartagena, this is an ideal spot for relaxation and rejuvenation. Owner María Fernanda runs the hotel and has information on mangrove tours, excursions and trips to Islas del Rosario and Volcán del Totumo. Amenities include a/c and fans, security box, Wi-Fi, minibar, restaurant, spa with massage, and a 2nd-floor terrace with hammocks. 10% discount for paying in advance. Highly recommended.

### Isla Barú

### $$$ Playa Manglares
*Km 16, Vía Playa Blanca, on a private beach on Isla Barú, T317-657 1315, www.playamanglares.com.*
Ecolodge, B&B, owned and run by Olga Paulhiac, organic food, yoga available, evening cocktails, attentive service, delightful.

### $ Hugo's Place
Hammocks with mosquito nets, fish meals served, camping.
Another place is **Mama Ruth** which is also recommended.

### Restaurants

There is a wide range of excellent, upmarket restaurants. All restaurants are busy during high season, when reservations are recommended. At cafés try *patacón*, a round flat 'cake' made of green banana, mashed and baked; it's also available from street stalls in Parque del Centenario in the early morning. At restaurants ask for *sancocho*, the local soup of the day made from vegetables and fish or meat. Stands serving tasty shrimp cocktails can be found just outside of El Centro. Also try *obleas* for a snack: biscuits with jam, cream cheese or caramel fudge (*arequipe*); and *buñuelos*, deep-fried cheese dough balls. Fruit juices are fresh, tasty and cheap in Cartagena: a good place is on the Paseo de los Pegasos (Av Blas de Lezo) from the many stalls alongside the boats. **Crepes y Waffles**, **Jeno's Pizza** and **Juan Valdez** have outlets in the centre, Bocagrande and elsewhere.

## Outer city: Getsemaní and La Matuna

With spiralling property prices Getsemaní is undergoing the same gentrification treatment as Centro and San Diego, which is reflected in the number of smart restaurants opening up in the area.

### $$ La Casa de Socorro
*C Larga, No 8B-112, T315-718 6666.*
This seafood restaurant is popular with locals and does very good *bandejas de pescado* and *arroz con camarones*. Take note that there are 2 rival restaurants of the same name on the same street. This one is the original. Friendly and recommended.

### $$-$ La Cocina de Pepina
*C Vargas, No 9A-6, T5-664 2944.*
A restaurant serving Colombian Caribbean cuisine, run by established chef and cookbook author María Josefina Yances Guerra.

### $$-$ Lunarossa
*C de la Media Luna y San Andrés.*
Italian restaurant and bar serving thin-crust pizza, pasta and other dishes.

### $ Café Lunático
*C Media Luna, No 10-81, T301-740 0642 (next door to Hostal Casa Baluarte).*
Interesting café with fresh juices, local and Indian dishes. Also sells weavings and blankets.

### $ El Coroncoro
*C Tripita y Media, No 39-22.*
More typical of the area, very popular at lunchtime with locals. It's atmospheric and offers *menús del día* from US$3.

### $ Este es el punto
*C San Andrés, No 30-35.*
Another popular restaurant, *comida corriente* at lunchtime, US$4, also serves breakfast.

## Inner city: El Centro and San Diego

**Plaza San Diego** has several good restaurants serving a variety of international cuisine.

### $$$-$$ Donde Olano
*C Santo Domingo, No 33-81, e Inquisición, T5-664 7099, www.dondeolano.com.*
Art deco restaurant serving French and Creole cuisine in a cosy atmosphere. Try their fantastic seafood platter, *Tentaciones de Zeus*. Well worth the price.

### $$ Balkoon
*C de Tumbamuertos, No 38-85, p 2 (above Zebra).*
Small restaurant with a nice balcony overlooking the Plaza de San Diego. Good atmosphere and good views.

### $$ Bistro
*C de los Ayos, No 4-46, www.el-bistro.com.*
German-run restaurant with a relaxed atmosphere, closed Sun. Sofas, music, Colombian and European menu at reasonable prices, German bakery. Recommended.

### $$ Juan del Mar
*Plaza San Diego, No 8-12, www.juandelmar.com.*
Offers 2 restaurants in one: expensive seafood is served inside, while fine thin-crust pizzas are available outside, though you are likely to be harassed by street hawkers.

### $$ Oh! La La
*C de los Ayos, No 4-48.*
Café/restaurant serving good French and Colombian food. Next door are **Jugoso** juice bar and **El Gallinero** for ice creams, yoghurts and snacks.

### $$ Teppanyaki
*Plaza San Diego, No 8-28.*
Serves sushi and Thai food in smart surroundings.

## $$ Zebra
*Plaza San Diego, No 38-34.*
Café with wide selection of coffees,
hot sandwiches and African dishes.

## $$-$ Casa Suiza
*C de la Soledad No 5-38.*
For breakfast, lunch such as lasagne,
salads, cheeses dishes, also does take-
away, Wi-Fi.

## $$-$ La Mulata
*C Quero, No 9-58, www.lamulata
cartagena.blogspot.com.*
A popular lunchtime venue with locals,
you get a selection of set menu dishes.
Try the excellent seafood casserole and
coconut lemonade. Wi-Fi.

## $$ Perú Fusión
*C de los Ayos, No 4-36.*
Good-value Peruvian-style food,
including ceviches.

## $ La Esquina del Pan de Bono
*San Agustín Chiquito No 35-78, opposite
Plazoleta San Agustín.*
Breads, *empanadas, pasteles* and juices,
popular for a quick snack.

## $ Pizza en el parque
*C 2a de Badillo, No 36-153.*
This small restaurant serves delicious
pizzas with some interesting flavours
(pear and apple) which you can
munch on while enjoying the
delightful atmosphere of Parque
Fernández de Madrid.

### East of the old city

## $$$ Club de Pesca
*Fuerte de San Sebastián de Pastelillo,
Isla Manga, T5-660 4594, www.club
depesca.com.*
Perhaps the most famous fish and
seafood restaurant in Cartagena.

Wonderful setting, though expensive.
Warmly recommended.

### Bocagrande

## $$$ Ranchería's
*Av 1A, No 8-86.*
Serves mainly seafood and meats
in thatched huts just off the beach.

## $$$-$$ Arabe
*Cra 3A, No 8-83, T5-665 4365, www.
restaurantearabeinternacional.com.*
Upmarket Arab restaurant serving
tagines, etc. A/c, indoor seating or
pleasant outdoor garden.

## $$$-$$ Carbón de Palo
*Av San Martín, No 6-40.*
Steak heaven (and other dishes),
cooked on an outdoor *parrilla.*

## $ La Fonda Antioqueña
*Cra 2, No 6-164.*
Traditional Colombian food served
in a nice atmosphere.

### Marbella and the northern beaches
There are good fish dishes in La Boquilla
and upscale dining options (including
a gourmet supermarket) at the turn-off
to Manzanillo.

## $$ Archie's Trattoria
*Km 9 via Manzanillo, T5-643 7070,
www.archies.co.*
Chain Italian restaurant serving delicious
thin-crust pizzas and a large selection
of pastas.

## $$ Hotel Kohsamui
*Trans 2 No 3-51, Manzanillo,
T317-648 9303.*
Chef Elbert runs the restaurant in the
hotel, serving up a variety of seafood
dishes, including fresh ceviches, *arroz
con mariscos* and fried fish. Probably
the best seafood on the beach.

## Bars and clubs

Cartagena boasts a lively dance scene and the atmosphere in the city after dark is addictive. Any one of the cafés next to the Santo Domingo church is a great place for a drink.

### Old city

Many of the hotels have evening entertainment and can arrange *chiva* (brightly coloured local bus) tours, usually with free drinks and live music on the bus. Most bars play crossover music and don't get going until after 2400, though the Cuban bar **Donde Fidel**, on Portal de los Dulces, and **Café Havana**, on C de la Media Luna in Getsemaní start a little earlier. C del Arsenal in Getsemaní hosts many clubs and you will probably wind up there if you are really giving the city's nightlife a go.

### Café del Mar
*Baluarte de Santo Domingo, El Centro.*
The place to go at sundown, where, surrounded by ancient canons, you can watch the sun set over the bay. Highly recommended, but very popular. Get here early to get a seat for the sundowners.

### Café Havana
*C de la Media Luna y C del Guerrero, Getsemaní, T310-610 2324, www.cafehavanacartagena.com. Thu-Sat and holidays 2030-0400.*
A fantastic Cuban bar and restaurant, which feels like it has been transported from Havana brick by brick. The walls are festooned with black-and-white portraits of Cuban salsa stars and it has live bands playing most nights. Note that it doesn't take credit cards. Highly recommended.

### Donde Fidel
*Portal de los Dulces, El Centro.*
Highly recommended if you want to hear Cuban salsa. Open during the daytime and the atmosphere is good even early on.

### Mister Babilla
*C Larga No 9B-127, Getsemaní.*
A popular, exclusive bar. Take something warm with you – they really like to blast the a/c here.

### Quiebra Canto
*C Media Luna at Parque Centenario, next to Hotel Monterrey, Getsemaní, www.quiebracanto.com.*
The best place for salsa. Nice atmosphere, free admission.

### Studio 54
*C Larga, No 8B-24, Getsemaní.*
Gay bar.

### Tu Candela
*Portal de los Dulces, next door to Donde Fidel, www.tucandela.co.*
A late-night option, open 2000-0400.

### Bocagrande
There are good local nightclubs in Bocagrande eg **La Escollera**, Cra 1, next to El Pueblito shopping centre, with other places nearby, including spontaneous musical groups on or near the beach most evenings.

## Entertainment

### Cinema
There are many cinemas in Cartagena. In Bocagrande there is one in the **Centro Comercial Bocagrande**, Cra 2, No 8-142, T5-665 5024. Others are in the **Centro Comercial Paseo de la Castellana** at C 30, No 30-31, www.paseodelacastellana.com, and in **Centro**

**Comercial La Plazuela**, Diag 31, No 71-130, www.multicentrolaplazuela.com.

### Dance

**El Colegio del Cuerpo**, *Campus Universidad Jorge Tadeo Lozano, Módulo 6, Km 13, Anillo Vial Zona Norte, T5-665 4081, www.elcolegiodel cuerpo.org*. A classical dance studio that works with children from Cartagena's slums. They perform internationally and occasionally in Cartagena.

## Festivals

Mid-Jan **Festival Internacional de Música**, www.cartagenamusicfestival. com. Classical music festival with associated education programme for young musicians.

End-Jan **Hay Festival Cartagena**, www.hayfestival.com. Franchise of the famous UK literary festival, with internationally renowned writers.

End-Jan **Cartagena de Indias Jazz Fest**, www.jazzcartagena.es.

Jan-Feb **La Candelaria**, religious processions and horse parades (see La Popa, page 148).

2nd week of Mar **International Film Festival**, www.ficcifestival.com. The longest running festival of its kind in Latin America. Although mainly Spanish American films are featured, the US, Canada and European countries are represented in the week-long showings.

1 Jun Celebrations commemorating the Foundation of Cartagena.

2nd week of Nov **Independence** celebrations: masked people in fancy dress dance to the sound of *maracas* and drums. There are beauty contests, battles of flowers and general mayhem.

## Shopping

Pricey antiques can be bought in C Santo Domingo and there are a number of jewellery shops near Plaza de Bolívar in Centro, which specialize in emeralds. The handicraft shops in the Plaza de las Bóvedas (see page 147) have the best selection in town but tend to be expensive– cruise ship passengers are brought here. Woollen *blusas* are good value; try the **Tropicano** in Pierino Gallo building in Bocagrande. Also in this building are reputable jewellery shops.

**Abaco**, *C de la Iglesia with C Mantilla, No 3-86, T5-664 8338, www.abacolibros. com.* A bookshop and popular hangout for local writers and poets. Delightful atmosphere and a café serving juices and snacks.

**Centro Comercial Getsemaní**, *C Larga between San Juan and Plaza de la Independencia.* A large shopping centre. Good *artesanías* in the grounds of the convent.

**El Centavo Menos**, *C Román, No 5-08, Plaza de la Proclamación.* Good selection of Colombian handicrafts.

**Exito**, *Escallón y del Boquete.* A supermarket, with a/c and cafeteria.

**Galería Cano**, *Plaza Bolívar No 33-20, www.galeriacano.com.co (and at the airport and Hotel Santa Clara).* Has excellent reproductions of pre-Columbian designs.

**H Stern**, *Pierino Gallo shopping centre and at the Hilton Hotel.* Jewellery shop.

**Librería Nacional**, *C 2 de Badillo, No 36-27, T5-664 1448, www.librerianacional.com.* A good bookshop with large stock.

**Santo Domingo**, *C Santo Domingo, No 3-34.* Recommended for jewellery.

**Upalema**, *C San Juan de Dios, No 3-99, www.upalema.com.* A good selection of handicrafts.

## Markets

The main market is to the southeast of the old city near La Popa off Av Pedro de Heredia (**Mercado Bazurto**). Good bargains in the **La Matuna** market, open daily including Sun.

### City tours

Many agencies, hotels and hostels offer city tours, US$22. There is also a hop-on, hop-off city sightseeing bus tour. A party tour on a *chiva* bus costs US$20. **Horse-drawn carriages** can be hired for for a trip around the walled city from Puerta del Reloj, about US$20 for up to 4 people. Or from opposite Hotel El Dorado, Av San Martín, in Bocagrande, to ride into town at night (romantic but a rather short ride). You can also rent **bicycles** for riding the city streets from places such as **Bike Flag**, www.facebook.com/BikeFlag; rates about US$2 per hr.

### Diving

Discounts are sometimes available if you book via the hotels. There is a recompression chamber at the naval hospital in Bocagrande.

**Diving Planet**, *C Estanco del Aguardiente, No 5-09, T320-230 1515 (English), www. divingplanet.org.* PADI training courses, PADI e-learning, snorkelling trips, English spoken. Associated hotel in Cartagena, Puertas de Cartagena, T5-664 6030.

**La Tortuga Dive Shop**, *Edif Marina del Rey, C 1, No 2-23, loc 4, Av del Retorno, El Laguito, Bocagrande, T5-665 6994, www.tortugadive.com.* Fast boat, which allows for trips to Isla Barú as well as Los Rosarios.

### Football

**Estadio de Futbol Pedro de Heredia**, *Villa Olímpica, south of the city.* Games are infrequent.

### Language schools

**Nueva Lengua School**, *T315-855 9551, 1-202 470 2555 (international), www. nuevalengua.com.* Offers courses ranging from ½-day schedules to a scheme that arranges volunteer jobs. There are even Spanish courses combined with dance, music, adventure, kitesurfing or diving.

### Tour operators

**Aventure Colombia**, *C del Santísimo, No 8-55, T5-664 8500, T314-588 2378, www.aventurecolombia.com.* Also with a branch in Bogotá. The only tour organizer of its kind in Cartagena, French/Colombian-run, offering alternative tours across Colombia, local and national activities and expeditions, working (wherever possible) with local and indigenous groups. The focus is on ecotourism and trekking, also organizes boat trips. Highly recommended.

**Ocean & Land**, *Cra 2, No 4-15, Edif Antillas, Bocagrande, T5-665 7772, 727, oceanlandtours_cartagena@hotmail.com.* Organizes city tours, rumbas in *chivas* (brightly coloured local buses) and other local activities.

### Yachting

**Club Náutico**, *Av Miramar No 19-50, Isla Manga (across the Puente Román), T5-660 4863, www.clubnauticocartagena.com.* Good for opportunities to charter, crew or for finding a lift to other parts of the Caribbean.

## Transport

### Air

**Rafael Núñez Airport** is 1.5 km from the city in the Crespo district and can be reached by local buses from Blas de Lezo, in the southwest corner of El Centro. A bus from the airport to Pl San Francisco costs US$0.90; a taxi to San Diego or the centre is US$5 and to Bocagrande, US$9. City buses can be very crowded so if you have a lot of luggage, a taxi is recommended. There is a *casa de cambio* (daily 0830-2000) at the airport, but rates are better in town. Travel agents have offices on the upper level. There are also a number of fast-food outlets.

There are direct flights daily to/from major Colombian cities and smaller places in the north of the country, as well as direct international flights to/from **Lauderdale**, **Miami**, **New York** and **Panama**. From Dec to Mar flights can be overbooked, so turn up at the airport early.

**Airline offices** **Avianca**, C del Arzobispado, No 34-52, T5-664 7376, Mon-Fri 0800-1200, 1400-1800, Sat 0800-1300; Av Venezuela 33, No 8B-05, Edif City Bank, loc B2, T5-664 7822; also in Bocagrande, C 7, No 7-17, L 7, T5-665 0287 and at the airport, T5-666 1175. **Copa**, Av San Martín Cra 2, No 10-54, Edif Sky II Bolívar (Bocagrade), T5-665 0428, Mon-Fri 0800-1800, Sat 0900-1300. **EasyFly**, T5-693 0400. **LAN**, Cra 3, No 4 -21 local 1, T1-800 094 9490. **Viva Colombia**, T5-642 4989.

### Bus

The **bus terminal**, known as the 'Terminal de Transportes' (www.terminaldecartagena.com) is at least 35 mins away from town on the road to Barranquilla. A Metrocar city bus to the terminal from the centre costs US$0.90,

or a taxi, US$15; agree your taxi fare before you get in.

Several bus companies run to **Barranquilla**, every 15 mins, 2-3 hrs, US$7-8; there's also a **Berlinastur** minibus service from Av 1, No 65-129, Crespo, T318-724 2424, and *colectivos* from C 70, Crespo, every 2 hrs, US$14 (centre-to-centre service). To **Santa Marta**, hourly, US$20, 4 hrs. Few buses go direct to Santa Marta from Cartagena, most stop in Barranquilla. To/from **Bogotá** via Barranquilla and Bucaramanga, daily, 21-28 hrs (depending on number of checkpoints), US$80-90, several companies. To **Medellín** 665 km, US$50-70, more or less hourly from 0530, 13-16 hrs; book early (2 days in advance at holiday times); the road is paved but in poor condition. To **Magangué** on the Río Magdalena (for connections to Mompós) with **Brasilia**, US$19, 4 hrs, or with **Cotransabanas Express** *colectivo* (Trans 54, No 94-06, Vía Estrella) from petrol station outside Cartagena bus terminal, 0600-1700, 4 hrs, US$22. To **Mompós**, direct bus with **Unitransco** or **Brasilia**, 0630, 8 hrs, US$40; **Toto Express**, T310-707 0838, totoexpress2@hotmail.com, runs a door-to-door *colectivo* service, 6-7 hrs, US$40. To **Riohacha**, US$33. To **Maicao** on Venezuelan border, every hour 0500-1200, 2 in the evening, 12 hrs, US$40, with **Brasilia**.

### Car hire

Several of the bigger hotels have car rental offices in their foyers, such as **Bechs**, Hotel Bahía, Bocagrande, C 4 at Cra 4, local 1, T5-665 0318. There are also car rental companies in Edif Torremolinos, Av San Martín, including **International Car Rentals**, T5-665 5399, and **National**, T5-655 1215; and on

Av San Martín: **Budget**, No 13-37 L-3, T5-664 1293; **Trans**, No 11-67, Edif Tulipana L-5, T5-665 2427. Multiple companies at the airport.

## Sea

For boat services to Cartagena's beaches and islands, see pages 148-150. Boats also go from Cartagena to the **San Blas Islands** (Panama); the journey takes 5 days in all, 2 sailing to the archipelago and 3 touring the San Blas islands. Trips usually end at Puerto Lindo on the mainland, from where you can continue to Colón and thence to Panama City. The fare, about US$550, includes food and passport stamps. Some boats are cheaper, but you get what you pay for, so take your time before choosing a boat. Some captains are irresponsible and unreliable. The journey is cramped so it's best to get on with the captain. There are many notices in hostels in Getsemaní advertising this trip, for example in **Casa Viena** and **Mamallena**. Also **Sailing Koala**, T312-670 7863, www.sailingkoala.com, which offers a trip to San Blas and Panama.

**Note** On the street, do not be tempted by offers of jobs or passages onboard a ship. Jobs should have full documentation from the Seamen's Union office and passages should only be bought at a recognized shipping agency.

## Taxi

There are no meters; journeys are calculated by zones and the minimum fare is US$2.50. (Bocagrande to Centro is 2 zones, US$4.) It is quite common to ask other people waiting if they would like to share, but, in any case, always agree the fare with the driver before getting in. By arrangement, taxis will wait for you if visiting more remote places. Fares go up at night.

## Trips from Cartagena

*choose mangroves and mud baths or beaches and coral reefs*

### Ciénaga la Caimanera

To the northeast, the coastline is characterized by *ciénagas* (mangrove swamps). At La Boquilla canoe trips can be made to explore the Ciénaga la Caimanera, a labyrinth of mangroves full of wildlife (motorboats are not allowed). Local guides cost US$15 per person, and they will catch oysters for you to eat. Further north near **Galerazamba** is the clay bath of **Volcán del Totumo** ① *entry to the cone US$2.50, mud bath US$2.50*. Climb up steep steps to the lip of the 20-m-high crater and slip into the grey cauldron of mud, which is a comfortable temperature. The crater is about 10 m across and reputed to be over 500 m deep. You wash off in the nearby *ciénaga*, in beautiful surroundings.

To get there, catch a bus from Cartagena bus terminal to the turn-off (US$7.50, 45 km), then take a mototaxi to the crater (US$ 1.50, 10 minutes). Taking a tour from Cartagena may cost more but will save a lot of time. Tours to the volcano last about six hours and cost between US$20 and US$40 depending on what is included (with or without lunch, trip to Manzanillo beach, etc). This has become a very popular excursion and the bath may be very busy.

## Mud volcanoes

The Caribbean coast is peppered with several geological curiosities popularly known as 'mud volcanoes'. These large mud pools are believed to be the result of underground oil and gas deposits, which combine with water, forcing the mud to ooze to the surface. Often they form conical mounds, hence the name. Many of these pools can be found between the Gulf of Urabá and Santa Marta. Turbo has several in its proximity (Rodosalín, El Alto de Mulatos and Caucal), as does San Pedro de Urabá. The Volcán del Totumo is a popular day trip from Cartagena, but the pick of the bunch is Arboletes, where an enormous 30-m-wide lake has formed a stone's throw from the beach.

Wallowing in the grey-black mud is a strange experience: it's impossible to sink, and attempts to swim are about as worthwhile as trying to battle your way across a vat of treacle. When you have had enough, clamber out and join the line of mud-caked figures waddling down to the Caribbean for a wash and a swim. The stuff is reportedly an excellent exfoliant and does wonders for the skin and hair.

★ Islas del Rosario

The Parque Nacional Natural Corales del Rosario y San Bernardo embraces the archipelago of Rosario, the mangrove coast of the long island of Barú to its furthest tip (see page 149) and the Islas de San Bernardo (see under Tolú, below).

The Islas del Rosario, 45 km southwest of the Bay of Cartagena, are picture-postcard coral islands, low lying and densely vegetated, with narrow strips of fine sand. **Isla Grande** is the largest and best conserved, with a profusion of aquatic and avian life. The island has access to some of the best coral reefs in the archipelago and diving and snorkelling are available. **Isla Grande** and some of the smaller islets are easily accessible for day trippers and those who wish to stay in one of the hotels. Permits are needed for the rest, many of which are privately owned. Day trips usually include a stop at the **Oceanario (aquarium)** on **San Martín de Pajarales** ⓘ *US$12.50, note that the price of entry is not included in boat fares*, and time at Playa Blanca on Isla Barú (see page 149).

Travel agencies and the hotels offer excursions from the Muelle Turístico in Cartagena, leaving 0700-0900 and returning 1600-1700, costing from around US$50 (free if staying at one of the hotels), lunch included; book in advance. Overnight trips can be arranged through agencies, but they are overpriced. Note that in addition to the tour and the national park fee (US$3), there is an additional 'port tax' of US$6 payable at the entrance to the Muelle or on the boat. For the cheapest rates, buy tickets direct from the boat owners (make sure they are the boat owners!) at the dockside. Groups of five or more people should try hiring their own boat for the day and bargaining for a fair price. This way you get to see what you want in the time available, rather than dodging the beach vendors around the tour boats. If you wish to enjoy the islands at your leisure there are several hotels.

## Where to stay

### Islas del Rosario

**$$$$ Kokomo Islas del Rosario**
*Caño Ratón-Isla Grande,*
*www.hotelkokomo.com.*
All-inclusive private beach resort, pool
and restaurant, transport to and from
the island.

**$$$$ Isla del Pirata**
*Book through Excursiones*
*Roberto Lemaitre, T5-665 2952,*
*www.hotelislapirata.com.*
Simple, comfortable *cabañas*, activities
include diving, snorkelling, canoeing
and petanque, good Caribbean
restaurant. Prices include transport
to the island, food and non-guided
activities. Highly recommended.

**$$$$ San Pedro de Majagua**
*Isla Grande; book at C del Torno,*
*No 39-29, Cartagena, T5-650 4460,*
*www.hotelmajagua.com.*

Everything from a 'pillow menu' to
Egyptian cotton bed sheets, this is a
lovely, luxurious place for utter relaxation.

**$$$ Ecohotel La Cocotera**
*Comunidad de Orika, Isla Grande,*
*www.ecohotellacocotera.com.*
Rooms with bath and solar power,
also has camping and hammocks,
restaurant, diving school.

## What to do

### Islas del Rosario
**Diving**
**Diving Planet** in Cartagena organizes
snorkeling, diving and various tours of
the coral reefs and mangroves. **Club
Isla del Pirata**, T5-665 5622, www.
hotelislapirata.com, has the best
boats and is near the top end of the
price range; **Yates Alcatraz** is more
economical; enquire at the quay.

# South of
Cartagena

Just a few years ago, the area south of Cartagena was a no-go zone. The road between Cartagena and Medellín was the scene of frequent kidnappings by guerrillas who would perform raids on passing traffic and quickly abscond into the region's network of densely vegetated hills. Today it's a different story and locals no longer sweat before making what was once a perilous journey. It is now even considered reasonably safe to travel between Cartagena and Medellín at night. That said, although towns such as Sincelejo and Montería are fine to pass through, we advise against staying there too long. Be warned, too, that drug smuggling is still very active in the area near the Panama border.

The improvement in security means that this area, rich in culture and natural wonders, has opened up to tourism. Southeast is the colonial town of Mompós (also spelt Mompox) stranded in a time warp on an island in the Río Magdalena. Due south of Cartagena is Tolú, gateway to the coral islands of San Bernardo (part of the Parque Nacional Natural Corales de Rosario y San Bernardo), while further along the coast is Arboletes, location of the largest mud volcano in the area. Further still is Turbo, a rough frontier town from where boats can be caught to the emerald green coastline of the Darién.

**time warp town in a unique riverine setting**

★The grand old Magdalena River splits in two just before Mompós. When the town was founded in 1540, Santa Cruz de Mompós was on the main branch of the river, and it became a major staging port for travellers and merchandise going to the interior. But at the beginning of the 20th century, the river silted up with mud and became unnavigable for large boats, so traffic was diverted to the Brazo de Lobo. As a result, Mompós became a backwater, and it has remained practically untouched ever since.

Part of Mompós' charm lies in the fact that it is still quite difficult to reach and so retains much the same atmosphere you might have experienced had you visited in the early 20th century. In 1995 UNESCO declared it a World Heritage Site for the quality of its colonial architecture and its fine churches. The town is also well known in Colombia for hand-worked gold and silver jewellery, especially filigree, as well as for its wicker rocking chairs. Today, in the evenings, as the sweltering heat begins to lessen and the bats start to swoop from the eaves of the whitewashed houses,

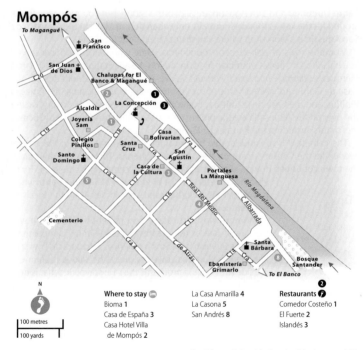

**Mompós**

To Magangué

San Francisco

San Juan de Dios

Chalupas for El Banco & Magangué

La Concepción

Alcaldía

Joyería Sam

Colegio Piñillos

Santa Cruz

Casa Bolívarian

San Agustín

Santo Domingo

Casa de la Cultura

Portales La Marquesa

Cementerio

Real del Medio

Rio Magdalena

Albarrada

C de Atrás

Santa Bárbara

Ebanistería Grimarlo

Bosque Santander

To El Banco

N

100 metres
100 yards

**Where to stay**
Bioma **1**
Casa de España **3**
Casa Hotel Villa de Mompós **2**

La Casa Amarilla **4**
La Casona **5**
San Andrés **8**

**Restaurants**
Comedor Costeño **1**
El Fuerte **2**
Islandés **3**

locals carry their rocking chairs out onto the streets to chat with neighbours and watch the world go by.

## Cartagena to Mompós

The highway towards Medellín goes southeast from Cartagena through **Turbaco**, 24 km, where there's a **botanical garden** ① *1.5 km before the village on the left, Tue-Sun 0900-1630*. At **Malagana**, 60 km, the road splits; to reach Mompós continue east and then south towards **San Jacinto**, known for its *cumbia* music using *gaitas* and for its hand-woven hammocks, and **El Carmen de Bolívar**, 125 km. After another 40 km, a road runs east from the highway to **Magangué**, on the western loop of the Río Magdalena, the port for the savannas of Bolívar. From here boats go to La Bodega where you pick up the road again to reach the small town of **Mompós**.

## Sights

The churches demonstrate the colonial origins of the town. **San Francisco** is probably the oldest, dating from the end of the 16th century, with an interesting interior. **Santa Bárbara**, on Calle 14 by the river, has a unique octagonal Moorish tower and balcony. Nearby on Calle 14, opposite Carrera 4, is a garden open to visitors (usually) with trees and flowering plants. **San Juan de Dios**, **La Concepción**, **Santo Domingo** and **San Agustín** are all worth visiting, but you may have to ask around for the key as they are normally only open during Mass. In the **Claustro de San Agustín** is a workshop where youngsters are taught local skills.

Mompós' rows of well-preserved buildings, some with balconies, have served as a backdrop in many Colombian films, including the adaptation of Gabriel García Márquez's *Chronicle of a Death Foretold* (1987). Among notable buildings are the **Casa de Gobierno**, once a home of the Jesuits and now the Alcaldía; the **Colegio Pinillos**, and the **Casa de la Cultura**, home of the local Academy of History. Facing the river on the Albarrada are the old customs house and the mansions of Spanish merchants, including the Portales La Marquesa.

The cemetery is of considerable historical interest; on one side of the central avenue lie the Conservatives; on the other, the Liberals. This political division of the town continued down Calle 18, running from the cemetery to the river. Try to visit the cemetery on the Wednesday of **Semana Santa** when it is illuminated by thousands of candles lit by the locals to honour the dead.

**Tip...**
Guides who approach you on the street can gain access to all the significant buildings and charge US$6 per hour for tours of the city on foot or by motortaxi.

Mompós was particularly dear to Simón Bolívar, as it was the site of one of the greatest victories in his campaign to expel the Spanish from South America. "If to Caracas I owe my life, then to Mompós I owe my glory," he said (a monument outside the Alcaldía proclaims this). He stayed in what is now called the **Museo Cultural Casa Bolivariana** ① *C del Medio y 17, no regular opening hours*, which houses memorabilia and some religious art exhibits.

**Boat trips** ① *3-4 hrs, US$15-20*, can be taken along the Río Magdalena and into the surrounding wetlands, which provide excellent opportunities for birdwatching. Alternatively take the small ferry across the river beyond the Parque Santander, US$0.50, and walk a little way up the track to where it meets another track. Turn sharp right and look for birds in the wet areas beyond the cattle pens; early morning or dusk are the best times. Beware of dogs. Ferocious mosquitoes and the odd bat are also a nuisance after dusk; take insect repellent and wear long sleeves.

## Listings Mompós *map p164*

### Where to stay

It is essential to book in advance for Semana Santa and other festival periods, when prices go up.

**$$$ Bioma**
*C Real del Medio (Cra 2), No 18-59, T5-685 6733, www.bioma.co.*
Boutique style, cool and fresh, courtyard garden with running water, jacuzzi on roof terrace and a small pool. Rooms are large, family rooms have 2 floors. There's a restaurant but reserve in advance.

**$$$-$$ La Casa Amarilla**
*Cra 1, No 13-59, T5-685 6326, www.lacasaamarillamompos.com.*
A block up from the Iglesia Santa Bárbara near the riverfront. Master suites, suites and cheaper 'colonial' rooms, all beautifully decorated. All rooms open onto a cloister-style colonial garden. English owner Richard McColl is an excellent source of information on Colombia. Laundry, book exchange, use of kitchen, roof terrace, bicycle hire, tours arranged to silver filigree workshops and to wetlands for birdwatching and swimming (US$10 pp). Recommended.

**$$ Casa de España**
*C Real del Medio (Cra 2), No 17A-52, T5-685 5373, www. hotelcasaespanamompox.com.*
White rooms, some for families, pool to be built.

**$ Casa Hotel Villa de Mompox**
*Cra 2, No 14-108, 500 m east of Parque Bolívar, T5-685 5208, casahotelvillademompox@yahoo.com.*
Charming, family-run, decorated with antique bric-a-brac. Also arranges rooms for families during festivals.

**$ La Casona**
*Cra 2, No 18-58, T5-685 5307, www.hotelmompos.com.*
Fine colonial building with delightful courtyards and plants.

**$ San Andrés**
*C Real del Medio (Cra 2), No 18-23, T5-685 5886, www.hotelsanandres mompox.com.*
Another fine, restored colonial building, with nice sitting room and garden. Rooms for 1-5 people, cheaper with fan, on a corridor off the garden, spacious, use of kitchen, meals extra. Same owner as **Islandés** restaurant and tour company (river tours).

### Restaurants

Every night stallholders sell freshly cooked food and fresh juices in Pl Santo Domingo.

**$$$-$$ El Fuerte**
*Parque Santander, T314-564 0566, www.fuertemompox.com.*
Serves gourmet pizza in a restored colonial building. It is the art gallery

of Walter Maria Gurth and displays his wooden furniture. Contact in advance.

**$ Comedor Costeño**
*On the riverfront between C 18 and C 19.*
Good local food, popular for lunch.

**$ Islandés**
*On the riverfront between C 18 and C 19.*
In same vein as **Comedor Costeño** and almost next door, same owner as **San Andrés** (see Where to stay).

## Shopping

Mompós is famous for its filigree gold and silver jewellery and its wicker rocking chairs. Several jewellers can be found on C del Medio (Cra 2). You can visit the workshops.

### Jewellery
**Filimompox**, *C 23, No 3-23, T5-685 6604*.
**Joyería Sam**, *C 23 No 3-04, T311-403 5492*.
Fine selection of beautifully worked gold and silver earrings, bracelets and brooches.
**Santa Cruz**, *Cra 2, No 201 132 T310-656 5568, tallersantacruz@yahoo.com*.
Another jewellery shop.

## Transport

Cars are rare here: the main forms of transport are bicycle, moped, auto-rickshaw – or on foot.

### Air
The closest airport is **Corozal** (near Sincelejo), which has regular connections with **Medellín** and **Bogotá**. It's 1 hr by *colectivo* from Corozal airport to Magangué, or 15 mins from Corozal to Sincelejo; then take a *colectivo* to Magangué, as below.

### Bus
Buses from Cartagena and Barranquilla travel to Mompós via Magangue for the river crossing (see below); buses from central Colombia travel via El Banco, while buses from Valledupar and Santa Marta travel via Bosconia.
**Note** Prices for public transport rise Dec-Jan and at Easter.

Direct services to/from **Cartagena** are run by **Unitransco** and **Brasilia**, 8 hrs, US$40. **Toto Express**, T310-707 0838, totoexpress2@hotmail.com, runs a door-to-door *colectivo*, 6-7 hrs, US$40. There are additional services between Cartagena and Magangué. **Asotranstax** runs a door-to-door *colectivo* service between Mompós and **Santa Marta**, 6 hrs, US$40. To **Medellín**, catch the **Brasilia** bus, 12 hrs, US$32.50, direct from Magangué, or travel from Magangué by *colectivo* to **Sincelejo**, US$10, 1½ hrs, then take a **Brasilia** or **Rápido Ochoa** bus from there, 8-10 hrs, US$40. To **Valledupar** (via **Bosconia**), door-to-door service with Lalo Castro, T312-673 5226, US$20; if he isn't going, **CotraNorte**, **Cotracol** or **Cootracegua** buses daily. To **Bogotá**, take a 4WD to El Banco, US$17 (US$20 a/c), 1 hr, then a **Copetran** or **Omega** bus to the capital, 14 hrs, US$70.

### Ferry
To get to Mompós from Magangué you have to travel to **La Bodega**, either by fast *chalupa* (motorized canoe, 20 mins, US$4, life jacket provided), or on the vehicle ferry (from 0600, 1 hr, food and drink on board), which leaves from Yati, about 2 km outside town. From La Bodega you continue by *colectivo* to Mompós (1¼ hrs, US$6).

## Tolú and around

Tolú, 35 km northwest of Sincelejo, on the coast, is a fast developing holiday town popular with Colombians and, increasingly, foreign tourists attracted by visits to the offshore islands and diving. Along the *malecón* (promenade), there are plenty of bars and restaurants. A distinctive feature of the town is the number of bicycle rickshaws armed with loud sound-systems blasting out *vallenato*, salsa and reggaeton; the rickshaw drivers spend much of their time trying to outdo each other with the volume of their music.

There are also two mud volcanoes to visit in the area. The closest one is in **San Antero**, 30 minutes' drive from Tolú; a six-hour tour, including other sites of interest and lunch, costs US$55. The other is in San Bernando del Viento (see below). Trips to the mangrove lagoons are also recommended.

## ★Islas de San Bernardo

Tolú is the main departure point for boat trips to the beautiful beaches of Múcura island or Tintipán in the **Islas de San Bernardo**. Club Náutico Maradentro ① *www. clubnauticomaradentro.com*, runs daily boats to Múcura at 0800, returning at 1600, which cost US$30 for a return trip. The beach is of fine white sand with beautiful, clear water, and there are a number of shacks serving seafood, including excellent barbecued lobster. Unfortunately, with several launches converging on the island at the same time, it can get crowded, and the number of beach vendors can detract from the beauty of the place. There is a charge for everything, including sitting at a table. To enjoy the islands at your leisure, it is better to stay overnight. It's also possible to reach the island from Cartagena, if you have a reservation at **Punta Faro** (one hour 45 minutes by boat, transfer included in the cost of accommodation).

## Coveñas and around

There are, perhaps surprisingly, good beaches at **Coveñas**, 20 km further southwest, the terminal of the pipeline from the oilfields in the Venezuelan border area. Coveñas is essentially a 5-km-long stretch of road peppered with *cabañas* and hotels. During high season (Easter, Christmas to mid-January, June and July) it is very popular with Colombians eager to hit the beach and party. To get there, take a bus or *colectivo* from Tolú. Further along the coast, 18 km southwest of Coveñas, turn right at Lorica to reach **San Bernardo del Viento** from where launches can be arranged to **Isla Fuerte**, an unspoilt coral island with fine beaches and simple places to stay. It's a good place to dive, but there are very limited facilities on the island. Enquire at travel agencies in Medellín and elsewhere for inclusive trips or negotiate in San Bernardo.

## ★Arboletes

As well as being a convenient stopover on the way to Turbo and the Darién coast, the otherwise unremarkable town of Arboletes has one extraordinary attraction: the largest mud volcano in the area. The **Volcán de Lodo** is a 15-minute walk from town on the road to Montería or a two-minute taxi ride (US$7 return; the driver will wait for you while you bathe; mototaxi US$2). Dipping into this swimming pool-sized mud bath is a surreal experience – like swimming in treacle. It's also very good for your skin. You can wash the mud off in the sea by walking to the beach 100 m below. There is a small restaurant and changing rooms (US$ 0.50), plus a locker room (US$1 per bag) and showers (US$0.50).

## Turbo

At the mouth of the Gulf of Urabá is the port of Turbo: a hot, rough, frontier community with a lawless feel about it. It is a centre for banana cultivation. The beach is nice enough, although like everywhere on this stretch of the coast, the sea is a muddy brown due to its proximity to the Gulf. There is little reason to stop here except to catch a boat to Capurganá and the Panamanian border.

## Listings The coast south of Cartagena

### Where to stay

#### Tolú

**$$ Alcira**
*Av La Playa, No 21-151, T5-288 5016,*
*www.hotelalcira.amawebs.com.*
Modern, on the promenade, with restaurant and parking.

**$$ Villa Babilla**
*C 20, No 3-40, Barrio el Cangrejo, T312-677 1325, www.villababillahostel.com.*
Run by a Colombian/German team.
3 blocks from the beach, well organized, dorms and private rooms, good restaurant, good information on diving and island tours. Recommended travellers' hostel.

**$$-$ Mar Adentro**
*Av La Playa 11-36, T5-286 0079,*
*www.clubnauticomaradentro.com.*
Belonging to the good tour agency of the same name. Nice rooms, cheaper with fan.

**$ El Turista**
*Av La Playa, No 11-20, T5-288 5145.*
The cheapest option in town and good value for money. Next to all the tour agencies.

#### Islas San Bernardo

**$$$$ Punta Faro**
*Isla Múcura, T318-216 5521 (Medellín),*
*www.puntafaro.com.*
Low-key luxury resort with 45 rooms in a gorgeous setting by the sea, inside Corales del Rosario National Park. Price includes all meals (buffet-style) and return boat transfer from Cartagena (boats leave once a day in high season and Mon and Fri only in low season). Massage treatments, hammocks on the beach, eco walks around the island and a good sustainability policy. Highly recommended.

#### Coveñas and around
There are plenty of hotels in Coveñas, many catering for family holidays.

**$$$ Porto Alegre**
*Primera Ensenada, T350-316 7554,*
*www.hotelportoalegre.com.co.*
Beachfront hotel, rooms for 2-5 people, with a/c, microwave, pool, jacuzzi, breakfast included, no restaurant but can arrange meals with nearby establishments, similarly tours.

**$$ pp Estado Natural Ecolodge**
*7 km from San Bernardo del Viento, T321-724 7888, www.estado-natural.com.*
Rustic cabins on a beach, composting toilets and other sustainable practices, meals not included but cabins have kitchen, activities include birdwatching, windsurfing, trips to Isla Fuerte, riding and guided tours.

**$$ La Candelita**
*Primera Ensenada de Punta Piedra, T314-561 6513.*
Simple cabins for 2 to 6 people, with a/c or fan, TV; principally a watersports centre, including kitesurfing lessons, kayaks, sailing, boat trips.

---

### Arboletes

**$$$-$$ El Mirador**
*C Principal, T4-820 0441, www.hotel elmiradordearboletes.com.*
Self-styled 'boutique' hotel with 14 rooms, some with bunk beds ($ pp), includes breakfast, restaurant and bar, jacuzzi, internet and parking.

**$ La Floresta**
*C Principal, T4-820 0034.*
This small hotel has simple rooms with private bathrooms and a/c. Ask for a street-facing room if you want a window.

---

### Turbo

**$$ Castilla de Oro**
*C 100, No 14-07, T4-827 2185, hotelcastilladeoro@hotmail.com.*
The best option in town has a/c, safety box, minibar, a good restaurant and a swimming pool. Modern building with reliable water and electricity. Friendly staff.

**$$ Simona del Mar**
*Km 13 Vía Turbo, T4-824 3729, www.simonadelmar.com.*

Turbo is not a safe place to walk around at night, so this option a few kilometres outside town is a safer choice. It has a number of *cabañas* in a tranquil setting near the beach. Good restaurant. A taxi to and from Turbo is US$10. You can also ask *colectivos* to drop you there.

### What to do

#### Tolú
**Tour operators**
Club Náutico Mar Adentro, *Av La Playa, No 11-36, T5-286 0079, www.clubnautico maradentro.com.* A good agency offering tours to the islands and diving. Also has its own 35-room hotel, connections with **Hotel Darimar** and can organize lodging at other hotels and *cabañas* in the area.

### Transport

#### Tolú
Tolú can be reached from Cartagena via **San Onofre**, or Toluviejo; continue from Toluviejo for 20 km to reach **Sincelejo**.

**Bus**
Brasilia hourly to **Cartagena** 0715-1730, US$15. 12 a day to **Medellín** with **Brasilia** and **Rápido Ochoa**, US$43, via Montería.

#### Turbo
**Bus**
To **Medellín**, buses every 90 mins, 10-12 hrs, US$22.50-35. To **Montería**, 4-5 hrs, US$20. Fewer to **Cartagena**. Check safety carefully before travelling by road to/from Turbo.

**Sea**
Turbo's port is known as El Waffe. Launches for **Capurganá**, T312-701 9839, leave daily at 0700-0900, 3 hrs, US$22.50. It's a spectacular journey that hugs the

Caribbean shoreline of Darién. Rush for a seat at the back as the journey is bumpy and can be painful in seats at the front. There is a 10-kg limit on baggage (US$0.25 per extra kilo). Make sure that all your belongings, especially valuables, are in watertight bags and be prepared to get wet. From mid-Dec to end Feb the sea is very choppy and dangerous. We advise you not to make the journey at this time.

## The Darién Gap → *Colour map 2, A1.*

**blissful beaches backed by impenetrable jungle**

The Darién Gap has long held a special place in travellers' lore as the ultimate adventure – and for good reason. This thin stretch of land, just 50 km wide and 160 km long, which links Central and South America, has some of the densest tropical jungle in the world – so dense that to date neither the Panamanians nor the Colombians have succeeded in building a road across it, and the only inland routes are by boat or on foot. At present, the Pan-American Highway, which stretches from Canada to Tierra del Fuego in Chile, stops at Yaviza in Panama, 60 km short of the frontier, and begins again 27 km west of Barranquillita, well into Colombia. The Darién is home to an incredible profusion of flora and fauna, as well as indigenous tribes who rarely see foreigners.

The trek across the Darién is held in high regard by adventurers but we strongly advise against it, not simply because it is easy (and fatal) to get lost, but also because bona fide travellers are not welcome (indigenous communities in Darién have never truly accepted trekkers passing through) and this area still has a heavy guerrilla presence. The Colombian government's successes against the FARC have pushed them to the extremes of the country, where they have come into conflict with those trafficking drugs from South to North America. Drug gangs find the density of the jungle a useful protection for running consignments and regard the area's infiltration by both FARC and ELN guerrilla groups as a threat to their land. As a result this has become a war zone, virtually deserted now by police and the military, and it is a hostile environment for any tourist. For the moment, only the foolhardy would attempt the land crossing. However, the Caribbean coastline, heavily patrolled by Colombian and Panamanian forces, is safe, though you should exercise caution if venturing into the forest beyond.

### Acandí

Acandí is a small fishing village on the Caribbean side of the Darién. It has a spectacular, forest-fringed bay with turquoise waters. To the south are other bays and villages, such as **San Francisco**. From March to June, thousands of leatherback turtles come here to lay their eggs. There are several cheap *residencias* to stay in.

### Capurganá

For many years, Capurganá and neighbouring Sapzurro (see below) have been among the best-kept secrets in Colombia. In this most isolated of Colombia's corners, a glistening, untouched shoreline of crystal waters and coral reefs backs onto quiet little villages where, at night, if you listen carefully, you can hear the howler monkeys calling to each other in the jungle-clad hills behind.

Capurganá has developed into a resort popular with affluent Colombians and is increasingly visited by foreigners, despite being somewhat difficult and expensive to get to. It is a quiet place: there are no banks or ATMs, nor are there any cars, just a couple of motorbikes. Taxi rides are provided by horse and carts, and someone has had the ingenious idea of attaching modified plastic seats.

There are two beaches in the village. **La Caleta** is at the northern end, beyond the pontoon, and is protected by a barrier reef, has golden sand and is the best for swimming. There are a couple of restaurants and several hotels and *cabañas* here. **Playa de los Pescadores**, south of the village, is fringed by palm and almond trees but has disappointing grey sand and is more pebbly. Ask the fishermen about fishing trips from here in rowing boats.

## Around Capurganá

Several half- and full-day trips can be made by launch to neighbouring beaches. **Aguacate** is a beautiful bay with clear, aquamarine water and a small beach. There is a rocky promontory with a blowhole and what locals call '*La Piscina*', a natural jacuzzi amongst the rocks which you can lower yourself into using a rope. Aguacate has good snorkelling, but **Playa Soledad** is perhaps the most attractive beach in the area and was recently used as the location for a Colombian reality TV programme. The beach has white sand and is fringed by palms. A return trip by launch boat costs US$15 per person, minimum five people. You can walk to Aguacate, 1½ hours along the coast, but not to Playa Soledad. Note that it can be difficult to obtain a return by launch if you walk.

A delightful half-day excursion is to **El Cielo** ⓘ *0600-1700, US$2; 40-min walk, take flip flops or waterproof boots for crossing a stream several times*, a small waterfall in the jungle. Take the path to the left of the airport and keep asking for directions. Just before the waterfall a small restaurant serves *patacones* and drinks. Alternatively, you can hire horses to take you there. Another horse-riding trip is to **El Valle de Los Ríos**, a valley in the jungle with several crystalline rivers and beautiful waterfalls (take a guide). The primary forest in this area is rich in wildlife; you might see, among other animals, sloths, howler monkeys, toucans, parrots, fishing eagles and several types of lizard and iguana. The trip includes lunch at a *ranchería*. For more details, enquire at **Capurganá Tours** (see page 175).

There is excellent diving and snorkelling around Capurganá. You are likely to see nurse sharks, moray eels, spotted eagle rays, trumpetfish, jewfish, barracuda and hawksbill turtles, among other species, as well as large brain and elkhorn coral. Several of the hotels organize diving, but the independent dive centre **Dive and Green** is recommended.

## Sapzurro

Reached by tours from Capurganá or by a beautiful four-hour hike along the coastline through jungle rich in wildlife, Sapzurro is a quiet little village in the Darién and the last outpost before Panama and Central America. Set in a shallow,

**Sapzurro–Miel**

This could qualify as the most relaxed border crossing in the world. The Colombian and Panamanian immigration officers share a hut and copy each other's notes. Ask at the **Migración Colombia** office in Cartagena (see page 444), Medellín (Calle 19, No 80A-40 in Belén La Gloria section, T4-345 5500) or Montería (Calle 28, No 2-27, T4-781 0841, cf.monteria@migracioncolombia. gov.co, Monday-Friday 0800-1200, 1400-1700) whether the immigration office in Capurganá is open. If entering Panama you must get your passport stamped before leaving Colombia and check with the Panamanian embassy (www. panamaenelexterior.gob.pa/colombia) or a consulate about current entry requirements. However, these formalities are not required for day trips to Miel.

horseshoe-shaped bay dotted with coral reefs, little happens in this village of less than 1000 inhabitants. There are no roads, let alone cars; the houses are linked by intersecting pathways bursting with tropical flowers. It has a couple of excellent little hostels and some good restaurants serving up home-cooked seafood. The bay is excellent for snorkelling, with a couple of underwater caves to explore.

You can make a day trip to the small village of **La Miel** over the border in Panama by walking up the forested hill behind the village. There are breathtaking views of Panama and back into Sapzurro at the border on the brow of the hill. Be sure to take your passport; they won't stamp it for visits to La Miel, but they will take your details (see also box, above).

La Miel has a gorgeous white-sand beach with beautiful, clear waters and a coral reef. The snorkelling is relatively good though a little low on fauna. There are a couple of shacks selling beer and food; try the sea snails in coconut sauce. You can arrange for a launch to pick you up and take you back to Sapzurro or Capurganá.

**Listings** The Darién Gap

### Where to stay

#### Capurganá
Accommodation and food are generally more expensive than in other parts of Colombia. Upmarket options include **Tacarcuna Lodge** (www.hotelesde costaacosta.com/capurgana) and **Bahía Lodge** (www.bahia-lodge.com).

**$$ Cabaña Darius**
*T314-622 5638, www.darius capurgana.es.tl.*
In the grounds of Playa de Capurganá, excellent value, simple, comfortable rooms in tropical gardens, fan, breakfast included.

**$$ Marlin Hostal**
*Playa de los Pescadores, T4-824 3611, capurganamarlin@yahoo.es.*

The best mid-range option in town, good rooms, also bunks ($), restaurant serving excellent fish.

**$ Hostal Capurganá**
*C del Comercio, T316-482 3665, www.hostalcapurgana.net.*
Comfortable, pleasant patio, well situated. Recommended.

**$ Posada del Gecko**
*T314-525 6037, www.posadadel gecko.com.*
Small place, 5 rooms with bath and 3 cabins, gardens, popular café/bar that serves good Italian food.

### Sapzurro

**$ Paraíso Sapzurro**
*T8-824 4115/313-685 9862.*
*Cabañas* on the beach at the southern end of the village, Chilean-run (ask for El Chileno), higher price includes dinner. Also has space for camping.

**$ Zingara Cabañas**
*Camino La Miel, T313-673 3291, www.hospedajesapzurrozingara.com.*
Almost the last building in Colombia, 2 lovely *cabañas* overlooking the bay. The owners have a herb and vegetable garden and sell home-made chutneys. This also doubles up as the village pharmacy.

## Restaurants

### Capurganá

**$$ Donde Josefina**
*Playa La Caleta.*
Josefina cooks exquisite seafood, served to you under a shady tree on the beach. Try the lobster cooked in garlic and coconut sauce.

## What to do

### Capurganá
**Diving**
Dive and Green, *near the jetty, T311-578 4021, www.diveandgreen.com.* Dive centre offering PADI and NAUI, lots of courses, snorkeling and excursions to San Blas. English spoken. Also has rooms to let.

**Tour operators**
Capurganá Tours, *C del Comercio, T316-482 3665, www.capurganatours.net.* Organizes walking tours with knowledgeable guides to nearby beaches and into the jungle as well as horse riding, diving and birdwatching. Also trips to San Blas Archipelago in Panama, possibly some of the most beautiful islands in the Caribbean. Can assist in booking flights from Puerto Obaldía to Panama City. English spoken. Highly recommended.

## Transport

### Acandi
**Air**
About 3 flights weekly to/from **Medellín** with **Aerolínea de Antioquia** (ADA, www.ada-aero.com), US$150 one way. These are twin Otter biplanes with just 16 passenger capacity, so be sure to book ahead. Baggage limit of 10 kg; your baggage may have to follow on a later plane if it's seriously overweight.

### Capurganá
**Sea**
Launches to **Turbo**, T312-701 9839, 3 hrs, US$22.50, 10 kg limit on baggage (US$0.25 per extra kg); we advise you not to make this journey from mid-Dec to end Feb. To **Acandí**, US$10. To **Sapzurro,** US$5, 30 mins. There are also launches

to **Puerto Obaldía** in Panama, US$15 (leaving at about 0700). From here it's possible to catch an **Air Panamá** flight to **Panama City** on Mon, Tue or Wed, cost US$81, www.flyairpanama.com. Essential to book in advance.

**Sea**
Launch to **Capurganá**, US$5, 30 mins; to **Puerto Obaldía**, 45 mins, US$15.

# Barranquilla
## & around

Barranquilla, Colombia's fourth-largest city, lies on the western bank of the Río Magdalena, about 18 km from its mouth. It's a seaport (though less busy than Cartagena or Santa Marta), as well as a river port, and a modern industrial city with a polluted but colourful central area near the river. Many people stay a night in Barranquilla because they can find better flight deals than to Cartagena or Santa Marta. It's worth a short stay as the city is growing as a cultural centre, safety has improved and there are several things to do and see. It's also a good place to buy handicrafts, which are the same as can be found elsewhere but cheaper.

First and foremost, however, Barranquilla is famed for its carnival, held 40 days before Easter (end of February/beginning of March). It's reputed to be second only to Rio de Janeiro in terms of size and far less commercialized. In 2003 UNESCO declared it a "masterpiece of the oral and intangible heritage of humanity".

The city is surrounded by a continuous ring road, which is called the 'Vía Cuarenta' from the north along the river to the centre; 'Avenida Boyacá' to the bridge (Puente Pumarejo) across the Río Magdalena for Santa Marta; and 'Circunvalación' round the south and west of the city. The long bridge over the Río Magdalena gives fine views.

The central square is Plaza San Nicolás. Here is the former cathedral of **San Nicolás** and a small statue of Columbus. The commercial and shopping districts are around Paseo Bolívar (Calle 34), the main boulevard, a few blocks north of the old cathedral, and west along Avenida Murillo (Calle 45). A cultural centre, **Parque Cultural del Caribe**, has opened at the Paseo Bolívar end of Avenida Olaya Herrera (Carrera 46). It contains the **Museo del Caribe** ① *C 36, No 46-66, T372-0581, www. culturacaribe.org, Mon-Thu, 0800-1700, Fri 0800-1800, Sat-Sun 0900-1800, last entry 1 hr before closing, closed 1st Mon of month, US$5.50*, an excellent introduction to the region. Displays are in Spanish only, but guided tours in English are available. Visits start on the top floor, at the Sala García Márquez, which has audiovisual displays and a library. Work your way down through floors dedicated to nature, indigenous people and cultures, to a video musical presentation at the end. Outside is a large open space for theatre and children's games, and the **Cocina del**

## 1 Barranquilla centre

➡ **Barranquilla maps**
1  Barranquilla centre, page 178
2  Barranquilla – El Prado, page 180

200 metres
200 yards

**Where to stay**
Cayenas 1
Girasol 3
San Francisco 5

**Restaurants**
La Cueva 1

Museo restaurant. Not far away is the restored customs house, **Antiguo Edificio de la Aduana** ⓘ *Vía 40 y C 36*, dating from 1919, which has historical archives.

West of the centre, opposite Parque la Paz, is the **Catedral Metropolitana** ⓘ *Cra 45, No 53-120*, which contains an impressive statue of Christ by the Colombian sculptor Arena Betancourt. To the northwest, the **Museo Romántico** ⓘ *Cra 54, No 59-199, Mon-Fri 0900-1200, 1430-1800, US$2.50*, covers the city's history with an interesting section on carnival. Visitors can also see some of García Márquez's old typewriters.

Stretching back into the northwestern heights overlooking the city are the modern suburbs of **El Prado**, Altos del Prado, Golf and Ciudad Jardín. There are good parks in these areas, including **Parque Tomás Suri Salcedo** on Calle 72.

Barranquilla also attracts visitors because the most important national and international football matches are held here in Colombia's largest stadium, **Estadio Metropolitano** ⓘ *Av Murillo, south of the city*. The atmosphere is considered the best in the country.

## Beaches

Regular buses from Paseo Bolívar and the church at Calle 33/Carrera 41 travel 19 km to the attractive bathing resort of **Puerto Colombia** ⓘ *www.puertocolombia-atlantico.gov.co*, with its pier built around 1900. This was formerly the ocean port of Barranquilla, connected by a railway. The beach is clean and sandy, though the water is a bit muddy. The **Hotel Pradomar** ⓘ *C 2, No 22-61, T309 6011, www.hotel pradomar.com*, has a good beach bar, **Climandario Sunset Lounge**, and restaurant. It also offers surfing lessons, as does surf school **Olas Puerto Colombia** ⓘ *T313-817 0111, www.olascolombia.com*. February to May is the best time for taking classes; the biggest waves are November to January. Nearby are the beaches of **Salgar**, and north of Barranquilla is **Las Flores** (2 km from the mouth of the Río Magdalena at Bocas de Ceniza); both are good places for seafood.

## Along the Río Magdalena

South along the west bank of the Magdalena, 5 km from the city, is the old colonial town of **Soledad**. The cathedral and the old narrow streets around it are worth seeing. A further 25 km south is **Santo Tomás**, known for its Good Friday street theatre and processions in which flagellants symbolically whip themselves as an Easter penance. The small town of **Palmar de Varela** is a little further along the same road, which continues on to Calamar.

**Vía Parque Isla de Salamanca** ⓘ *US$16.50 for non-nationals, US$3.75 for Colombians*, is a national park, across the Río Magdalena from the city, comprising the Magdalena Delta and a narrow area of beaches, mangroves and woods that separates the Ciénaga Grande de Santa Marta (see page 192) from the Caribbean. Its purpose is to restore the mangroves and other habitats lost when the highway to Santa Marta was built, blocking off the channels that connect the fresh and salt water systems. There is lots of wildlife, but it is not yet geared up for tourism.

## Tourist information

Tourist information is provided by **Secretaría de Cultura**, Patrimonio y Turismo, C 34, No 43-31, p 4, T5-339 9450, www.barranquilla.gov.co/cultura. It is also available at the main hotels. The best place for carnival information is the official office **La Casa de Carnaval**, Cra 54, No 49B-39, T319-7616, www.carnavaldebarranquilla.org. The **tourist police** can be found in the botanical gardens, Cra 13C, at C 41.

## Where to stay

Hotel prices rise significantly during carnival; it's essential to book well in advance. Most people stay in the north zone, beyond the Catedral Metropolitano, C 50. There are also a few hotels in the business zone, Cra 43-45, C 42-45.

### $$$$-$$$ El Prado
*Cra 54, No 70-10, T5-330 1530/40, www.hotelelpradosa.com.*
A landmark in Barranquilla, this enormous hotel with 200 rooms has been around since 1930 and still retains some of its old-fashioned

**Barranquilla – El Prado**

➡ **Barranquilla maps**
1 Barranquilla centre, page 178
2 Barranquilla – El Prado, page 180

N

400 metres
400 yards

**Where to stay** ●
Barranquilla Plaza 1
El Prado 2
Majestic 4
Meeting Point Hostel 3

**Restaurants** ●
Arabe Gourmet 1
Arabe International 2
Firenze Pizza 3
La Parilla Libanese 4

Los Helechos 5

**Bars & clubs** ●
Froggs Leggs 6
Henry's 7

service. Fantastic pool shaded by palm trees, various restaurants, tennis courts and a gym.

### $$$$-$$$ Sonesta
*C 106, No 50-11, T5-385 6060, www.sonesta.com.*
Overlooking the Caribbean, a 1st-class business hotel with fitness facilities and restaurant to match. There is a shopping centre and nightclub nearby.

### $$$ Barranquilla Plaza
*Cra 51B, No 79-246, T5-361 0333, www.hbp.com.co.*
A deluxe hotel popular with Colombian businessmen, it's worth visiting just for the 360° view of the city from its 26th-floor restaurant. It has all the other amenities you would expect of a hotel of this standard, including gym, spa, sauna and Wi-Fi.

### $$$ Majestic
*Cra 53, No 54-41, T5-349 1010, www.hotelmajesticbarranquilla.com.*
An oasis of calm in the city, with large, fresh rooms. It has a fine pool and a restaurant serving the usual fish and meat dishes and sandwiches.

### $$ Girasol
*C 44, No 44-103, T5-379 3191, www.elhotelgirasol.com.*
Safe, central with a helpful manager, it has a restaurant and a functions room.

### $$ San Francisco
*C 43, No 43-128, T5-351 5532, www.sfcol.com/barranquilla.html.*
Bright rooms, courtyard full of songbirds, a good, safe bet, with restaurant.

### $ Cayenas
*C 43, No 44-136, T5-370 6912, hotelcayenas@yahoo.com.*
A simpler option, welcoming, rooms are cheaper with fan.

### $ Meeting Point
*Cra 61, No 68-100, El Prado, T5-368 6461, www.themeetingpoint.hostel.com.*
Very helpful and congenial Italian/Colombian-owned hostel – the best choice for budget travellers. Mixed dorms or women only, US$13-17, cheaper with fan and shared bath, also has a private room. Eating places and cultural centres nearby. Warmly recommended.

### Restaurants

In Barranquilla you'll find places to suit all tastes and budgets. Many upmarket restaurants can be found along Cras 52-54 from C 70 to 93. There are numerous good Middle Eastern restaurants, especially Lebanese, in Barranquilla, due to waves of immigration in the 20th century; also Chinese restaurants and pizzerias.

### $$$-$$ Arabe Gourmet
*Cra 49C, No 76-181.*
More formal and expensive than other Arabic restaurants. There are others in the same chain.

### $$$-$$ La Cueva
*Cra 43, No 59-03, T5-379 0342, www.fundacionlacueva.org.*
This cultural centre was formerly a high-class brothel and a favourite haunt of Gabriel García Márquez and his literati friends during the 1950s. Its bohemian charm may have gone, but its bar/restaurant is recommended for a visit. Good typical food, live music and other events.

### $$$-$$ La Parrilla Libanesa
*Cra 61, No 68-02, T5-360 6664, near Meeting Point.*
Well-regarded Lebanese place, colourful, indoor and terrace seating.

**$$ Arabe Internacional**
*C 93, No 47-73, T5-378 4700.*
Good Arab cuisine in an informal setting.

**$$ Firenze Pizza**
*C 68, No 62-12, El Prado, T344 1067, www. firenzepizza.com.co near Meeting Point.*
Eat in or take-away.

**$$-$ Los Helechos de Carlos**
*Cra 52, No 70-70, T5-345 1739.*
Offers *comida antioqueña* in a good atmosphere.

## Bars and clubs

Cra 8 is a popular nightlife area, but you'll need to take a taxi there and back.

**Frogg Leggs**
*C 93, No 43-122, T5-304 8973, www.frogg.co.*
Popular bar, good atmosphere.

**Guararé**
*Cra 8 at C 35. Open until 0400.*
A good spot for salsa dancing.

**Henry's Café**
*C 80, No 53-18, CC Washington, T5-345 6431. Daily from 1600.*
Popular US-style bar and restaurant.

## Entertainment

Teatro Amira de la Rosa, *Cra 54, No 52-258, T5-369 2410, www.banrepcultural.org/amira-de-la-rosa*. This modern theatre offers a full range of stage presentations, concerts, ballets, art exhibitions and more throughout the year.

## Festivals

**Jan/Mar Carnival**. Carnival is a long-standing tradition in Barranquilla and is comparable to the carnivals in Rio de Janeiro and Trinidad. Pre-carnival parades and dances throughout Jan until an edict that everyone must party is read out. Carnival itself lasts from Sat, with the Batalla de las Flores, through the Gran Parada on Sun, to the funeral of Joselito Carnaval on Tue. The same families have been participating for generations, keeping the traditions of the costumes and dances intact. Prepare for 4 days of intense revelry and dancing with very friendly and enthusiastic crowds, spectacular floats, processions, parades and beauty queens. Tickets for the spectator stands are sold in major restaurants and bars. As always on such occasions, take special care of your valuables. For more information, contact **La Casa de Carnaval**, www. carnavaldebarranquilla.org.

## Shopping

There is a good-value handicrafts market near the old stadium, which is at Cra 46 y C 74 (at the end of Transmetro). **Portal del Prado**, www.portaldelprado.com, is one of the larger and more popular shopping complexes in the city.

## Transport

### Air
**Ernesto Cortissoz Airport**, www. aerocivil.gov.co, is 10 km from the city. The airport has an ATM outside the terminal entrance, a *casa de cambio* in the hall (closed after 1900) and a tourist information desk. A city bus from the airport to town costs US$0.90 (more on Sun). Only take buses marked 'centro'; you can catch them 200 m from the airport on the right. Taxis are booked at the central taxi kiosk; tell them your destination and you will be given a ticket with the price to pay the driver at end of ride. A taxi to the centre costs US$12.50 and takes about 30 mins.

From town, the bus to the airport (marked Malambo) leaves from Cra 44, travels up C 32 to Cra 38, then along C 30 to the airport.

Daily flights to **Bogotá**, **Cali**, **Cúcuta**, **Medellín**, **Bucaramanga**, **Montería** and **Valledupar**. International flights to **Miami** and **Panama City**.

**Airline offices** Avianca, C 53, No 46-38, T5-351 8344, and Cra 46, No 85-152, T5-378 6579, at airport T5-334 8396; **Copa**, C 72, No 54-49, loc 1 y 2; **LAN**, C 75 No 52-56 local 3; **EasyFly**, T5-385 0676, www.easyfly.com.co; **Viva Colombia**, T5-319 7989.

## Bus

**Local** Within the city, the **Transmetro** is a dedicated bus service with 2 routes: *Troncal Murillo* and *Troncal Olaya Herrera*. It takes prepaid cards; single journey US$0.90 (US$0.95 on Sun and holidays). Taxis for trips within town should cost US$2.50-4.

**Long-distance** The main long-distance bus terminal, Km 1.5 Prolongación Murillo, www.ttbaq.com.co, is south of the city near the Circunvalación.

To **Santa Marta** with **Brasilia**, US$5-6, 2 hrs. To **Valledupar**, 5-6 hrs, US$14.50. To **Bogotá**, 24 hrs, frequent, US$40 direct. To **Maicao**, US$17.50, 6 hrs (with **Brasilia**, frequent). To **Cartagena**, 2½-3 hrs, US$5-6, several companies. **Brasilia Van Tours** (Cra 35, No 44-63, T5-371 5226, as well as at the bus terminal) and **Berlinastur** (Cra 43, No 74-133, T318-396 9696, and other offices) have minibus services to **Cartagena** and **Santa Marta** (US$7.50).

# Santa Marta
## & around

Santa Marta, the capital of Magdalena Department, was the first town created in Colombia by the conquistadors. It does not have the same concentration of colonial beauty as Cartagena, but what it lacks in architecture, it makes up for in character and activity. The Samarios are some of the most welcoming and gregarious people you will find anywhere in Colombia.

The area around Santa Marta has much to offer, including a number of beaches. Head west to the family resort of Rodadero, or north to the former fishing village of Taganga. Backpackers love Taganga's lazy charm; it's a convenient stopping point en route to Tayrona and a good place to organize treks to Ciudad Perdida in the Sierra Nevada de Santa Marta. Southeast is Ciénaga de Santa Marta, 4000 sq km of wetlands with all types of waterbirds.

When leaving Santa Marta, most travellers will make a beeline for Tayrona National Park and its wild coastline of golden sands, secluded coves and tropical jungle. But there are other options. If the heat of the coast becomes too much, the rural village of Minca, in the foothills of the Sierra Nevada, will provide welcome respite. From Santa Marta you can also reach Aracataca, birthplace of Colombia's most famous writer, Gabriel García Márquez.

*Colour map 1, A3.*

## Sights
**lively city close to beaches and mountains**

Santa Marta lies at the mouth of the Río Manzanares, one of the many rivers that drain the Sierra Nevada de Santa Marta, on a deep bay with high shelving cliffs at each end. The city's fine promenade, Avenida R de Bastidas, offers good views of the bay and is lined with restaurants, accommodation and nightlife, though none is of a very high quality. At the southern end, where the main traffic turns inland on Calle 22, is a striking sculpture dedicated to the indigenous heritage of the region, La Herencia Tairona. The main commercial area and banks are mainly on Carrera 5, which has many kerbside stalls, and Calle 15, which leads to Plaza Bolívar. Carrera 3 is the hub of nightlife in the centre and is largely pedestrianized, as is Calle 19.

### City centre
In the city centre, well-preserved colonial buildings and early churches still remain and more are currently being restored. The focal point is the pleasant and leafy Plaza Bolívar, which leads down to the seafront. It is complete with statues of Bolívar and Santander, and a bandstand. On the north side is the **Casa de la Aduana/ Museo de Oro** ① *C 14, No 2-07*, which became the Custom House when Santa Marta was declared a free port in 1776. Previously it belonged to the Church and was used as the residence of the Chief Justice of the Inquisition. The house dates from 1531 and was probably the first built of brick and stone in Colombia. An upstairs garret, added in 1730, offers an excellent view

## Essential Santa Marta and around

### Getting around

Local bus services cost US$0.75 (this is a flat fee all the way to the airport and Rodadero); a taxi to Rodadero is US$5-6. Many of the buses coming from Barranquilla and Cartagena stop at Rodadero on their way to Santa Marta. There are also local minibuses to Taganga and Tayrona. Boats from Santa Marta, Rodadero and Taganga visit beaches along the coast.

### When to go

Santa Marta is always hot, although it can be marginally cooler in August and September. The driest months are December to April. October is the low season for tourists, but it is also the wettest month.

### Time required

You will need at least four days to see Santa Marta and Parque Tayrona; extend this to a week to trek to Ciudad Perdida.

### Tip...

The north end of town near the port and the section beyond the old railway station are dangerous and travellers are advised not to go there alone, as it's rife with drugs, and prostitution is common. South of Rodadero Beach has also been reported unsafe.

of the city and the bay. Simón Bolívar stayed here briefly in December 1830 and lay in state on the second floor from 17th to 20th December, before being moved to the cathedral. The Custom House now displays an excellent archaeological collection, with four rooms of exhibits mainly dedicated to the indigenous Tayrona.

# Santa Marta

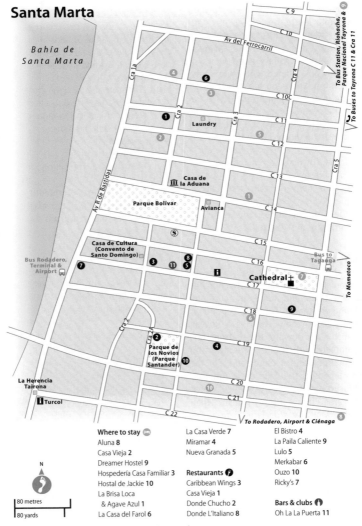

**Where to stay** ⊜
Aluna **8**
Casa Vieja **2**
Dreamer Hostel **9**
Hospedería Casa Familiar **3**
Hostal de Jackie **10**
La Brisa Loca
   & Agave Azul **1**
La Casa del Farol **6**

La Casa Verde **7**
Miramar **4**
Nueva Granada **5**

**Restaurants** 🍴
Caribbean Wings **3**
Casa Vieja **1**
Donde Chucho **2**
Donde L'Italiano **8**

El Bistro **4**
La Paila Caliente **9**
Lulo **5**
Merkabar **6**
Ouzo **10**
Ricky's **7**

**Bars & clubs** 🍸
Oh La La Puerta **11**

# BACKGROUND
## Santa Marta

This part of the South American coastline was visited in the early years of the 16th century by Spanish settlers from Venezuela. At this time, many indigenous groups were living on and near the coast, trading with each other and with communities further inland. The dominant group were the Tayrona.

Santa Marta was founded in 1525 by Rodrigo de Bastidas, who chose it for its sheltered harbour and its proximity to the Río Magdalena and therefore its access to the hinterland. The *indígenas* represented a potential labour force, and the gold in their ornaments suggested fortunes could be made in the area. Within a few years, the Spanish settlement was consolidated and permanent buildings, such as the Casa de la Aduana, had been constructed. Things did not go well, however. The *indígenas* did not 'cooperate', and there was continual friction amongst the Spaniards, all of whom were expecting instant riches. Bastidas' successor, Rodrigo Alvarez Palomino, attempted to subdue the *indígenas* by force, with great loss of life and little success. The *indígenas* that survived took to the hills, where their successors, the Kogi, remain to this day.

By the middle of the 16th century, a new threat had appeared. Encouraged and often financed by Spain's enemies (England, France and Holland), pirates realized that rich pickings were to be had, not only from shipping, but also by attacking coastal settlements. The first raid took place around 1544, captained by the French pirate Robert Waal with three ships and 1000 men. He was followed by many privateers – the brothers Côte, Drake and Hawkins – who all ransacked the city. Forts were built on a small island at the entrance to the bay and on the mainland, but before the end of the century more than 20 attacks had been recorded; the pillage continued until as late as 1779, and the townsfolk lived in constant fear. Caches of treasure have been unearthed in old walls and floors around Santa Marta – testimony to the population's fear of looting during those troubled times. Cartagena, meanwhile, had become the main base for the conquistadors and much had been invested in its defences (see page 144). Santa Marta was never fortified in the same way and declined in importance.

Two important names connect Santa Marta with the history of Colombia. Gonzalo Jiménez de Quesada began the expedition here that led him up the Río Magdalena and into the highlands to found Santa Fe de Bogotá in 1538; and it was here that Simón Bolívar, his dream of Gran Colombia shattered, came to die. Almost penniless, he was given hospitality at the *quinta* of San Pedro Alejandrino, see below, where he died on 17 December 1830, at the age of 47.

Especially interesting is the model of Ciudad Perdida, the most important of the Tayrona cities. Contained within the building is the **Museo de Oro (Gold Museum)** ⓘ *T5-421 4336, Mon-Sat 0900-1700, Sun 1000-1500*, which holds a number of pre-Columbian gold artefacts in its vault.

The original building on the site of the **cathedral** ⓘ *Cra 4, C 16/17, Mass Mon-Fri 1200 and 1800, Sun 0700, 1000, 1200 and 1800,* was completed a few years after the founding of the city and was probably the first church in Colombia, as proclaimed by the inscription on the west front. The present building is mainly 17th century with many additions and modifications, hence the mixture of styles. There are interesting shrines along the aisles, a fine barrel roof and chandeliers, and a grey Italian marble altar decorated in red and brown. Look out for monument to Rodrigo de Bastidas, founder of the city, to the left of the main entrance, and the inscription by the altar steps commemorating the period when Bolívar's remains rested here from his death in 1830 to 1842 when they were transferred to the Pantheon in Caracas.

The **Convento de Santo Domingo** ⓘ *Cra 2, No 16-44, Mon-Fri 0800-1800, Sat 0800-1300,* now serves as the Centro Cultural Universidad Magdalena and houses a library as well as the **Museo Etnográfico de la Universidad del Magdalena**, which has good displays tracing the history of Santa Marta, its port and the Tayrona culture.

### Quinta de San Pedro Alejandrino
*5 km southeast of the city. Daily 0900-1700. US$6, discounts for students and children. To get there, take a bus or colectivo from the waterfront, Cra 1 C, towards Mamatoca and ask for the Quinta, US$0.75.*

This early 17th-century villa on a sugar plantation is where Simón Bolívar lived out his last days; the simple room in which he died, with a few of his personal belongings, can be visited. Other paintings and memorabilia of the period are on display in the villa, and there's a contemporary art gallery featuring works by artists from Venezuela to Bolivia (the countries associated with Bolívar's life) and an exhibition hall in the grounds. The estate and gardens, with some ancient cedars, *samanes*, dignified formal statues and monuments, are worth a stroll. It is an impressive memorial to the man most revered by Colombians.

## Listings Santa Marta *map p186*

### Tourist information

The **tourist office**, Consejo Municipal C 16, No 4-15, T5-438 2587, has friendly staff but not much information. The **national parks office**, C 17, No 4-06, Plaza de la Catedral, www.parques nacionales.gov.co, has information for each of the 4 local parks.

### Where to stay

Do not stay at the north end of town near the port and beyond the old railway station. It's essential to book ahead during high season, particularly weekends, when some hotels increase their prices by 50%.

**$$$$ La Casa del Farol**
*C 18, No 3-115, T5-423 1572,*
*www.lacasadelfarol.com.*
A luxury boutique hotel with 6 rooms, each with its own style, all modern conveniences, laundry service, beauty salon with massages and roof terrace with pool. Price includes breakfast.

### $$$ La Casa Verde
*C 18, No 4-70, T5-431 4122,*
*www.casaverdesantamarta.com.*
Only 5 rooms, standard or suite, in
attractive 'boutique' style, safe, with
Wi-Fi, cable TV, small jacuzzi pool and
juice bar. A *desayuno típico* is available.

### $$$ Nueva Granada
*C 12, No 3-17, T5-421 1337,*
*www.hotelnuevagranada.com.*
This charming old building in the historic
quarter has rooms round a pleasant
courtyard, quiet. Shared rooms with fan
are cheaper ($). Safety-deposit boxes in
rooms, small pool with jacuzzi, includes
breakfast and welcome drink. Reductions
in low season. Recommended.

### $$ Aluna Casa y Cafe
*C 21, No 5-72, T5-432 4916,*
*www.alunahotel.com.*
Pleasant and large Irish-run hostel in
a converted 1920s villa, central and
convenient. It has private rooms and
dorms (US$12.50-17.50 pp), with roof
terrace. Breakfast is extra. There's a café,
extensive book exchange, and a good
noticeboard. Recommended. Under the
same ownership is **Finca Entre Ríos**, 1 hr
from Santa Marta, a working farm with
rooms to stay, full board $$ pp.

### $$ Casa Vieja
*C 12, No 1C-58, T5-431 1606,*
*www.hotelcasavieja.com.*
$$$ in high season. Has a Spanish
feel about it with white tiling and
simple, clean rooms and a/c.
Cheaper with fan, welcoming.

### $$ pp The Dreamer Hostel
*Cra 51, No 26D-161 Diagonal, Los Trupillos,*
*Mamatoco, T5-433 3264, or T300-251*
*6534, www.thedreamerhostel.com.*
Travellers' hostel in a residential district
15 mins from the centre, 5 mins by taxi

from the bus station. All rooms are set
around a sunny garden and pool, dorms
for 4-10 people and private rooms with
and without bath ($$), fan or a/c, bar,
good Italian restaurant, tour information
and activities, good atmosphere. All
services close at hand, including a huge
shopping mall, San Pedro Alejandrino and
the bus stop for Tayrona. Recommended.

### $$-$ La Brisa Loca
*C 14, No 3-58, T5-431 6121,*
*www.labrisaloca.com.*
US-owned lively hostel, with dorms from
US$11 pp, or US$26 for a/c private rooms,
all with shared bath. Meals extra. Also
bar, swimming pool and billiard room.

### $ Hospedería Casa Familiar
*C 10C, No 2-14, T5-421 1697, www.*
*hospederiacasafamiliarfreeservers.com.*
Run by an extremely helpful family,
rooms with fan, roof terrace where you
can cook your own food, bicycles for
hire. Has its own dive shop and organizes
trips to Tayrona and Ciudad Perdida.

### $ Hostal de Jackie
*C 21, No 3-40, T5-420 6944,*
*www.elhostaldejackie.com.*
Backpacker place with dorms for
4-12 people, US$10.50-14 pp, also a
double dorm and private rooms with
and without bath ($$). It has a kitchen for
guests' use, serves breakfast, small pool.

### $ Miramar
*2 blocks from Malecón, C 10C, No 1C-59,*
*www.hosteltrail.com/hotelmiramar/.*
Very knowledgeable and helpful staff
at this backpacker favourite. Can be
crowded. Simple dorms and some
nicer more expensive private rooms
(US$16.50), motorbike parking, cheap
restaurant. Often full. Reservations
via the internet are held until 1500 on
the day of arrival. Tours to the Ciudad

Perdida, Tayrona, Guajira and local sites are available with the in-house operator. Airline tickets also sold here.

## Restaurants

### $$$-$$ El Bistró
*C 19, No 3-68, T5-421 8080. Daily 1100-2300, happy hour 1700-2000.*
Meat dishes, pastas, salads, burgers, sandwiches and set lunches, neither a big place nor an extensive menu, wine list, Argentine influence throughout.

### $$ Donde Chucho
*C 19, No 2-17.*
A little expensive but well situated in the corner of Parque Santander. Serves mostly seafood.

### $$ Donde L'Italiano
*Cra 3, No 16-26. Mon-Sat 1130-1430, 1800-2230.*
Tasty Italian fare at reasonable prices, generous portions.

### $$ La Paila Caliente
*C 18, No 4-60.*
Delightful restaurant with good Colombian/Caribbean food, à la carte at night, excellent value lunch, US$5.

### $$ Ouzo
*Cra 3, No 19-27, www.ouzosanta marta.com.*
Mediterranean restaurant and bar with seating on the street, popular.

### $$ Ricky's
*Cra 1a, No 17-05.*
Beachside restaurant serving international food, including Chinese. Reasonably priced.

### $$-$ Caribbean Wings
*C 17, No 2-59.*
Small *parilla* near the water with a sports-bar vibe. Popular for American-style chicken wings. Great option on a budget.

### $$-$ Lulo
*Cra 3, No 16-34, www.lulocafebar.com.*
Café and bar serving *arepas*, wraps, paninis, fresh juices, coffee and cocktails.

### $ Merkabar
*C 10C, No 2-11. Opens early for breakfast.*
Pastas, great pancakes, good juices and seafood. Family-run, good value and provides tourist information. Recommended.

## Bars and clubs

Santa Marta is a party town; new clubs, discos and bars open every week. In the evening wander along Cra 3 and C 17 and 18 either side of it to see what's going on.

### Agave Azul
*C 14, No 3-58, www.agaveazul santamarta.com.*
In the same building as **La Brisa Loca**.

### Oh La La Puerta
*C 17, No 2-29.*
Excellent bar and atmosphere in a colonial house. Recommended.

## Festivals

**Jul Festival Patronal de Santa Marta.** Celebrates the founding of the city with parades and musical performances.
**Jul Fiestas del Mar.** Aquatic events and a beauty contest.

## Shopping

**Craft shops**
The **market** is at C 11/Cra 11, just off Av del Ferrocarril and has stalls with excellent selections of hammocks. There are several good handicraft

shops on Parque Bolívar. Also try **Artesanías Sisa**, Cra 4, No 16-42 on the Plaza Catedral, T5-421 4510, which sells local handicrafts including clothes, bags, hammocks and sombreros.

## What to do

For guided trips to Quinta San Pedro Alejandrino and other local points of interest, ask at your hotel, travel agencies or the tourist office. For trips to Ciudad Perdida and the Sierra Nevada, see under the relevant destination below.

**Tour operators**
Tours to Ciudad Perdida are run by just 4 authorized agencies in Santa Marta: **Turcol** (see below), **Magic Tour** (C 16, No 4-41, T5-421 5820, www. magictourcolombia.com), **Expotur** (C 18, No 2A-07, T5-421 9577, www.expotur-eco.com) and **Wiwa Tour** (Cra 3, No 18-49, T5-420 3413, www.wiwatour.com).

New Frontiers Adventures, *C 27, No 1C-74, close to Playa Los Cocos, T318-736 1565/317-648 6786, www.colombia. newfrontiersadventures.com.* Trekking to Ciudad Perdida, birdwatching, diving and other adventures and ecotours, with English-speaking guides. Turcol, *C 13, No 3-13, CC San Francisco Plaza loc 115, T321-838 5185, www. buritaca2000.com.* Arranges trips to Ciudad Perdida, Tayrona, Pueblito, Guajira and provides a guide service.

## Transport

**Air**
**Simón Bolívar Airport** is 20 km south of the city. A bus to town costs US$0.75; a taxi is US$12-50, less to Rodadero; beware of taxi drivers taking you to a hotel of their choice, not yours.

There are daily flights to **Bogotá**, **Bucaramanga**, **Cali** and **Medellín** for connections to other cities. During the tourist season, get to the airport early and book well ahead (the same goes for bus reservations).

**Airline offices** Avianca, Cra 2A No 14-17, Edif de los Bancos, loc 105, T5-421 4958, T5-432 0106 at airport. **Copa**, CC Rex, Cra 3, No 17-27, loc 2. **EasyFly**, T5-435 1777. **LAN**, C 23, No 6-18, loc 2.

**Bus**
The **bus terminal** is southeast of the city, towards Rodadero. A minibus to the centre of Santa Marta costs US$0.75; taxi to the centre US$2.50, or US$5 to Rodadero.

**Local** To **Aracataca**, US$5 with **Berlinas**. Buses to **Taganga** can be picked up on Cra 5; buses to **Rodadero** leave from the waterfront. Buses to **Tayrona** leave from the corner of C 11/Cra 11 in the market area, every 15 mins, US$3.

**Long distance** To **Bogotá**, 7 daily, 16 hrs, US$80, **Brasilia** or **Berlinas del Fonce**. **Berlinas** and **Brasilia** to **Bucaramanga** about 9 hrs, US$45-50, frequent departures 0700-2200. Buses to **Barranquilla**, frequent, 2 hrs, US$6. To **Cartagena**, 5 hrs, US$20, with **Brasilia**. To **Riohacha**, 3 hrs, US$15. Frequent buses to **Maicao**, 4-5 hrs, US$21 a/c, cheaper non a/c. **Asotranstax** runs a door-to-door *colectivo* service to Mompós, which leaves Santa Marta 0300 and 1100, 6 hrs, US$40.

All along this stretch of coast are rocky headlands, sandy bays and coves, surrounded by hills, green meadows and shady trees. To the south, the bus from the airport passes by Playa Pleno Mar, one of the more tranquil and recommended beaches in the area. The best beaches east of Santa Marta are in Tayrona National Park, see page 196.

## Around the bay

Santa Marta is the largest bay on this stretch of coast, with **Punta Betín**, a promontory, protecting the harbour to the north and a headland to the south on top of which are the ruins of an early defensive fort, Castillo San Fernando. There is a marine ecosystem research centre, run by Colombian and German universities, near the end of Punta Betín. If you wish to visit, you will need a boat or a permit to pass through the port area, so ask for guidance. The rugged **Isla El Morro** lies 3 km off Santa Marta and is topped by a lighthouse. The proximity of the port and the city means the beaches on the bay are not recommended for bathing.

## Rodadero and around

Rodadero Beach, 4 km southwest of Santa Marta, is one of the best along this coast and is a popular destination for family holidays. It is part of the municipality of **Gaira**, a small town 2 km inland on the Río Gaira, which flows into the Caribbean at the southern end of Rodadero Beach. The main part of the beach has high-rise hotels of all standards, but it is attractive, tree lined, relatively clean and pleasant for bathing. Behind the promenade are restaurants, cheaper accommodation and other services. Nearby are a number of holiday flats and other facilities. Rodadero has a waterpark that's popular with kids, but it was closed indefinitely at the time of writing.

Launches leave Rodadero Beach at the end of Calle 12 for the 10-minute trip to the **Aquarium** ① *Cra 1 No 7-69, T5-422 7222, www.acuariorodadero.com, daily 0920-1600, US$16 including boat transport*, north along the coast at Inca Inca Bay, where you'll find sharks, dolphins, seals and many colourful Caribbean fish. The aquarium is linked to a small museum housing relics from Spanish galleons sunk by pirates, and a collection of coral and seashells. From the aquarium, you can walk (10 minutes) to **Playa Blanca** and swim in less crowded conditions. There is also food available at this beach.

## Ciénaga de Santa Marta

South of Rodadero the paved coast road between Santa Marta and Barranquilla passes salt pans and skirts the Ciénaga Grande de Santa Marta. The wildlife sanctuary, recognized by UNESCO and RAMSAR, is not open to visitors, but many water birds, plants and animals can be seen on and around the lake. The construction of the coast road blocked the egress from the lake to the sea and killed large areas of mangrove, but a National Environment Programme is working to reopen the channels and restore the area. There are two villages built on stilts in the lake, **Nueva Venecia** and **Buenavista**. Boatmen from the village of Tasajera will take visitors out on the lake; ask at the **Santuario de Flora y Fauna Ciénaga Grande de Santa Marta** desk in the national parks office in Santa Marta (see page 188) for information. On the east shore of the lagoon is **Ciénaga**, which is famous for *cumbia* music.

## Taganga and around
*From Santa Marta it takes 15-20 mins by minibus (US$0.80) or taxi (US$5-6).*

Close to Santa Marta is the former fishing village and beach of Taganga, where most people now make a living from tourism. Set in a tranquil semi-circular bay surrounded by scorched hills dotted with cacti, Taganga attracts its fair share of backpackers and has become quite a party resort, especially at weekends. It is laid back and welcoming, but beaches to the east of Tayrona National Park are becoming more favoured as 'in' places on the backpacker circuit (see page 198). The swimming is good, especially on **Playa Grande**, 25 minutes' walk round the coast, but do not leave your belongings unattended. Boat trips along the coast for fishing, and to the many bays and beaches, are run by hotels and by a syndicate of boatmen along the beach.

Half an hour north of Taganga is **Isla de la Aguja**, a good fishing zone. **Playa Granate** is nearer and has excellent places to snorkel and dive around the coral reefs, although lately the reefs have been showing signs of bleaching.

# Around Santa Marta

## Tourist information

### Rodadero
In Rodadero, **Fondo de Promoción Turística**, C 10, No 3-10, T5-422 7548, can provide local information and advice on hotels.

## Where to stay

### Rodadero
There are numerous resort hotels and holiday apartments; ask at the tourist information for a complete list. Do not stay in the area south of Rodadero Beach.

### Taganga

**$$$ Bahía Taganga**
*C 8, No 1B-35, T5-421 0653,*
*www.bahiataganga.com.*
Up on a hill at the north end of the bay with an unmissable sign on the cliff face. It has commanding views over the village and is tastefully decorated with clean rooms. Breakfast is served on a lovely terrace, hospitable, a/c, more expensive in the new building.

**$$$ La Ballena Azul**
*Cra 1, No 18-01, T5-421 9009,*
*www.hotelballenaazul.com.*
Attractive hotel with French riviera touch, decorated in cool blues and whites. Comfortable, spacious rooms with sea views open onto a central atrium with hanging bougainvillea and a palm tree. Also runs boat tours to secluded beaches, horses for hire. Nice restaurant on the beach, terrace bar.

**$$ Casa Blanca**
*Cra 1, No 18-161, T5-421 9232, at the*
*southern end of the beach, www.*
*casablancahosteltaganga.com.*
Characterful. Each room has its own balcony with hammock, US$19 in dorm. The roof terrace is a fine place to pass the evening, drinking beer with fellow guests. Also has a tour desk.

**$$ Techos Azules**
*Sector Dunkarinca, Cabaña 1-100,*
*T5-421 9141, www.techosazules.com.*
Off the road leading into town, *cabañas* with good views over the bay, private rooms and dorm US$12.50 pp (low season prices), free coffee, laundry service.

**$$-$ Bayview**
*Cra 4, No 17B-57, T5-421 9560,*
*www.hosteltrail.com/bayview.*
With a technicolour façade, pleasant rooms, cheaper dorms (US$10 pp), kitchen, barbecue area, lounges with DVD player.

**$$-$ Hostal Moramar**
*Cra 4, No-17B-83, T5-421 9202.*
2 blocks uphill from beach opposite football pitch. Bright, airy patio area, Wi-Fi, breakfast and laundry extra, attentive owners, welcoming.

**$$-$ La Casa de Felipe**
*Cra 5A, No 19-13, 500 m from beach*
*behind football field, T316-318 9158 (mob),*
*T5-421 9101, www.lacasadefelipe.com.*
Cosy traveller place run by knowledgeable French team of Jean-Phillipe and Sandra Gibelin. Good kitchen facilities, excellent restaurant run by a French chef, hospitable, relaxing hammock and expanisve roof with terrace with sea views, studio apartments (**$$$-$$**), dorms (US$8-12.50) and rooms with

private bath. Good information on trips to Tayrona (maps provided), English spoken.

**$ pp Divanga B&B**
*C 12, No 4-07, T5-421 9092, also Casa Divanga, C 11, No 3-05, T5-421 9217, www.divanga.com.*
French-owned hostel, doubles with private bath or 3-person dorm, includes great breakfast, comfortable, 5-mins' walk from beach, nice views, attentive service, lovely atmosphere, good pool, HI affiliated. Recommended.

**$ Pelikan Hostal**
*Cra 2, No 17-04, T5-421 9057, www.hosteltrail.com/hostalpelikan.*
Rooms with fan for 2-7 people, restaurant.

## Restaurants

### Taganga
Fresh fish is available along the beach and good pancakes can be found at the crêperie at the **Hotel La Ballena Azul.**

**$$ Babaganoush**
*Cra 1C 18-22, 3rd floor next to the Tayrona Dive Center.*
Serves up international dishes. Great steaks and a generous half-off happy hour from 1700-2200.

**$$ Bitácora**
*Cra 1, No17-13.*
Seafood, pastas, burgers, steaks and salads, has a good reputation.

## Bars and clubs

### Taganga

**El Garaje**
*C 8, No, 2-127, T5-421 9003.*
Plays hip hop and electronica. Starts late, finishes late.

**Mirador**
*C 1, No 18A-107.*
Rooftop bar and disco that strikes a nice balance between in- and outdoor fun.

**Mojito Net**
*C 14, No 1B-61.*
Live music, open mic sessions, wine, cocktails, food and internet.

**Sensation**
*C 14, No 1-04.*
Dance club that's open till 0300 at weekends.

## What to do

### Rodadero
In addition to trips to the aquarium, evening and day-long boat tours are offered (US$15-25), as well as swimming with dolphins (US$75).

### Taganga
**Adventure tours**
Elemento, *C 18. No 3-31, T5-421 0870.* Mountain biking, hiking and other tours in the Sierra Nevada, Minca and Tayrona.
Magic Tours, *C 14, No 1b-50, T5-421 9429, www.magictourcolombia.com.* Authorized agency for tours to Ciudad Perdida.
Vergel Tours, *T304-571 1425, www.vergel tours.com.* Christine Vergel organizes a number of excursions from Tagonga, including trips to Ciudad Perdida, scuba outings, snorkelling and cliff jumping.

**Diving**
There are several dive shops in Taganga.
Oceano Scuba, *Cra 2, No 17-46, T5-421 9004, www.oceanoscuba.com.co.* PADI, NAUI, TDI and other courses, 2, 3 and 4 days.
Poseidon Dive Center, *C 18, No 1-69, T5-421 9224, www.poseidondivecenter.com.* PADI courses at all levels and the only

place on the Colombian Caribbean coast to offer an instructor course. German owner, several European languages spoken. Own pool for beginners, also has rooms to rent ($ pp), Wi-Fi.

Tayrona National Park is named after the Tayrona (also spelt Tairona) culture, one of the most important in pre-colonial Colombia. It extends from north of Taganga along 85 km of rugged coastline much of it fringed with coral reefs. The beaches are what you would expect of a tropical paradise: thick jungle teeming with wildlife spills over onto golden sand. You will see monkeys, iguanas and, possibly, snakes. Some beaches have pounding surf, while others are small, secluded bays, excellent for swimming and sunbathing.

There is something of the prehistoric about Tayrona. Half-close your eyes, and, with a little imagination, the flocks of pelicans that glide overhead could be pterodactyls; the bright-tailed lizards that scurry across the forest paths are reminders of their extinct cousins, and the enormous boulders that stand guard over the beaches look like they have been there since the beginning of time. However, time and tourism have caught up with Tayrona and it is becoming increasingly popular. Prices have rocketed and there is now a steady stream of visitors, especially during the national holidays: Semana Santa, July/August and December/January.

### The western park

Many of the bays closest to Santa Marta are accessible by road, including the beautiful beach at **Villa Concha**, 5 km east of the city. Surrounded by tree-covered hills and with several restaurants nearby, the bay is popular with locals at the weekend and makes a good day trip during the week. Tours from Santa Marta visit this beach as well as **Neguanje** and **Playa Cristal** (a 10-minute boat ride from Neguanje). Neguanje can also be reached by *colectivos* from Santa Marta market, which leave at 0700 and return at 1600.

### El Zaino and the eastern park

El Zaino, 35 km from Santa Marta, is the main access point for the eastern end of the park. From there, a road leads 4 km to the administrative and visitor centre at **Cañaveral**, where there is a gift shop, car park, a museum (closed at the time of writing), campsite, juice bar and a short trail to a mirador (about 30 minutes there and back).

It is a one-hour walk on a forest trail from Cañaveral to **Arrecifes**. The trail is mostly level, apart from a couple of short, steep sections; horses can be hired at Cañaveral for those that don't want to walk. At Arrecifes, beyond the cabins, campsites and eating places, is a long beach backed by mangroves. On no account be tempted to swim here as the tides and surf are treacherous. Every year, people drown because they do not heed the warnings.

# Essential Parque Nacional Natural Tayrona

## Access

The park has two entrances: **Calabazo** for Pueblito and Cabo San Juan de Guía, and **El Zaino**, at the east end of the park, 35 km from Santa Marta, for Cañaveral and Arrecifes (El Zaino is the most commonly used). The park is open daily 0800-1700; tickets cost US$19 for foreigners (regardless of age), US$7.75 for Colombians (US$3.75 children); parking is extra.

Tours can be arranged at several hotels and agencies in Santa Marta. Guides, who charge US$20 or more per person, are also available, but you will not need one for the main trail from Cañaveral to Arrecifes and beyond.

## Getting around

In the wet, the paths are very slippery, so hiking boots are recommended.

From the gate *colectivos* make the 4-km journey to the visitor centre at Cañaveral (see below), US1.50, or it is possible to walk (approximately 30 minutes). You can hire horses to carry you and your luggage from Cañaveral to Arrecifes, US$8; La Piscina, US$13, or Cabo San Juan, US$16.50 (one way). It is possible to do a circuit Santa

### Tip...

There are food and drink stands in the park, or you can take your own food and water. If you are staying overnight in one of the campsites or hammock places, remember to take all supplies with you as there is only a small store in the park at Cañaveral. However, only take essential valuables, as robbery has been a problem. Littering was a big issue in the past, but there are now camouflaged litter bins along all the main trails and around the campsites. In the wet, the paths are very slippery, so hiking boots are recommended. Beware of falling coconuts and omnivorous donkeys in the campsites. Mosquitoes and other insects can also be a problem; take insect repellent.

Marta–Cañaveral–Arrecifes– Pueblito–Calabazo–Santa Marta in one day, but you will need to leave by 0700 at the latest. It is easier (more downhill) to do the circuit in reverse, so ask to be dropped at Calabazo.

It is advisable to inform park guards when walking anywhere in the park other than the main trail.

Walk on from Arrecifes to **La Piscina**, 40 minutes further. You pass a little beach, **La Arenilla**, two-thirds of the way along, with a cevichería and juice stall. La Piscina also has a couple of places selling drinks and food. The beach is narrow, but the swimming after the walk is divine and there is excellent snorkelling. From La Piscina you can walk on to **Cabo San Juan de Guía**, 45 minutes, which also has excellent bathing, places to eat and a popular campsite.

From Cabo San Juan you can return the way you came, take the boat to Taganga, or walk 1½ hours on a clear path up to the ruins of the ancient Tayrona settlement of **Pueblito**. A guided tour around the site is free, every Saturday, or as arranged with a park guard. There are still indigenous people at Pueblito; do not photograph them. From Pueblito you can continue for a pleasant two-hour walk up to Calabazo on the Santa Marta–Riohacha road.

### East of Tayrona
Beyond El Zaino on the Santa Marta–Riohacha road is **Playa Los Angeles**, a fine empty stretch of coastline that's excellent for surfing. Ten minutes' walk west is the mouth of the Río Piedras, which forms the border of Tayrona National Park and is good for bathing. A short drive east of Tayrona, 5 km inland from Playa Costeno, is the **Quebrada de Valencia** , several natural swimming pools amid waterfalls, with good views. From the marked roadside entrance, it is a pleasant 20-minute walk along a clear path to the falls, with drinks and snacks available along the way. Note that the falls can get overcrowded during high season.

## Listings Parque Nacional Natural Tayrona

### Tourist information

The address of the national parks office in Santa Marta is given on page 188. Information can also be found at www.colombia.travel and www.parquesnacionales.gov.co.

### Where to stay

#### Eastern park
#### Cañaveral
Comfortable upmarket cabins with thatched roofs (*ecohabs*) for 1-4 people cost from US$60 for 2 people half board (4 people sharing, US$100 full board). Book through **Aviatur** (Av 19, No 4-62, Bogotá, T1-587 5181, www. concesionesparquesnaturales.com).

Camping is US$10 pp in 5-person tent; hammocks US$7.50.

#### Arrecifes
Cabins for 1-5 people cost from US$60 pp (other packages available); book through **Aviatur** (as above). The cabins offer privacy as well as great views over the sea and jungle. Camping is US$10 pp in 5-person tent; hammocks US$7.50. Various other places offer double tents with mattress and hammocks; these include **Bukaru**, T310-691 3626, and **El Paraíso**, T317-676 1614.

#### Cabo de San Juan de Guía
There is a small restaurant with hammocks for hire (US$10-12.50) and

2 *cabañas* (US$60). Pitching your own
tent costs US$10; double tent hire, US$25.

**East of Tayrona**

There is an ecohostel called **Yuluka**
about 1 km from El Zaino entrance
on the main road.

**$$$ Cabañas Los Angeles**
*Los Angeles, www.cabanasanta*
*martalosangeles.com.*
The owner is Nohemi Ramos who also
offers tours and hires out surfboards.

**$$$ Zenduka**
*Km 60, T312-583 3908, pipeludo@*
*hotmail.com.*
Owner Felips offers a lovely cabin for up
to 4 people at this ecolodge. There are
a number of activities and excursions,
including visits to the Coquitos tribe,
walks through Palomino, night fishing
and marine turtle viewing.

**Restaurants**

There are decent restaurants at both
Cañaveral and Arrecifes, as well as
smaller eateries at many of the beaches.

## Parque Nacional Natural Sierra Nevada de Santa Marta

**an unmissable jungle trek to the Lost City**

The Sierra Nevada, covering a triangular area of 16,000 sq km, rises abruptly
from the Caribbean to 5800-m snow-capped peaks in about 45 km, a gradient
comparable with the south face of the Himalaya and unequalled along the world's
coasts. Pico Colón is the highest point in the country. Here can be found the most
spectacular scenery and most interesting of Colombia's indigenous communities.
The area is a drugs-growing, processing and transporting region, and also shelters
guerrilla and paramilitary groups, so some local *indígenas* have been reluctant
to welcome visitors, but the situation is improving and limited activities are now
possible, such as the unmissable trek to Ciudad Perdida. It is also possible to enter
the sierra from Valledupar with permission from community leaders.

### ★Ciudad Perdida → *Colour map 1, A3.*

*Entry to the park is US$10.25 for non-Colombians and is included in the price of a*
*tour to Ciudad Perdida (about US$300 pp). Travelling to Ciudad Perdida alone is not*
*permitted. Only 4 agencies are licensed to take tours to Ciudad Perdida (listed under*
*What to do, page 191), although other tour operators and hotels in Santa Marta or*
*Taganga can make arrangements. Under no circumstances should you deal with*
*unauthorized guides; check with the tourist office if in doubt.*

Ciudad Perdida (Lost City) is the third of the triumvirate of 'must-sees' on Colombia's
Caribbean coast (the other two being Cartagena and Tayrona). The six-day trek is
right up there with the Inca Trail in Peru and Roraima in Venezuela, as one of the
classic South American adventures and is a truly memorable experience.

Ciudad Perdida was called Teyuna by the Tayrona, meaning 'mother nature', and
served as their political and trading centre. It was built around AD 700 at 1100 m
on the steep slopes of Cerro Corea, which lies in the northern part of the Sierra

Nevada de Santa Marta. The site covers 400 ha and consists of a complex system of paved footpaths and flights of steps linking a series of terraces and platforms on which were built cult centres, warehouses and residences housing between 1400 and 3000 people. Sophisticated irrigation systems and walls were constructed to prevent erosion. By around 1600 the Tayrona had been almost wiped out by the conquistadors and the few who survived were forced to flee. For the next four centuries, Teyuna disappeared under the forest growth. In 1973, tomb looters searching for gold, known to exist in burial urns and graves, rediscovered the city by chance. By 1975, the city was attracting local and international anthropologists and archaeologists who started to excavate, leading to the first tourist groups in 1984. Today the area is a protected indigenous reserve, where three main indigenous groups, the Koguis, Arhuacos and Arsarios (Wiwa), continue to live.

The 20-km trek to the Lost City is perhaps as spectacular as the archaeological site itself. At times gruelling and challenging, it is not a leisurely walk, but is well worth the effort for a rewarding and memorable experience. Tours run all year, so be prepared for heavy rain. As well as lush tropical humid and dry forests rich in flora and fauna, there are crystal-clear rivers, waterfalls and natural swimming pools. Along the way, you will pass friendly Kogui villages. The final section is climbing some 1200 steep, slippery steps to the summit of the city. Watch out for snakes.

All tours include transport to and from the start and end of the trail at Machete Pelao (aka El Mamey), a settlement three hours east of Santa Marta; sleeping in hammocks with mosquito nets at organized camps or cabin sites; food; insurance; guides and entrance fees. The companies list the clothes and equipment you should take, such as sleeping bag, insect repellent, water bottle, etc. Don't forget that Ciudad Perdida is in a national park: it is strictly forbidden to damage trees and collect flowers or insects. Leave no rubbish behind and encourage the guides to ensure no one else does.

## Minca
*Catch a bus from C 11 with Cra 11 in Santa Marta (30 mins, US$3.50). A taxi will cost US$25.*

If the heat of the coast becomes too much then a stay up in Minca is a refreshing alternative. Some 20 km from Santa Marta in the foothills of the Sierra Nevada, this small village, surrounded by coffee fincas and begonia plantations, is a popular excursion and offers several cheap and truly charming places to stay. Horse riding, birdwatching and tours further into the Sierra Nevada can be arranged from here.

About 45 minutes' walk beyond the village is **El Pozo Azul**, a local swimming spot under a waterfall. Popular at weekends but almost always empty during the week, it's well worth a visit. El Pozo Azul was a sacred indigenous site where purification rituals were performed and on occasion it is still used by the Kogi of the Sierra Nevada.

## San Lorenzo
Beyond Minca, the partly paved road rises steeply to San Lorenzo which is surrounded by a forest of palm trees. On the way to San Lorenzo is **La Victoria**, a large coffee finca which offers tours to demonstrate the coffee-making process. It is possible to stay in *cabañas* run by the park authorities close by.

## ON THE ROAD
## The Lost City

From the first day we set out on the trail toward the mysterious Colombian Lost City, until day six when the remarkable adventure into the heart of the sierra came to an end, I was blown away by the crystal-clear rivers that cascaded down from the upper reaches of the mountains and treated us to amazing natural swimming pools, beautiful waterfalls and a much welcomed respite after hours of hiking amidst the endless jungle landscape. There are 18 or so river crossings en route to the Lost City, river pools to swim in each day and 1200 stone steps to climb at the very end of the third day that take you above the gorgeous river valleys to the high ridges blanketed in green. While the site alone is impressive, and its mysterious history and late discovery only add to its splendour, the surrounding mountain peaks dominate the endless landscape. What else lies undiscovered and hidden among such wild, rugged and beautiful terrain?

Although there was a kidnapping incident on the trail in 2003, the region is currently considered safe and is heavily patrolled by the Colombian Army. The site is guarded day and night by about 40 friendly soldiers who pass their two-month assignment on site by asking visitors for cigarettes in exchange for odd looking nuts that they have picked up off the jungle floor. They will also obligingly pose for photos, which they seem to enjoy more than anything else.

There is more than one option when it comes to choosing a route, some little more difficult and with longer days, but the rewards will outweigh the fatigue. Starting and finishing the hike in different places will give you the chance to see more of the remote landscape and travel to less visited parts of this unique mountain range.

*Craig Weigand*

Near San Lorenzo is the **El Dorado Bird Reserve**, the perfect place to see the majority of the 19 bird species endemic to the Sierra Nevada de Santa Marta. It is managed by **ProAves** ⓘ *Cra 20, No 36-61, Bogotá, T1-340 3229, www.proaves.org*, a Colombian NGO dedicated to the conservation of biodiversity, especially birds at risk of extinction. There is a lodge at the reserve and all visits must be arranged through ProAves. They run multi-day tours which include Minca and Guajira, or more specialist itineraries at set times.

**Listings** Parque Nacional Natural Sierra Nevada de Santa Marta

### Tourist information

For the latest information, check with national parks offices in Santa Marta and Bogotá.

**Fundación Pro Sierra Nevada**, C 17, No 3-83, Santa Marta, T5-431 0551, www.prosierra.org is also helpful. For archaeological information, contact

**ICANH**, C 12, No 2-41, Bogotá, T1-444 0544, www.icanh.gov.co.

## Where to stay

### Minca

**$$$ Minca**
*On the hill to the right as you enter Minca, T317-437 3078, www.hotelminca.com.*
Converted convent with views of the valley below, formerly called La Casona, fully remodelled, with breakfast, bath, fan, hot water, restaurant and bar, various activities including birdwatching.

**$$ Sans Souci**
*Minca, T313-590 9213, sanssouciminca@ yahoo.com.*
Rambling house in a beautiful garden, German-owned, rooms in the house or separate apartments, swimming pool, kitchen, discount in exchange for gardening. Stunning views.

**$$ Sierra's Sound**
*C Principal, Minca, T311-600 1614, www.mincahotelsierrasound.com.*
Italian-owned, overlooking a rocky river, hot water, home-made pasta, tours into the Sierra Nevada.

There are many more places to stay in town.

## What to do

### Minca
**Semilla Tours**, *Minca, T313-872 2434, www.semillatours.com.* Community tourism company offering tours in the region and elsewhere in Colombia. Also volunteering opportunities. Has its own guesthouse, **Finca La Semilla**, www. fincalasemilla.blogspot.co.uk.

## Inland from Santa Marta
*a detour for fans of Colombian literature and music*

### Aracataca
Aracataca, 60 km south of Ciénaga and 7 km before Fundación, is the birthplace of Gabriel García Márquez. It was fictionalized as Macondo in some of his novels, notably in *One Hundred Years of Solitude*. His home is now a **Casa Museo** ⓘ *take Cra 5 away from plaza at corner with Panadería Delipán, the museum is next to La Hojarasca café, daily 0900-1300, 1400-1700.* Different rooms have objects and quotations from his work in Spanish and English to provide an overview of his family life. You can also visit the **Casa del Telegrafista**, which houses a few dusty items. **Finca Macondo** (named after a type of tree) is possibly the inspiration for García Márquez' choice of the name. It is 30 minutes from town and can be visited independently in the afternoon, or as part of a tour (see What to do, page 206). Other sites related to the stories are the river, where you can swim, and the railway station, through which coal trains pass.

### Towards Valledupar
South of Aracataca and Fundación is the important road junction of Bosconia (80 km). The main road continues to Bucaramanga, while a road west heads towards the Río Magdalena; turn off this road at La Gloria to reach Mompós (see Transport, below). The easterly route, meanwhile, heads towards Maicao and the Venezuelan border reaching **Valledupar** after 89 km. Continuing on this road takes you **Cuestecitas**, where you can turn north to Riohacha, or carry on to Maicao.

## ON THE ROAD
### Gabriel García Márquez

More than any other Colombian, Gabriel García Márquez, or Gabo as he is affectionately known, has shaped the outside world's understanding of Colombian culture. His books champion the genre of magical realism where the real and the fantastical blur so naturally that it is difficult to discern where one ends and the other begins.

But is this what life in Colombia is really like? Schoolteachers-turned-dictators who fashion a town's children into an oppressive army, a woman so beautiful she causes the death of anyone who courts her and a child born with his eyes open because he has been weeping in his mother's womb seem improbable, especially to sceptical Western sensibilities. Yet many of the places, events and characters are based on real life. Macondo, a place which features in so many of his stories, is modelled on his town of birth, Aracataca. Cartagena is easily recognizable as the unnamed port that is the setting for *Love in the Time of Cholera*, while Fermina Daza and Florentino Ariza's love affair is based on his own parents' marriage. Events in *Chronicle of a Death Foretold* and *The Story of a Shipwrecked Sailor* were inspired by real life stories lifted from newspaper articles.

Despite his death in April 2014, Marquez's legacy of combining fantasy and reality continues to be a defining characteristic of Colombia's artistic identity. And who can challenge Gabo's interpretation of the truth when Colombia has produced real life characters such as Pablo Escobar? Where else in the world are there villages that host donkey beauty contests or elect a mayor who dresses up as a superhero? Sometimes Colombian reality is stranger than Gabo's fiction.

### Valledupar and around

Located on the plain between the Sierra Nevada de Santa Marta and the Sierra de Perijá, Valledupar is capital of César Department and the home of *vallenato* music and culture (see box, page 204). On the main Plaza Alfonso López Pumarejo is the cultural centre, **Compai Chipuco** ⓘ *C 16, No 6-05, T5-580 8710, tiendacompaichipuco@festivalvallenato.com*, a good place for information. It sells handicrafts, books and music and has a bar, restaurant and a photographic exhibition about Consuelo Araujonoguera, known as *'La Cacica'*, one of the founders of Valledupar's famous music festival (see page 206), who was murdered by FARC in 2001. Also of interest are **La Academia de Musica Vallenata Andrés Turco Gil** ⓘ *C 31 No 4-265*, with photos of events and famous personalities, and **Casa Beto Murgas** ⓘ *Cra 17 No 9A-18, US$5*, which has a collection of photographs, indigenous instruments and accordions.

Also on the Plaza Alfonso López Pumarejo is the **Iglesia Nuestra Señora de la Concepción** and the fine balconied colonial façade of the **Casa del Maestre Pavejeau**, in front of which is a dramatic statue of 'La Revolución en Marcha' by Rodrigo Arenas Betancourt. Around the city are many other statues, some to symbols and instruments of *vallenato*.

## ON THE ROAD

### Música tropical

No country in South America has a greater variety of musical genres than Colombia, and nowhere is music more abundant than in the fertile breeding grounds of the north coast. The diversity of musical expression comes from a mixture of African, indigenous and European influences.

On the coast, *música tropical* is an umbrella term used to encompass the many hybrids that have arisen over the years. Most popular among these is *vallenato*, a form of music that originated with farmers around Valledupar. Its primary instruments are the accordion; the *guacharaca* (a tube made from the trunk of a small palm tree, with ridges carved into it), which when scraped with a fork produces a beat, and the *caja vallenata* (a cylindrical drum brought over by African slaves).

*Vallenato* has its roots in a more ancient genre, *cumbia*, which is believed to derive from Guinean *cumbe* and began as a courtship dance practised among the slave population; it later mixed with European and indigenous instruments, such as the guitar, the accordion and the *gaita*, a type of flute used by the *indígenas* of the Sierra Nevada de Santa Marta. *Cumbia* is celebrated for bringing together Colombia's three main ethnic groups and was used as an expression of resistance during the campaign for Independence from the Spanish. *Cumbia* has many other derivatives, such as *porro*, *gaita*, *fandango* and *bullerengue*.

The newest genre to emerge is *champeta*. This is the most African of the genres; it takes its influence from *soukous* and *compas*, and is characterized by very sensual dancing. It gained popularity among the black population of Cartagena and San Basilio de Palenque in the 1980s.

The Río Guatapurí runs cold and clear from the Sierra Nevada past the city. The **Balneario Hurtado**, by the bridge just past the Parque de la Leyenda, is a popular bathing spot, especially at weekends, although the water is muddy after heavy rain. A statue of a mermaid overlooks the bathers from the trees, and there's food, drink and music on offer. To get there from the centre, take Carrera 9, the main commercial avenue, or, if cycling, the quieter Carrera 4. Across the bridge is **Ecoparque Los Besotes** (9 km), a dry forest wildlife reserve, good for birdwatching.

**Casa Indígena** ⓘ *Av Simon Bolivar, just past the accordion statue at end of Cra 9*, is where the indigenous communities from the sierra gather. Go here if you need permission to visit remote places. A good excursion is to the Arhuaco community of **Nabusímake** ⓘ *to get there take a bus at 0600 from Carrera 7A where it splits from Carrera 7 (beyond 5 esq) to Pueblo Bello (1½ hrs), then a jeep to Nabusímake (2-2½ hrs, US$5)*, one of the most important centres of indigenous culture in the Sierra Nevada de Santa Marta. You will have to stay the night as there is only one jeep each day and it comes straight back. Another full-day tour from the city is to **La Mina** (20 km), a natural swimming pool by magnificent rocks, also popular at weekends.

## Where to stay

### Aracataca

**$$-$ Hotel Milán**
*C 7 No 8-24.*
Most people visiting the town stay in
neighbouring Fundación. **Restaurant
El Patio Mágico de Gabo y Leo Matiz**
occasionally organizes rooms.

### Valledupar

**$$$ Sonesta**
*Diag 10, No 6N-15, T5-574 8686,
www.sonesta.com.*
Business-class hotel, next to
CC Guatapurí Plaza, it has all the
usual amenities including a pool
and restaurant.

**$$$-$$ Casa de Los Santos Reyes**
*C 13C No 5 esq, T5-580 1782.*
Centrally located, this restored colonial
home, run by the same people who run
**Hostal Provincia**, has been turned into
a boutique hotel. Its 5 spacious rooms
have all mod cons.

**$$$-$$ Vajamar**
*Cra 7, No 16A-30, T5-573 2010,
www.hotelvajamar.com.*
This smart city centre hotel, whose
rooms are cheaper at weekends.
Pool and an expensive restaurant.

**$$ Aqua Hostal**
*Cra 7 No 13A-42, T5-213 9142.*
Opened in 2013, this hostel has
private rooms as well as 12-bed
dorms. Wi-Fi throughout.

**$$ Hostal Provincia**
*C 16A, No 5-25, T5-580 0558,
www.provinciavalledupar.com.*
Private rooms and cheaper dorms
for 6 ($ pp). A very good choice, with
a nice atmosphere. Bike rental, Wi-Fi
throughout, hammocks, barbecue
and bar, lots of information, helpful
staff can organize tours and excursions
to local indigenous communities.
Warmly recommended.

## Restaurants

### Aracataca

**$$ El Patio Mágico de Gabo y Leo Matiz**
*C 7 No 4-57.*
Central option offers Italian and local
dishes in an open-air courtyard. Also
has vegetarian options.

**$ La Hojarasca**
*Next to the Casa Museo. Daily 1800-2200.*
Juices, snacks and drinks, clean
and pleasant.

### Valledupar
There are some cafés on the Pl Alfonso
López, but all types of restaurants on
Cra 9 from C 15 down, heading towards
Pl del Acordeón.

**$$ Varadero**
*C12 N0 6-56, T5-570 6175,
www.varadero.com.co.*
Simply put: the best seafood in town.

**$ Café de Las Madres**
*Pl de las Madres, Cra 9, No 15-19.*
A nice shady place, with a limited
selection: coffee, beer, ices.

## Entertainment

### Valledupar

Palenke Cultura Bar, *Cra 5 No 13C 52*.
A good spot offering dance classes, free
cinema nights and other cultural events.

## Festivals

### Valledupar

**6 Jan** The anniversary of the founding
of Valledupar. There's dancing and
accordion music in the streets.
**Apr Festival de la Leyenda Vallenata.**
The festival celebrating *vallenata* music
and culture draws thousands of visitors.
It is focused around Parque de la Leyenda.
Contact the cultural centre (C 16, No 6-05,
T5-580 8710, www.festivalvallenato.com)
for information. There are other cultural
events throughout Sep.

## Shopping

### Valledupar

Centro Artesanal Calle Grande,
*C 16, block 7*. Lots of stalls selling
handicrafts and local artwork, including
distinctive hats (US$15-US$150),
indigenous bags, jewellery, hammocks
and some musical instruments.

Compai Chipuco on the plaza sells
books and music CDs of the region, as does
**La Casa de la Música**, Cra 9, No 18-85.

## What to do

### Aracataca

Primacho, *T321-593 7330*. Arranges
5-hr tours of the town and
surroundings, US$25.

### Valledupar

Paseo Vallenato Tour, *Cra 18 No 14-33,
T313-571 9025, www.paseovallenato.com*.

Offers cultural tours in and around
Valledupar as well excursions to the
river and indigenous communities.
Recommended.

## Transport

### Aracataca
#### Bus

To **Santa Marta**, US$5 with **Berlinas**.
To **Barranquilla**, US$6. To **Valledupar**,
3 hrs 45 mins, US$6.50 with **Cootracosta**.
There may be a long stop in Fundación,
but you don't have to change bus. To
go to **Bucaramanga** (US$25) or **Bogotá**
(US$35), you have to catch a bus coming
from Santa Marta at the toll station
(*peaje*) outside town 1½ hrs after the
bus has left Santa Marta. Be at the toll
30 mins early. For information on all
buses, go to the **Berlinas** office.

### Valledupar
#### Air

The airport is 3 km southeast of the town,
close to the bus station (taxi, US$5).

Flights to **Barranquilla** (30 mins)
and **Bogotá** (1½ hrs) with **Avianca**
(T01-8000-953434) and **LAN** (Av Hurtado
Diag 10N-6N, 15, CC Guatapuri, p 1,
Plazoleta Juan Valdez).

#### Bus

The bus terminal is near the airport
(taxi, US$5).

To **Aracataca**, US$6.50. To **Santa
Marta**, 4 hrs, US$11.50. To **Barranquilla**,
5-6 hrs, US$12.50. To **Cartagena**, US$17.50.
To **Mompós** (via Bosconia) door-to-door
service with **Lalo Castro**, T312-673 5226,
US$20; if he isn't going, **CotraNorte**,
**Cotracol** or **Cootracegua** buses leave
every morning. There are also door-to-
door services to **Riohacha**, US$15.

# Riohacha
## & Guajira

Along the coast from Santa Marta the lush vegetation of the foothills of the Sierra Nevada gives way to flat expanses of scorched earth where only a scrub-like tree known as trupillo (*Prosopis juliflora*) and the cactus survive. The change in landscape marks the beginning of the Guajira Peninsula, home to the Wayúu, one of Colombia's best-preserved indigenous cultures. It is also the northernmost tip of South America and certainly feels like the end of the world: an arid and unforgiving terrain that is nonetheless home to vast flocks of flamingos and other birds.

Riohacha may be a departmental capital but it feels more like a sleepy fishing village, though it livens up considerably at the weekend and on public holidays. Musichi and Manaure, with their flamingos and salt works, will be of interest to nature lovers, and Cabo de la Vela, with its turquoise waters that lap against a desert landscape, is a sight to behold. If you have the time and energy, Parque Natural Nacional Macuira, an oasis of tropical green sprouting out of the semi desert, and Punta Gallinas, the northernmost point of the continent, will cap off a trip into this strange and ethereal land. The difficulties in transport only add to the sense of adventure this peninsula presents. *Colour map 1, A5-A6.*

# Essential Riohacha and Guajira

## Finding your feet

The Guajira Peninsula is bordered by the Gulf of Venezuela and the Caribbean Sea. Trips to the region are best arranged in Riohacha, but can also be organized in Bogotá, Cartagena and Santa Marta.

## Getting around

Early morning is best for travel, as transport is scarce in the afternoon. Getting to Cabo de la Vela independently is a time-consuming and at times uncomfortable experience, particularly during the wet season, although it can be done: *colectivos* and taxis make the journey on the paved road to Uribia and Manaure, and from there on dirt tracks to Cabo de la Vela (two or three hours). Beyond Cabo de la Vela we advise you take a tour or at least contract your own jeep and guide. **Aventure Colombia** in Cartagena (see page 159) arranges trips here from time to time.

## When to go

Rainy season is September to November; dirt tracks can become impassable at this time. To enjoy the deserted beaches around Cabo de la Vela, avoid Christmas and Easter when it is crowded and full of cars. The **Wayúu Indian Festival** in Uribia takes place in May.

## Time required

Most tours of the peninsula last three days; add another couple of days' beach time to your itinerary.

## Riohacha and around
### fishing and flamingos

Riohacha, 160 km east of Santa Marta, is capital of La Guajira Department. Formerly a port, today it has the ambience of a provincial fishing town. *Riohacha y Los Indios Guajiros* by Henri Candelier, a Frenchman's account of a journey to the area 100 years ago, has very interesting depictions of the life of the Wayúu.

### Palomino

The paved coastal road from Santa Marta crosses into Guajira Department at increasingly popular **Palomino**, halfway to Riohacha, which has a fine beach, a river running into the sea and views of the Sierra Nevada, including snow-capped Pico Bolívar. There are hotels, hostels and *cabañas* here, with more under construction.

### Santuario Los Flamencos

*95 km east of Santa Marta and 25 km west of Riohacha, www.parques nacionales.gov.co. Take a colectivo from the roundabout between the water tower and bus station in Riohacha to Camarones, US$3.*

The Santuario de Fauna y Flora Los Flamencos covers 7000 ha of saline vegetation, including mangroves and lagoons, separated from the Caribbean by sand bars. The two large saline lagoons (Laguna Grande and Laguna de Navío Quebrado) are fed by several intermittent streams which form deltas at the south point of the lakes and are noted for their colonies of flamingos. Some are there all year; others gather during the wetter months between November and May, when some fresh water enters the lagoons. The birds are believed to migrate to and from the Dutch Antilles, Venezuela and Florida. There is also plenty of other birdlife throughout the year.

Laguna Grande is near **Camarones**, which is just off the main road. From here another road leads to the park entrance at Guanebucane (3.5 km). At the northern end of **Laguna de Navío Quebrado** is a community-run visitor centre called **Los Mangles** (www.ecoturismosantuario.weebly.com), with *cabañas*, hammocks ($) and camping. Beware that it gets very windy and sleeping in hammocks can be uncomfortable. Meals are also available. The centre arranges birdwatching trips on foot or by boat (US$5 per person). Take plenty of water if walking. There are several bars/restaurants and two shops on the beach.

# Riohacha

**Where to stay**
Almirante Padilla 1
Arimaca 2
Castillo del Mar 7
Internacional 4

Yalconia del Mar 6

**Restaurants**
El Malecón 1
La Tinaja 2

## BORDER CROSSING
## Colombia–Venezuela

**Paraguachón**
The border is 8 km east of Maicao at Paraguachón. With all the right papers, the crossing is easy.

**Entering Venezuela** There is no Venezuelan consul in Maicao, so if you need a visa, get it in Cartagena or Barranquilla (see page 444). There is also a consulate in Riohacha (Carrera 7, No 3-08, p7-B, T5-727 4076, conve.corha@mppre.gob.ve, Monday-Thursday 0800-1200, 1400-1700, Friday 0800-1300), but it is not always easy to get a visa here, and you should check all requirements for your nationality before arriving. Note that a transit visa will only suffice if you have a confirmed onward ticket to a third country within three days.

*Colectivos*, known as *por puestos* in Venezuela, run from Maicao to Maracaibo, US$10 per person, or there is an infrequent microbus, US$3.50. There are very few buses to Venezuela after 1200. Brasilia bus company has its own security compound, where you can change money, buy bus tickets and food before your journey; non-passengers are not allowed in. *Por puestos* wait here for passengers to Maracaibo; it is a very easy transfer.

**Entering Colombia** If travelling by *por puesto* make sure the driver stops at the Colombian entry post. If not you will have to return later to complete formalities. Minibuses or *busetas* can be caught from the terminal de Maracaibo (T0261-723 9084) to Maicao for US$15, but they only run from 0400 to 0800. *Carritos*, taxis shared with three other passengers, continue to leave Maracaibo until 1500 (US$20 per person). **Migración Colombia**, Calle 5, No 4-48, Riohacha, daily 0800-1200, 1400-1700.

## Riohacha

The city was founded in 1545 by Nicolás Federmann and became a centre for oysters; the pearls were valuable enough to tempt Drake to sack it. Pearling almost ceased during the 18th century and the town was all but abandoned. The town has two good white-sand beaches lined with coconut palms and divided by a long wooden pier. The sea is clean, despite the dark silt stirred up by the waves. A couple of blocks inland is the cathedral, where José Prudencio Padilla is buried. He was born in Riohacha and commanded the Republican fleet that defeated the Spaniards in the Battle of Lago Maracaibo in 1823. There is a statue of him in the central park that bears his name. Also worth visiting are the town's two busy markets: the old market in the centre and a newer one further south. At weekends Riohacha fills up, with bars and music springing up all over the place; it is a good place to take stock before pushing on to Venezuela or into the more remote areas of La Guajira.

## Maicao

The paved Caribbean coastal highway continues from Riohacha inland to Maicao, 78 km, close to the Venezuelan border. Maicao is hot, dusty and has a strong Arab presence, with several mosques and restaurants selling Arabic food. Clothing and white goods make up much of the business, but the city has a reputation for black-market activities. Most commercial premises close early and after dark the streets are unsafe.

**Listings** Riohacha and around *map p209*

## Tourist information

**Dirección de Turismo de Guajira**, C 1, Av de La Marina, No 4-42, T5-727 1015, has some information, but you may find out more if you ask tour operators. The University of the Guajira has an excellent resource centre related to the region and the Wayuú culture (ID is necessary to get in). The provincial website is www.laguajira.gov.co and the municipal site is www.riohacha-laguajira.gov.co.

## Where to stay

### Palomino

**$$ Finca Escondida**
*T315-610 9561, www.chillandsurf colombia.com.*
Double rooms, dorms at US$17.50 pp in high season, also camping and hammock space, direct access to the beach, which has good surf (surfing lessons and board rental available) and beach sports, bar-restaurant, prices rise in high season.

**$ pp The Dreamer on the Beach**
*Playa Donaire, T300-609 7229, www. onthebeach.thedreamerhostel.com.*
Sister hostel to **The Dreamer** in Santa Marta, dorms and private suites ($$$), gardens, pool, restaurant, mini-market and access to activities.

### Riohacha

**$$$ Arimaca**
*C 1, No 8-75, T5-727 3481.*
Impressive high tower with clean, light and spacious rooms, some with reception room, all with balconies and magnificent sea views. There is a fine swimming pool on the 2nd floor, a good restaurant and buffet breakfast is included.

**$$ Castillo del Mar**
*C 9A, No 15-352, T5-727 5043.*
Pleasant hotel by the sea, a bit rough around the edges but very reasonably priced. Large rooms with a/c or fan. Tour operator on site. Recommended.

**$ Almirante Padilla**
*Cra 6 y C 3a, T5-727 2328.*
Crumbling but with character. Has an inviting patio and a restaurant with cheap *almuerzo*. It's clean, friendly, large and very central. Some rooms with a/c.

**$ Internacional**
*Cra 7, No 13-37, T5-727 3483.*
A friendly option down an alleyway off the old market, with a pleasant restaurant on the patio. Free iced water. Recommended.

**$ Yalconia del Mar**
*Cra 7, No 11-26, T5-727 3487.*
Rooms with bath, cheaper with fan, clean, safe, friendly, helpful, halfway between the beach and the bus station.

## Maicao

**$$$-$$ Hotel Maicao Internacional**
*C 12, No 10-90, T5-726 7184.*
Rooms with a/c, plus rooftop pool
and bar. A good option in Maicao,
attentive staff.

**$$ Los Médanos**
*Cra 10, No 11-25, T5-726 7523.*
Large rooms, a bit dark, minibar,
restaurant and disco.

**$$ Maicao Plaza**
*C 10, No 10-28, T5-726 6597.*
Modern, central, with spacious rooms.

## Restaurants

### Riohacha
Many ice cream stalls, juice bars and
small *asados* serving large, cheap
selections of barbecued meat can be
found at the western end of the seafront.
There is also a row of picturesque,
brightly painted huts serving ceviche
and fresh seafood. The eastern end has
more restaurants for sit-down meals.

**$$ El Malecón**
*C 1, No 3-47.*
Good selection of seafood and meats
served in a palm-thatched barn looking
out to sea. There is music and dancing
in the evenings. A good place for
people-watching.

**$$ La Tinaja**
*C 1, No 4-59.*
Excellent seafood in a light, breezy
restaurant. Try the tasty and
substantial *delicias de la casa* rice dish.
Recommended.

## Festivals

### Riohacha
Mar **Festival Francisco el Hombre.**
*Vallenato* festival.

## Shopping

### Riohacha
Good hammocks sold in the new
market, 2 km from town on the
road to Valledupar. The best place
for buying local items is **La Casa
de la Manta Guajira**, Cra 6 y C 12.
Be prepared to bargain.

## What to do

### Riohacha
**Tour operators**
Trips to the Guajira Peninsula are best
arranged in Riohacha where there are
several operators. Tours to Cabo de la
Vela, 1-2 days, usually include Manaure
(salt mines), Uribia, Pilón de Azucar
and El Faro. Afternoon tours to Wayúu
*rancherías* include a typical goat lunch.

**Cabo de la Vela Turismo**, *T5-728 3684,
www.cabodelavela.turismo.co.* Runs tours
throughout the region.
**Comfaguajira**, *T5-727 0204, www.
comfaguajira.com. Mon-Fri 0800-1200,
1400-1700.*
**Kaí Ecotravel**, *Hotel Castillo del Mar, C 9A,
No 15-352, www.kaiecotravel.com.* Based
in Uribia and run by a network of Wayúu
families, this operator organizes 2-day
tours to Cabo de la Vela (US$210 pp),
4-day tours to Parque Natural Nacional
Macuira (US$835 pp) and 3-day tours to
Punta Gallinas (US$545 pp). Prices are
pp for 2 people and include transport,
accommodation and food; discounts for
larger groups.

## Transport

### Riohacha

#### Air

The **José Prudencio Padilla Airport** is south of the town towards Tomarrazón.

There are 2 flights a day to **Bogotá**, 1 hr 35 mins, with **Avianca** (C 7, No 7-04, T727 3624), for connections to other cities.

#### Bus

The main bus terminal is on C 15 (Av El Progreso)/Cra 11. Some *colectivos* for Uribia and the northeast leave from the new market, 2 km southeast on the Valledupar road. It is best to travel from Riohacha in a luxury bus, in the early morning, as these are less likely to be stopped and searched for contraband.

**Brasilia** runs Pullman buses to **Maicao**, frequent service, 1-1½ hrs, US$6.50; also to **Santa Marta**, US$15, 3 hrs, and **Cartagena**, US$33.50, every 30 mins. There are no direct buses to **Cabo de la Vela**; travel to **Uribia** and wait for a jeep (see below).

#### Taxi

**Coopcaribe Taxis** travel throughout the region and can be picked up almost anywhere in town, especially close to the old market area near the **Hotel Internacional** or outside **Drogas La Rebaja**. They charge US$10 to either **Uribia** (1½ hrs) or **Manaure** (1¾ hrs) and leave when full (4 people); be prepared to pay slightly more if there are no other travellers.

### Maicao

#### Bus

There is a bus terminal to the east of town with frequent services to **Riohacha**, US$6.50; **Santa Marta**, 3 hrs, US$21; **Barranquilla**, 4-5 hrs, US$29, and **Cartagena**, 6 hrs, US$40. Those who decide against taking a flight to Venezuela via Panama can opt for a taxi or bus from Riohacha to Maicao and then a *colectivo* to Maracaibo (see box, page 210).

## Guajira Peninsula

**beautiful and remote indigenous outpost**

★Beyond Riohacha to the east is the arid and sparsely inhabited Guajira Peninsula, with its magnificent sunsets. The indigenous peoples here, the Wayúu, fish, tend goats and collect *dividivi* pods from a strangely wind-bent tree (the *Caesalpina coriaria*), which are mainly used for tanning. (Look out for the coloured robes worn by the women.) This is a semi-self governing zone, but increasingly, thanks to government schemes, the Wayúu are also involved in tourism. The local language is Wayuunaiki; beyond Cabo de Vela little Spanish is spoken.

### Manaure and Musichi

Manaure (www.manaure-laguajira.gov.co) is known for its salt flats southwest of the town. Hundreds of workers dig the salt and collect it in wheelbarrows: a bizarre sight against the glaring white background. If you walk along the beach for an hour, past the salt works, there are several lagoons where flamingos gather.

Around 14 km from Manaure in this direction is **Musichi**, a protected area for the flamingos. Note that the birds may be on the other side of the lagoon and difficult to see, so take binoculars. To get there, hire a moto-taxi or rent a bicycle in Manaure. Take plenty of sunblock and water, and remember a torch for returning in the evening.

## Uribia

Uribia is known as the indigenous capital of Colombia, but it doesn't really live up to its name. You can buy authentic local handicrafts by asking around, but it's also full of Venezuelan contraband and has a rough and ready feel to it. There is a **Wayúu Festival** here annually in June at which *alijunas* (white people) are welcome, but ask permission before taking photographs.

### Cabo de la Vela

The journey from Uribia to Cabo de la Vela via Puerto Bolívar is uncomfortable and slow, as passengers are dropped off at their various *rancherías*, but it is also spectacular; the final few kilometres are a bumpy ride across a shimmering, dried-out salt lake that generates mirages. Cabo de la Vela, known as 'Jepirra' in Wayuunaiki, is where the Wayúu believe their souls go after death. The barren landscape of shrubs and cacti only serves to accentuate the colour of the water, which glimmers in a dozen shades of aquamarine. At night, don't forget to look up for spectacular starry skies. In recent years tourism has really taken off here, and there are now more hostels in Cabo de la Vela than in Riohacha itself, all of them following the two-mile bay. There are excursions from Cabo de la Vela to Pilón de Azúcar mountain, with lovely views of the sea, and to a beautiful beach and lighthouse.

### Parque Nacional Natural Macuira

*Entry US$17.50, Colombians US$6, children US$3.75. Registration and 30-min compulsory induction at Nazareth park office, guides US$20.*

Towards the northeast tip of the Guajira Peninsula is the Serranía de Macuira, named after the Makui people, ancestors of the Wayúu. The 25,000-ha park is entirely within the Wayúu reservation and consists of a range of hills over 500 m, with microclimates of their own creating an oasis of tropical forest in the semi-desert. The highest point is **Cerro Palúa**, 865 m, and there are two other peaks over 750 m. Moisture comes mainly from the northeast, which forms clouds in the evening that disperse in the early morning. The average temperature is 29°C and there is 450 mm of mist/rain annually providing water for the streams that disappear into the sand once they reach the plains.

Macuira's remoteness has resulted in some interesting flora and fauna; notable wildlife includes the cardinal bird and 15 species of snake, including coral snakes. There are also Wayúu settlements little affected by outsiders, where the indigenous people cultivate cashew nuts, coconuts and plantains, as well as collecting *dividivi* pods. The rangers are all locals and are very friendly.

## Hammocks

There's no better way to enjoy Colombia's beaches than to relax in a hammock, using conveniently located palm trees as supports. Plenty of places hire them out, but for true comfort it's best to buy your own.

The hammocks developed by the Wayúu are made up of intricately woven threads of cotton that form a crocheted net. These are known as *chinchorros* and are larger than the average hammock, with wrap-around sides that serve as a blanket and elaborate tassels. The best places to buy chinchorros are the market in Riohacha and Uribia's handicraft shops in La Guajira.

The other most common style uses brightly coloured woven cotton or wool to form a large stretch of material. These can be bought in San Jacinto, a couple of hours south of Cartagena, which is the capital of Colombia's hammock industry and the best place to find a bargain. The market in Santa Marta also has a good selection.

To reach the Parque Natural Nacional Macuira you must travel northeast from Uribia along the mineral railway, then either round the coast past Bahía Portete, or direct across the semi-desert, to Nazareth on the east side of the park. There are no tourist facilities anywhere nearby and no public transport, though trucks may take you from Bahía Portete to **Nazareth** (seven to eight hours in the dry season), if you can find one. Nazareth is a Wayúu village and the location of the park office where you must register, pay and undergo an induction before entering the park. Someone may let you stay the night in a hammock here; otherwise, there is camping beside the park office.

Spending a few days exploring the park is a remarkable and rewarding experience. The landscape, usually arid and desolate, turns a bright shade of green after the rainy season and there are gorgeous bays for swimming and chilling. It's also the best place for getting closer to Wayúu culture and traditions. A recommended walk is a visit to the 40-m-high **El Chorro waterfall**, a delightful lush, green area. At the tip of the park, spectacular **Punta Gallinas** is the northernmost point in South America. When the road is bad, it can only be reached by a two- to three-hour boat ride from near Cabo de la Vela, often choppy and very wet. Nearby is **Taroa**, where sand dunes drop directly into the sea. It's a dramatic spot for a swim, but beware the powerful waves and strong currents.

**Tip...**

The Guajira Peninsula is not a place to travel alone; you are strongly advised to join a tour group, but if travelling independently, then parties of three or more are recommended. Always check the situation before setting out. The roads are mostly dirt tracks and can be in very bad condition or even impassable during the wet season. Also remember it is hot; it is easy to get lost; there is limited phone reception and very little water.

## Where to stay

### Manaure and Musichi

**$$ Palaaima**
*Cr 6, No 7-25, T5-717 8455/314-581 6789.*
Comfortable, cool rooms with a/c or fan.
There are always Wayúu locals hanging
around the hotel who are eager to talk
about their culture and traditions.

### Uribia
There are other cheap, somewhat
grotty options.

**$ Hotel Juyasirain**
*Diagonal 2A No 2B-02, T5-717 7284.*
The only slightly more upmarket hotel
in Uribia. Large, light and airy with a
patio restaurant.

### Cabo de la Vela
There are now some 60 hostels along
the beach, all offering roughly the
same set-up for the same cost: fried
fish, coconut rice and a place to sling
a hammock for US$5-10. Try **Playa
Bonita**, in the main cluster of houses
and shops, or **Pujurú**, further up the
beach towards Pilón de Azúcar.

### Parque Nacional Natural Macuira

**$ Luz Mila**
*Punta Gallinas.*
A lonely but friendly little hostel and
restaurant run by the Wayúu, where

**Kai Ecotravel** (see below) has a base for
their tours. Recommended.

## What to do

### Uribia
**Kaí Ecotravel**, *Diagonal 1B, No 8-68,
T5-717 7173/311-436 2830, www.kaieco
travel.com.* Run by a network of Wayúu
families, this operator organizes 2-day
tours to Cabo de la Vela (US$210),
4-day tours to Parque Natural Nacional
Macuira (US$835) and 3-day tours to
Punta Gallinas (US$545). Prices are pp
for 2 people and include transport,
accommodation and food; discounts
for larger groups
**Kaishi**, *T5-717 7306/311-429 6315, www.
kaishitravel.com.* Speak to Andrés
Delgado. Jeep tours around La Guajira.

## Transport

### Manaure and Musichi
Early morning *busetas* to **Uribia**,
30 mins, US$3.

### Uribia
All transport leaves from the market.
*Busetas* to **Maicao**, 1 hr. Also *busetas*
to **Puerto Bolívar**, daily until 1400
(fewer on Sun), for onward transport
to **Cabo de la Vela** (US$6-10 for the
whole journey). The journey is slow
as passengers are dropped off at their
various *rancherías*.

# San Andrés
## & Providencia

San Andrés and Providencia are destinations most Colombians dream about visiting at least once in their lifetime. Closer to Nicaragua than to the Colombian mainland – there is a running dispute between the two countries over sovereignty – these Caribbean islands have what locals have dubbed 'the sea of seven colours', though it often seems like more. At 32 km in length, the Old McBean Lagoon barrier reef off Providencia is the third largest in the world. The waters around this archipelago play host to a variety of marine life, and the clarity of the sea makes this one of the best diving destinations in the Caribbean. In 2000, UNESCO declared the archipelago a World Biosphere Reserve, christened 'The Seaflower'.

San Andrés and Providencia share a coastline rich in coral reefs, white-sand cays and waters of extraordinary colours, but are in fact very different. San Andrés, the larger island, is a popular mass tourism destination, replete with resort hotels and discos. Providencia has quietly observed its big sister's development, decided it does not want to follow the same path, and has put in place certain restrictions to halt the encroachment of package tourism. *Colour map 1, inset.*

# Essential San Andrés and Providencia

## Finding your feet

The islands are 770 km north of continental Colombia, 849 km southwest of Jamaica and 240 km east of Nicaragua. A cheap way to visit San Andrés is on a package from Bogotá or another major city, with flights, accommodation and food included; look for supplements in the Colombian newspapers and adverts on the internet. Alternatively, you may wish to opt for a cheap airfare and choose where to stay when you get there. On arrival in San Andrés, you must buy a tourist card, US$22.50; it is also valid for Providencia, so don't lose it. You must also have an onward or return ticket. Visitors to Providencia can arrive by air from San Andrés (20 minutes) or by sea on launches and boats that ferry goods over. Beware that the sea can be choppy on this trip.

## Getting around

Cars, motorbikes, bicycles and golf buggies can all be hired on San Andres, but they may be in poor condition. Buses ply the route along the east coast and there are taxis, too. On Providencia, transport is provided by *chivas* and *colectivos* or by hiring a moped or golf buggy. Boats go to offshore cays.

## When to visit

The islands have a typical Caribbean climate that includes hurricane season from roughly June to November. The best weather is from December to April, but these months also attract the largest crowds.

## San Andrés and around
**popular tourist island**

San Andrés is a coral island, 11 km long, rising at its highest to 120 m. The town, commercial centre, major hotel sector and airport are at the northern end. A good view of the town can be seen from El Cliff. San Andrés is a popular, safe and local holiday destination for Colombians.

### Sights

San Andrés and Providencia are famous in Colombia for their different styles of music: the local form of calypso, soca, reggae and church music, as well as schottische, quadrille, polka and mazurka, the musical legacies of the various European communities that settled here. A number of good local groups perform on the islands and in Colombia. Look out for concerts at the **Coliseo San Luís** on the east coast and the cultural centre in San Andrés town. There is also a **Museo Casa Isleña** ⓘ *Av Circunvalar Km 5, daily 0900-1800, US$3.50*, housed in a small historic building with displays relating to the culture of the island, including food, music and dance.

The eastern side of the island has beautiful cays and beaches backed by hotels and resorts; perhaps the best is at **San Luís** and **Bahía Sonora** (Sound Bay). If you can tear yourself away from the sand, visit **Hoyo Soplador** at the southern tip of the island, a geyser-like hole through which the sea spouts into the air when the wind is in the right direction. The west coast is less spoilt, but there are no beaches on this side. Instead there is **El Cove**, the island's deepest anchorage, and **Cueva de Morgan** (Morgan's Cave), reputedly a hiding place for pirate's treasure, which is penetrated by the sea through an underwater passage. Next to Cueva de Morgan is a **Pirate Museum** ⓘ *US$5*, with exhibitions telling the history of the coconut, lots of paraphernalia salvaged from wrecks around the island and a replica pirate ship. About 1 km south of Cueva de Morgan is **West View** ⓘ *daily 0900-1830*, an excellent place to see marine life as the sea is very clear. There is a small jetty, with a diving board and slide, and a restaurant opposite the entrance.

From El Cove, you can cross the centre of the island back to town. Here you will find some life as it was before San Andrés became a tourist destination, with clapboard houses and traditional music. You'll also pass **La Laguna**, a freshwater lake 30 m deep, home to many birds and surrounded by palm and mango trees. Just to the north is **La Loma**, the highest point on the island at 120 m. On the town side of La Loma is the first **Baptist Church** to be built on the island (1847), which serves as a beacon to shipping. The church has a Sunday service 1000-1200 with gospel singing. If you take a turning just before the church you will reach the **Mirador Escalona**, a lookout point on someone's unfinished roof (US$1.50), from which there are spectacular views of the island.

## 1 San Andrés Island

### Offshore cays

Boats leave from Tonino's Marina or from Muelle Casa de la Cultura on Avenida Newell in San Andrés between 0930 and 1100 daily for El Acuario and Haynes Cay, and continue to Johnny Cay (frequently spelt Jhonny) in the afternoon (US$10), returning at 1530. **El Acuario** has crystalline water and is a good place to snorkel and see eagle and manta rays. You can wade across the water to **Haynes Cay** where there is good food and a reggae bar at **Bibi's Place** ⓘ *daily 0930-1530*. **Johnny Cay** has a white beach where parties are held every Sunday. These are popular tours; if you want to avoid the crowds a good option is to hire a private boat (US$150 for the day) and do the tour in reverse.

Other cays and islets in the archipelago are **Bolívar**, **Albuquerque**, **Algodón** (included in the Sunrise Park development in San Andrés), **Rocky**, the **Grunt**, **Serrana**, **Serranilla** and **Quitasueño**.

**Where to stay** 🛏
Casa Harb **1**
Sunset **2**

**Restaurants** 🍴
Bibi's Place **1**

➡ **San Andrés maps**
1 San Andrés island, page 219
2 San Andrés town, page 222

# BACKGROUND
## San Andrés and Providencia

Columbus spotted the islands on his fourth trip to the Caribbean in 1503. Their early colonial history was dominated by the conflicts between Spain and England, though the Dutch also occupied Providencia for some years. English Puritans arrived on Providencia from Bermuda and England in 1629 and later moved to San Andrés. The English left in 1641, but Creole English remained the dominant language until recent times and is still widely spoken. Surnames such as Whittaker, Hooker, Archbold, Robinson, Howard and Newell are also common. Providencia later became a pirate colony, shared between the Dutch and the English, before it was taken by the Spanish and assigned to the Vice Royalty of New Granada (modern-day Colombia) in 1803. In 1818 French Corsair Louis-Michel Aury successfully invaded Providencia and declared it part of the United States of Argentina and Chile, using it to capture Spanish cargo to bolster the burgeoning Latin American Independence movement. Finally, in 1822 San Andrés, Providencia and Santa Catalina were incorporated into the newly independent state of Gran Colombia.

The inhabitants of the islands are mostly the descendants of Jamaican slaves brought over by English pirates such as Henry Morgan, although the frequent comings and goings of English, Dutch, French and Spanish settlers over the years has led to an extraordinary genealogical mix. Today, about 50% of the population of San Andrés is made up of immigrants from mainland Colombia, and there are also Lebanese and Turkish communities. Immigration is less pronounced in Providencia. The islands' proximity to Nicaragua (just 240 km west) has led that country to claim them from Colombia in the past. Battleships now patrol San Andrés to guard against any invasion.

### Diving

Diving off San Andrés is very good; the depth varies from three to 30 m, visibility from 30 to 60 m. There are three types of site: walls of seaweed and minor coral reefs; large groups of different types of coral, and underwater plateaux with much marine life. It is possible to dive in 70% of the insular platform. The **Pared Azul (Blue Wall)** is excellent for deep-water diving. **Black Coral Net** and **Morgan's Sponge** are other good sites.

### Listings San Andrés *maps p219 and p222*

### Tourist information

Staff at the **tourist office**, Av Newball, opposite **Restaurante La Regatta**, T8-512 5058, securismosai@yahoo. com, Mon-Fri 0800-1200, 1400-1800, are helpful and speak English. They can provide maps and hotel lists. There's also a **tourist kiosk** at the end of Av 20 de Julio, across from the sea, daily 0800-2000. The municipal website is www.sanandres.gov.co and the island's newspaper, the *San Andrés Hoy*, www.sanandreshoy.com, has some information in Spanish.

## Where to stay

Hotels quote rates per person, but we list prices for double rooms. Prices include half board, but most can be booked without meals. Most raise prices by 20-30% on 15 Dec. This also applies to Providencia. The **Decameron** group has 5 hotels on San Andrés, www.decameron.com.

### $$$$ Casa Harb
*C 11, No 10-83, La Rocosa, T8-512 6348, www.casaharb.com.*
Just outside town, this boutique hotel takes its inspiration from the Far East and is the most stylish location on the island. Each room is individually decorated with antique furniture. The baths, made of solid granite, are enormous. A former family home, this mansion has an infinity pool and offers home-cooked meals.

### $$$$ Lord Pierre
*Av Colombia, No 1B-106, T8-512 7541, www.lordpierre.com.*
It boasts a magnificent pier on the tip of the *malecón*, but some of the services are a bit dated. Rooms are large with heavy furniture.

### $$$ Portobelo
*Av Colombia, No 5A-69, T8-512 7008, www.portobelohotel.com.*
Occupies a couple of buildings on western end of the *malecón*. Rooms have large beds, a/c and cable TV. Breakfast included. ($$$$ in high season).

### $$$ Sunset Hotel
*Ctra Circunvalar, Km 13, T8-513 0420, www.sunsethotelspa.com.*
On the western side of the island, this is the perfect place to stay if you want to do some serious diving – or just want to escape the crowds. It has bright, fresh rooms with high ceilings, all set around a saltwater swimming pool. With a restaurant serving a mixture of international and regional food in a typical clapboard house and a dive shop next door, this is one of the best places to unwind in San Andrés.

### $$ Hernando Henry
*Av Las Américas, No 4-84, T8-512 3416, www.hotelhernandohenry.com.*
At the back of town, this hotel has shoddy but passable rooms. TV and laundry service. Rooms are significantly cheaper with fan.

### $$ La Posada D'Lulú
*Av Antioquia, No 2-28, T8-512 2919/523 6308.*
This brightly coloured hostel with its clean and comfortable rooms is one of the best mid-range options in town. There are 2 apartments to rent for longer stays and an excellent restaurant serving home-cooked food. Recommended.

### $$ Posada Doña Rosa
*Av Las Américas con Aeropuerto, T8-512 3649, www.posadarosa.blogspot.com.*
A 2-min walk from the airport, this is a reasonable and economical option. It has clean rooms with private bathrooms and a small patio with potted plants. There is a kitchen and TV room, and it's a short walk from the beach. Also has 2 apartments to rent.

### $$-$ pp El Viajero Hostel
*Av 20 de Julio No 3A-122, T8-512 7497, www.elviajero hostels.com/hostel-san-andres.*
A member of the South American El Viajero hostel chain. It has private rooms and dorms (US$16 per bed) all with ensuite bath, a/c and safe

boxes. Breakfast included in the price, bicycles can be hired, rooftop bar and scuba certification courses. There's a tourist office at reception that books all tours and excursions. Like its sister hostel in Cartagena, El Viajero is for the party crowd.

## Restaurants

**$$$-$$ La Regatta**
*Av Newball, next to Club Náutico, T8-512 0437, www.restaurantelaregatta.com.*
Seafood restaurant on a pier, fine reputation.

**$$$-$$ Margherita e Carbonara**
*Av Colombia, No 1-93, opposite the Lord Pierre Hotel.*
Italian-owned restaurant decorated with photographs from Italian films. Good pizzas.

**$$ Bibi's Place**
*Haynes Caye.*
Reggae bar and restaurant on cay next to **El Acuario** serving seafood, including crab and lobster. Organizes full moon parties and civil and rasta weddings.

**$$ Niko's**
*Av Colombia, No 1-93.*
Bills itself as a seafood restaurant though its steaks are actually better. Lovely setting by the water.

## Festivals

**Apr Festival del Cangrejo.** Celebrating the crab and all the many ways it can be prepared to eat, plus music and dancing.
**20 Jul Independence,** which incorporates a **Festival del Mar.**
**Late Oct Green Moon Festival.** A popular music festival that has been revived after several years' absence.
**End-Nov Reinado del Coco.** The crowning of the Coconut Queen coincides with the festival of the island's patron saint.

## What to do

### Canopying
**Canopy La Loma,** *Vía La Loma-Barrack.* A site at the top of the hill in San Andrés. 3 'flights' over the trees (450 m, 300 m and 200 m above sea level) with spectacular views out to sea. Good safety precautions and equipment.

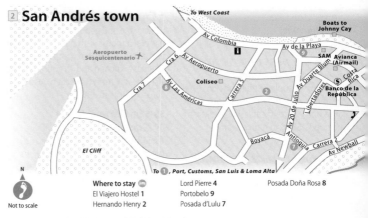

**2 San Andrés town**

Not to scale

| Where to stay | Lord Pierre 4 | Posada Doña Rosa 8 |
| El Viajero Hostel 1 | Portobelo 9 | |
| Hernando Henry 2 | Posada d'Lulu 7 | |

## Diving

**Banda Dive Shop**, *Hotel Lord Pierre, Local 102, T8-513 1080, www.bandadiveshop. com*. PADI qualified, offers various courses. Fast boat and good equipment. **Sharky Dive Shop**, *Ctra Circunvalar Km 13, T8-512 0651, www.sharkydiveshop. com*. Next to **Sunset Hotel**, Sharky's has good equipment and excellent, English-speaking guides. PADI qualifications and a beginners' course held in the Sunset's saltwater pool.

## Watersports and boat trips

**Cooperativa Lancheros**, *on the beach in San Andrés town*. Fishing trips, windsurfing, jet skiing and kitesurfing. Snorkelling equipment can be hired for US$5. **Galeón Morgan**, *Centro Comercial New Point Plaza, T8-512 8787*. Boat tours to El Acuario.

Transport

## Air

The airport is 15 mins' walk from town. Buses to the **centre** and **San Luis** go from across the road; a taxi is US$5.50-7.50, a *colectivo*, US$0.90.

➡ **San Andrés maps**
1 San Andrés island, page 219
2 San Andrés town, page 222

**Restaurants** ⦿          Niko's **3**
La Regatta **1**
Margherita e Carbonara **2**

It is essential to confirm flights to guarantee a seat. Schedules change frequently. To **Providencia,** twice daily with **Satena** (San Andrés, T8-512 1403; Providencia, T8-514 9257) and **Searca** (booked through Decameron); bookable only in San Andrés. Flights to **Bogotá**, **Cali**, **Medellín** and **Cartagena** with **Avianca** (Av Colón, Edif Onaissi local 107, T8-512 3212; airport T8-512 3216); **Satena** and **Searca. Copa** (Av Newball, No 4-141, Torre Sunrise Beach, local 125-B6) has a daily flight to **Panama City**.

## Boat

Cruise ships and tours visit San Andrés but there are no other official passenger services to the island by sea.

To **Providencia**, **Catamaran Sensation**, www.catamaranelsensation.com, sails Mon, Wed, Fri, Sun 0730, returning at 1500, US$32.50 one way, 3¼ hrs. Alternatively, cargo boats make the journey 3 times a week, 4 uncomfortable hrs, US$65 (return); they usually leave at 0600-0700, arriving at 1130. *Miss Isabel*, *Doña Olga* and *Raziman* make the trip regularly; speak directly to the captain at the port on Bahía San Andrés.

## Bus and taxi

Buses run every 15 mins along the eastern side of the island, US$0.90, and more often at night and during the holidays. Taxis around the island cost US$15-20, but in town fares double after 2200.

## Vehicle and bicycle hire

Cars, motorbikes, bikes and golf buggies can all be hired, up to US$40 per day. A licence is required to hire cars and motorbikes, and a passport may be required as deposit.

Providencia, also called Old Providence, 80 km to the north-northeast of San Andrés, is 7 km long and 3.5 km wide. The island is more mountainous, rising to 360 m, and considerably more verdant than San Andrés due to its volcanic origin. There are waterfalls, and the land drops steeply into the sea in places.

Providencia is striving to retain its cultural identity. Hotels must be constructed in the typical clapboard style of the island and cannot be built higher than two storeys; mainland operators cannot manage them directly, but must work in

# Providencia

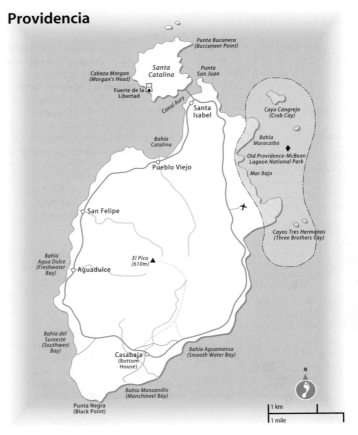

Punta Bucanera
(Buccaneer Point)

Santa Catalina

Punta San Juan

Cabeza Morgan
(Morgan's Head)

Fuerte de la Libertad

Canal Aury

Santa Isabel

Cayo Cangrejo
(Crab Cay)

Bahía Catalina

Bahía Maracaibo

Old Providence-McBean
Lagoon National Park

Pueblo Viejo

Mar Bajo

San Felipe

Bahía Agua Dulce
(Freshwater Bay)

El Pico
(610m)

Aguadulce

Cayos Tres Hermanos
(Three Brothers Cay)

Bahía del Suroeste
(Southwest Bay)

Casabaja
(Bottom House)

Bahía Aguamansa
(Smooth Water Bay)

Bahía Manzanillo
(Manchineel Bay)

Punta Negra
(Black Point)

N

1 km
1 mile

## ON THE ROAD

### The black crabs of Providencia

With the arrival of the first rains between April and June, Providencia is the scene of a spectacular natural phenomenon. Each night during the wet season thousands of black crabs (*Gecarcinus lateralis*) descend from the forests of High Hill and release their eggs in the waters between South West Bay and Freshwater, wriggling their abdomens in the surf to deposit their eggs. The hatchlings are born in the sea and return to the hills one month later.

During the migration the road that encircles the island is closed to traffic, thus allowing the crabs free access to the beaches without the risk of being run over. Coralina (www.coralina.gov.co), the government's environmental agency on the archipelago, has banned the capture and eating of crabs during the breeding season and anyone caught disobeying the ban risks a heavy fine equivalent to three months of the minimum wage.

Many of the islanders make a living from crab fishing, but during this time the hunters turn protectors, as they are employed as enforcers of the ban, thus ensuring that Providencia's black crab population will continue to thrive.

partnership with local owners; only locals are allowed to buy property on the island, and outsiders can stay no longer than six months at a time.

### Parque Nacional Natural Old Providence – McBean Lagoon

In 1996 part of the east coast and offshore reefs and coral islands were declared a national park (entry US$7.75 for non-nationals). **Cayo Cangrejo** (Crab Cay) is a beautiful place for swimming and snorkelling; at the southern end of the national park is **Cayos Tres Hermanos** (Three Brothers Cays). Recommended diving spots on the Old McBean Lagoon reef are **Manta's Place**, a good place to see manta rays; **Felipe's Place** where there is a submerged figure of Christ; and **Stairway to Heaven**, which has a large wall of coral and big fish.

The land position includes Iron Wood Hill (150 m), whose tree species include cockspur (*Acacia colinsii*), which has large conical-shaped needles that are home to a species of ant (*Pseudo-myrmex ferruginea*) with a very painful sting.

In the south of the island, there are superb views from **Casabaja** (Bottom House) or **Aguamansa** (Smooth Water). From here, a climb to the summit of El Pico (610 m) will take about one hour and cost US$15 with a guide. You will see relics of the fortifications built on the island during its disputed ownership.

### Santa Catalina

Boat trips can be made to Santa Catalina, an old pirate lair separated from Providencia by a channel cut for better defence. Santa Catalina is joined to the main island by a 100-m wooden bridge, known as the **Puente de los Amantes** (Lovers' Bridge). An ATM is tucked away just before the bridge, on the road to Santa Catalina. On the west side of Santa Catalina are the ruins of an old fort, built by the English to defend their pirate colony. Formerly known as Fort Warwick, it was rechristened **Fuerte de la Libertad** after the island was retaken by the Spanish in the 17th century. The fort still has the original canons and it is rumoured that there is a secret cave below that was used by Henry Morgan to escape to the sea (probably untrue). Beyond the fort is **Playa del Fuerte**, a fine beach, excellent for snorkelling, with caves with air chambers and lots of starfish. Further still is a rock formation called **Morgan's Head**; seen from the side it looks like a man's profile. The path beyond Morgan's Head leads through thick forest to the top of the mountain and an abandoned house formerly belonging to a drug trafficker.

## Beaches

The largest, most attractive and least developed beach is **Bahía Manzanillo** (Manchineel Bay) at the southern end of the island, which is named after the *manzanillo* trees found on its edges. (The fruit is like a miniature apple; it is sweet-smelling but has an acid taste and is poisonous.) It has a couple of restaurants, including **Roland's Roots Bar**. A good walk over Manchineel Hill from Bottom House (Casa Baja) will take you 1.5 km through tropical forest, with fine views of the sea, to **Bahía del Suroeste** (South West Bay); many types of bird can seen on the route, along with iguanas and blue lizards. South West Bay is fringed by almond trees, palms and has bottle-green water. On Saturday afternoons the local boys hold bareback horse races here. To the north, **Bahía Agua Dulce** (Freshwater Bay) has a small strip of beach and several sea-front hotels. Between Aguadulce and San Felipe is **Alan's Bay**, which is very secluded and seldom visited.

## Listings Providencia *map p224*

### Tourist information

The **tourist office** is in the Centro Administrativo Aury, T8-514 8054.

### Where to stay

Rooms can be rented at affordable prices in local houses (*posadas nativas*). The Decameron group, www.decameron.com, represents 5 properties on the island, including **Cabañas Miss Elma**, T8-514 8229, www.hotelmisselma.com and **Cabañas Miss Mary**, T8-514 8454, www.hotelmissmary.com at Aguadulce.

$$$$ Deep Blue Hotel
*Maracaibo Bay, T8-514 8423,*
*www.hoteldeepblue.com.*
Luxury 'boutique' hotel set in tropical forest.It offers splendid views of Crab Caye and the Caribbean. There's a restaurant by the sea and visitors get complimentary use of the hotel's sea kayaks. It has an infinity pool and staff can arrange scuba diving and other excursions. Good sustainability and environmental policies. Recommended.

$$$ Posada del Mar
*Aguadulce, T8-514 8168, www.*
*posadadelmarprovidencia.com.*

Pink and purple clapboard house with comfortable rooms, each with a terrace and hammock looking onto the bay. The sea laps at the edge of the garden. Has cable TV, a/c, minibar and hot water. Recommended.

### $$$ Sirius
*South West Bay, T8-514 8213, www.siriushotel.net.*
Large, colourful house set back from the beach, run by a Swiss family. The rooms are large and light, some have balconies with hammocks. Kitchen available for guests. Also dive centre, kayaks, wakeboarding, horse riding, massage. The owner speaks German, Italian and English. Half-board and diving packages available.

### $$$ Sol Caribe Providencia
*Agua Dulce, www.solarhoteles.com.*
Bright chain hotel offering 2- to 5-night packages, with pool, sea views, a/c, TV, fridge.

### $$ Hotel Old Providence
*Diagonal Alcaldía Municipal, Santa Isabel, T8-514 8691, www. hoteloldprovidence.com.*
Above supermarket **Erika**, rooms are basic but clean and have a/c, cable TV, fridge and private bathroom.

## Restaurants

Local specialities include crab soup and *rondón*, a mix of fish, conch, yucca and dumplings, cooked in coconut milk. Corn ice cream is also popular – it tastes a little like vanilla but sweeter. Breadfruit, a grapefruit-sized fruit with a taste similar to potato, is the archipelago's official fruit.

As well as hotel restaurants, good places include: **Arturo**, on Suroeste beach, next to Miss Mary, and **Café Studio**, between Agua Dulce and Suroeste, which serves great pies and spaghetti.

### $$ Caribbean Place (Donde Martín)
*Aguadulce.*
*Bogoteño* chef Martín Quintero arrived for a brief stay in 1989 and has never left. He uses local ingredients. Specialities include lobster in crab sauce, fillet of fish in ginger, and corn ice cream.

## Shopping

**Arts and Crafts Café**, *Agua Dulce, T8-514 8297.* French owners sell local crafts and delicious home-made cookies and ice-cream.

## What to do

### Diving
**Felipe Diving**, *South West Bay, T851 8775, www.felipediving.com.* Mini and full courses, also rents snorkel equipment, can arrange lodging. Owner Felipe Cabeza even has a diving spot on the reef named after him. Warmly recommended. See also **Hotel Sirius**, above. PADI qualifications.

### Snorkelling and boat trips
Snorkelling equipment can be hired from numerous outlets or on board. Day tours are arranged through hotels around the island, stopping typically at Cayo Cangrejo to swim and snorkel. Other recommended snorkelling sites include the waters around Santa Catalina, where there are many caves to explore as well as **Morgan's Head** and lots of starfish; **Hippie's Place** on the northwest coast, which has a little bit of everything; and **El Faro** (The Lighthouse), at the end of the reef before it drops into deep sea, some 14 km from Providencia.

### Tour operators

Body Contact, *Aguadulce, T8-514 8283*. Owner Jennifer Archbold organizes excursions, fishing and hiking trips, currency exchange, accommodation, and more. Recommended.

## Transport

*Chivas* (brightly coloured buses) circle the island at more or less regular intervals; the standard fare is US$2. *Colectivos* can also be found on the island and charge much the same. Agua Dulce is 10 mins by motor taxi (US$1) from the centre or a 1-hr walk. Suroeste is a 20-min walk from Agua Dulce. Mopeds and golf buggies are available for hire (up to US$40 per day).

# Northwest Colombia

**an intoxicating mixture of diverse landscapes and people**

*Paisas*, as people from Antioquia are known, are enterprising individuals, who have made this corner of Colombia the country's industrial heartland. They are known for their distinctive accent, gregarious nature and generous hospitality.

Their boundless optimism has seen Medellín, for so long associated with drugs and violence, undergo an extraordinary transformation into a city buzzing with new ideas, art and culture. Outside Medellín are delightful *paisa* villages, such as Santa Fe de Antioquia.

To the west, the department of Chocó could not be more different. This area's relentless rainfall and dense jungles have hampered attempts to build any significant roads, and, as a result, it is one of the poorest places economically but one of the richest culturally. The population is proud of its African heritage and distinctive music. Bahía Solano and Nuquí boast beautiful, untouched beaches, as well as a chance to see one of the great whale migrations.

South of Medellín, the Zona Cafetera is Colombia's main coffee-producing region. Surrounding the three main cities – Manizales, Pereira and Armenia – are delightful fincas, pretty villages, banana groves and coffee plantations. Moreover, the icy peaks of Los Nevados, the wax palms of the Valle de Cocora, and the birdlife at the Río Blanco reserve make this an excellent destination for nature lovers.

**Best** for
Coffee ■ Landscapes ■ Wildlife

# Footprint
## picks

★ **Nightlife in Medellín**, page 252

Learn to dance the tango in a back-street bar.

★ **Medellín's Flower Festival**, page 253

Soak up the sights and smells of this extraordinary floral event.

★ **Metrocable**, page 257

Ride Medellín's cable cars and discover their effect on the social fabric of the city.

★ **El Peñol**, page 259

Climb the monolithic rock.

★ **Zona Cafetera**, page 277

Stay on a coffee finca to learn about Colombia's black gold.

★ **Los Nevados**, page 291

Trek among snow-covered volcanic peaks.

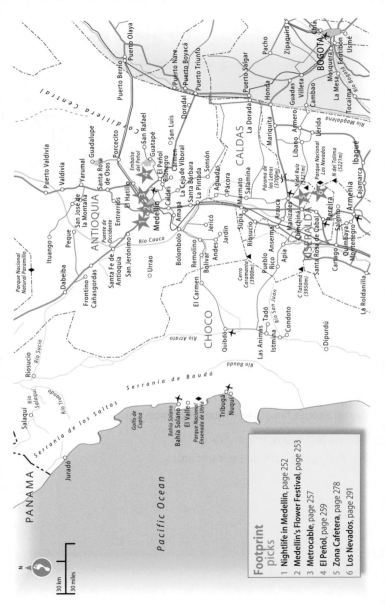

## Footprint picks

1 Nightlife in Medellín, page 252
2 Medellín's Flower Festival, page 253
3 Metrocable, page 257
4 El Peñol, page 259
5 Zona Cafetera, page 278
6 Los Nevados, page 291

# Medellín

Medellín, capital of Antioquia Department, is a dynamic, contemporary city, considered by many to be the engine of Colombia. Previously the home and headquarters of notorious drug-trafficker Pablo Escobar, Medellín has since shaken off its association with drugs and violence in what is one of the most remarkable turnarounds in Latin America. Medellín is now a fresh, vibrant and prosperous city, known for its progressive social politics, art, culture and partying. It is one of the main industrial cities of Colombia, and its inhabitants are known for their canny business sense as well as the pride they take in their city.

In the centre, the new has driven out much of the old and few colonial buildings remain. However, many large new buildings incorporate modern works of art which, together with plazas and parks, monuments and sculptures, make for an interesting walking tour. Music, arts and gastronomy festivals attract many visitors, and the flower festival, the *Desfile de Silleteros*, in August is the most spectacular parade in Colombia. *Colour map 2, B3.*

# Essential Medellín

## Finding your feet

Note that maps of the city are not generally available in shops; try the tourist office or the **Instituto Geográfico Agustín Codazzi** in the basement of the Fundación Ferrocarril building, Carrera 52, No 42-43, T4-381 0561, www.igac.gov.co, Monday-Friday 0730-1545.

### Streets

Medellín's central streets have names as well as numbers. Our maps show both numbers and names, but in addresses we give the Calle (C) and Carrera (Cra) numbers only for easy reference. Particularly important are: Carrera 46, part of the inner ring road, which has several names but is known popularly as 'Avenida Oriental'; Carrera 80/Carrera 81/Diagonal 79, the outer ring road to the west, which is called 'La Ochenta' throughout; Calle 51/52, east of the centre is 'La Playa'; and Calle 33, which crosses the Río Medellín to become Calle 37, is still called 'La Treinta y Tres'.

## Getting around

The best way to get around the city is by metro, which serves the three main sectors of Medellín: centre, south and west. It is efficient and safe; most of the track in the centre is elevated and none of it is underground, so you can get a good overview of the city. A single ticket, US$1 is valid for the whole network, including the three Metrocable (cable car) lines. Town bus services are marginally cheaper and are smart and comfortable, but slower because of the volume of traffic. *Colectivos* operate on certain main routes, US$0.75-0.80. There are plenty of taxis. Pasaje Junín (Carrera 49) is pedestrianized from Parque de Bolívar to Parque San Antonio (Calle 46). This gives walkers pleasant relief from traffic in the busy heart of the city. If driving in Medellín, check for rules that restrict the use of hire cars.

## When to go

Known as 'The City of Eternal Spring', Medellín has a pleasant, temperate climate: warm during the day and cool in the evening. It is often cloudy, however, and rain can come at any time over the Cauca valley from Chocó, which is only 100 km to the west. The city's festivals draw many visitors from the rest of Colombia and abroad.

## Time required

Three to four days is enough to see the best of the city and its surroundings.

## Weather Medellín

| Month | Temp (high) | Temp (low) | Rainfall |
|---|---|---|---|
| January | 26°C | 17°C | 50mm |
| February | 26°C | 18°C | 60mm |
| March | 26°C | 18°C | 100mm |
| April | 26°C | 18°C | 180mm |
| May | 26°C | 18°C | 190mm |
| June | 26°C | 18°C | 130mm |
| July | 26°C | 17°C | 110mm |
| August | 26°C | 17°C | 130mm |
| September | 26°C | 17°C | 150mm |
| October | 25°C | 17°C | 200mm |
| November | 25°C | 17°C | 140mm |
| December | 25°C | 17°C | 80mm |

Medellín (population 2,700,000) is located at 1495 m in the comparatively narrow Aburrá valley surrounded by high mountain barriers of the Cordillera Central in nearly all directions. The built-up metropolitan area now extends from Copacabana in the north to Sabaneta in the south, more than 25 km. The city is centred around the old and new cathedrals, the former on Parque Berrío and the latter overlooking Parque de Bolívar. The main commercial area is three blocks away on Carrera 46, with shopping and hotels throughout the area. In the south, El Poblado has become an upmarket commercial and residential area with many of the best hotels, restaurants, bars and nightclubs, especially around Parque Lleras, known as the Zona Rosa. Also favoured is the area west of the centre between Cerro El Volador and the Universidad Pontificia Bolivariana. Around Carrera 70 and Calle 44 are busy commercial and entertainment sectors with many new hotels, shopping centres and the huge Atanasio Girardot sports stadium nearby.

## Plaza de las Esculturas and San Benito
*Metro Parque de Berrío.*

The focus of the city is the **Plaza de las Esculturas** (also known as Plaza Botero, Calle 52 y Carrera 52), which has 23 sculptures donated by Fernando Botero, Colombia's leading contemporary artist, as well as two fountains designed by him. The sensuous pieces depicting rotund characters invite visitors to touch them. On the north side of the plaza is **El Palacio de la Cultura Rafael Uribe**, an extraordinary Gothic building, built by Belgian architect Agustín Goovaerts between 1929 and 1937. It was formerly the governor's office and is now a cultural centre and art gallery (free entry). Opposite is the **Museo de Antioquia** ⓘ *Cra 52, No 52-43, T4-251 3636, www.museode antioquia.co, Mon-Sat 1000-1730, Sun and hols 1000-1630, US$5.* It has contemporary pictures and sculptures, including the best collection of works by Botero, and a room of paintings by Francisco Antonio Cano. There's an auditorium and film screenings, as well as a good gift shop selling clothes by up-and-coming Colombian fashion designers, postcards and *molas* (colourful, painted fabrics).

The oldest church in the centre of Medellín is believed to be the **Iglesia de la Veracruz**, originally started in 1682 by early Spanish settlers. It was only finally completed around the end of the 18th century. Pablo Chávez was commissioned to decorate the interior and the main altar was brought directly from Spain. It has an attractive *calicanto*-style façade. In the square outside, there is a statue of Atanasio Girardot, a hero of the War of Independence.

The area west of Plaza Botero, especially Calle 55, is increasingly seedy with down-and-outs, drug addicts,

> **Tip...**
> Travellers should take the same safety precautions as they would in any large city, particularly at night. Medellín is, nevertheless, a friendly place. For all police services: T123.

prostitutes and homeless people. It has an edgy feel even during the day. However, there are two churches that are worth a visit in this area: **San Juan de Dios**, in colonial style, and **Iglesia de San Benito**, which was founded in about 1685, but whose present baroque style dates from 1802.

## 1 Medellín

## Parque de Berrío and La Candelaria
*Metro Parque de Berrío.*

Three blocks from Plaza Botero, **Parque de Berrío** is bounded on one side by the **Señora de la Candelaria** church. The original building on this site dated

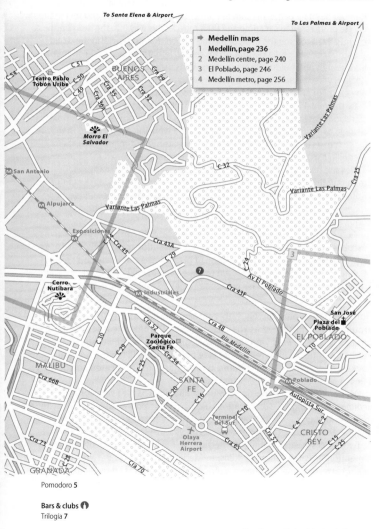

Pomodoro **5**

Bars & clubs
Trilogía **7**

## ON THE ROAD

### Pablo Escobar

Pablo Emilio Escobar Gaviria, one of the world's most notorious outlaws, was born in 1949 into a middle-class family in the Antioquian town of Rionegro. Rumour has it he began his criminal career stealing tombstones and selling them on. He progressed to car crime and then muscled his way into the drug business, eventually becoming the head of the most powerful drug cartel in the world.

Escobar developed a reputation for casual, lethal violence, often kidnapping his enemies and holding them for ransom. His trademark technique for dealing with the authorities became known as *plata o plomo* (cash or lead); any judge or official who refused his bribes was shot.

By the mid-1980s his drug organization was so lucrative that he owned 19 residences in Medellín alone, each with its own heliport, as well as boats, planes, banks and properties throughout the world. In 1989, Forbes magazine listed him as the seventh richest man on the planet, estimating that the Medellín cartel was pulling in US$30 billion a year.

Despite his brutal methods, he was incredibly popular. A master at manipulating public opinion, he actively cultivated an image as the '*paisa* Robin Hood', raising money to build roads and put up electricity lines, build roller-skating rinks, football pitches and even a housing development for the poor, known as Barrio Pablo Escobar.

At the height of his popularity he ran and was voted into Congress. But Escobar's forays into public life also brought attention to his nefarious activities. Following the assassination of presidential candidate Luis Carlos Galán (in which Escobar is believed to have been involved), President César Gaviria ordered his arrest. He went on the run for several years, using a string

---

from the latter part of the 17th century. The present church was finished around 1767 and served as the city's cathedral from its consecration in 1776 until 1931. The towers were built five years later and the cupola in 1860; the clock was donated by Tyrell Moore (see below) in 1890. It has a fine flat-roofed nave and interesting altar gilding by local artisans dedicated to the patron saint of Medellín.

Overlooking Parque Berrío is **Museo Filatélico** ⓘ *4th floor of Banco de la República building, C 50, No 50-21, T4-576 7402, Mon-Fri 0800-1700*, with an interesting stamp collection and special displays connected with postal services. There is also a music room with concerts on video in the afternoons.

Two blocks east of Parque de Berrio, the modern **Edificio Coltejer** deserves a mention. It is the tallest building in Medellín (35 floors) and was built as the headquarters of the **Compañía Colombiana de Tejidos**, thus symbolizing the importance of textiles to the city. It is in the form of a needle, with the 'eye' clearly visible near the top. The building contains offices, a commercial centre and various other public facilities for cultural events.

of hideouts in Medellín and Antioquia before he eventually tired and negotiated very favourable terms of surrender.

Escobar was allowed to design and have constructed a luxurious prison on a hill outside Medellín, known as La Catedral. It had a football pitch and gym and the rooms were like hotel suites, with jacuzzis, giant TVs and bars. He hosted lavish parties and came and went as he pleased, often attending football matches in Medellín; on these occasions his motorcade was accompanied by a police escort that blocked traffic to ensure smooth passage.

Eventually the government decided to transfer him to a 'real' prison, but in the resulting siege of La Catedral, Escobar slipped through the cordon of an entire army battalion and went on the run for a further 18 months.

In the meantime a vigilante group known as *Los Pepes* (*Los Perseguidos por Pablo Escobar* – People Persecuted by Pablo Escobar), believed to be funded by his rivals, the Cali cartel, and to be colluding with the government, began a campaign in which 300 of his business associates were assassinated, severely hampering his cash flow. He was eventually tracked down and shot by special forces in December 1993 while attempting to escape across the rooftops of a Medellín suburb.

During his three-decade career he is believed to have been responsible for the death of more than 4000 people, including 30 judges and 457 policemen, and he is also charged with being the single figure most responsible for Colombia's reputation for drugs, kidnappings and pitiless violence. Today, the Pablo Escobar tour has become one of the more popular in Medellín, taking in his family home, the house where he was shot, as well as his final resting place. Morbid tourism perhaps, but it does provide insights into the life and death of one of the most influential men in Colombia's history. For tour information, visit www.seecolombia.travel.

Two blocks further, **Iglesia de San José** was begun in the 17th century but modified several times up to 1903. It was the last work done by the Nicaraguan architect Félix Pereira and houses a painting of San José by Carlos Hefritter and the oldest painting in the city – of San Lorenzo, the first patron saint of Medellín. Nearby, the Franciscan church of **San Ignacio** was begun in 1793 and has a colonial interior with a barrel-vaulted central nave and a splendid red and gold altar. It was later taken over by the Jesuits and formed part of the original group of buildings of the Universidad de Antioquia. This complex includes the auditorium (*paraninfo*) of the university, which was declared a National Monument in 1982 and reopened in 1997 after careful restoration; there is a great view of the city from the top of the tower.

## Villanueva and El Prado
*Metro Prado.*

The city's main business area is **Villanueva**. It is interesting for its blend of old and modern architecture, including many skyscrapers. **Parque de Bolívar** is dominated by the new **Catedral Metropolitano**, built between 1875 and 1931. It is one of the largest (sun-dried) brick structures in the world and claims to be the largest cathedral in South America. It is impressive inside, with marble used only for the pulpit, the altar canopy and some statuary around the nave. The Spanish stained-glass windows are

### 2 Medellín centre

Cementerio San Pedro

Hospital

Fomento y Turismo de Medellín

Parque de Bolívar

EL PRADO

**Catedral Metropolitana**

VILLANUEVA

Hospital San Vicente de Paul

JESÚS NAZARENO

Juan del Corral

Carabobo

Universidad de Antioquia

Plazuela Nutibara

Plaza Botero

La Veracruz

Museo de Antioquia

EL CHAGUALO

Av de Greiff

Punto Zero

SAN BENITO

San Benito

San Juan de Dios

Alfonso

Río Medellín

Metro Service Link

Universidad Nacional de Colombia

Biblioteca Pública Piloto para América Latina

Av del Río

Museo de Arte Moderno

Edificio Suramericana de Seguros

Cerro El Volador

SURAMERICANO

N

200 metres
200 yards

**Where to stay**
Botero Plaza **1**
Gran **2**

Nutibara **4**

**Restaurants**
1,2,3... Cazuelas **5**
Café Botero **6**

a good example of the period. There are several paintings by Gregorio Vázquez de Arce. In the square outside is a plaque to Tyrell Moore, the Englishman who donated land to the city for the Parque de Bolívar. On the first Saturday of the month there is a craft market in the park, known as the **Mercado de San Alejo**.

Deli Lunch **8**
Hacienda Real **7**
Hato Viejo **9**

Fonda Parque Boívar **10**
Salon de Té Astor **11**
Versalles **12**

**Bars & clubs** 🎵
La Boa **13**
La Papayara **14**

Salón Málaga **15**

## BACKGROUND

## Medellín

Though the Valle de Aburrá was discovered early on by the Spaniards (1541), there were few settlements here until early in the 17th century. The town is thought to have been founded in 1616 as 'San Lorenzo de Aburrá', on the site of what is now El Poblado. It was given the official title of town (*villa*) in 1675 by Queen Mariana of Austria and named after Don Pedro Portocarrero y Luna, Count of Medellín. The town established itself around the Basílica de La Candelaria (now known as the Old Cathedral), which was built at the end of the 17th century. Medellín was declared a city in 1813 and in 1826 became the capital of Antioquia.

The industrialization of Medellín followed the coffee boom. The first looms arrived in 1902, and the textile industry remains an integral part of Medellín and a major export to this day. Other major local industries are brick-making, leather goods and plastics. There has been limited immigration from overseas since the original settlement, but the natural growth in population has been extraordinary. A positive manifestation of this rapid expansion is the fine metro system, which connects all areas of the city.

To the north across Calle 58, is **El Prado**, originally a finca named La Polka, where there were many fine old houses, most of which have been replaced or are in decay. Some, however, have been restored and the area attracts artists and musicians.

### Parque San Antonio
*Metro San Antonio.*

Among the city's many sculptures, don't miss the works of **Fernando Botero** in **Parque San Antonio** (between Calles 44/46 and Carrera 46), including the *Torso Masculino* (which complements the female version in Parque Berrío), *La Mujer Inclinada* and the *El Pájaro de Paz (Bird of Peace)*, which was severely damaged by a guerrilla bomb in 1996. At the request of the sculptor, it has been left unrepaired as a symbol of the futility of violence, with a new *Bird of Peace* placed alongside. There is a garden beyond the plaza and a useful footbridge for crossing the busy Calle 44 (San Juan). The church after which the park is named was designed by Benjamín Machiantonio and built between 1884 and 1902. It was inspired by San Antonio de Padua, a 13th-century Venetian church, and has one of the biggest domes in the country.

> **Tip...**
> An unusual attraction is the **Punto Cero** (Point Zero), an elegant steel double arch with a pendulum marking the 'centre of the city'. It was the initial idea of students at the neighbouring Universidad Nacional and straddles the river where it is crossed by Calle 67.

On the other side of the metro at Carrera 52 and Calle 48 is the **Palacio Nacional**, designed by Agustín Goovaerts in the Romantic style. Built

If you visit Medellín, you'll be hard pushed to miss the enormous sculptures adorning several parts of the city, including one of the main squares, known as Plaza Botero. These imposing works were created by local-born Fernando Botero, one of Latin America's best-known sculptors and artists. Botero, who has spent many years living abroad, donated these works to the city of Medellín, perhaps, one might guess, because he found them too difficult to pack on his departure. His striking rotund figures tower impressively over the viewer in Botero's own characteristic style: disproportionately large, bulbous and voluptuous. Despite first leaving the country in 1952 and spending most of his time in Paris, Botero returns to his roots every year, spending a month in his native Colombia. His works have been exhibited worldwide, from Tokyo and New York, to Mexico City and Athens.

in 1925, it is now a commercial centre, recognizable by its brass-coloured domes, stylishly renovated with sweeping marble staircases and spacious hallways.

### Corazón de Jesús
*Metro Alpujarra/Cisneros.*

Government of the city and department is now conducted from **La Alpujarra** administrative centre, a nine-block area at Calle 44 and Carrera 52. Within the complex is the fine old Medellín railway station building designed in 1914 by Enrique Olarte. Other public services in Medellín concentrate their administrative operations in a highly energy-efficient building to the south, known as the **Edificio Inteligente** ⓘ *Cra 58, No 42-125*, completed in 1996. Nearby is the **Parque de los Pies Descalzos** (Barefoot Park) ⓘ *C 42B, No 55-40*, an excellent example of urban planning. It is designed to encourage local workers to relax during their lunch break; sand pits, fountains, a Zen garden and a bamboo forest actively promote strolling about shoeless. It has several restaurants and internet cafés, as well as the interactive **Museo Del Agua EPM** ⓘ *T4-380 6954, Mon-Fri 0830-1730, Sat-Sun 1030-1630, US$3.*

### North of the centre
One of the city's more unusual sights is the **Cementerio San Pedro** ⓘ *Cra 51, No 68-68 (metro Hospital), T4-516 7650, www.cementeriosanpedro.org.co, daily 0800-1300, 1400-1700.* Built in 1828, it has the dubious honour of being the resting place of many notorious drug dealers, guerrillas and the like, as well as of the city's richest families. One particularly elaborate tomb is reserved for the Muñoz family who were some of Pablo Escobar's most ruthless *sicarios* (assassins). Also of note is the tomb of Jorge Isaacs, celebrated author of the romantic novel *María*. Even for Latin America, some of the tombs are spectacular, and the small chapel has some of the most colourful stained glass in Antioquia. It also houses some unique sculptures, such as *Dolor de Madre*, a replica of Michelangelo's *La Pietà* depicting the anguish

## ON THE ROAD

## Tango in Medellín

Tango may have originated in the barrios of Buenos Aires and Montevideo but it has been whole-heartedly adopted by Medellín.

How tango arrived in the city is unclear, but by 1919 it was gaining widespread popularity. A short story written by local poet Ciro Mendía references tango star Carlos Gardel's *Mi Noche Triste* in a tale that revolves around a fallen woman who is assassinated by her jealous lover in the red-light district of the city.

By 1922, North American record companies such as RCA Victor and Columbia had picked up on tango's increasing popularity and began to distribute tango songs for the Colombian market, while tango films featuring Argentine starlets such as Libertad Lamarque drew large crowds to the city's cinemas. In Medellín, tango was concentrated around the working-class barrio of Guayaquil, where cantinas and cafés played songs by Argentine stars.

It was after the tragic death of Carlos Gardel in 1935 in a plane accident at Medellín's Olaya Herrera airport that tango really took off. The death crystallized tango's connection with the city in the local imagination, and in the following decades tango became intrinsic to Medellín's distinctive cultural identity. By the 1950s Medellín was hosting large-scale tango concerts with many of Argentina's biggest tango stars coming to perform and even settle in the city.

Today, tango culture is still strong in Medellín. Bars such as Salón Málaga and La Boa (where the novel *Aire de Tango* was written) are popular venues for tango aficionados (see page 252), and the city also hosts monthly *Tangovías*, in which entire streets are given over to tango dancing events; Carrera 45 (Avenida Carlos Gardel) in Barrio Manrique is normally the focus of activity. Each June, the Festival de Tango takes place with over 60 events, including dance competitions and concerts. There's also a museum dedicated to Carlos Gardel (see below).

of a mother losing her young son. Each month during the full moon there are nocturnal tours of the cemetery with violin music, dancing and storytelling.

**Joaquín Antonio Uribe botanical gardens** ⓘ *entrance at Cra 52/C 78 (metro Universidad), T4-444 5500 ext 120, www.botanicomedellin.org, daily, 0900-1800 (last entry 1700), free,* was formerly the **Finca Edén** and was turned into a garden by the owner, the botanist Joaquín Antonio Uribe. It was rescued from developers in 1972 and converted into a public garden with 5500 species of plants and trees. There is a lake with various lilies on display – a cool and restful place. In March an international orchid show takes place in the gardens in a covered exhibition area; Medellín's gastronomy festival in August has also been hosted here. There are two restaurants, one pricey and one more economical, with nice views of the gardens, plus facilities for children, a library and an open-air auditorium.

East of the botanic gardens is a museum, **Museo Casa Gardeliana** ⓘ *Cra 45, No 76-50, T4-213 5965, Mon-Fri 0900-1700, Sun 1000-1600,* commemorating tango legend Carlos Gardel who died in a plane crash in Medellín in 1935. Opposite the botanical gardens, meanwhile, is the **Parque Explora** ⓘ *Cra 52, No 73-75 (metro Universidad), T4-516 8300, www.parqueexplora.org, Tue-Fri 0830-1730 (last entry 1600), Sat, Sun and hols 1000-1830 (last entry 1700), up to US$10*, a science and technology museum. With more than 300 interactive scientific puzzles and games spread over 20,000 sq m, this is fun for adults and heaven for kids. It has four state-of-the-art rooms, each of which takes one to two hours to explore: the latest technological advances in **Territorios Digitales**; geology and climate in **Colombia Geodiversa**; the natural world in **Conexión de la Vida** and **Física Viva**. There is also a 3D cinema. It's one of the highlights of a visit to Medellín.

Nearby is the **Parque Norte J Emilio Valderrama** ⓘ *Cra 53, No 76-115 (metro Universidad), www.parquenorte.gov.co, Tue-Fri 0930-1700, Sat, Sun and hol 1030-2000, entry US$2.50, attractions and funfair from US$9.50*, a recreational park with a lake and children's playground. Next to it is the old railway station **El Bosque**, now restored and converted into a recreation centre for the elderly.

Also in this area is the **Planetario** ⓘ *Cra 52, No 71-117, T4-516 8300, Tue, Wed, Fri 0830-1700, Thu 0830-1800, Sat-Sun 1000-1800*, which has a 300-seat projection room, an auditorium for 200, a library and exhibition hall. Slightly further north is the **Casa Museo Maestro Pedro Nel Gómez** ⓘ *Cra 51B, No 84-24 (metro Universidad), T4-233 2633, www.museopedronel.tumblr.com, Mon-Sat 0900-1700, Sun 1000-1600 (may be closed during school hols), donations welcome*, house of the Colombian painter and sculptor (1899-1984) with many of his artworks, and a specialist library.

## South of the centre and El Poblado

The **Parque Zoológico Santa Fe** ⓘ *Cra 52, No 20-63 (metro Industriales, then 10-min walk), T4-444 7787, www.zoologicosantafe.com, daily 0900-1700, US$5, children half price*, houses mainly South American animals and birds and is concerned with the protection of threatened local species, including the spectacled bear and the Andean condor. There are special exhibits of Caribbean fauna and a butterfly section. Within the complex is the **Museo Santa Fe** which has displays of furniture and pictures of Medellín's past, including the Antioquia railway and the construction of La Quiebra Tunne.

The Spanish first settled in the Aburrá valley in the area called El Poblado to the south of the city. The church **Iglesia San José** is located on the central park here and is the third on the site; the architect Agustín Goovaerts was involved in its construction. There are commemorative plaques in the park. The area to the east, around Parque Lleras, is commonly known as the Zona Rosa and is the centre for eating and nightlife in the city.

Further south, **Museo El Castillo** ⓘ *C 9 Sur, No 32-269, T4-266 0900, www.museo elcastillo.org, Mon-Fri 0900-1200, 1400-1800, Sat-Sun 1000-1700, US$5*, was formerly a landowner's home, constructed in 1930 in neo-Gothic style. It has interesting collections of paintings, sculptures, porcelain and furniture, and is set in beautiful grounds with a 250-seat concert hall. To get there take a bus to Loma de los Balsos in El Poblado, then walk 1 km up the hill until you see the road lined with pine trees to the right.

## West of the centre

South of the Río Medellín is the **Museo de Arte Moderno** ⓘ *Cra 44N, No 19A-100 (metro Suramericana), T4-444 2622, www.elmamm.org, Mon-Fri 0900-1730, Sat 1000-1730, Sun 1000-1700, US$4.* It has a small collection of paintings, collages and photographs, including particularly good paintings by Débora Arango. It also shows films and has a coffee shop.

Nearby is the **Biblioteca Pública Piloto para América Latina** ⓘ *Cra 64, No 50-32, T4-460 0590, www.bibliotecapiloto.gov.co, Mon-Fri 0830-1900, Sat 0900-1800.* This is one of the best public libraries in the country, with several branches in Medellín. It was set up by UNESCO and the Colombian government in 1952 and has links to the **Biblioteca Luis Angel Arango** in Bogotá. It hosts art and photo exhibitions, author readings and foreign film screenings.

**Museo Etnográfico Miguel Angel Builes** ⓘ *Cra 81, No 52B-120 (metro Floresta and then 10-min walk), T4-444 4144, Mon-Fri, 0800-1200, 1400-1700, Sat 0800-1200, free but donations welcome,* was originally founded in 1963 in Yarumal, Antioquia, by missionaries and moved to Medellín in 1972. The fine building houses an extensive collection of artefacts from indigenous cultures: two floors are

**Medellín maps**
1 Medellín, page 236
2 Medellín centre, page 240
3 **El Poblado, page 246**
4 Medellín metro, page 256

**Where to stay** 🛏
Black Sheep Hostal 1
Casa Kiwi 2
Dann Carlton 3
Geo Hostel 7
Global Hostel 4
Hostel Casa Blanca 10
La Habana Vieja 5

Park 10 **6**
Pitstop Hostel **8**
Tiger Paw Hostel **9**

**Restaurants** 🍴
Basílica 2
Donde Paco 3
Le Bon 4

Thaico **6**
Tony Roma's **7**
Triada **5**

**Bars & clubs** 🍸
Blue Bar **9**

500 metres
500 yards

dedicated to Colombia, one to other Andean countries, including Peru and Bolivia, and another floor to Africa. There are models of indigenous houses, a library and a bookshop.

Further west, the **Museo de la Madre Laura** ① *Cra 92, No 34D-21 (metro, T4-252 3017, Tue-Fri 0900-1200, 1400-1700*, has a good collection of indigenous costumes and crafts from Colombia, Ecuador and Guatemala collected by a community of missionary nuns.

## Medellín's hills

You will notice three prominent hills within the Aburrá valley. The first, **Cerro Nutibara** (across the river from Exposiciones and Industriales metro stations) has an outdoor stage for open-air concerts, a sculpture park (the idea of former President Belisario Betancur), a miniature Antioquian village (known as **Pueblito Paisa**), souvenir shops and restaurants. There is a statue of Chief Nutibara near the village. Every month, on the night of the full moon, there is a party here with music, dancing, food stalls and tango show, organized by the Department of Sports and Recreation. To get there, either catch bus 173 from Parque Berrío to the bottom of the hill then walk (1.5 km), or take a taxi from Industriales or Exposiciones metro stations to the village (US$2.50).

**Cerro El Volador** lies to the northwast of the centre and can be seen on the left as the metro turns between Universidad and Caribe stations. It is tree-covered and is the site of an important indigenous burial ground.

East of La Candelaria is **Morro El Salvador**, with a cross and statue on top designed by Arturo Longas in 1950. This hill and its small public park have been absorbed into building developments and are not recommended for visits on foot.

## ★Metrocable to Santo Domingo Savio

No visit to Medellín would be complete without riding its cable cars. The Metrocable is integrated into the transport system and is one of the city's proudest achievements (see box, page 257). There are three lines: Line **J** from San Javier to La Aurora in the west; Line **K**, which runs from Acevedo metro (northeast of the centre) up the mountain slopes to Santo Domingo Savio, and **Línea L**, which continues from Santo Domingo further up the mountains to Arví. The panorama from the cable cars is outstanding, giving you a bird's eye view of the entire city.

Santo Domingo Savio was formerly one of the city's most dangerous and crime-ridden barrios, but you can now walk around the neighbourhood safely (although it's best not to flash cash or expensive cameras). Its library, **Parque Biblioteca de España**, a short walk down from the metro station, was opened by the King and Queen of Spain in March 2007 and is worth a look. Designed by Colombian architect Giancarlo Massanti, it has seven floors with thousands of donated books and over a hundred computers: all this in what was once one of the most notorious areas of Medellín.

## Tourist information

The **Oficina de Turismo de Medellín**, C 41, No 55-80, in the convention center, T4-261 7277, has helpful staff. **Burbuja informative**, Plaza Botero, Cra 51 52A-48, T4-511 1211, burbujainformativa@ comfenalcoantioquia.com, www. conexionciudad.com, Mon-Sat 0900-1700, also has very helpful staff and an email response service in Spanish, English and French.

## Where to stay

### Central Medellín
Medellín has transformed beyond recognition in the last decade and one of the changes is that much of the accommodation has moved out of the centre. Many of the cheaper hostels in this part of town are now *acostaderos* or pay-by-the-hour brothels with questionable security that we advise you to avoid.

**$$$ Botero Plaza**
*Cra 50A, No 53-45, T511 2155,*
*www.hotelboteroplaza.com.*
Just 1 min's walk from Parque Botero, this hotel is convenient as it is on the street where the *busetas* leave for the airport. It has clean rooms, an internet café, sauna, gym and Turkish bath but is also located in a slightly seedy area that can be dangerous at night.

**$$$ Gran**
*C 54, No 45-92, T513 4455,*
*www.granhotel.com.co.*
A 1970s structure often used for business conventions, the **Gran** is 5 blocks east of Parque de Las Esculturas. It has a swimming pool, room service, free internet, parking and a restaurant

serving steak, fish and pastas. Nominally cheaper if paying by cash.

**$$$ Nutibara**
*C 52A, No 50-46, T511 5111,*
*www.hotelnutibara.com.*
This grand old lady of Medellín was the city's first major hotel, built in 1945. Its best days may be behind it, but it retains a certain art deco charm and has all modern amenities, including a pool, sauna, Turkish bath, an internet room, Wi-Fi in the lobby and a new lobby bar.

### South of the centre and El Poblado

**$$$$ Dann Carlton**
*Cra 43A, No 7-50, Av El Poblado,*
*T4-444 5151, www.danncarlton.com.*
Enormous block of brick that towers over Av El Poblado, the **Dann Carlton** has all the usual amenities, including a pool, spa, sauna, beauty parlour and Wi-Fi throughout. Features include a computer in every room and a revolving restaurant on the top floor. **Aviatur** office on the premises.

**$$$$ Park 10**
*Cra 36B, No 11-12, T4-310 6060,*
*www.hotelpark10.com.co.*
In a quiet and green corner of El Poblado, the **Park 10** has a cultured air with wooden floorboards and smartly dressed bellboys. All rooms have a reception area and safes. It also has a sauna, gym, Wi-Fi and the travel agency **Aviatur** in the same building.

**$$$ Global Hostel**
*Cra 35, No 7-58, T4-311 5418.*
In a city that has a poor selection of mid-range hotels, this is an excellent option close to the Zona Rosa. The owners have

gone for a minimalist, boutique look and generally succeed. Breakfast is included and there's Wi-Fi throughout.

### $$$ La Habana Vieja
*C 10 Sur, No 43A-7, T4-321 2557, www.hotellahabanavieja.com.*
Tucked away just off Av Poblado, this is about the only colonial hotel you will find in Medellín. Has TV, minibar and balconies for rooms on 2nd floor. Breakfast included.

### $$$-$$ Hostel Casa Blanca
*Transversal 5A, No 45-256, T4-586 5149, www.casablancamedellin.com.*
Large private rooms as well as a 5-bed dorm and a 15-bed dorm ($), storage, kitchen, laundry, free Wi-Fi. Spanish classes once a week. Close to the Zona Rosa.

### $$ Geo Hostel
*Cra 35 8A-58, T4-311 7150, www.geohostel.com.*
Pleasant, light and airy hostel near la Zona Rosa. Private rooms or dorms ($) available. Internet, kitchen and laundry, disabled access and a small shop selling arty, crafty things.

### $$-$ Tiger Paw
*Cra 36, No 10-49, T4-311 6079, www.tigerpawhostel.com.*
A variety of rooms and dorms ($), US-owned, free internet and Wi-Fi, laundry service, tourist packages, sports bar and lots of activities.

### $ The Black Sheep Hostal
*Transversal 5a, No 45-133, T4-311 1589 or T317-518 1369 (mob), www.blacksheepmedellin.com.*
Run by New Zealander Kelvin, **The Black Sheep** is a very comfortable backpackers' hostel on the site of an ex-hospital. With Wi-Fi, a kitchen, Spanish classes and a barbecue, it is a great place to unwind and plot excursions around Antioquia. Bunks in dorms ($) also available. Quieter private rooms at the back. Recommended.

### $ Casa Kiwi
*Cra 36, No 7-10, T4-268 2668, www.casakiwihostel.com.*
A maze of living areas, games rooms and outdoor patios, **Casa Kiwi** is one of the most comfortable backpackers' hostels in Colombia. The rooms are tastefully decorated, while a couple of dorm rooms with bunks ($) provide an economical alternative. It has Wi-Fi, several computers, a pool table, DVD collection and is just a couple of blocks from the bars and restaurants of Parque Lleras. There's also a roof terrace with pool, hammocks and a bar. Recommended.

### $ Pitstop Hostel
*Cra 43E, No 5-110, T4-352 1176, www.pitstophostel.com.*
The biggest hostel in Medellín, located close to Parque Lleras as well as the Metro station. Amenities include free Wi-Fi in every room, swimming pool, Irish bar, steam room, volleyball and basketball court, pool table and a huge outdoor area. The expansive grounds, large pub and central courtyard provide a good vibe conducive to meeting other travellers. Organizes tours and events, including the Pablo Escobar tour. Friendly staff speak English and Spanish. Recommended.

---

### West of the centre
Cra 70, next to metro Estadio, is replete with hotels, all of a similar standard and with similar prices. There are also a number of eateries lining the same road.

### $$$ Florida
*Cra 70N, No 44B-38, T4-260 4900, www.hotelfloridamedellin.com.*

Standard hotel on Cra 70. Internet room, Wi-Fi, laundry service, car park and restaurant. Some rooms lack windows.

### $$$ Lukas
*Cra 70, No 44A-28, T4-260 1761, www.lukashotel.com.*
Clean and crisp rooms with all the necessary amenities, including safe, a/c, cable TV, minibar, an internet room and Wi-Fi throughout. Breakfast included.

### $$$ Parque 70
*C 46B, No 69A-11, T4-260 3339, www.hotelparque70.com.*
Good little mid-range hotel in a quiet cul-de-sac off Cra 70. Clean rooms with minibar, stereo, TV and Wi-Fi. Just 1 block from the Estadio metro station.

### $$ Hotel Villa Real
*Cra 70 45E-153, T4-414 4905, www.hotelvillarealmedellin.co.*
Comfortable, modern hotel with a/c, TV, telephone for local calls and private bath.

### $$ Plaza 70
*Cra 70, No 45E-117, T4-412 3266, www.hotelplaza70.com.co.*
This functional hotel has clean but dark and small rooms with cable TV. Wi-Fi.

### $ Hostal Medellín
*C 44B, No 69-13, T4-260 2972, www.hostalmedellin.com.*
Spacious hostel run by a German and Colombian couple, popular with bikers for its large garage. Has a fine little garden with a hammock, pool table and organizes tours to Guatapé and Santa Fe de Antioquia.

### $ Palm Tree Hostal
*Cra 67, No 48D-63, T4-444 7256, www.palmtreemedellin.com.*
Backpackers' hostel in a central location, which ticks all the boxes in terms of facilities, including a kitchen, Wi-Fi, TV and DVD room, bike hire, book exchange and hammocks. Private and dormitory rooms ($) available. Helpful staff speak English. Recommended.

## Restaurants

### Central Medellín

### $$ Café Botero
*Cra 52, No 52-43 esq.*
Excellent lunchtime venue next to the Museo de Antioquia. Fish, fine steaks and delicious puddings. Recommended.

### $$ Hacienda Real
*Cra 49 52-98 (next door to Salón de Té Astor).*
Pleasant restaurant with balcony seating, overlooking Pasaje Junín.

### $$ Hato Viejo
*Cra 47, No 52-17, 2nd floor.*
Overlooking Av La Playa, Hato Viejo serves typical dishes such as *ajiaco*, *bandeja paisa*, *sudao* and *mondongo* as well as the usual steaks and fish.

### $$ Versalles
*Pasaje Junín No 53-59, www.versallesmedellin.com.*
Argentine-run restaurant, famous in Medellín for being the epicentre of the Colombian nihilism movement of the 1960s. *Parrillas*, pastas and pizzas in a room filled with photographs of renowned Latin American philosophers. Tasty food in an atmospheric setting.

### $$-$ 1,2,3… Cazuelas
*CC Unión, Cra 49, No 52-107, local 219.*
Fast food *cazuelas* in what was once the Union Club, Medellín's most exclusive social club.

### $$-$ Salón de Té Astor
*Cra 49, No 52-84.*
A delightful traditional tea house, famous throughout Colombia for its chocolate

## ON THE ROAD

## Gastronomic Medellín

Of Colombia s three main cities, Bogotá, Cali and Medellín, it is Medellín that has arguably succeeded in turning itself into the gastronomic centre of Colombia, hotly contested by the other two, to be sure. Colombia has yet to gain a reputation as a gourmet destination, but the days when you were presented with the sole option of rice, meat and an *arepa* are long gone, at least in the cities.

Many of Medellín s best restaurants are centred around Parque Lleras in El Poblado district, which is buzzing any evening of the week. Everything from Thai to Mexican, and from Peruvian to Italian can be found here, but Medellín is also the place to try some traditional Colombian fare. The *bandeja paisa* is the regional dish to sample, containing sausages, pork crackling, rice, beans, avocado, *arepa*, black pudding and more. Try to finish it all and you'll be positively groaning.

Medellín hosts a food festival, *Otro Sabor*, on the last weekend of August.

delicacies and excellent pastries. Try the *besitos de negro*. Lasagne, sandwiches and salads also served.

**$ Deli Lunch**
*CC Plaza Orquídeas, Cra 49, No 52-81, local 99-15.*
Creole food at economical prices. *Menú ejecutivo* US$5. Several similar places nearby.

**$ Fonda Parque Bolívar**
*C 55, No 47-27.*
Just off the Parque Bolívar, this popular lunchtime venue is festooned with antiques. *Menú ejecutivo* US$4.

### El Poblado

The area around Parque Lleras is positively heaving with bars and restaurants, with more springing up each year. Below is just a selection, mostly long-runners with a good track record, but there are many others to try out from Mexican to sushi.

**$$$ Basílica**
*Cra 38, No 8A-42, www. restaurantebasilica.com.*

Thick Argentine steaks, sushi and Peruvian dishes on an open terrace on Parque Lleras.

**$$$ Tony Roma's**
*Cra 43, No 7-50.*
Revolving restaurant on top of the **Hotel Dann Carlton**, serving ribs and steak. Worth visiting just for the view.

**$$$ Triada**
*Cra 38, No 8-03.*
Enormous restaurant/bar/club in the heart of the Zona Rosa. Huge steaks, sushi, salads and Tex Mex are the order of the day. It even has a bell on each table for calling the waiter. Good atmosphere with open terrace.

**$$ Thaico**
*C 9, No 37-40.*
Good Thai food with fresh ingredients. A popular spot for watching televized sports (or just people strolling through Parque Lleras). 3-for-1 happy hour cocktails until 1900.

## $ Donde Paco
*Cra 35, No 8A-80.*
Economical Colombian or Oriental food in a good atmosphere.

## $ Le Bon
*C 9, No 39-09.*
French café serving omelettes, pancakes, fruit salads and coffees and teas from around the world.

### West of the centre

## $$ La Margarita No 2
*Cra 70, No 45E-11.*
Antioquian dishes in a pleasant atmosphere: *bandeja paisa* and *cazuelas*.

## $ Opera Pizza
*C 42, No 70-22, www.operapizza.jimdo.com.*
*Paisas* swear these are the best pizzas in town. Italian-owned restaurant with a wood-fired oven. Recommended.

## $ ¡Orale!
*C 41, No 70-138.*
Excellent little Mexican canteen with tables on the street. Burritos, tacos and fajitas. Recommended.

## $ Pomodoro
*C 42, No 71-24, www.restaurantepomodoro.com.*
This little Italian restaurant serves lots of different pastas and sauces at reasonable prices. *Menú ejecutivo* good value.

## ★ Bars and clubs

### Central Medellín
In the centre, the area around the Parque de Los Periodistas attracts a bohemian crowd of goths, punks, and students. Be careful how you go, however, as this area is considerably seedier than the upmarket Zona Rosa.

### La Boa
*C 53, No 43-59.*
This bar has been around for more than 40 years and is famous for its tango and jazz. The book *Aire de Tango* by Manuel Mejía Vallejo was written here. It claims to be the only bar in Medellín where there has never been a fight!

### La Papayara
*C 53, No 42-55.*
Those interested in salsa should head here. It's an institution in the neighbourhood. Popular with foreigners, it still hasn't lost its authenticity with live salsa on Tue and Thu nights.

### Salón Málaga
*Cra 51, No 45-80, T4-231 2658, www.salonmalaga.com.*
This is one of Medellín's oldest tango bars and its owner, Gustavo Arteaga, is considered one of the principal collectors of tango in Colombia.

### West of the centre
You will find plenty of bars along Cra 70 and the adjacent streets.

### South of the centre: El Poblado
In the south, the best nightlife options are in the Zona Rosa, around Parque Lleras. Try **Blue Bar**, C 10, No 40-20, which plays rock and Colombian music Thu-Sat. **Triada** (see Restaurants, above) is another popular spot with a bar and disco upstairs. Between the centre and El Poblado, in Barrio San Diego, **Trilogía**, Cra 43G, No 24-08, T4-262 6375, www.trilogiabar.com, attracts an older crowd and has live cover bands playing a mix of rock and Colombian music. Arrive before 2230 on Fri and Sat.

Further afield, an alternative after-hours location is **Sabaneta**, 11 km from the centre of Medellín (metro

La Sabaneta, taxi US$10-15 from El Poblado). This suburb has an attractive plaza and fills up in the evenings with a mixed crowd of young and old. Try **El Viejo John**, Cra 45, No 70 Sur-42, a popular local spot with strings of chorizo hanging from the ceiling; **Fonda Sitio Viejo**, C 70 Sur, No 44-33, another bar full of character, or **La Herrería**, Cra 45, No 70 Sur-24, which is crammed with pictures, sombreros, saddles and bananas.

## Entertainment

### Cinema

Multiplexes showing the latest releases can be found in the following shopping centres: **CC Oviedo**, Cra 43A, No 7 Sur-170, T4-321 6116, www.oviedo.com.co; **CC Unicentro**, Bolivariana 66B, No 34A-76, T4-350 750, www.unicentromedellin. com.co; **Parque Comercial El Tesoro**, Cra 25A, No 1A Sur-45, T4-321 1010, www. eltesoro.com.co, and **CC Los Molinos**, C 82, No 30A-24, T1-800 093 5777, www. losmolinos.com.co. For independent, foreign-language and arthouse films, try the **Centro Colombo Americano**, Cra 45, No 53-24, T4-204 0404, www. colomboworld.com, **Universidad de Antioquia** and **Universidad de Medellín**; also check the local press.

### Music and dance

Monthly concerts by the **Antioquia Symphony Orchestra** are held in the **Teatro Metropolitano** (see below). Band concerts and other entertainment take place in the Parque de Bolívar every Sun. See also Tango in Medellín, page 244.

### Theatre

**Teatro Metropolitano**, *C 41, No 57-30, T4-232 2858, www.teatrometropolitano. com.* A modern-style brick building close to the river, 1600 capacity, symphony concerts, opera, ballet, tango shows, etc. **Teatro Pablo Tobón Uribe**, *Cra 40, No 51-24, T4-239 7500, www.teatropablo tobon.com.* Traditional theatrical presentations, 880 capacity. There are many other theatres of all types in the centre and barrios of the city. See local press for details.

## Festivals

**Easter Semana Santa** (Holy Week) has special Easter religious parades.
**Jun International Tango Festival**.
**Jul International Poetry Festival**, held on Cerro Nutibara in the open-air Carlos Vieco. For information, see www. festivaldepoesiademedellin.org.
**Jul Feria de Artesanías**, handicrafts of all kinds from all over the country, held in the Atanasio Girardot stadium complex.
**Jul Colombiamoda**, Colombia's largest fashion and designer fair.
★**Aug Feria de las Flores/Desfile de Silleteros** (flower fair), held annually in the 1st half of the month, for several days ending on the Sat with parades and music. The parade goes from Cra 55 across the Puente Colombia to the Atanasio Girardot Stadium. The flowers are grown at Santa Elena in the Parque Ecológico de Piedras Blancas, 14 km from Medellín (bus from Plaza Las Flores). A horse *cabalgata* is a special feature: in 2006, 8223 riders took part, taking 4 hrs to pass by: a Guinness World Record. For more information, visit www. feriadelasfloresmedellin.gov.co.
**End of Aug, Otro Sabor** gastronomy festival, 3 days, usually held in the lovely setting of the botanical gardens.
**2nd Sat in Sep Amor y Amistad**, in true *paisa* style, this equivalent of St Valentine's day lasts for a whole week!

**Dec** **Christmas** starts with a fantasy parade and dancing on 7 Dec to coincide with the switching on of the Christmas lights.

### Books

Centro Colombo Americano, *Cra 45, No 53-24, T4-204 0404, www.colomboworld.com.* Good selection of books in English for sale (including *Footprint*).
La Anticuaria, *C 49, No 47-46, T4-511 4969.* Antique and second-hand books, including those in English, helpful.
Librería Científica, *C 51, No 49-52, T4-251 8929, www.libreriacientifica.com.co.* Has another 3 branches and stocks a large selection, including some foreign books.

### Handicrafts

Try the *artesanía* shops at the top of Cerro Nutibara, or **Salvarte** in CC Oviedo. There is a small handicrafts market at C 52 near Cra 46 with many hippy stalls.

### Markets

Mercado San Alejo, *Parque Bolívar.* Feb-Dec 1st Sat of month, 0800-1800.

### Shopping centres

Centros Comerciales (CC) can be found in all the main areas of the city. The most notable are: **Camino Real**, Cra 47/ C 52, www.caminoreal.com. co; **El Diamante**, C 51/Cra 73, www. ccdiamante.com; **El Tesoro**, between Cras 7-8, www.eltesoro.com.co; **Junin La Candelaria**, Cra 49/C 50; **Monterrey**, C 14, www.monterrey.com.co/home/; **Obelisco**, Cra 74/C 48, www.obelisco. com.co; **Oviedo**, Cra 43A/ C 7 Sur, www. oviedo.com.co; **Sandiego**, C 36/Cra 43 www.sandiego.com.co; **Unicentro**, Cra 66B/ C 34A, www.unicentromedellin.

com.co; **Villanueva**, C 57 y C 56, www. centrocomercialvillanueva.com.

### Textiles

Many of the textile mills have discount-clothing departments attached offering good bargains. Ask at your hotel for more info.
Aluzia Correas y Cinturones, *Cra 55 No 29B-62.* For an incredible selection of belts.

### Bullfighting

If it isn't outlawed at the time of your visit, bullfighting takes place at the bullring of La Macarena, C 44A/Cra 63, T4-260 7193, in Jan and Feb; tickets from US$25, usually fully booked.

### Dance lessons

Academia Dance, *Cra 46, No 10 sur-36, T4-444 8582, www.danceas.com.* Salsa, merengue and rumba among other styles. **Black Sheep Hostal** guests get a 10% discount. Individual classes from US$19. Good reports.
Salón Málaga, *Cra 51, No 45-80, T4-231 2658.* One of Medellín's oldest tango bars.

### Spanish classes

Eafit University, *Cra 49, No 7 Sur 50, T4-448 9500, www.eafit.edu.co.* US$445 for a 4-week course, popular, well-organized, good reports.
Medellín Spanish School (part of **Black Sheep Hostal**), *Transversal 5A, No 45-133, T4-311 1589.* From US$6 per hr in a group, US$7.50-12.50 for individual classes.

### Stadium

Estadio Atanasio Girardot, *Cra 73, C 48 (metro Estadio).* Was enlarged in 1978 for the Pan American games and has facilities for over 50 sports including football, baseball, swimming and cycling.

## Tour operators

Destino Colombia, C 50, No 65-42, Centro Comecial Contemporáneo, Local 225, T4-260 6868, www.destinocolombia.com. Tours to attractions in Antioquia and nationwide. Very well-informed English-speaking guides. Can also arrange flights. Very helpful. Recommended.

## Trekking

Instituto de Deportes y Recreación (Inder), T4-379 9000, www.inder.gov.co. Offers walking tours around Medellín Jan-Nov.

Transport

## Air

There are 2 airports serving Medellín; when leaving by air, make sure you go to the correct one.

José María Córdova international airport (sometimes called Rionegro airport, T4-444 2818, www.airplan.aero) is 28 km east of Medellín (40 mins via the new highway) and 9 km from Rionegro. A taxi to central Medellín is US$25-30, or there is a frequent buseta service (US$4-5, 1 hr) to Cra 50A/C 53, next to Hotel Botero Plaza. Busetas will also drop off in El Poblado on request. A taxi from the airport to Rionegro is US$8-10, bus US$2.

There are frequent flights to Bogotá, 25 mins with Avianca, Lan or Copa. To Cali, 1 hr, Avianca and Lan, some requiring a change in Bogotá. To Barranquilla, Bucaramanga, Cartagena, 1hr, 1 daily, with Avianca, Lan and Copa.

Some internal flights arrive at Enrique Olaya Herrera metropolitan airport (T4-365 6100, www.aeropuertoolayaherrera.gov.co), located in the Santa Fe district of the city, near El Poblado. A taxi from this airport to the centre (10 mins) or El Poblado costs US$7.50, or you can take the metro for US$1. Taxis between the airports cost US$25-30. National flights only to Bogotá, several a day with Satena. To Cali, with Satena. To Quibdó, with easyfly or Aerolíneas de Antioquia (ADA). To Bucaramanga, with Satena. To Acandí with ADA.

For non-scheduled charter flights to coastal resorts (eg San Andrés), and elsewhere, check with travel agents. To get the best price, shop around.

Airline offices   Aerolíneas de Antioquia, C 10, No 35-32, T4-444 4232, www.ada-aero.com, or at Olaya Herrera airport; Avianca, Cra 43A, No 1A Sur-108, T4-266 8789, www.avianca.com, and at both airports; Copa Air, Cra 43A No 34-95, of 099 CC Almacentro, T1-800 011 2600, www.copaair.com; Lan, CC Premium Plaza, 1-800 094 9490, www.lan.com, and at both airports. Satena, Cra 42 No 9-24, T4-444 2185, www.satena.com, and at Olaya Herrera airport.

## Bus

Long distance   For buses going north and east, Terminal del Norte is at Cra 64C (Autopista del Norte), No 78-58, T4-444 8020, about 3 km north of the centre, with shops, cafés, left luggage, ATMs and other facilities. It is well policed and quite safe, though best not to tempt fate. Metro Caribe; taxi to the centre, US$7.50.

To Bogotá, 9-12 hrs, US$27.50, every 20 mins or so, with multiple companies. To Cartagena, multiple companies, 15 hrs, US$52.50, road paved but poor. To Santa Marta, 18 hrs, US$52.50. To Sincelejo, 9½ hrs, US$41.50. To Arboletes, Rápido Ochoa, US$36, 12 hrs. To Turbo,

US$30, with **Gómez** (best), 14 hrs. To **Santa Fe de Antioquia**, 1½ hrs, US$5 with multiple companies. To **Magangué**, US$51.50, with **Rápido Ochoa** or **Brasilia**. To **Doradal**, 3 hrs, US$13.50.

**Terminal del Sur**, Cra 65, No 8B-91, is alongside the Enrique Olaya Herrera airport. To get there, take a bus No 143 marked 'Terminal del Sur' from C 47 (in front of the Edic del Café) along Cra 46 or the metro to Poblado on Línea A, from where you will probably need a taxi for the remaining 1.5 km to the bus station.

**To Manizales**, 4-7 hrs US$18.50, frequent services 0430-1930 with **Empresa Arauca**, also **Flota Ospina** US$17.50, faster service in minivans. To **Pereira**, 6-8 hrs, US$16.50-18.50 with **Flota Occidental Pullman** or **Empresa Arauca**. Many buses to **Cali**, eg **Flota Magdalena**, US$25, 7-8 hrs. To **Popayán** (US$37.50, 12 hrs), **Pasto** (US$52.50, 18 hrs) and **Ipiales** (US$54, 22 hrs) with **Expreso Bolivariano**. To **Quibdó**, 11-13 hrs, US$33, daily with **Rápido Ochoa**. To **El Retiro**, US$2.75, with **Sotra Retiro**. To **La Ceja**, US$3.75, every 20 mins, with **Transportes Unidas La Ceja**. To **Jardín**, 4-5 hrs, US$9, daily with **Rápido Ochoa** or **Transportes Suroeste**.

### Car
**Car hire** **Milano**, C 10 No 43B-80, T4-604 6903, www.milanocar.com; **Hertz**, Cra 43A, No 1A Sur-69 of 101, T4-319 1010, www. hertz.com. Other offices and vehicles are located at the international airport.

### Metro
The metro has 2 lines: **Línea A** from Niquía to La Estrella; and **Línea B** from San Javier to San Antonio, where they intersect. The Metro links up with 3 cable car lines: **Línea J**, **Línea K** and **Línea L**. A single journey (anywhere on the system) is US$1. The system operates Mon-Sat 0430-2300, Sun and hols 0500-2230.

## ④ Medellín Metro

## ON THE ROAD

### ★ The Metrocable

Medellín's cable car, the Metrocable, has become one of the symbols of this city's remarkable renaissance. It is the first cable car in the world designed primarily as a public transport system, although its success as a tool for social change has made it a popular tourist attraction.

The Metrocable connects the *comuna nororiental* (northeastern area), a slum full of brick and corrugated-iron shack communities constructed haphazardly on the side of the hill, with the metro station at Acevedo. During the 1980s and 1990s this was one of the most notorious slums in Latin America, the *zona de cultivo*, or cultivation area, for drug trafficker Pablo Escobar's army of *sicarios* (assassins).

In terms of transportation, it was a difficult place to leave. Narrow streets clogged with traffic meant that it could take up to two hours to get into town by bus. Back in the 1990s the area was highly segregated, with sectors at war with each other. The bridge between the communities of La Francia and Andalucía, for example, was a no-go area. Today, residents walk freely between the two neighbourhoods over what has been rechristened the 'Bridge of Reconciliation'.

Part of the local government's drive to propagate 'participatory democracy', the Metrocable's aim is to allow the city's very poorest to take an active role in society and to 'de-ghettoize' the area. Commuting time has been reduced to 45 minutes, allowing easier access for those looking for employment in the centre, and it has significantly improved congestion in the area. Most importantly, it has restored a sense of pride to the community.

The Metrocable is just one cog in a movement that has allowed the people of this neighbourhood to reclaim public space from criminals. Other initiatives include the Biblioteca de España, which brings books, computers and spaces for social and artistic activities to one of Latin America s most deprived communities.

The success is measurable. Violent deaths in the neighbourhood fell from 6349 in 1994 to 373 in 2005, while individual living space grew from less than half a square metre to between two and three squares metres per person.

The cable car's success is being replicated across Colombia and the region. A second line was inaugurated in 2008 to link La Aurora district with San Javier metro station, and a third opened from Santo Domingo Savio as far as Arví, near Lake Guarne. There is even talk of building a connection with the airport in Rionegro. Elsewhere in Colombia, the villages of Guatapé near El Peñol and San Agustín in Huila have expressed an interest in building their own systems, while Caracas in Venezuela opened its own cable car system in 2010.

**Taxis**

Taxis have meters, so make sure they are used; minimum charge US$2.50.

Radio taxis include **Flota Bernal**, T4-444 8882 and **Taxi Andaluz**, T4-440 0200, www.taxandaluz.co.

# **Around** Medellín

By the time they reach Antioquia, the Andes have almost petered out, yet their foothills can still reach heights of up to 3000 m. This gives the rolling green countryside around Medellín an agreeable temperate climate in which all types of flowers and fruit thrive, and the typical villages of the region make for popular day trips from the departmental capital.

East of the city is the network of artificial lakes known as the Embalse del Peñol, above which towers an extraordinary granite rock that bears an uncanny resemblance to Río de Janeiro's Sugar Loaf Mountain. On the shores of the lake is Guatapé, a sleepy town that livens up at weekends. Further east still, as the road drops down towards the Río Magdalena and temperate turns to tropical, hidden in the jungle is the Río Claro Nature Reserve, where a crystalline river with a marble bed has cut a path through an enormous rock, creating a 150-m canyon. Just a few kilometres on is Hacienda Napoles, former home of drug baron Pablo Escobar, now a theme park with *Jurassic Park* pretensions.

Due south is the beginning of coffee country. Enchanting villages such as Jardín, Jericó and Andes are seldom visited: a just reward for the intrepid traveller.

Santa Fe de Antioquia, to the north, was once the departmental capital, but fortunately for architecture lovers, it was eclipsed by Medellín, allowing it to take on a new role as Antioquia's very own time capsule.

Climbing east out of the valley of Medellín, the landscape becomes increasingly more attractive, with carefully cultivated hills bursting with an abundance of coffee, tomatoes, corn and beans. This is Antioquia's breadbasket, and its many colonial towns and typical *paisa* villages are a popular weekend excursion for Medellín's well-heeled. The Circuito de Oriente includes the towns of El Retiro, La Ceja and Rionegro and passes through some of the most expensive property in Colombia, including that of former Colombian president Alvaro Uribe.

### Circuito de Oriente → *Colour map 2, B3.*

El Retiro, 33 km southeast of Medellín, is a quiet colonial town with a fine plaza dominated by a 100-year-old ceiba tree. The pretty church, **Nuestra Señora del Rosario**, built in 1774, has an interesting stained-glass dome. There is an even older adobe mud chapel, the Capilla de San José, where a document to free local slaves, the first in South America, was signed in 1813. The **Fiesta de los Negritos** is held in late December to mark the event. El Retiro is also known for its furniture-making; you can have almost any piece of furniture copied here.

Beyond El Retiro is the pretty town of **La Ceja**, which has an attractive church dedicated to Nuestra Señora de Chiquinquirá. The main industry in town is flower-growing and there's a local flower festival held annually in December. Any of the surrounding hills offer excellent views of the area; one of the best known is **Cerro Capiro**.

The **Circuito de Oriente** continues its loop through several pretty colonial towns including **Carmen de Viboral**, known for its pottery; there are several factories north of the market place.

Five kilometres from Medellín airport in a delightful valley is **Rionegro**, where the western circuit of the Circuito loops back towards Medellín. In town, the Casa de Convención and cathedral are worth a visit. There are colourful processions in Easter week. Near Rionegro, on the road southwest to El Retiro, is **La Fe** reservoir, with a fine public park, **Parque de los Salados**, that's popular at weekends for aquatic sports amid pine forests.

### ★ El Peñol → *Colour map 2, B3.*

East of Rionegro, and not to be missed, is El Peñol, an extraordinary, 200-m-high, bullet-shaped granite rock, which towers above a series of interlocking artificial lakes known as the Embalse del Peñol. A spiral staircase has been built into a crack in the rock from the base to the summit – climbing the 649 steps to the top will take about 30 minutes – from where there are impressive views across the aquamarine lakes (entrance fee US$5). On the side of the rock you will notice the letters GI carved in white. This was originally meant to spell

**Tip...**

If driving out of Medellín, check routes carefully before leaving; there are few signs and information from officials and petrol stations is often less than clear.

'GUATAPE', an effort by residents of that town to claim the rock as their own, a claim that is vociferously rejected by the residents of El Peñol. The painters were caught in the act and prosecuted, though the graffiti is yet to be removed.

The original town of El (Viejo) Peñol was founded in 1714 on an indigenous site known as Sacatín. In 1978, it was submerged by the new reservoir and El Peñol

# Around Medellín

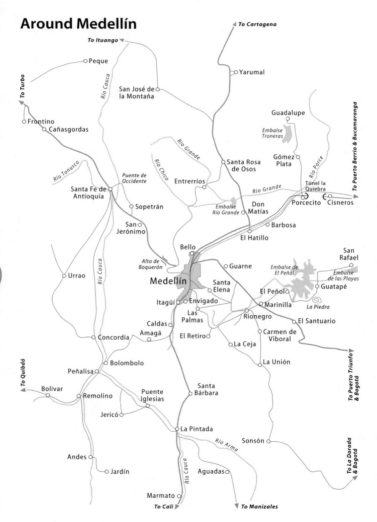

Nuevo was built to replace it. The new town, about 1 km from the original site, is of little interest, although it does have a strange-looking church modelled on the rock (and the only ATM in the area). If you walk down to the lake you can still see the spire of the original church sticking out of the water.

## Guatapé → Colour map 2, B4.

An entirely more agreeable place to stay in is Guatapé, 3 km beyond the rock, a pretty lakeside town with brightly coloured colonial houses and a pleasant plaza with a white and red Greco-Roman church, the **Parroquia Nuestra Señora del Carmen**. If you look closely you will notice that the Roman numeral '4' on the church clock has been executed incorrectly.

At the weekend Guatapé is thronged with visitors from Medellín, and the *malecón* (promenade) along the lake shore tends to fill up with pleasure boats blasting out music. There is also a zip wire (known as 'canopy') across a section of the lake. During the week, however, it's a quiet town with several economical accommodation options. Aside from the rock and the pleasure boats, Guatapé is known for the brightly painted *zócalos* that adorn the lower portion of the houses. Although *zócalos* were originally a Spanish import, Guatapé is unique in that the residents have chosen to embellish theirs with intricate sculptures depicting local families and political events. **Calle de los Recuerdos**, a couple of blocks from the main plaza, has the best examples of these fascinating public works of art.

Guatapé has two religious orders nearby. One is a Benedictine monastery, which holds Eucharistic services with Gregorian chanting every Sunday at 1100. The other, **Las Adornadas del Divino Paráclito**, is a convent that holds 24-hour vigils. Its nuns produce and sell honey and royal jelly. You can visit both by taking a mototaxi from the Parque Principal.

## Reserva Natural Cañón del Río Claro → Colour map 2, B4.
*www.rioclaroelrefugio.com. Free.*

The Medellín–Bogotá road eventually descends into hot tropical forest before it meets the Río Magdalena at Puerto Triunfo. About three hours' drive and 152 km from Medellín is Reserva Natural Cañón del Río Claro, one of Colombia's first national parks, founded in 1970 by local landowner Juan Guillermo Garcés. A 450-ha conservation area based around a 150-m-deep limestone canyon, the park has spectacular walks along jungle paths following a crystal-clear river with a marble bed. There are several caves that show the geological history of the area and a couple of sandy beaches. The reserve is noted for its incredible biodiversity, with over 50 new species of plant discovered and more than 370 different species of bird identified since its foundation.

## Doradal → Colour map 2, B4.

About 15 km beyond Río Claro is Doradal. Hotels and restaurants line the busy Medellín–Bogotá trunk road, but there's also an attractive plaza with palm trees and a beautiful church if you venture into the town proper. It is a convenient place to

## ON THE ROAD

### Discovering Reserva Natural Cañón del Río Claro

Before the main Bogotá–Medellín trunk road was completed, this majestic 150-m-deep limestone canyon was known only to jaguars and other animals of the forest.

Eduardo Betancourt, a *campesino* from a nearby finca, first discovered the gorge in 1964. Tracking a jaguar that had been killing his livestock, it took him six weeks to follow it back to the canyon. The animal eventually escaped him but not before leading him to the site, which locals refused to enter, believing it to be bewitched.

He returned home empty-handed but told his landowner, Juan Guillermo Garcés, about the canyon. Garcés was fascinated, but nothing was done for a further six years until, in 1970, a government engineer spotted it from a helicopter while searching for a suitable place to build a bridge across the river for the new road.

Garcés was inspired to see it for himself, so he set out with his brother and Betancourt. It took them two days to hack through the jungle, and they had to enter the canyon itself by pulling themselves upriver on a raft. They remained at the site for several months, building shelters in the caves under the steep walls of the canyon. The diversity of species Garcés discovered during his stay inspired him to develop it into a private nature reserve to ensure its protection.

The canyon gained some publicity from journalists who were staking out nearby Hacienda Nápoles belonging to Pablo Escobar, and on the first weekend after the completion of the new road, 1500 visitors descended on the reserve. Garcés decided that it would be impossible to keep people away and that the best way of protecting the canyon was to develop a sustainable tourism reserve. He named it 'El Refugio', in memory of its former role as a jaguar refuge.

stay for visits to both the Río Claro Nature Reserve and Hacienda Nápoles. A couple of kilometres away is **Aldea Doradal**, a small community that has been entirely modelled on a Greek town, complete with whitewashed houses and narrow, windy streets. It could be a theme-park nightmare, but somehow it works, partly due to the fact that locals have bought properties and injected some life into the place.

#### Hacienda Nápoles

*Medellín–Bogotá, Km 165, T4-444 2975/Freephone 01800-051 0344, www.hacienda napoles.com. Tue-Sun 0900-1700. US$16-30.*

About 20 km beyond Río Claro is Hacienda Nápoles, former country retreat of the notorious drug baron Pablo Escobar, now a theme park with a wildlife reserve full of exotic animals. Hacienda Nápoles was notorious throughout Colombia for the private zoo that Escobar put together and opened up for free to the public. Many of the animals – along with huge quantities of drugs – were flown into the estate via the 1280-m private runway, which is long enough to land a Boeing 747.

As the war between Escobar and the Colombian government escalated in the late 1980s, the estate was abandoned and subsequently pillaged for secret stashes of money and drugs. Many of the animals died or were stolen; some even escaped: it is believed that two of the hippos are now roaming free in the Magdalena river.

Today the nature reserve is home to a herd of hippos as well as elephants, water buffalo, ostriches, llamas, wild cats, monkeys and a butterfly sanctuary. In a slightly surreal turn, there is also a collection of life-size dinosaur models, originally built for Escobar and recreated for the reserve by the same model makers. You enter the reserve through gates with lettering uncannily similar to that used for the film *Jurassic Park*.

It is also possible to visit Escobar's old house, which has been left in a state of disrepair, with holes in the swimming pool where bounty hunters excavated for buried treasure. The house, especially Escobar's bedroom, is remarkably small considering *Forbes* magazine placed Escobar as the seventh-richest man in the world in his heyday. Other attractions include the runway and a Coliseum, used by Escobar as his private bullring, which now holds cultural events and exhibitions.

There are luxury hotels in the hacienda, a camping zone within the grounds, as well as several hotel options in nearby Doradal (see Where to stay, page 264).

## Listings East of Medellín

### Where to stay

#### Circuito de Oriente
There are various hotels ($$-$) and many places to eat in and near the plaza in Rionegro.

#### $$$ El Gran Chaparral
*Km 2 Vía La Fe, T4-541 2451.*
Just outside El Retiro, this beautiful horse ranch and trout farm has fine rooms in a converted stable. The horses across the yard are not for hire but riding can be arranged on request. There is a large pond full of rainbow trout for fishing and a restaurant serving enormous Angus beef steaks or fish. Rooms have cable TV and hot water.

#### $$ El Zaguán
*C 21, No 22-08, El Retiro, T4-541 2534, hotelzaguan@gmail.com.*
Modern brick building with 6 large, very clean rooms. Rooftop has good views of the town and a small bar showing occasional films. Laundry service, TV and hot water.

#### $ Casa Campesina
*Cra 20, No 22-43, El Retiro, T4-541 0692.*
This slightly run-down establishment near the Parque Principal has an extraordinary pulley system for opening the front door. Despite being a bit shabby, it has good beds and several dorms.

#### Guatapé
Rooms for hire in houses ($) can be found through calling the local tourist office on T4-861 0555 ext 30 or T312-873 0302 (mob).

#### $$$ Hotel Guatatur
*C 31, No 31-04, T4-861 1212, www.hotelguatatur.com.*
Located in a modern building just off the plaza, this hotel has crisp, airy rooms with large windows and comfortable beds. The suites have lovely elevated

jacuzzis with good views out to the lake. Restaurant, plasma-screen TV, minibar, room service. Breakfast included.

### $ El Descanso del Arriero
*C 30, No 28-82, T4-861 0878, www.eldescansodelarriero.com.*
An *arriero* is a mule driver, and this pleasant hostel has a suitably rustic feel. It has clean rooms with private bath and hot water, some with a view to the church.

### $ Hotel Portal del Lago
*C 32 No 22-39, T4-861 0985.*
Good mid-range option located right on the *malecón*. Expansive rooms and large beds.

## Reserva Natural Cañón del Río Claro

### $$$ El Refugio
*T4-268 8855 (Medellín), www.rioclaroelrefugio.com.*
Swiss Family Robinson-style wooden structures perched high above the river. All rooms have a balcony open to the elements and include all meals. There is also a small hostel ($) at the entrance to the reserve, with rooms with private bath, as well as a campsite ($).

## Doradal

### $$$ Doradal Mediterráneo
*Aldea Doradal, T4-834 2129, http://hoteldoradalmediterraneo.blogspot.com.*
The hotel, at the top of the village, has airy, a/c rooms with tiled bathrooms, a swimming pool and jacuzzi and Wi-Fi. Breakfast included.

### $$$ El Lago
*200 m east of Doradal on Bogotá–Medellín road, T311-382 7635.*
*Cabañas* with a/c and private bathrooms and a fine pool, though a little noisy with all the traffic.

### $ Hotel Yahaya
*On the Bogotá–Medellín road, T4-834 2177, www.hotelyahaya.com.*
Clean, comfortable rooms with fan, TV, private bathroom and balcony as well as a good swimming pool. Restaurant serves typical dishes.

## Restaurants

### Circuito de Oriente
In addition to **El Gran Chaparral** (see Where to stay), there are several good places to eat on the Parque Principal in El Retiro, where there is also an ATM.

### $ Fonda de los Recuerdos
*Western end of El Retiro, on the main road to Medellín.*
More antique junkyard than restaurant. Food served is served to a backing track of old boleros, tango and 1940s ballads. It is reportedly a favourite with local politicians; there is a photograph of President Alvaro Uribe with eccentric owner Chepe on the wall.

### Guatapé
There are several places to eat on the Parque Principal. Trout is a local speciality.

### Doradal

### $$ Asados del Camino
*On main road at west end of Doradal, www.asadosdelcamino.com.*
*Bandeja paisa*, burgers and hotdogs in a large ranch.

## What to do

### Circuito de Oriente

Club Hípico Los Malos, *Cra Santander, No 18-07, El Retiro, T316-825 5479.* Hire horses from US$30 per day with optional *burroteca* (a donkey with a music sound system attached).

___

## Reserva Natural Cañon del Río Claro

**El Refugio**, *T4-268 8855 (Medellín)*, *www.rioclaroelrefugio.com*. Organizes rafting expeditions, Grade I and II, scenic rather than adventurous. There is also a series of zip wires ('canopy') across the canyon and you can hire rubber rings for floating down the river.

### Transport

Although the area east of Medellín is mountainous, with many twists and turns, the bus and minivan system is extensive. Daily buses run to all towns and pueblos east of Medellín, including Guatape.

Buses from the Terminal del Norte in Medellín to **Doradal** take 3 hrs and cost US$13.50. There are buses to **El Retiro**, from Terminal del Sur, US$2.75, with **Sotra Retiro**.

___

## South of Medellín → *Colour map 2, B3.*

**beautiful countryside and appealing towns west of the Río Cauca**

### Towards Manizales

**Santa Bárbara** (altitude 1857 m) is 57 km south of Medellín on the main road via the town of Caldas, with stunning views of coffee, banana and sugar plantations, orange-tiled roofs and folds of hills, in every direction. There are hotels and restaurants on the main plaza; the bus from Medellín costs US$3. A further 26 km is **La Pintada** (camping; hotels $). Here the road crosses the Río Cauca, then splits. To the east is the particularly attractive road through Aguadas, Pácora and Salamina, all perched on mountain ridges, to Manizales in the Zona Cafetera.

Alternatively, from La Pintada, the main road goes up the Cauca valley through beautiful countryside to **Marmato** (see page 287) and **Riosucio**. Beyond, at Anserma, the road turns east to Manizales via Arauca.

### Southwest of Medellín

Shortly after Caldas, a road to the right (west) descends through Amagá to cross the Cauca at Bolombolo. From here, several attractive towns can be visited.

**Jericó** is an interesting Antioquian town with a large cathedral, several other churches, two museums and a good view from Morro El Salvador. **Andes** is a busy coffee-buying centre; it has several places to stay and to eat on Carrera 50/51, and there are pretty waterfalls nearby.

**Jardín** is 16 km southeast of Andes. This pretty Antioquian village is surrounded by cultivated hills and trout farms. It was founded in 1863 on the site of an indigenous settlement (of the Embera-Katío group), who worked the naturally iodized salt in the river there. There is still a reservation of the Cristianías community in the locality. It is a delightful place that lives up to its name, with an attractive fountain in the plaza, surrounded by flowering shrubs and trees. The neo-Gothic church, **Templo Parroquial de la Inmaculada Concepción**, is a National Monument. It has a fine façade built of dark dressed stone, an striking altar of Italian marble and an eight-pointed star in the ceiling of the apse. The

Fiesta de las Rosas takes place in January. The small museum in the **Casa Cultura** has paintings and local artefacts, not to mention a bank that accepts Visa cards. Just outside Jardin, is **Hacienda Balandú ($$$)**, Vía Jardín Río Sucio, which has comfortable rooms, pool, gardens, lake, spa, sports, good restaurant.

## North of Medellín → *Colour map 2, B3-A2.*

mountain scenery on the long road to Cartagena

### Santa Rosa de Osas and around

About 21 km north of the city is **Santa Rosa de Osos**, 2550 m, founded in 1636 and with several surviving colonial buildings, including the Humildad chapel. There are sculptures by Rodrigo Arenas Betancur and Marco Tobón Mejía. About 15 km southwest is **Entrerríos**, in attractive steep country between the Río Grande and the Río Chico; it's somewhat extravagantly called the 'Switzerland of Colombia'. Nearby is a 75-m *peñón*, El Monolito, which is of archaeological interest.

### Towards Parque Nacional Natural Paramillo

About 25 km north of Santa Rosa, a road to the west leads to **San José de la Montaña**, 2550 m, in the Páramo de Santa Inés, surrounded by cloudforest, caverns and waterfalls. The rough road continues over the gorge of the Río Cauca, 75 km beyond, to **Ituango** at 1550 m, a town with simple accommodation, banks, pharmacies and a supermarket. From Ituango, rural transport is available to Badillo in the **Parque Nacional Natural Paramillo**, 460,000 ha of forest that stretches from the plains of the Río Sinú and the Río San Jorge to the headwaters of both rivers. The national park has *páramo* (moorland) over 3000 m – the highest point is 3960 m – and a wide range of flora and fauna: caiman and turtles in the lower areas; monkeys and many varieties of trees and birds at all levels.

### Northern Antioquia

The main road north of Santa Rosa climbs to **Yarumal**, 122 km from Medellín, a friendly town in a cold mountain climate with fine views from Parroquia La Merced. There is a museum of religious art in the town hall and an interesting chapel, **Capilla de San Luis**, nearby. There is a natural bridge 1 km from the town and several *peñoles* in the neighbourhood. *Hosterías* can be found on the main plaza and Calle Caliente.

A further high pass, **Alto de Ventanas**, follows, then a drop to **Valdivia**, 159 km from Medellín. There are a number of good walking and riding trails around here, including to the **Quebrada Valdivia** and **Quebrada El Oro** and to two waterfalls: **Cascadas de Santa Inez** and **Chorros Blancos**. There are *residencias* ($) on the main road and several restaurants. The main road continues north, leading eventually to Cartagena, 665 km north of Medellin.

a colonial time-warp town

About 78 km northwest of Medellín is Santa Fe de Antioquia, or Santa Fe as it is frequently called. It was founded as a gold mining town by Mariscal Jorge Robledo in 1541, the first in the area, and still retains its colonial atmosphere, with interesting Christmas and New Year fiestas. For a time in the 19th century it was the capital of the department and retains much grandeur and character from that time, little affected by changes since then. It has some beautiful colonial mansions with wooden balconies and narrow cobbled streets.

## Santa Fe de Antioquia

Nuestra Señora de Chiquinquirá

To Turbo

Plazuelita (Plaza Menor)

Palacio Arzobispal

Cra 13

Cra 12

La Casa Negra

Cra 11

Cra 10

Cra 9

Plaza Mayor

Cathedral

Museo Juan de Corral

Plazuela de Santa Bárbara

Santa Bárbara

Cra 8

Casa de la Cultura

Cra 7

Cra 6

Jesús Nazareno

To Coliseo & Puente de Occidente

To Río Cauca & Medellín

To Río Cauca & Medellín

To Río Cauca & Medellín

100 metres

100 yards

**Where to stay** 
Alejo 1
Caserón Plaza 2
Guaracú 3
Hostal Tenerife 4
Hostería de la Plaza Menor 5
Hostal Plaza Mayor 6
Las Carnes del Tío 7
Mariscal Robledo 8

**Restaurants** 
Don Roberto 1
La Comedia 2
La Plazuela 3
Macías 4

## Sights

The **Plaza Mayor** is particularly attractive, with an imposing cathedral and *artesanía* stalls selling tamarind products, nuts, honey and dried fruits. The square is dominated by the fountain, which has been supplying water to the town for 450 years and incorporates a bronze statue of Juan del Corral, who was the President of Antioquia during its few years of Independence between 1813 and 1826. The **Catedral Metropolitana** is on the site of the first modest church that was built in the town in the late 16th century. A second church was completed in 1673, with three naves and other embellishments, including chapels, added in the next 100 years. This, in turn, was replaced in 1799, and the present building was consecrated in 1837. It has an imposing white and coloured stone/brick façade (a style called *calicanto* seen in a number of local buildings). There is a fine 17th-century Christ figure as the centrepiece of the high altar, and a notable Last Supper sculpture from the 18th century. The shrine, with embossed-silver ornamentation, was the work of local artists, but unhappily, several fine gold pieces, also of local workmanship, were stolen from the Treasury in 1986. The tower was used as a prison in times past.

Northeast of the Plaza Mayor, the **Iglesia de Santa Bárbara** ⓘ *C 11, No 8-53*, is also on the site of at least one previous building, which was passed to the Jesuits in 1728. They found it too small, and the present three-nave church was finished by Juan Pablo Pérez de Rublas at the end of the 18th century. The interior walls and arches are in *calicanto* style, as is the broad west front, crowned with turrets and bells. An interesting woodcarving of the Virgin is enshrined in the Altar of San Blas, which is the oldest altar in Santa Fe. The font, in rococo style, is also older than the building. Next to the church is the **Museo Juan del Corral** ⓘ *C 11, Mon-Fri 0900-1200, 1400-1730, Sat and Sun 1000-1700*, which contains an interesting collection of historical items, including paintings and gold objects, from colonial and more recent times.

The church of **Jesús Nazareno** is another classical-style building, this one from the 19th century, and is notable for the wood sculptures of Jesus on the cross and the Crown of Thorns.

West of the main square, Plaza José María Martínez Pardo has a statue of **Mariscal Robledo** at its centre and is overlooked by a hotel of the same name. Opposite is the church of **Nuestra Señora de Chiquinquirá**, which was built in the late 19th century on the site of a 17th-century Franciscan temple. An old painting of the Virgin of Chiquinquirá is built into the modern marble altar. This church, too, was used in the past as a prison. On the south side of the square is the **Palacio Arzobispal**, in Republican style, well worth a look inside. Opposite is a music school, further evidence of the cultural life of the town.

There are many fine colonial houses in the town; take a look inside where you can. Typical of the *calicanto* style are the **Casa de la Cultura** and **La Casa Negra** (the birthplace of Fernando Gómez Martínez).

## Puente de Occidente

A trip to the Puente de Occidente, a fine slender suspension bridge across the Río Cauca, is worthwhile. It is about 3 km downstream from the main (new) bridge and about 6 km from the centre of Santa Fe. You can walk, drive or take a taxi; hitching is difficult as there is little traffic. Leave the town northeast on Carrera 9, cross the main Turbo road, and follow the signs to the 'Coliseo'. The paved road winds through the suburbs of the town, then drops down steeply through dry scrub to the river. The single-track bridge with wooden cross slats is 300 m long and was designed and constructed by José María Villa, who studied in the USA, between 1887 and 1895; it was declared a National Monument in 1978. Small vehicles are allowed to cross the bridge, but it is abundantly clear why this is not encouraged!

## Where to stay

### $$$ Guaracú
*C 10, No 8-36.*
Gorgeous colonial mansion with a restaurant set around a courtyard full of mango trees and palms. Beautiful antique furniture, gramophones, cameras and pistols interspersed throughout the building. There is even a large pet tortoise that wanders around the corridors. Rooms are very comfortable with TV and stereo.

### $$$ Hostal Tenerife
*Cra 8, No 11-50, T4-539 1965,*
*www.hotelcasatenerife.com.co.*
This beautifully decorated colonial house has 7 rooms, each equipped with a/c, cable TV and a minibar. There's free use of house bikes, internet access and a gorgeous pool in one of the courtyards. Breakfast is included in the price. Recommended.

### $$$ Mariscal Robledo
*C 10, No 9-70, T4-853 1563,*
*www.hotelmariscalrobledo.com.*
Former home of José María Martínez Pardo, former governor of Antioquia, this colonial mansion has a large swimming pool and commanding views across the valley. Staff can organize horse-riding trips and guided tours of the town.

### $$$-$$ Caserón Plaza
*Plaza Mayor, C 9, No 9-41, T4-853 2040,*
*www.hotelcaseronplaza.com.co.*
Large colonial building on the main plaza, decorated with African carvings and potted plants. Comfortable rooms, some with balconies looking onto large pool. Has a fine sun deck with fantastic views across the valley. Internet room,
Wi-Fi, bike hire, a/c and can arrange guides for local tours.

### $$$-$$ Hostería de la Plaza Menor
*C 9A, No 13-21, T4-853 1133,*
*www.hosteriadelaplazamenor.com.*
Tucked away round the corner from the Plaza Menor, this hotel has 26 comfortable rooms and offers a swimming pool, Turkish bath, gym and a children's playground.

### $$ Las Carnes del Tío
*C 10, No 7-22, T4-853 3385.*
A restaurant that also offers some good rooms with vaulted ceilings and enormous bathrooms. Also dorms and shared baths.

### $ Hostal Plaza Mayor
*C 9, No 10-59, T4-853 3448.*
Right on the main square, this is a popular choice with backpackers. There are hammocks, a small pool and a small *cabaña* with bunk beds ($). The owner also has a Mexican ranch outside town where he will take guests for a barbecue.

### $ Alejo
*C 9, No 10-56, T4-853 1091.*
Well placed just 1 block from the Plaza Mayor, it has small and basic but clean rooms with their own TV and bathroom. The restaurant serves cheap food.

## Restaurants

### $$ Guaracu
*C 10, No 8-36, in the hotel of the same name (see Where to stay).*
The speciality is fish, especially trout.

### $ Don Roberto
*C 10, No 7-37, T4-853 2294.*
In a large colonial building with a swimming pool out the back (US$5

for the day), this restaurant has a simple menu of typical dishes, such as *bandeja paisa* and *sancocho de bagre*, as well as fast food. Delicious juices: try the *guandolo* – bitter orange with brown sugar.

### $ La Comedia
*C 11, No 8-03, T4-853 1243.*
On the corner of Plazuela Santa Bárbara, this restaurant has a novel concept: you can buy any of the furniture or utensils you use while you eat, all of which are made by *artesanos* from Barichara. Jazz music and exhibitions of work by local artists give it a bohemian atmosphere. Colombian and international arthouse films are shown every Thu evening, projected either in the bar or in the square outside.

### $ La Plazuela
*C 10, No 5-63.*
Bar and restaurant serving pizza by the slice, plus sandwiches and desserts.

### $ Las Carnes del Tío
*C 10, No 7-22.*
Steaks and fish in the sunny courtyard of a fine colonial building.

### $ Macías
*Plaza Mayor.*
This small restaurant has been serving locals for over 35 years, so it must be doing something right. The menu is a mixture of regional and national dishes.

## Festivals

**Mar/Apr  Holy Week** is a major celebration here, and is followed by another week of festivities between the 2nd and 3rd Sun after Easter when there are many children's parades. This is known as **Semana Santica**.
**11 Aug  Antioquian Independence** is celebrated.
**Early/mid-Dec**  Film festival for 5 days, www.festicineantioquia.com.
**22-31 Dec  Fiesta de los Diablitos**, with folk dancing, parades, bullfights, etc.

## Shopping

**Artesanías Antiguedades**, *Cra 10, No 10-71.* Antique clocks, locks, cameras and typewriters as well as beautiful papier mâché figurines.
**Guarnielería**, *C 10, No 7-66.* Leather products, especially *carriel paisa*, a man's handbag replete with secret pockets for hiding your gun, now often used by women too.
**Joyería Leydi**, *C 10, No 8-58.* Excellent filigree gold jewellery.

## What to do

**Gimnasio Life**, *C 10, No 7-09, T4-853 4177.* Only in Santa Fe would you find exercise bikes and weights in the courtyard of a beautiful colonial building.

## Transport

### Bus
The bus station is on the road to Turbo at the north end of Cras 9 and 10.

To **Medellín**, US$5 with **Sotraurabá**, 1 hr, or US$4 with **Rápido Ochoa**, 5 a day; also *colectivos*, US$7. To **Turbo**, US$20-25, 8 hrs, every 2 hrs or so.

# Chocó
## Department

Undoubtedly one of the rainiest and most biodiverse locations on the planet, the Pacific coast of Colombia's Chocó region is overlooked and under-visited. Fearing tales of kidnapping and guerrilla activity, tourists are understandably quick to avoid this region of Colombia; but the security situation has been improving, and, with a little research and some good faith, there are several parts of Pacific Chocó that are no longer out of bounds. Having said that, it is recommended that you check in with the local authorities before visiting and exercise caution while you are there.

Stretching like a ribbon for 400 km between the Cordillera Occidental and the Pacific coast, from Panama to Valle del Cauca, Chocó is one of Colombia's least-developed and most beautiful departments. In the northern three-quarters of the department, the mountain ranges of the Serranía de Los Saltos and Serranía del Baudó rise directly from the ocean to reach a height of about 500 m. The scenery of pristine rainforest descending the mountain slopes to the sea is spectacular.

# Essential Chocó Department

## Finding your feet

The easiest and most convenient way to get to the Pacific coast is to fly from Medellín or Bogotá via Quibdó to either Nuquí or Bahía Solano, with Satena (www.satena.com) and Aerolínea de Antioquia (www.ada-aero.com). You can travel by bus from Medellín to Quibdó with Rápido Ochoa, but the journey is arduous and not recommended. Note that banking services and currency exchange are limited in Chocó; best to buy pesos in larger centres before arriving.

### Tip...
Exercise extreme caution if travelling overland beyond Quibdó. The former governor of Chocó was kidnapped at gunpoint just outside the city in 2013.

## Getting around

Travelling on from Quibdó you are strongly recommended to fly straight to Nuquí or Bahía Solano; until the road to Tribugá is completed, overland journeys to the coast involve a three-day trek through the jungle and should not be undertaken lightly in this volatile region. River trips north along the Río Atrato are also risky. Once on the coast, sea taxis will take you to beaches and villages.

## When to go

Choco is very warm and very wet year round. Try to coordinate your visit with whale-watching season from July to November.

## Time required

Three to five days is enough time to enjoy the scenery and wildlife.

| Weather Chocó Department (Quibdó) | | | | | |
|---|---|---|---|---|---|
| **January** | **February** | **March** | **April** | **May** | **June** |
| 30°C 23°C 554mm | 30°C 23°C 517mm | 30°C 23°C 524mm | 31°C 23°C 660mm | 31°C 23°C 719mm | 32°C 23°C 755mm |
| **July** | **August** | **September** | **October** | **November** | **December** |
| 31°C 23°C 816mm | 31°C 23°C 840mm | 31°C 23°C 682mm | 32°C 23°C 638mm | 32°C 23°C 719mm | 32°C 23°C 580mm |

**see humpback whales and turtles along this unspoiled coastline**

## Quibdó → *Colour map 2, B2.*

Quibdó, the capital of the department, is an unlovely and underwhelming city on the frontline. It is the jumping-off point for most military operations in this stretch of the country and it is not uncommon to see brigades of soldiers returning war-weary from the jungle, while the new batch ready themselves for their next outing. The few Western faces you are likely to see are aid workers or delegates from Médecins Sans Frontières. There is little to keep you here save for the warmth and curiosity of the locals regarding your choice of tourist destination, and the unstoppable partying during the city's fiestas. Hordes of birds fly in to roost at dusk and locals gather on the waterfront promenade, El Malecón, to watch the magnificent sunsets.

## Nuquí → *Colour map 2, B1.*

Construction is continuing on a road from Las Animas (south of Quibdó) to Nuquí on the coast, which will eventually connect the port planned for Tribugá with the interior. It is presently a strenuous three-day trek along a jungle trail through several indigenous villages to Nuquí. Once there, Nuquí town has very little to offer the visitor aside from a serviceable runway and some poorly stocked shops. It is to the north and south of the town where the real attractions lie in the form of award-winning ecolodges.

## El Valle → *Colour map 2, B1.*

Some 50 km north of Nuquí along the coast, El Valle has the best bathing and surfing beaches in the area, although tourism development has gone hand in hand with a decline in friendliness. As yet there is no access to El Valle for regular vehicles, so most people arrive either by air to Bahía Solano and then by truck, or by boat from Nuquí. The entrance to El Valle's harbour is very tricky at ebb tide and many boats have been swept onto the rocks here. If hiring boats privately, check carefully and make sure there are life jackets for any sea journeys.

**El Almejal**, north of town, is the best beach and has *cabañas* (see Where to stay, page 275). Another beautiful and isolated beach, **El Tigre,** can be visited by boat, or on a three-hour walk. Near El Valle, the **Fundación Natura** runs a *tortugario*, known as **Estación Septiembre** ① *www.natura.org.co*, where turtle eggs are protected from predators in season; check the website for visiting opportunities. Guides are available in El Valle for tours by canoe up the Río Baudó, and to other places of interest along the coast; El Nativo has been recommended.

**Parque Nacional Natural Ensenada de Utría** → *Colour map 2, B1.*
*US$18. Boat from El Valle to park headquarters, 1 hr, US$16 return; from Nuquí, 1½ hrs, US$24.*

Between Nuquí and El Valle is Parque Nacional Natural Ensenada de Utría. This 54,000-ha park was created in 1987 to preserve several unique aquatic and terrestrial habitats. The park is named after a large inlet (*ensenada*), which is home to two varieties of whale, plus corals, needlefish and many other aquatic species. This is one of the best places on the west coast of South America to see humpback whales migrating from late July to mid-October. The park headquarters is located halfway up the inlet; motorboats are not allowed further than this and the area is best appreciated if you paddle through in a canoe. Steep mountains covered in pristine rainforest drop down to the ocean to create dramatic scenery, and there are several magnificent white-sand beaches. Across the inlet from the headquarters is a private research station run by **Fundación Natura** as a base for biologists.

Day trips by boat may be arranged from El Valle, Nuquí or Bahía Solano (weather and sea conditions permitting) and special permits are sometimes granted for longer stays by the national parks office in Bogotá. The ranger welcomes volunteers to help clear rubbish from the beaches and other tasks (also best arranged in advance from Bogotá). The launch that runs from Nuquí to El Valle will sometimes (depending on tides) stop at Playa Blanca, a small, privately owned island near the park boundary, with good snorkelling and fishing. The park headquarters are five minutes away by motorboat and you can generally hitch a ride with fishermen or park employees. There is also a road and trail leading through the jungle from El Valle to the head of the inlet (9 km, four to five hours, can be very muddy), but you must arrange for a boat to pick you up as it is not possible to reach the park headquarters on foot.

The park headquarters has a visitor centre with maps, good information and a display of whale bones and other exhibits, plus a small restaurant. There are several well-marked trails from here. Fresh fish can sometimes be purchased, but all other provisions should be brought from town. Mosquito nets are essential for protection against insects and vampire bats.

## Bahía Solano → *Colour map 2, B1.*

A road runs 18 km from El Valle to Bahía Solano (passing the airport on the way into town). During the annual migration of the humpback whales – their breaching can be seen from the shore – the town is overrun with holidaymakers from Medellín. Outside this period Bahía Solano is a functional fishing town with a side trade in collecting discarded packages of cocaine on their way north. This industry is so lucrative to local fishermen, who stand to earn a lifetime's pay in one swoop, that it has become their principal activity. Excursions include diving a scuttled naval ship, hiking to waterfalls, sports fishing and visiting neighbouring beaches. Check out the **Hotel Balboa Plaza** – you can't miss it as it's the only three-storey building in town – a folly and luxury pad built by Pablo Escobar that's now falling into disrepair.

## Where to stay

### Quibdó
Quibdó is not overwhelmed with decent places to stay, but centrally located and safe is the **Hotel Malecón**, Cra 1 No 26A-60, T4-671 2725.

### Nuquí
Close to Nuquí, **Piedra Piedra** (T4-204 0671, www.piedrapiedra.com), **Pijiba Lodge** (T574-474 5221) and **Morromico** (T312-795 6321, www.morromico.com) are environmentally aware, award-winning and design-oriented lodges that can organize fishing trips, surfing outings and kayak rental. Communication is scant out here so it is imperative to book ahead through the main offices in Medellín; the staff will be providing you with 3 sumptuous meals each day and will need to stock up in advance.

### El Valle
There are several large but simple tourist complexes at El Almejal, with rooms and cabins ($ range), as well as bars and restaurants; they are deserted Mon-Thu off-season. Other cheap accommodation includes **Carmen Lucía** or **Nativo y Rosa;** ask around.

### $$$ Cabañas El Almejal
*T4-412 5050 (Medellín),*
*www.almejal.com.co.*
The best cabins, clean with private bath. Friendly staff. Full board available.

### $$-$ El Morro
*El Almejal.*
Full board or with breakfast only.

### $ Cabinas Villa Maga
*Between El Valle and El Almejal.*
Friendly, safe, family-run.

### Ensenada de Utría
**$** Simple but comfortable accommodation for about 15 people is provided in a guest house at US$6 per night and there's an outdoor kitchen with a wood stove, meals US$3, but camping is prohibited. Food and hammock space is also provided at Playa Blanca by Sr Salomón Caizamo (US$2 for up to 5 hammocks).

### Bahía Solano
**$$$ Mapara Crab Hotel Bahía Solano**
*T314-700 4824, www.maparacrab.com.*
Run by the affable and knowledgeable Nancy and Enrique Ramírez, this is a small, comfortable family enterprise offering private rooms with fan and breakfast. Enrique is a master sports fisherman and diving enthusiast.

## Restaurants

### Nuquí
There are several small restaurants on the road to the airport serving mostly fish. Shops are well stocked with basic goods, but prices are somewhat higher than in Quibdó.

### El Valle
A local product in El Valle is *borojo* marmalade, made from a local fruit that tastes like tamarind. There are several restaurants and bars at El Almejal.

### Bahía Solano

There's good food at **Las Delicias** and at the restaurant run by Señora Ayde near the **Balboa** hotel.

## Festivals

### Quibdó

**Sep-Oct Fiesta de San Pacho** (www.sanpachobendito.org) has parades and a San Francisco de Asís procession.

## Transport

### Quibdó
#### Air

To **Medellín**, with **Lan** and **Avianca**, 2 daily. To **Bogotá**, **Lan** and **Satena**; to **Bahía Solano** and **Nuquí**, daily, with **Satena**. Enquire about other non-scheduled flights at holiday times.

#### Boat

From Buenaventura on the Río San Juan to **Istmina** and then by road to Quibdó; infrequent services. An irregular cargo service on the Río Atrato takes passengers to Turbo and Cartagena, 4 days; take drinking water. Deal directly with boatmen. There are also 20-seater power boats, 7 hrs to Turbo, about US$30. Note that the lower Atrato can be a very dangerous area, so caution and detailed advance enquiry are strongly recommended.

#### Bus

**Rápido Ochoa** to **Medellín**, via El Carmen and Bolívar, 3 daily, 10-12 hrs, US$30-32.50 luxury coach, US$16 by regular bus. **Transportes Arauca** to **Manizales**, via Tadó, Pueblo Rico, La Virginia and Pereira, Tue, Thu, Sat, Sun 0600, 14-17 hrs, US$26. **Flota Occidental** along same route to **Pereira**, daily at 0700, 8-10 hrs, US$30. There are occasional buses to **Cali**, US$32; otherwise change at La Virginia. To **Bogotá**, US$53. There are local services to **Santa Cecilia** and **Tadó**.

### Nuquí
#### Air

To **Quibdó**, with **Satena**, 20 mins. Some extra flights at Christmas and Easter time.

#### Boat

There are launches south to **Arusi** (Mon, Wed, Fri) and north to **El Valle**. The twin-engined *Magdalena* runs to **Jurubidá**, **La Esperanza** (US$4) and **El Valle** (US$8) on Mon, Wed and Fri, returning Tue, Thu and Sat. There are also occasional coastal vessels (usually small fuel barges) to **Buenaventura**, about US$40. Sea taxis will take you to beaches and villages along the coast.

### El Valle

Jeeps to **Bahía Solano** leave every morning, 1 hr, US$3; tickets can be purchased 1 day in advance.

### Bahía Solano
#### Air

To **Medellín**, daily with **Satena,** 40 mins. To **Quibdó**, daily with **Satena**. Reconfirm return flights and arrive at the airport early before departure.

#### Boat

Some coastal cargo vessels travel north to **Juradó** and south to **Buenaventura** (eg *M/V Fronteras*), US$75, including food and a cramped bunk, 36 hrs.

# La Zona
## Cafetera

★Since the middle of the 19th century, the departments of Caldas, Risaralda and Quindío have been the country's sweet spot for coffee production. The region enjoys a tropical climate at high altitude, which allows coffee plants to thrive. Plantations in the area have altered their production methods very little over the decades, and the beans are still picked by hand, but now the coffee farmers supplement their income by opening their doors to tourists, offering a glimpse of the whole process, from cultivating the plants, to roasting the beans, to making the perfect cup of espresso. The surrounding countryside is mountainous, fertile and rich in wildlife. And the high peaks of Los Nevados National Park are visible to the east.

# Essential La Zona Cafetera

## Finding your feet

The three departmental capitals of La Zona Cafetera lie close to each other, flanked to the east by the massif of Los Nevados: Manizales (Caldas) in the north, Pereira (Risaralda), 50 km away in the centre, and Armenia (Quindío) a similar distance to the south. All three can be reached from Bogotá by crossing the Cordillera Central. The most direct route (309 km) heads west through Facatativá and Honda and then over the Páramo de las Letras pass (3700 m, the highest main road pass in Colombia); the alternative is through Girardot to Ibagué and over the high crest of the Quindío pass (3250 m). Both routes involve long winding climbs and descents amid superb scenery.

## Getting around

Road and transport facilities are good, although landslides on the steep hills around Manizales can cause significant travel difficulties during the rainy season. The three main cities are connected by the fast Autopista del Café toll road, which has cut journey times. Much of the local transport in this region is by *chiva* (literally 'goat'), simple, brightly coloured buses and jeeps, often called by the historic name 'Willys'; they're usually ancient but lovingly maintained. To get off the beaten track, a hire car is recommended.

### Best coffee fincas

**Hacienda Guayabal**, page 284
**Hacienda Venecia**, page 284
**Hacienda San José**, page 297
**Hacienda Bambusa**, page 306
**El Carriel**, page 307
**El Delirio**, page 307
**Finca Villa Nora**, page 307

## When to go

Because of the altitude, the climate in this region is generally very agreeable. The best months of the year are from mid-December through to early March. In Los Nevados national park the dry seasons are January to February and June to September, but even in those months it can rain for days or be very foggy. The whole upland area is subject to wide temperature changes during the day, depending on cloud cover, and very cold nights.

## Time required

You'll need a week to explore this area; add three to four days for trekking in Los Nevados.

## Weather Manizales

| | | |
|---|---|---|
| **January** 22°C 11°C 98mm | **February** 22°C 12°C 92mm | **March** 22°C 12°C 134mm |
| **April** 22°C 12°C 167mm | **May** 21°C 13°C 154mm | **June** 21°C 12°C 91mm |
| **July** 22°C 12°C 64mm | **August** 22°C 12°C 75mm | **September** 21°C 12°C 138mm |
| **October** 21°C 12°C 190mm | **November** 21°C 12°C 167mm | **December** 21°C 11°C 125mm |

Manizales is a comparatively new city, founded in 1848 by a group of settlers from Antioquia looking for a peaceful place at a time of civil disturbances further north. As a result, Manizales has the feel of a late 19th-century city with Republican architecture and a fierce pride in '*Los Fundadores*', the founders of the city. However, this area is unstable geologically and was struck by severe earthquakes in 1875 and 1879, followed by fires that swept through the city in 1925 and especially 1926, severely damaging the centre. As a result, much of the architecture is modern with high-rise office and apartment blocks, although traditional 19th-century architectural styles are still seen in the suburbs and the older sections of the city. The city's dramatic location on a narrow saddle at 2150m that falls away sharply into adjacent valleys to the north, west and south has forced it to expand to the east, along precipitous ridges between the Río Chinchiná and Quebrada Olivares using every available piece of flat land; surrounding villages, such as Villa Maria, are gradually being absorbed by the city. The warm, wet climate means the area around the city is prodigiously fertile, with flowers lining the highways to the north and south. Frequently the city is covered in cloud but when it is clear, there are brilliant views in every direction. With luck, you may see the snows of the Nevados to the southeast.

The centre of Manizales is pleasant and convenient for walking, though narrow streets can create traffic problems. The key thoroughfare is Carrera 23, which runs the full length of the city (it's know as Avenida Santander in the east), leading eventually to La Nubia airport, Honda and Bogotá. Lined with shops and eateries, it's busy any day of the week. East of the centre, **El Cable** is the city's Zona Rosa and has the best restaurants and bars. Further east again is **Barrio Milán**, another popular nightlife area.

### Centro

The centre of the city is the **Plaza de Bolívar** with two ceramic murals by Guillermo Botero and a central plinth on which stands an extraordinary bronze statue of **Bolívar Condor** (1991) by Rodrigo Arenas Betancur. It depicts Bolívar as a condor, his head dismembered from his body and protruding into the plaza. On the north side of the plaza is the departmental government building, **La Gobernación**, an imposing example of neo-colonial architecture, built in 1926 around a central garden patio. The building was declared a National Monument in 1984. Opposite is the enormous modern **cathedral**, which dominates the city. Two previous cathedrals on the site were destroyed and even this one suffered during an earthquake in 1979. It was designed in neo-Gothic style by Italian architects after the fires of 1925 and 1926 and is constructed mainly of reinforced concrete, with an elegant spire over 100 m high. It now has four towers, one each dedicated to saints Inés, Francis, Mark and Paul. Inside, look out for the finely decorated altar cover with a suspended cross above; the wooden choir stalls, and the colourful stained-glass windows, including a fine rose window at the west end. There is also a simple but elegant marble font to the left of the west door. One-hour tours including a climb up the cathedral spire take place daily, US$5.

Nearby, the **Banco de la República** ⓘ *Cra 25, No 52-40, Mon-Fri 0830-1800, Sat 0830-1300, free,* has a gold and anthropology museum, a good reference library, records and videos.

Other churches in the centre include **Iglesia de los Agustinos** ⓘ *Cra 19,* which has a colonial-style façade and numerous spires, and the neo-Gothic **Iglesia de la Inmaculada Concepción** ⓘ *Cra 22/C 30, overlooking Parque Caldas,* built 1903-1921, with cedarwood pillars and stained-glass windows. Nearby, the **Teatro de los Fundadores** ⓘ *Cra 23/C 33,* is a good example of local modern architecture and is well worth a visit; it has some fine murals and metal sculptures in the foyer and upper floors, including works by Guillermo Botero (see below).

### West of the centre

Avenida 12 de Octubre is bordered on its west side by a park with magnificent views across the city to the east and over coffee country to the west, down towards the Río Cauca. It is much frequented by locals at weekends. Stalls along the promenade sell *obleas*, large wheat wafers, served with *arequipe* and coconut that are well worth a try. The large water tower known as **El Tanque** is a local landmark. At the end of the avenue is an impressive sculpture, the **Monumento a los Colonizadores** ⓘ *daily 1100-1900, free,* made from keys collected locally and melted down. There is also a tourist information point here. **Chipre** is a suburb in

**Manizales**

Where to stay
Bolívar Plaza 1
Carretero 4
Escorial 5
Estelar Las Colinas 6
Manizales Hostel 8
Mountain House 7
Roma Plaza 9
Regine's 10
Varuna 12

Restaurants
El Zaguán Paisa 1
Frisby 2
Pollos Asados Mario 3

the northwest of the city and has, in its centre, the **Nuestra Señora del Rosario church**, which is a replica of the previous city cathedral.

Southwest of the centre, the **bull-ring** ① *Av Centenario, T6-883 8124, tickets US$10-30*, was built around 1950 in traditional Moorish style and is an impressive copy of the one in Córdoba, Spain. It holds 20,000 people. Bullfights take place in late January, and again in June and July with young bulls and no kills.

## East of the centre and El Cable

Just east of Centro, **Universidad de Caldas** ① *C 65 No 26-10, www.ucaldas.edu.co, Mon-Fri 0830-1200, 1415-1800; 'Fatima' bus from Centro*, has a natural history museum with a good selection of butterflies, moths and birds. Also on the campus is the **Centro de Museos** ① *Cra 23, No 58-65, T6-886 2720, Mon-Fri, 1000-1800*, which has an art gallery and exhibitions on geology and archaeology. Further east, the **University of Manizales** ① *off Cra 23 at C 40*, is housed in a fine building (originally the railway station) of considerable historic interest. Further east, **La Galería del Arte** ① *Av Santander (Cra 23) at C 55*, has exhibitions and sale of works by local artists.

Heading out on Avenida Santander (Cra 23) to Bogotá, you will see the tower of the old aerial cableway terminal at Calle 65. The cableway once stretched 75 km from Manizales to Mariquita and was used from 1922 till the 1960s to carry coffee, thus avoiding the difficult journey over the Alto de Las Letras pass (3700 m). From Mariquita the coffee was taken by road and rail to the Río Magdalena for shipment and export. The cableway has given its name to this popular district of the city, **El Cable**, where many bars and restaurants are located.

## Parque Ecológico Río Blanco

*Contact Aguas de Manizales T6-887 9770, www.aguasdemanizales.com.co, for permission to enter the park; US$13 for groups up to 16 people.*

A short distance northeast of Manizales is the **Parque Ecológico Río Blanco**, a 4343-ha protected cloudforest, considered by the World Wildlife Fund to be the best place for birdwatching in Colombia. To date, 335 species of bird have been identified, including 33 species of hummingbird, a sub-species of the rusty-faced parrot, the royal woodpecker and four types of toucan. There are also 350 species of butterfly and 40 types of orchid, as well as rare mammals, such as spectacled bears, ocelots and white-tailed deer. There are several hikes through the park of between 20 minutes and eight hours.

The park is owned by **Aguas de Manizales**, which manages the water from the Río Blanco and provides Manizales with 35% of its drinking water, believed to be some of the purest in the world. The **Fundación Ecológica Gabriel Arango Restrepo** conducts scientific investigations in the park with the support of WWF. Before the area was turned into a reserve it was inhabited by *campesino* families, who have been allowed to stay and have been trained as rangers. The rangers' hut has a feeding station that attracts 22 species of hummingbird. Birdwatchers, photographers and hikers can stay at the hut; contact Technical Director Sergio Ocampo, T6-887 9770, sergiofundegar@gmail.com.

## Chinchiná and the coffee fincas

Visits to coffee farms in the area are warmly recommended. They are often included in local tours arranged by agencies or through hotels, but the best way to experience them is to stay the night. Some 22 km southwest of Manizales is **Chinchiná**, one of the main coffee-producing towns in Colombia. The surrounding hills are carpeted with coffee bushes and on roasting days the smell of coffee hangs in the air. Just outside the town (taxi US$4) is the **Hacienda Guayabal**, www.haciendaguayabal.com, a coffee finca owned by the Londoño family since 1959. It is one of the best places to observe the growing and production process. See box, opposite, and Where to stay, page 284.

## Listings Manizales and around *map p280*

### Tourist information

**Manizales**
There are 3 **tourist information points** in Manizales, 1 at the bus terminal, 1 on the corner of Cra 22 and C 31 (daily 0700-1900) and 1 in Edif La Licorera on Pl Bolívar. The website www.culturayturismomanizales.gov.co is useful. For Los Nevados and other national parks, try **Unidad de Parques Nacionales**, Cra 23, No 7A-44, T6-887 227.

### Where to stay

In Jan, during the Feria de Manizales, hotel prices are considerably increased.

**Centro**

**$$$$-$$$ Estelar Las Colinas**
*Cra 22, No 20-20, T6-884 2009,*
*www.hotelesestelar.com.*
Part of the Estelar chain of hotels, Las Colinas has large rooms with cable TV and Wi-Fi. It also has a sauna. Significant discounts at weekends.

**$$$ Bolívar Plaza**
*C 22, No 22-40, T6-884 7777,*
*bolivarplaza@hotmail.com.*
Just round the corner from Pl Bolívar and the cathedral, this hotel has cable TV, Wi-Fi, laundry service and a restaurant.

**$$$ Escorial**
*C 21, No 21-11, T6-884 7696,*
*www.hotelesmanizales.com.*
Smart hotel with good, clean rooms, including a junior suite and some 5-bedded rooms. Extra services include Wi-Fi, parking, cable TV and a restaurant serving local and international food. Breakfast is included in the price.

**$$$ Roma Plaza**
*C 21, No 22-30, T6-884 7442,*
*www.hotelesmanizales.com.*
Around the corner from the Bolívar Plaza with simple, clean rooms, cable TV, Wi-Fi, free local calls and breakfast included.

### East of the centre and El Cable

**$$$ Carretero**
*C 23, No 35A-31, T6-887 9190,*
*www.hotelcarretero.com.*
Well placed, halfway between the centre and El Cable, the Carretero has a smart, glassy lobby and large, comfortable rooms. Breakfast is included in the price and it has Wi-Fi throughout as well as a sauna. Can also organize car hire.

## ON THE ROAD
## Coffee in Colombia

The wild coffee plant originally came from East Africa, possibly first discovered near Kaffa (Kefa) in Ethiopia. A favourite legend is that an Arab goatherd noticed his flock behaving oddly after eating the berries of the bush, so he tried it himself, was exhilarated by the experience and proclaimed his discovery to the world. Coffee was first cultivated in South Arabia in the 15th century, and, in spite of a period when it was decreed intoxicating and therefore prohibited by the Koran, it gained increasing popularity, first among the Arabs and their neighbours, then in Europe, Asia and the Americas. Coffee houses started to open in London and Paris in about 1650, and in North America by about 1690, giving the drink a social dimension. By the end of the 17th century, production was being extended from Arabia (principally Yemen) to Ceylon, Indonesia and the West Indies (about 1715), Brazil (1727) and, towards the end of the century, Colombia.

The two principal types of coffee are arabica and robusta, the latter cultivated mostly in Asia and the Indian sub-continent. Arabica varieties are milder, having about half the level of caffeine, but are less tolerant of warm humid climates and more susceptible to disease. They are however more popular with western coffee drinkers and have brought prosperity to many countries in Latin America including Colombia, which grows virtually no *robusta* coffee. It is believed that coffee was brought into Colombia by Jesuit priests who first set up cultivation in Santander Department. Later it was tried in Cauca, and it wasn't until about 1850 that serious production started to take place in what is now known as the Zona Cafetera.

Colombia's coffee has been hit by several serious diseases, notably *roya* (a leaf fungus) and *broca* (a bug that attacks the bean). The latter was particularly destructive in the 1990s, but counter measures including the breeding of resistant plants have improved the situation. The other critical element is the world coffee price which fluctuates wildly. Coffee production in Colombia is done by hand, with an emphasis on quality over quantity. The country can't compete with machine-manufactured, mass-produced coffee sold by such countries as Brazil. So, when the coffee price slumped in 1992 and again in 2002, Colombia was one of the nations that was left struggling, and coffee growers in Caldas, Risaralda and Quindío were forced to diversify into other crops. In 1994, Quindío's tourism board, emulating the success of Spain's countryside haciendas, proposed to the region's finca owners an alternative source of income, and the idea of opening up coffee farms to tourism was born.

From stately post-colonial Antioquian mansions to some pretty primitive accommodation, no two fincas are the same. Some still produce their own coffee – and offer tours where you can learn about the process of coffee-growing – while others have retired that part of the business altogether and give guests the chance to relax, lounge around pools and appreciate the incredible richness of flora and fauna of the region. For our list of recommended fincas, see page 278. For further details, visit www.clubhaciendasdelcafe.com.

### $$$ Regine's Hotel
*C 65A, No 23B-113, T6-887 5360,*
*www.regineshotel.com.*
Located in a quiet suburban street
behind El Cable, Regine's has good, clean
rooms and computers for internet access,
Wi-Fi, cable TV and laundry service.
The free breakfast can be served in a
small garden out the back where there
are also some smaller, cheaper rooms.
Lovely views and room 1 has a nice
balcony. An excellent mid-range option.
Recommended.

### $$$ Varuna
*C 62, No 23C-18, T6-881 1122,*
*www.varunahotel.com.*
A newer hotel with a slick, minimal
look and a good restaurant, Tabil,
serving international food. The rooms
are large and comfortable with hydro
massage showers and Wi-Fi throughout.
Recommended.

### $ Manizales Hostel
*Av Santander, No 67-23A, T6-887 0871,*
*www.manizaleshostel.com.*
A sister hostel to **Mountain Hostel** (see
below), this Belgian/Colombian-run hostel
offers a good introduction to Manizales
and the region at check-in, including
a 'What to do in Manizales' info sheet.
There are dorms and private rooms,
a nice patio for socializing, kitchen, and
Wi-Fi. Friendly and recommended.

### $ Mountain Hostel
*C 66, No 23B-91, T6-887 4736,*
*mountainhostels@gmail.com.*
One of few backpacker options in town,
**Mountain Hostel** is a suburban home
with 10 private rooms and 6 4- to 6-bed
dorms with bunks. It has a pool table
and a terraced garden with a barbecue,
also offers use of a kitchen and access to
an internet-enabled computer. There is

Wi-Fi throughout, a cosy TV room and
laundry service.

---

## Chinchiná and the coffee fincas

### $$$ Hacienda Guayabal
*Km 3 Vía Chinchiná–Santa Rosa, T314-
772 4856, www.haciendaguayabal.com.*
Working coffee finca 30 mins outside
Manizales. Set in 64 ha of gorgeous
rolling fields brimming with coffee
plants as well as a botanist's note-book
full of flowers and trees. One of the best
places to do a coffee tour in the region.
Guests can stay at the Londoño family
home in private bedrooms or dorms.
The price includes accommodation,
3 excellent home-cooked meals, a fine
swimming pool and the tour. Coffee is
free, of course (see box, page 283).

### $$$ Hotel Tinamu
*30 mins west of Manizales in Vereda San
Peregrino, T314-7771 1557,*
*www.hoteltinamu.com.*
Just outside Manizales lies this
former coffee plantation turned
nature reserve. Avid birders can
relax and snap photos of the some
188 avian species that can be found in
the area. Hiking trails with opportunities
to spot local wildlife abound.

### $$$-$$ Hacienda Venecia
*3.5 km off the Chinchiná autopista, T320-
636 5719, www.haciendavenecia.com.*
Delightful 4th-generation working
coffee finca in a beautiful location with
2 different types of accommodation:
hostel with private or shared rooms,
or the main hacienda; both include
breakfast, and other meals can be
arranged. Attentive, English-speaking
hosts. Swimming pools on site as
well as riding and various tours.
Highly recommended.

## Restaurants

Apart from the hotels, the best restaurants are around Cra 23 in El Cable (La Zona Rosa) and in Barrio Milán, in the eastern part of the city.

### Centro

**$$-$ El Zaguán Paisa**
*Cra 23, No 31-27 (almost directly opposite the cablecar station).*
You enter this cosy, reasonably priced restaurant through a long bamboo corridor (hence the name). Typical Caldense dishes, *bandeja paisa,* and a set lunch menu for US$4.

**$ Frisby**
*Cra 23, No 23-01.*
Colombian chain serving fried chicken à la Kentucky and other meat dishes.

**$ Pollos Asados Mario**
*C 23 at Cra 22.*
Traditional Colombian *asadero* with the best rotisserie chicken in downtown. Also does burgers and steaks.

### East of the centre and El Cable

**$$$-$$ Bologninis**
*C 77, No 21-116, Loc 2.*
Italian-Argentine restaurant with good pasta, good steak and good wines.

**$$ Spago**
*C 59, No 24A-10, Loc 1.*
Tasty Italian food and a good variety of pastas.

**$$ Valentino**
*Cra 23, No 63-128. Open until 0200.*
Gourmet dining with artisan chocolates for dessert. Turns into a late-night bar serving excellent cocktails.

**$ Don Juaco Snacks**
*C 65A, No 23A-44.*
Sandwiches and burgers as well as typical dishes such as *ajiaco* and *mondongo.*

**$ Il Forno**
*Cra 23, No 73-86.*
Italian restaurant in pleasant surroundings serving pastas, pizzas and salads. Good vegetarian options.

**$ Juan Valdez**
*Cra 23, No 64-55.*
Part of the ubiquitous coffee chain, this one is in a good position next to the old cablecar line, has free Wi-Fi.

**$ La Cuatro Estaciones**
*C 65, No 23A-32.*
Good selection of pastas and pizzas. Be sure to order big as portions can be a bit small.

**$ La Ricura**
*C 62, No 24-38.*
The best spot for breakfast *buñuelos* and fresh juices.

### Chinchiná and the coffee fincas

**$$ Punta de Anca**
*on the Autopista de Café, 3 km from Chinchiná.*
Worth the trip for the excellent cuts of meat and a hearty *bandeja paisa.*

## Bars and clubs

Manizales' Zona Rosa is El Cable, around the old cable car station on Cra 23. The 2nd nightlife area, a little smaller and a taxi ride from Cable Plaza, is Barrio Milán. For a more rough-and-ready Colombian experience, the area of Alto Tablazo, southwest of the centre, is worth a visit (best reached by taxi, US$4). This is where many locals gather at the weekends for a beer, a dance and very occasionally a brawl. The views around here are stunning, with Manizales lit up below. Beware of steep *quebradas* nearby and go easy on the fire water. Most nightclubs have a cover charge of between US$2.50 and US$5 per person, some include a few free drinks. Most clubs don't get going until 2300 or later.

### East of the centre and El Cable

Barcelona Bar Manizales
*Av Santander, No 71-72.*
Cocktail bar and tapas restaurant featuring the occasional DJ.

Bar La Plaza
*Cra 23B, No 64-80, Loc 1.*
Playing pop and rock, this bar also does deli platters and substantial (2-litre) jugs of sangría.

Juan Sebastián Bar (JSB)
*Cra 23, No 63-66. Mon-Sat 1900-0200.*
Plays jazz, blues, Brazilian and Cuban rhythms. Good Margaritas and dry Martinis.

Salsoteca Yare
*Cra 23, No 62-57. Thu 2100-0100 and Fri 2100-0200.*
Lively salsa club, no cover charge.

### Entertainment

### East of the centre
**Cinema**
**Cable Plaza Cinema** in El Cable has all the latest releases but few films in English. **Universidad Nacional** shows free films on Fri.

### Festivals

### Manizales
Early Jan **Feria de Manizales**, includes a coffee festival, bullfights, beauty pageants and folk dancing as well as general partying.
Sep/Oct **Jazz and Theatre Festival**, events at the Centro Cultural y

Convenciones los Fundadores, Cra 22 with C 33, www.ccclosfundadores.com, and other location.

### Shopping

### Manizales
Try **Cable Plaza,** Av Santander (Cra 23), No 65-11, www.cableplaza.com.co, for more expensive shops or **Centro Comercial de Parque Caldas**, Cra 22, No 29-29, www.parquecaldas.com.co, for cheaper shopping.

### What to do

### Manizales

Colombia57, *T6-886 8050, www. colombia57.com.* Ex-pats Simon Locke, Russell Coleman, Brendan Rayment and team organize tailor-made trips for individuals or groups around the coffee zone and the rest of Colombia. Well-planned, thoroughly researched with a commitment to sustainability and quality. Highly recommended.

### Transport

### Manizales
**Air**
Manizales has a small airport, **La Nubia**, 7 km east of the centre, overlooking the city; bus, US$1; taxi, US$4. There are several daily flights to **Bogotá** (50 mins), **Cali** and **Medellín** (30 mins) with **Avianca** (Hotel Las Colinas, Cra 22, No 20-20, Loc 1, T6-884 7427), **Lan, Copa** and **Aerolínea de Antioquia** (**ADA**), though due to the altitude and humidity, services can sometimes be delayed by fog.

**Bus**
The bus terminal is at Cra 43, No 65-100, T6-878 7858, www.terminaldemanizales. com, and is connected to the town

centre by a cablecar (US$1 single, 10 mins, one midway stop at Betania). Alternatively a taxi to the centre costs US$2.50; to El Cable, US$3-4.

To **Medellín**, daily 0430 to 2000, 6 hrs, US$17.50 with multiple companies; by *kia* (7-seater minivan), 4½ hrs, US$17.50. For **Cartagena**, **Santa Marta** and **Turbo**, change at Medellín. To **Bogotá**, Expreso Bolivariano, US$22.50, 9 hrs, hourly 0600-2300. To **Honda**, US$10.50, with **Expreso Bolivariano**. To **Cali**, with multiple companies, 6 hrs, US$17.50, hourly 0400-2100; also by *kia*, 4½ hrs, US$18, daily 0630-1830. To **Pereira**, with **Expreso Palmira** or **Arauca**, every

30 mins, 2 hrs, US$4.50, or in *kia*, hourly 0600-2000, 1½ hrs. To **Armenia**, 3 hrs, US$9, hourly 0600-2000. To **Ibague**, 5 hrs, US$17, with **Expreso Palmira**. To **Buenaventura**, 7 hrs, US$22.50, with **Ruana Azul**. To **Marmato**, 3 buses a day with **Flota Occidental**, at 0615, 0830 and 1600, US$7.50, 2½ hrs. To **Supía**, 1½ hrs, US$6; in *colectivo*, US$7, with connections every 40 mins to Marmato.

**Car**
**Car hire** **Thrifty Car Rental**, in Hotel Carretero, Cra 23, No 35A-31, T6-893 0300, Ext 327.

## North of Manizales → *Colour map 2, B3.*

**a unique gold-mining town in splendid mountain scenery**

The Pan-American highway runs north from Manizales to Medellín through picturesque scenery dotted with small villages perched on the fertile mountainsides of the Cordillera Occidental. The road runs alongside the Río Cauca until it reaches a fork: you can take the left turn to Supía and Riosucio (see page 289), or stay on the main road for a further 14 km and then take an unpaved road west for some 7 km to Marmato.

### Marmato

Situated on top of a mountain at 1350 m, 80 km from Medellín, Marmato is a village with a colourful history, steeped in myths and legends. Since the 16th century, it has been the focus of foreign exploitation by the Spanish, German and English because of its gold mines. Today local gold prospectors dynamite and excavate the mountain much in the same way they would have done 400 years ago. Entire chunks of the mountain have been gouged out in the pursuit of gold, or have fallen away in frequent landslides. Buckets full of gold ore extracted from the mines zip up and down on wires that criss-cross the valley, while lorries trundle through its steep, narrow streets. Some of the houses have retained their traditional *tapia pisada* architecture and afford spectacular views down into the valley below, but other parts of town are not so picturesque, although they are no less fascinating to explore. Marmato is not a village geared towards tourism. There is little infrastructure and it is a difficult place to reach. The locals are friendly and helpful, but they do have a reputation for heavy drinking and philandering: on Friday afternoons, busloads of prostitutes are shuttled in to satisfy the miners' needs.

## ON THE ROAD

## The legends of Marmato

Marmato is known as the 'cradle of Colombian gold'. It is believed that gold has been mined here for more than 500 years. When Sebastián de Belalcázar and Jorge Robledo arrived in 1536, they found the local indigenous Cartamas already mining the mountain and fashioning beautiful *huacas* out of its gold. Belalcázar and Robledo took the Cartamas' bounty and then returned to Marmato in 1539, bringing black slaves from Cartagena to work the mines. Word spread about the fortune under the mountain, and shortly afterwards German mercenaries, who had joined the Spanish hunt for El Dorado, arrived and built their own mines in San Juan, a village just up the mountain from Marmato. In the 19th century, the British came to Marmato at the behest of the Colombian government, which used the gold mines here as collateral to secure funding for its fight for Independence against the Spanish.

Marmato is a place steeped in myth, legend and superstition. A cross at the mountain's peak is meant to ward off beautiful flying witches who have the power to entrance any man. Locals say the witches persuaded the foreign gold prospectors in days gone by to drink from the enchanted waters of the Cascabel spring, so that they would fall in love with the women of Marmato and never want to leave.

The slaves brought in by the Spanish to work the mines brought their own distinct myths. Legend has it that they practised a sacred ritual under an ancient ceiba tree in which they formed a ring around the most beautiful slave girl and made her drink the blood of a sacrificial goat while she undressed. The local Catholic priest, shocked by the practice, denounced the slaves as devil worshippers and cursed them. The ceiba tree is believed to have fallen away in a landslide following the priest's damnation. This is not the only example of divine intervention. The 16th-century Iglesia de Santa Bárbara has collapsed and been rebuilt several times, some say because the town priest cursed the village for its heavy drinking and prostitution; there is an ongoing belief here that the more you drink, the more gold you will find.

The most interesting sights are above the village. Walk past the church and its square, along the main street. Beyond a row of shops there is a narrow cobbled street to the left. Keep climbing past the primary school and you will reach the secondary school where helmets and Wellington boots can be hired (essential if you are going to visit one of the mines). Beyond the school is the main plaza and *alcaldía* (currently abandoned). There are spectacular views from here down into the village and the valley below, and some interesting murals depicting the legends of Marmato (see box, above). In 2006 the town plaza and *alcaldía* were buried under a landslide, but fortunately no one was killed.

Exiting the plaza to the right you will notice several abandoned houses. Step inside to see how these homes incorporated former German mines as kitchens or pantries.

A narrow path (prone to landslides) leads from here to a viewpoint over a muddy stream. This is the source of the **Aguita de Cascabel**, a magical spring. It is said that once someone has drunk from its waters, they will never leave Marmato. Looking further down, beyond a former water mill, you can see several stone buildings pegged to the side of the hill opposite. These were prison cells used to punish slaves.

Below the plaza to your left is a colonial building with a small park. This is the **Parque de los Mineros**, which houses a small library and ingenious statues of a miner, a witch and a slave girl made from miners' tools and nuts and bolts. It also has the original bell that was used to call the slaves to work, although someone has stolen the clapper! You can reach the park by leaving the plaza opposite the *alcaldía* and turning right beyond a group of buildings housing a small silver studio where the workers will sell pieces of silver at reasonable prices.

Retracing your footsteps from the Parque de los Mineros past the silver studios, you will reach a small gold mine, owned by the town mayor. Here there are several pulley systems bringing down gold ore from mines further up. The crushed rock is siphoned off with water to separate the gold. The mine can be visited free of charge although a tip of US$5 for the miner who accompanies you is appreciated. Health and safety is not a priority in Marmato. The miners can provide head torches, but the mines are narrow, muddy and airless. Do not enter if you suffer from claustrophobia. This is a working mine; you are likely to hear dynamite blasts in other parts of the mountain. You enter at your own risk.

## Supía
*Supía is 77 km from Manizales and can be reached off the main Manizales–Medellín highway.*

A spectacular unpaved road runs over the mountain from Marmato to Supía, passable by *chiva*, jeep or on foot. With its backdrop of resplendent rolling green hills and an agreeable temperate climate, this small town at 1183 m is an excellent place for hiking. It is known throughout the region for its *colación*, a sweet delicacy made from sugar cane.

The town is a mixture of colonial and modern architecture and has an impressive church with two imposing towers. There is an interesting little museum displaying religious artefacts at the back of the church, where you'll also find tourist information on the surrounding area. The picturesque Parque Principal has palms and ceiba trees covered in Spanish moss, or *tillandsia*, as well as several attractive bird houses.

Beyond Supía, **Riosucio** is a delightful town with fine views, a large church and many restaurants and shops.

## Salamina
Perched atop a mountain deep in Caldas lies this little-known Colombian gem. Located about three hours north of Manizales by van or mini-bus, Salamina is notable for its sweeping vistas of the surrounding tall peaks. The town was declared a national monument in 1982 because of its well-preserved colonial architecture, but its remote location means that it does not attract the tourist hordes who flock to Salento to the south. There's not much to do here, but it's a beautiful place for a relaxing weekend.

## Where to stay

**Marmato**
There is no accommodation available
in Marmato but nearby Supía has
several options.

### Supía

**$$ Hotel Campestre La Vina**
*C 33, No 5-07, T312-871 8229,*
*www.hotelcampestrelavina.com.*
A good choice.

**$$ Hotel Premium Biss**
*Av Guayabal (Cra 10) No 29-65, T311-*
*631 7032, www.hotelpremiumbiss.com.*
Another good-value new hotel with very
clean rooms, a/c and cable TV. You pay a
little more for rooms with windows that
look out onto the street.

### Salamina

**$ Hotel Colonial**
*C 5, No 6-74, T312-649 6355.*
Smaller hotel on the plaza, located
just above Tierra Paisa, a good local
restaurant run by the same people
who own **La Casa de Lola García**.

**$ La Casa de Lola García**
*C 6, No 7-54, T312-864 1571,*
*www.lacasadelolagarcia.com.*
Charming colonial hotel located a block
and a half away from the plaza. Has all
mod cons, including flatscreen TVs and
rainwater showers. Breakfast included.
Can organize tours and excursions.
Friendly owners.

## Restaurants

**Marmato**
There is a small restaurant in the plaza
opposite the church, serving whatever
is available.

### Supía
There are several good places to eat on
the Parque Principal.

**$ La Casona**
*Cra 6, No 33-36.*
Good *bandejas* in pleasant surroundings.

## Festivals

**Marmato**
Late Oct **Feria de Oro** is a raucous event
involving the consumption of copious
quantities of beer and *aguardiente*.

**Supía**
End Jun **Feria de Colación** is a biannual
festival celebrating sugar cane.

## Transport

**Marmato**
Buses to **Manizales** with **Flota
Occidental** leave at 1200, 1500 and 1600,
2½ hrs. Alternatively, **Colombia57** (see
What to do, page 286) can arrange tours
from Manizales, providing transport and
knowledgeable local guides. To **Supía**,
*chivas* and Willys take the high road over
the mountain via San Juan. Alternatively,
you can walk to Supía in 5 hrs.

★Los Nevados are a compact range of volcanic peaks in central Colombia and the nearest and most accessible mountains to Bogotá. The park is home to three huge volcanoes: Nevado del Ruiz, Nevado de Santa Isabel and Nevado del Tolima, and a further three high peaks without snow cover: Paramillo del Cisne, Paramillo de Santa Rosa and Paramillo del Quindío. The highest of all, Nevado del Ruiz (5321 m) erupted in 1985, completely destroying the village of Armero under a mud stream and killing more than 25,000 people. At the time of writing Nevado del Ruiz was again displaying seismic activity and excursions in the park were therefore limited. Nevado del Tolima is also active but hasn't shown major changes recently. In addition to the high peaks, the park has volcanic lakes, hot springs and high-altitude volcano vegetation, with *frailejones* up to 12 m, all combining to create an unmissable landscape. There are several treks within the park, the longest and toughest of which is from south (Ibagué) to north (Manizales) in six days.

From Manizales the main route to the park is via a right turn off the Manizales–Bogotá highway at La Esperanza, from where it is 17 km to the park entrance at Las Brisas. It is also possible to reach the park entrance by car from the Termales del Otoño, southeast of Manizales. If you arrive on foot or on horseback, then you can visit the western and southern areas of the park independently from Santa Rosa, Pereira (via the Parque Ucumari; see page 295), Salento (via the Valle de Cocora; see page 300) and Ibagué (following the Río Combeima; see page 309).

### Nevado del Ruiz and the northern sector
*Entry to the park is US$12 for non-Colombians. Beyond the park entrance you must be accompanied to Ruiz and El Cisne by an official guide (included in the entry price) or visit as part of an organized tour (try De Una, based in Bogotá, www.deunacolombia.com).*

The northern sector of the park is the easiest to access and therefore the most popular with visitors. From the entrance at **Las Brisas** a road runs to a car park at the base of Nevado del Ruiz and continues (4WD only) as far as Laguna del Otún. **Nevado del Ruiz** is the highest of the three volcanoes. It is an easy climb to a viewpoint at 5100 m, but this has been closed since 2011. With a special permit and gear it is also possible to climb to the top (5321 m), providing seismic conditions are favourable.

### Tip...
The three volcanoes can normally be climbed, but visiting any portion of the park above 4300 m has been restricted since 2011 due to seismic activity. Check with the park office for the latest information regarding current restrictions; **Mountain Hostel** in Manizales is also a good source of information. There has been no problem with safety in the park in recent years.

Further south on the main route through the park, there is a visitor centre with accommodation at **El Cisne** (4200 m). From here, you can trek to Laguna Verde, a beautiful green lake at 4300 m between Paramillo el Cisne and **Nevado de Santa Isabel**.

Nevado de Santa Isabel is the lowest of the three volcanoes at 4965 m and inactive. It can be climbed (when permitted) from **Laguna del Otún** to the southwest. At the

# Los Nevados National Park

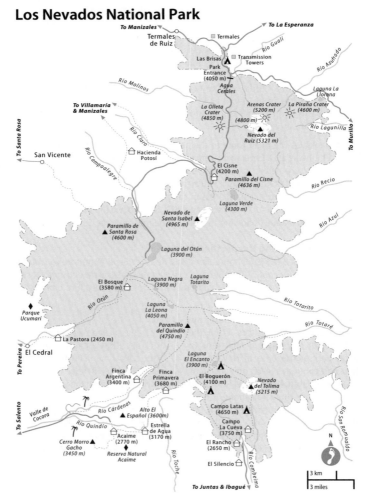

summit there is an amazing view on clear days of Nevado del Ruiz to the north and Nevado del Tolima to the south. Laguna del Otún is the biggest lake in the park and full of trout (April to August); fishing gear is available to rent.

There are comfortable *cabañas* at El Cisne ($$$ pp) and camping nearby ($ pp); those wishing to camp will need to bring all equipment with them. Note that temperature can drop below 0°C at night as most of the park lies above 3800 m.

▸▸ *For information on the southern sector of the park, including Nevado del Tolima, see page 300.*

▸▸ *For information on the southern sector of the park, including Nevado del Tolima, see page 300.*

## Pereira and around → *Colour map 2, C3.*

### service capital for the coffee zone

Capital of Risaralda Department, Pereira is situated on a small plateau 56 km southwest of Manizales, within sight of the peaks of the Cordillera Central. It is bounded to the south by the Río Consota and to the north by the Río Otún, which lies about 140 m below the city. Beyond the Otún is Dosquebradas, an industrial town, now virtually part of the city and dramatically linked by a viaduct.

A settlement was established here around 1541 by Mariscal Jorge Robledo but around 1700 it was moved to the present site of Cartago on Río La Vieja after continuing difficulties with a tribe of indigenous Quimbaya. Francisco Pereira from Cartago set out to re-establish a town here in the 19th century but died before achieving his objective. His friend, the priest Remigio Antonio Cañarte, tried again successfully in 1863 and named the town after him.

Pereira is now the largest city in this part of Colombia and acts as the centre of the Zona Cafetera with the appropriate range of official and commercial institutions and services. It has a very pleasant climate, punctuated by short, sharp showers that allow the cultivation of a wide variety of local agricultural produce; you will notice the high quality of the food available here. Unfortunately this is also an active seismic zone and earthquakes periodically damage Pereira, notably in 1995 and January 1999. The city has also grown rapidly and suffers from the attendant ills of high unemployment, petty crime and prostitution in some areas.

The city is centred around Plaza de Bolívar and most points of interest are within walking distance. The centre is safe (subject to the usual common sense precautions) but the semi-derelict area between Carrera 10 and 12 is not a place to linger. The same applies to the streets heading east, starting with Calle 14.

### Sights

The central square is the **Plaza de Bolívar**, noted for its *El Bolívar Desnudo*, a striking sculpture of the nude general on horseback by Rodrigo Arenas Betancur to commemorate the city's centenary in

> **Tip...**
> An interesting throwback to Spanish colonial customs can be found in the centre of Pereira, on Calle 19 by the post office. *Los Escribanos* are scribes who help locals with legal documents and official forms, working on the street with their typewriters during office hours.

1963. It caused a stir when unveiled and brought a whole new meaning to the term 'liberator', but it is now accepted with pride by the local citizens. Enthusiasts of Arenas Betancur can find three of his other works in the city: *Monumento a los Fundadores* on Avenida Circunvalar/Calle 13; *El Prometeo*, in Universidad Tecnológico de Pereira (south on Calle 14), and *Cristo Sin Cruz* in the **Capilla de Fátima** (Avenida 30 de Agosto/Calle 49), towards the airport. There are many other examples of public art on display; look for works by Jaime Mejía Jaramillo and Leonidas Méndez, and for an interesting bronze of Benito Juárez, Mexico's first president of indigenous origin, on Avenida 30 de Agosto.

Also in Plaza de Bolívar is the **cathedral**, unimpressive from the outside but with an interesting and elegant interior. After the 1999 earthquake, extensive restoration work was carried out, uncovering the original wooden interior, which has been left bare. There are also fine chandeliers down the central nave, two large mosaics depicting baptism and the Eucharist, and a fine dome with roof paintings. Also interesting are the two Lady Chapels and the stained-glass windows.

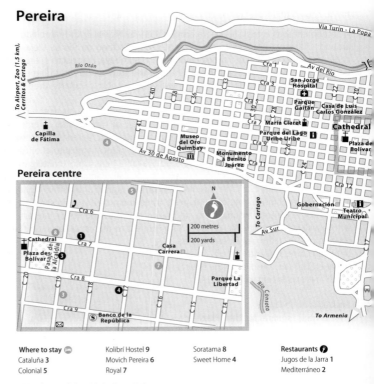

## Pereira

### Pereira centre

| Where to stay | Kolibrí Hostel **9** | Soratama **8** | Restaurants |
|---|---|---|---|
| Cataluña **3** | Movich Pereira **6** | Sweet Home **4** | Jugos de la Jarra **1** |
| Colonial **5** | Royal **7** | | Mediterráneo **2** |

The city has three other parks with attendant churches. The **Parque del Lago Uribe Uribe**, west of the centre, is the most picturesque with an artificial lake and a fountain illuminated at night. **Parque Gaitán** and **Parque La Libertad** (with its striking mosaic by Lucy Tejada) are also worth a visit. Opposite the Meliá Pereira hotel is the **Templo Nuestra Señora del Carmen**, a Gothic-style church with a dull grey concrete exterior but with some good sculptures and stained glass inside. Two early 20th-century houses of architectural interest are **Casa de Luis Carlos González** ① *Cra 6, No 21-62*, and **Casa Carrera** ① *Cra 7, No 15-58*. Both have been declared National Monuments.

The impressive road bridge over the Río Otún connecting Pereira with Dosquebrados, is known as **El Viaducto César Gaviria Trujillo**. It was built by Colombian, German and US contractors to Italian designs.

Some way from the city centre, but worth a visit, is the small **Museo del Oro Quimbaya** ① *Av 30 de Agosto, No 35-08, free*, which features many Quimbaya pottery and gold items including three exquisite 2-cm-high face masks. Alongside is a library and a music auditorium with a daily programme of classical music. On the campus of Universidad Tecnológica de Pereira, the **botanical garden** ① *T6-321 2523, www.utp.edu.co, Mon-Fri 0800-1200, 1400-1800, Sat 0900-1300, Sun and hols 1100-1700, US$10 including compulsory 2-hr tour; book in advance*, is good for birdwatching and has bamboo forests and two-hour nature walks.

## Around Pereira

Halfway between Pereira and Manizales is Santa Rosa de Cabal, from where a 9-km unpaved road leads to **Termales de Santa Rosa/Los Arbeláez** ① *0900-2300, US$16 (early morning chiva or taxi, US$11 to entrance)*. The hot baths are surrounded by forests and waterfalls, and are understandably packed at the weekend.

Northwest of Pereira, 30 km towards the Río Cauca, is **Marsella** and the **Alexander von Humboldt Gardens**, a carefully maintained botanical display with cobbled paths and bamboo bridges.

## Parque Ucumari

*Park office, T6-325 4781; day visits free. To get there, catch a chiva from C 12, No 9-40, in Pereira (daily 0900 and 1500, with Transporte Florida) to the village of El Cedral; it's a 2½-hr walk from there to the visitor centre at La Pastora.*

From Pereira it is possible to visit the beautiful Parque Ucumari, which borders Parque Nacional Los Nevados (see page 291). It is one of the few places where the Andean spectacled bear survives. The park visitor centre is at **La Pastora**, where there is a refuge (US$8.50 per person) and excellent camping (US$2.50 per person), meals extra. From La Pastora it is a steep, rocky one- to two-day hike to **Laguna de Otún** in Los Nevados through beautiful scenery of changing vegetation. The **Otún Quimbaya Flora and Fauna Sanctuary** forms a biological corridor between Ucumari and Los Nevados, protecting the last remaining area of Andean tropical forest in Risaralda.

### Filandia
*There are frequent buses from Pereira and Armenia. If travelling from Salento, take a bus towards Pereria and change at Las Cruces on the highway.*

The road from Pereira to Armenia passes through the heart of the Zona Cafetera. The coffee here grows up to about 2000 m, above which forests provide the communities with an alternative livelihood. There are some pleasant places to eat, as well as art galleries and craft centres. **Filandia**, a pleasant village 7 km off the main road, has excellent examples of *paisa* architecture, with doorways, windows and balconies painted in primary colours. A fire destroyed a corner of the town near the central plaza in 1996, but the unusual grey and white **Iglesia de la Inmaculada Concepción**, dating from 1892, was not harmed.

Founded in 1878 by colonizers from Antioquia, Filandia is rumoured to take its name from Finland (Finlandia in Spanish), but it was misspelt as Filandia. The village was used for the popular local soap opera (*telenovela*) *Café con Aroma de Mujer*. Baskets for coffee picking are made here.

Because it is higher than the land to the east, Filandia offers splendid views of the Nevados; they look especially dramatic if the weather is unsettled or after a recent storm, when you may well see snow well below the normal permanent snowline at about 4800 m. A **mirador** ① *daily 1000-2100, US$1*, has been constructed next to the cemetery, 1 km from the Parque Principal; it's a bit of an architectural disaster made from mangrove wood imported from San Bernardo del Viento, but it nonetheless affords expansive views of Pereira, Armenia, Cartago and Quimbaya.

## Listings Pereira and around *map p294*

### Tourist information

**Pereira**
Information can be obtained from the **Centro Cultural Lucy Tejada** (Cra 10, No 6-16, T6-311 6544, www.

pereiraculturayturismo.gov.co, Mon-Thu 0730-1200 and 1400-1830, Fri 0800-1200, 1400-1800) and from **Corporación Autónoma Regional de Risaralda**, Carder; Av de las Américas y C 46, No 46-40, T6-311 6511, www.carder.gov.co.

For park permits, contact **Aviatur**, C 14
No 13, T6-326 3630, www.aviatur.com.

## Where to stay

### Pereira

**$$$$ Hotel Movich Pereira**
*Cra 13N, No 15-73, T6-311 3333,*
*www.movichhotels.com.*
Pereira's grandest hotel has a spacious
lobby and excellent service. Well located
3 blocks from the centre, it has good
rooms with plasma TVs, Wi-Fi and a great
pool. It has a travel agency within the
building and a sauna, gym and Turkish
bath. Discounts available at weekends.

**$$$$-$$$ Soratama**
*Cra 7, No 19-20, T6-335 8650,*
*www.hotelsoratama.com.*
Hotel on the Plaza Bolívar with helpful
staff and lots of services available,
including parking, free local calls,
Wi-Fi, massage therapist and spa.
Breakfast included. Discounts available
at the weekend.

**$$$-$$ Hotel Cataluña**
*C 19, No 8-61, T6-335 4527,*
*www.hotelcatalunapereira.com.*
The Cataluña has clean and airy rooms
with balconies and private bathrooms
with hot water. There are plasma-screen
TVs and a popular restaurant serving
fixed meals. Good value for money.

**$$ Hotel Colonial**
*C 17, No 5-50, T6-333 7206,*
*www.hotelcolonialpereira.com.*
Hotel with clean rooms and good
security, though none have windows.

**$ Hotel Royal**
*C 16, No 5-78, T6-335 2501, www.*
*hotelroyalpereira.blogspot.com.*
Near the Plaza Bolívar, this hotel has
clean, basic rooms with cable TV.

**$ Kolibrí Hostel**
*C 4, No 16-35, T6-331 3955,*
*www.kolibrihostel.com.*
Newer hostel close to the center
offering dorms, privates with ensuite
bath and even an apartment for up to
8 people. Organizes bike tours through
**RetroCiclas** (see What to do, page 299).

**$ Sweet Home**
*C 42, No 10-37, T6-345 4453,*
*www.sweethomehostel.com.*
Slightly out of town, but worth the trek.
3 dorms, 1 private room, use of kitchen,
Wi-Fi, hot water and breakfast. Handy
for the airport.

### Around Pereira

**$$$$ Hacienda San José**
*Entrada 16 cadena El Tigre,*
*Km 4 Vía Cerritos, T6-313 2612,*
*www.haciendahotelsanjose.com.*
Breakfast included. One of the oldest
houses in the region, this *bahereque*
hacienda built by Franciso Mejía
Jaramillo in 1888 is simply breathtaking.
Today it is run as a hotel and almost
all of the features have been
painstakingly preserved. Popular
activities include: horse riding through
sugarcane, coffee and livestock fields,
visits to one of the largest bamboo
reserves in the region, and a trapiche
where you can see how *panela*,
unrefined sugarcane, is processed.

**$$$$-$$$ Hotel Sazagua**
*Km 7, Via Cerritos T6-337 9895,*
*www.sazagua.com.*
This boutique hotel located just outside
town is one of Pereira's oldest and
swankiest options. Amenities include
a spa and massage services, and there
is a restaurant serving upscale takes on
regional dishes.

$$$ Hotel Termales de Santa Rosa de Cabal
*Attached to the hot springs, T6-364 5500, www.termales.com.co.*
Comfortable chalet-style hotel, with restaurant.

$$$-$$ Castilla Casa de Huéspedes
*Km 10, Vía Cerritos, T6-337 9045, www.haciendacastilla.com.*
Beautiful colonial hotel with pool and gardens. Wi-Fi available.

$$ Ecohotel Los Lagos
*Just outside Marsella, T6-368 5298, www.ecohotelloslagos.com.co.*
Previously a gold mine, then a coffee hacienda, and now restored as a hotel and nature park with lakes.

### Filandia

$$$-$$ La Posada del Compadre
*Cra 6, No 8-06, Filandia, T313-335 9771.*
This beautifully preserved *paisa* building has several good rooms of variable price, depending on size, and a gorgeous terrace with fine views out toward Salento. All rooms have en suite bathrooms that jar a bit with the rest of the architecture. Cable TV and breakfast included. Recommended.

$$ Hostal Tibouchina
*C 6, No 5-05, T6-758 2646, Filandia.*
Fine old hostel on the corner of the plaza with a beautiful gallery looking out on the street. Comfortable, wooden panelled rooms with private bathrooms, cable TV and breakfast included.

$ Cabaña del Recuerdo
*Km 5 Vía Filandia–Montenegro, T311-628 5149, reservaselrecuerdo@hotmail.com.*

A few kilometres outside Filandia, this chalet on a Colombian family's finca is surrounded by banana and coffee plantations. It has a swimming pool and ping pong table, and there are great walks in a *guadua* bamboo forest with a swimming hole in its midst. Free pick up from Filandia with enough notice.

## Restaurants

### Pereira

$$ Mediterráneo
*Av Circunvalar, No 4-47.*
Steaks, seafood, fondus and crêpes in a relaxed atmosphere on an open terrace.

$$-$ Pasaje de la Alcaldía
A narrow alleyway next to the Alcaldía with a number of cheap eating options including French, Italian, Colombian and a few cafés.

$ Jugos La Jarra
*Cra 7, No 18-12.*
Fresh fruit juice chain with simple snacks. The juices are served *con ñapa* (with an extra top-up free of charge). 2 more outlets in the centre.

$ Terracita Paisa
*C 17, No 7-62.*
Typical regional food served on a 2nd-floor terrace decorated with antiques.

## Entertainment

### Pereira
There are several cinema complexes within 2 blocks of Plaza de Bolívar. The **Teatro Comfamiliar**, Cra 5/C 22, www.comfamiliar.com, has cultural activities, while the **Teatro Municipal Santiago Londoño**, in the Centro Comercial Fiducentro, in Av 30 de Agosto/C 19, T6-335 7724, stages major productions.

**Pereira**
**Aug** Fiestas de la Cosecha
(Harvest Festival).

## What to do

**Pereira**
**Living Trips**, *Entrada 16, Via Cerritos, T6-312 8671, www.livingtrips.com.* Offers a number of multiple-day excursions in the region, such as rafting and coffee tours.
**RetroCiclas**, *T310-540 7327, www. retrociclas.co.* Bike tour agency that runs city tours as well as adventure trips through surrounding areas. Can also be booked through **Kolibrí Hostel**.

## Transport

**Pereira**
**Air**
**Matecaña airport** is 5 km to the west of the city and is well-equipped.
    To **Bogotá**, around 15 flights a day with **Lan** and **Avianca** (Cra 10, No 17-55, Edif Torre Central, L 301 and at the airport). To **Medellín**, usually 4 daily with **Avianca**, **Lan** and **Copa** (Av Cir No 8b-51, Edif Bancafe, T01-800 011 2600). To **Cali**, frequent via Bogotá and Panama with **Avianca**, **Lan** and **Copa**. To **Ibagué**, frequent via Medellín and Bogotá with **Lan** and **Avianca**. Less frequent flights

to **Bucaramanga** and the **north coast** with **Lan**, **Avianca** and **Copa**. Local airlines fly to the **Chocó**.

**Bus**
Local taxi and bus services, including the **Megabus**, www.megabus.gov.co, modelled on the **TransMilenio** in Bogotá, are of good quality. The bus terminal (C 17, No 23-157, www.terminalpereira. com) is 12 blocks (1.5 km) south of the centre. It has a luggage store.
    There are frequent bus services to/ from other major Colombian cities. To **Cali**, US$15.50, 4½-5 hrs, *colectivo* by day, bus by night, same price. To **Medellín**, 6-8 hrs, every hour, US$18.50. To/ from **Bogotá**, US$27, 7 hrs (route is via Girardot, Ibagué – both cities bypassed – and Armenia), hourly from 0630. To **Buenaventura**, daily with **Expreso Trejos**, US$22. To **Quibdó**, US$30, 8 hrs. To **Armenia**, 1 hr, every 20 mins from 0600, US$5, a beautiful trip. To **Salento** with **Flota Alcalá** multiple times a day, or take any bus towards Armenia, get off at Ciscaria/entrada Salento (US$3.50, 40 mins) and change to a minibus to Salento (US$1).

**Car**
**Car rental** **Hertz**, Mataceña airport, T6-314 2678, www.hertz.com; **RentaCar**, Av 30 de Agosto, No 73-51, Loc 22, T311-635 1133, www.rentacarpereira.com.

Well into the foothills of the Cordillera Central, on a promontory above the valleys that lead up to the Nevado de Tolima and Paramillo de Quindío, is the little town of Salento at 1985 m. It is the oldest settlement in Quindío and was established on 5 January 1842 as the epicentre of the Antioquian colonization of the region. It's prone to a lot of rain, as evidenced by the abundance of crops and flowers; low-lying clouds often drape themselves over the mountains like loosely flung scarves, but on a clear morning you can see the snowy peaks of Los Nevados to the east.

## Salento

Salento used to be a sleepy village, but tourism has really taken off in recent years; the days when you could hear a dog's bark resonate across the valley are long gone. It is now a popular weekend resort for Colombians for walking, riding and trekking, although it is quieter during the week. Salento is still a charming place, which has retained its village feel, despite being firmly on the backpacker trail with plenty of hostels, shops, bars and restaurants to choose from.

The town has some of the best examples of *bahareque* architecture in the coffee region. The main plaza is especially impressive, with a curious grey and white church, **Nuestra Señora del Carmen**, which contrasts with the surrounding buildings. From the plaza, walk up Calle Real (Carrera 6), which has further beautiful examples of post-colonial architecture, and then climb the 250 steps to an outstanding viewpoint overlooking the upper reaches of the Quindío and Cardenas rivers, known as the Valle de Cocora; there are 14 stations of the cross to measure your ascent and a military guard is usually stationed at the top. This is one of the finest views in Colombia, with many kilometres of the Cordillera Occidental visible to the west.

## Valle de Cocora and Acaime Natural Reserve

This fertile valley east of Salento, in the upper reaches of the ríos Quindío and Cardenas, has an enchanting landscape of pines and eucalyptus towered over by famous wax palms, Colombia's national tree. It makes for an extraordinary sight: the palms looming over the valley like sentinels on guard, with the crystal-clear waters of the Río Quindío, rich in freshwater trout, dissecting the valley. There are some breathtaking walks in this area.

Beyond the small hamlet of Cocora, at the end of the vehicular track (20 minutes by jeep), is **Finca La Montaña**, where there is a nursery for the wax palm overlooked by Cerro Morro Gacho (see below). From here you can make your way on foot for 2 km down across the infant Río Quindío and up the other side to the **Acaime Natural Reserve** at 2770 m, with a visitor centre, ponies for hire, accommodation for 20 (US$5.50 per person) and a small restaurant. This reserve borders Los Nevados National Park and is the most important wax palm zone in Colombia;

many varieties of humming bird, parrot, toucan and other wildlife can be seen feeding on the fruit of the palm.

Above Acaime are many trails into the high mountains. Day trips include steep walks through the forest of the reserve to **Cerro Morro Gacho** (3450 m) and **Alto El Español** (3600 m). The hike to **Paramillo del Quindío** (4700 m), one of the principal mountains in the national park, takes three to four days via **Finca Argentina** (3400 m); it's a total of 12 hours' ascent from Cocora to the top. This is an exposed rocky summit but not technically difficult. There are the remnants of a crater on the summit and climbers occasionally pitch their tents here on the grey/yellow sand. Other fincas/campsites can be used on this trip.

## Nevado del Tolima

Nevado del Tolima (5215 m) is the most beautiful but also the toughest summit in Los Nevados national park. The crater is spectacular, and a walk around it in the snow is unforgettable. There are several routes to climb to the top, but some are only for experienced climbers with good equipment. Route-finding in this featureless country can be especially difficult in mist, and guides are strongly recommended (about US$50 per day).

From Acaime, the ascent (ice axe and crampons required) normally takes three days, with accommodation at **Finca Primavera** (3680 m), followed by a two-day descent. This area is known as the Valley of the Lost because it is easy to wander off the track, so call ahead to Finca Primavera and request a guide (US$8-15) to shepherd you through this section. Again there are variants, including camping at **Laguna El Encanto** midway between Tolima and Quindío, from which both can be climbed.

Tolima can also be climbed from **El Rancho** (2600 m), an area of hot springs in the south of the park, accessed from Ibagué. From here, the climb to the summit takes two to three days and requires ice gear and sturdy camping equipment, as you will be camping at least one night over 4000 m. A *lechero* (milk truck) leaves Ibagué marketplace for El Silencio, just south of El Rancho, between 0630 and 0730, US$2.50, two hours. A guide in Ibagué is **Maklin Muñoz** ⓘ *Cra 1, No 5-24, T8-261 5865, T300-675 6216 (mob)*.

### Tourist information

#### Salento
Details of accommodation, guides and transport to the southern sector of Los Nevados are available from the **Alcaldía de Salento**, Parque Principal, T6-759 3105, www.salento-quindio.gov.co.

**Ecoaventuras Cocora Extremo**, C6 4, No 34, T310-566 9980, www. ecoaventurascocoraextremo.blogspot. com, also offers free tourist information and sells an excellent map of the area for US$3. **Plantation House**, www. theplantationhousesalento.com, is another good resource.

## Where to stay

### Salento

**$$$ Casa Alto del Coronel**
*Cra 2, No 1-61, T6-759 3760, www.*
*casahotelaltodelcoronel.com.*
Obscured by bushes of bougainvillea,
this *bahareque* house has beautifully
kept gardens and a summer house
with fine views over the town and
surrounding area. The 4 rooms are good,
if a bit heavy on the floral wallpaper.
Breakfast is included. It is possible to
rent the whole house for larger parties.

**$$$ Posada del Café**
*Cra 6, No 3-08, T6-759 3012,*
*www.laposadadelcafe.webs.com.*
This traditional house has rooms set
around a beautiful garden brimming
with flowers. The rooms are nicely
decorated and there is a larger family
room for 5. Friendly, English-speaking
owner. Recommended.

**$$ Balcones del Ayer**
*C 6, No 5-40, T6-759 3273.*
Great position half a block from the
plaza, recently expanded with improved
rooms and facilities. Most rooms have
balconies with lovely views, private bath,
hot water, parking and cable TV. Friendly
and family-run with good restaurant
attached. Recommended.

**$$ Posada del Angel**
*C 6, No 8-47, T6-759 3507.*
Sweet little place with clean rooms and
great balcony with fine views. Cheaper
midweek ($).

**$$-$ Hostal Ciudad de Segorbe**
*C 5, No 4-06, T6-749 3794, www.*
*hostalciudaddesegorbe.com.*
Friendly hostel not far from the
main square. Rooms all have private

bathrooms, including the spacious dorm.
Music, TV and reading room, breakfast
included and there is 1 room with
disability access. Recommended.

**$ Camping Monteroca**
*Km 4 Vía Pereira–Salento, T315-413 6862*
*(mob), www.campingmonteroca.com.*
Owner Jorge has run this site at the
bottom of the hill next to the Río Quindío
for over a decade and knows the area
well. The place is well maintained with
clean bathrooms, showers, a communal
cooking area and TV lounge. There is also
a serpentarium and an eclectic museum
filled with fossils and meteorites as well
as a room dedicated to Simón Bolívar,
who is reported to have stayed a night
there. As well as the campsite, there are
some themed cabins, including a jungle
tree house and the 1960s-inspired Hippie
Hilton. All cabins offer good privacy, a
stove and hot showers, and there is a
jacuzzi nearby.

**$ Las Palmas**
*C 6, No 3-02, T311-540 3828.*
This small, traditional hostel has
8 comfortable rooms with en suite
bathrooms and hot water. Kitchen,
cable TV, internet access and roof
terrace. Good value for money.

**$ The Plantation House**
*C 7, No 1-04, T316-285 2603, www.*
*theplantationhousesalento.com.*
The first backpackers' hostel in town
now has 2 houses, a number of private
bedrooms and several dorms with
bunks. English owner Tim and his
Colombian wife, Cris, have the best
information in town on the local area
and also offer bikes to rent and tours to
coffee plantations. Pick up from airports
can be arranged for a fee with advanced
warning. Recommended.

**$ Tralala Hostel**
*Cra 7, No 6-45, T314-850 5543,*
*www.hosteltralalasalento.com.*
Dutch-run hostel with dormitories,
as well as 3 private rooms (one with
bathroom), 2 kitchens, laundry service,
hot water and Wi-Fi. Cosy DVD/reading
room, great views, Wellington boot hire.
Recommended.

## Valle de Cocora

**$$$ Las Palmas de Cocora**
*Km 10, Vía Cocora, T310-455 5400,*
*www.laspalmasdecocora.com.*
Wooden 2-storey chalet with
comfortable rooms, sleeping 2-4. Also
has a restaurant serving trout (**$$**).
Horses for hire (US$4 per ½ hr, guide
US$7.50 per hr).

**$$-$ Bosques de Cocora**
*Km 11, Vía Cocora, T6-746 3515,*
*www.bosquesdecocora.com.*
Accommodation at a nearby finca, or
camping next to the restaurant. Hires
out tents, mattresses, sheets, blankets
and pillows. Shower facilities and free
coffee and hot chocolate offered. Good
restaurant. Try the *canelazo* to warm
up – *agua de panela* with cinnamon.

**$ Finca San José**
*Km 11, Vía Cocora, T310-0227 5091.*
Finca San José is a 100-year-old farm,
which sits above the hamlet of Cocora.
With basic but characterful rooms and
a delightful veranda with shuttered
windows opening up onto spectacular
vistas. An excellent place to stay while
hiking the hills of the Cocora Valley. Also
runs the **Living Trips** tour agency (see
What to do).

### Salento
Salento has an increasing variety of
restaurants. Make sure you try the
local speciality, trout.

**$$ Balcones del Ayer**
*C 6, No 5-40 (see Where to stay).*
Hotel restaurant specializing in trout
and meat dishes. Family-run and
friendly. The only restaurant in
Salento with disability access.

**$$ El Rincón Campestre**
*Mirador de Salento.*
Just outside Salento, at the top of
the lookout point, this restaurant is
a treat. Although specializing in trout,
they also do excellent meat, which
makes a nice change.

**$ Café Jesús Martín Bedoya**
*Cra 6, No 6-14.*
Excellent little café serving coffee from the
family finca (see also What to do, below).

**$ El Rincón de Lucy**
*Cra 6, No 4-02.*
Lovely little eatery with good
breakfasts and economical
dishes typical of the region.

### Salento

#### Craft courses
**Aldea del Artesano**, *book*
*through Alejandro, T320-782 9128,*
*aldeadelartesano@gmail.com.* This
community of artisans lives on the
outskirts of Salento in 4 large houses,
each family practising a number of
crafts. Try your hand at bamboo craft,
candle-making, gardening, jewellery-
making and much more. Full-day

courses include lunch cooked in the outdoor kitchen. There is also a small shop. Highly recommended.

**Tours**
Ecoaventuras Cocora Extremo, *C6 4-34, T310-566 9980, www. ecoaventurascocoraextremo.inf.travel.* Tours of the area and extreme sports. Jesús Martín, *Cra 6, No 6-14 (coffee shop), T316-620 7760, www.cafejesusmartin.com.* 1-hr tours of local coffee-roasting factory, US$17.50, fun and informative. Also 4- to 5-hr tours to a coffee finca in Quimbaya, tour of the plantation with full explanation of the coffee-making process and coffee and a brownie in the Salento coffee shop (see page 303) US$67.50, minimum 2 participants. Recommended.

**Valle de Cocora**

Marino Toro Ospina, *matoros432@ hotmail.es.* Organizes tours, walks and horse riding in Valle de Cocora, where he works daily 0800-1800. He is particularly good on historic information about the area and the park.

## Transport

**Salento**
Microbuses to **Armenia** every 20 mins, US$3, 50 mins; taxi US$10. To **Pereira,** Mon-Fri only, US$3.50, 1 hr. To **Medellín,** *colectivos* daily, US$21, 5 hrs. To **Valle de Cocora**, jeeps from the plaza, Mon-Fri 0610, 0730, 0930, 1130, 1600, US$1.75, 35 mins (last return 1700); more departures at the weekend. Jeeps can also be hired.

# Armenia and Quindío → *Colour map 2, C3.*
**busy city with recommended coffee fincas nearby**

Armenia, capital of Quindío Department, was founded in 1889 and named in memory of the massacres by Turkish Ottomans that took place in Armenia in the 19th century. The city has had its own tragedies to contend with, due to the area's seismic activity, most devastatingly in January 1999, when an earthquake destroyed about 30% of the city centre. In spite of this, Armenia is a busy place, more so than both Pereira and Manizales. New construction is of a high quality and hotels and restaurants are fresh and comfortable.

The surrounding Quindío countryside is characterized by coffee plantations and wax palms, although you will also see many other agricultural crops and activities. To appreciate your surroundings more fully, stay at a coffee finca (see box, page 283).

The interesting part of the city is within walking distance of the Plaza de Bolívar. There are important attractions in Quindío outside the city, for which buses, taxis, tours or your own transport will be required.

## Sights
The central square, **Plaza de Bolívar**, has a fountain and two bronze sculptures, a conventional Bolívar by Roberto Henau Buritacá, and a fine example of Rodrigo Arenas Betancur's work, the *Monumento al Esfuerzo*, which poignantly portrays

the positive attitude of the local population. The plaza has lost many of the surrounding buildings, including part of the Quindío administration building. The striking modern **cathedral** was badly damaged but has been faithfully restored to its former triangular shape. Inside, the nave continues the form and has a light, airy feeling, accentuated by fine stained glass. There is an impressive bronze figure of Christ. Also worth a look is the church of **San Francisco**, which has some notable stained-glass windows. The church overlooks the market, covering four blocks in the centre of the city, with stalls selling local *artesanía*, particularly basket work, at good prices. From Plaza Bolívar, Carrera 14 has been pedestrianized as far as Parque Sucre to the northwest, a colourful square with an ancient ceiba tree and a bust of Marshal Ayacucho. North from here, **Museo del Oro Quimbaya** ① *Av Bolívar, C 40 Norte 80, Tue-Sat, 0900-1700, free*, is worth a visit, while **Parque de la Vida**

**Armenia**

To ②①②③④⑤⑥⑨,
Museo Quimbaya
& Pereira

To Calarcá & Bogotá

To ⑩,
Bus Station
(7 blocks)
& Airport

To Cali

N

200 metres
200 yards

**Where to stay** 🛏
Armenia 2
Bolívar Plaza 3
Café Plaza 4
Café Real 5
Centenario 6
Hacienda Bambusa 10

Imperial 7
Zuldemayda 8

**Restaurants** 🍴
Anis 1
Café Quindío 3
El Rancho Argentino 4
Keizaki 5
La Fogata 6
La Fonda Antioqueña 7
La Puerta Quindiana 8
Natural Food Plaza 9

has bamboo structures, waterfalls and a lakeside theatre. Southeast of Plaza Bolívar, meanwhile, in the oldest part of the city, is **Parque Uribe Uribe** where concerts are held from time to time.

## Montenegro and around

Northwest of Armenia near **Montenegro** is the **Parque Nacional del Café** ① *1 km from Pueblo Tapao, T6-741 7417, www. parquenacionaldelcafe.com, high season daily 0900-1800, low season Wed-Sun and hols 0930-1800, US$11.50 or US$18.50-28 incl activities and rides, parking US$1.* The park has restaurants, a Juan Valdez coffee shop, a botanical garden, ecological walks, a Quimbaya cemetery, a tower with a fine view and an interesting museum which covers all aspects of coffee. A cableway links to a children's theme park with rollercoasters and water rides.

Beyond Montenegro is **Quimbaya**, known for its **Festival of Light** (Fiesta de Velas y Faroles) in December each year. About 7 km away is the **Parque Nacional de la Cultura Agropecuaria (PANACA)** ① *T01-800 012 3999, www. panaca.com.co, Tue-Sun 0900-1800, US$14.50-28*, an educational theme park, with many varieties of horse, cattle and other animals on display. It makes a good family outing.

## Tourist information

Information is available from **Fondo Mixto de Promoción del Quindío**, C 20, No 13-22, T6-741 7700, www. turismocafeyquindio.com. Also try **Corporación de Cultura y Turismo**, Centro Administrativo Municipal CAM, p 4, T6-741 2991. **Corporación Autónoma Regional de Quindío (CRQ)**, C 19N, No 19-55, T6-746 0600, www. crq.gov.co, has information on parks and natural reserves. For maps and information, visit **Instituto Geográfico Agustín Codazzi**, Cra 17, No 19-29, pisos 2 and 3, www.igac.gov.co, Mon-Fri 0730-1130, 1400-1630.

## Where to stay

### Armenia

**$$$$-$$$ Armenia**
*Av Bolívar, No 8N-67, T6-746 0099, www.armeniahotel.com.co.*
Impressive hotel in the northern part of Armenia, opposite the Parque de la Vida. It has a cavernous lobby and enormous rooms with beds made from *guadua* bamboo as well as all the expected services: sauna, gym, swimming pool, Wi-Fi and a restaurant with Chilean and Argentine wines. Discounts available at weekends. English spoken.

**$$$$-$$$ Hacienda Bambusa**
*Km 93, Vía El Caimo– Portugalito, T311-506 9915, www.haciendabambusa.com.*
South of the city, this enchanting traditional hacienda sits hidden in a labyrinth of banana plantations. This is very much a place to relax, but there are plenty of activities for the restless, including canopying in a bamboo forest, horse riding, birdwatching or swimming in the majestic pool. Has cable TV, restaurant and free pick up from airport or bus station.

**$$$ Bolívar Plaza**
*C 21, No 14-17, T6-741 0083, www.bolivarplaza.com.*
Just off the Plaza Bolívar, this hotel's rooms are a bit dark and musty, though they do have large beds. It also has parking, Wi-Fi and an internet room, free local calls and breakfast included.

**$$$ Café Real**
*Cra 18, No 21-32, T6-744 3055, www.hotelcafereal.com.*
Modern hotel with bright but slightly pokey rooms. Sauna, gym, Turkish bath and jacuzzi. Wi-Fi and breakfast included in the price.

**$$$ Centenario**
*C 21, No 18-20, T6-744 3143, www.hotelcentenario.com.*
Modern hotel with airy, bright rooms and attentive staff. Has Wi-Fi throughout and a small internet room as well as cable TV, parking and breakfast included.

**$$$ Zuldemayda**
*C 20, No 15-38, T6-741 0580.*
Popular business hotel with facilities such as Wi-Fi, internet room and parking. Breakfast included.

**$$ Café Plaza**
*Cra 18, No 18-09, T6-741 1500, hotelcafeplaza@hotmail.com.*
Near the Plaza Bolívar, this hotel is a little noisy but has simple but clean rooms with en suite bathrooms, cable TV and breakfast included.

**$ Imperial**
*C 21, No 17-43, T6-744 9151.*
This hotel has basic but clean rooms with cable TV and good security. No hot water, however.

## Montenegro and around

**$$$ Casa de Campo El Delirio**
*Km 1 Vía Montenegro–Parque del Café, T6-744 9955, casadelirio@hotmail.com.*
This beautiful, traditional finca has been restored with immaculate taste and decorated with original mahogany furniture, wrought-iron beds and black-and-white photographs of bullfighters. It's a perfect place to unwind, boasting a pool, large gardens with a coffee plantation at the bottom and delicious home-cooked food.

**$$$ Finca Villa Nora**
*Vereda La Granja, Km 1, Ctra Antigua vía Quimbaya– Montenegro, T311-422 6335, www.quindiofincavillanora.com.*
The rooms at this finca all have the same fittings as they would have when Antioquian settlers built it in the 19th century and its spacious veranda is decorated with original Quimbaya artefacts. It has an excellent kitchen serving up home-cooked food and a pleasant pool for relaxing after a tour of its working coffee farm. Also has Wi-Fi.

**$$$ Hostería Mi Monaco**
*Km 7, Vía Armenia–Pueblo Tapao, T310-374 5643, www.mimonaco.net.*
On the side of a hill with a bamboo copse that plunges down to a stream, **Mi Monaco** has comfortable rooms with crisp, white sheets in a traditional 60-year-old *bahareque* house. With a good pool, jacuzzi, and professional mountain bike guides, it's an excellent place to relax.

**$$$ Hotel del Campo**
*Km 7 contiguo a Panaca, T6-741 5222, www.hoteldelcampo.com.co.*
Set on the lip of a steep valley surrounded by banana, yucca and alfalfa plantations, this hotel is ideally located just 500 m from the Panaca park. It has good rooms with interesting bathrooms, a kidney-shaped pool and a restaurant. Wi-Fi in reception.

**$$ El Carriel**
*Km 1, Vía Quimbaya–Filandia, T6-746 3612, elcarriel@hotmail.com.*
This is an excellent option if you are looking for an economic way to stay on a working coffee finca. The rooms are simple but comfortable with private bathrooms and hot water, and there's a good little restaurant. The excellent coffee tour encourages visitors to pick coffee grains and follow the whole process from plant to cup.

## Restaurants

### Armenia

**$$ Café Quindío**
*Cra 19, No 33N-41, www.cafequindio. com.co.*
Gourmet coffee shop and restaurant, serving recipes such as chicken or steak in coffee sauce as well as international dishes (Thai, French, Italian). It also sells coffee products from its own farm and even has a school where you can learn about all aspects of coffee. The menu includes 29 varieties of coffee.

**$$ El Rancho Argentino**
*Av Bolívar, No 13N-47.*
Another popular restaurant in the fashionable northern part of Armenia, this restaurant serves mainly *parrillas* but pastas too.

### $$ Keizaki
*Cra 13, No 8N-39, www.keizaki.com.*
Restaurant serving sushi and other Asian dishes. There are several other good restaurants on the same block.

### $$ La Fogata
*Cra 13, No 14N-47.*
One of Armenia's most popular high-end restaurants, **La Fogata** serves all sorts of cuts of thick, juicy steaks as well as pork chops and typical dishes like *ajiaco*.

### $$-$ Anis
*C 10N, No 13-94.*
This excellent little restaurant has a varied menu cooked to a high standard. The steaks are thick and cooked to perfection. There are also salads, sandwiches, crêpes and other brunch options. It has a pleasant sunny patio with a wood-fired oven and even makes its own pasta. Recommended.

### $ La Fonda Antioqueña
*Cra 13, No 18-59.*
Pleasant *paisa* restaurant on a 2nd floor gallery festooned with antiques. Serves the usual dishes, such as *bandeja paisa*, etc.

### $ La Puerta Quindiana
*C 17, No 15-40.*
This restaurant serves cheap *comida corriente* for US$3, with dishes such as *sancocho* a speciality, as well as good fruit juices.

### $ Natural Food Plaza
*Cra 14, No 18N-40.*
Vegetarian restaurant with a varied menu that includes veggie burgers, crêpes, salads, Mexican, *tamales* and fruit juices. Also has a wholefood shop.

## What to do

### Armenia

**Territorio Aventura**, *Cra 14, No 14N-6, Edif Acuarium, loc 1, T310-422 0596, www. territorioaventura.com.co.* Organizes rafting, kayaking, parapenting, horse riding and zip wiring in local area.

### Montenegro and around

**Balsaje Los Remansos**, *C 16, No 6-12, Quimbaya, T314-775 4231, adal161@ hotmail.com.* Organizes *balsaje* excursions (punting down rivers on bamboo rafts) on the Río La Vieja.

## Transport

### Armenia

### Air
**Airport El Edén** is 13 km from city (taxi 15 mins, US$7.50). Scheduled direct flights to **Bogotá**, frequent, with **Avianca** (C 21, No 13-23, L 4, T6-741 4842, and at the airport, T6-747 9911). To **Medellín**, 3 daily, with **Avianca**, **Lan** and **Copa**.

### Bus
The bus station is south of the city at C 35, No 20-68, www.terminalarmenia. com. There are comprehensive bus services to/from major Colombian cities.
   Daily buses to **Bogotá**, 7-9 hrs, US$24. To **Cali**, 3-4 hrs, US$15.50. To **Medellín**, 6-7 hrs, US$22.50. To **Popayán**, 5-6 hrs, US$26. To **Ipiales**, 14 hrs, US$54. To **Pasto**, 12 hrs, US$47. To **Manizales**, 3-4 hrs, US$9. To **Neiva**, 6-7 hrs, US$26. To **Pitalito/San Agustín**, 10 hrs, US$42. To **Buenaventura**, 5-6 hrs, US$19.50. To **Cartagena**, US$75. To **Bucaramanga**, 12-13 hrs, US$50.

The main road from Armenia to Ibagué heads east over the Cordillera Central via the Quindío Pass (3350 m) at Km 105; the pass is also known as La Línea after the power lines that cross the mountains. On the east side is Cajamarca, a friendly town in a beautiful setting at 1900 m. Bar El Globo, on the corner of the main plaza, serves excellent coffee and there's an interesting market on Sunday.

Ibagué, capital of Tolima Department, lies at the foot of the Quindío mountains. Parts of the town are old: visit the **Colegio de San Simón** for its architecture and the market for its *tamales*. The **Parque Centenario** is pleasant, and there is a famous **Conservatory of Music**. Try the local alcoholic drink called *mistela*. Just outside town, off the Armenia road, a dirt road leads up the Río Combeima to El Silencio and the slopes of the Nevado del Tolima in the Parque Nacional Los Nevados (see page 301). Beyond Ibagué, the main road continues via Giradot to Bogotá.

### Listings Ibagué and around

### Tourist information

**Tourist office** is on Cra 3 between C 10 and 11, p 2, T6-262 5264, www.tolimaturismo.gov.co. The **tourist police** at the bus terminal are helpful.

### Where to stay

**$$$ Ambalá**
*C 11, No 2-60, T6-261 3888, www.hotelambala.com.*
Business hotel, includes breakfast, and has rooms with TV, a pool, sauna, parking, and a restaurant.

**$ San Remo**
*C 16, No 2-88, T8-261 3339.*
Rooms with fan and TV.

### Restaurants

**$$ El Fogón Antioqueño**
*Cra 6, No 26-03, www.elfogonantioqueno.com.*
Good local dishes.

**$$ La Vieja Enramada**
*Cra 8, No 15-03.*
Local and international dishes.

### Festivals

Jun **National Folklore Festival**, www.festivalfolclorico.com
Jun **San Juan** (24 Jun) and **San Pedro y San Pablo** (29 Jun). Commemorated by the departments of Tolima and Huila with bullfights, fireworks, and music.
Dec Biannual **choral festival**.

### Transport

**Air**
Daily **Avianca**, **Copa** and **Lan** flights to **Bogotá**, **Cali** and **Medellín** and **Pereira**.

**Bus**
Terminal is at Cra 2 No 20-89, www.terminalibague.com. Frequent services to **Bogotá**, US$17, 4 hrs. To **Neiva**, US$18.50, 5 hrs, and many other places.

# Southern Colombia

stone statues, sulphur pools and salsa in the steamy south

Much of Southern Colombia is characterized by the three mountain ranges that eventually join up to form the high Andes, South America's spine. The people of this region have adapted to the physical obstacles these mountains present, while inaccessibility has kept at bay the cultural dilution that comes with modern advancements.

The sensual city of Cali has branded itself as the capital of salsa music and sits in the tropical, sugar cane-rich plains of the Valle del Cauca. To the west lies the port of Buenaventura, gateway to the Pacific coast and its isolated beaches and islands. The Pan-American Highway continues south to Popayán, known for its dazzling white colonial buildings and its solemn Easter processions. East of Popayán are the mysterious archaeological sites of Tierradentro and San Agustín, while next to the Magdalena river lies the geographical anomaly that is the Tatacoa Desert.

From Popayán, the Cordillera Occidental reaches ever higher, rising up to the highland towns of Pasto and Ipiales, ideal places to observe indigenous ways of life. If you're crossing into Ecuador, the extraordinary Gothic cathedral that straddles a gorge at Las Lajas is worth a visit.

**Best** for
Archaeology ▪ Festivals ▪ Volcanoes

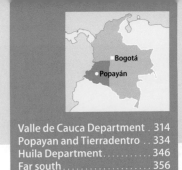

# Footprint picks

★ **Cali's nightlife**, page 322

Dance the night away in a *salsateca*.

★ **The journey to San Cipriano**, page 329

Ride a *brujita* along the rails through thick jungle to this isolated village.

★ **Pre-Columbian archaeology**, pages 342 and 350

Admire the burial mounds at Tierradentro and the carved megaliths at San Agustín.

★ **Parque Nacional Natural de Puracé**, page 344

Soak in the sulphur pools or climb to the summit of a volcano.

★ **Desierto de Tatacoa**, page 347

Spend a night in the desert under countless stars.

★ **Carnaval de los Blancos y Negros**, page 361

Get very messy at these lively festivals in Pasto.

★ **Las Lajas**, page 364

Join thousands of pilgrims at the neo-Gothic sanctuary.

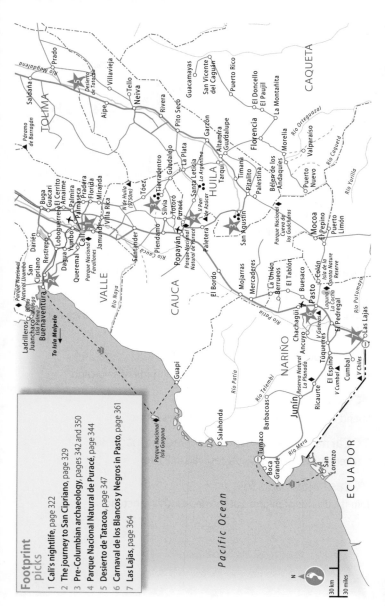

## Footprint picks

1 Cali's nightlife, page 322
2 The journey to San Cipriano, page 329
3 Pre-Columbian archaeology, pages 342 and 350
4 Parque Nacional de Puracé, page 344
5 Desierto de Tatacoa, page 347
6 Carnaval de los Blancos y Negros in Pasto, page 361
7 Las Lajas, page 364

# Essential Southern Colombia

## Finding your feet

The Pan-American Highway provides the quickest access to Cali from the north, continuing to Popayán, Pasto and the Ecuadorean border. Another major route heads southwest from Bogotá, following the Río Magdalena to Neiva, Pitalito (for access to San Agustín) and Mocoa. There are airports at Cali, Popayán and Pasto. Note that there is a malaria risk along the Pacific coast and in the southeast towards Amazonia.

## Getting around

Walking is the best way to get around town centres, including Cali, but you'll need taxis to reach the outlying suburbs. Long-distance buses travel around the region; busetas and *colectivos* are more expensive but significantly faster and may be the only option in more remote areas.

## When to go

Cali and its surroundings are warm throughout the year, with little climate variation. It is hot and humid at midday but a strong breeze that blows up in the afternoon makes the evenings cool and pleasant. Rain can come at more or less any time, although the city is shielded from the heavy rainfall on the Pacific coast by the Cordillera Occidental. To the east, Huila department can be swelteringly hot year round, but the upland areas around Popayán, San Agustín and Tierradentro are noticeably cooler, particularly in the evenings; temperatures drop still further in mountainous regions near the Ecuadorean border. Around San Agustín, the rainy season is April to June/July, but since the weather often comes up from the Amazon to the southeast, it can rain at any time, hence the beautiful green landscape. Festivals are a big deal throughout the region; the biggest celebrations take place in early January in Cali, Popayán and especially Pasto; at Easter in Popayán, and in June in Neiva and San Agustín.

## Time required

Spend two to three days in Cali and two to three weeks exploring the rest of the region.

## Weather Southern Colombia (Cali)

| Month | High | Low | Rainfall |
|---|---|---|---|
| January | 28°C | 19°C | 50mm |
| February | 24°C | 19°C | 60mm |
| March | 24°C | 19°C | 100mm |
| April | 23°C | 19°C | 140mm |
| May | 23°C | 19°C | 110mm |
| June | 23°C | 19°C | 60mm |
| July | 23°C | 18°C | 30mm |
| August | 24°C | 18°C | 50mm |
| September | 23°C | 18°C | 60mm |
| October | 23°C | 18°C | 120mm |
| November | 23°C | 18°C | 110mm |
| December | 23°C | 19°C | 70mm |

# Valle de Cauca
## Department

South from Pereira and Armenia the Pan-American Highway drops to the hot, sugar-rich Valle del Cauca, a narrow strip of flat plains abundant in wheat, pineapple, livestock and sugar cane, flanked on either side by the slender fingers of two mountain ranges, the Cordillera Occidental and the Cordillera Central. Capital of the valley is Cali, a sweltering, sexy city and self-appointed capital of salsa music. The road continues south to Popayán and eventually to Ecuador, while from Cali a road and railway run west high over mountains down to the port of Buenaventura, the largest settlement on the Pacific coast.

## Cali → *Colour map 3, A3.*

**sensual party city**

With a population of nearly three million, Cali may be second to Bogotá and Medellín in terms of size, but this vibrant, prosperous city is very much *número uno* when it comes to partying. Cali has proclaimed itself salsa capital of the world. The sensuous, tropical rhythms are ubiquitous, seemingly seeping out of every pore of the city. Cali's other major claim, rather more contentious, is that it boasts the most beautiful women in Colombia.

Through the centre of the city runs the Río Cali, a tributary of the Cauca, with grass and exotic trees on its banks. North of the river, all streets have the suffix 'N', and Carreras become Avenidas. The city extends southwards 15 km from the Río Cali. The centre of the city is comparatively small, however, and most places of interest to the visitor are within comfortable walking distance.

### Central Cali

The city's centre is the **Plaza de Caicedo**, with a statue of the Independence leader Joaquín de Caycedo y Cuero and some notably tall palms. Facing the square is the **Catedral Metropolitana**, a large three-aisle church, with a clerestory, elaborate aisle niches and stained-glass windows. The original church on the site dated from around 1539; the present building is mid-19th century. The **Palacio Nacional** is on the eastern side of the plaza, a French neoclassical style building (1933), now the city archive.

Among the most interesting buildings in Cali are the church and monastery of **San Francisco, just west of the cathedral along Carrera 6**. The brick church originates from 1757 and was structurally renovated inside in the 19th century and most recently in 1926. It has a fine ceiling and many 17th- and 18th-century images, carvings and paintings. The altar came from Spain. A second church in the complex is the **Capilla de la Inmaculada**, with a long nave, well lit *reredos* and gold-headed columns. The adjoining 18th-century monastery has a splendidly proportioned domed bell tower in the *mudéjar* style known as the Torre Mudéjar. On the opposite side of the square is the imposing 20-floor **Gobernación** building.

Cali's oldest church, **La Merced** ⓘ *Cra 4, No 6-117, T2-880 4737*, dates from 1545 and was constructed on the symbolic site of the founding of the city nine years earlier. It is in the classical style with a fine altar. It has been well restored by the Banco Popular. The adjoining convent houses two museums: **Museo de Arte Colonial** (which includes the church), a collection of 16th- and 17th-century paintings, and the **Museo Arqueológico** ⓘ *Cra 4, No 6-59, T2-885 4675, Mon-Sat 0900-1300, 1400-1800, US$2*. This houses a good pre-Columbian pottery collection highlighting Calima and other southwest Colombian cultures. By the well in the courtyard is a replica of a Tierradentro tomb. Opposite La Merced on the corner of Carrera 4 and Calle 7 is the **Casa Arzobispal**. This is one of the earliest buildings in Cali and the only surviving two-storied house of the period. Bolívar stayed here in 1822.

Nearby, in the Banco de la República building is the **Museo Calima (Museo de Oro)** ⓘ *C 7, No 4-69, T2-883 4352, Tue-Fri 0900-1700, Sat 1000-1700, free*. This is another of Colombia's national gold museums, of the usual high standard and well worth a visit. In addition to pre-Columbian gold work, well presented, with some exquisite tiny items magnified, it has an excellent pottery collection. There is a music room and library in the basement and exhibition halls.

Another church the visitor cannot fail to notice is **La Ermita by the river at Carrera 1 and Calle 13**. The original church was built here in 1602, but was totally destroyed by the 1925 earthquake. It was rebuilt between 1926 and 1942 with funds from public subscription, with Cologne cathedral in mind. The neo-Gothic blue and white exterior is striking, and there's a fine marble altar

> **Tip...**
> Although Cali is still associated with drug and anti-drug operations, the atmosphere is quite relaxed. Violent crime can be a problem in the city's barrios but is less of a threat in more affluent areas. However, carry your passport (or photocopy) at all times and be prepared for police checks. At night, do not walk east or south of Calle 15 and Carrera 10. Do not change money on the street under any circumstances and avoid all people who approach, offering to sell. Take advice on where and where not to go.

inside. The painting *El Señor de la Caña*, reflecting the local importance of sugar cane, was one of the few items that survived the earthquake. In the pleasant plaza in front of the church you can sit next to life-size figures of notable *caleños* of the past, including Joaquín de Caycedo and Jorge Isaacs. Nearby is an example of the older architecture of the city, the ornate Colombiana de Tabaco building.

Cross the river by the delightful, pedestrianized **Puente Ortiz**, built in the 1840s. On the north side, Calle 12 becomes **Paseo Bolívar**, with a bronze statue of *El Libertador* and a sculpture honouring Jorge Isaacs, the romantic 19th-century novelist, depicting the characters of his novel *María*. Alongside is the Centro

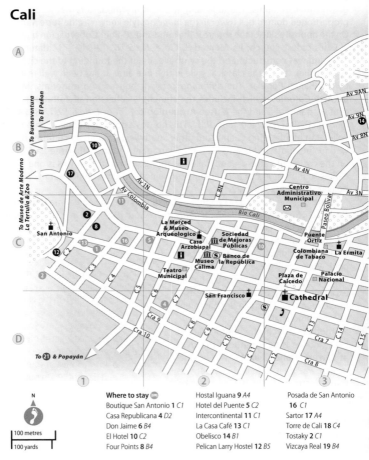

# Cali

**Where to stay** 🛏
Boutique San Antonio **1** *C1*
Casa Republicana **4** *D2*
Don Jaime **6** *B4*
El Hotel **10** *C2*
Four Points **8** *B4*

Hostal Iguana **9** *A4*
Hotel del Puente **5** *C2*
Intercontinental **11** *C1*
La Casa Café **13** *C1*
Obelisco **14** *B1*
Pelican Larry Hostel **12** *B5*

Posada de San Antonio
**16** *C1*
Sartor **17** *A4*
Torre de Cali **18** *C4*
Tostaky **2** *C1*
Vizcaya Real **19** *B4*

Administrativo Municipal (CAM) and the main post office. North of here is the Barrio Granada, with numerous hotels and restaurants.

A special feature of the centre of Cali is the ribbon of green along the river, lined with exotic and ancient trees that always give a freshness to the heat of the day. Several sculptures commissioned in the late 1990s line the banks: look out for *María Mulata*, a black bird seen everywhere along the coasts of Colombia, and the splendid bronze *El Gato del Río* by Hernando Tejada, inaugurated in 1996. Cali prides itself on its trees, and several are marked out for conservation, including the huge ceiba on Avenida 4N at Calle 10, by the viaduct.

**Restaurants** 🍴
Archie's Pizza **3** *B3*
Bahareque **2** *C1*
Carambolo **5** *B3*
D'Toluca **4** *B4*
El Solar **6** *B4*

Granada Faro **7** *B4*
La Tartine **10** *B1*
Ojo de Perro Azul **12** *C1*
Pampero **13** *A4*
Rosa Mezcal **8** *C1*
Solsticio **14** *B3*

Taisu **16** *B4*
Tortelli **17** *B1*

**Bars & clubs** 🍸
Talbert's Pub **18** *A4*
Tin Tin Deo **21** *D1*

Zaperoco **22** *B4*

# BACKGROUND

## Cali

After the collapse of the Incas in 1533, Sebastián de Belalcázar left Pizarro's army in Peru and came north, founding Quito in 1534. He established Popayán and (Santiago de) Cali in 1536, intending to continue northwards and establish other new settlements. But around Cali he encountered stiff resistance from the indigenous locals, which delayed him for several years, so that other conquistadors founded Antioquia and Bogotá.

The first site of the city was beside the Río Lili near the present Ciudad Universitaria and Ciudad Jardín, but it was moved north to its present location in 1539. Cali remained a dependency of Popayán and was dominated by Quito for 250 years, due to the fact that north–south communications along the line of the cordillera were so much easier than across the mountain ranges. Indeed, Cali remained a leisurely colonial town until 1900 and the arrival of the railway, when it rapidly expanded into an industrial complex serving the whole of southern Colombia.

The railway has since been eclipsed by road and air links, but today Cali is economically closely tied with the rest of Colombia as the capital of the rich agricultural Valle del Cauca Department, which produces sugar, cotton, rice, coffee and cattle. It sits on the main route north from Ecuador along the Río Cauca and controls the passage to the only important port on Colombia's Pacific coast, Buenaventura. Thanks to the port and the sugar industry, many Afro-Caribbeans and other groups of people have come to the valley over the years and now contribute to the city's wealth and entertainment.

In the early 1990s Cali achieved international notoriety because of its highly successful drug cartel. Known as the 'Gentlemen of Cali', thanks to their high society background, the Rodríguez Orejuela brothers and their associate José Santacruz Londoño profited from Pablo Escobar's war with the government, rising to supersede his Medellín organization. But in 1995, six of the seven heads were arrested, and in 2006 the Rodríguez Orejuela brothers were extradited to the United States, effectively bringing this drug-trafficking cartel to an end.

### San Antonio and further west

A popular morning 'run' is up the hill to the west of the city to the 18th-century church of **San Antonio**, built around 1747. It is a favourite place for weddings. There are some attractive colonial-style houses on the way and pleasant parkland with lovely trees and fine views of the city, though partly obstructed by high-rise buildings.

North of here, along the river from the city centre, is the **Museo de Arte Moderno La Tertulia** ① *Av Colombia, No 5-105 Oeste, T2-893 2939 Ext. 101, www.museolatertulia.com, Tue-Sat 0900-1900, Sun 1000-1700, US$2.50*, which has exhibitions of South American art, including local, modern works.

**Zoológico de Cali** ① *Cra 2A Oeste/C 14, entrance on the south bank of the Río Cali about 3 km west of the centre, T2-488 0888, www.zoologicodecali.com.co, daily*

*0900-1630, US$7.50 adults, US$5 children*, has an interesting and well-organized collection of South American animals, birds and reptiles, and makes very good use of the river as it enters the city. There is a small aquarium, a primate display and an 'ant' auditorium.

For a full view of the city, go to the huge **Monumento Cristo Rey**, at 1470 m to the west of the city. This statue can be seen for 50 km across the Río Cauca.

### North and east of the centre

There are more panoramic views from the **Monumento Las Tres Cruces**, at 1450 m, to the northwest of the city, a traditional pilgrimage site in Holy Week. It is also worthwhile going up the skyscraper of the Hotel Torre de Cali (see Where to stay), but you may have to buy an expensive meal as well.

The orchid garden, **Orchideorama** ① *Av 2N, No 48-10, T2-664 3256, www. caliorquideas.com, free, closed Sun*, is worth seeing. Located to the east of the city, it hosts a major international flower show in mid-November.

A popular family park is **Acuaparque de la Caña** ① *Cra 8, No 39-01, El Troncal (about 4 km east of the centre), T2-438 4812, daily 0900-1700 in high season (closed Mon in low season), adults US$7.50, children US$5.50*, with family entertainment, sports, swimming, riding and children's amusements. It also has a small sugarcane museum.

## Listings Cali *map p316*

### Tourist information

**Punto de Información Turística**, Cra 4 C 6 esq, Mon-Fri 0800-1200 and 1400-1700, Sat 0800-1300, housed inside the large red-brick **Cultural Centre** has pamphlets but otherwise isn't much help. The centre also has free exhibitions in the hallways. Don't bother with the **Secretaría de Cultura y Turismo**, Cra 5, No 6-05, sala 102, T2-885 4777 ext 102, www.cali.gov.co. See www.laguiadecali. com for news, history, entertainment, music and tourist information. The **National Parks Office**, C 29N, No 6N-43, Santa Mónica, T2-667 6041, is very helpful for information on Los Farallones de Cali and other parks. For information on the many privately owned nature reserves in this part of Colombia, enquire at **Asociación Red Colombiana de**

**Reservas Naturales de la Sociedad Civil**, C 2A, No 26-103, T2-558 5046, www.resnatur.org.co. For maps, try the **Instituto Geográfico Agustín Codazzi, IGAC**; Cra 6, No 13-56, T2-885 5611, www.igac.gov.co.

### Where to stay

#### Central Cali

**$$$ Casa Republicana**
*C 7, No 6-74, T2-896 0949,*
*www.hotelcasarepublicana.com.*
Gorgeous Republican-era building with a lovely courtyard full of large plants. Has good rooms with cable TV, Wi-Fi and a good restaurant serving lunch and dinner. Can be noisy early mornings when stallholders set up outside, but friendly and welcoming. Recommended.

## $$ El Hotel

*C 9, No 3-13, www.elhotelcali.com.*
Hotel in the centre. Wi-Fi and American
breakfast included in the price, so very
good value for money. There is a bar and
business centre. Recommended.

## San Antonio and further west

### $$$$ Hotel Boutique San Antonio

*Cra 6, 2-51, T2-524 6364, www.
hotelboutiquesanantonio.com.*
Charming hotel with sound-proofed
rooms, HD TVs, own security system
and Wi-Fi.

### $$$$ Intercontinental

*Av Colombia, No 2-72, T2-882 3225,
www.intercontinental.com.*
The most expensive hotel in town,
the Intercontinental has all the services
you would expect and more: a half-size
Olympic pool, sauna, Turkish bath, spa,
large rooms with plasma TVs and a 24-hr
casino. Additionally, it is well placed
on the edge of San Antonio. Prices
drop at weekends.

### $$$ Obelisco

*Av Colombia, No 4 Oeste-39, T2-893 3019,
www.hotelobeliscocali.com.*
One of Cali's traditional upmarket hotels,
the **Obelisco** offers a pool, sauna,
rooftop bar and Wi-Fi in its pizzeria.

### $$ Posada de San Antonio

*Cra 5, No 3-37, T2-893 7413, www.
posadadesanantonio.com.*
With rooms set around a couple of
sunny, leafy patios and decorated
with Calima indigenous artefacts,
this *bahareque* building dating back
to 1906 represents good value for
money. Wi-Fi and 3 different breakfast
menus to choose from. 10% discount
for Footprint readers.

### $$-$ Hotel del Puente

*C 5, No 4-36, T2-893 8484, www.
hoteldelpuentecali.blogspot.com.*
A little noisy and lacking some basic
things such as loo seats but it's well
situated on the edge of San Antonio.

### $ La Casa Café

*Cra 6, No 2-13, T2-893 7011,
www.lacasacafecali.blogspot.com.*
Nice backpackers' hostel cum café
in San Antonio. The hostel has
simple rooms with high ceilings
and wooden floor-boards and
the café hosts cultural evenings.
There is a kitchen and DVD room.

### $ Tostaky

*Cra 10, No 1-76, T2-893 0651,
www.cafetostaky.blogspot.com.*
Situated at the bottom of San Antonio
park, this sweet backpackers' hostel with
13 rooms is run by a French/Colombian
team and has airy rooms above a café
open only to guests, serving French
breakfasts and snacks. Facilities include
use of a kitchen, a TV room with DVDs,
and hot water in shared bathrooms.
Recommended.

## North and east of the centre

### $$$$ Four Points

*C 18 Norte, No 4N-08, T2-685 9999,
www.fourpointssheraton.com.*
Slick hotel with lots of steel, glass
and brick with a swimming pool,
gym, Wi-Fi and à la carte restaurant.

### $$$$-$$$ Vizcaya Real

*C 20 Norte, No 5AN-30, T2-683 1000,
www.hotelvizcayareal.com.*
Located on a palm-lined avenue, with
good facilities, including a small pool,
gym, Turkish bath and an internet room;
the beds are a bit short, though. Free
airport transfers included in price.

### $$$ Don Jaime
*Av 6 Norte, No 15N-25, T2-667 2828,*
*www.hoteldonjaime.com.*
Large but dated hotel on the noisy
Av 6 with a/c, cable TV, Wi-Fi and
breakfast included. Restaurant and
terrace bar in bustling Av 6 Norte.

### $$$ Torre de Cali
*Av de las Américas, No 18N-26, T2-683
3535, www.hoteltorredecali.com.*
From its imposing 41-floor tower, the
**Torre de Cali** has one of the best views in
town. The rooms are large with big TVs
and there are significant discounts
at weekends.

### $$ Sartor
*Av 8 Norte, No 20-50, T2-668 6482,*
*www.hotelsartor.com.*
The rooms are basic; they have hot water
in the en suite bathrooms but small
beds. Wi-Fi, cable TV and laundry service.

### $ Hostal Iguana
*Av 9 Norte, No 22N-22, T313-768 6024,*
*www.iguana.com.co.*
Spread over 2 pleasant suburban
houses on the edge of the fashionable
Barrio Granada, this has long been
Cali's best-known backpackers' hostel.
Several private rooms, some with
en suite bathrooms, a kitchen, garden,
TV room with DVDs, Wi-Fi, free coffee,
Spanish and salsa classes (1st hr free)
and great local information. Run by
Urs from Switzerland.

### $ Pelican Larry
*C 20 Norte, No 6AN-44, T2-392 1407,*
*www.hostelpelicanlarry.com.*
Rooms with and without bath, and
dorms. Close to Barrio Granada's
restaurants and bars, 15 mins' walk from
bus terminal and centre. Hot water,
laundry (use service at **Hotel Sartor**
when raining), Wi-Fi throughout, kitchen,

Spanish classes and free salsa lessons
arranged, bicycle rental, TV room,
helpful staff. Warmly recommended.

## Restaurants

Cali has a good restaurant scene.
In the centre, the areas of El Peñón
and San Antonio have an excellent
selection of restaurants serving all
types of international food. The
Mercado Alameda in the southwest
of the city has a concentration of
seafood restaurants as well as ladies
preparing tamales. Also in the south of
the city is **$ La Colina** (C 9, No 72-75),
which serves pizzas that one traveller
described as the best he had eaten in
Central or South America. North of the
centre, the sheer volume of eateries in
Barrio Granada, particularly on C 14N
and 15N, makes for some difficult
dining dilemmas.

### San Antonio and further west

### $$$ La Tartine
*C 3 Oeste, No 1-74, T2-893 6617.*
Classic French-owned restaurant
serving delicacies such as snails and
*chateaubriand* in eccentric surroundings.

### $$$ Tortelli
*C 3 Oeste, No 3-15, T2-893 3227,*
*www.restaurantetortelli.com.*
Little Italian restaurant serving
home-made pasta.

### $$ Rosa Mezcal
*C 2, No 4-63, T2-893 6597,*
*rosamezcalrestaurante.jimdo.com.*
Restaurant in the style of a Mexican
cantina, complete with live mariachi
bands. Happy hour specials change daily.

### $ Bahareque
*C 2, No 4-52.*

This laid-back restaurant has a lounge feel. Ultra-friendly owners Marly and José are a wealth of information on the local music and dance scene. It serves typical Colombian food as well as salads.

### $ Ojo de Perro Azul
*Cra 9, No 1-27.*
Bright bohemian hangout with cards, dominoes, chess – a place to chat, eat and drink. Serves mostly *picadas* and *tostadas* but has a few traditional Colombian mains on the menu. The funky animal-print furniture is mostly fake but at least one zebra died to decorate the floor.

**North and east of the centre: Barrio Granada**

### $$$ Carambolo
*C 14 9N-18/28, T2-667 5656, www.carambolocali.com.*
Excellent themed restaurant with Latin and Mediterranean dishes. Friendly and recommended.

### $$$ El Solar
*C 15 Norte, No 9N-62B, T2-661 2451, www.faroelsolar.co.*
A great atmosphere thanks to an open-air gravel patio shaded by trees, and a varied international menu of Asian, Italian and Mexican cuisines. Popular *caleño* choice.

### $$$ Granada Faro
*Av 9 Norte, No 15AN-02, T2-667 4625, www.granadafaro.com.*
Another Cali culinary fixture, the **Granada Faro** serves Mediterranean-Peruvian fusion.

### $$$ Solsticio
*Av 9 Norte, No 13-76, T2-661 2951, www.solsticio.com.co.*
Colombian and world food in pleasant setting. Occasionally live music in the evenings.

### $$$-$$ Archie's Pizza
*Av 9 Norte, No 14N-22, T2-524 4414 for delivery, www.archies.co.*
Quite simply the best pizzas in Cali. Part of a gourmet pizza chain. Pricey, but worth it.

### $$ Pampero
*C 21N, No 9-17, T2-661 3117.*
Pitch-perfect Argentine steaks on pleasant terrace with good service. Recommended.

### $$ Taisu
*C 16N, No 8N-74, T2-661 2281, www.restaurantetaisu.com.*
**Taisu** serves a variety of Asian cuisines, including sushi, *teppanyaki* and various stir-fried dishes.

### $ D'Toluca
*C 17N, No 8N-46, T2-661 8390, www.dtoluca.com.*
Good (for South America) Mexican restaurant serving fajitas, tacos and burritos at reasonable prices.

### ★ Bars and clubs

Cali is legendary for its nightlife and especially for its *salsatecas* or salsa-playing discos. The most popular with *caleños* can be found on Av 6 Norte where there are dozens of venues to choose from, including bars playing rock, jazz, blues and electronic music as well. Bars in town close by 0300, after which many people head to the range of *salsatecas* in Zona Juanchito in the western outskirts of the city or Barrio Menga in the north. It is worth visiting just to watch the couples dancing even if you don't dare to join in. Go with locals and couples; groups of foreign male tourists might have a hard time getting in. It's advisable to

## ON THE ROAD
### Salsa

Salsa may have its roots in Cuba and have developed its sound in the Latin barrios of New York, but the people of Cali claim that it's in their city that it has found its true home. It can be heard everywhere – on radios, in taxis, bars and nightclubs. So all-pervasive is its reach that it can be said that this horn-led music with its complex, syncopated beats has, literally, become part of the rhythm of everyday life.

Local groups such as Orquesta Guayacán, Grupo Niche and Jairo Varela have helped develop a distinctive sound, which is mirrored on the dancefloor by a style that is characterized by an upright upper body and intricate movements of the feet.

'No salsa, no dates', say the locals. At the weekend, sexual attraction is measured in moves on the dancefloors of Juanchito's enormous *salsatecas*. But salsa purists also head for traditional salsa bars nearer the centre, such as **Zaperoco**, where the dancing is the most important thing.

take a registered radio taxi there and back (15 mins).

**Escondite Nightclub Tequendama**
*Cra 37, No 5-14, Barrio Estadio.*
Crossover music. Sometimes stays open (illegally) on Sat nights until 0400 if enough people are there. Reasonably priced.

**Club Living**
*Cra 40, No 11-83, Barrio Menga.*
Lively salsa in a raging nightclub.

**Talbert's Pub & Bourbon St**
*C 17N and Cra 8N, Barrio Granada, www.talbertspub.tripod.com.*
English- and American-themed bars, owned by the same person. Good live bands on Fri, and convivial atmosphere in general.

**Tin Tin Deo**
*C 5, No 38-71, T2-514 1537, www.tintindeo.com.*
*Salsateca* that attracts a liberal crowd of students and teachers and is more forgiving on salsa beginners than some other places.

**Zaperoco**
*Av 5N, No 16-46, Barrio Granada, www.zaperocobar.com.*
The place for real salsa purists.

### Entertainment

**Cultural centres**
All give language classes, show films and have other events; enquire for programme: **Alianza Colombo Francesa** (Av 6N, No 21-34A, T2-661 3431, www.alianzafrancesa.org.co); **Centro Cultural Colombo-Americano** (C 13N, No 8-45, T2-687 5800, www.colomboamericano.edu.co); **Centro Cultural de Cali** (Cra 5, No 6-05, T2-885 8855); **Centro Cultural Comfandi** (C 8, No 6-23, T2-334 0000, ext 1302).

**Performing arts**
Teatro Aire Libre Los Cristales, *Cra 14A Oeste, No 6-00, T2-558 2009*. All kinds of musical and artistic presentations.

Teatro Experimental, *C 7, No 8-63, T2-884 3820*. Weekend theatre productions by the resident company.
Teatro Jorge Isaacs, *Cra 3, No 12-28, T2-889 9322, www.teatrojorgeisaacs. com.co*. Neoclassical 1930s building declared a National Monument in 1984. Hosts jazz and pop music events as well as comedy nights.
Teatro La Máscara, *Cra 10, No 3-40, T2-893 6640, www.teatrolamascara.com*. Feminist theatre ensemble that stages alternative productions.
Teatro Municipal, *Cra 5, No 6-64, T2-881 3131, www.teatromunicipal.gov.co*. Has been hosting major cultural activities since 1918, including opera, ballet and weekly classical concerts and is also home to the Cali Symphony Orchestra.

## Festivals

**25 Dec-3 Jan Feria Internacional de Cali**. Centred on Plaza Cañaveralejo on C 5 but engulfing the whole city, with bullfights, horse parades, masquerade balls, sporting contests and salsa competitions everywhere. Groups come from all over the world.
**Jun Feria Artesanal**. At Parque Panamericano, C 5, handicrafts and excellent leather goods.
**Aug Festival de Música del Pacífico Petronio Alvarez**. Champions music from Colombia's Pacific coast. Recommended.
**Sep AjazzGo** festival, www.ajazzgo festival.com. International artists.
**Sep Festival Internacional de Arte**. Painting, sculpture, theatre and music.

## Shopping

### Books

There are pavement bookstalls on Cra 10 near C 10.

Librería Nacional, *Cra 5, No 11-50, www. librerianacional.com*. Bookshop with a café, almost next to the cathedral on Plaza de Caicedo. Other branches at the airport and in all major shopping centres.

### Handicrafts

Artesanías Pacandé, *Av 6N, No 17A-53*. Typical regional handicrafts.
Centro Artesanal, *Parque La Loma de la Cruz, C 5 entre Cra 14 y 16*. Permanent handicraft market (daily 0900-2200) in a nice secure setting, pleasant neighbourhood, cafés around the park.
Cerámicas Palomar, *Cra 12, No 2-41, www.ceramicaselpalomar.com*. Good pottery.
La Caleñita, *Cra 24, No 8-53, www. lacalenita.com*. Good selection of typical handicrafts.

### Jewellery

Platería Ramírez, *many outlets including CC Unicentro, www.plateriaramirez.com*. Good selection of jewellery, lessons offered in jewellery making.

## What to do

### Bullring

Plaza de Toros Cañaveralejo, *www. portal.plazatoroscali.com, is 5 km from the city centre along C 5*. Bullfights take place end Nov-Jan.

### Cycling

**Ciclovía** On Sun 0700-1400, C 9 is closed from north to south to allow people to cycle, run and exercise on the roadway.

### Dance classes

Academia El Manicero, *Cra 39, No 9-56, piso 2*. Classes for individuals or groups. Also enquire at **Hostal Iguana** and **Pelican Larry**, see page 321.

### Diving

Contact **Rafael Lozano**, T313-767 6099 (mob), for diving trips. Speaks English, lots of experience and very responsible. Recommended.

Casco Antiguo Diving Centre, *Cra 34, No 3-89 (Parque del Perro), www.casco antiguocolombia.com.* PADI certified.

### Football

Cali's 2 major football teams, América de Cali and Deportivo Cali both play at the **Pascual Guerrero Stadium**, which holds 50,000 people.

### Parapenting

Speak to **Rob Ottomani**, T314-678 7972. German and English spoken.

### Tour operators

Panturismo, *C 18N, No 8N-27, T2-668 2255, www.panturismo.com.co and other branches.* All-inclusive trips.

Vela, Cra 4, C 18, No 118-241, of 305, T2-555 1723, www.velatours.com. Student travel agency, cheap tickets. Recommended.

Transport

### Air

**Alfonso Bonilla Aragón airport**, 20 km northeast of city, T2-442 2624, has banks and ATMs, international telephone facilities and a tax-exemption office. Internet is available. The best way to reach the city is by minibus from the far end of the road outside Arrivals to the bus terminal on the edge of the centre, every 15 mins, 0430-2020, 30 mins, US$2.50. From here taxis to any destination in the city cost around US$2.50-3.50. Alternatively, take a taxi all the way from the airport, US$25-30, 30 mins. (Note: Minibuses marked 'Aeropuerto' leave from the 2nd floor of the bus terminal.)

Frequent flights to **Bogotá**, **Medellín**, **Cartagena**, **Ipiales** and other Colombian cities with **Satena** (Cra 5 No 8-12, T2-885 7709) and **Avianca** (Av 6N, No 23N-05, T2-398 2000 or Cra 6, No 11-42). International flights to **Miami**, **New York**, **Ecuador** with TAME (C 5D, No 38-35, Edif Vida Centro Profesional, T2-554 5161) and **Panama**. Copa Air (Cra 44, No 8A-03); LAN (C 25N, No 6B-36).

### Bus

Cali has an integrated rapid transit bus system, with services running north–south and west–east, US$0.90 per journey; you can prepay at stations. Transport by both bus or taxi can be tedious because of the density of the traffic.

The **bus terminal**, C 30N, No 2AN-29, T2-668 3655, www.terminalcali.com, is 25 mins' walk from the centre following the river along Av 2N, and about 15 mins from Barrio Granada (leave terminal by the taxi stands, take 1st right, go under railway and follow river to centre, or go through tunnel, marked 'túnel' from the terminal itself). There are 3 floors: ground floor has most of the shops, restaurants and services, including hotel information, left luggage (US$1.35 per item for 12 hrs), banks and currency exchange (cash only). The 2nd floor has showers (US$2) and also most of the ticket offices for long-distance buses, while the 3rd floor has taxis and more bus company offices. There are plenty of local buses between the bus station and the centre (US$0.90). A tunnel connects the terminal with C 25, from where it's cheaper to get a taxi to the centre (US$4).

*Busetas* (**Velotax** and others) charge 50% more than buses but save time; *taxi-colectivos* are about 2½ times more expensive than buses and even quicker. To **Popayán**, US$6-7, 2½-3 hrs. To **Pasto**, US$32.50, 8-9 hrs. To **Ipiales** (direct), US$39, 12 hrs; to **San Agustín**, 9 hrs, US$14-16. To **Cartago**, 3½ hrs, US$15. To **Armenia**, US$15.50. To **Ibagué**, US$23, 6-7 hrs. To **Manizales**, US$22, 7 hrs. To **Medellín**, US$36, 8-10 hrs. To **Bogotá**, 10-15 hrs, US$22-30 (sit on the left of the bus). To **Buenaventura**, 3 hrs with **Expreso Palmira**, US$10.

### Taxi
Cali's taxis have meters (make sure that these are used) and can be flagged in the street, or ordered by telephone (US$2 minimum fare; extra at night). Some have helpful translations of common phrases on display in Spanish and English. Radio taxis include **Taxis Libres**, T2-444 4444, and **Taxis Valcali**, T2-333 3333.

### Train
There are no longer any passenger services running from Cali.

### Car hire
**Hertz**, Av Colombia No 2-72 (Hotel Intercontinental), T2-892 0437, and at airport, T2-666 3283. **Colombia Rent a Car**, Av 8, No 16N-50, Of 1. **National**, C 5, No 39-36, T2-524 4432; airport, T2-666 3016.

## Cauca Valley north and south of Cali → Colour maps 2, C3-3, A3.
### colonial towns and handicrafts

From Cali the Pan-American Highway follows the route of the Cauca Valley north to Cartago and south to Popayán. There it mounts the high plateau between the Western and Central Cordilleras and goes through to Ecuador.

### Buga
Buga, some 73 km north of Cali, has been firmly on the radar of most Colombians for decades and attracts large numbers of pilgrims a year to its cathedral, **Basílica del Señor de los Milagros**. Slowly but surely it's beginning to attract more foreign visitors and now even boasts a hostel. The pleasant town with its imposing cathedral is surrounded by beautiful countryside; day excursions can be made to several nearby nature reserves, including **Bosque de Yotoco** and **Laguna de Sonso**. The area is perfect for hiking or biking with plenty of picturesque waterfalls and natural swimming pools.

### Cartago
Cartago lies at the northern extreme of the Department, 177 km north of Cali and just 25 km southwest of Pereira. Founded in 1540, it still has some colonial buildings, particularly the very fine **Casa del Virrey** on Calle 13, and the **cathedral**. The town is noted for its embroidered textiles. From Cartago, roads run east to Pereira and Armenia in the Zona Cafetera (see page 304).

### Santander
From Cali it is 135 km south to Popayán. The road crosses the Río Cauca, then rejoins the main east bank route south at Villa Rica. About 17 km along the main road is Santander, an attractive town with a colonial chapel, Capilla de Dominguillo, that is worth a visit. Ceramics and *fique* handicrafts are sold here.

## Where to stay

### Buga

**$ Buga Hostel and Holy Water Ale Café**
*Cra 13 4-83, Buga, T2-236 7752,*
*www.bugahostel.com.*

German/Colombian-run hostel with their own microbrewery and the **Holy Water Ale Café**. Dorm beds and a private room with balcony. Rooftop terrace with lovely views. They can organize tours of the area. Recommended.

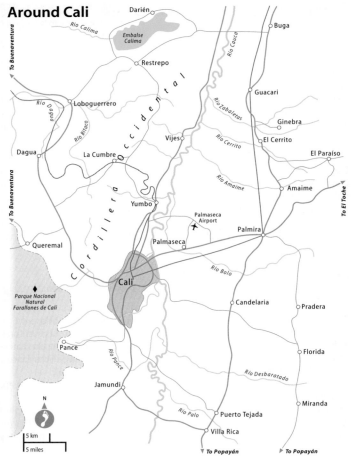

**Around Cali**

**Cartago**

Many hotels in area around bus terminals (Cra 9) and railway station (Cra 9 y C 6).

**$$ Don Gregorio**
*Cra 5, No 9-59, T6-211 5111,*
*www.hoteldongregorio.net.*
Rooms with a/c (cheaper with fan). Also has pool, sauna and includes breakfast.

**Cartago**
To **Cali**, US$15, 4 hrs. To **Armenia**, US$5, 2 hrs. To **Pereira**, US$3.50, 1 hr. To **Medellín**, US$21, 5-7 hrs.

## West of Cali → *Colour map 3, A3.*

*from the mountains to the jungle*

To the west of Cali is the northeast/southwest line of the Cordillera Occidental, which rises here to over 4000 m. A large section of this area and down to 200 m on the Pacific side is the Farallones de Cali National Park (see below). North of this are the road and rail links to Buenaventura. Both the paved toll road (US$3.50, included in bus tickets) and the old road out of Cali give beautiful views of mountains and jungle. The road first climbs 12 km to Saladito, which attracts *caleños* to its roadside restaurants thanks to its fresh climate, 10°C cooler than the city. The highest point is reached at Km 18, where the old road turns off left towards El Queremal (see below).

**Dagua** (828 m), 46 km from Cali, is in a semi-arid pineapple-growing zone, a good place for refreshments. Here the railway comes alongside the road, both following the Río Dagua to the coast. Further down, the route is lined with tropical forests. Traffic is heavy, but there are several places to stop and bathe on the way, including San Cipriano and Córdoba, where you can rent small *cabañas* in the forest, swim in the rivers and visit the rainforest. They are busy at weekends and holidays but quiet otherwise.

### Parque Nacional Natural Farallones
*Information: Av 4N, No 37AN-37, Cali, T2-664 9334, www.fundacionfarallones.org.*
*Entrance to the park, US$1.70.*

There are two ways to access the park. The first is from **El Queremal**, a pleasant local mountain village at 1460 m, about an hour west of Cali (3½ hours from Buenaventura). A dirt road leads south from the plaza in El Queremal to the park. The alternative access is via **Pance**, which lies southwest of Cali (one hour by *colectivo*). From Pance a path leads to the environmental centre at El Topacio (about 30 minutes).

There is good walking and bathing in the park and peaks to climb. It's a steep, slippery scramble for 2½ hours to the top of Pico de Loro, but worth it for the views and the sound of the swooping birds. The park is busy at weekends. Camping is possible at El Topacio or at Quebrada Honda, near the Río Pance (US$8.50 for six people), but you will need a permit from the national parks office in Cali. It is best to go with a guide.

# ★San Cipriano

The expression 'the journey is the destination' could have been coined for San Cipriano. Sitting in steaming jungle next to a shallow river, 20 km east of Buenaventura, San Cipriano was founded in the 18th century as a base for hunting, tree felling and gold panning. The village is only accessible by the railway line between Cali and Buenaventura and this is used only for cargo. To compensate for the lack of official transport to their village, the locals have come up with their own ingenious system, consisting of carts mounted on the railway line between Córdoba and San Cipriano, which are punted along using large poles. The whole effect resembles a witch riding a broomstick, hence the name, *brujita*. Lately, they have started using motorbikes to power the carts: the bike is strapped onto the cart with its back wheel on the line. There are no brakes to speak of, so the 10-minute descent through thick jungle from Córdoba to the village can be hairy, and if a train comes along it's a desperate scramble to get the cart off the line. You can get a bus from Cali to Córdoba, from where the *brujitas* to San Cipriano depart (US$2.50).

The village and its environs were declared a national reserve in 1979. **Fundación San Cipriano** has 8564 ha of protected forest, through which runs the San Cipriano river. It is noted for the rich variety of animal life that can be seen and heard, including spectacled bears, spider monkeys, toucans and several varieties of hummingbird. On arrival at the village you will have to pay US$1 at the Fundación San Cipriano office to enter the reserve. Enquire here about guides for walks in the forest, including to La Cascada Veinteadora. Most houses near the river hire out inflatable rubber rings for floating down the river, US$2.50. Take insect repellent.

## Listings West of Cali

### Where to stay

**San Cipriano**

Accommodation in San Cipriano is about as basic as it gets, though there is running water and electricity.

**$ Cabañas Carvajal**
Simple *cabañas* near the river.

**$ Hotel David**
*Towards the end of the village.*
Run by the lovely Luz Mari and her family. Basic rooms, including a chalet above her restaurant, with clean showers and fan provided. She guarantees that if you get bitten by mosquitoes during the night, she won't charge!

Colombia's only important port on the Pacific is Buenaventura, 145 km by road from Cali over a pass in the Western Cordillera. South of the town a swampy coast stretches as far as Tumaco (see page 363); to the north lies the beautiful coastline of the Bahía de Málaga (see below) and deeply jungled Chocó Department, with its abundant wildlife and some good beaches (see page 271).

### Buenaventura → *Colour map 3, A2.*

The commercial centre of the city is now entirely paved and has some impressive buildings, including the cathedral, but the rest of the town is very poor, with unpaved streets lined with wooden shacks. Buenaventura handles 80% of Colombia's coffee exports and 60% of the nation's total exports, including sugar and frozen shrimp. However, it is also one of Colombia's main drug- and people-trafficking centres and has severe poverty, leading to high levels of violent crime and homicide. In 2014 it was judged the most dangerous city in Colombia by *The Economist* online. We strongly advise you to visit Buenaventura only as a transit point for other destinations; move on as quickly as possible, or, if you must stay, pre-book your accommodation and go straight to the hotel once you arrive.

### Parque Nacional Natural Uramba Bahía Málaga → *Colour map 3, A2.*

North of the city is the Bahía Málaga, where rocky promontories sag under the weight of thick tropical vegetation; squadrons of pelicans patrol its glassy green waters, and from a boat you will catch glimpses of some inviting golden sand beaches. The bay was incorporated into a national park in 2010. It boasts the greatest plant biodiversity on the planet: 265 species per hectare. Just as impressive is the number of animals: there are 60 species of amphibian, 114 reptiles, 148 types of fish and over 400 species of bird. In its eastern corner is the waterfall **Las Sierpes**, which falls 65 m directly into the sea. Some 3500 people subsist primarily as fishing communities on its various islands. The bay also has some fine beaches, including **Playa Dorada** (golden sand), **Juan de Dios** (white sand) and **Chucheros**, which has a waterfall falling onto the beach, creating a freshwater pool. All these are accessible by *lancha* from Buenaventura or Juanchaco.

### Juanchaco, Ladrilleros and around

**Juanchaco**, one hour on a *lancha* from Buenaventura, has cheap accommodation and restaurants, but its beach is polluted and its streets muddy. **Ladrilleros** is just around the headland and has much better beaches, albeit a bit grey, backed by picturesque cliffs and with many sea caves and freshwater falls to explore. The village itself is quiet and pretty, with rickety clapboard houses and dirt tracks for streets.

Partly because of the richness of the water in this region, this is a great location to watch dolphins and humpback whales on their migration south with their calves from July to early October each year. There are also all kinds of sea birds, including pelicans and frigate birds. A good place is near the Isla Palma, an island off Juanchaco owned by the Colombian Navy.

Another worthwhile activity near Ladrilleros is a tour round the inland sea canals. This network of tidal mangrove rivers, consisting of 90% fresh water, winds its way through thick jungle with encroaching vines. A tour by canoe or motorboat includes a visit to a swimming hole fed by a waterfall. For details, see What to do, page 333.

## Parque Nacional Natural Isla Gorgona → *Colour map 3, A1.*

*For information, contact Aviatur, T01-900-331 2222/382 1616, www.concesiones parquesnaturales.com. Entrance fee US$17.50 for foreigners. To get there: fly to Guapi with Satena from Cali or Popayán, then catch a launch to the island, 1½ hrs; or contract a launch from Buenaventura, 4 hrs. Book transport and accommodation well in advance during high season.*

Until 1984 the island of Gorgona was Colombia's high-security prison (a sort of Alcatraz). The prison is derelict but some parts can still be seen. Convicts were dissuaded from escaping by the island's poisonous snakes (after whom Francisco Pizarro named the island) and the sharks patrolling the 46 km stretch of water to the mainland (both snakes and sharks are still there).

The national park protects a wealth of flora and fauna. There is an abundance of birds (pelicans, cormorants, geese, herons) that use the island as a migration stopover, and from the paths you can see monkeys and iguanas. (Rubber boots are recommended.) The island also boasts many unspoilt, deserted sandy beaches. Snorkelling and diving are rewarding, with many exotic fish and turtles to be seen; equipment can be hired but take your own if possible. Killer whales visit the area from July to September.

> **Tip...**
> Visits to the island are normally managed and run by **Aviatur**. However, in 2014, violent FARC activity on the island increased and **Aviatur** suspended trips. **Embarcaciones Asturias** is still offering excursions to the island (see page 332), but you are strongly advised to check all safety notices from government agencies before even considering a trip to Isla Gorgona.

## Isla Malpelo

*Contact the national parks office in Bogotá for more information, T1-353 2400.*

Declared a UNESCO site in 2006, Isla Malpelo is located 506 km from Buenaventura in the Pacific Ocean and is an acclaimed birdwatching haven with great diving opportunities. The island is considered to be one of the world's best places to observe hammerhead sharks in great numbers. The voyage from Buenaventura takes 36 hours and can be rough. There are no places to stay on the island and camping is not allowed.

## Where to stay

### Buenaventura

If you can't avoid staying in Buenaventura, these are the best options. Most hotels have their own restaurants; eat there rather than wandering around town.

### $$$$-$$$ Hotel Estelar Estación
*C 2, No 6-08, T2-243 4070,*
*www.hotelesestelar.com.*
With its white neoclassical façade, the 80-year-old **Estación** gleams in comparison to the rest of Buenaventura. Smartly dressed bellboys and sculpted gardens add to the old world charm. Swimming pool, sauna, cable TV and a restaurant serving *criollo* food. Healthy discounts available, especially at weekends. The hotel can organize whale-watching trips to Bahía de Málaga (see below).

### $$-$ Los Delfines
*C 1, No 5A-03, T2-241 5449, 4 blocks up the hill from the muelle.*
This hotel is good value with clean rooms, a/c, cable TV, private bathrooms and a breezy terrace.

### $$-$ Titanic
*C 1, No 2A-55, T2-241 2046.*
Handily located about a block from the *muelle turístico*, this hotel has clean rooms with en suite bathrooms and beds with crisp, white sheets. Its 6th-floor restaurant has great sea views. There's cable TV and a safe in each room.

### Juanchaco, Ladrilleros and around

### $$$ Cabañas Reserva Aguamarina
*Ladrilleros, T311-728 3213,*
*www.reservaaguamarina.com.*
Colourful wooden *cabañas* set amongst lush tropical gardens. Fan, cable TV and en suite bathrooms. 2 meals included in price. Owner John Janio also runs **Eco-guías**, which organizes whale-watching tours (from US$24) and other activities.

### $$$ Palma Real
*Ladrilleros, T310-820 0026, www.*
*hotelpalmarealcolombia.com.*
Up on a cliff, this hotel affords spectacular glimpses of the sea through a canopy of trees. It has a good pool and jacuzzi and private access down a jungle path to the beach below. The rooms, in a clapboard house, are a bit small and the walls a little flimsy, but there are 2 meals at its restaurant included in the price.

### $ Doña Francia
*Ladrilleros, T2-246 0373.*
This little place has a couple of good, clean rooms with fan and a shared bath. Ask at the restaurant of the same name around the corner.

## What to do

### Buenaventura

**Embarcaciones Asturias**, *Muelle Turístico, T2-240 4048, barcoasturias@ hotmail.com.* Boat trips around Buenaventura, including a weekend trip to Isla Gorgona, US$600 per person, including accommodation, food, permit and snorkelling equipment. (Check with the authorities before booking this or any other trip to Gorgona.) Also an 8-day diving trip to Isla Malpelo.

**Hotel Estación**, *T2-243 4070, www.hotel esestelar.com*. Whale-watching tours to Bahía Málaga mid/late Jul-end Sep, including accommodation (3 nights), all meals and transport, US$264 per person.

---

**Juanchaco, Ladrilleros and around**
**Eco-Guías**, *T2-347 5736, www.ecoguias. com*. Whale watching, boat trips, diving, snorkelling and kayaking excursions.

---

**Buenaventura**
**Air**
Flights to **Cali** and **Bogotá** with **Satena**.

**Bus**
The **bus terminal** is at Cra 5/C 7; don't hang around here longer than is absolutely necessary. To **Cali**, US$9, 4 hrs; also *colectivos* every 30 mins.

**Sea**
Slow and uncomfortable cargo boats leave from the Puente del Piñal, stopping at **Nuquí**, 18 hrs, and **Bahía Solano**, 24 hrs, 1-2 per week, US$55 single.

# Popayán
## & Tierradentro

South of Cali is Popayán, one of the country's oldest Spanish settlements, which gleams like a beacon in the crisp sunshine of the Cordillera Central's mountain air. Its colonial centre suffered severe damage after an earthquake hit the region in March 1983, but an extensive restoration programme has left little sign of the tragedy, and the city's dazzling white buildings appear much as they would have to the Spanish sugar plantation owners who first came here to escape the heat of the Cauca Valley. Popayán has a cultured air about it, no doubt aided by its large student population. Maybe there is something in the water, as it has produced more Colombian presidents than any other city and has also been home to many notable painters, writers and composers. Its famously austere Semana Santa celebrations are second in size only to those of Seville in Spain.

To the Spanish, Popayán was a strategic link between Lima and Quito in the south, and Bogotá and Cartagena further north. For today's traveller, the city makes a convenient jumping-off point for visiting the remote archaeological sites of Tierradentro and San Agustín, and the indigenous market at Silvia, or as a break from the heat and partying in Cali.

**restored colonial city and birthplace of presidents**

Popayán is the capital of the Department of Cauca. To the north, south and east the broken green plain is bounded by mountains; to the southeast is the cone of Volcán Puracé (4650 m). The Río Cauca rises near Puracé and flows past Popayán a few kilometres to the north; its tributary, the Río Molino, runs through the town. The city has managed to retain its colonial character, which is remarkable given that it was partially destroyed by the March 1983 earthquake and extensively restored. Many of the streets are cobbled and the two-storey buildings are in rococo Andalusian style, with beautiful old monasteries and cloisters.

### Sights

The **cathedral**, at Calle 5 and Carrera 6, was built around 1900 and is the third on the site; it was beautifully restored after the 1983 earthquake. It has a fine marble Madonna sculpture behind the altar by Buenaventura Malagón.

There are several other interesting churches in the centre. **San Agustín**, two blocks south of the cathedral, is notable for its gilt altarpiece and the unusual statue of Christ

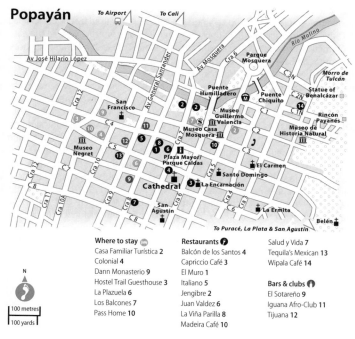

**Popayán**

| Where to stay | Restaurants | Salud y Vida 7 |
|---|---|---|
| Casa Familiar Turística 2 | Balcón de los Santos 4 | Tequila's Mexican 13 |
| Colonial 4 | Capriccio Café 3 | Wipala Café 14 |
| Dann Monasterio 9 | El Muro 1 | |
| Hostel Trail Guesthouse 3 | Italiano 5 | Bars & clubs |
| La Plazuela 6 | Jengibre 2 | El Sotareño 9 |
| Los Balcones 7 | Juan Valdez 6 | Iguana Afro-Club 11 |
| Pass Home 10 | La Viña Parrilla 8 | Tijuana 12 |
| | Madeira Café 10 | |

# BACKGROUND

## Popayán

Popayán was founded by Sebastián de Belalcázar, Francisco Pizarro's lieutenant, in 1536, in the valley of the Pubenza. After establishing their sugar estates in the hot, damp Cauca valley, early settlers retreated to Popayán to live. The city was high enough to give it a delightful climate, and it was surrounded by a peaceful landscape of palm, bamboo and the sharp-leaved agave. After the conquest of the indigenous Pijao, Popayán became the regional seat of government, subject until 1717 to the Audiencia of Quito, and later to the Audiencia of Bogotá.

Popayán has given no fewer than eleven presidents to the Republic. It is also the birthplace of the scientist Francisco José de Caldas (1768-1816), who discovered how to determine altitude by variations in the boiling point of water. It was to him that Mutis (of the famous *Expedición Botánica*) entrusted the directorship of the newly founded Observatory at Bogotá. Caldas was a passionate partisan of Independence and was executed in 1815 during Morillo's 'Reign of Terror'.

kneeling on the globe. **La Encarnación**, one block east of the cathedral, dates from 1764 and has a fine retable; it is used for religious music festivals. Nearby, **Santo Domingo** has some fine wood carvings; the church is now used by the Universidad del Cauca whose building next door on Carrera 5 is also worth a visit. To the east, **El Carmen** is a monastery church constructed about 1730 with *mudéjar* influences. **La Ermita**, on Calle 5 at Carrera 2, was built in the 16th century on the site of the first chapel established by Sebastián de Belalcázar. Three blocks west of the Plaza Mayor, **San Francisco** dates from about 1775, but has been frequently damaged by earthquakes; it is now partly restored. Note the fascinating figures on the pulpit stairs.

**Museo de Historia Natural** ① *Cra 2, No 1A-25, daily 0900-1200, 1400-1700, US$1.50, children US$1*, has good displays of archaeological and geological items, with sections on insects (particularly good on butterflies), reptiles, mammals and birds. Other museums celebrate Popayán's famous sons: **Museo Negret** ① *C 5, No 10-23, Tue-Sun 0800-1200, 1400-1800, free*, contains the art, photographs and furniture of the sculptor Edgar Negret, plus works by Spanish and Latin American artists; **Museo Guillermo Valencia** ① *Cra 6, No 2-69, Tue-Sun 1000-1200, 1400-1700, free*, was the birthplace of the poet, and **Museo Casa Mosquera** ① *C 3, No 5-14, Tue-Sun 0800-1200, 1400-1800, free*, was the home of General Tomás Cipriano de Mosquera, four times President of Colombia. There is also a **Museum of Religious Art** ① *C 4 No 4-56, T2-824 2759, Tue-Fri 0900-1230, 1400-1800, Sat 0900-1400, contribution welcome*. During Holy Week it opens up its vaults and displays several large emeralds, including one the size of an avocado.

Beyond La Ermita (see above), a pleasant walk east will take you past stations of the cross to **Belén chapel** and a fine view of the city. From there, you could continue to **El Cerro de las Tres Cruces**, if you have the energy, and on to the equestrian statue of Belalcázar on the **Morro de Tulcán**, which overlooks the city centre. This hill is the site of a pre-Columbian pyramid. Next to El Morro is **Rincón Payanés**, also known as El Pueblito Patojo, which has scale models of the town's landmarks and a number of handicraft stalls and cafés. Although the area around the Belén chapel is reasonably safe at Mass times, take care of your belongings at other times, and be discreet with cameras, phones and wallets.

A fine arched bridge built in 1868, **Puente del Humilladero** crosses the Río Molino at Carrera 6. Public presentations and concerts are given in the gardens below. It is said that Bolívar marched over the nearby **Puente Chiquito**, built in 1713. Take care if you cross any of the bridges over the river going north, especially at night.

## Silvia

*Tourist information is 1½ blocks up from the plazuela on the right-hand side. Getting there: catch a bus towards Cruce Pisimbalá and change to a colectivo (US$1) at Totoró (see Transport).*

The little town of Silvia lies in a high valley northeast of Popayán. The local Guambianos wear typical blue and fuchsia costumes, and are very gregarious and friendly. You can watch them spinning and weaving their textiles, although the town's Tuesday market seems to be full of indigenous Otavalo from Ecuador and their goods. The market is at its best between 0600 and 0830; there's not much to buy, but it's very colourful. Silvia has a small **Museo de Artesanías** ⓘ *Cra 2, No 14-39*, with exhibits of local crafts, past and present.

There are beautiful places to walk and ride around Silvia, including several indigenous settlements. **La Campana**, for example, is up in the hills, 45 minutes on the bus from town; you can return on foot (2½ hours' walk downhill). Note: it is not safe to park cars in the street at night in Silvia.

## Coconuco and around

About 25 km from Popayán, on the road to San Agustín, is **Coconuco**, a particularly beautiful spot, surrounded by green hills and cascading waterfalls. The village is famous for its hot springs. **Aguas Hirviendas** ⓘ *Tue-Sun 24 hrs, US$2.50, jeep (US2.50) or mototaxi (US$1) from the village*, has several concrete pools, one of which has water hot enough to boil an egg in five minutes. It is a popular spot at weekends but quiet during the week. Further up the valley is **Aguas Tibias** ⓘ *US$12*, whose waters are warm rather than hot. These pools, run by an indigenous family, have a rather more rustic feel to them and include a waterslide and therapeutic mud bath.

## Listings Popayán and around *map p335*

### Tourist information

**Punto de Información Turística**, known as PIT; Cra 7, No4-36, T2-824 3625, www. cccauca.org.co, daily 0800-1200, 1400-

2000, is next door to the **Cámara de Comercio de Cauca, Cultura y Turismo** on the Plaza Mayor and has a reasonable selection of maps and brochures.

## Where to stay

Hotel prices include taxes, but are subject to a 100% or more increase in some cases for Holy Week and festivals, eg 5-6 Jan.

### $$$ Hotel Dann Monasterio
*C 4, No 10-14, T2-824 2191, www. hoteldannmonasteriopopayan.com.*
Run by the ubiquitous **Dann** group, this 17th-century Franciscan monastery, with its cobbled courtyards and fountains, emanates tranquillity. The rooms are comfortable and it has a swimming pool and sauna. Staff can be a bit snooty.

### $$$-$$ La Plazuela
*C 5, No 8-13, T2-824 1084, www.hotellaplazuela.com.co.*
This beautiful colonial building has good-sized rooms with antique furniture set around a colonnaded, cobbled courtyard, opposite a church. There is Wi-Fi throughout the building, cable TV and breakfast included.

### $$$-$$ Los Balcones
*Cra 7, No 2-75, T2-824 2030, www. hotellosbalconespopayan.com.*
**Los Balcones** is a mixed bag. It has some enormous rooms, including one in the attic with stained glass skylights, while others are small. Ancient TVs and antique furniture give it a certain charm while Wi-Fi and a free internet room are the hotel's concession to modernity.

### $$-$ Hotel Colonial
*C 5, No 10-94, T2-831 7848, hotelcolonial@hotmail.es.*
This hotel has clean – if a little dark – rooms with comfortable beds. It has a restaurant serving home-cooked food, cable TV, hot water, Wi-Fi, safe and free local calls.

### $$-$ Pass Home
*C 5, No 10-114, T2-824 3725, hotelpasshome@gmail.com.*
Friendly hotel with a relaxing atmosphere. Private rooms or dorms for 4 with private bathrooms, hot water, cable TV and Wi-Fi. Use of kitchen, free laundry service with a 3-day stay. Can arrange pick-up from airport or bus terminal for a charge. Recommended.

### $ Casa Familiar Turística
*Cra 5, No 2-07, T2-824 4853.*
Another popular backpackers' choice, this little place has simple rooms with incredibly high ceilings and thin walls. It has good notice boards with information and messages from other travellers, and there is Wi-Fi throughout.

### $ HostelTrail Guesthouse
*Cra 11, No 4-16, T314-696 0805, www.hosteltrailpopayan.com.*
This excellent backpackers' hostel is efficiently run by Scottish couple Tony and Kim. The rooms are comfortable and clean (most with shared bathroom) and have Wi-Fi access; there are also cheap dorms with bunks, good communal areas, a kitchen, DVD room, book sale and lockers. Tony and Kim have extensive knowledge of the local area, including the Southern Loop, and run a good bike tour to the thermal springs at Coconuco. Spanish lessons with university graduates, US$5 per hr.

## Restaurants

Popayán has a tradition of good food. In 2005 the city was named a UNESCO City of Gastronomy, and each year it hosts a gastronomy festival. Local specialities include *tamales de pipián*.

## $$ Balcón de los Santos
*Cra 7, No 5-06, T2-832 0050,*
*www.balcondelosantos.com.*
This 2nd-storey eatery sits on the corner
of the plaza and has good views of the
action going on below. Offers traditional
fare such as trout.

## $$ La Vina Parilla
*C 4, No 7-07.*
A *parillada* serving an enormous
selection of juicy, Argentine-style
steaks accompanied by fries and salads.

## $$-$ Restaurante Italiano
*C 4, No 8-83, T2-824 0607.*
Swiss-run restaurant that has been
serving an excellent selection of pastas,
pizzas, crêpes and fondues since
1995 with much love and attention.
Recommended.

## $$-$ Salud y Vida
*C 8, No 7-19, T2-822 1118.*
Popular vegetarian option serving cheap
lunch options for around US$2.50.

## $$-$ Tequila's
*C 5, No 9-25.*
Mexican-run cantina with solid Mexican
food, reasonably priced. Also good
cocktails. Go straight for the crispy
*al pastor* tacos. Recommended.

## $ El Muro
*Cra 8, No 4-11, T2-824 0539.*
This little place serves vegetarian
*almuerzos* (US$2.50), with daily menus
ranging from quinoa salad to pizzas
and veggie burgers. At night it converts
into a dimly lit bar.

## $ Jengibre
*Cra 7, No 2-71 and 2-38, T2-820 5456.*
Good breakfast venue; the restaurant
opposite with the same name
serves *almuerzos* for US$4 as well
as à la carte options.

## Cafés
Popayán has a thriving café culture,
with many of them located in gorgeous
colonial buildings. There are good
options on Cra 5 between C 1 and 4.

## Capriccio
*C 5, No 5-63.*
Popular with the locals, this café
has excellent hot drinks, some
with potent shots added, as well
as brownies and ice creams.

## Juan Valdez
*Cra 7, No 4-36/49.*
Part of the ubiquitous chain, this one
is housed in a beautiful courtyard with
4 enormous palm trees. Large selection
of coffees and merchandise on sale.
Has Wi-Fi.

## Madeira Café
*C 3, esq con Cra 5.*
Good selection of coffees, milkshakes,
brownies, fruit juices and cheesecakes.

## Wipala
*Cra 2, No 2-38.*
Art and café in lovely surroundings.

## Bars and clubs

## El Sotareño
*C 6, No 8-05.*
Run by an elderly couple from San
Agustín, this eccentric bar plays old
tango LPs from the 1940s and 50s
as well as *bolero* and *ranchero* music.

## Iguana Afro-Club
*C 4, No 9-67.*
Good music, jazz, salsa, friendly owner.

## Tijuana
*Cra 9, No 4-68.*
Mix of music, popular.

## Festivals

**5-6 Jan Día de los Negros** and **Día de los Blancos**. Like the celebrations in Pasto, but a lot less wet.

**Mar/Apr Semana Santa** (Holy Week). The processions, every night until Good Fri, are spectacular, but the city is very crowded. It's easier to get a view of the children's processions during the following week, when the children assume all the roles of the official processions to the delight of parents and onlookers. There is also an international sacred music festival, founded in 1964, with orchestras and groups from around the world.

**Sep Festival Gastronomia**. For 1 weekend in Sep food stalls serve the traditional cuisine of the area, including *tamales*.

## Shopping

During the week, the city's open markets are interesting. For handicrafts, try the stands at Rincón Payanés, next to El Morro.

**Mercado Bolívar**, *C 1N, Cra 5*. Best in the early morning for local foods such as *pipián*, *tamales* and *empanadas*.
**Mercado Esmeralda**, *C 5 and Autopista, west of the centre*. A little bigger and also worth a visit.

## What to do

A great trip is the 5-day circuit known as the Southern Loop, taking in San Agustín, Tierradentro, the Tatacoa desert and more.

**Health spa**
Vida Sana, *Km 6, Vía Popayán–Pasto (nr La Bomba de Bohío)*, *T311-605 9766, www.centrovidasana.org, Sun-Fri, treatments*

*from US$9, book in advance.* Health and spiritual centre in lovely surroundings, with treatments, accommodation, meals and eco walks available.

**Tour operators**
Aviatur, *C 4, No 8-69, T2-820 8674.*
Luna Paz Tours, *C 8, No 7-61, T315-513 9593.* Organizes tours to Tierradentro as well as further afield.
Popayan Tours, *www.popayantours. com, based at Hostel Trail (see above).* Tony runs tours to Tierradentro and does the Southern Loop.

## Transport

**Air**
The **airport** is a 20-min' walk from the centre (taxi US$2). To **Bogotá** with **Avianca** (Cra 7, No 5-77) daily.

**Bus**
Popayán's **bus terminal** is near the airport, 15 min' walk from the centre (taxi US$2 daytime or US$2.50 at night). Luggage can be stored safely (receipt given); there is a charge to use the toilets. To **Silvia**, hourly with **Coomotorista** and **Belalcázar**, plus *busetas* in the morning, US$3-3.50, 90 mins. To **Coconuco**, every 30 mins 0600-1800, US$2, 1 hr. To **Bogotá**, **Expreso Bolivariano**, daily 1900 and 2000, US$41, 12-16 hrs, also Flota Magdalena and Velotax.

> **Tip...**
> Avoid travelling at night between Popayán and San Agustín. The roads are in very bad condition and can be dangerous. There have been reports of theft on the buses between these towns; do not trust 'helpful' strangers and do not put bags on the luggage rack.

To **Cali**, US$6-7, 2½-3 hrs; *colectivos* leave from the main plaza. To **Pasto**, US$17, 4-6 hrs, spectacular scenery (sit on right). To **Ipiales**, **Expreso Bolivariano**, hourly, US$17, 7-8 hrs, many buses arrive full from Cali, so book in advance. To **San Agustín**, **Cootranslaboyana**, **Cootranshuila** or **La Gaitana**, hourly, US$15, 7-8 hrs, sit on the left for the best views. To **Cruce de Pisimbalá** (also known as Cruce de San Andrés or San Andrés de Pisimbalá) for **Tierradentro**, 4 daily, 0430-1300, US$12, 4-6 hrs; bus continues to **La Plata**, US$15, 5 hrs, with **Cootranshuila** and **Sotracauca**. To **Puracé**, **Cootranshuila and Sotracauca**, hourly, US$5, 2-2½ hrs; bus continues to La Plata.

## Tierradentro → *Colour map 3, B4.*

**mysterious tombs in stunning mountain scenery**

Tierradentro is one of Colombia's great pre-Columbian attractions. Scattered throughout the area are man-made burial caves dating from the sixth to the 10th centuries AD. The tombs were intended for the elite of Tierradentro society and are decorated with red, black and white geometric patterns. Some are shallow, others up to 8 m deep. The surrounding hills are spectacular, and there are many small indigenous villages to explore (get exact directions before setting out). For many years the unforgiving mountains of this region were a FARC stronghold, which stunted any kind of tourism development. Today, the guerrilla presence is no more, and the number of visitors is steadily increasing, especially around Easter.

### Tierradentro

To Santa Rosa

El Duende (1700m)

Segovia (1650m)

Quebrada Los Guasos

Quebrada Chaqueis

El Tablón (1700m)

Quebrada La Virgen

San Andrés de Pisimbalá

Quebrada San Andrés

Alto de San Andrés (1750m)

Museum & Administration

To La Pirámide

To El Cruce, Inzá & La Plata

Quebrada El Escaño

El Aguacate (2000m)

N

500 metres
500 yards

### Towards Tierradentro

The road from Popayán to Tierradentro is extremely rough, but you will be compensated by the beautiful scenery. At **Totoró** a road heads north to Silvia (see above). Continuing east, 67 km beyond Totoró is **Inzá**, which has several indigenous stone statues in its new plaza. About 9 km beyond Inzá is the **Cruce de Pisimbalá**, sometimes known as the Cruce de San Andrés or simply El Cruce, where the road turns off towards **San Andrés de Pisimbalá** at the far end of the archaeological park. The park administration and museum are 2 km along this road; the village is 20 minutes' further on.

★**Tierradentro Archaeological Park**

The **Tierradentro Museum** ① *daily 0800-1630 (may close at lunchtime), US$10 for the museum and all sites,* is a well-maintained museum in two parts. The archaeological section has a model of the Tierradentro region with details of the sites and what has been found. The second floor is dedicated to an overview of the Páez and their culture, past and present. This is all very well worth seeing before you go to the sites themselves; the staff are very helpful and can provide local information.

**Tip...**

An excellent guide to the Páez and their culture is *Valores Culturales de Tierradentro* by Mauricio Puerta Restrepo, published by the Instituto Colombiano de Antropología (available from AbeBooks.com).

You can hire horses to ride around the burial sites (US$3 an hour or US$24 per day with guide; make sure they are in good condition) from opposite the museum or in San Andrés. It is also quite possible to walk, although you should take a hat and plenty of water. Women are advised not to wander around alone at night. There are five burial sites to explore: Segovia, El Duende, El Tablon, Alto de San Andrés and El Aguacate. The main caverns are lit, but a torch (your own or one borrowed from the park administration) is advisable.

**Segovia** (15 minutes' walk up behind the museum across the river) has around 30 tombs, five of which are lit: Nos 9, 10 and 12 have the best decorations; Nos 8 and 28 are also impressive. The guard is very informative (Spanish only) and turns lights on in the main tombs; check if photography is permitted. Some 15 minutes up the hill beyond Segovia is **El Duende**, which has four tombs, two of which are very good. From El Duende continue directly up to a rough road that descends to Pisimbalá (40 minutes). **El Tablón**, with eight stone statues, is just off the road after 20-30 minutes' walk downhill. **El Alto de San Andrés** is 20 minutes beyond Pisimbalá; tombs 1 and 5 are the best here, and the guard is very helpful. From the back of El Alto it's 1½ hours up and down hills, with a final long climb to **El Aguacate**. Only one tomb is maintained here, although there may be 30 more. The views from El Aguacate are superb. You can continue from El Aguacate back to the museum, or do the whole route in reverse; either way, it is a splendid walk.

## San Andrés de Pisimbalá and around

Located about 2 km beyond and up the hill from the museum, this is a charming village, peaceful and friendly. It has a unique and beautiful **colonial missionary church** with a thatched roof, dating back to the 17th century. Around the cobbled square, the locals lay their coffee to dry on the grass outside their chocolate-box houses, while chickens wander in and out of the church and swallows dive between its eaves.

Try to spend a few days around Tierradentro to allow yourself time to walk in the hills and enjoy the spectacular night skies. The people are very friendly and hospitable, and you can stop at almost any house to buy *guarapo*, a local slightly fermented sugarcane drink. The markets at **Inzá** and **Belalcázar** (both Saturday from 0600) are good places to experience the local Páez culture. The whole area is also recommended for birdwatching. For a longer hike, ask about the Páez reserve at **Tumbichutzwe**, a strenuous three- to four-day walk, or less on horseback.

## Tourist information

The **Casa de Cultura**, in a building just as you enter San Andrés, has good information and is helpful. The staff can organize guides to local indigenous villages.

## Where to stay

**$$ Hotel Albergue El Refugio**
*T321-811 2395.*
Upscale cottages situated around a large swimming pool. Private bathrooms with hot water.

**$$ Residencias Pisimbalá**
*Near the museum, T311-612 4835 (mob).*
The **Pisimbalá** has rooms with private bathrooms and hot water as well as the cheaper option of shared cold-water bathrooms. It has a good little restaurant.

**$ Hospedaje La Maria**
*In the village.*
Family home with rooms to rent. Moto pickups available on request.

**$ Hospedaje Lucerna**
*Next to the museum.*
Run by a lovely old couple, this little place has clean, basic rooms and very good hot showers (with 30 mins' forewarning).

**$ Hospedaje Ricabet**
*Near the museum, T312-795 4636 (mob).*
This little *hospedaje* has a bright courtyard bursting with colourful flowers and clean rooms and en suite bathrooms with hot water. Rooms with a shared bath are a little cheaper.

**$ La Portada**
*www.laportadahotel.com.*
Bamboo building at the jeep/bus stop in village, with basic rooms, popular.

**$ Los Llanos**
*100 m past the church.*
Pleasant colonial building with clean, basic rooms and a colourful courtyard.

## Restaurants

**$ La Portada** serves *almuerzos* for around US$2.50; **Pisimbalá** also has good, cheap food and is recommended. For both, see Where to stay, above.

## Transport

**Bus**
There are daily buses from Popayán (see Transport, page 335) to **Cruce Pisimbalá**. It's best to take the early buses, otherwise you will arrive at El Cruce in the dark. There are also *colectivos* from La Plata, which leave when full (US$4 per person). To **La Plata**, buses leave from San Andrés, passing by the museum at 0500, 0600 and 0800. If you miss these, you must walk to El Cruce for buses and *camionetas*, US$4, 4-5 hrs (en route to San Agustín) or more frequent *colectivo* jeeps, US$6. If you cannot get a direct Cruce–La Plata bus, take one going to **Páez** (Belalcázar; US$1) and alight at Guadualejo, 17 km east of Inzá, from where there is a more frequent service to La Plata.

★Located east of Popayán, the national park covers an area of 86,600 ha and contains Volcán Puracé (4646 m), Pan de Azúcar (4670 m), with its permanently snow-covered peak, and the line of nine craters known as the Volcanes los Coconucos. Virtually all the park is over 3000 m, and a strenuous two-day hike can be made around the summits. The park also encompasses the sources of four of Colombia's greatest rivers: the Magdalena, Cauca, Caquetá and Patía. The park's fauna includes the spectacled bear and mountain tapir. The Andean condor is being reintroduced into the wild here from Californian zoos, and there are many other birds to be seen. Although much of the park is *páramo*, there are also many species of orchid to be found. For those who do not wish to make the climb up Volcán Puracé, there are waterfalls, lakes and some technicolour sulphur pools to visit further down.

### Around the park
*The standard park entrance fee is US$10.25.*

From Popayán a road crosses the Cordillera Central heading to Garzón on the paved highway south of Neiva. After 18 km a road turns south towards Coconuco (see page 337) and San Agustín (see page 349). The road east, meanwhile, climbs to the small town of **Puracé**, at Km 12 (30 km from Popayán), which has several old buildings. Behind the school a path leads for 500 m to the **Chorrera de las Monjas** waterfalls on the Río Vinagre, notable for their milky white water due to concentrations of sulphur and other minerals.

Continuing east, look for the spectacular San Francisco waterfall on the opposite side of the valley at Km 22. At Km 23 is the turning to the Puracé sulphur mines (6 km), which can be visited by applying through the Popayán tourist office. About 1 km along this side road is a left turn leading 1.5 km to **Pilimbalá**, a good base from which to explore the northern end of the park, where there are Páez settlements. A standard car will struggle to make it up the last stretch to the centre of the village, but it is an easy 2.5-km walk from Km 23. The walk to the **Cascada de San Nicolás** from Pilimbalá is recommended. Turn right when you see the abandoned cabin and continue steadily uphill through very muddy terrain (rubber boots advisable). The waterfall is spectacular, but take care on the slippery, overhanging rocks.

Back on the main road to La Plata, there is a viewpoint for **Laguna Rafael** at Km 31, the **Cascada de Bedón** at Km 35 and the entrance to the most northerly part of the national park at Km 37. The **visitor centre** here has a decent geology/ethnology museum, a scale model of the park, picnic shelters, a good restaurant (rainbow trout a speciality) and three *cabañas* that hold eight, US$13, with a shared (cold water) bathroom and a small fireplace. Sleeping bags or warm clothing is recommended to supplement the bedding provided. Camping costs US$2 per person. The rangers are very helpful.

Half an hour's walk beyond the visitor centre, on the road to La Plata, are the **Termales de San Juan**. The toxic, sulphurous gases released by these hot pools mean that swimming is not advisable, but a walkway allows for a tour through the colourful mosses and algae surrounding the bubbling, multi-coloured pools and along the milky white streams that run off them. There's a basic place to eat where the bus stops and a cabin with information about the national park. Buses are not regular but up until 1700 there should be something every hour or so. Hitching a lift should also be possible.

### Climbing Volcán Puracé

A marked trail goes from behind the park office and eventually joins a road leading to a set of telecommunications antennae. These installations are no longer guarded by the military, but the area around them is mined, so don't take shortcuts. The summit is about one hour beyond the military buildings and is a demanding hike, as loose ash makes it hard to get a foothold. The total time from Pilimbalá is at least four hours up and 2½ down, and you may need to take shelter if there is a sudden storm, so start the trek early in the day; rangers will not allow you to start after 1200. An alternative route is from the sulphur mine (at 3000 m), or driving, with permission, to the military base. It is also possible to walk round the crater (30 minutes). Avoid getting downwind of the fumaroles, and do not be tempted to climb down into the crater. Although the best weather is reported to be December to March and July to August, this massif creates its own climate, and high winds, rain and sub-zero temperatures can come in quickly at any time. Rope and crampons are useful above the snowline. If you want to continue to Pan de Azúcar and the Coconucos, high-altitude camping and mountaineering equipment are required and a guide is strongly recommended. A descent over the *páramo* to Paletará on the Popayán–San Agustín road is also possible.

## Listings Parque Nacional Natural Puracé

### Transport

There are several buses daily between Puracé and **Popayán**; the last bus returning to Popayán in daylight leaves at about 1700. The bus service can be erratic so be prepared to spend a cold night at 3000 m.

# Huila
## Department

Huila is a largely agricultural region that nonetheless encompasses very diverse terrain. There are snow-capped mountains in the west, miles of featureless plains in the centre, a sweltering capital city on the banks of the Magdalena to the east and a surreal desert in the north. It is also the location of one of Colombia's most impressive archaeological sites, San Agustín, which lies in subtropical scenery in the south of the Department.

### Northern Huila and the Desierto de Tatacoa → *Colour map 3, A5.*

go star-gazing in the desert

Driving through the plains and mountains of Huila it might be difficult to imagine that a desert sits just around the corner. But just 50 km north of Neiva is the Tatacoa desert, a 370-sq-km area of scrub and surreal rock formations dotted with candelabra and prickly pear cacti.

#### Neiva

Capital of the Department of Huila, Neiva is a hot, modern city on the east bank of the Río Magdalena, surrounded by arid cattle plains. The snow-capped Nevado del Huila (5365 m) looms large to the west. It has a series of pleasant plazas and hosts a raucous folklore festival to celebrate the fiestas of San Juan and San Pedro in June.

Neiva was founded in 1539 when Sebastián de Belalcázar came east from Popayán on his quest for El Dorado. By the riverside a monument by Rodrigo Arenas Betancur has been erected to commemorate Colombia's struggles for Independence. The cathedral was destroyed in an earthquake in 1967.

#### Rivera

A 30-minute drive south from Neiva is the pretty little town of Rivera, famous for its thermal springs. At the weekend it's a popular destination for locals wishing to escape the heat of Neiva, with plenty of activity around its picturesque plaza. There are several hotels in town ($$-$).

The springs are 5 km north of the town. There are several options but the most popular, **Termales de Rivera** ⓘ *daily until 2400, US$3.60-9; tuk-tuk or taxi, US$2.80*, are set around exuberant tropical gardens and have two restaurants, accommodation ($$$), changing rooms and lockers, a cold swimming pool and an excellent waterslide.

## Villavieja

Villavieja lies on the edge of the Desierto de Tatacoa, 45 km north of Neiva. It was founded in 1550 by the Spanish conquistador Juan Alonso, who named it San Juan de Nepomuceno. It was later razed to the ground by the indigenous locals but was rebuilt by Diego de Ospina y Medinilla in 1562 as **Villavieja**. The town played an important role in the 1000-Day War at the turn of the 20th century when a battle between the Liberals and Conservatives was fought nearby.

Villavieja has a particularly charming Parque Principal, surrounded on all sides by 18th-century colonial buildings and with a replica of a Megatherium in the centre, an elephant-sized sloth that existed in this region in the Pleistocene epoch. The **Capilla de Santa Bárbara** was built by Jesuit priests in 1630, making it the oldest church in Huila. It has been restored, but the local priest keeps it under lock and key and it is difficult to gain access. Next to the church is the **Palaeontological Museum** ⓘ *US$1*, with displays of fossils of armadillos, turtles and crocodiles found in the desert, mainly from the Miocene epoch. Also worth visiting is the railway station, decommissioned since 1975, a reminder of Villavieja's former role as an important staging post on the Bogotá–Neiva line.

## ★ Desierto de Tatacoa

The **desert** itself begins 10 km outside Villavieja. Named after a snake that used to thrive in its unforgiving conditions, the desert is wedged between two mountain ranges that absorb the region's rainfall, starving it of moisture. The desert presented a challenging obstacle to the Spanish conquistador Juan Alonso on his quest for El Dorado. He was following the Magdalena river and looking for a route to Popayán when he stumbled across the desert, which he named 'El Valle de las Tristezas' (The Valley of Sorrows).

On top of a small incline some 15 minutes' drive from Villavieja is the **Observatorio Astronómico de la Tatacoa** ⓘ *www.tatacoa-astronomia.com*, run by stellar enthusiast Javier Fernando Rua. Tatacoa's clear skies and almost non-existent light pollution make it perhaps the best place in Colombia for star-gazing. Javier gives an excellent talk every evening at 1900 on the observatory roof, with telescopes and a laser to point out individual constellations, US$10 per person. There are also daytime observances of solar flares and eruptions, US$2.

Opposite the observatory is a viewpoint looking out over **El Cuzco**, a labyrinthine landscape of ochre red hillocks and plateaux that would not look out of place in an episode of *Star Trek*; pop star Shakira filmed one of her early music videos here. You can walk down into the miniature valley, which is particularly spectacular at sundown. It is possible to walk from Villavieja to El Cuzco in about one hour, but bear in mind that temperatures can reach up to 49°C, so be sure to take lots of water, a hat and sun cream.

Some 8 km beyond El Cuzco, is **Los Hoyos**, which has similar topography but grey earth. Enterprising locals have built a **swimming pool** ① *US$1.50 (pay at the estadero)*, amongst the rock formations, fed by water from a natural spring.

## Listings Northern Huila and the Desierto de Tatacoa

### Tourist information

**Villavieja**
**Asociación de Operadores Turísticos**
on the Parque Principal, T313-804 9580 (mob), can arrange guides, transport and accommodation in the desert.

### Where to stay

**Neiva**

**$$$-$$ Hotel Neiva Plaza**
*C 7, No 4-62, T8-871 0806,*
*www.hotelneivaplaza.com.*
This has been Neiva's smart hotel for nearly 60 years. It has good, comfortable rooms, a restaurant and a swimming pool.

**$$ Andino**
*C 9, No 5-82, T8-871 0184.*
This centrally located hotel's rooms are a little small and dark but nonetheless clean and with cable TV.

**$$-$$ Tayronas**
*C 8, No 3-46, T8-871 2371.*
You'll be greeted by the smell of incense and a reception covered in pre-Columbian artefacts as you enter this hotel, which has dark, small rooms with en suite bathrooms.

**Villavieja**

**$ La Casona**
*C 3, No 3-60, T8-879 7636,*
*hostellacasonavillavieja@yahoo.es.*
Simón Bolívar once stayed the night at this gorgeous old building on the Parque Principal. It has a shady backyard for dining. The monastic rooms are crammed with beds but the owner won't fill them up if you ask for privacy. Recommended.

**Desierto del Tatacoa**
Camping is permitted next to the observatory (US$3.50); Javier hires tents or bring your own. There are showers, and good food is prepared with advance notice. There are also several *posadas nativas* run by local families.

### Restaurants

**Neiva**

**$$-$$ Tierra y Mar**
*C 9, No 1G-41.*
Serves up local meat and seafood specialities.

**$ Confucio**
*Cra 6, No 9-34.*
Popular Chinese restaurant.

**$ Frutería y Heladería Alaska**
*Cra 6, No 8-40.*
This little fruit and ice cream spot does delicious fruit salads, though be sure to inform them if you don't want ice cream with your breakfast.

### Festivals

**Neiva**
**Jun** **Festival Folclórico y Reinado Nacional del Bambuco**. A raucous affair

incorporating the fiestas de San Juan and San Pedro, it involves Bambuco dancing competitions and various parades in which bikini-clad beauty queens float downriver on boats and up to 5000 (often) drunken women ride horses through the streets. It culminates in the crowning of a Bambuco queen.

## What to do

### Desierto del Tatacoa
For transport and guides, contact the **Asociación de Operadores Turísticos de La Tatacoa**, T313-804 9580 (mob), on the Parque Principal in Villavieja. Alternatively, the manager of the observatory, **Javier Fernando Rua**, T8-879 7584/T310-465 6765 (mob), can make arrangements.

## Transport

### Neiva
**Air**
Several flights daily to/from **Popayán** with **Avianca**, 3 hrs with stop.

**Bus**
To **Bogotá**, 5½ hrs, US$15, with **Bolivariano** (5 a day) or **Coomotor**. To **Rivera**, *colectivo*, US$1.50, 25 mins. To **Villavieja**, *colectivo*, US$4, up to 1 hr. To **La Plata**, *colectivo*, 2 hrs, US$5.50.

### Villavieja
To **Neiva**, US$4, 1 hr, from the Parque Principal. Transport the **desert**, to is expensive: US$11 per person as far as El Cuzco, 15 mins. To **Bogotá**, take a *colectivo* to Neiva and transfer there. Alternatively, it is possible to hail buses on the main Neiva–Bogotá highway from the town of Aipe on the other side of the Río Magdalena. To get there from Villavieja, walk past the cemetery down to the river and cross by motorized canoe (US$1; shout for attention if they're on the other side). Then it's a 1.5-km walk along the path until you reach the edge of Aipe. Walk up C 5, past the Parque Principal, and continue for about 250 m to the main road. A taxi from the centre of Aipe to the main road is US$2 (recommended).

## San Agustín and around → *Colour map 3, B3.*
### mysterious megaliths above the raging Magdalena river

Famed for its enigmatic pre-Columbian stone figures of men, animals and gods, the little town of San Agustín is also a great place to enjoy the rural landscape of Colombia at its finest. The statues uncovered in this wild, spectacular countryside were hewn from stone between 3300 BC and the arrival of the Spanish and represent the largest collection of religious monuments and megalithic sculptures in South America. Little is known about the culture that produced them, further adding to their mystery. Many of the figures have been moved to an archaeological park just outside the town, but you can also visit some in their original locations, ensconced in rolling green hills, surrounded by subtropical flowers and tumbling brooks.

★**Parque Arqueológico**
*Daily 0800-1700 (last entry 1600). US$10 for park, museum and Alto de los Ídolos.*

The nearest archaeological sites to town are in the Parque Arqueológico, about 2.5 km from San Agustín and less than 1 km from the **Hotel Osoguaico**. The park, which was declared a World Heritage Site by UNESCO in 1995, incorporates the **Bosque de las Estatuas**. The statues in the park are in situ, though some have been set up on end and fenced in. Those in the Bosque de las Estatuas have been rearranged and are linked by gravel footpaths.

At the entrance to the park is a **museum** displaying pottery, artefacts and a good scale model of the local sites that gives an excellent idea of the topography of the area. Apart from the distinctive statues of gods and mythical animals in various styles, the most notable features of the San Agustín site are the **Mesitas** (barrows). These large, vertical stone slabs, standing in circular enclosures about 25 m in diameter, were probably originally roofed over with statues set inside and out. There is some doubt whether they primarily served as places of ceremony or as tombs. There are four Mesitas: Mesita D is beside the museum area near the entrance to the park; you will visit B, A and C by following the trail. Beyond Mesita C is **Fuente de Lavapatas**, where water runs through man-made channels carved with the shapes of animals and people. This is arguable the most interesting site in the park and was used for religious ceremonies and ritual bathing. The park authorities have reduced the water flow to the Fuente to limit erosion and it is now easier to see the engravings. The **Alto de Lavapatas**, above the Fuente, has an extensive view. There are snack stalls at Fuente and on the way up to Lavapatas.

You can get a very good idea of the park, the Bosque and the museum in the course of three hours' walking, or add in El Tablón and La Chaquira (see below) for a full day. The whole site leaves an unforgettable impression thanks to the size and strangeness of the statues and the great beauty of the rolling green landscape.

**Tip...**
The best books on the subject are *Exploraciones Arqueológicas en San Agustín*, by Luis Duque Gómez (Bogotá, 1966, 500 pages), *San Agustín, Reseña Arqueológica*, by the same author (1963, 112 pages) and the more recent *El Mundo del arte en San Agustín*, by Efrain Sanchez (Villegas Editores, 2012). The **Colombian Institute of Archaeology** has also published a booklet (English/Spanish) on San Agustín and Tierradentro, which may be available at the museum in San Agustín.

**Other sites around San Agustín**
In the town is the **Museo Arqueológico Julio César Cubillos** ① *Cra 11, No 3-61, Mon-Fri 0800-1200, 1300-1800*, with a good library, videos in Spanish and English, and light refreshments. From San Agustín head up Carrera 14, over the brow of the hill and on for 250 m to a marked track to the right, then head down to the left to reach **El Tablón**, where five sculptures have been brought together under a bamboo roof. Continue down the path, muddy in wet weather, ford a stream and follow signs to the Río Magdalena canyon; **La Chaquira**, which has figures carved

on the rocks, is dramatically set halfway down to the river. Allow two hours for the return trip. Plenty of houses offer refreshments as far as El Tablón. There are many pleasant paths to follow in this area; ask locally for ideas.

Continue along the road from San Agustín for the site of **La Pelota**, where two painted statues were found in 1984. It's a three-hour return trip, or six hours if you include El Tablón and La Chaquira on the way (15 km in all). Other archaeological discoveries from 1984/1986 include some unique polychromed sculptures at **El Purutal** near La Pelota and a series of at least 30 stones carved with animals and other designs in high relief. These are known as **Los Petroglifos** and can be found on the right bank of the Río Magdalena, near the **Estrecho** (narrows); access is by jeep from San Agustín.

Also part of the UNESCO site is **Alto de los Idolos** ⓘ *10 km northeast of San Agustín, daily 0800-1630, US$5 or US$8 combined with park and museum*. It's a lovely, if strenuous, walk, steep in places, via **Puente de la Chaquira** to this hill overlooking San Agustín, where there are more statues in a different style. They are known as *vigilantes* and each guards a burial mound; one is an unusual rat totem. The few mounds that have been excavated have revealed large stone sarcophagi, some covered by stone slabs bearing a sculpted likeness of the occupant.

## San José de Isnos and around

Alto de los Idolos can also be reached from San José de Isnos, a village 5 km to the northeast and 27 km by road from San Agustín. This road passes the **Salto del Mortiño**, a dramatic 170 m waterfall about 7 km before Isnos, which lies 500 m off the road.

About 6 km north of Isnos is **Alto de las Piedras**, which has a few interesting tombs and monoliths, including the famous 'Doble Yo' statue, which is supposed to represent a dual being. Only slightly less remarkable than the statues are the orchids growing nearby. Bordones is 8 km further on; turn left at end of the village to reach parking for the **Salto de Bordones** waterfalls.

## Pitalito and beyond

Southeast of San Agustín is the little town of Pitalito. It has little to offer the tourist, except as the place where the brightly painted, imaginative ceramics are made so often used in tourist advertisements for southern Colombia. Most popular are the extravagantly decorated *chivas*, the ubiquitous country buses of the region.

An unpaved road from Pitalito goes southwest through remote jungle, crossing the Río Caquetá 25 km before Mocoa. From Mocoa, you can travel west to Pasto and then south to Ecuador. This is a faster way to get to the border than travelling back via Popayán. Until recently security was poor on this route due to guerrilla activity and drug-trafficking, but lately it has improved, though the road still suffers from many landslides and accidents.

### Parque Nacional Natural Cueva de los Guácharos

*Permission to visit the park must be obtained from the National Parks Office, Cra 4, No 4-21, Pitalito. US$18.50 for foreigners. To get there: take a bus from Pitalito to Palestina (US$2, 1 hr), then walk for 6 hrs along an eroded muddy path.*

South of Pitalito, this 9000-ha park extends to the crest of the Cordillera Oriental, rising to over 3000 m, and is mostly rain and cloudforest with an abundance of wildlife. Much of the park is inaccessible, but there are three caves that can be visited in the valley of the Río Suárez if you're feeling intrepid. The Suárez is a tributary of the Magdalena and flows through limestone gorges. **Cueva Chiquita** is near the park entrance; **Cueva del Indio** is 740 m long with interesting calcium formations, and further upstream is **Cueva de los Guácharos**, with a natural bridge over the river. Between December and June swarms of oilbirds (*guácharos*) may be seen; they are nocturnal, with a unique radar-location system. The reserve also shelters the unusual and spectacular cock-of-the-rock. The rangers are particularly friendly, providing tours and basic accommodation.

## Listings San Agustín and around

### Tourist information

**San Agustín**

There are several tour agencies that pose as 'tourist offices'. While they may well give out useful advice, they are often contracted to particular hotels and other operators around town. For impartial advice and a leaflet in English on the archaeological sites, visit the **Oficina Municipal de Turismo** on the Plaza Cívica, or the **Oficina de Policía de Turismo**, C 3, No 11-86.

### Where to stay

**San Agustín**

**$$$ Yalconia**
*Vía al Parque Arqueológico, T8-837 3013, hotelyalconia@hotmail.com.*
The only mid-range hotel in town, the Yalconia is a modern building with cleanish rooms, although some of the paintwork is starting to deteriorate.

**$$ Hacienda Anacaona**
*Vía al Estrecho, T311-231 7128, www.anacaona-colombia.com.*
This traditional finca has comfortable, spacious rooms and a colourful garden with fine views into the hills as well as a restaurant serving typical regional food such as trout and *sancocho*.

### $$-$ Casa de Nelly
*Km 2, Vía Parque Arqueológico por
Vereda La Estrella, T310-215 9067 (mob),
www.hotelcasadenelly.co.*
On top of the hill on the road to the
archaeological park, this lovely old
house has colourful rooms and *cabañas*
set in a gorgeous garden bursting with
subtropical flowers and bushes. There's a
kitchen serving home cooked pastas and
pizzas as well as a thatched kiosk with
hammocks for taking in the atmosphere.

### $$-$ El Jardín
*Cra 11, No 4-10, T8-837 3455,
www.hosteltrail.com/eljardin.*
In town, this colonial house has a
colourful patio decorated with hanging
baskets, snake skins and animal pelts as
well as a couple of chirpy songbirds. The
rooms are simple but clean and it has a
restaurant. There are also dorms ($).

### $ Casa del Sol Naciente
*1 km from the village along Cra 13,
T311-587 6464.*
This rustic retreat has a several *cabañas*,
including 2 with spectacular views down
into a gorge of the raging Magdalena
river. With a vegetable and herb garden
and an open air bath, this is a place for
nature lovers, though it's best not to opt
for a room in the main house, which is
a little dark. There is also camping from
US$4 per person.

### $ El Maco
*1 km from town, 400 m past Piscina Las
Moyas, T8-837 3437, www.elmaco.ch.*
Welcoming Swiss-owned, working
organic farm with colourful gardens,
cosy cabins and a tepee. Rustic and
peaceful setting. Basic kitchen facilities,
internet, laundry service, very good

restaurant (reserve in advance), excellent
local information; see **Chaska Tours**,
below. Recommended.

### $ La Casa de François
*200 m on the way to El Tablón, T314-358
2930 (mob), www.lacasadefrancois.com.*
Just outside town, this French-run hostel
has private rooms with bathrooms as
well as dorms set in 2 ha of gardens
blooming with orchids and other
flowers. There's a kitchen that's free to
use or there's a varied menu of home-
made food, as well as crêpes and home-
baked bread. Other pluses include bike
and horse hire and Wi-Fi.

### Camping
Next to **Yalconia** is **Camping San
Agustín**, a clean, pleasant, safe (guards)
site with showers, toilets, lights, laundry
service, horse hire. US$1.60 per person
with own tent, US$5.50 to hire.

## Restaurants

### San Agustín
Within the park children sell various
things including *guama* fruit, which
comes in a large pea-like pod. It has a
refreshing moist flavour, but do not eat
the black seeds! Tap water in San Agustín
is not safe to drink.

### $$-$ Pepenero
*C 5, No 18-287, T319-258 4556.*
Red-checkered tablecloths and Italian
fare in a homely environment. Decent
wine selection.

### $ Brahama
*C 5, No 15-11.*
This small restaurant serves up the
usual Colombian fare as well as
some good vegetarian options.

### $ Donde Richard
*C 5, No 23-45, T312-432 6399.*
On the outskirts of town, this is one of the better restaurants in San Agustín, with excellent quality steak, chicken and fish dishes cooked in agreeable surroundings and accompanied by soups and salads.

### $ El Fogón
*C 5, No 14-30.*
Festooned with local trinkets and antiques, **El Fogón** does à la carte and *comidas corrientes*, including fish, steaks, and *patacón*.

### $ El Maco
*T8-837 3437.*
It's an appetite-inducing 1-km walk from town to **El Maco** for some of the best food in San Agustín, including excellent Thai curries and pastas as well as organic options. Recommended.

### $ Surabhi
*C 5, No 14-09, T313-9294 5368 (mob).*
Tasty regional specialities.

## Festivals

**San Agustín**
Mid-Jul **Santa María del Carmen**.
24 Jun **San Juan**. Fiesta with horse races and dances.
29 Jun **San Pedro**. Horse races, dances, fancy dress, competitions and other events.
1st week of Oct **La Semana Cultural Integrada** is celebrated in the Casa de Cultura, with many folklore events from all parts of the country.
End Oct/beginning Nov **Feria de San Agustín**. Livestock shows and horse displays.

## Shopping

**San Agustín**
Leather goods are beautiful and priced reasonably. Many local shops make boots to your own design (double-check the price beforehand). C 5, No 14-25 is a good place for handicrafts by local leatherworker Angélica.

## What to do

**San Agustín**
**Guides**
There are countless guides in town offering tours of the various sites. Some give a better service than others, so enquire at your hotel or at the tourist office for advice. Recommended names are **Marino Bravo** (T313-221 4006), speaks good English; **Gloria** (T312-440 2010) and **Carlos Bolaños** (T311-459 5753).

**Rafting**
The Río Magdalena is at its angriest here, kicking and screaming into life as it begins its journey through the heart of Colombia towards the Caribbean coast.

**Magdalena Rafting**, *C 5 No 16-04, T311-271 5333, www.magdalenarafting.com.* French-run adventure sports company specializing in whitewater rafting (all grades of rapids and experience available, from US$24 pp), as well as kayaking and caving.

**Riding**
You are strongly advised to hire horses for trips around San Agustín through hotels (about US$6 per hr, per rider, or US$25 per day with guide.) **Pacho** (T311-827 7972, pachitocampesinito@ yahoo.es) comes highly recommended as a riding guide and can be contacted

through **La Casa de Nelly**. As well as the various archaelogical sites, he also does rides to Lago Magdalena, the source of the Río Magdalena.

### Swimming
**Piscina Municipal**, *behind the Yalconia*. A clean swimming pool, with water fed from a natural spring, busy at weekends, US$1 per day.

### Tour operators
Chaska Tours, *T8-837 3437, www.chaska tours.net*. Run by Swiss René Suter (who also owns the hostel **El Maco**), this agency organizes tours around San Agustín as well as to Tierradentro, Puracé and the Tatacoa desert. English and German spoken. Recommended.

### Vehicle tours
Jeeps for 4-5 people cost about US$20 per day; try bargaining for a lower price.

## Transport

### San Agustín
#### Bus
To **Bogotá,** daily by *buseta* with **Taxis Verdes** (C 17, No 68D-54, Bogotá, T1-411 1152 or C 3, No 11-27, San Agustín, T8-837 3068, www.taxisverdes.net), US$25, 9 hrs; more frequent services depart from Pitalito (see below). To **Neiva**, daily with **Coomotor** and **Cootranshuila**,

6 hrs, US$15.50. To **Pitalito** by *colectivo*, 1½ hrs, US$4-5, or on any bus to Neiva. To Popayán, you may have to take a *colectivo* to Km 5 on Popayán–Pitalito road and catch a bus from there. To **Tierradentro**, take early transport to Pitalito for connections to La Plata. **Note** Bus times change constantly. Enquire at bus station or hotel before setting out.

### Pitalito
Frequent *colectivos* to **San Agustín**, US$4-5. To **Bogotá** (more frequent than from San Agustín) with **Coomotor** (www.coomotor. com.co) or **Cootranshuila** (www. cootranshuila.com), US$30-40, 8-10 hrs. To **Tierradentro**, take a direct bus to **La Plata** (US$15), and then a *colectivo* to Tierradentro (US$5); if you miss the service to La Plata, go via Garzón (this road is in much better condition). To **Pasto**, travel to **Mocoa** by bus, minivan or SUV (US$12), then by bus from Mocoa, US$20. This is a far quicker route to Pasto (11 hrs in total) than going via Popayán and it is now relatively safe from guerrilla activity. However, you should take local advice before travelling this route and do not make the journey at night. There have been reports of thefts and hijackings, and the road is prone to landslides and traffic accidents.

# **Far** south

From Popayán to Ecuador the Pan-American highway travels through arguably the most spectacular scenery in Colombia, at first dipping into humid agricultural land before rising again as it nears the highland city of Pasto, where the landscape becomes increasingly dramatic. At times, the road lies in the shadow of the Western Cordillera and waves of small hills roll out towards its edges like crumpled sheets on an unmade bed. Beyond Pasto the road snakes its way ever upward, clinging to the edges of steep escarpments painstakingly planted with maize, peas and wheat, overlooking deep gorges that plunge down to raging rivers.

The area is dominated by volcanoes, some of which are active, especially those around the border town of Ipiales. Near Pasto is Laguna La Cocha, which has a small national park on the Isla de Corota. Just outside Ipiales is the extraordinary Gothic church of Las Lajas, which straddles a deep gorge and is a magnet for miracle-seekers and pilgrims. To the west it's a long ride down to the Pacific coast at Tumaco, where salt marshes and mangroves have created a distinct ecosystem. On the way, the private nature reserve of La Planada has a unique population of native birds and a conservation programme of special interest to ecologists.

The capital of the Department of Nariño stands upon a high plateau at 2534 m in the southwest of the country, 88 km from Ecuador. Pasto (full name San Juan de Pasto) enjoys a very attractive setting, overlooked from the west by Volcán Galeras (when not in cloud) and from the east by green hills not yet suburbanized by the city.

The city was founded in 1539 by Lorenzo de Aldana, who came here from Quito, and it is therefore one of the oldest cities in Colombia. During the Wars of Independence, it was a stronghold of the Royalists and the last town to fall into the hands of the patriots; Simón Bolívar directed the bloodiest battle of the Independence War against the forces of Basilio García on 7 April 1822 from his headquarters in nearby Bomboná. Today, the city still retains some of its colonial character, including several notable churches, but its aesthetics have not been helped by several serious earthquakes. Pasto is a centre for the agricultural and cattle industries of the region, and Pasto varnish (*barniz*) is mixed locally to embellish strikingly colourful wooden bowls. The people of Pasto have a reputation throughout the rest of Colombia for being very stupid and are the butt of many jokes; travellers are more likely to find that they are extremely friendly and not averse to a good party, especially in the festive period around New Year.

### Sights

On the main plaza (Parque Antonio Nariño), the **Gobernación** has an interior courtyard with two tiers of colonnaded balconies. Also on the square, the church of **San Juan Bautista** (St John the Baptist) is the oldest in Pasto; the finely decorated building dates from 1669 and is a replacement for the original 1539 structure which was damaged by earthquakes. Just north, the **cathedral** is a large but undistinguished building, sombre in its appearance and austere inside. East of the main square, the church of **Cristo Rey** at Calle 20, No 24-64, has a striking yellow stone west front with octagonal angelic turrets. **La Merced** on the corner of Calle 18 and Carrera 22 is also worth a look for its rich decoration and gold ornamentation. From the church of **Santiago Apóstol** at Carrera 23 and Calle 13, there is a good view of the green mountains beyond the city. Four blocks to the north at Calle 12 and Carrera 27 are the green tiled domes of the church of **San Felipe** and the monastery of the **Inmaculada Concepción**.

The **Museo de Oro del Banco de la República** ① *C 19, No 21-27, T2-721 5777, Tue-Fri 1000-1700, Sat 0900-1700 free*, has a small well-displayed collection of pre-Columbian pieces from the cultures of southern Colombia, a library and auditorium. Another museum in the city centre is the **Museo Alfonso Zambrano** on Calle 20, No 29-78, which houses a private collection of indigenous and colonial, especially *quiteño* (from Quito) art. Alfonso Zambrano was a renowned local woodcarver. The **Museo Maridíaz** ① *C 18, No 32A-39*, is mainly concerned with religious art and relics from the region.

## Volcán Galeras

The Galeras volcano (4276 m), quiescent since 1934, erupted in 1989 and again in 2005 and 2010. It has been closed to the public since 1995, and the area is reportedly now mined to discourage unauthorized visitors, at least one of whom has died as a result. The volcano itself has claimed several victims, including the

**Pasto**

To Sandoná
To Cali
To Volcán Galeras
Av Agustín Aqualongo
Museo Maridíaz
Av Los Estudiantes
Río Pasto
Museo Alfonso Zambrano
Artesanía-Mercado Bomboná
Plaza de Bomboná
DAS
Cra 28
Cathedral
Cra 27
San Felipe
Ecuadorian Consulate
Cra 26
Cra 25
San Juan Bautista
Parque Antonio Nariño
Cristo Rey
Cra 24
Gobernación
To Mercado Los Dos Puentes
Parque Santiago
Santiago Apóstol
Cra 23
Cra 22
La Merced
Museo de Oro
Av Santander
Cra 21
Cra 2B
Cra 20
Av Las Américas
Cra 19
To Laguna la Cocha
200 metres
200 yards
N
Av Boyacá
Av Panamericana
Av Julián Buchell
Teatro Agustín Aqualongo
Av Colombia
Av Champagnat
Cra 14
Parque Bolívar & Sports Centre

**Where to stay**
Canchalá 1
Casa Madrigal 2
Chambú Plaza 3
Don Saúl 4
Fernando Plaza 5
Galerías 6
Koala Inn 7
Loft 8
María Belén 9
Metropol 10
Morasurco 11

Libertad Stadium
Cra 11
Av Chile
To Ipiales
To Bus Terminal

**Restaurants**
Guadalquivir Café 2
Inca Cuy 3
Loto Verde 4
Parrilla Chipichape 5
Picantería Ipiales 6

British geologist Geoffrey Brown, who died in an eruption in 1993. Brown was setting up equipment to measure gravity changes which, it was hoped, would help to predict volcanic activity. A road climbs up the mountain to a ranger station and police post at 3700 m where you will be stopped, although a rough track does continue to the TV relay station near the summit.

On the north side of the volcano lies the village of **Sandoná** where Panama hats are made. Sandoná's market day is Saturday and it is easily accessible from Pasto by frequent daily buses, 1½ hours, US$3. There are good walks on the lower slopes through Catambuco and Jongovito.

## Laguna La Cocha

About 25 km east of Pasto, on the road to Mocoa, is **Laguna La Cocha** (sometimes called Lago Guamuez), which at 14 km long and 4.5 km wide, is the largest lake in southern Colombia. The lake lies at 2760 m and is surrounded by forested mountains. Near its north end (10 minutes by boat from the **Hotel Sindamanoy**) is the **Santuario de Fauna y Flora Isla de la Corota** ⓘ *daily 0800-1700, US$0.50.* This nature reserve is the smallest protected area administered by the Colombian National Parks service and can be visited in a day. The island was the ritual centre for Quillacinga and Mocoa cultures for several centuries. There is now a small chapel on the island, as well as a research unit and an interesting information centre. A marked path allows visitors to see the island's many varieties of trees, small mammals and birds, and there are good views over the lake.

Around the lake are 15 or 20 private nature reserves run by the local **Asociación para el Desarrollo Campesino** ⓘ *C 10, No 36-28, Pasto, T2-723 1022, www.adc. org.co,* to protect prime forest areas and the *páramo* of the Guamuez river, which is part of the Putumayo river system. Several reserves have trails for visitors; take (rubber boots) and wet-weather clothing if you plan to hike.

Back on the road to Mocoa, beyond El Encano there is a steep climb over the Sierra, where a large statue of the Virgin marks the entry into the Putumayo. The road then descends steeply to Sibundoy and Mocoa. For many years this has been a drug-growing and processing area with much guerrilla activity. However, security has improved markedly in recent times, and the journey between Pasto and Mocoa is relatively safe. That said, you should take local advice before travelling this route and do not make the journey at night. There have been reports of thefts and hijackings, and the road is prone to landslides and traffic accidents. Travellers are advised not to head south towards Puerto Asís on the border with Ecuador.

## Tourist information

### Pasto

The **tourist office**, just off the main plaza, C18, No 25-25, T2-723 4962, www.turismonarino.gov.co, Mon-Fri 0800-1200, 1400-1800, is friendly and helpful and will advise on money changing. **Instituto Geográfico Agustín Codazzi**, in the Banco de la República building, C 18A, No 21A-18) has a limited selection of maps.

## Where to stay

### Pasto

**$$$-$$ Morasurco**
*Cra 40/Av de los Estudiantes with C 20, T2-731 3250, www.hotelmorasurco.co.*
Located on the northern outskirts of town, Pasto's most expensive hotel has rooms with large beds, cable TV, Wi-Fi, parking and a Turkish bath.

**$$ Casa Madrigal**
*Cra 26, No 15-37, T2-723 4592, www. hotelcasamadrigal.blogspot.com.*
This hotel has spacious rooms with good beds and cable TV, parking, a restaurant and Wi-Fi, and breakfast is included.

**$$ Chambu Plaza**
*Cra 20, No 16-14, T2-721 3129, www.hotelchambuplaza.net.*
This hotel has clean, basic rooms and good extras, such as Wi-Fi, parking and a restaurant serving *menú del día*, as well as friendly staff.

**$$ Don Saúl**
*C 17, No 23-52, T2-722 4480, www.hoteldonsaul.com.*
This hotel stays close to its Jordanian owner's roots with murals depicting

Arabic scenes and a restaurant serving Middle Eastern food. It has very large beds, a sauna, Turkish bath, cable TV and Wi-Fi; breakfast is included in the price.

**$$ Fernando Plaza**
*C 20, No 21B-16, T2-729 1432, www.hotelfernandoplaza.com.*
Smart hotel with lots of good details such as beds with orthopaedic mattresses and stereos and Wi-Fi in every room. It also has a restaurant serving steak and seafood.

**$$ Hotel Galerías**
*Cra 26, No 18-71, p 3, T2-723 7390, www.hotel-galerias.com.*
Situated in the town's main shopping centre, the **Galerías** has good-sized rooms as well as Wi-Fi, parking and a decent restaurant with a typical Colombian menu.

**$$ Loft Hotel**
*C 18, No 22-33, T2-722 6737, www.lofthotelpasto.com.*
Comfortable hotel with minimalist decor and amenities including Wi-Fi and a spa. Sleek and stylish.

**$ Canchalá**
*C 17, No 20A-38, T2-721 3965.*
This hotel has clean but small rooms with private bathrooms, but its position on a busy street makes it a little noisy.

**$ Koala Inn**
*C 18, No 22-37, T2-722 1101.*
This creaky hostel is the best backpackers' option in town. It has an enormous central atrium, large, antiquated rooms, some with private bathrooms, and good information on the local area. There is a small café serving decent breakfasts for US$2.

$ **María Belén**
*C 13, No 19-15, T2-723 0277.*
Basic but passable hotel with cable TV, en suite bathrooms with hot water and grumpy staff.

$ **Metropol**
*C 15, No 21-41, T2-720 0245.*
Decent hotel with small but clean rooms with cable TV and en suite bathrooms.

### Laguna la Cocha

There are cheap and friendly places to stay in and near El Encano (sometimes shown on maps as 'El Encanto') on the main road, with many restaurants serving trout.

$$ **Chalet Guamuez**
*By the lake, 3 km from the main road, T2-721 9307, www.chaletguamuez.com.*
Recommended chalet accommodation, with boats and jeep trips.

$$ **Hotel Sindamanoy**
*T2-721 8222, www.hotelsindamanoy.com.*
Government-run chalet-style hotel with good views. Camping allowed with manager's permission.

## Restaurants

### Pasto

$ **Guadalquivir Café**
*C 19, No 24-84, www.guadalquivir cafe.com.*
A Pasto stalwart for more than 35 years, this atmospheric café serves up home-made snacks such as *tamales*, *empanadas de añejo* and *envueltos de choclo*.

$ **Inca Cuy**
*C 29, No 13-65, T2-723 8050.*
Tucked down a narrow corridor behind the Plaza de Bombona. A large statue of a guinea pig makes clear this restaurant's speciality. Be warned that fried *cuy* takes an hour to prepare, so it's best to phone ahead.

$ **Loto Verde**
*Cra 24, No 13-91.*
This Hare Krishna-run café serves up vegetarian lunches.

$ **Parrilla Chipichape**
*C 18, No 27-88, T2-729 1684.*
This is one of Pasto's most popular restaurants, renowned for its barbecued steaks and pork steamed in aluminium foil. On Sun it serves *ajiaco santafereño* and *sancocho de pollo*.

$ **Picantería Ipiales**
*C 19, No 23-37, T2-723 0393, www.picanteriaipiales.com.*
Despite its modern decor this restaurant specializes in typical food from Nariño, specifically pork-based dishes such as *lapigancho*.

## ★Festivals

### Pasto

**25 Dec-6 Jan** Lively seasonal festivities, including:
**28 Dec Fiesta de las Aguas.** Anything that moves gets drenched with water from balconies and even from fire engines' hoses. All towns in the region are involved in this legalized water war.
**31 Dec Concurso de Años Viejos,** in Pasto and also in Ipiales. Huge dolls representing the old year are burnt. The figures sometimes lampoon local people.
**4 Jan Llegada de la Familia Castañeda.** Parades commemorate this peasant family who came from El Encano to Pasto in 1928.
**5 Jan Día de los Negros.** People cover their hands in black grease and smear each other's faces (nice!)

6 Jan **Día de los Blancos**. People throw talc or flour at each other. Local people wear their oldest clothes.

5 Feb **Fiesta de las Aguas**. More water.

## Shopping

### Pasto
The shopping centre on the main plaza (C 19 y Cra 25) has many retail and food outlets. Mercado Los Dos Puentes (Cra 24 with C 21) sells fruit, vegetables and flowers.

### Handicrafts
Leather shops are on C 17 and 18. For other handicrafts, including varnished wooden bowls, try **Artesanía-Mercado Bomboná** (C 14 y Cra 27); **Artesanías Mopa-Mopa** (Cra 25, No 13-14); **Artesanías Nariño** (C 26, No 18-91) and **Casa del Barniz de Pasto** (C 13, No 24-9); www.barnizdepasto.com is also a good resource.

## What to do

### Pasto
Emproturn, *C 19, No 31B-44, T2-731 0975, emproturn@gmail.com*. Tours in and around Pasto. Can arrange private transport from Cali.

## Transport

### Pasto
#### Air
The **airport** is at Cano, 35 km north of Pasto; US$2 by *colectivo* or US$15 by taxi (45 mins, beautiful drive). There are no currency-exchange facilities, but the airport shop will change US$ at a poor rate.

To **Bogotá**, daily flights with **Satena** (C 18, No 27-47, T2-722 0623) and **Avianca** (Centro Comercial Belalcázar, T2-723 2320 or at the airport), 1 hr 55 mins. To **Cali**, 1 flight daily with **Avianca**, 50 mins.

#### Bus
All interurban buses leave from the new terminal (Cra 6, C 16), 4 km from the centre; taxi, US$2, or take city bus No 4 from the centre.

To **Bogotá**, 8 daily, US$60, 18 hrs. To **Ipiales**, frequent, US$7, 2 hrs; sit on left hand side for the views. To **Popayán**, US$20. To **Cali**, US$32.50, 8½-10 hrs. To **Bucaramanga**, 27 hrs, US$95. To **Medellín**, 18 hrs, US$67.50. To **Mocoa**, 8 hrs, US$20.

---

## Pasto to the coast → *Colour map 3, B2-B1.*

**a detour for the determined or foolhardy**

The 250 km road west from Pasto to Tumaco is paved, but is subject to landslides – check in Pasto. It leaves the Panamericana 40 km south of Pasto at El Pedregal, passing brick factories on the high plains of the Cordillera Occidental.

At **Túquerres** (3050 m) the Thursday market is good for ponchos. A short distance beyond Túquerres a track to the right leads up to the Corponariño cabin (2½ hours), where you can stay the night, and then continues for a further 1½ hours to the spectacular **Laguna Verde**, which is fed by sulphur springs. The lake is located in the crater of Volcán Azufral (4070 m), which is still intermittently active, so beware of fumaroles. For information on walking and climbing in this area, enquire in Túquerres.

The road continues to El Espino (no hotels) where it divides, left 36 km to Ipiales on the Ecuador border, and right to Tumaco.

## Reserva Natural La Planada
*T310-45 5284, www.reservalaplanada.blogspot.com, www.fundacionfes.org.*

About 90 km from Túquerres, before the town of Ricaurte, is the village of **Chucunez**. A dirt road branches south here and, after crossing the river, climbs for 7 km to Reserva Natural La Planada, a private 3200-ha nature reserve created in 1982 by **Fundación FES La Planada**. This patch of dense cloudforest on a unique flat-topped mountain is home to a wide variety of flora and fauna and is believed to have one of the highest concentrations of native bird species in South America. The foundation has initiated a programme to reintroduce the spectacled bear to the reserve. There are also many orchids and bromeliads to be seen from the nature trails. Check at the tourist office whether it is safe to climb the mountain and whether you need a permit. The visitor centre has maps and details of nature trails. There is accommodation on site in comfortable cabins, with hot water and three meals (US$12.50 per day); camping is not permitted. **Fundación FES** has published a fine illustrated book on the reserve, US$25; proceeds help conservation.

## Tumaco and around → *Colour map 3, B1.*
The coast of Nariño is noted for archaeological finds associated with the Tumaco culture. The landscape is mangrove swamp, with many rivers and inlets on which lie villages and settlements. The movement of the tides governs most of the activities in the area, especially transport. The climate is excessively humid, with very high rainfall and a yearly average temperature of about 30°C.

Tumaco itself suffers from high unemployment, poor living conditions, poor roads and problems with water and electricity supplies. The northern part of the town is built on stilts out over the sea (safe to visit only in daylight). A natural arch on the main beach north of town is reputed to be the hiding place of Henry Morgan's treasure. Swimming is not recommended from the town's beaches, which are polluted and populated by poisonous rays. You can negotiate with boatmen for a visit to the swamps, across the bay to Salahonda and beyond, or to the island tourist resort of **Boca Grande**. However, you should bear in mind that this area is known for its coca plantations, and to make matters worse, violence perpetrated by FARC rebels has devastated the region over the last few years. Take official advice and consider the dangers carefully before visiting.

Buses on the paved Pan-American Highway cover the 84 km from Pasto to Ipiales in 1½ to two hours. The road crosses the spectacular gorge of the Río Guáitara at 1750 m, near El Pedregal, where *choclo* (corn) is cooked in many forms by the roadside.

## Ipiales → *Colour map 3, C2.*

Ipiales, 'the city of the three volcanoes', stands close to Colombia's main border crossing with Ecuador (see box, page 367) and is famous for its colourful Friday morning indigenous market. The **Catedral Bodas de Plata** is worth visiting and there is a small museum, set up by Banco de la República. The city's main attraction, however, lies 7 km east on a paved road.

### ★Sanctuary of the Virgin of Las Lajas

*7 km from Ipiales (1½ hrs' walk). Mass Mon-Fri 0600, 0700, 0900, 1100, 1500 and 1700, Sun hourly 0600-1200, 1500-1700, US$0.55. Ipiales town buses going 'near' the Sanctuary drop you 2.5 km away; instead take a colectivo from the bus station (US$1pp) or a taxi (US$5).*

Pilgrims come from all over Colombia and Ecuador (very crowded at Easter) to this sanctuary, which was built in the first half of the 20th century and declared a National Monument in 1984. Seen from the approach road, looking down into the canyon, it is a magnificently executed architectural vision, heavily ornamented in Gothic Revival style and built on a bridge over the Río Guáitara. The altar is set into the rock face of the canyon where the Virgin Mary appeared in 1754 (see box, opposite). This forms one end of the sanctuary, with the façade facing a wide plaza that forms a bridge over the canyon. It is a 10- to 15-minute walk down to the sanctuary from the village, along a path lined with plaques giving thanks for the miracles rendered by the Virgin. There is also a statue of Manuel de Rivera, a blind man cured by the Virgin who walked through Ecuador begging for alms as thanks. He raised 388 pesos and seven reales. In the vaults of the church is an interesting museum telling the history of the construction of the church and displaying religious artefacts and some interesting taxidermy: the 'two-headed' and 'eight-legged' sheep are meant to be examples of further miracles but are clumsily stitched together from many animals. Walks to nearby shrines pass through dramatic scenery.

## ON THE ROAD

### Las Lajas

In 1754 María Mueces de Quiñonez was travelling from the village of Potosí to Ipiales with her deaf-mute daughter Rosa when she stopped to rest by a cave next to the Guaitara river. Rosa escaped her clutches and ran into the cave. Some moments later she emerged and spoke for the first time in her life, saying: "Mother, look at the *mestiza* over there holding a boy in her arms". María did not look in the cave but grabbed Rosa and continued on her way. When she reached Ipiales, she recounted what had happened, though no one took what she said seriously.

A few days later, Rosa disappeared from home. María guessed that her daughter must have gone to the cave, as Rosa had often said that the Lady was calling her. María ran to Las Lajas and found her daughter in front of a lady and playing with a child. María fell to her knees before the Virgin Mary and Baby Jesus.

From that day, she and Rosa often went to the cave to place wild flowers and candles in the cracks in the rocks. One day Rosa fell gravely ill and died. A distraught María decided to take her daughter's body to Las Lajas to ask the Lady to restore Rosa to life.

The Virgin resurrected Rosa, and María returned home brimming with joy. Crowds began to visit the cave, curious about what had happened. They discovered a picture of the mysterious Lady on the wall of the grotto that is still there to this day.

That same year Fray Gabriel Villafuerte returned to the cave and built a straw church. As more pilgrims visited the miraculous spot, a new cathedral was planned on the other side of the river. The first stone was laid in 1899 and the extraordinary Gothic Revival structure was finally finished in 1949. Today it is a popular destination for religious believers from all parts of Latin America.

### Listings South to Ecuador

#### Where to stay

**Ipiales**
There are several basic hotels and a small number of restaurants at Las Lajas. You can also stay at the convent; simple but cheerful.

**$$ Angasmayo**
*C 16, No 6-38, T2-773 2140, www. hotelangasmayo.amawebs.com.*
The slick, minimalist lobby of this hotel is misleading as it appears to be the only part of the building that has seen a lick of paint in the last 10 years. However, the rooms are passable, and it also has internet access, parking, a restaurant with breakfast included, and a disco.

**$$ Santa Isabel 2**
*Cra 7, No 14-27, T2-773 4172.*
Smart, centrally placed hotel with good services, including Wi-Fi in reception, an internet room, parking and a restaurant.

### $ Belmonte
*Cra 4, No 12-11, T2-773 2771.*
Basic but clean hotel offering rooms with cable TV and shared bathrooms.

### $ Emperador
*Cra 5, No 14-43, T2-725 2413.*
Good clean rooms with cable TV and private bathrooms with hot water. This hotel is the pick of the budget options. Also has parking and is well placed 1 block from the Parque Principal.

### $ Metropol
*Cra 2, No 6-10, T2-773 2311.*
Opposite the bus station, this basic hotel has passable rooms with cable TV and en suite bathrooms with hot water as well as a small café in reception. Take care walking around at night.

## Restaurants

### Ipiales
Try local guinea pig (*cuy*) and boiled potatoes for lunch; or, maybe, guinea-pig betting in the central plaza is more to your taste.

### $ Mi Casita
*C 9, No 6-18, T2-773 2754.*
A local favourite, this canteen-style restaurant serves up typical Colombian specialities such as *mondongo* and several variations of *bandeja*.

### $ Rancho Grande
*Cra 7, No 14-51, T2-773 2665.*
With an interior built primarily in bamboo, **Rancho Grande** is an agreeable place to enjoy steaks, chicken, seafood and fast food.

## Transport

### Ipiales
**Air**
**San Luis airport** is 6.5 km out of town; taxi to centre, US$8.

To **Bogotá**, **Medellín** and **Puerto Asis** with **Satena**.

**Bus**
Buses to most destinations leave from the terminal at Cr 3 and C 6. It has good facilities with a 24-hr left-luggage facility and toilets (US$0.25). Most buses leave from here but **Bolivariano** and **Transipiales** have kiosks at the border (see box, opposite) and will collect passengers from here for destinations further into Colombia.

To **Popayán**, hourly 0730-2030, with **Expreso Bolivariano**, **Transipiales** or **Cootranar**, US$20, 7½ hrs; sit on the right-hand side for best views. To **Cali**, US$39, 10-12 hrs. To **Pasto**, frequent, US$7, 1½ hrs. To **Bogotá,** with Bolivariano, 24 hrs, US$67.50. To **Medellín**, **Expreso Bolivariano**, 22 hrs, US$75, 3 a day.

# BORDER CROSSING
## Colombia–Ecuador

### Tumaco–San Lorenzo

The adventurous can travel to Ecuador by boat from Tumaco. Part of the trip is by river, which is very beautiful, and part on the open sea, which can be very rough; a plastic sheet to cover your belongings is essential. Take sun cream. Obtain an exit stamp for Colombia from Migración Colombia, Avenida Estudiantes, No 3-74, Pasto, T2-727 1692, Monday-Friday only. Entry stamps for Ecuador must be obtained once you arrive in San Lorenzo.

### Ipiales–Tulcán

Ipiales is 2 km from the Rumichaca bridge across the Río Carchi which forms the border with Ecuador. All Colombian formalities are handled in a single modern building at the border, 24 hours daily: immigration, customs, vehicle permits and plant/animal quarantine. There is also a restaurant, Telecom for long-distance phone calls, clean bathrooms (ask for key, fee payable) and ample parking. The Ecuadorean side is older and more chaotic than the Colombian complex, but adequate. It has a modern Andinatel office for phone calls. There are many moneychangers near the bridge on both sides; travellers report better rates on the Colombian side, but check all calculations as they may take advantage of you if the banks are closed.

**Transport** *Colectivos* run from Calle 14/Carrera 11 in Ipiales to the border when all seats are full, US$0.90. A taxi frrom Ipiales airport to the border costs US$6-8. A *colectivo* from the border to Tulcán (Parque Ayora near the cemetery, six blocks from the centre) costs US$0.75, or to Tulcán bus station, US$1; taxi, US$3.50.

**Entering Ecuador** Get an exit stamp at Migración Colombia, and if you're leaving Colombia by car, show your vehicle entry permit to the INTRA officials on the Colombian side and get your papers stamped. On entering Ecuador, ask for 90 days if you need it, otherwise you will be given 30 days. There is an **Ecuadorean consulate** in the Migración office in Ipiales (Carrera 7, No 14-10 esquina Calle 14 piso 3, Monday-Friday 0900-1200, 1400-1700), which can issue visas.

**Entering Colombia** You are not allowed to cross from Tulcán to Ipiales for the day without having your passport stamped; both an Ecuadorean exit stamp and a Colombian entry stamp are required. No one will stop you at the border, but you risk serious consequences in Colombia if you are caught without your documents 'in order'. If you bring a private vehicle into the country, it is supposed to be fumigated against diseases that affect coffee plants at the ICA office on the Colombian side of the border; the certificate must then be presented in El Pedregal, 40 km beyond Ipiales on the road to Pasto. (This fumigation process is not always carried out; contact www.aduana.gob.ec for further information). In addition, car owners must present title deeds to the vehicle with a photocopy, and the vehicle's chassis and engine number. You can buy Colombian car insurance at Banco Agrario, in the plaza in Ipiales.

# Eastern Colombia

empty plains and teeming jungle

A map of Colombia reveals that an immense area east of Bogotá, with barely a town or road to be seen, makes up more than a quarter of the country. This is the Llanos, fertile cattle plains that stretch from the edge of Boyacá almost as far as the Amazon river and from the mountains of Bogotá to Venezuela (and beyond).

Empty of people and inaccessible by road, the Llanos have provided effective and convenient cover for guerrillas and cocaine-production factories, and it is here that the government's war with armed groups such as the FARC continues. Significant gains by the government in the last few years have made some of this cowboy country safe to visit again, particularly the main city, Villavicencio, and its immediate surroundings.

Further south, the grassy pastures make way for seemingly infinite hectares of pristine jungle, accessible only by boat or plane. The city of Leticia sits on the Amazon river and forms a three-pronged frontier with Brazil and Peru. Amacayacú national park and the village of Puerto Nariño allow travellers to observe some of this majestic river's wildlife at close range. Even better is a quick excursion to the Yavarí river in Brazil, whose private nature reserves are excellent for birdwatching, sports fishing and dolphin and caiman spotting.

**Best** for
Adventure ■ Isolation ■ Wildlife

# Footprint picks

⭐ **Ruta del Amanecer Llanero**, page 373

Head east to watch magnificent sunsets over the river in Puerto Gaitán.

⭐ **Río Ariari**, page 374

Go whitewater rafting or float gently downstream.

⭐ **Fincas**, page 375

Unleash your inner cowboy on a *llanero* cattle ranch.

⭐ **Puerto Nariño**, page 379

Use this tranquil riverside village as a base for spotting pink dolphins or visiting the Tikuna tribe.

⭐ **Río Yavarí**, page 385

See the Amazon's incredible flora and fauna on a private nature reserve.

VENEZUELA

Puerto Wilches
Cúcuta
Villa Rosario
Pamplona

Bucaramanga
Chitaga
Barrancabermeja
Parque Nacional Tamá
Sierra Nevada del Cocuy
San Gil
SANTANDER
Barbosa
BOYACA
Duitama
Chiquinquirá
Sogamoso
El Pretexto
Tunja
Yopal
Nemocón
BOGOTA
Parque Nacional Natural Chingaza
Restrepo
Cumaral
Acacías
Villavicencio
Guamal
Puerto López
Parque Nacional Natural Sumapaz
Granada
Mesetas
San Juan de Arama
Vista Hermosa
Parque Nacional Natural Serranía de la Macarena
San José del Guaviare
La Macarena
Calamar
GUAVIARE

ARAUCA
Río Arauca
Arauca
Tame
Río Casanare
Pore
Trinidad
CASANARE
Oracué
San Pedro de Arimena
San Miguel
Puerto Gaitán
META
Río Meta
Río Meta
La Primavera
VICHADA
Río Tomo
Santa Rita
Río Vichada
Río Guaviare
Río Vaupés
VAUPES
Mitú

Puerto Carreño
Casuarito
Río Tuparro
Río Orinoco
Puerto Inírida
GUAINIA
Río Infreda
Río Guainia
Bocas de Casiquiar

CAQUETA
Río Mesay
Río Apaporis
Río Caquetá
Araracuara
Puerto Santander
AMAZONAS
La Chorrera
Río Igara Parand
Río Cahuinari
Bocas de Cahuinari
San Rafael
El Encanto
Río Putumayo

PERU

Tarapaca

Puerto Nariño
Parque Nacional Amacayacú
Río Amazonas
Leticia
Río Yavarí

BRAZIL

N

100 km
100 miles

# **Los** Llanos

The vast plains that unfurl eastwards towards Venezuela like a green carpet from the mountainous folds of central Colombia make up almost a quarter of the country. These are the Llanos, comprising the departments of Arauca, Casanare, Vichada, Guainía, Meta, Vaupés and Guaviare – a land of cattle ranches, cowboys, *música llanera* and spectacular sunsets. For many years this area has been at the heart of the guerrilla war and a centre of drug production. Much of it still is, but certain parts are beginning to open up thanks to increased security. Villavicencio and its immediate surroundings are particularly safe, and many Colombians take their holidays on the numerous cattle fincas that have been converted into very comfortable rental homes and hotels. With the construction of the Buenavista tunnel (Colombia's longest), down the mountain from Bogotá, 'Villavo', as the locals call it, is a convenient 1½-hour drive from the capital.

# Essential Los Llanos

### Finding your feet

A spectacular 110-km road runs southeast from Bogotá to Villavicencio, at the foot of the eastern slopes of the Eastern Cordillera. A tunnel has reduced the journey by road from Bogotá to 1½ hours. Villavicencio is a good centre for visiting the Llanos, which stretch 800 km east as far as Puerto Carreño and Puerto Inírida on the Orinoco.

### Getting around

From Villavicencio, three roads run further into the Llanos. Buses operate along the main routes but a private 4WD will allow you to explore more fully. Roads tend to be tracks left by previous vehicles; they are easy to follow from late December till early April and almost impassable for the rest of the year. If driving, carry plenty of spare fuel as there are few service stations; also take food and plenty of water. You will be able to hang up your hammock or pitch your tent almost anywhere, but mosquito nets are a must; fishing tackle could also be useful. We recommend you get advice from the **Gobernación del Departamento de Meta** before driving around the Llanos independently.

### Tip...

At the time of writing, the area of La Macarena national park near Río Caño is safe to visit and some agencies run tours there. However, the FARC maintains a presence in outlying areas of the park. Check with local authorities before visiting, and don't venture beyond the organized tour routes.

### When to go

The plains are very hot all year round, with heavy rainfall from April to November, especially from April to July. Visit in June/July or October to experience Villavicencio's *llanero* festivals.

### Time required

One week is enough to explore the main routes out of Villavicencio and spend some time on a ranch.

## Weather Los Llanos (Villavicencio)

| January | February | March | April | May | June |
|---|---|---|---|---|---|
| 32°C 21°C 40mm | 32°C 22°C 90mm | 31°C 22°C 140mm | 31°C 21°C 500mm | 30°C 21°C 520mm | 30°C 21°C 500mm |

| July | August | September | October | November | December |
|---|---|---|---|---|---|
| 30°C 20°C 450mm | 30°C 21°C 380mm | 31°C 20°C 400mm | 32°C 21°C 380mm | 31°C 20°C 350mm | 32°C 20°C 160mm |

Locally shortened to Villavo (Vee-a-bo), Villavicencio is the capital of Meta Department and a good centre from which to visit Los Llanos. This is where *llaneros* come to stock up on provisions and blow off a little steam in the city's bars and clubs. Founded in 1840 by Esteban Aguirre, it was originally a staging post on the way to Bogotá and a market for the ranching activities of the plains.

### Sights
The attractive central **Parque de Los Libertadores** (also called Parque Santander) has busts of Francisco Santander and Simón Bolívar and many ancient ceiba trees. It is overlooked by the mid-19th-century cathedral of **Nuestra Señora del Carmen**. Southwest of the city, the **Monumento a Cristo Rey**, off Calle 40, has good views. In the same direction, on the road to Acacias, is the **Monumento a Los Fundadores**, a sculpture by Rodrigo Arenas Betancur. There is a **botanical garden** 2 km from the centre.

### Ruta del Piedemonte Llanero
To the north is a popular route known as the **Ruta del Piedemonte Llanero**, with parks, indigenous communities and hot springs to visit.

Around 3 km northeast of Villavicencio is the **Bioparque Los Ocarros** ⓘ *Km 3 via Restrepo, T300-815 6222, Mon-Thu 0900-1600, Fri-Sun 0900-1700, US$5, children US$3.50,* a 5.5-ha thematic park set around lakes and forests with nearly 200 species endemic to the Llanos. The park runs educational talks and workshops.

Further along the road is the pleasant town of **Restrepo**, famous for its salt mines and its pretty church. Beyond is **Cumaral,** which has palm tree plantations and is known as the best place to eat meat in the Llanos. A few kilometres north of Cumaral, near Barranca de Upía, is the **Reserva Natural Aguas Calientes**, which has a natural pool set in exuberant forest.

### ★Ruta del Amanecer Llanero
On the road east towards Puerto López is the **Eco Etnoturismo El Maguare** ⓘ *office at Cra 33 No 34A-46 Lc 1, Villavicencio, T8-682 4345, www.resguardoindigenamaguare. com*, a community project set up and managed by the Uitoto. The community puts on ancestral dances in a traditional *maloca* as well as talks about Colombia's indigenous people and workshops on how to use some of their traditional tools and weapons. Some of the proceeds go towards supporting displaced and marginalized indigenous groups.

The road east passes through the Apiay oil field before reaching **Puerto López** on the Río Meta. A few kilometres beyond Puerto López is the 21-m-high **El Obelisco** at Alto Menegua, built to mark the geographic centre of Colombia. This colourful monument, built in 1993, displays elements of local prehistory, cultural heritage and a relief map of Colombia. From here there are wonderful views of the

## ON THE ROAD
### Cowboy culture

*Llaneros* have a distinct culture, worlds apart from the rest of Colombia. In fact, they share far more in common with their fellow ranchers across the border in the Venezuelan Llanos.

The first cowboys in the Americas, preceding both the gauchos of the Argentine *pampas* and the cattle herders of North America, the *llaneros* are predominantly a mixture of indigenous and Spanish heritage. They are known for their hardiness, appearing impervious to heat and cold and often riding their horses barefoot. They live an isolated life on these vast savannahs, tending their cows and returning to the few cities only for provisions and a spot of drinking.

*Llaneros* played an important part in the South American War of Independence, initially siding with the Spanish, who exploited their distrust of the aristocratic *criollos*, until Simón Bolívar, recognizing their value as skilled horsemen, went to live among them and won them over. They nicknamed him *culo de hierro*, or 'iron buttocks' for his feats of endurance in the saddle.

Today *llanero* culture is known for its distinctive music whose main instruments are the harp, maracas and a small guitar called a *cuatro*. The *joropo* has become the national dance of Venezuela and the regional dance of the Llanos and is celebrated during festivals such as the Torneo Internacional del Joropo in Villavicencio in late June/July.

Most important are the cattle. There are an estimated 12 million cows on the Llanos of Colombia and Venezuela, spread out over an area of 451,474 sq km. *Llaneros* are proud of their cattle-herding skills, and there are annual tournaments that test their prowess at *coleo*, a kind of rodeo in which cowboys on horseback attempt to fell cattle by grabbing their tails and twisting them until they tumble. Villavicencio hosts the Encuentro Mundial de Coleo each October.

Llanos. A further 150 km east is **Puerto Gaitán**, where there are good views and excellent sunsets to be seen from the bridge across the Río Manacacías. North of town, the Manacacías reaches the Río Meta where there are some beautiful white-sand beaches.

### ★Ruta del Embrujo Llanero

Running south from Villavicencio, the Ruta del Embrujo Llanero passes through **Acacias**, **Guamal** and **San Martín**, a cattle town. From Guamal a road leads southwest to the village of **Cubarral** and the **Río Ariari**, on the edge of the Parque Nacional Natural Sumapaz. This area is increasingly popular for adventure sports, including paragliding and abseiling. Whitewater rafting is particularly recommended, as well as *balsaje* (floating downriver on bamboo rafts); contact **Vergel Tours** in Villavicencio.

The road, meanwhile, eventually leads to **San Juan de Arama**, gateway to the **Parque Nacional Natural Serranía de la Macarena**, which encompasses a remote mountain range similar to the *tepuis* of Venezuela. The Caño Cristales river runs through the park; depending on the time of year and the amount of algae found in its waters, the river has an incredible technicolour sheen.

## Listings Villavicencio

### Tourist information

Information on the Llanos can be obtained from the **Instituto de Turismo del Meta**, Km3, Vía Camino Gandero, Parque Las Malocas, T310-207 8600, www.turismometa.gov.co, and from the office of the **Gobernación del Departamento de Meta**, www.meta.gov.co.

### Where to stay

**$$$ Don Lolo**
*Cra 39, No 20-32, T8-670 6020,*
*www.donlolohotel.com.*
This hotel is no beauty. Rooms have cable TV, Wi-Fi, a/c, minibar and room service but are a little frayed round the edges. Restaurant and pool.

**$$$ Hotel del Llano**
*Cra 30, No 49-77, T8-671 7000,*
*www.hoteldelllano.com.*
Tucked under the forested hills of the Cordillera Oriental, this is Villavo's smartest option with good rooms and a host of extras such as a spa, sauna, pool, restaurant, tour agency and Wi-Fi throughout.

**$$$ María Gloria**
*Cra 38, No 20-26, T8-672 0197,*
*www.hotelmariagloria.com.*
In an ugly building, rooms feel a bit antiquated but have services such as a/c, flatscreen TV and Wi-Fi. Price includes breakfast. Good pool area with sauna and Turkish bath.

**$$ Hotel Oriental Plaza**
*C 15, No 9-65, T313-816 4180.*
Good, large rooms, minibar, room service and en suite bathrooms. Cheaper rooms have fan instead of a/c. Good security.

**$$ San Jorge**
*C 38, No 31-21, T8-662 1682.*
Good clean rooms, a/c and cable TV.

**$$ Savoy**
*C 41, No 31-02, T8-662 2666.*
Clean, simple rooms with a/c, cable TV and en suite bathrooms. Vegetarian restaurant downstairs.

**$ Delfín Rosado**
*C 35, No 23-15, T8-662 6896.*
The rooms may open up off dark corridors but they are comfortable with fan and cable TV, and there's a restaurant serving decent breakfasts.

**$ El Caporal**
*C 39, No 33-35, T8-662 4011.*
Clean, simple rooms in a small hotel 1 block from the Parque Principal.

**$ Turista del Llano**
*C 38, No 30A-42, T8-662 6207.*
Rooms are a bit musty, but it's in the centre of town, with cable TV, private bathrooms; towels and soap provided.

### ★Fincas
One of the best ways to get to know the Llanos is to stay on one of the cattle ranches, where you'll get the chance to go hiking, wildlife-

spotting and riding. Check out www.
alquilerfincasenlosllanos.com, which
has multiple listings.

## Restaurants

**$$ Chop Suey**
*C 38, No 30A-44.*
Popular Chinese restaurant.

**$ Asadero La Llanerita**
*C 35, No 27-16, T8-662 3001.*
Slow-roasted meats cooked on an open
barbecue, including *falda de Costilla*.

**$ Fonda Quindiana**
*Cra 32, No 40-40, T8-662 6857.*
One of Villavo's oldest restaurants,
with a great atmosphere. Typical
dishes such as *frijoles* and *lengua
en salsa* as well as *parrillas*.

**$ La Posada del Arriero**
*C 41A, No 30-08, T8-664 1319.*
This restaurant serves typical dishes such
as *mondongo* and *frijolada* as well as fish,
chicken and steak, on a pleasant terrace
painted orange and green.

**$ Toy-Wan**
*C 40A, No 28-79, T8-664 1347,
www.restaurantetoywan.com.*
Smart oriental restaurant, does
spring rolls and stir fries.

## Festivals

**Jun-Jul Torneo Internacional del
Joropo**, involving parades, singers
and over 3000 couples dancing the
*joropo* in the street.

**Mid-Oct Encuentro Mundial de Coleo**,
www.mundialcoleo.com.co. *Coleo* is a
sport similar to rodeo in which cowboys
tumble young calves by grabbing their
tails and twisting them until they lose
their balance.

## Shopping

**Almacenes Ley**, *C 37, No 29-83*. A good
place to stock up with provisions.

## What to do

### Tour operators
**Vergel Tours**, *Hotel del Llano, Cra 30,
No 49-77, T8-682 5353, www.vergel
aventura.com.* Runs adventure-sport
activities, including whitewater rafting,
paragliding, horse riding and visits to
hot springs. Recommended.

## Transport

### Air
The airport, **La Vanguardia**, is 4 km
northwest of the town.
   To **Bogotá**, daily flights with **LAN**,
**Avianca** and **Satena**. To **Puerto Carreño**,
with **Satena** several a week. Satena also
flies to a number of other destinations
in Los Llanos.

### Bus
The **bus station** is on Av del Llano, the
ring road to the east of town; taxi US$2.
   To **Bogotá**, *colectivos* and minivans
leave multiple times a day, US$10,
1½ hrs. Also regular services with
**Expreso Bolivariano**, **Arimena**
and **Flota La Macarena**.

# Amazonia

The Colombian Amazon forms part of the largest ecosystem on the planet. More than one third of all the species in the world live in the Amazon rainforest, which covers an area of more than 5,400,000 sq km. Its lifeline is the Amazon river, the largest river in the world, which begins its journey in the Andes of Peru and Ecuador and flows for over 6000 km across almost the entire width of the continent before reaching the Atlantic in Brazil. By the time it passes Leticia, capital of Colombian Amazonas, it is already well into its stride, and this section of the Amazon provides plenty of opportunities for nature lovers to observe its flora and fauna up close. From Leticia, vast swathes of forest run northwards with little human activity to interrupt their quiet splendour. There are no roads, and indigenous communities live off the fishing and transport provided by tributaries that feed into the Amazon.

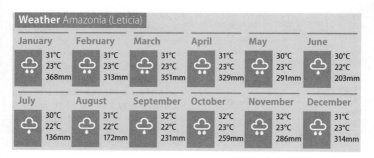

**Weather** Amazonia (Leticia)

| | January | February | March | April | May | June |
|---|---|---|---|---|---|---|
| High | 31°C | 31°C | 31°C | 31°C | 30°C | 30°C |
| Low | 23°C | 23°C | 23°C | 23°C | 23°C | 22°C |
| Rain | 368mm | 313mm | 351mm | 329mm | 291mm | 203mm |

| | July | August | September | October | November | December |
|---|---|---|---|---|---|---|
| High | 30°C | 31°C | 32°C | 32°C | 32°C | 31°C |
| Low | 22°C | 22°C | 22°C | 23°C | 23°C | 23°C |
| Rain | 136mm | 172mm | 231mm | 259mm | 286mm | 314mm |

Leticia is a port town on the Amazon that shares a border with both Brazil and Peru. The city is clean, modern and safe, though run-down near the river. It is rapidly merging with neighbouring Tabatinga in Brazil. Leticia is a good place to buy typical indigenous Amazonian products, and tourist services are better than in Tabatinga or Benjamin Constant.

## Sights

There's precious little in the way of sights around town, but the **Banco de la República** ① *Cra 11, No 9-43*, is housed in a beautiful building and has a museum that covers local ethnography and archaeology, with various workshops and talks, as well as a library and a terrace overlooking the Amazon. Agencies run overnight tours with full board to **Monkey Island (La Isla de los Micos)** upriver. There are not many monkeys on the island now, and those left are semi-tame, but visits can be made to indigenous Yagua and Ticuna communities. The price depends on the number of people in the group.

**Parque Nacional Natural Amacayacú**
*60 km upstream from Leticia. Daily 0700-1700. US$17.50. Boat from Leticia with Tres Fronteras, 0800, 1000 and 1400, US$14.50 one way, 1½-2 hrs; boats go on to Puerto Nariño.*

Some 60 km up the Amazon, at the mouth of Quebrada Matamatá, is the entrance to the Amacayacú National Park, which stretches 100 km from north to south and covers a total of nearly 300,000 ha. It is bounded by several rivers flowing into the Putumayo and Amazon systems. At one point it touches the border with Peru. It is claimed that there are over 500 species of bird to be seen in the park, and 150 or so species of mammal, including pink dolphin, danta and manatee. The smallest monkey in the world, the pygmy marmoset (*Cebuella pygmaea*), may also be seen. There is a jungle walk to a lookout (guides will point out plants, including those to avoid) and a rope bridge over the forest

**Leticia**

To Airport & Tarapaca
Stadium
To Iquitos (Peru)
Río Amazonas
To Manaos (Brazil)
MA
Brazilian Consulate
Banco de la República Museum
Parque Santander
Migración
Almacen Uirapuru
Productos Naturales del Trapecio Amazonico
Peruvian Consulate
BRAZIL
To Marco & Tabatinga
N
200 metres
200 yards

**Where to stay**
Amira 1
Decalodge Ticuna 2
Fernando Real 3
Hospedaje Los Delfines 5
Mahuta Guesthouse 6
Mochileros 7
Yurupary 8

**Restaurants**
El Cielo 1
Tierras Amazónicas 2
Tierras Antioqueñas 3

canopy, with wonderful views over the surrounding jungle (US$25). There are various other guided day treks through the jungle, and boats go to a nearby island to see Victoria Regia water lilies. Note that the park is flooded for much of the year so activities are restricted and sometimes it is closed altogether; check with Aviatur.

### ★ Puerto Nariño

The Colombian Amazon's second largest settlement after Leticia, this tranquil riverside village has banned all motorized traffic. Its streets are no more than pathways, immaculately swept and lined with flowers and herbaceous borders, while most of its houses are brightly painted with carefully tended gardens. There's an emphasis on good environmental practice here; Puerto Nariño has plans to become Colombia's first environmentally sustainable town.

Be sure to visit **Fundación Natutama** ⓘ *www.natutama.org, Wed-Mon 0800-1700, free but contributions appreciated*, which works to preserve the marine life in this part of the Amazon by organizing educational programmes with local communities. At their visitor centre by the river there's an informative display of underwater life, with life-size models of the various Amazonian fish and reptiles, as well as videos. This is a good way to inform yourself about the Amazon's ecosystems before venturing out to see it in person.

Just beyond the village is **Lago de Tarapoto**, a popular place for seeing pink river-dolphins and caimans. Excursions in a *peque peque* (motorized canoe) cost about US$70 per person. Another, less well-known excursion is to **Lago San Juan**

## Essential Amazonia

### Finding your feet

Leticia lies in the far southeast of Colombia on the border with both Brazil and Peru; crossing between these countries is straightforward as long as your paperwork is in order (see box, page 384). There are onward boat services to Manaus (Brazil) and Iquitos (Peru). Transport to/from elsewhere in Colombia is by air or boat only. There is an obligatory US$9.50 environment tax payable on arrival in Leticia. You may also be asked for a yellow fever certificate, although this is only compulsory if you're travelling from Peru. Take water-purification tablets with you since almost all the water here is taken from the river.

### Getting around

You can get around Leticia on foot. River taxis or organized boat tours travel to destinations on the Amazon.

### When to go

The Colombian Amazon is very hot all year round. The best time to visit the area is from June to August, during the early months of the dry season. The river is at its highest level in May, when some areas may be flooded and inaccessible. The river is lowest in September. At weekends, accommodation may be difficult to find.

### Time required

One week is enough to explore the area around Leticia, but you'll need more time if you want to venture into Brazil or Peru.

It may all look the same from above as you fly into Leticia, but the Amazon has three types of tropical forest, each with distinct ecosystems. *Terra firme*, which is dry all year round and characterized by an abundance of tropical hardwoods, is where you are most likely to see large mammals. *Várzea*, which is flooded for half the year, contains fewer mammals but an abundance of birds. *Igapo*, which is always flooded and grows to a height of 3 m, is where you are likely to see reptiles such as anacondas, caimans, boa constrictors and large fish.

The area immediately around Leticia is characterized by *várzea* and *igapo* forests; for *terra firme* you will have to venture inland from the river or into Brazil or Peru.

del Socó, a smaller lake that offers a better chance of seeing wildlife due to Tarapoto's increasing popularity.

There are also guided walks from Puerto Nariño to various indigenous communities such as **San Martín de Amacayacú**, which is home to the Tikuna tribe who will talk about their customs. The Tikuna have built a fine viewing tower in the village for wildlife spotting.

## Around Leticia

## Tourist information

### Leticia

For general information, contact the **tourist office**, C 10, No 10-47, T8-592 8065. **Aviatur (Ecodestinos)**, Cra 10, No 6-67, T317 441 5529, will give information and arrange transport to Parque Nacional Natural Amacayacú; it can also arrange lodging in nearby Puerto Nariño. For a good account of the local ecology and cultures of the northwest Amazon, see *The Forest Within: World View of the Tukano Amazonian Indians* (Gerardo Reichel Dolmatoff, UK 1996).

## Where to stay

### Leticia

**$$$$ Decalodge Ticuna**
*Cra 11, No 6-11, T8-592 6600,*
*www.decameron.com.*
Leticia's smartest hotel, run by the hotel chain **Decameron**, has comfortable rooms with a/c, cable TV and a large swimming pool, but there have been reports of poor service. Can arrange stays in Amacayacu National Park and trips to Monkey Island. All-inclusive packages available.

**$$$ Amira**
*Cra 9, No 9-71, T8-592 7767.*
This modern hotel has clean, comfortable rooms with a/c (almost half-price with fan), cable TV and private bathrooms with hot water.

**$$$ Fernando Real**
*Cra 9, No 8-80, T8-592 7362.*
This hotel has an intimate atmosphere with rooms opening up onto a patio bursting with heliconias. The bathrooms are a little small.

**$$$ Yurupary**
*C 8, No 7-26, T8-592 4743,*
*www.hotelyurupary.com.*
A good mid-range option, the Yurupary has large rooms with private bathrooms and hot water as well as a lovely pool, fringed with tropical plants. Also arranges tours into the Amazon.

**$$ Hospedaje Los Delfines**
*Cra 11, No 12-85, T8-592 7488,*
*losdelfinesleticia@hotmail.com.*
This hotel has a lovely patio bursting with tropical plants and rooms with private bath, fan and Wi-Fi.

**$ Mahatu Guesthouse**
*C 7, No 1-40, T8-592 7384.*
A comfortable and well organized backpackers' hostel. It has 1 private room in a *maloca* in an overgrown garden out back and a couple of dorms with bunks, as well as a pool, kitchen and bike hire. Owner Gustavo René Alvarado speaks English, Flemish, French and Portuguese and organizes alternative tours of the Amazon.

**$ Mochileros**
*Cra 5, No 9-117, T8-592 5491.*
Basic hostel designed specifically for backpackers with bunks-only rooms and shared bathrooms. Organizes economical tours.

### Tabatinga (Brazil)
Reais or pesos accepted.
In Mar 2015 R$1 = COP$796.

**$$$ Takana**
*Rua Osvaldo Cruz, 970, T973-412 3557,*
*takanahotel@hotmail.com.*
The lobby of this hotel is festooned with wooden figurines of Amazonian animals,

while the rooms are comfortable and clean with private bathrooms with hot water and a/c. Recommended.

### $$ Vitoria Regia
*Rua da Patria, 820, T973-412 4145, https://portaltabatinga.com.br/ hotelvitoriaregia.htm.*
Basic rooms with cable TV and private bathrooms. Prices negotiable.

### $$-$ Hotel Santiago
*Rua Pedro Teixeira 49, T973-412 4680.*
Very basic but large rooms with private bathrooms.

### $ Hotel Pajé
*Rua Pedro Teixeira 367, T973-412 2774.*
Next to the **Santiago**, this hostel is a little cheaper and a little cleaner.

## Puerto Nariño

### $$$ Casa Selva
*Cra 6, No 6-78, T311-201 2153, www.casaselvahotel.com.*
Very comfortable hotel with a fresh, airy feel about it. Rooms are spotless and it has a fine viewing platform on the roof. Can organize trips to nearby Lago de Tarapoto.

### $ El Alto del Aguila
*20 mins' walk from the village or 5 mins by boat.*
Héctor, a local school teacher/missionary, has cabins and will arrange trips to indigenous communities and to see dolphins at Lago Tarapoto. He has pet monkeys, parrots, *gavilanes* and a pair of young *caiman*.

### $ Hospedaje Manguaré
*Cra 5, No 5-52, T311-276 4873.*
This small hotel has comfortable cabin-style rooms with fans and shared bathrooms. It also doubles up as the town chemist.

### $ Lomas del Paiyü
*C 7, No 2-26, T313-268 4400, hotellomasdelpaiyu@yahoo.com.*
Small but clean rooms off a long corridor. Ventilation could be a problem.

### $ Malocas Napú
*C 4, No 5-72, T310-488 0998, www.malocasnapu.blogspot.com.*
This *maloca* has a couple of comfortable private rooms with fans as well as the cheaper option of hammocks. Staff are very helpful and run trips to Lago San Juan del Socó. Recommended.

## Restaurants

### Leticia

### $$ El Cielo
*C 7, No 6-50.*
Leticia's only 'gourmet fusion' restaurant does interesting things with local ingredients such as pirarucu fish (the largest freshwater fish in South America). Yuca pizza is on offer as well.

### $ Tierras Amazónicas
*C 8, No 7-50, T8-592 4748.*
This restaurant has a good atmosphere, artisan decor and a varied menu of fish, chicken and steak dishes.

### $ Tierras Antioqueñas
*C 8, No 9-19.*
Good *almuerzos* of steak, chicken and *piracucu*. *Bandeja paisa* is a speciality of the house.

### Tabatinga (Brazil)
Reais or pesos accepted.
In Mar 2015 R$1 = COP$796.

### $ Te Contei
*Av da Amzide, 1813, Centro.*
Pay-by-the-kilo barbecued meats and salads from a buffet. By night they cook up excellent pizzas.

**$ Tres Fronteras Do Amzonas**
*Rua Rui Barbosa, Barrio San Francixe.*
Excellent restaurant with dining in a
series of *malocas*. The menu is a mix
of Brazilian, Peruvian and Colombian.

**Puerto Nariño**
There are cheap restaurants near
the waterfront, opposite the mini
football pitch.

## Shopping

**Leticia**
Almacén Uirapuru, *C 8, No 10-35, T8-592
7056.* Enormous shop selling handicrafts
from the Amazon region. It also has a
small museum at the back with free
entry if you buy *artesanía*.
Productos Naturales del Trapecio
Amazónico, *C 8, No 9-87, CC Shopping
Center Centro, local 16-17, T8-592 4796.*
This natural chemist's is packed with
powders and herbs gathered from the
forest. Ethno-botanist José Raúl Cuéllar
has been making treatments from the
Amazon's plants for more than 30 years
and sells them all over the world.

## What to do

If you choose to go on an organized
tour, do not accept the 1st price and
check that the equipment and supplies
are sufficient for the length of the
tour. On night excursions to look for
caiman, the boat should have powerful
halogen lamps.

**Leticia**
**Swimming**
You can swim in the Amazon and its
tributaries, but do not dive as this
disturbs the fish. Do not swim at sunrise
or sunset when the fish are more active,
nor when the water is shallow in dry

season, nor if you have a wound that
may open up and bleed.

**Tour operators**
Amazonas Jungle Tours, *Cra 9,
No 11-56, T313-265 1778, www.amazonas
jungletours.com.* Tailor-made tours in
and around Leticia.
SelvAventura, *Cra 9, No 6-85, T311-287
1307 (mob), www.selvaventura.org.* This
small operator does something a little
different from the norm, with tailor-
made trips to the Río Tacana to meet
indigenous communities, sleeping in
*posadas* and opportunities for kayaking,
caiman spotting and observation of the
forest from canopy platforms. Prices start
from US$90 pp. English, Portuguese and
Spanish spoken.
Steve McAlear, *T313-313 1106,
stevemcalear@hotmail.com.* Englishman
Steve McAlear runs personalized
tours to some of the area's more
remote locations.

**Puerto Nariño**
**Tour guides**
For trips to Lago San Juan del Socó,
ask for Ismael or Sergio León at
**Malocas Napü**, T315-607 4044. Ever
Sinarahua, Clarindo López and Milciades
Peña are recommended for their
local knowledge of flora and fauna
and indigenous customs; enquire
through **Casa Selva**. Pedro Nel Cuello
at **Fundación Natutama**, www.
natutama.org, is also recommended.

## Transport

**Leticia**
**Air**
The airport is 1.5 km from town, taxi
US$2.50. It's a small terminal with few
facilities. Expect to be searched before

## BORDER CROSSING
### Colombia–Brazil and Colombia–Peru

**Leticia–Tabatinga (Brazil) and Santa Rosa (Peru)**
In this frontier area, carry your passport at all times. You can travel freely between the three border towns for 24 hours after which time you will need an entry stamp. For entry into Brazil, formalities are done in Tabatinga; for Peru, in Santa Rosa (upstream); for Colombia, in Leticia.

**Colombian immigration** Migración is at Calle 9, No 9-62, Leticia, T8-592 5930, and at the airport. Exit stamps to leave Colombia are given only at the airport, so if you're flying into Leticia in order to travel to Brazil or Peru, get an exit stamp before you leave the airport. If you are entering Colombia at Leticia and plan to stay for longer than 24 hours, you must complete immigration and customs formalities. Those who fail to do so and who stay past the 24-hour window can be fined US$400. If coming from Peru, you must have a Peruvian exit stamp and a yellow fever certificate to enter Colombia. Tourist cards for Colombia are available at the consular office in Tabatinga and from the Colombian consulate in Iquitos.

**Brazilian immigration** If visiting Brazil beyond Tabatinga you should get your passport stamped at Leticia airport before you go to the border and then pass through Brazilian immigration at the federal police building on Avenida Da Amizade in Tabatinga (the main throroughfare from Leticia); it's open 0800-1200, 1400-1700 daily. Proof of US$500 or an onward ticket may be asked for. There are no immigration facilities in Benjamin Constant.

**Peruvian immigration** Entry/exit formalities take place at Santa Rosa, upstream towards Iquitos; every boat leaving Peru stops here. There is a Colombian consulate in Iquitos at Malecón Tarapacá 382.

leaving Leticia airport, and on arrival in Bogotá from Leticia.

**LAN** and **Avianca** (T8-592 6021) each fly to/from **Bogotá** (using Tabatinga airport if Leticia's is closed). For good deals on Bogotá–Leticia flights with **Satena**, we recommend: **Vivir Volando**, Cra 16, No 96-64, Bogotá, T310 411 9953, www.vivirvolando.co.

### Boat
To **Parque Nacional Amacayacú**, with **Tres Fronteras**, 0800, 1000 and 1400, US$14.50 single, 1½-2 hrs, continuing to **Puerto Nariño**; buy your ticket early to secure a seat and check return days

and times. There are no public river transport services up the Río Yavarí. **Reserva Natural Palmarí** (see below) can organize private transport from Leticia, including transfer from the airport and stops at immigration to get your passport stamped. The boat trip takes 2½ hrs in a fast boat and 5 hrs in the slower, more scenic wooden boat, US$75. Alternatively, it is possible to make your own way there by catching a river taxi from Tabatinga to Benjamin Constant, 15 mins, US$8, followed by a *colectivo* on the road to Atalaia do Norte, 40 mins, US$7.50, where the reserve will arrange a pick-up for the final hour's journey by boat, US$40. This is quicker and cheaper than making the whole journey by boat, but less scenic. Onward transport to Heliconia is by *peque peque* from Palmari.

Boat services into Brazil and Peru are from **Benjamin Constant** on the south side of the river, opposite Leticia and Tabatinga; river taxi, US$8. Boats from **Manaus** (Brazil) take 8 days to Tabatinga and Benjamin Constant and usually wait 1-2 days in both before the 3-day return trip downriver; you can stay on board.

Boats sail from **Iquitos** (Peru) to a mud bank called **Islandia**, on the Peruvian side of the creek near Benjamin Constant. The journey time is a minimum of 2 days upstream, 8-36 hrs downstream, depending on the speed of the boat. All passengers to/from Peru must visit immigration at **Santa Rosa** when the boat stops there en route (see box, opposite).

**Taxi and colectivo**
To **Tabatinga**, US$6-12 (depending if you want to stop at immigration offices or exchange houses). Beware of drivers who want to rush you (expensively) over the border before it 'closes'. *Colectivo*, US$2 (more after 1800).

immerse yourself in the wildlife of the Brazilian Amazon

★West of Benjamin Constant, the Río Yavarí (one of the Amazon's main tributaries) forms the border between Peru and Brazil. This is one of the best places to observe wildlife on this section of the Amazon. There are several privately owned reserves here, with comfortable accommodation and excellent facilities for birdwatching, and dolphin and caiman spotting.

### Reserva Natural Palmarí
*T1-610 3514 (Bogotá), www.palmari.org (very informative website), US$70 per person, includes all food and alcohol, most activities and Wi-Fi. For transport from Leticia, see above.*

The reserve has access to all three types of Amazon forest within a 10-minute walk (see box, page 380). It employs over 20 guides and has equipment for birdwatching, fishing (over 20 species of gamefish, including peacock bass and *arowana*) and kayaking. Within its 40 ha there are canopy platforms and natural pools for swimming and fishing. The jungle lodge is set on a raised bank looking out over the Javarí (in Portuguese) river and has been designed to maximize the visitor's chances of seeing as many types of flora and fauna as possible. With jungle walks ranging from one to 72 hours, this is one of the best places in the area to observe the Amazon's wildlife up close.

Colombian/German owner Axel Antoine-Feill has set up the **Instituto de Desenvolvimiento Socioambiental do Vale do Javarí** (www.idsavj.org) to work with local indigenous communities. All employees of the reserve come from five settlements close by and some of Palmarí's profits are invested back into these communities. The reserve also takes a strong stance on responsible environmental practice, with only eco-friendly shampoos and soaps allowed during the visitor's stay. Accommodation is in simple cabins or a large communal *maloca*, connected by wooden gangways and with a viewing platform for observing wildlife immediately behind.

### Reserva Natural Heliconia
*T311-508 5666 (Leticia), www.amazonheliconia.com. US$32.50 per night per person.*

Up a small tributary of the Javarí, about an hour by *peque peque* from Palmarí, this jungle lodge is about as isolated as you can get. It has several very comfortable *cabañas* (with bathrooms open to the forest behind) set around a jungle garden awash with heliconia plants. The reserve organizes night-time caiman-spotting excursions as well as trips to visit local indigenous communities such as Santa Rita in nearby Peru. The forest behind provides opportunities for excellent walks, including a visit to an enormous ceiba tree; there are also special birdwatching and fishing tours.

# Background
# Colombia

# History

## Pre-Columbian

Colombia was inhabited by various indigenous groups before the Spanish conquest. The most highly developed were the **Tayronas**, who had settlements along the Caribbean coast and on the slopes of the Sierra Nevada de Santa Marta. The Tayronas had a complex social organization, with an economy based on fishing, agriculture and commerce. They built paved roads, aqueducts, stone stairways and public plazas for ceremonies.

Another major group were the **Muisca**, a Chibcha-speaking people who dominated the central highlands of Colombia at the time of the conquest. Muisca and Chibcha can be considered the same language. Philologists identify the 'Chibchan' language as referring to a series of dialects extending from Nicaragua in Central America to Ecuador, almost all of which have now disappeared. Carbon dating places their earliest settlements at around BC 545. Their village confederation was ruled by the **Zipa** at Bogotá, and the **Zaque** at Hunza (now Tunja). The Zipas believed that they were descended from the Moon, and the Zaques from the Sun. Their livelihood came from trading at markets in corn, potatoes and beans. They were also accomplished goldsmiths, and traded emeralds, ceramics and textiles with other societies.

The **Sinú** had their chiefdoms in the present-day Department of Córdoba and parts of Antioquia and Sucre. They farmed yucca and maize on artificial mounds in the local marshlands with complex drainage systems to make the best use of high and low water levels. They also cultivated reeds used for textiles and basket-weaving, as well as working with gold. Much wealth was plundered from their tombs, known as 'guacas', by the Spaniards during the conquest.

The **Quimbayas** inhabited parts of the Valle del Cauca. They had a class system and society similar to that of the Muisca and Tayronas, except that some evidence suggests they practised ritual cannibalism.

'Calima' is a term used to classify the other indigenous groups living in the department of Valle del Cauca. They include the **Liles** (based near present-day Cali) and the **Gorrones** (based in the Cordillera Occidental). They were organized into small chiefdoms with economies based on fishing, hunting and cultivating beans, yucca and corn. They traded in gold, salt, textiles and slaves. Two other significant groups prospered in San Agustín and Tierradentro, in what is now the south of Colombia. Both left fascinating monuments but they had disappeared well before the conquest.

## Spanish colonization

The first permanent Spanish settlement in Colombia was established in 1500-1507 by **Rodrigo de Bastidas** (1460-1527). He reached the country by sailing south along the Caribbean coast. After his return to Spain to face trial for insubordination, he was given permission to establish a colony. In 1525 he founded Santa Marta and named the river Magdalena. Cartagena was founded in 1533 by **Pedro de Heredia** and used as a central stockpile for the growing Spanish collection of treasure. Massive fortifications were built to protect it from pirate attacks. Santa Fe de Bogotá was founded by **Gonzalo Jiménez de Quesada** (c.1495-1579) in 1538. He arrived in Santa Marta in 1535 and continued up to the high plateau of Sabana de Bogotá with his men: 200 made the trip by boat, 670 by land. **Sebastián de Belalcázar** (c 1480-1551), the lieutenant of Francisco Pizarro, was given instructions to explore southern Colombia and the Cauca Valley in 1535. He founded Cali and Popayán in 1536 and 1537 respectively, and was made governor of Popayán in 1540. **Nicolás Federmann** (1506-1541), acting on behalf of the Welser financiers of Germany, led an expedition east to Coro and Cabo de la Vela, then back to Barquisimeto and Meta. He arrived in the Sabana de Bogotá in 1538, where he met Belalcázar and Jiménez de Quesada.

Jiménez de Quesada named the territory he had conquered Nuevo Reino de Granada, because it reminded him of Granada in Spain. Santa Fe de Bogotá was named after the city of Santa Fe in Granada. The first secular government to be established after the conquest was the Audiencia de Santa Fe de Bogotá, in 1550. After 1594, it shared ruling authority with the president of the New Kingdom of New Granada, the name given to the whole conquered area, which included Panama. The presidency was replaced in 1718 by a viceroyalty at Bogotá, which also controlled the provinces now known as Venezuela; it was independent of the viceroyalty of Peru, to which this vast area had previously belonged.

### Independence from Spain

In 1793, a translation of *Rights of Man* was published in Colombia by **Antonio Nariño** (1765-1823), an administrator and journalist, known as 'el Precursor' for his important role in the Independence movement. He was imprisoned in Spain in 1794, but escaped and returned to Nueva Granada (as Colombia was then called) in 1797. He joined the patriot forces in 1810 and became president of Cundinamarca in 1812. In 1813 he led a military campaign in the south and was again imprisoned by the Spanish. Meanwhile **Simón Bolívar** (1783-1830) was leading a campaign for Venezuelan Independence. Following the collapse of the First Republic of Venezuela in 1812, he joined the Independence movement in Cartagena and had early successes in his 1812 Magdalena Campaign, which ended in Caracas, where the Second Republic was proclaimed. Again, the patriots lost control and Bolívar returned to Colombia, but was forced to flee to the West Indies when **General Pablo Morillo** launched the Spanish re-conquest.

Changes in Europe were also to affect the situation in Colombia. In 1808, Napoleon replaced Ferdinand VII of Spain with his own brother Joseph. The New World refused to recognize this, and several revolts erupted in Nueva Granada, culminating in a revolt at Bogotá and the establishment of a junta on 20 July 1810. Cartagena also bound itself to a junta set up at Tunja.

Simón Bolívar returned to the Llanos in 1816 and formed a new army. Their campaign for liberation involved a forced march over the Andes, in the face of incredible hardship. After joining forces with **Francisco de Paula Santander**'s Nueva Granada army, he defeated the royalists at the Battle of the Pantano de Vargas in July of 1819, winning the decisive victory at the Battle of Boyacá on 7 August. From 1819 to 1828 Bolívar was president of Gran Colombia, the new name for the union of Colombia, Venezuela, Panama and Ecuador, which lasted until the 1830s.

After the fall of Napoleon in 1815, the Spanish set about trying to reconquer the independent territories. The main Spanish general behind the task was Pablo Morillo (1775-1837), known as 'the Pacifier'. During his reign of terror (1816-1819), more than 300 patriot supporters were executed. Morillo set up the 'Consejo de Guerra Permanente' and the 'Consejo de Purificación'. The latter's aim was to punish crimes of treason. There was also a board of confiscations known as the 'Junta de Secuestros'. Morillo was linked to the re-establishment of the Inquisition, which saw many priests tried in military courts in South America.

The Spaniards created a considerable legacy in Colombia. Their main objective was to amass riches, notably gold, and ship everything back to Spain. Protecting what they had collected from their English, French and Dutch rivals led to the massive fortifications of their main port, Cartagena. Most of what they built is still intact and has to be experienced to be fully appreciated. However, they also brought with them culture and lifestyle, and some of their best colonial public and domestic architecture can be found in Colombia. Furthermore they brought their language, religion and many institutions, including universities, that continue to thrive today. The towns they planned and built are now being preserved. What they did not create, however, were political institutions, and the search for a durable formula continues, 200 years after Independence.

### Gran Colombia

La República de Gran Colombia was established by the revolutionary congress at present-day Ciudad Bolívar (Venezuela) on 17 December 1819. A general congress was held at Cúcuta on 1 January 1821, and it was here that the two opposing views that later sowed such dissent in Colombia first became apparent. Bolívar and Nariño were in favour of centralization; Santander, a realist, wanted a federation of sovereign states. Bolívar succeeded in enforcing his view and the 1821 Constitution was drawn up, dividing Gran Colombia into 12 departments and 26 provinces. New laws were introduced to abolish the slave trade and allow free birth for the children of slaves born in Colombia, to redistribute indigenous lands and to abolish the Inquisition. This constitution lasted until 1830 when, following the breakaway of Venezuela and Ecuador, a new constitution was drawn up.

The next president after Bolívar was Francisco de Paula Santander, from 1832 to 1837. Formerly the vice-president, he had led a campaign of dissent against the alleged dictatorship of Bolívar, culminating in an assassination attempt on Bolívar on 25 September 1828. Suspected of having had a hand in the attempt, Santander was sentenced to death, but pardoned by Bolívar himself and instead sent into exile. later returning to hold the presidency. He played an important role in establishing the administrative structure of the new republic of Colombia, and went on to become leader of the congressional opposition from 1837 to 1840.

## Colombia's civil wars

The new country, which still included present-day Panama, was the scene of much dissent between the centralizing pro-clerical Conservatives and the federalizing anti-clerical Liberals. The Liberals were dominant from 1849, and the next 30 years saw countless insurrections and civil wars. In 1885 the Conservatives imposed a highly centralized constitution that was not modified for over 100 years. Civil war had a disastrous effect on the economy, leading to the Paper Money Crisis of 1885, when Colombian currency suffered a dramatic fall in value and circulation had to be reduced to 12 million pesos in notes. Gold was not established as the standard for currency until 1903.

A Liberal revolt of 1899 against the rigidly partisan government of the Conservatives turned into the 'War of the Thousand Days', also known as 'La Rebelión'. It lasted from 17 October 1899 to 1 June 1903. The first Liberal victory was at Norte de Santander in December 1899, when government forces were defeated by rebel leader General Benjamín Herrera. The Battle of Palonegro, 11-26 May 1900, was won by the government forces, led by General Próspero Pinzón. This proved to be the decisive victory of the 'War of a Thousand Days'. 100,000 people had died before the Liberals were finally defeated.

During the Independence Wars, Panama remained loyal to Spain. Although it had been a state in Nueva Granada since 1855, it was practically self-governing until 1886, when the new Colombian constitution reduced it to a mere department. A bid for Independence in 1903 was supported by the USA. The revolution lasted only four days (3-6 November) and by 18 November the USA had signed a treaty allowing them to build the Panama Canal.

The authoritarian government of General **Rafael Reyes** (1850-1921), from 1904 to 1909, was known as the Quinquenio dictatorship. He created his own extra-legal national assembly in 1904. His territorial reorganization and his negotiations with the USA over Panama increased his unpopularity, leading to an assassination attempt in 1906. The new president from 1910 to 1914, **Carlos Eugenio Restrepo** (1867-1937), restored a legal form of government and began negotiations with the USA for the Urrutia-Thomson Treaty of 1914. This resulted in a US$25 million indemnity payment to Colombia over US involvement in the Panamanian Revolution.

Colombia was also engaged in a dispute with its southern neighbour, Peru, over Leticia, capital of the Commissariat of Amazonas. Peru had repudiated the Salomón-Lozano Treaty of 1922 by occupying Leticia, a part of Colombia according to the treaty. The dispute was submitted to the League of Nations in 1933, who took over the Leticia area and handed it back to Colombia in 1934.

## La Violencia

The late 1940s to mid-1960s were dominated by a period known as 'La Violencia', incited by the assassination of the socialist mayor of Bogotá, **Jorge Eliécer Gaitán**, on 9 April 1948. The riots that ensued were known as the 'Bogotazo'. La Violencia was characterized by terrorism, murder and destruction of property. Simultaneous, though uncoordinated, outbursts persisted throughout the 1950s. Among the many victims were Protestants, who were persecuted 1948-1959. Some 115 Protestants were murdered and 42 of their buildings destroyed. Other contributing factors to La Violencia were anti-communist sentiments, economic deprivation and the prevailing partisan political system. In 1957 a unique political truce was formed, putting an end to the violence. The Liberal and Conservative parties became the Frente Nacional, a coalition under which the two parties supported a single presidential candidate and divided all political offices equally between them. Political stability was maintained for 16 years. Ultimately the Conservatives gained more from this accord, and unforeseen opposition was provoked in parties not involved in the agreement.

## Guerrilla movements

One of the biggest guerrilla organizations active after La Violencia was the Movimiento 19 de Abril, known as M19. Their political wing was the Alianza Nacional Popular (ANAPO), founded by followers of the dictator **General Gustavo Rojas Pinilla** (1900-1975). His Peronist tactics during his 1953-1957 presidency had resulted in his trial by national tribunal and he was overthrown on 10 May 1957. ANAPO opposed both Liberals and Conservatives. They became a major protest force during the late 1960s and 1970s, believing that the 1970 presidential elections, in which Rojas Pinilla was a candidate, had been rigged, and that fraudulent results had placed **Misael Pastrana Borrero** in power. MI9 took their name from the date of the election, 19 April 1970.

M19's agenda was to achieve a democratic socialist society. Seeking to identify themselves with the legacy of the hero of the Independence movement, their first public act was the theft of Bolívar's sword from Quinta de Bolívar in Bogotá. They also kidnapped José Rafael Mercado, president of the Confederation of Workers, in 1976, accusing him of fraud and misconduct in office, for which they tried and executed him. They then kidnapped Alvaro Gómez Hurtado, Communist Party leader and son of earlier president Gómez, to publicize demands for renewed talks with the government.

It was not until the late 1980s that negotiations got under way. A peace accord was reached in late 1989. The following year, M19 members surrendered their weapons and turned themselves into a bona fide political party, named Alianza Democrática, or M19-AD, with which they gained a significant percentage of the vote in the 1990 elections.

The other main terrorist organization after La Violencia was Fuerzas Armadas Revolucionarias de Colombia (FARC). Formed in 1964 under leader **Pedro Antonio Marín**, known as Manuel Marulanda or 'Tirofijo' ('Sureshot'), they were aligned with the Communist Party. After 20 years of guerrilla activity they signed a truce with the government on 24 May 1984. FARC joined forces with the legitimate Unión Patriótica and went on to win 10 seats in the 1986 election, while the Liberals took the majority.

In 1985 many of Colombia's guerrilla movements merged into the 'Coordinadora Guerrillera Simón Bolívar' (CGSB), together with all organizations that had refused to sign the government amnesty offered by **President Belisario Betancur** in 1985. Their aim was to co-ordinate their actions against the government and the armed forces. Most of their actions were based along the upper Río Cauca and the department of Antioquia. Peace talks with the government in the early 1990s collapsed, followed in 1992-1993 by several indecisive but destructive offences on the part of both the guerrillas and the armed forces.

The 1994 presidential elections were won by another Liberal, **Ernesto Samper**. The main thrust of his programme was that Colombia's current economic strength should provide resources to tackle the social deprivation that was causing drug use and insurgency. He placed emphasis on bringing the FARC and the other main guerrilla group, the **Ejército de Liberación Nacional** (**ELN**), to the negotiating table, while also increasing public spending on social welfare. Revelations during 1995-1997 that Samper's election campaign had been financed partly by a US$6 million donation from the Cali cartel saw the government's popularity decline. In 1996 further charges were brought against the president for links with the drugs mafia, although he was acquitted. The charges led to political instability and the attempted killing of Samper's lawyer. With the assassination of opposition leader Alvaro Gómez, Samper declared a state of emergency.

When it was revealed that other ministers had links with the drugs mafia, suspicion arose that Samper's acquittal had only been to protect their own positions. International confidence was lost. The USA decided, in March 1996, to remove (decertify) Colombia from its list of countries making progress against drug trafficking. This made Colombia ineligible for US aid.

Colombia was decertified for the second time in March 1997 partly because the Cali leaders were continuing their business from prison, having been given light sentences. Whatever progress was being made to eradicate drugs plantations and stocks, the denial of US aid permitted little scope for the establishment of alternative crops. Many rural communities were therefore left without any means of support.

In May 1997 the government admitted for the first time to the escalating problem of paramilitary groups and their links with members of the armed forces. The most infamous of these is 'Autodefensas Campesinas de Córdoba y Urabá' (ACCU), who receive financial support from drugs cartels. The state department admitted that 48% of violent episodes in 1997 were carried out by paramilitaries. This was confirmed by the annual report of the Inter-American Human Rights Commission in June 1997. In March 1998, congressional elections were relatively peaceful; and the US withdrawal of decertification restrictions the same month, were a welcome boost of confidence. Two rounds of presidential elections in May and June 1998 also passed without excessive guerrilla disruption. The new president, **Andrés Pastrana**, voted in on a promise to find a formula for peace, immediately devoted his efforts to bringing the guerrilla groups to the negotiating table. After a long, tortuous process with FARC, a large *zona de despeje* (demilitarized zone), was conceded, centred on San Vicente del Caguán in Caquetá. Not everyone was in favour of Pastrana's initiative, not least because FARC violence and extortion did not cease. In April 2000, the government proposed the ceding of a similar but smaller demilitarized zone to the ELN, situated on the west side of the Río Magdalena in the department of Bolívar and a small section of Antioquia, a *zona de encuentro*. Local communities of this agricultural area were dismayed and peacefully demonstrated by closing roads and causing disruption.

After a series of high-profile guerrilla terrorist actions, including the hijacking of a plane, attacks on several small towns and cities, and the kidnapping of several political figures, Pastrana ended the peace talks on 21 February 2002 and ordered the armed forces to start retaking the FARC-controlled zone.

# Modern Colombia

## Recent history

**Alvaro Uribe** succeeded Andrés Pastrana as president in May 2002, holding office for two terms, until 2010. A Harvard- and Oxford-educated lawyer, he came to power promising to eradicate the left-wing guerrillas' and right-wing paramilitaries' hold on the country.

To a large extent he succeeded. Using US funding from Plan Colombia (see below) and helped by the CIA, he boosted spending on the military, targeted FARC leaders and armed peasants in vulnerable regions. He held formal peace talks with far-right paramilitaries and managed to bring security to most of the urban areas of the country within the mountainous centre. In so doing he effectively pushed the guerrillas, who at one point held territory within an hour of Bogotá, to the margins of the country – to the dense jungles around the borders with Venezuela, Ecuador and Panama.

In terms of the state's fight against the FARC, which has been going on for more than 40 years, 2008 was Colombia's *annus mirabilis*. Three major successes – each of which would have been considered a major, standalone coup in their own right – have shifted the balance of the conflict overwhelmingly in favour of the government.

In March of that year, the Colombian army executed a raid just over the border into Ecuador in which Luis Edgar Devia Silva (normally known by his nom de guerre, Raúl Reyes), the FARC's spokesperson and a member of the Secretariat, was killed.

In May, it was revealed that the FARC's founder and leader, Pedro Antonio Marín Marín, aka Manuel Marulanda or Tirofijo ('Sureshot'), had died of a heart attack.

Then in July came the biggest blow of all – the dramatic rescue of Senator Ingrid Betancourt, who had been kidnapped six years previously while campaigning for the presidency. In many ways, Betancourt's imprisonment had come to symbolize the potency the FARC held over Colombia and her rescue severely dented the rebels' bargaining power.

These three strikes put the FARC firmly on the defensive. Alfonso Cano took over command after Marulanda's death, but Colombia has continued to target high-level FARC leaders and decimate rebel camps through airstrikes. The FARC officially entered peace talks with the Colombian government in Havana, Cuba in 2012, which gave many Colombians hope that five decades of conflict might soon come to an end. However, despite releasing 10 of the longest-held hostages in the world in 2012, the FARC continues to kidnap and bomb, with major incidents occurring in 2008 and 2013. This continuing rebel activity, however intermittent, has led Colombian President Juan Manuel Santos to suspend peace talks at various points and is further proof that, however diminished the FARC may be, they are likely to continue to disrupt civilian life for years to come.

Successes notwithstanding, Uribe was not without his critics. A Human Rights Watch report released in October 2008 concluded that President Uribe's government had put obstacles in the way of the Supreme Court's efforts to investigate the paramilitaries' mafia-like networks, and his cousin Mario Uribe was charged for alleged links to paramilitary groups.

In spite of these scandals, Uribe did manage to improve security in most areas in Colombia during his eight years in office. His successor, Santos, a Harvard economist and former minister, took office in August 2010 and appears to be following in Uribe's footsteps in terms of national security policies, while also recommencing a long-awaited land redistribution programme.

## Relations with neighbours

In the last few years, diplomatic relations between Colombia and her neighbours have been at best frosty, at worst volatile. While much of Latin America has experienced a swing toward socialism and anti-American sentiment, Colombia has strengthened its ties with the USA and pursued a neo-liberal economical model. Uribe and the former president of Venezuela, Hugo Chávez, one of the more outspoken critics of US 'imperialism', displayed a barely disguised disdain for each other and their diametrically opposed ideologies. New president Santos is working to improve neighbourly relations with the country, having met frequently with Chávez before his death. Border relations with Ecuador and Panama have at times also been fraught, due to guerrilla and drug-trafficking activities in the border areas, particularly after the Colombian incursion into Ecuador in 2008.

## Plan Colombia

Plan Colombia is a US-Colombian initiative designed to reduce the flow of cocaine into the USA. Conceived during the presidency of Andrés Pastrana, the original Plan Colombia asked for US aid to address the problem of social exclusion that has plagued Colombia since Independence from the Spanish and that has forced peasant farmers to cultivate coca, giving birth to guerrilla movements like the FARC in the first place.

A second draft, presided over by US President Bill Clinton's advisers, had an entirely more militaristic slant and aimed to reduce the drug supply by providing extra firepower to the Colombian army in its pursuit of drug-traffickers and supplying equipment and civilian agents for the destruction of coca plantations.

The plan has come under heavy criticism for its fumigation policy, which has seen farmers' legal crops destroyed alongside illegal ones, as well as causing adverse health effects on those exposed. NGOs also claim that the money provided by the US government, which tallies up to several billion dollars, has funded Colombian army units involved in extra judicial killings and other human rights abuses.

Despite the billions of dollars ploughed into the project, the plan has failed in its primary objective. A UN analysis has found that the eradication of coca plantations has been on a smaller scale than anticipated. What's more, the market price of cocaine has not increased significantly, something that would be expected if there were a shortage of the drug on the streets of the USA. Critics of the plan also argue that any eradication of coca production in Colombia would simply push cultivation back to countries such as Bolivia and Peru.

But the initiative has had a huge tangential success in that the money provided by the US government has helped the Colombian army in its victories over the FARC and for that has gained much approval in the eyes of many Colombians. The Plan Colombia budget for 2011 was being cut by 50 million dollars and it's uncertain how this will affect its future execution, but it remains in operation.

## The drugs trade

In Medellín and Cali, two cartels transformed Colombia's drugs trade into a major force in worldwide business and crime. Their methods were very different; Medellín's was violent and ostentatious, while Cali's was much more low-key. The Medellín cartel processed and distributed 60-70% of cocaine exported to the USA during the 1980s. It was headed by **Pablo Escobar Gaviria** (see box, page 238) and **Jorge Luis Ochoa Vásquez**. In the late 1980s both Jorge Luis Ochoa and Pablo Escobar were listed as billionaires by *Forbes Magazine*.

In 1981, **Marta Nieves Ochoa Vásquez**, Jorge's sister, was kidnapped. M19 were believed responsible. In response to the kidnapping, 'Muerte a Secuestradores' (Death to Kidnappers) was formed by leaders of the drugs trade. Their strong anti-Communist beliefs led to alleged support from factions of the military. In 1984 Muerte a Secuestradores assassinated Carlos Toledo Plata, an ANAPO congressman who had later joined M19.

**President César Gaviria Trujillo**, the Liberal candidate who had won the 1990 presidential election, put into motion a pacification plan to end the drugs cartels' offensive and establish a peace agreement with the guerrillas. In a further display of reformist government, he appointed **Antonio Navarro Wolff**, former guerrilla leader now of the M19-AD, to the post of health minister.

As a result of the reform of the constitution in 1991, a further general election was held in October 1991 and the Liberals retained a majority in the Senate and the House of Representatives. By 1991 the government had secured the surrender, under secret terms, of senior members of the Medellín cartel, namely Pablo Escobar and Jorge Luis Ochoa. One of the publicized conditions for their surrender was immunity from extradition and reduced sentences. Some of the senior traffickers and murderers got only five to eight years. President Gaviria received international support, including from the USA, for his stance against the drugs problem, which contrasted with previous president Barco's tougher and unsuccessful stand.

In the National Constituent Assembly elections of 1991 the M19-AD won 19 of the 70 contested seats; the Liberals won 24; combined Conservative factions won 20. These results were followed by attempts to legitimize and modernize the political system, in an effort to deny remaining guerrilla groups any cause for protest and therefore lead to peace. The judicial system was strengthened and extradition was banned. However, the early 1990s saw high abstention rates in elections: 60-70% of the electorate didn't vote. This was blamed on loss of confidence in the political system and disruption of voting by guerrillas in some rural areas.

During the Gaviria term, it was reported that Pablo Escobar was continuing to direct the Medellín cartel from inside his purpose-built prison at Envigado.

## ON THE ROAD
### Colombian entrepreneurism

Colombia is a nation of small businesses. Millions make their living by hawking their wares on the street: street artists, photographers, people hiring out their mobile phones by the minute, and countless street stalls selling everything from fruit juices to iguana eggs.

Step onto one of the colourful buses and you'll want for nothing. Fizzy drinks and snacks will keep you nourished, while you listen to a travelling salesman delivering a carefully prepared sales pitch. Don't switch off from the sales talk, as some of the products are really quite useful! By the time the bus reaches the outskirts of town the salesman has usually sold a few items and can hop off the bus with a few thousand pesos in his back pocket.

The Cali cartel's trade was in turn growing in the wake of reduced activity by the Medellín cartel. In July 1992, Escobar escaped during a transfer to army barracks. Drug-related violence in Bogotá increased in 1993; thought to be Escobar's way of persuading the government to offer better surrender conditions for him. A paramilitary vigilante group was formed, called 'Perseguidos Por Pablo Escobar' (Los Pepes). This was allegedly made up of relatives of Escobar's murder victims and members of the Cali cartel, and it targeted Escobar's family. Escobar was finally shot by the armed forces on 2 December 1993 in Medellín, giving a temporary boost to the government's popularity. The Cali cartel capitalized on the death of Escobar and the dismantling of his empire. By the mid-1990s they controlled 70% of the world market in cocaine. But in June and July 1995, six of the seven heads of the cartel were arrested. In 2006, the Rodríguez brothers, Gilberto and Miguel, were extradited to the USA and pleaded guilty in Miami, Florida, to charges of conspiracy to import cocaine. This put an end to cartel control over the Colombian drug trade and it has now splintered into many individual groups, including paramilitary and guerrilla forces, although this has not stopped production in any significant way.

### Government

Senators and Representatives are elected by popular vote. The Senate has 102 members, and the Chamber of Representatives has 166. The president, who appoints his 13 ministers, is elected by direct vote for a term of four years, but cannot succeed himself in the next term. Every citizen over 18 can vote. Reform of the 1886 Constitution was undertaken by a Constituent Assembly in 1991 (see History, above). Administratively, the country is divided into 32 departments and the Special Capital District of Bogotá. Liberty of speech and the freedom of the press are in theory absolute but in practice more limited. The official language of Colombia is Spanish. Its religion is Roman Catholicism. There is complete freedom for all other creeds not contravening Christian morals or the law.

# People

The regions vary greatly in their racial make-up. Antioquia and Caldas are largely of European descent; Nariño has more indigenous roots; while people from the Cauca Valley are more African, descending from the slaves brought to the area when sugar was introduced. Afro-Caribbeans are also prominent in the rural area near the Caribbean and the northwest Pacific coastline. No colour bar is legally recognized but is not entirely absent in certain centres.

The birth, death and infant mortality rates vary greatly from one area of the country to another, but in general they are similar to those of neighbouring countries. Hospitals and clinics are few in relation to the population. About 66% of the doctors are in the departmental capitals, which contain about half of the population, though all doctors have to spend a year in the country before they can get their final diploma. The best hospitals, notably in Bogotá and Medellín, are well equipped and have fine reputations attracting patients from other countries of Latin America.

An estimated 800,000 tribal peoples, from 84 ethnic groups, live in Colombia. Groups include the Wayúu (in the Guajira), the Kogui and Arhauco (Sierra Nevada de Santa Marta), indigenous Amazonians such as the Huitoto, the nomadic Nukak and the Tikuna, indigenous Andean and groups of the Llanos and in the Pacific coast rainforest.

Although the national and official language of Colombia is overwhelmingly Spanish, many indigenous groups still use only their own languages. The largest ethno-linguistic group are the 150,000 Chibchas. On the Caribbean coast, especially the islands, English or Creole are widely spoken. The diversity and importance of indigenous peoples was recognized in the 1991 constitutional reforms when Indigenous Colombians were granted the right to two senate seats; the National Colombian Indian Organization (ONIC) won a third seat in the October 1991 ballot. State recognition and the right to bilingual education has not, however, solved major problems of land rights, training and education, and justice.

The vast majority of Colombians (90%) are nominal Roman Catholics, though observance is not particularly high. As elsewhere in Latin America, Protestant Evangelical Churches have made some progress in Colombia in recent years.

## Indigenous cultures

Santa Marta — Guajira
Barranquilla — (Wayúu)
Cartagena — Tayrona
(Kogi)
(Arhuaco)
PANAMA
(Cuna) — Sinú — Cúcuta
(Embera-Wunan) — Sinú
(Cholo) — Muisca — Bucaramanga
Medellín — Chibcha — (U'wa)
Quimbaya — Tunja
Pereira — Calima — Tolima — □ BOGOTA
Cali — (Páez) — Maypure
(Guambiano) — Tierradentro — (Pijhave)
Tumaco — Popayán — Neiva
Tumaco — San Agustín
Pasto
VENEZUELA
ECUADOR
BRAZIL
(Huitoto)
N
PERU
(Tikuna) — Leticia
Guajira...... Pre-Columbian
Not to scale (Wayúu)..... Present day

# Culture

## Arts and crafts

With the wide variety of climate, topography and geology, it is not surprising that Colombia has virtually all the materials, fibres, minerals and incentives to create useful and artistic products. Many of the techniques practised today have been inherited from the indigenous peoples who lived here before the conquest, some indeed have not changed much in the intervening centuries and are as appropriate now as they were then.

### Gold

Gold is very much associated with Colombia. It was gold that brought the Europeans to the New World, and where they found it first. The indigenous peoples had been using it for many centuries though not as a simple 'store of value'. Only when it had been made into jewellery, body ornaments or items to be used for sacrificial rites for their gods did gold have value for them. It must have seemed incomprehensible to them, as well as a tragedy for posterity, when the Spaniards melted down the gold they obtained in order to ship it back to Europe.

Many of the *sierras* in the west of the country have traces of gold in the strata. Through erosion in the rainy climates of the region, panning for gold in the rivers was productive and has probably been practised here since around 800 BC. Even some deep shaft mines have been found in west Colombia.

The Quimbaya of the Cauca Valley produced 24 carat gold containers, helmets and pendants in their ascendancy from 1000-1500 AD and also worked with *tumbaga*, a gold-copper alloy. The Tolima of the Magdalena Valley made artefacts of pure gold, while the Wayúu of the Guajira made string beads, sometimes covered with gold, a tradition that continues today. When the Spaniards arrived, the Muisca of the Boyacá/Bogotá area were modelling figures in wax and covering them with clay. They then fired them, removed the melted wax and filled the mould with gold. By carefully prizing open the mould, they were able to make many replicas, thus inventing an early form of mass production.

Virtually all of today's techniques of the goldsmith were known to the early peoples of Colombia and there is a fine presentation on this subject at the museum in the Parque Arqueológico in Sogamoso, Boyacá, see page 99.

There are some good gold item bargains to be had in Colombia, notably in Bogotá and Cartagena. Perhaps the most interesting place, however, is Mompós, Bolívar, where there is a tradition of fine gold filigree work.

No one visiting Colombia should miss the Banco de la República's wonderful gold museums. The central collection of gold artefacts is in Bogotá but there are other smaller presentations in the main cities around the country, always worth a visit.

## Textiles

Although Colombian textiles cannot rival those of Guatemala or Peru in terms of design and spectacular colour, certain areas of the country have very fine traditions. For the Wayúu, *'ser mujer es saber tejer'* (to be a woman is to know how to weave). Cotton was available in north Colombia and textiles were traded for wool from the Santa Marta *sierra* nearby, also used as a raw material. The Cuna of northwest Colombia still make the decorative panels for garments known as *molas*. A speciality is the *mola* made of many layers of coloured cloth sewn together, then cut out using the different colours to create a pattern or motif.

One striking costume is found in the south near Silvia, Cauca, where the indigenous Guambiano weave their own blue and fuchsia costumes as well as many other wool garments and blankets.

## Basketry

By its nature, articles made of vegetable fibres do not survive for very long, but we know that the Spaniards found many examples of indigenous work in Colombia. The basket- weaving techniques of the Muisca have continued in Tenza, Boyacá, where people still use the giant reed *caña de castilla* (Arundo donax), which is easier to work with than bamboo. The whole local village works in this cottage industry.

Another similar community enterprise is in Sandoná, Nariño, where, in addition to basket weaving, Panama hats are a speciality. Panama hats are so named for where they were initially sold and shipped from, rather than where they were made. The workers on the canal in the early part of the 20th century were the first customers, followed by those passing through. They were made in Ecuador and in Sandoná where the local *iraca* palm fibre is used. Hats are also made in Sampués, Sucre, from 'arrowcane' which grows in the river lowlands nearby and good basket weaving using palma iraca can be found at Usiacurí, south of Barranquilla.

The finest quality basket weaving in the country is to be found along the northwest Pacific coast of Chocó where the women of the indigenous Waunana use *werregue* palm to weave a texture so fine that the finished product can look like clay and be used to carry water. They have a flourishing trade nowadays in coarser but more colourful palm weaving products.

## Wood

The indigenous people of Chocó also make interesting 'healing sticks', said to have magical as well as healing powers. These are about 50 cm long with a pointed end and carved figures above. Held against the stomach of the patient, they can drive away evil spirits and cure illnesses. Carved wooden masks are a feature of indigenous crafts in the Sierra Nevada de Santa Marta in the north and the Sibundoy people of Putumayo in the extreme south of the country, used them for festivities and rituals. Interesting wood carvings are made by the Puinave people near Inírida. Wooden masks appear in the carnival in Barranquilla.

Perhaps the most important wood *artesanía* is found in Chiquinquirá (Boyacá). Carved musical instruments are a speciality and many other items including all sorts of items made of *tagua* nuts gathered in the forests of Chocó and Amazonas. Guitars are also found in Marinilla near Medellín.

## Leather
Leather and woodwork often go together, and the arrival of cattle brought the necessary raw material. Now, finely engraved leather covering carved wooden chairs and other furniture is made in Pasto (Nariño), an important centre.

## Barniz
An additional craft is that of the resin locally called *barniz*. This comes from seed pods of *Eleagia Utilis*, which grows at altitudes of over 2000 m in Putumayo. Nowadays, the resin is extracted by passing through a mill or by hammering. Previously this was done by chewing the seeds, commonly known as *mopa-mopa*, supposedly because of the strange sound made by the chewers attempting to speak as well as chew at the same time. After extraction, the resin is dyed and expertly stretched to paper thin sheets into which designs are cut to decorate wooden objects including masks, each colour produced individually, finally covered with a protective lacquer. Pasto is the most important centre for *barniz*.

## Pottery
The best known pottery centre in Colombia is Ráquira, Boyacá. A large selection of products is made for household and ornamental use including many small items, all sold here and in surrounding towns. The large earthenware pots made here today are identical to those made by the Chibcha centuries ago. A similar pottery centre across the country, Carmen de Viboral, Antioquia, also produces ceramics that are known throughout Colombia.

Imaginative and amusing ceramics are made in Pitalito, Huila. This form of popular art, pottery adorned with scenes of everyday life, is typified by representations of the *chiva*, the omnipresent brightly coloured bus seen in many parts of Colombia.

A more unusual line of production is the 'blackware' made at La Chamba, Tolima. This small village, beside the Río Magdalena near Guamo, is not generally marked on maps. The process involves using closed kilns, thus cutting down the use of oxygen which thereby causes the iron in the clay to turn from red to black. La Chamba is now a household name in Colombia and is also becoming better known abroad.

## Fine art and sculpture

The colonial art of Colombia is rich and diverse, perhaps reflecting its geographical position between the Caribbean and the Pacific, but also because of the early rivalry between the two first important colonial settlements of Bogotá and Tunja. Both cities boast numerous museums and religious foundations with good collections of painting, sculpture and decorative arts. Throughout the colonial period works of art were imported from Europe and elsewhere in the Spanish territories, particularly from Quito in the south. Artists came from far afield to work in the wealthy Colombian centres. In contrast to colonial practices in Mexico and Ecuador there seems to have been little attempt to train native craftsmen in the dominant European artistic modes of painting and sculpture, perhaps because indigenous expertise lay in pottery and metalwork rather than carving or painting.

## Early art from Spain

The conquerors brought the Christian religion and, along with it, Christian art. The cathedral sacristy in Bogotá preserves what must be one of the first European imports: a fragile silk standard traditionally believed to have been carried by Jiménez de Quesada's troops at the foundation of Bogotá in 1538, and known as the **Cristo de la Conquista**. The emaciated, bloody figure of Christ is in a mixture of paint and appliqué, with a swirling length of loin cloth around his hips. This seems to billow in the breeze, an impression that would have been all the stronger in its original context. It is hard to imagine anything more alien to native beliefs or native forms of art. Other early Christian images, especially pictures of the Virgin, must have tapped into local beliefs because they soon became the focus of popular cults: the **Virgen de Monguí**, for example, is a 16th-century Spanish painting, which tradition holds was sent over by Philip II, while the **Virgen de Chiquinquirá**, the patron saint of Colombia, was painted by the Andalucían **Alonso de Narváez** who settled in Tunja in the 1550s. Neither is outstanding as a work of art but both have been attributed with miraculous powers and versions can be found all over Colombia.

Although religious commissions dominated artistic production throughout the colonial period some remarkable secular wall paintings survive in Tunja that show another side to colonial society. In the late 16th and 17th centuries the houses of the city's founder, Gonzalo Suárez Rendón, of poet Juan de Castellanos and of city notary Juan de Vargas were decorated with colourful murals based on a wide range of printed sources. Those in the **Casa Vargas** are the most sophisticated, the combination of mythological figures, exotic animals, grotesques, heraldic cartouches and occasional Christian monograms resulting in a complex humanistic programme, probably devised by Castellanos. The diversity of styles reflects the diversity of sources, which can be traced to French, Flemish, German and Spanish originals. The rhinoceros, for example, is derived from Dürer's famous woodcut of 1515 but reached Tunja via a Spanish architectural treatise by Juan de Arfe, published in Seville in 1587. The murals in the **Casa Suárez Rendón** derive in part from those in the Casa Vargas, but are less philosophical, more straightforwardly decorative. Nevertheless, these paintings imply that a highly cultured society imported the most-up-to-date books and prints from Europe.

## Woodcarvings and sculpture

The new religious foundations in the Americas created a huge market for paintings and sculptures with which to adorn their altarpieces, and workshops in Andalucía flourished as a result. An outstanding example of imported polychrome sculpture is the dignified Crucifixion group of 1583 on the high altar of the chapel of the wealthy Mancipe family in the cathedral in Tunja, sent by **Juan Bautista Vázquez** (died 1589) from his workshop in Seville. Sculpture workshops were soon established in the Americas, however, and Colombian churches preserve a wealth of carved and polychrome wooden altarpieces, choir stalls, confessionals and pulpits, as well as decorative wooden ceilings, screens and wall panels. An early example is the ambitious high altar of the church of San Francisco in Bogotá. The central bays were redesigned in the late 18th century but the wings date from about 1620. The tightly ordered Renaissance structure frames panels of relief carving in two distinctive styles: in the upper storey each has a single, clearly defined saint, while in the lower storey the panels contain crowded narrative scenes, overflowing with energy (the torso of the figure of St Jerome leans right out towards the high altar) and lush vegetation. The unknown artist was probably trained in Andalucía.

Such altarpieces usually involved several different craftsmen. The carvings for that in the Jesuit church of San Ignacio in Bogotá (1635-1640), for example, were by an Italian, **Gian Battista Loessing**. Another important sculptor working in Colombia in the 17th century was **Pedro de Lugo Albarracín**, whose devotional images of the suffering Christ appealed to popular piety, and several, such as the powerful figure of the fallen Christ known as **El Señor de Monserrate** (1656) in the eponymous shrine on the hill above Bogotá, have become pilgrimage destinations. Records of other sculptors with the same surname working in Bogotá and Tunja in the 17th century suggest that Pedro de Lugo was the father of a dynasty of craftsmen. **Lorenzo de Lugo**, for example, executed the eight large reliefs for the high altar of the chapel of Rosary in Santo Domingo, Tunja (c 1686). The architectural frame of this outstanding altarpiece includes numerous anthropomorphic supporting figures, *atlantes*, a common feature of colonial church furnishings in Colombia, and a chance for craftsmen to indulge in fanciful invention constrained by Christian orthodoxy. A famous example is the androgynous figure on the pulpit stairs in San Francisco, Popayán, a basket of exotic fruit on its head, and a pineapple in its hand, but grotesque figures, sometimes semi-angelic, sometimes semi-demonic, can be spotted amongst the fronds of tropical foliage on almost any baroque altarpiece. In the 18th century, figure sculptor **Pedro Laboria** from Andalucía introduced a new lightness of touch with his sinuous, almost dancing saints and angels (examples in Tunja cathedral and Santo Domingo, Bogotá).

## Early paintings

As with sculpture, the demand for painting was met from a variety of sources. Works were imported from Europe, particularly from Andalucía and from the Netherlands. In the 17th century, enterprising sea captains would find room in their holds for a roll or two of canvases from the workshops of Zurbarán or Rubens to sell in the colonial ports. Itinerant artists worked their way round the viceregal centres in pursuit of lucrative commissions such as **Angelino Medoro** (c 1567-1631) from Rome who also worked in Quito and Lima before returning to Europe (see the two large canvases in the Mancipe chapel in Tunja cathedral, 1598). Quito was an important source both of artists and of works of art. Born in Quito, the

Dominican **Pedro Bedón** (c 1556-1621) worked in Tunja in the late 16th century and his influence can be seen in the *bogotano* miniaturist **Francisco de Páramo** (active in the early 17th century), while **Miguel de Santiago** (c 1625-1706) sent numerous works to Colombia, including his esoteric 'Articles of the Faith' paintings now in Bogotá's cathedral museum.

Santiago was an important influence on Colombia's best 17th-century artist, **Gregorio Vásquez de Arce y Ceballos** (1638-1711) who trained in the workshop of the extensive Figueroa family of painters but who was working independently by the time he was 20. A prolific and eclectic artist, Vásquez drew on a variety of sources: sometimes his stiff, hieratic figures reveal his debt to popular prints, sometimes his soft landscapes and sweet-faced Virgins demonstrate his familiarity with the work of Zurbarán and Murillo (good examples in the Museo de Arte Colonial, Bogotá). 18th century painting in Colombia follows the well-trodden paths of earlier generations of artists, with none of the confident exuberance found in sculpture. You will find his work in many of Bogotá's churches.

## After Independence

Independence from Spain did not bring independence from the traditions of colonial art. A survey of the galleries of ponderous churchmen and other civic dignitaries in the various museums suggests a more or less seamless production from the 17th to the 19th centuries: some appear sophisticated, some brutish, and the artist is not necessarily to blame. But if artistic style changed little the struggle for independence did provide some new subject matter. Bolívar is endlessly celebrated in painting. An inventive example is that of 1819 in the Quinta de Bolívar in Bogotá, by **Pedro José Figueroa** (1770-1838), where he stands with a protective arm around the shoulders of a diminutive female figure personifying the new and newly tamed republic, dressed in a silk gown, but still with bow, arrows and feather headdress, and seated on a caiman. The events of the Wars of Independence are recorded by **José María Espinosa** (1796-1883) in a series of paintings of the 1813-1816 campaigns (examples in the Quinta de Bolívar and the Academia de Historia, Bogotá). The painting of the death of General Santander in 1840 by **Luis García Hevia** in the Museo Nacional is sincere in its naïveté, whereas **Alberto Urdaneta** (1845-1887) who studied in Paris with Meissonier and is a much more versatile artist, sometimes makes his subjects from recent history seem artificial and melodramatic (*Caldas marchando al patíbulo*, Museo Nacional). But Urdaneta is also remembered as an uncompromising caricaturist, so much so that on one occasion he was expelled from the country. The Museo Nacional in Bogotá has two contrasting portraits of the heroine Policarpa Salavarrieta, executed by the Spanish in 1817; one a popular anecdotal version shows her *en route* to the scaffold, the other attributed to **Epifanio Garay** (1849-1903) nicely contrasts the formal society portrait with the drama of the event: she sits poised and beautiful while the ominously shadowy figure of a soldier appears in a doorway behind.

Interest in Colombia's natural resources produced scientific missions that, although organized by foreigners (the first by the Spanish botanist **Celestino Mutis** in the 18th century and the next by the Italian geographer **Agustín Codazzi** in the 19th), nevertheless helped to awaken an appreciation of the landscape, peoples and cultures of Colombia, past and present. The Venezuelan **Carmelo Fernández** (1809-1887) worked for Codazzi in 1851, producing carefully observed watercolours of the peoples and traditions of different provinces (examples in the Biblioteca Nacional). **Manuel María Paz** (1820-1902) held the same position in 1853 and his drawings of the pre-Columbian culture of San Agustín are the first of their kind. **Ramón Torres Méndez** (1809-1895) was not a member of the mission, but like them he travelled extensively in the countryside and his scenes from everyday life helped to make *costumbrista* subjects respectable.

## 20th century

During the first decades of the 20th century Colombian artists preferred to ignore the upheavals of the European art scene and hold on to the established traditions of academic figure and landscape painting. Almost the only interesting figure, **Andrés de Santa María** (1860-1945), spent most of his life in Europe and developed a style that owed something to Cezanne and something to 17th-century Spanish art, but with an over-riding concern for a thickly textured painted surface that is entirely personal (*Self-portrait*, 1923, Museo Nacional, Bogotá). During the 1930s the more liberal political climate in Colombia encouraged the younger generation of Colombian artists to look for a more socially and politically relevant form of art which, conveniently, they found in the Mexican muralists. Instead of having to embrace the violent rupture with the past represented by modern European movements such as Cubism and Futurism, the muralists offered a way of continuing in a figurative tradition but now with a social conscience expressed in images of workers and peasants struggling against the forces of oppression. **Pedro Nel Gómez** (1899-1984) was the first to paint murals inside public buildings, particularly in his native Medellín, and he was followed by others such as **Alipio Jaramillo** (1913-1999) and **Carlos Correa** (1912-1985). The sculptor **Rómulo Rozo** (1899-1964) was also influenced by the rhetoric of the Mexican muralists, as well as by forms of Aztec and Mayan sculpture, and strove to achieve a comparable combination of simplicity and monumentality.

Only in the 1950s did Abstraction have any impact in Colombia. Born in Munich, **Guillermo Wiedemann** (1905-1969) arrived from Germany in 1939 and after a spell painting tropical landscapes began to experiment with an expressionist form of abstraction, full of light, space and colour. **Eduardo Ramírez Villamizar** (1922-2004) also began painting in a figurative mode but moved into abstraction in the 1950s and subsequently into sculpture, to create, alongside his contemporary **Édgar Negret** (born 1920), some of the most interesting Constructivist work in Latin America. Both work in metal and have produced large, often brightly painted pieces for public spaces. Another important artist of this generation was Barcelona-born **Alejandro Obregón** (1920-1992), who avoided pure abstraction, preferring instead to include colourful figurative references with nationalistic overtones: carnations, guitars, condors. The slightly younger and internationally famous **Fernando Botero** (born 1932) has also tended to favour national themes. Working both as a painter and a sculptor he takes figures from Colombian society – dictators, drug barons, smug priests, autocratic matrons, prostitutes, spoilt children – and inflates them to ludicrous proportions. His gigantic bronze figures and the angular, two-dimensional sheets of metal of Negret and Ramírez Villamizar represent the two poles of 20th-century artistic expression.

For the subsequent generation of artists Colombia's turbulent political history remains a recurrent preoccupation. **Luis Caballero** (1943-1995) was a masterful draughtsman who expressed his sympathy for the victims of officially sanctioned violence by the tender attention he devotes to their tortured, naked bodies. **Beatriz González** (born 1938) uses a pop idiom to present military and political leaders as big and bold but essentially empty. **Juan Camillo Uribe** (born 1945) manipulates the paraphernalia of popular religion – prayer cards, plastic angels, metallic trinkets – to construct wittily disturbing collages. Younger artists are exploring the tensions between the national and international demands of art, and are experimenting with a tremendous diversity of styles and media. There is certainly no shortage of talent. Many cities in Colombia now boast a lively art scene with regular public exhibitions of contemporary art and a good range of commercial galleries.

**Rodrigo Arenas Betancur** (1919-1995) followed in Rozo's footsteps (see above) to become Colombia's best known sculptor of nationalistic public monuments. His gigantic and often rather melodramatic bronzes can be found in towns and cities throughout the country, as, for example his heroically naked *Bolívar* in Pereira, *Monumento a la Vida* in the Centro Suramericano in Medellín and the complex *Lanceros del Pantano de Vargas* near Paipa which must have been quite a challenge to the foundrymen. His sculptures are eminently worth seeking out.

## Literature

The indigenous Colombian written language was discovered to be at its earliest stages at the time of the Spanish conquest in the 16th century. Consequently there are practically no records of pre-conquest literature. The poetic tradition was oral; one of the few transcribed examples of spoken poetry is 'El Yurupay', an oral epic gathered from *indígena* in the Vaupés region in the 16th century, though not published until 1890.

The literature produced during the colonial period (1500-1816) was mainly by an ecclesiastical elite, written for the benefit of an upper-class minority. The predominant themes were the conquest itself, Catholicism and observations of the New World. The two major writers of this period had themselves been renowned conquistadors. **Gonzalo Jiménez de Quesada** (1495-1579), the founder of Bogotá in 1538, wrote *Antijovio* in 1567. The main purpose of this book was to defend Spain's reputation against accusations made by the Italian Paolo Giovio in his *Historiarum sui temporis libri XLV* (1552). Quesada sought to put the record straight on matters concerning the behaviour of his nation during the conquest of the New World.

**Juan de Castellanos** (c 1522-1607) wrote a lengthy chronicle of the conquest called *Elegías de varones ilustres de Indias* (*Elegy of Illustrious Men of the Indies*, 1589). It was written in the Italian verse style popular at the time, and has been called one of the longest poems ever written, 113,609 verses. The most important piece of narrative prose written during this period was *El carnero* (*The Butcher*, 1638) by **Juan Rodríguez Freyle** (1566-1640). This is a picaresque account of a year in the life of Santa Fe de Bogotá, using a blend of historical fact and scandalous invention to create a deliciously amoral book for its time. Mystic writing was also popular during the middle years of the conquest. **Sor Francisca Josefa de Castillo y Guevara** (1671-1742) was a nun who wrote baroque poetry, but was best known for her intimate spiritual diary *Afectos espirituales* (date unknown). Another Baroque poet of renown was **Hernando Domínguez Camargo** (1606-1659), who chronicled the life of Saint Ignatius in his epic *Poema heróica de San Ignacio de Loyola* (*Heroic Poem of St Ignatius of Loyola*, 1666).

The first major Colombian writer after the declaration of Independence in 1824 was **Juan José Nieto** (1805-1866). His *Ingermina, o la hija de Calamar* (*Ingermina, or the Child of Calamar*, 1844) is a historical novel about the conquest of the Calamar Indians in the 16th century. The mid-19th century saw the publication in Bogotá of *El Mosaico*, a review centred around a literary group of the same name, founded by **José María Vergara y Vergara** (1831-1872). The prevailing style in the capital was *costumbrismo*, the depiction of local life and customs in realistic detail. Major *costumbrista* novels were *Manuela* (1858) by **Eugenio Díaz** (1803-1865) and *María* (1867), by **Jorge Isaacs** (1837-1895). Romantic poetry also defined the early years of Independence, reflecting the strong influence Europe still had over Colombia. One of the exceptions was a poet from Mompós, **Candelario Obeso** (1849-1884), the first Colombian poet to use Afro-American colloquialisms in poetry. His *Cantos populares de mi tierrra* (*Popular Songs of my Land*, 1877) marked a progressive shift from the Romantic style, into a poetic language which reflected the true variety of Colombia's indigenous population.

An important region in the development of Colombian literature was Antioquia, the main city of which is Medellín. This region spawned the first crop of writers who were not of the upper-class elite which had dominated Colombian letters until the late 19th century. **Tomás Carrasquilla** (1858-1940) produced three major novels which reflected his humble middle-class background, and used a casual, spoken style to portray local customs and speech, and above all a love of the land. Another Antioquian of renown was **Samuel Velásquez** (1865-1941), whose novel *Madre* (*Mother*, 1897) gives a strong sense of the simple life of the countryside coupled with the religious passion of its inhabitants.

The beginning of the avant-garde in Colombia is marked by the publication of *Tergiversaciones* (*Distortions*) in 1925 by **León de Greiff** (1895-1976), in which he experimented with new techniques to create a completely original poetic idiom. Another important Modernist poet was **Porfirio Barba-Jacob** (the pseudonym of Miguel Angel Osorio, 1883-l942), who was influenced by the French Parnassian poets and published melancholic verse, typified by *Rosas negras* (*Black Roses*, 1935).

Other novelists of the same era were pursuing a much more social realist style than their avant-garde counterparts. *La voragine* (*The Vortex*, 1924) by **José Eustasio Rivera** (1888-1928) deals with the narrator's own struggle for literary expression against a backdrop of the Amazonian rubber workers' struggle for survival. **César**

Uribe Piedrahita (1897-1951) also chronicled the plight of rubber workers, and in *Mancha de aceite* (*Oil Stain*, 1935) he looks at the effects of the oil industry on the land and people of his country. The problems facing indigenous people began to get more attention from socially aware writers and **Bernardo Arías Trujillo** (1903-1939) examined the lives of Afro-Americans in Colombia in *Risaralda*.

The late 1940s to the mid-1960s in Colombian society were dominated by La Violencia (see History, page 392). Literary output during this intensely violent period reflected the political concerns which had led to the violence; among the novels to stand out from the many personal tales of anger and disbelief was *El jardín de las Hartmann* (*The Garden of the Hartmanns*, 1978) by **Jorge Eliécer Prado** (born 1945), which charts the history of La Violencia in Tolima, one of the most severely affected regions. What makes this book readable is the lack of historical facts and figures, typical of books set during La Violencia, and a more generalized view of the troubles.

Two important poetry movements to come out of La Violencia were the 'Mito' group and the 'Nadaistas'. *Mito* was a poetry magazine founded in 1955 by **Jorge Gaitán Durán** (1924-1962). It included **Eduardo Cote Lemus** (1928-1964), **Carlos Obregón** (1929-1965) and **Dora Castellanos** (born 1924). Their influences were contemporary French writers such as Genet and Sartre, and the Argentinean José Luis Borges. *Mito* came out during the dictatorship of Rojas Pinilla, and was one of the few outlets for free literary expression in the country. The Nadaista group was concerned with changing the elitist role of literature in the face of the violent conflict which affected everyone, and they felt should be addressed directly; they used avant-garde styles and techniques to achieve this.

By far the biggest influence on Colombian fiction was the publication, in 1967, of *Cien años de soledad* (*A Hundred Years of Solitude*) by **Gabriel García Márquez** (1927-2014). He had published many short stories and novels in the 1950s and early 1960s. Among the most significant were *La hojarasca* (*Leaf Storm* in 1955) and *El coronel no tiene quien le escriba* (*No one Writes to the Colonel*, 1958), a portrayal of a colonel and his wife struggling to cope with the tropical heat, political oppression and economic deprivation in their final years. But it was with *Cien años de soledad* that he became recognized as the major exponent of a new style generic to Latin American writers. Events were chronicled in a deadpan style; historical facts were blended with pure fantasy, the latter written matter-of-factly as if it were the truth; characters were vividly portrayed through their actions and brief dialogues rather than internal monologues. The style came to be known as Magical Realism in English, a translation of the Spanish 'Lo real maravilloso'. In 1975 Márquez published *El otoño del patriarca* (*The Autumn of the Patriarch*), which was a return to a favourite theme of his, the loneliness that power can bring. *Crónica de una muerte anunciada* (*Chronicle of a Death Foretold*, 1981) was set in an unnamed coastal city, but no doubt not far from Márquez's birthplace of Aracataca. It captures the docility and traditional stubbornness of the people of Colombia's Caribbean seaboard, an area in which Márquez had worked as a journalist in the 1950s. *El amor en los tiempos de cólera* (*Love in the Time of Cholera*, 1985) is set at the turn of the century, and depicts the affair between a couple of septuagenarians against the backdrop of another fictional city; Márquez skillfully blends Cartagena, Barranquilla and Santa Marta into one coastal town. Márquez published 23 works in total, as well as articles, essays and an autobiography.

Other important writers in the 1970s and 1980s include **Fanny Buitrago** (born 1945) and **Manuel Zapata Olivella** (1920-2004). In novels such as *Los Pañamanes* (1979) and *Los amores de Afrodita* (*The Loves of Aphrodite*, 1983), Buitrago contrasts the legends and culture of the Caribbean coast with the needs of young people to move on, at the risk of being swallowed up by modern North American culture. Zapata Olivella has published a monumental novel, *El fusilamiento del diablo* (*The Shooting of the Devil*, 1986) covering the six centuries of African and Afro-American history.

Colombian post-modern literature has followed European theoretical trends, with many of Colombia's more avant-garde writers living and working in Europe. While retaining the Magical Realist tradition of dispensing with a subjective, authoritative narrator, the post-modernists have greatly distanced themselves from the Colombian tradition of orally based, colloquial storytelling. Despite these developments it is García Márquez who continues to dominate the public imagination. By borrowing from Colombian traditions with a modernist approach, he created a style that made him an internationally renowned literary figure and a national icon in both life and death.

## Music and dance

No South American country has a greater variety of music than Colombia, strategically placed where the Andes meet the Caribbean. The four major musical areas are: the mountain heartland; the Pacific coast; the Caribbean coast; and the Llanos or eastern plains.

### Mountain heartland

The heartland covers the Andean highlands and intervening valleys of the Cauca and Magdalena rivers and includes the country's three largest cities, Bogotá, Medellín and Cali. The music here is relatively gentle and sentimental, accompanied largely by string instruments, with an occasional flute and a *chucho* or *carángano* shaker to create the rhythm. The preferred instrument of the highlands and by extension Colombia's national instrument, is the *tiple*, a small 12-stringed guitar, most of which are manufactured at Chiquinquirá in Boyacá. The national dance is the **bambuco**, whose lilting sounds are said to have inspired Colombian troops at the Battle of Ayacucho in 1824. This dance can be found throughout the country's heartland and has long transcended its folk origins. The choreography is complex, including many movements, such as Los Ochos, La Invitación, Los Codos, Los Coqueteos, La Perseguida and La Arrodilla. Other related dances are the **torbellino**, where the woman whirls like a top, the more stately Guabina, the Pasillo, Bunde, Sanjuanero and the picaresque **rajaleña**. Particularly celebrated melodies are the *Guabina Chiquinquireña* and the *Bunde Tolimense*. The following fiestas, among others, provide a good opportunity to experience the music and dancing: **La Fiesta del Campesino**, ubiquitous on the first Sunday in June, the **Fiesta del Bambuco** in Neiva and **Festival Folclórico Colombiano** in Ibagué later in the month, the **Fiesta Nacional de la Guabina y el Tiple**, held in Vélez in early August, the **Desfile de Silleteros** in Medellín in the same month and **Las Fiestas de Pubenza** in Popayán just after the New Year, where the Conjuntos de Chirimía process through the streets.

## Pacific coast

On Colombia's tropical Pacific coast (and extending down into Esmeraldas in Ecuador) is to be found some of the most African sounding black music in all South America. The **currulao** and its variants, the **berejú** and **patacoré**, are extremely energetic recreational dances and the vocals are typically African-style call-and-response. This is the home of the *marimba* and the music is very percussion driven, including the upright *cununo* drum plus *bombos* and *redoblantes*. Wakes are important in this region and at these the **bundes**, **arrullos** and **alabaos** are sung. Best known is the 'Bunde de San Antonio'. The **jota chocoana** is a fine example of a Spanish dance taken by black people and turned into a satirical weapon against their masters. The regional fiestas are the **Festival Folclórico del Litoral** at Buenaventura in July and **San Francisco de Asís** at Quibdó on 4 August. Quibdó also features a **Fiesta de los Indios** at Easter.

## Caribbean coast

The music of Colombia's Caribbean lowlands became popular for dancing throughout Latin America more than 30 years ago under the name of **Música Tropical** and has much more recently become an integral part of the Salsa repertoire. It can be very roughly divided into cumbia and vallenato. The **cumbia** is a heavily black influenced dance form for several couples, the men forming an outer circle and the women an inner. The men hold aloft a bottle of rum and the women a bundle of slim candles called *espermas*. The dance probably originated in what is now Panama, moved east into Cartagena, where it is now centred and quite recently further east to Barranquilla and Santa Marta. The most celebrated cumbias are those of Ciénaga, Mompós, Sampués, San Jacinto and Sincelejo. The instrumental accompaniment consists of *gaitas* or *flautas de caña de millo*, backed by drums. The *gaitas* ('male' and 'female') are vertical cactus flutes with beeswax heads, while the *cañas de millo* are smaller transverse flutes. The most famous conjuntos are the Gaiteros de San Jacinto, the Cumbia Soledeña and the Indios Selectos. Variants of the cumbia are the **porro**, **gaita**, **puya**, **bullerengue** and **mapalé**, these last two being much faster and more energetic. Lately cumbia has also become very much part of the vallenato repertoire and is therefore often played on the accordion. Cumbia has been superseded by vallenato in Colombia and today is probably heard more outside the country than in it, with Colombian migrants taking it with them to cities like Buenos Aires, Mexico City, Los Angeles – even London. While it has travelled, it has picked up influences to create new sub-genres such as **techno-cumbia** and **cumbia villera**, both popular in Peru and Argentina. **Vallenato** music comes from Valledupar in the department of César and is of relatively recent origin. It is built around one instrument, the accordion, albeit backed by *guacharaca* rasps and *caja* drums. The most popular rhythms are the paseo and the merengue, the latter having arrived from the Dominican Republic, where it is the national dance. Perhaps the first virtuoso accordionist was the legendary 'Francisco El Hombre', playing around the turn of the century. Today's best known vallenato names are those of Rafael Escalona (1927-2009), Alejandro Durán (1919-1989), Los Gigantes del Vallento and Calixto Ochoa. In April the **Festival de la Leyenda Vallenata** is held in Valledupar and attended by thousands.

Barranquilla is the scene of South America's second most celebrated **carnival**, after that of Rio de Janeiro, with innumerable traditional masked groups, such as the *congos*, *toros*, *diablos* and *caimanes*. The **garabato** is a dance in which death is defeated. Barranquilla's carnival is less commercialized and more traditional than that of Rio and should be a 'must' for anyone with the opportunity to attend. Other important festivals in the region are the **Corralejas de Sincelejo** with its bullfights in January, **La Candelaria** (Candlemas) in Cartagena on 2 February, the **Festival de la Cumbia** in El Banco in June, **Fiesta del Caimán Cienaguero** in Ciénaga in January and **Festival del Porro** in San Pelayo (Córdoba). To complete the music of the Caribbean region, the Colombian islands of San Andrés and Providencia, off the coast of Nicaragua, have a fascinating mix of mainland Colombian and Jamaican island music, with the calypso naturally a prominent feature. More recently two other genres have gained increasing popularity. **Champeta** originates in Cartagena and has roots in soukous, compas and reggae. It is characterized by very provocative dancing. **Reggaeton** has become a phenomenon throughout Latin America. Believed to have originated in Panama, it blends a merengue beat with rapping and influences from reggae and ragga.

## Llanos

The fourth musical region is that of the great eastern plains, the so-called Llanos Orientales between the Ríos Arauca and Guaviare, a region where there is really no musical frontier between the two republics of Colombia and Venezuela. Here the **Joropo** reigns supreme as a dance, with its close relatives the **galerón**, the slower and more romantic **pasaje** and the breathlessly fast **corrido** and **zumba que zumba**. These are dances for couples, with a lot of heel tapping, the arms hanging down loosely to the sides. Arnulfo Briceño (1938-1989) and Pentagrama Llanera are the big names and the harp is the only instrument that matters, although normally backed by *cuatro*, guitar, *tiple* and *maracas*. Where to see and hear it all is at the **Torneo Internacional del Joropo** at Villavicencio in December.

# Land &
# environment

## Geology and landscape

Colombia is the fourth largest in size of the 10 principal countries of South America, slightly smaller than Peru and slightly larger than Bolivia at 1,142,000 sq km. In terms of Europe, that is the size of France and Spain combined. The latest estimate of population is 44.6 million, marginally more than Argentina and second only to Brazil in the continent. The people are concentrated in the western third of the country: nevertheless the population density of 39.3 per sq km is only greater in Ecuador within South America. To the east, it is bounded by Venezuela and Brazil, to the south, by Peru and Ecuador and in the northwest by Panama. It is the only South American country with a coastline on the Pacific (1306 km) and the Caribbean (1600 km), with two small offshore islands in the Pacific. In the Caribbean, there are various coastal islands including the Rosario and San Bernardo groups and the more substantial San Andrés/Providencia archipelago off the coast of Nicaragua, plus several cays towards Jamaica.

Its greatest width east-west is 1200 km and it stretches 1800 km north-south, from 12°N to 4°S of the equator, with virtually all of one of its departments, Amazonas, south of the equator. The borders of Colombia have been stable since 1903 when Panama seceded, though Nicaragua occasionally revives a claim for the San Andrés group of islands and there are three minute uninhabited reefs claimed by Colombia and by the USA: Quita Sueño Bank, Roncador Cay and Serrana Bank.

### Structure

As with other countries on the west side of the continent, Colombia is on the line of collision between the west moving South American Plate, and the Nasca Plate, moving east and sinking beneath it thus creating the Andes. Almost 55% of the country to the east is alluvial plains on top of ancient rocks of the Guiana Shield dating from the Pre-Cambrian era over 500 million years ago. This was at one time part of the landmass called 'Pangea' which geologists believe broke up between 150 and 125 million years ago and the Americas floated away from what became Africa and Europe. It is presumed that prior to this, what is now the Caribbean Sea was an extension of the Mediterranean Sea and in the course of time this expanded to separate the two halves of the Americas. During the Cretaceous period, around 100 million years ago, the Atlantic was undoubtedly connected to the Pacific Ocean, at least from time to time, but by the end of the Cretaceous, the Tertiary mountain building had begun and the emergence of Central America and eventually the Isthmus of Panama, sealed off the connection.

All the rest of Colombia to the west, apart from the islands, is the product of the Andean mountain building activity, which continues today. This began earlier in the Jurassic and Cretaceous eras with intense volcanic activity, but the maximum was in the late Tertiary (around 25 million years ago). Large areas of molten material were formed beneath the surface and were pushed up to form the large high plateaux with peaks formed from later volcanic activity. Some areas were folded and contorted and the original rocks metamorphosed to lose their former identity. In general, it is the mountain ranges to the west that were most affected in this way. Continuous weathering, especially during the ice ages of which the most recent was in the Pleistocene up to 10,000 years ago, has been responsible for deep deposits in the valleys and the plains of north Colombia and in the inland slopes of the Andes towards the Orinoco and Amazon.

Other than the coral islands just off the north coast, the Colombian islands of the Caribbean are all on a submarine ridge, which extends from Honduras and Nicaragua to Haiti, known as the Jamaica Ridge, which separates the Cayman Trench from the Colombia Basin, two of the deepest areas of the Caribbean Sea. Providencia is probably volcanic in origin but San Andrés has a less certain past, perhaps being an undersea mount which has been colonized by coral for millions of years, evidenced by the white sands and the limestone features. Little is known about the other reefs, banks and cays that belong to Colombia. The two Colombian island groups in the Pacific are quite different. Isla Gorgona is one of the few islands off the South American Pacific coast which is on the continental shelf and no more than 30 km from the mainland. There is evidence of past volcanic activity on the island and it may represent a point on an otherwise submerged ridge parallel to the coast. By contrast, the Isla de Malpelo is on one of the structural lines of the east Pacific which runs due south from west Panama along the line of longitude 81°W which peters out off the coast of Ecuador. There is a deep trench between this line and the coast with depths down to 5000 m and clear signs of tectonic activity along the ridge including Malpelo which is the top of a volcanic structure. Further to the west there is another ridge running south from Central America, the Cocos Ridge, which leads to the Galápagos Islands.

## Andes

To the south of Colombia, the Andes of Ecuador are a single high range with volcanic peaks up to nearly 5000 m, but north of the border they quickly split into three distinct cordilleras named Occidental, Central and Oriental. The first two are close together for 400 km but separated by a fault line occupied by the Río Patía in the south and the Cauca in the north. The Cordillera Oriental gradually pulls eastwards creating a valley basin for Colombia's most important river, the Magdalena. This range crosses the northeast border into Venezuela and continues as the Cordillera de Mérida. A subsidiary range, called the Sierra de Perijá, continues north within Colombia to reach the Caribbean at Punta Gallinas on the Península de Guajira, the northernmost point of the South American mainland. Near this point is the Santa Marta massif, one of the biggest volcanic structures in the world with the highest mountain peak in Colombia at 5775 m.

All three of the cordilleras have peaks, mostly volcanic, over 4000 m, the Central and Oriental over 5000 m, with permanent snow on the highest. Many are active and have caused great destruction in the past, both with gas and ash explosions and by creating ice and mud slides. The whole of the western half of the country is subject to earthquakes, demonstrating the unstable nature of the underlying geology, and the significant situation of the country at the point where the Andes make a dramatic turn to the east. Also, in the northwest, another range to the west of the Cordillera Occidental appears, the Serranía de Baudó, which becomes the spine of the Darién isthmus of Panama, eventually continuing westwards. Thus north Colombia is at the tectonic crossroads of the Americas.

## Valleys

A glance at the map of Colombia will show the physical dominance of the cordilleras and the human dependence on the valleys between them. The fact that they run more or less north-south was a great advantage to the earlier explorers interested in finding gold and silver and the later settlers looking for good arable land. Even the earliest inhabitants were interested in the protection that the rugged land offered them but also in ways to migrate further south. As a consequence, the eastern half of the country has, until very recently, been ignored and still remains largely unexplored.

The valleys are structural basins between the cordilleras and not simply products of river erosion. In some places they are many kilometres broad, as for example between Cali and Popayán, yet the Patía and Cauca rivers flow in opposite directions. Elsewhere, the rivers go through narrow passages, eg near Honda on the Magdalena where rapids interrupt river navigation. However, the basins have been filled many metres thick with volcanic ash and dust which has produced very fertile terrain. This, together with the height above sea level has made for an agreeable environment and one of the most productive zones of the tropics worldwide.

By contrast, the cordilleras create formidable obstacles to lateral movements. The main routes from Bogotá to Cali and Manizales must cross the Cordillera Central by passes at 3250 m and 3700 m respectively, and virtually all the passes over the Cordillera Oriental exceed 3000 m. Many of the volcanic peaks in these ranges are over 5000 m and are capped with snow, hence the name *nevados*. Such is the nature of the terrain that no railway was ever built to cross the cordilleras, except from Cali to Buenaventura.

The rivers themselves do not provide the most attractive human corridors as can be seen by the frequent diversions from the rivers by the main trunk roads. Fortunately, the surrounding countryside is frequently dominated by plateaux. These make good level sites for towns and cities (Bogotá itself is the best example). They also give long stretches of easy surface travel but are interrupted by spectacular descents and climbs where there are natural rifts or subsidiary river gorges. This makes for dramatic, but time-consuming scenic trips by road throughout this area of Colombia.

## Caribbean lowlands

From the Sierra de Perijá and the Sierra Nevada de Santa Marta westwards are the great plains of the lower Magdalena, which collects most of the water flowing north in Colombia to the Caribbean. The Cordilleras Central and Occidental finish at about 4°N, 350 km from the mouth of the river at Barranquilla. About 200 km from the sea, both the Magdalena and the Cauca flow into an area of swamps and lagoons which becomes a vast lake when water levels are high. This lowland is the result of the huge quantities of alluvium that has been brought down over the years from the mountains in the south of Colombia. While not comparable in length with the major rivers of the world, the average discharge at the mouth of the Magdalena is 7500 cu m per second similar to that of the Danube or about one third of that of the Orinoco. To the north, the land slopes gently to the sandy beaches of the Caribbean and a string of inshore islands of considerable touristic appeal.

Beyond Barranquilla to the east, a sandbar encloses a salt lake that was formerly part of the Magdalena delta, now abandoned by the river which flows to the sea further west. On the far side of the lake, the Santa Marta massif comes down to the sea creating an interesting stretch of rocky bays and headlands. Further east again, the flatter land returns extending finally to the low hills of the Guajira peninsula at the northernmost tip of the continent. This is a sandy, arid region, and the modest northern end of the Cordillera Oriental.

At the west end of this section is the Gulf of Urabá and the border with Panama. The Río Atrato, which drains most of the area between the Cordillera Oriental and the Serranía de Baudó, reaches the sea here via another large swampy area where no land transport is possible. It is probable that this was formerly linked to the Gulf of Urabá which is itself now being filled up with material brought down by the Atrato and many other small streams. This was also probably an area where, in a much more distant past, the Atlantic was joined to the Pacific, a point not lost on the Colombians who periodically quote this as the site of a future rival to the Panama Canal. There is little seismic activity in this region though there are occasional earthquakes and the mud lakes near Arboletes, Galerazamba and elsewhere near the coast are volcanic in origin.

## Pacific coast

The Serranía de Baudó runs from Panama south to 4°N just north of Buenaventura. The basin between it and the Cordillera Occidental is drained by the Río Atrato to the north and the San Juan to the south with another river, the Baudó assisting the centre. This is an area of very high rainfall and access by any means is difficult. This coastline is very different from the north coast. Most of it is heavily forested but with very attractive small beaches interspersed with rocky stretches and affected with a wide tidal range, absent from the Caribbean. It has only recently been 'discovered' by the tourist industry and remains quiet owing to the difficulties and cost of getting there.

South of Buenaventura, there is another 300 km of coastline to Ecuador, but reasonable access is only possible at Buenaventura, and Tumaco in the extreme south. Rainfall here is still copious with many short rivers coming down from the

Cordillera Occidental and creating alluvial plains along the coast typically with mangrove swamps, which continue into Ecuador. This part of the Colombian coast is also remote and unspoilt with a few fishing communities though tourism is beginning to take hold at the end of the two access roads. Further inland there are a few mineral deposits and gold mines which have attracted interest. There is no range of Tertiary hills here between the Andes and the coastline as in Ecuador.

## Eastern plains

This section, representing more than half of Colombia, is divided into two parts. In the north are the grasslands known as *los llanos*, which stretch from the Cordillera Oriental across into Venezuela and on to the mouth of the Orinoco. Around 40% of the *llanos*, which means 'plains', are in Colombia. They are noted in both countries for the quality of the land for cattle raising which has been going on since the 16th century and are second only to the *Pampas* in Argentina for ranching in South America. Several important rivers, eg the Meta, flow from the mountains through this region to the Orinoco and act as transport routes. Slowly roads are being made into the interior but all-weather surfaces are virtually non-existent and land transport in the wet season is impossible. All important towns and villages and many fincas have their own airstrips. In the extreme north of the area, near the border with Venezuela, oil was found some years ago and new finds are still being made.

The southern part of the section is tropical forest associated with the Amazon Basin. As far as the vegetation is concerned, the transition is, of course, gradual. However, the Río Guaviare is the southernmost tributary of the Orinoco and, with headwaters (here called the Guayabero) rising near Neiva in the Cordillera Oriental, has its source some 350 km further from the sea than those of the official source of the Orinoco in the Sierra Parima on the Brazil/Venezuela border. Two important rivers join to form the Guaviare near the town of San José, the Guayabero and the Ariari. Between them is an extraordinary geological anomaly, the Serranía de Macarena. It is a huge dissected block of crystalline rocks partly covered with stratified later formations, 140 km long and 30 km wide, that stands isolated 2000 m above the surrounding undulating forest and has been identified as a chunk of the Guiana Shield, the rest of which is hundreds of kilometres to the east, forming the border area between The Guianas, Venezuela and Brazil. Although there are some other low formations in this area of the country which are founded on the ancient basalt rocks, as a remnant of 'Pangea', Macarena displays by far the oldest exposed rocks of Colombia.

South of the Guaviare Basin, all the waters of the region flow into the Amazon system. However, in the extreme east of the country, the Río Guainía drains the south part of the department of the same name which connects with another geographical curiosity, discovered by the great explorer Alexander von Humboldt. Some 250 km before joining the Guaviare, the Orinoco divides, with part of its flow going southwest as the 'Brazo Casiquiare', which eventually joins the Guianía to form the Negro and thence the Amazon. Other Colombian rivers feed the Negro, in particular the Vaupés, the longest tributary. Colombia therefore has the distinction of providing the true sources of the Orinoco and the Negro.

In the southern area, the climate becomes progressively wetter. Thick jungle covers much of it, though Colombia is no exception to the gradual destruction of the environment. The rivers Caquetá and Putumayo are important water routes to the Amazon proper but there is virtually no tourist traffic.

In the extreme south of Colombia is Leticia, on the Amazon itself, a reminder of the original drawing of the maps which allowed all the western countries of South America except Chile to have access to the river and an exit to the South Atlantic.

## Climate

Temperatures in Colombia are mainly affected by altitude and distance from the north and west coasts. The highest average temperatures in South America are in the Maracaibo lowlands of which Colombia has the southwest corner and the northwest extension into the Guajira Peninsula. Average annual temperatures in the Caribbean Lowlands are typically in excess of 25°C, modified downwards on the coast, yet, within sight of the coast are the permanent snows of Sierra Nevada de Santa Marta due to its altitude of over 5500 m. The temperature becomes oppressive where there is also high humidity.

Rainfall depends on the migrating northwest and southeast trade wind systems, the effect of the Andes acting as a weather barrier and also on local situations along the coasts. There is high rainfall in the southeast where the southeast trade winds bring moisture all year into the Amazon Basin that is continually recycled to produce heavy daily precipitation all along the east edge of the Andes. This however tails off northwards into the *llanos* especially November to March when the wind systems move south and the southeast Trades are replaced by the northeast system. This is less effective in bringing moisture into the area because of the protection of the Venezuelan Andes. The rainfall in the lower reaches of the Magdalena Basin is also high, aided by the large swampy area which keeps the air saturated. The highest rainfall in the country is in the northwest near the border with Panama, brought about by the convergence of the trade wind systems interacting with warm, saturated air coming in from the Pacific. Here it rains daily most of the year with some respite from January to March but with a total on average of 10,000 mm. This is one of the highest in the world. This heavy rain belt extends down the coast tailing off as Ecuador is approached. Unlike further south, the ocean here is warm and air over it readily condenses when it moves on to the land. However, this is a generalized pattern only.

Aberrations in the weather systems between November and March, when less rain normally falls, now labelled the *El Niño* phenomenon, also affect the western part of Colombia at least as far east as Bogotá. Large parts of the country, particularly the Caribbean coast and la Zona Cafetera, suffered from unusually heavy and prolonged rains in the autumn and winter of 2010, leading to extensive flooding, mud- and landslides.

Inland local features often determine the level of precipitation. To the east of Nevado de Huila (5750 m), for example, there is a small area of near desert caused by the effect of rain shadow. Near desert conditions also can be found on the tip of the continent, between Riohacha and Punta Gallinas which is probably caused by descending air collecting rather than expelling moisture. Although there are occasional storms here (Colombia was marginally affected by the heavy rains that brought disaster to the Venezuelan coast in 1999), the normal Caribbean hurricane track fortunately passes well to the north of the Colombian coast.

## Wildlife and vegetation

This neotropical zone is a land of superlatives. It contains the most extensive tropical rainforest in the world; the Amazon has by far the largest volume of any of the world's rivers and the Andes are the longest uninterrupted mountain chain. The fauna and flora are to a large extent determined by the influence of those mountains and the great rivers, particularly the Amazon and the Orinoco. There are also huge expanses of open terrain, tree-covered savannahs and arid regions. It is this immense range of habitats which makes Colombia one of the world's regions of high biodiversity.

This diversity arises not only from the wide range of habitats available, but also from the history of the continent. South America has essentially been an island for much of its geological past, joined only by a narrow isthmus to Central and North America at various times between 50 million and 25 million years ago. The present connection has been stable only for a few million years. Land passage played a significant role in the gradual colonization of South America by both flora and fauna from the north. When the land-link was broken these colonists evolved into a wide variety of forms free from the competitive pressures that prevailed elsewhere. When the land-bridge was re-established a new invasion of species took place from North America, adding to the diversity but also leading to numerous extinctions. Comparative stability has now ensued and guaranteed the survival of many primitive groups like the opossums.

There are three cordilleras of the Andes dominating the western part of Colombia. The rivers draining the area are referred to as white water (although more frequently brown because they contain a lot of sediment). This is in contrast to the rivers that drain the Guiana shield in neighbouring Venezuela, which are referred to as black or clear waters. The forests of the latter are of considerably lower productivity than those of the Andean countries.

### Llanos

Northeast of the Andes and extending almost to the Caribbean coast, the lowland habitat characterized by open grasslands and small islands of trees is called the *llanos*. Poor drainage leads to the alternation between standing water and extreme desiccation, leading to large areas being devoid of trees except for some species of palm. Fire has also been responsible for maintaining this habitat type. Above 100 m this gives way to predominantly dry forest with seasonal rainfall and a pronounced drought. Gallery forest persists only in the regions surrounding rivers and streams. In contrast, arid conditions are also found in the vicinity of the northern Caribbean coast.

## ON THE ROAD

## Floral Colombia

An overabundance of floral species has helped make Colombia the world's second largest exporter of flowers, with over US$1 billion in sales annually. You name it, Colombia has it, everything from garden-variety roses and carnations to more exotic species like the bird of paradise and the heliconia. However, this country's undisputed crown jewel is the orchid. Over 3000 species of orchid are known to exist in Colombia, including the national flower, the majestic *Flor de Mayo*. A passion for these flowers led botanist Tom Hart Dyke into the treacherous Darién Gap in 2000, a harrowing journey, including kidnap by guerrillas, that he recounts in his bestselling book, *The Cloud Garden*. For those who do not wish to risk life and limb to experience the best of Colombia s flora, check out the José Celestino Mutis Botanical Gardens in Bogotá or the Joaquín Antonio Uribe Botanical Gardens in Medellín. The latter is particularly spectacular and contains a newly built orquideorama that is not to be missed by orchid lovers. If you are lucky enough to be in Medellín during August, be sure to check out the flower festival that the city hosts every year.

## Pacific West

The wet forests of the Pacific slopes of the western Andes provide an interesting contrast with the Amazon region by virtue of their high degree of endemism – species unique to an area. The region is often referred to as the Chocó and extends from the Darién Gap in Panama to northern Ecuador. The natural vegetation is tropical wet forest. Clouds that hang over the forest provide condensation, and this almost constant drenching by mist, fog and rain leads to a profusion of plants with intense competition for space, such that the trees and shrubs are all covered with a great variety of epiphytes – orchids, mosses, lichens and bromeliads. The area has been referred to by birders as the 'tanager coast', owing to the large mixed flocks of these colourful birds. There are many other species of endemic birds here apart from the tanagers. At La Planada, between Pasto and Tumaco, there is one of the highest concentrations of native birds in the continent and the forest reserve contains an immense diversity of orchids.

Overall, the fauna shows some interesting biogeographic patterns. Some species found here are those more common to Central and North America than to South America. The westernmost range defines a coastal strip with a fauna similar to Panama. Meanwhile, to the southeast, the fauna south of the river Guaviare is more typical of the upper Amazon Basin of Brazil and Peru.

## High Andes

From about 3600 m to 4400 m, the high Andes are covered by *páramo* typified by the grass (*Stipa-ichu*) or *pajonal* which grows here. *Páramo* is a distinct type of high-altitude moorland vegetation comprised of tall grasses and *frailejones (Espeletia)* a member of the Compositae family, which are only found in the Colombian cordilleras and the Sierra Nevada de Mérida in Venezuela. These extraordinary plants that grow as high as 12 m, also frequently attract hummingbirds such as the black-tailed trainbearer and the great sapphirewing. Lakes and marshes are also a common feature since the ground is generally level. Interspersed among the grasses are clumps of club-moss and chuquiraguas. In the zone of the high *páramo* there are many lakes. Birds frequently seen in this area include the Andean teal, Andean coot and a variety of hummingbird species. **Andean condor** (*Vultur gryphus*) the largest land bird, weighing 12 kg and with a wingspan of 3 m, may be seen effortlessly gliding on the updraft from the warmer valleys below.

Some protection from the severe climate and the icy winds that can blast this harsh environment may be provided in the deeply incised gorges. Here there may be a lush growth of shrubs, orchids, reeds and dwarf trees providing a marked visual contrast to the superficially drier *páramo*. In the favourable sheltered micro-climatic conditions provided in the gaps between the tall clumps of grass, there nestle compact colonies of gentians, lupines and prostrate mosses. There is little evidence of mammal life here save for the occasional paw print of the Andean fox. **White-tailed deer**, once common has been over-hunted.

Under 3600 m, the condensation of the moisture-laden upwelling air from the warm humid jungles to the east creates cloudforest, with a similar wide variety of epiphytes as found near the west coast. Both giant and dwarf tree ferns are characteristic. These are highly resistant to fire, the traditional manner of maintaining grazing lands. Pollination is effected by a variety of agents. Fragrant odours and bright colours are used by some orchids to attract nectivorous birds, including some species of humming birds and insects. Others exude putrid smells to attract flies to carry out the same process. Tangled stands of bamboo intermingled with the *polylepis* forest are the dominant vegetation feature.

At high altitude *polylepis* forest clothes the deeply incised canyons and sides of the valleys. This is a tangled, lichen and fern be-decked world, dripping water from the moisture-laden air on to a mid-storey of tangled bamboo and lush tree ferns. A plentiful supply of bromeliads provide food for **spectacled bears**, now an endangered species. The steep slopes of the gullies are clothed in a dense blanket of giant cabbage-like paraguillas or umbrella plant. Tracks of mountain tapir are commonly found along river beaches, and the prints of the diminutive **pudu**, a small **Andean deer**, are also occasionally found. Mammals are rarely seen on the *páramo* during the day since most seek refuge in the fringing cloudforest, only venturing out on the open moors at night or under the protection of the swirling mists. But their presence is demonstrated by the tracks of **Andean fox** and marauding puma. Birds of the *páramo* include the mountain **caracara** and a variety of other raptors such as the **red-backed hawk**. Andean swifts, tapaculos, hummingbirds, finches and thrushes are common.

Masked **trogons** are also abundant in the *aliso* (birch) forests, evidence of recent colonization of areas devastated by the frequent landslides. Colourful tanagers and tiny hummingbirds are often encountered flitting between the myriad of flowers. At night the hills reverberate with the incessant croaks of frogs and toads.

## Eastern slopes of the Andes

The cloudforests of South America are found in a narrow strip that runs along the spine of the Andes from Colombia, through Ecuador and into Peru. On the western side of the Central Cordillera between 2000 m and 3000 m are the remaining stands of the **wax palm** (*Ceroxylon alpinum*), the tallest variety of palm tree that grows dramatically above the surrounding forest and often appears above the cloud blanket. On the eastern side of the Cordillera Oriental the dense,

# National parks & reserves

often impenetrable, forests clothing the steep slopes protect the headwaters of the streams and rivers that cascade from the Andes to form the mighty Amazon as it begins its slow 8000 km journey to the sea. A verdant kingdom of dripping epiphytic mosses, lichens, ferns and orchids grow in profusion despite the plummeting overnight temperatures. The high humidity resulting from the 2 m of rain that can fall in a year is responsible for the maintenance of the forest and it accumulates and leaks from the ground in a constant trickle that combines to form myriad icy, crystal-clear tumbling streams that cascade over precipitous waterfalls. In secluded areas flame-red Andean **cock-of-the-rock** give their spectacular display to females in the early morning mists. **Woolly monkeys** are also occasionally sighted as they descend the wooded slopes. Mixed flocks of colourful tanagers are commonly encountered, and the golden-headed **quetzal** and Amazon umbrella bird are occasionally seen.

At about 1500 m there is a gradual transition to the vast lowland forests of the Amazon Basin; surprisingly less jungle-like but warmer and more equable than the cloudforests clothing the mountains above. The daily temperature varies little during the year with a high of 23-32°C falling slightly to 20-26°C overnight. This lowland region also receives some 2 m of rainfall per year, most of it falling from November to April. The rest of the year is sufficiently dry, at least in the lowland areas, to inhibit the growth of epiphytes and orchids which are so characteristic of the highland areas. For a week or two in the rainy season the rivers flood the forest. The zone immediately surrounding this seasonally flooded forest is referred to as *terra firme* forest.

## Colombian Amazonas

The lowland Amazon region can be seen at its best as the river passes the Amacayacu National Park. Flood waters from the Peruvian catchment area inundate the forest for a short period starting in January in its upper reaches

200 km
200 miles

to create a unique habitat called *várzea*. *Várzea* is a highly productive seasonally inundated forest found along the banks of the whitewater rivers; it is very rich as a consequence of the huge amount of silt and nutrients washed out of the mountains and trapped by the massive buttress-rooted trees. One of the commonest trees of the *várzea*, the Pará rubber tree, is the source of latex. The Brazilian rubber industry foundered in the 19th century when seeds of this tree were illegally taken to Asia to form the basis of huge rubber plantations and flourished in the absence of pest species. In the still-flowing reaches of the *várzea*, permanently flooded areas are frequently found where vast carpets of floating water lilies, water lettuce and water hyacinth are home to the Amazonian manatee, a large herbivorous aquatic mammal which is the fresh-water relative of the dugong of the Caribbean. Vast numbers of spectacled caiman populate the lakes feeding on the highly productive fish community.

In the lowland forests, many of the trees are buttress rooted, with flanges extending 3-4 m up the trunk of the tree. Among the smaller trees stilt-like prop roots are also common. Frequently flowers are not well developed, and some emerge directly from the branches and even the trunk. This is possibly an adaptation for pollination by the profusion of bats, giving easier access than if they were obscured by leaves.

The vast river basin of the Amazon is home to an immense variety of species. The environment has largely dictated the lifestyle. Life in or around rivers, lakes, swamps and forest depend on the ability to swim and climb; amphibious and tree-dwelling animals are common. Once the entire Amazon Basin was a great inland sea and the river still contains mammals more typical of the coast, for example manatees and dolphins.

## National parks

Colombia established its first protected area in 1960 (Cueva de los Guácharos) and now has 57 reserves comprising National Nature Parks (PNN), Flora and Fauna Sanctuaries (SFF), National Nature Reserves, a Vía Parque, a Fauna Sanctuary and a Unique Natural Area (ANU), spread throughout the country and in virtually every department. They vary in size from the tiny island of Corota in the Laguna de la Cocha near the border with Ecuador to large areas of forest in the eastern lowlands. All the significant mountain areas are National Parks including the Sierra Nevada de Santa Marta, El Cocuy, El Nevado de Huila, Los Nevados (Tolima and Ruiz) and Puracé. There are 15 on or near the Caribbean and Pacific coasts including the off-shore islands.

All except the smallest parks normally have one or more centres staffed with rangers (*guardaparques*) who offer information and guidance for visitors. Most, however, are remote with difficult access and few facilities. Unlike some Latin American countries, many national parks in Colombia are virtually free of 'tourism' and are thus of particular interest to those looking for unspoilt natural surroundings.

For various reasons, unlike many countries where the main problem for national parks is visitor overcrowding, many of the parks in Colombia are difficult to visit.

Unfortunately, because of their remoteness, some have been sanctuary to guerrilla groups or drug traffickers, some are sensitive indigenous territories and many are of difficult access and have few or no facilities. Lovers of wilderness, however, will enjoy the richness of the natural attractions and the freedom from oppressive tourism.

Apart from the national parks, there are a considerable number of private nature reserves, some exclusively for research, others open to the general public. Many of these are worth visiting: details are given in the text.

# Practicalities
## Colombia

# **Getting** there

International flights arrive principally at Bogotá and Cartagena, but there are also direct flights to Medellín, Cali, Pereira, Barranquilla and San Andrés; information on all these airports is given in the relevant chapters. Fares are significantly lower outside the peaks times of Easter, July, August and December to mid-January. You no longer need to reconfirm most flights, especially if booked online, but double check with your travel agent at the time of booking. On departure, allow at least two hours for checking in and going through the comprehensive security procedures.

### From Europe
There are direct flights to Bogotá from Paris with **Air France** (www.airfrance.com), from Frankfurt with **Lufthansa** (www.lufthansa.com), from Madrid with **Avianca** (www.avianca.com) and **Iberia** (www.iberia.com). Flights from London go via one of these continental hubs or via the USA.

### From North America
**United** (www.united.com) has direct flights from New York, Cleveland, Los Angeles and Houston. **Delta** (www.delta.com) has flights from New York, Atlanta and Cleveland. **Avianca** and **LAN** (www.lan.com) fly direct from Miami to Bogotá. **Spirit Air** (www.spiritair.com) has flights from Miami to Cartagena, Medellín and Bogotá. **Air Canada** (www.aircanada.com) flies direct to Bogotá and San Andres Island from Toronto.

### From Australia and New Zealand
**LAN** and **Avianca** have connections with Auckland and Sydney via Santiago in Chile.

### From Latin America
**Avianca** has direct connections with Bogotá from Buenos Aires, Caracas, Lima, Mexico City, Panama City, Quito, Santiago and San José. **Copa** (www.copaair.com) has direct flights from Panama City. **Aerolíneas Argentinas** (www.aerolineas. com.ar) has four flights a week between Buenos Aires and Bogotá. **LAN** has direct connections from Santiago.

## River

Colombia shares borders with Brazil and Peru at Leticia on the Amazon. It is possible to cross into Colombia from these countries by ferry, but the journey can be time consuming: eight days from Manaus (Brazil); eight (by speedboat, US$80) to 36 hours (by cargo boat, US$40) from Iquitos (Peru). For further details, see Transport, page 384, and the border box, page 384.

## Road

The main overland Venezuela–Colombia crossings are at San Antonio–Cúcuta (page 131) and Paraguachón–Maicao (page 210). There are plenty of buses from Maracaibo (Venezuela) to Maicao, Santa Marta and Cartagena. The border with Ecuador is crossed at Rumichaca–Ipiales (page 367). **Cruz del Sur** and **Expreso Internacional** offer direct bus services from Quito to Bogotá, but it takes 36 hours. The 20-hour ride from Quito to Cali is a popular alternative. For details of this and other international services, see www.andestransit.com. ➤➤ *See also Visas and immigration, page 444.*

### Driving

To bring a car into Colombia, you must have documents proving ownership of the vehicle, and a tourist card/transit visa. These are normally valid for 90 days and must be applied for at the Colombian consulate in the country that you are leaving to enter Colombia. A *carnet de passages* is recommended when entering with a European registered vehicle. When you cross an overland border into Colombia, make sure you keep any vehicle papers you are given as you will be asked to produce them when you leave.

### Foot

If travelling independently on foot, there are many more places for entering Colombia, including from Panama via Sapzurro in the Darién (page 173). The border crossings from Ecuador at Puerto Asís, and from Venezuela across the Río Orinoco are not advised at the moment due to security concerns.

## Sea

Colombia can be reached from Ecuador via Tumaco (page 363). There are various ways to reach Colombia from Panama by sea but only the Puerto Obaldía–Capurganá route is currently considered safe (page 175).

# **Getting** around

## Air

Colombia has a well-established national airline network with several competing airlines. Internal flights are increasingly competitively priced and if you're short of time, flying may be your best option. **Avianca**, **Satena**, **Viva Colombia** and **Easyfly** are the main carriers; the latter two are low-cost airlines, with an expanding network of routes. There are also several regional airlines, such as **Aerolíneas de Antioquia (ADA)**, which serve smaller destinations.

Travel agents often have discount arrangements with certain airlines: **Vivir Volando** ① *T1-601 4676, www.vivirvolando.co*, in Bogotá, and **Destino Colombia** ① *www.destinocolombia.com*, in Medellín and Cartagena, are recommended. Otherwise, book online for advance purchase fares and last-minute deals. A useful search engine for sourcing cheap flights is www.despegar.com.

**Domestic airlines**

**Avianca**, El Dorado airport, Bogotá, T1-587 7700, ext 1875, www.avianca.com. The country's national airline, with offices in every major city in Colombia, **Avianca** flies to most destinations. The drawback is that all connections must go via Bogotá.

**Copa Airlines**, Cra 10, No 27-51, Loc 165, Bogotá, www.copaair.com. Colombia's 2nd-largest airline is owned by Panamanian carrier **Copa**. Flies to most of the main destinations.

**Easyfly**, T1-414 8111, www.easyfly. com.co. Budget airline with cheap flights to obscure destinations near popular tourist cities.

**Satena**, Av El Dorado 103-08, Entrada 1, interior 11, Bogotá, T1-423 8530/ T01-800 091 2034, www.satena.com. Government-owned airline with flights to most destinations.

**Viva Colombia**, T1-319 7989 (Bogotá), vivacolombia.co. Newer budget airline serving Medellín, Cali, San Andrés and Bogotá. It is cheap, but there are no ticket offices and they won't accept most foreign credit cards for payment.

## Rail

Colombia used to have an extensive railway system but due to lack of funding most of the lines have fallen into disrepair or are used purely for cargo. The one exception is the tourist train that runs at weekends north from La Sabana station in downtown Bogotá, stopping at Usaquén and continuing to the salt cathedral at Zipaquirá and Cajicá. See www.turistren.com.co for more information and page 71.

## Road

While there are few motorways, the main roads in Colombia are mostly in good condition and journeys are generally comfortable, although landslides frequently close roads after rains.

From Bogotá two roads run north towards the coast. To the northeast, a road (45A) heads high over the mountains of Boyacá and up to Bucaramanga before straightening up as it makes for the Sierra Nevada de Santa Marta. Another road forks northeast from here toward Cúcuta and the Venezuelan border. The second road (50) leaves Bogotá to the northwest and joins the Magdalena river valley at Honda. It follows the river until it reaches a fork at Puerto Triunfo. The eastern artery cuts back towards Bucaramanga. The western branch leads to Medellín.

Medellín is on the route of the Pan-American Highway (Panamericana). This single continuous road links most of the countries in the Americas, beginning in Canada and ending in Chile (interrupted only by the Darién Gap jungle between Panama and Colombia). In Colombia, after Darién, it begins again at Turbo and runs due south, passing through Medellín, the Zona Cafetera, Cali, Popayán, Pasto and reaches Ecuador via Ipiales.

There are two further main roads exiting Bogotá. One (40) runs southeast over (and under) high mountain passes towards Villavicencio and the Llanos. The other (45) heads south towards Neiva. It eventually joins up with the Pan-American Highway at Pasto but not before tackling some treacherous terrain around Mocoa.

### Bus and minibus

On the main routes, the bus network is comprehensive and buses are generally comfortable and efficient. Arriving at one of the large bus stations, the huge choice of carriers can be daunting, but it also has its advantages in that there are frequent services and competition between different companies can sometimes allow for a bit of haggling. The cost of tickets is relatively high by Latin American standards; fares shown in the text are middle of the range but should be treated as no more than a guide. Some of the best known operators include: **Berlinas del Fonce**, www.berlinasdelfonce.com; **Bolivariano**, www.bolivariano.com.co; **Copetran**, www.copetran.com.co; **Expreso Brasilia**, www.expresobrasilia.com, and **Expreso Palmira**, www.expresopalmira.com.co.

There is usually a variety of services on offer, with varying levels of price, quality and speed. The cheapest, *corrientes*, are essentially local buses, stopping frequently, uncomfortable and slow but offering plenty of local colour. *Pullman*

## TRAVEL TIP

### Driving in Colombia

If there is one rule that is always adhered to on Colombian roads it is that 'might is right'. Colombians may have impeccable manners in personal exchanges, but when they step into a car, like Dr Jekyll, their character transforms. Overtaking around blind corners, ignoring traffic lights – anything goes. The worst culprits are truck drivers who seem to treat their job as a permanent rally. They are closely followed by bus drivers, with the rest not far behind. In cities, especially Bogotá, pedestrians have few rights, so mind how you go. Look both ways twice when crossing the road, sit tight on the bus or in a taxi, and cross your fingers. The upside may be that after a week of travelling around the country by bus, you will be cured of any fear of flying – air travel is never more attractive than after just a few days on Colombia's roads.

or *servicio de lujo* (luxury) are long-distance buses, usually with air conditioning, toilets and DVDs (mostly rom-coms, but occasionally other films dubbed into Spanish). *Colectivos*, also known as *vans* or *busetas*, are usually 12- to 20-seat vehicles but also seven-seater cars, pick-up trucks or taxis; they are rather cramped but fast, saving several hours on long journeys. *Busetas* may also be known as *por puestos* (pay-by-the-seat) and will not leave until all the places have been filled. Some *colectivo* companies will offer a '*puerta-a-puerta*' (door-to-door) service.

### Car

With a good road network, self-driving is becoming an increasingly popular way of seeing Colombia. It's an especially good way of exploring rural areas such as the Zona Cafetera where public transport will only take you between the main cities. However, driving in these rural areas is a test of nerve, as speeding cars and buses frequently pass one another on blind corners.

The kind of motoring you do will depend on your car of choice. While a normal car will reach most places of interest, a high-clearance vehicle is useful for badly surfaced or unsurfaced roads and for fording rivers. Four-wheel drive vehicles are recommended for flexibility in mountain and jungle territory. Wherever you travel you should expect to find roads that are badly maintained, damaged or closed during the wet season; expect delays because of floods and landslides from time to time. There is also the possibility of delays due to major roadworks so do not plan your schedule too tightly.

There are *peajes* (toll stations) every 60-100 km or so on major roads: tolls depend on distance and type of vehicle, but start around US$3. For excellent information in Spanish and English, including all the toll costs, see www.viajaporcolombia.com. Fuel prices are around US$4 per gallon for standard petrol, US$4.50 per gallon for super and US$5.50 per gallon for diesel. Prices are likely to fluctuate in the current economic climate.

**Safety** Before taking a long journey, ask locally about the state of the road and check if there are any safety issues. Roads are not always signposted. Avoid night journeys, as the roads may not be in good condition, lorry and bus drivers are notoriously reckless, and animals often stray onto the roads. Police and military checks can be frequent in troubled areas, so keep your documents handy. In the event of a vehicle accident in which someone is injured, all drivers involved are usually detained until blame has been established; this may take several weeks.

Spare no ingenuity in making your car impenetrable to deter the determined and skilled thief. Be sure to note down key numbers and carry spares of the most important ones (but don't keep all spares inside the vehicle). Avoid leaving your car unattended except in a locked garage or guarded parking space (*parqueadero*), especially at night; the better hotels all have safe parking. Only park in the street if there is someone on guard; adult minders or street children will generally protect your car fiercely in exchange for a tip, US$0.50.

**Documents** Carry driving documents with you at all times. National or international driving licences may be used by foreigners in Colombia. For information on bringing a car into Colombia, see page 428. Bringing a car in by sea or air is much more complicated: you will usually be required to hire an agent to clear it through customs, which can be a slow and expensive process.

Insurance for the vehicle against accident, damage or theft is best arranged in the country of origin, but it is getting increasingly difficult to find agencies who offer this service.

**Car hire** Car hire is convenient for touring Colombia, though it is relatively expensive, especially if you are going to the more remote areas and need a 4WD or specialist vehicle. The main international car rental companies are represented at principal airports but may be closed on Saturday afternoons and Sundays. There are also local firms in most of the departmental capitals. In addition to passport and driver's licence, a credit card may be asked for as additional proof of identity (Visa, MasterCard, American Express) and to secure a returnable deposit to cover any liability not covered by the insurance. Check the insurance carefully; it may not cover you beyond a certain figure, nor for 'natural' damage such as flooding. Ask if extra cover is available. You should be given a diagram showing any scratches and other damage on the car before you hire it.

## Maps

A decent map can be difficult to find in Colombia. There are few road maps, although the *Guía Rutas de Colombia* (www.rutascolombia.com in Spanish), available at all toll booths, is relatively decent. The **Instituto Geográfico Agustín Codazzi** (www.igac.gov.co) produces general and specialist maps of the country but is receiving increasingly less funding from the government and many of its maps may be out of date. Tourist offices should be able to provide town maps. Try also major bookstores such as **Pan-Americana**.

# Essentials A-Z

## Accident and emergency

Contact the relevant emergency service and your embassy in Bogotá. Make sure you obtain police/medical reports in order to file insurance claims.

**Emergency services**
**CAI Police**: T156 (to report a crime and obtain the necessary paperwork); **Fire**: T119; **Police**: T112 or 123 (from mobiles); **Red Cross ambulance**: T132; **Traffic accidents**: T127.

## Children

Travelling with children can bring you into closer contact with Colombian families and presents no special problems. In fact your trip may be even smoother, since officials are sometimes more amenable where children are concerned and are particularly pleased if your child knows a little Spanish. Local comic strips are a good way for older children to get to grips with the language. For more detailed advice on travelling with children, see Footprint's *Travel with Kids*.

**Facilities**
Despite genuine good will towards younger visitors, Colombia's tourist industry does not generally offer dedicated family-friendly or children's facilities. Large, upscale chain hotels are likely to have babysitting or nanny services but you should not expect any independent hotels or haciendas to offer these. Baby-changing facilities can be found only in the larger airports.

On the plus side, many museums and attractions offer discounts for children.

**Bus travel**
On long-distance buses you pay for each seat and there are no half-price fares. For shorter trips it is therefore cheaper, if less comfortable, to seat small children on your knee. Sometimes there are spare seats that children can occupy after tickets have been collected. Local buses are often crowded and uncomfortable. Remember that a lot of time can be spent waiting around in bus stations and airports; take your own reading material to while away the hours since children's books are difficult to find and expensive in Colombia. Reading on the bus itself, especially on winding mountain roads, is not recommended!

**Food**
It is better to take food with you on longer trips rather than to rely on meal stops. Stick to simple things like bread and fruit while you are on the road. In restaurants, you may be able to buy a *media porción* (half portion), or divide a full-size helping between 2 children.

**Health**
Be extra vigilant to avoid sun burn and heat exhaustion.

## Customs

Travellers can bring up to US$1,500 worth of the goods into the country. Customs checks take place at airports and land frontiers for all arriving and departing travellers (see Visas and immigration, page 444). There are sometimes additional checks at the flight gate before departure. Do not carry drugs or firearms of any kind and take care that no-one tampers with your baggage. When entering the country, you will be given a copy of your DIAN (customs) luggage declaration. Keep it safe; you may be asked for it when you leave. On departure, foreigners must pay an exit tax of around US$30.

## Disabled travellers

Provision for the disabled in Colombia is limited, but increasing. Wheelchairs and assistance are available at major airports; modern public buildings are provided with ramps and lifts, and some streets have pavement breaks that are usually adequate for wheelchairs. An increasing number of hotels and restaurants (in the upper price range) now have disabled access, rooms and toilets.

Some travel companies specialize in exciting holidays, tailor-made for individuals with a variety of disabilities. For general information, consult the **Global Access – Disabled Travel Network**, www.globalaccessnews.com, and www.disabledtravelers.com.

## Drugs

As is all too well known, Colombia is a major drug-producing and smuggling nation that produces roughly 80% of the world's cocaine. Police and customs activities have greatly intensified in recent years, and criminals increasingly try to use innocent carriers to smuggle drugs out of the country. Pack all luggage yourself; do not leave any bags unattended, and under no circumstances carry packages for other people without checking the contents; indeed taking

any suspicious-looking packages or gift-wrapped presents through customs should be avoided, even if they are your own. Be very polite to customs staff and policemen, particularly if your hotel room is raided by police looking for drugs. Colombians who offer you drugs may well be framing you for the police, who are very active on the north coast, on San Andrés island and at other tourist resorts. Any foreigner caught using any drug can expect to face prison, fines and/or deportation.

## Electricity

110 volts AC, alternating at 60 cycles per second. A converter may be required if your device does not run on 110 volts. Most sockets accept both continental European (round) and North American (flat) 2-pin plugs.

## Embassies and consulates

For a list of both Colombian embassies abroad, and foreign embassies/consulates in Colombia, see http://embassy.goabroad.com. Note that only the UK embassy in Bogotá has public attention duties.

## Health

See your GP or travel clinic at least 6 weeks before departure for general advice on travel risks and vaccinations. Try phoning a specialist travel clinic if your own doctor is unfamiliar with health conditions in Colombia. Make sure you have sufficient medical travel insurance, get a dental check, know your own blood group and if you suffer a long-term condition, such as diabetes or epilepsy, obtain a Medic Alert bracelet/necklace (www.medicalert.

co.uk). If you wear glasses, take a copy of your prescription.

## Vaccinations

Confirm that your primary courses and boosters are up to date. It is advisable to vaccinate against polio, tetanus, typhoid, hepatitis A, and also rabies if going to more remote areas. Vaccinations for diphtheria, hepatitis B and yellow fever should also be considered. Although a yellow fever certificate is not compulsory for visiting Colombia, if you travel to the Amazon you are likely to be asked for one at the airport in Leticia. You may well be turned away if you can't produce one, or you will be made to have the vaccination on the spot (not recommended). The bus terminal in Bogotá now offers professional and free yellow fever vaccinations for foreigners.

## Health risks

The most common cause of **traveller's diarrhoea** in Colombia is eating contaminated food. Tap water in the major cities is in theory safe to drink, but it may be advisable to err on the side of caution and drink only bottled or boiled water. Avoid having ice in drinks unless you trust that it is from a reliable source. Swimming in sea or river water that has been contaminated by sewage can also result in stomach upset; ask locally if water is safe. Diarrhoea may also be caused by a virus, bacteria (such as E-coli), protozoal (such as giardia), salmonella and cholera. It may be accompanied by vomiting or by severe abdominal pain. Any kind of diarrhoea responds well to the replacement of water and salts. Sachets of rehydration salts can be bought in most chemists and can be dissolved in boiled water. If the symptoms persist, consult a doctor.

Travelling in high altitudes can bring on **altitude sickness**. On reaching heights above 3000 m, the heart may start pounding and the traveller may experience shortness of breath. Smokers and those with underlying heart or lung disease are often hardest hit. Take it easy for the first few days, rest and drink plenty of water; you will feel better soon. It is essential to get acclimatized before undertaking long treks or arduous activities.

Mosquitoes are a nuisance and some are carriers of serious diseases. **Malaria** and **dengue fever** are a danger in the Amazon and in other tropical areas along the Pacific coast including the Darién and Chocó. Take specialist advice on the best anti-malarials to use, and try to avoid being bitten as much as possible by sleeping off the ground and using a mosquito net and some kind of insecticide. Mosquito coils release insecticide as they burn and are available in many shops, as are tablets of insecticide, which are placed on a heated mat plugged into a wall socket.

Finally, remember that the sun in tropical areas and at high altitude can be fierce, so take precautions to avoid **heat exhaustion** and **sunburn**.

## If you get sick

Contact your embassy or consulate for a list of doctors and dentists who speak your language, or at least some English. Your hotel may also be able to recommend good local medical services. Good-quality healthcare is available in the larger centres of Colombia, but it can be expensive, especially hospitalization. Make sure you have adequate insurance (see below).

## Useful websites

**www.cdc.gov** US government site that gives excellent advice on travel health and details of disease outbreaks.

**www.fco.gov.uk** British Foreign and Commonwealth Office travel site has useful information on each country, people, climate and a list of UK embassies/consulates abroad.

**www.fitfortravel.scot.nhs.uk** A-Z of vaccine/health advice for each country.

**www.travelhealth.co.uk** Independent travel health site with advice on vaccination, travel insurance and health risks.

## ID

It is highly recommended that you photocopy your passport details, including entry stamps which, for added insurance, you can have witnessed by a notary. Always carry your passport or a photocopy with you, as you may be asked for identification at any time. A photocopy is a valid substitute for most purposes but not, for example, for cashing TCs or getting a cash advance on a credit card. A driving licence, provided it is plastic, of credit card size and has a photograph, is generally an acceptable form of ID (eg to enter government buildings). For more information, check with your consulate.

## Insurance

Travel insurance is a must for all visitors to Colombia. Always take out insurance that covers both medical expenses and baggage loss, and read the small print carefully before you set off. Check that all the activities you may end up doing are covered; diving, kayaking, mountaineering (especially at high altitude), whitewater rafting, etc, may require additional or specialist insurance. Check if medical coverage includes air ambulance and emergency flights back home.

Be aware of the payment protocol: in Colombia you will have to pay out of your own pocket and later request reimbursement from the insurance company. Before paying for any medical services, insist on getting a fully itemized invoice. In case of baggage loss, have the receipts for expensive personal effects like cameras and laptops on file, take photos of these items, note the serial numbers and be sure to leave unnecessary valuables at home. Keep the insurance company's telephone number with you and get a police report for any lost or stolen items.

## Internet

The internet has largely replaced postal and telephone services for the majority of travellers. Public internet access is available in most areas of Colombia, although the cost and speed of access varies. Small towns and villages may not have connectivity, or it may be slow; the best service is generally available in the largest cities. Most hotels and major airports now have free Wi-Fi, as do cafés, bars, restaurants and some public spaces, but connectivity can be erratic. Keep your wits about you if using Wi-Fi spots outdoors; not all are safe. Likewise, cyber cafés sometimes get crowded and noisy, so keep an eye on your belongings.

## Language

→ *For a list of useful Spanish words and phrases, see page 447.*

The official language of Colombia is Spanish and it is spoken by the majority of the population. However, there are also some 60 aboriginal languages spoken by the indigenous communities. A form of creole English is spoken on the islands of San Andrés and Providencia. An increasing number of Colombians can speak and understand a little English, even in more remote areas, but a basic knowledge of Spanish will infinitely enhance your journey and make communication that much easier. It's well worth learning the basics before you arrive or taking a course at the start of your trip (see below). Language exchanges with students wishing to learn English are also popular. Note that if you are intending to do any formal language or other studies, then you must get a student visa (see Visas and immigration, page 444), which can be obtained once you're in the country.

### Language courses
**Amerispan**, 1334 Walnut St, 6th floor, Philadelphia, PA 19107, USA, T215-7511100/T1-800-511 0179, www.amerispan.com. Spanish immersion and volunteer programmes throughout Latin America, including in Bogotá, Cartagena and Medellín.
**Cactus Language Travel Holidays**, T0845-130 4775 (UK), www.cactus language.com. Spanish language courses often combined with activities such as salsa or gastronomy in different parts of Colombia, including Bogotá, Cartagena and Leticia.

Universities in Bogotá also provide Spanish language courses: **Pontificia**

**Universidad Javeriana**, T1-320 8320 ext 4563, www.javeriana.edu.co; **Universidad de los Andes**, T1-339 4949, www.uniandes.edu.co (US$250 for 180 hrs tuition); **Universidad Nacional**, T1-316 5000, www.unal.edu.co (high-quality intensive courses for about US$500, group discount available); **Universidad Pedagógica**, C 72, No 11-86, T1-594 1894.

## LGBT travellers

Colombia has some of the most progressive laws regarding homosexuality in Latin America. While same-sex marriages and civil unions are yet to be legalized, common-law marriage (registered partnership), property rights and inheritance rights for same-sex couples were approved by the Constitutional Court in 2007. Since then the courts have often ruled in favour of gay plaintiffs and the Constitutional Court continues to be progressive on the subject of gay rights. Most of the big cities have gay neighbourhoods; Bogotá in particular has a large and thriving gay scene, centred around Chapinero. Gay travellers should not experience any difficulty booking a double room, say, in most hotels around the country. However, it may be wise to be discreet and respect local sensibilities in more conservative, remote locations.

## Media

### Newspapers and magazines
Bogotá has an excellent English-language magazine, *The City Paper*, www.thecitypaperbogota.com, distributed in hotels, hostels and bars. The best national magazine is probably *Semana*, www.semana.com. Most of the major cities have their own newspaper,

usually with a regional bias; most of these have an online presence.

**Bogotá**: *El Tiempo*, www.eltiempo.com; *El Espectador*, www.elespectador.com; *La República*, www.larepublica.com.co.

**Cartagena**: *El Heraldo*, www.elheraldo.co.

**Cali**: *El País*, www.elpais.com.co; *Nuevo Diario Occidente*, www.diariooccidente.com.co; *El Pueblo*.

**Medellín**: *El Mundo*, www.elmundo.com; *El Colombiano*, www.elcolombiano.com.

### Radio

Colombia has a wealth of radio stations. Try **W Radio**, www.wradio.com.co, for up-to-the-minute news. You may be able to pick up the **BBC World Service** or **Voice of America** with a long-wave or digital radio.

### Television

Colombia has some 25 TV stations including regional ones, but the 2 principal stations are **RCN** (state owned) and **Caracol** (private). All of the major stations have websites which enable live streaming and on-demand viewing. Colombian TV is well known for its 'soaps' (*telenovelas*), which are exported to other Spanish-speaking countries. Satellite TV with access to **CNN** and **CNN en Español** is available in even the cheapest hotels.

### Money

→ *US$1 = COP$2670; UK£1 = COP$3949; €1 = COP$2814 (Mar 2015). See www.xe.com.*

Colombia's currency is the *peso* (\$). Banknotes are available in the following denominations: 50,000, 20,000, 10,000, 5000, 2000 and 1000, as well as coins worth 500, 200, 100 and 50. Large bills may be hard to use in small towns so carry notes in small dominations (10,000 and below). Watch out for forged notes.

The 50,000-peso note should smudge colour if it is real; if not, refuse to accept it.

There is a variety of ways for visitors to bring their funds into Colombia; you are strongly advised to combine 2 or more of these, so as not to be stuck without money. Always carry some US$ cash, which can be used when and where all else fails. Avoid carrying large quantities of cash on your person.

### ATMs and credit cards

Credit cards are widely used, especially MasterCard and Visa; Diners Club is also accepted, but American Express (Amex) is only accepted in upmarket places in Bogotá. Many banks accept Visa (Visaplus and ATH logos) and Cirrus/MasterCard (Maestro and Multicolor logos) for peso cash advances; these cards can also be used in ATMs. There are ATMs for Visa and MasterCard everywhere, including in **Carulla** and **Exito** supermarkets, but you may have to try several machines before you find one that works.

Note that ATMs in Colombia do not retain your card during the withdrawal. Insert your card for scanning and withdraw it immediately, then proceed as normal. If your card is not given back straight away, do not proceed with the transaction and do not type in your pin number. Money has been stolen from accounts when cards have been retained. Only use ATMs in supermarkets, malls or where a security guard is present. Don't ask a taxi driver to wait while you use an ATM. Be particularly vigilant around Christmas time when thieves may be on the prowl.

ATMs dispense a frustratingly small amount of cash at a time. The maximum withdrawal is often 300,000 pesos (about US$150). You can make several withdrawals each day, but this will accrue heavy transaction charges over a period of time. For larger amounts try: **Davivienda** (occasionally 500,000 pesos per visit) and **Bancolombia** (400,000 pesos per visit).

If planning to use credit and debit cards abroad, be sure to warn your bank back at home in advance to prevent them blocking your card. It is also worth finding out how much your bank charges for foreign withdrawals; some banks have much higher fees than others. In case of credit card loss or theft, call your bank or contact Visa T0800-847 2911, or MasterCard T0800-627 8372.

### Currency exchange

Cash (preferably US\$ or euros) and TCs can, in theory, be exchanged in any bank, except the **Banco de la República**. Take your passport (a photocopy is not normally accepted) and, in smaller places, get there early. It can be difficult to buy and sell large amounts of pounds sterling, even in Bogotá.

In most sizeable towns there are *casas de cambio* (exchange bureaux), which are quicker to use than banks but may charge higher commission. US\$ and Euro are readily accepted but other international currencies can be harder to change. Hotels usually give very poor rates of exchange, especially if you are paying in dollars. On Sunday currency exchange is virtually impossible except at Bogotá airport. Do not be tempted to change money on the streets; it is dangerous and you may well be given counterfeit pesos. Counterfeit US\$ bills are also in circulation.

When leaving Colombia, try to sell your pesos before or at the border, as it may be difficult to change them in other countries.

### Traveller's cheques

Traveller's cheques are a secure but time-consuming and impractical way to obtain cash. They are not normally accepted in hotels, restaurants or shops in Colombia, and banks in remote areas may be unwilling to change them, so always have some local currency (and US\$ for emergencies). When changing TCs, you will need to show your passport and you may be asked for a photocopy too (take a supply of photocopies with you). The procedure is always slow, sometimes involving finger printing and photographs. The best currency to take is US\$, preferably in small denominations; sterling TCs are practically impossible to change. To change Amex TCs you may have to provide proof of purchase. Obtaining reimbursement for lost Amex TCs can be straightforward if you have the numbers recorded. You may be asked for proof of purchase, as well as a *diligencia de queja* (police certificate) explaining the circumstances of loss; apply to the Amex representative, **Expreso Viajes & Turismo** in Bogotá at C 19 No 70, T1-593 4949, Mon-Fri 0800-1800, Sat 0900-1200.

### Cost of living

Prices are generally lower than Europe and North America for services and locally produced items, but more expensive for imported and luxury goods. Modest, basic accommodation costs about US\$15-25 per person per night in Bogotá, Cartagena, Santa Marta and colonial cities like Villa de Leiva, Popayán or Santa Fe de Antioquia, but is cheaper elsewhere. A *menú del día* (set lunch) costs about US\$2-3 and breakfast US\$1.75-2. A la carte meals are usually good value as fierce competition keeps prices relatively low. Internet cafés charge US$1-2 per hr.

## Opening hours

**Business hours** are generally Mon-Fri 0800-1200, 1400-1700, and Sat 0900-1200. A longer siesta may be taken in small towns and tropical areas. **Banks** in larger cities do not close for lunch. Most businesses, such as banks and **airline offices**, close for official holidays, while **supermarkets** and street markets may stay open. This depends a lot on where you are, so enquire locally. The best time to visit **churches** for sightseeing is before or after Mass (not during).

## Police and the law

You are required to carry your passport at all times; you will seldom be asked for it outside border areas but police and military checks on main roads are increasing. In general, most police are helpful to travellers and you are unlikely to experience any hassle as long as you are polite and cooperative. Remain calm and courteous if your hotel room is raided by police looking for drugs. Never offer to bribe a police officer; if an official suggests that a bribe must be paid before you can proceed on your way, be patient and they may relent.

Note that if you are the victim of theft or other forms of crime, contact a **Centro de Atención Inmediata (CAI)** office for assistance, T156, not a standard police station. The CAI police office is the only place that will carry out the relevant paperwork. In Bogotá there are **CAI** offices at Cra 24, No 82-77, Downtown, T1-552 4840; at C 60 y Cra 9, Downtown, T1-217 7472, and at Cra 7 y C6, La Candelaria.

## Post and courier

There are 2 parallel services: **Deprisa**, operated by the national airline **Avianca**, and **4-72**, previously known as Correos de Colombia or Adpostal. Both have offices in major cities but only **4-72** can be found in small towns and rural areas. Both offer an overseas parcel service; anything important should be registered. **Servientrega**, DHL and **Fedex** also handle overseas parcels. **Portal Oficial**, 4-72 Diagonal 25G No 95A-55B, T1-472 2000, www.4-72. com.co. Bogota's main postal centre.

## Public holidays

Public holidays are known as *puentes* (bridges).

1 Jan   New Year's Day
6 Jan   Epiphany*
19 Mar   St Joseph*
Mar/Apr   Maundy Thu; Good Fri
1 May   Labour Day
May   Ascension Day* (6 weeks and a day after Easter Sun)
May/Jun   Corpus Christi* (9 weeks and a day after Easter Sun)
29 Jun   St Peter and St Paul*
30 Jun   Sacred Heart*
20 Jul   Independence Day
7 Aug   Battle of Boyacá
15 Aug   Assumption*
12 Oct   Columbus' arrival in America*
1 Nov   All Saints' Day*
11 Nov   Independence of Cartagena*
8 Dec   Immaculate Conception
25 Dec   Christmas Day

* When these do not fall on a Mon, the public holiday is held on the following Mon.

Travellers confirm that the vast majority of Colombians are polite, honest and will go out of their way to help visitors and make them feel welcome. In general, anti-gringo sentiments are rare. However, visitors should always keep in mind that Colombia is part of a major cocaine-smuggling route and take suitable precautions; for specific advice on drugs in Colombia, see page 434.

### Drug-based scams

There have been reports of travellers being victims of *burundanga*, a drug obtained from a native white flower, which is used to contaminate cigarettes, food or drink. It is almost impossible to see or smell but leaves the victim helpless. Usually, the victim is taken to an ATM to draw out money. At present, the use of this drug appears to be confined to major cities. Be wary of accepting cigarettes, food and drink from strangers at sports events or on buses. In bars watch your drinks very carefully. Other Colombian scams may involve fake police and taxicabs; there are variations in most major cities. For advice on safety in Bogotá, see page 37.

### Guerrillas

The government has had considerable success in its fight against left-wing guerrillas such as the **FARC**, but the internal armed conflict in Colombia is almost impossible to predict and the security situation changes from day to day. For this reason, it is essential to consult with locals for up-to-date information. Taxi and bus drivers, local journalists, soldiers at checkpoints, hotel owners and Colombians who actually travel around their country are usually good sources of reliable information. Since 2002, incidents of kidnapping and homicide in major cities have been declining. Travelling overland between towns, especially during the holiday season and bank holiday weekends, has become much safer due to increased military and police presence along main roads. However, the government has launched a major offensive against the guerrillas (especially in the south) with the result that, in some areas, fighting between the armed forces and guerrilla groups has intensified. In 2014, for example, Isla Gorgona experienced a surge in violence and Aviatur suspended trips to the island; visitors are recommended to bypass it altogether.

### Hotel security

The cheapest hotels are usually found near markets and bus stations but these are also the least safe. Look for something a little better if you can afford it; if you must stay in a suspect area, try to return to your hotel before dark. If you trust your hotel, then you can leave any valuables you don't need in their safe-deposit box, but always keep an inventory of what you have deposited. An alternative to leaving valuables with the hotel administration is to lock everything in your pack and secure that in your room; a light bicycle chain or cable and a small padlock will provide at least a psychological deterrent for would-be thieves. Even in an apparently safe hotel, never leave valuable objects strewn about your room.

### Theft

Pickpockets, bag snatchers and bag slashers are always a hazard for tourists, especially in crowded areas such as markets or the downtown cores of major cities. There have been reports of assaults in the Candelaria area of Bogotá, especially at night. Keep alert and avoid crowds of people. You should likewise avoid deserted areas, such as parks or plazas after hours. Be especially careful around bus stations, as these are often the most dangerous areas of town and are obvious places to catch people carrying a lot of important belongings.

To limit your chances of being robbed, leave unnecessary documents and valuables at home. Those you bring should be carried in a money-belt or pouch, including your passport, airline tickets, credit and debit cards. Hide your main cash supply in several different places. If one stash is lost or stolen, you will still have the others to fall back on. Never carry valuables in an ordinary pocket, purse or day-pack. Keep cameras in bags or day-packs and generally out of sight. Do not wear expensive wrist watches or jewellery. If you are wearing a shoulder-bag or day-pack in a crowd, carry it in front of you.

#### Women travellers

Unaccompanied foreign women may be objects of curiosity in Colombia; don't be unduly scared – or flattered – but do take sensible precautions. Avoid arriving anywhere after dark. Remember that for a single woman a taxi at night can be as dangerous as wandering around alone. During the day, a good general rule is to always look confident and pretend you know where you are going, even if you do not. If you accept a social invitation, make sure that someone knows the address of where you are going and the time you left; ask if you can bring a friend (even if you do not). Watch your alcohol intake at parties, especially if you are on your own, and keep a close eye

on your drink. Don't tell strangers where you are staying.

### Student travellers

If you are in full-time education you are entitled to an **International Student Identity Card (ISIC)**, which is sold by student travel offices and agencies in 70 countries. The ISIC may give you special prices on transport and access to a variety of other concessions and services, although these are relatively uncommon in Colombia. Teachers are entitled to an **International Teacher Identity Card (ITIC)**. Both are available from www.isic.org. If undertaking any form of study in Colombia, you will need a student visa (see Visas and immigration, page 444).

### Tax

**Departure tax** is US$31, and is not included in any airline tickets. The Revenue stamp can be paid in Colombian pesos, at the equivalent current exchange rate for IATA dollars for the day.

**VAT/IVA** is 16%. Ask for an official receipt if you want it documented. Some hotels and restaurants add IVA onto bills, but foreigners do not officially have to pay (see page 24).

### Telephone → *Country code +57.*

To call a landline in Colombia from outside the area, dial the 1-digit area code, followed by the 7-digit number. To make an international call from Colombia, dial the IDD code of the carrier — Orbitel 005; ETB 007; Telecom 009 — followed by the country code.

Phone boxes are widespread but are not recommended for long-distance calls. Instead, national and international calls can be made from the many public phone offices found in all major cities (eg in the **Tequendama Hotel** complex in Bogotá, Cra 13, No 26-45) and even in rural towns. You are assigned a cabin, place your calls and pay on the way out. There is usually a screen that tells you how much you are spending. Prices vary considerably. You can also make calls from street vendors who hire out their mobile phones (usually signposted *'minutos'*). Another cost-effective way to make an international call is to use Skype (www.skype.com), available in most internet cafés.

It is relatively inexpensive to buy a pay-as-you go SIM card for your mobile phone. Calls are on the whole cheap but making international calls from mobiles can be complicated.

## Time

GMT -5 all year round.

## Tipping

A voluntary charge is added to most bills but you can ask to have this taken off if you are not happy with the service. Otherwise a 10% tip is customary.

## Tourist information

Contact details for tourist offices and other information resources are given throughout the text. The Colombian government is making a big push to promote tourism and most *alcaldías* (municipalities) have some sort of tourist office, whose staff are invariably very well meaning. However, the qualifications of the staff, the resources available and the standards of service vary enormously in smaller towns. Keep your expectations modest and you may be pleasantly surprised. For further information, contact the **Colombia Tourist Board – Proexport**, C 28, No 13A-15, piso 36, Bogotá, T1-427 9000, www.colombia.travel; its website is useful, comprehensive and up to date. For information on the national parks, see box, page 22.

## Useful websites

**www.clubhaciendasdelcafe.com** Extensive list of coffee fincas in the Zona Cafetera.

**www.colombianhostels.com.co** Network of Colombian backpackers' hostels. Also publishes a thorough guidebook, available for free in most major hostels.

**www.conexcol.com** Colombian search engine (Spanish only).

**www.despegar.com** Cheap flights website for travel within Latin America.

**www.gobiernoenlinea.gov.co** Government website with information on new laws and citizen rights, in Spanish and English.

**www.hosteltrail.com/colombia** Reviews of hostels, tour agencies and destinations.

**www.ideam.gov.co** Weather and climate information.

**www.igac.gov.co** Instituto Geográfico Agustín Codazzi Official maps of Colombia.

**www.invias.gov.co** Instituto Nacional de Vías (National Road Institute). Current details on the state of the roads with maps, etc.

**www.lab.org.uk** Latin American Bureau site, based in the UK. Publishes books and holds talks on Latin American issues.

**www.quehubo.com** Listings site.

## Tour operators

### In the UK
**Dragoman**, T01728-862211, www.dragoman.co.uk.
**Exodus Travels**,T0845-805 5459, www.exodus.co.uk.
**Exploratory Overland Expeditions**, T01865-573987, www.eoe.org.uk.
**Explore**, T01252-883 790, www.explore.co.uk.
**Intrepid Travel**, T0808-274 5111, www.intrepidtravel.com.
**Journey Latin America**, T020-3432 9346, www.journeylatinamerica.co.uk.
**LATA (Latin American Travel Association)**, T020-3713 6688, www.lata.org. Useful country information and listing of UK operators specializing in Latin America.
**South America Travel**, T0800-011 9170, www.southamerica.travel.

### In North America
**GAP Adventures**, T1-416 260 0999, www.gapadventures.com.
**See Colombia Travel**, 11491 SW 20th St, Miami Fl, 33025-6639, T1-800-553-8701 (toll free), T020-7101 9467 (UK), www.seecolombia.travel.
**South America Travel**, T1-800-747 4540, www.southamerica.travel.

### In South America
**Colombian Highlands Tours & Expeditions**, Av Cra 10-21, Finca Renacer, Villa de Leiva, Colombia, T310-552 9079, www.colombianhighlands.com.
**De Una Colombia Tours**, Cra 24, No 39b-25, of 501, La Soledad-Bogotá, Colombia, T1-368 1915, www.deunacolombia.com.
**Surtrek**, Av Amazonas 897 y Wilson, Quito, Ecuador, T1-866 978 7398 (US) T080 8189 0438, www.surtrek.com.

## Visas and immigration

### Before you go
Always double-check visa regulations before leaving your home country. Nationals of Bulgaria, Russia and the Middle East (except Israel), Asian countries (except Japan, South Korea, Philippines, Indonesia and Singapore), Haiti, Nicaragua and all African countries need a visa to visit Colombia. Visas are issued only by Colombian consulates abroad. If a visa is required you must present a valid passport, 3 photographs on white background, the application form (in duplicate), US$13-40 or equivalent (price varies according to nationality), onward tickets and a photocopy of all the documents. Allow 2 weeks for your visa to be processed.

All other nationals with a valid passport are issued a standard 90-day tourist visa on arrival. If you intend to stay more than 90 days, extensions can be granted through **Migración Colombia** (www.migracioncolombia.gov.co; see below).

### On arrival
When entering the country, you will be given a copy of your DIAN (customs) luggage declaration. Keep it safe; you may be asked for it when you leave. Normally, passports are scanned by a computer and stamped on entry; sometimes a landing card is issued. If you receive an entry card when flying in and lose it while in Colombia, apply to any **Migración Colombia** office (see below) who should issue one and re-stamp your passport for free. It is highly recommended that you photocopy your passport details, including entry stamps which, for added insurance, you can have witnessed by a notary. Always carry

a photocopy of your passport with you (see page 436).

## Visa extensions

If you wish to stay longer than 90 days as a tourist, go to a **Migración Colombia** office in any major city with your onward ticket and they will usually grant you a free extension (*salvoconducto*) on the spot. You may be asked to prove that you have sufficient funds for your stay. The *salvoconducto* is only issued once for a period of 30 days, costs around US$23.50 and is usually processed within 24 hrs. It is best to apply 2-3 days before your tourist stay expires. Bring 2 recent photos and copies of your passport. Arrive early in the morning; expect long queues and a painfully slow bureaucratic process. Migración Colombia now accepts cash and credit card payments on site.

Alternatively, if you have good reason to stay longer (eg for medical treatment), you should apply to the Colombian embassy in your home country before leaving for Colombia.

If you overstay on any type of visa without an official extension, you will be charged a fine, minimum US$55 up to thousands of dollars.

## Student and business visas

If you are going to take a Spanish course, you must have a student visa; a tourist visa is not valid for study. A student visa can be obtained once you're in Colombia on a tourist visa. You must be enrolled on a course at a bona fide university and have proof of sufficient funds; US$400-600 for a 6-month stay is usually deemed sufficient.

Various business and other temporary visas are needed for foreigners who wish to reside in Colombia for a length of time. The **Ministerio de Relaciones Exteriores** (not **Migración Colombia**), C 10 No 5-51, Palacio de San Carlos, T01800-097 9899 or 382 6999, www.cancilleria.gov.co, Mon-Fri 0730-1600, processes student and some work visas, but in general, Colombian work visas can only be obtained outside Colombia at the appropriate consulate or embassy.

You must register work and student visas at a **Migración Colombia** office within 15 days of obtaining them; otherwise you will be liable to pay a hefty fine. Visas must be used within 3 months. Supporting documentary requirements for visas change frequently, so check with the consulate in good time before your trip.

## Leaving Colombia

To leave Colombia you must get an exit stamp. These are issued automatically at the airport as long as you haven't overstayed your visa. If you're leaving overland, get the exit stamp from a **Migración Colombia** office, but bear in mind that they may not have an office at the small border towns, so try to get your stamp in a main city.

## Migración Colombia offices

**Barranquilla** Cra 42, No 54-77, T5-351 3401.
**Bogotá** C 26, No 59-51, Edif Argos Torre 3, Piso 4, T1-605 5454, Mon-Fri 0800-1600.
**Cali** Av 3N, No 50N-20, T2-397 3510.
**Cartagena** Cra 20B, No 29-18, T5-670 0555, daily 0800-1200, 1400-1700.
**Cúcuta** Av 1, No 28-57, T7-572 0033, daily 0800-1130, 1400-1700; also at the airport.
**Ipiales** Cra 7, No 14-10 esq C 14 piso 3, Mon-Fri 0900-1200, 1400-1700. There's also an Ecuadorean consulate here.

**Leticia** C 9, No 9-62, T8-592 5930; also at the airport.

**Manizales** C 53, No 25A-35, T6-887 9600, cf.manizales@migracioncolombia. gov.co, Mon-Fri 0800-1200, 1400-1700.

**Medellín** C 19, No 80A-40, Belén La Gloria, T4-340 5800; and at airport, T4-562 2903.

**Pasto** C 29-76. Will issue exit stamps if you are going on to Ecuador.

**Riohacha** C 5, No 4-48, daily 0800-1200, 1400-1700.

**Santa Marta** C 22, No 13A-88, Santa Marta, T5-421 7794. Mon-Fri 0800-1200, 1400-1700.

### Volunteering

Volunteers can apply to work as park rangers at some national parks (see box, page 22). Other agencies offering volunteer placements include:

**Colombia Ministry of the Environment**, www.minambiente. gov.co. Environmental legislation and general information.

**Conservation International**, www. conservation.org. Click on 'Get Involved' of 'Join Us' to start the process.

**Fundación Natura**, www.natura.org. co. For scientific information on several national parks where they have projects.

**Goals for Peace**, www.goalsforpeace. com. **Kasa Guane** hostel in Bucarmaranga runs a social project dedicated to improving opportunities for low-income children in the city. Local and international volunteers can get involved with teaching, coaching, mentoring and administrative work.

**Institute Von Humboldt**, www. humboldt.org.co (in Spanish). Probably the most important environment research organization in Colombia. An excellent site with descriptions of the different ecosystems in the country and details of projects with ethnic communities.

**International Union for the Conservation of Nature**, www.iucn.org. One of the best sites for information on biodiversity protection worldwide with links to South America/Colombia including projects in protected areas and national parks.

**Survival International**, www.survival international.org. Information on indigenous communities in Colombia.

### Weights and measures

Colombia uses the metric system, but uses US gallons for petrol.

# **Basic** Spanish for travellers

Learning Spanish is a useful part of the preparation for a trip to Latin America and no volumes of dictionaries, phrase books or word lists will provide the same enjoyment as being able to communicate directly with the people of the country you are visiting. It is a good idea to make an effort to grasp the basics before you go. As you travel you will pick up more of the language and the more you know, the more you will benefit from your stay.

## Colombian Spanish

Colombians display a sometimes excessive inclination for politeness. Nowhere is this more evident than in their language, which is characterized by a punctilious, sometimes archaic, courteousness. Step inside any shop or taxi in the interior (the coast has its own rules, separate from the rest of the country) and you are likely to be bombarded by forms of address such as '*a la orden*' (at your service), '*que esté bien*' (may you be well), '*con mucho gusto*' (with pleasure); in departments such as Boyacá, you may even be addressed as '*su merced*' (your mercy). And politeness isn't only for strangers. They even use the third person, formal *usted* (you) with their children or spouses.

Although more and more Colombians speak a few phrases of English, you shouldn't rely on this, particular in more remote or rural areas. Instead, make the effort to learn some Spanish, either before you arrive or by signing up for a language course as part of your trip. Without any language skills, you will feel like someone peering through a keyhole at the country. But Colombians are so gregarious that with just a modest knowledge of the language you will soon be engaged in conversation, and, helpfully, the Colombian accent is one of the easiest to understand, save for the more choppy intonations heard on the coast.

### General pronunciation

Whether you have been taught the 'Castilian' pronunciation (*z* and *c* followed by *i* or *e* are pronounced as the *th* in think) or the 'American' pronunciation (they are pronounced as *s*), you will encounter little difficulty in understanding either. Regional accents and usages vary, but the basic language is essentially the same everywhere.

### Vowels
*a*   as in English *cat*
*e*   as in English *best*
*i*    as the *ee* in English *feet*
*o*   as in English *shop*
*u*   as the *oo* in English *food*
*ai*  as the *i* in English *ride*
*ei*  as *ey* in English *they*
*oi*  as *oy* in English *toy*

### Consonants
Most consonants can be pronounced more or less as they are in English. The exceptions are:
*g*   before *e* or *i* is the same as *j*
*h*   is always silent (except in *ch* as in *chair*)
*j*    as the *ch* in Scottish *loch*
*ll*   as the *y* in *yellow*
*ñ*   as the *ni* in English *onion*
*rr*   trilled much more than in English
*x*   depending on its location, pronounced *x*, *s*, *sh* or *j*

## Spanish words and phrases

**Greetings, courtesies**

hello *hola*
good morning *buenos días*
good afternoon/evening/night
  *buenas tardes/noches*
goodbye *adiós/chao*
pleased to meet you *mucho gusto*
see you later *hasta luego*
how are you? *¿cómo está?/¿cómo estás?*
I'm fine, thanks *estoy muy bien, gracias*
I'm called... *me llamo...*
what is your name? *¿cómo se llama?/*
  *¿cómo te llamas?*
yes/no *sí/no*
please *por favor*
thank you (very much) *(muchas) gracias*

I speak Spanish *hablo español*
I don't speak Spanish *no hablo español*
do you speak English? *¿habla inglés?*
I don't understand *no entiendo/*
  *no comprendo*
please speak slowly *hable despacio*
  *por favor*
I am very sorry *lo siento mucho/disculpe*
what do you want? *¿qué quiere?/*
  *¿qué quieres?*
I want *quiero*
I don't want it *no lo quiero*
good/bad *bueno/malo*
leave me alone *déjeme en paz/*
  *no me moleste*

**Questions and requests**

Have you got a room for two people?
  *¿Tiene una habitación para dos personas?*
How do I get to_? *¿Cómo llego a_?*
How much does it cost?
  *¿Cuánto cuesta? ¿cuánto es?*
I'd like to make a long-distance
  phone call *Quisiera hacer una llamada*
  *de larga distancia*
Is service included? *¿Está incluido*
  *el servicio?*

Is tax included? *¿Están incluidos*
  *los impuestos?*
When does the bus leave (arrive)?
  *¿A qué hora sale (llega) el autobús?*
When? *¿cuándo?*
Where is_? *¿dónde está_?*
Where can I buy tickets?
  *¿Dónde puedo comprar boletos?*
Where is the nearest petrol station?
  *¿Dónde está la gasolinera más cercana?*
Why? *¿por qué?*

**Basics**

bank *el banco*
bathroom/toilet *el baño*
bill *la factura/la cuenta*
cash *el efectivo*
cheap *barato/a*
credit card *la tarjeta de crédito*
exchange house *la casa de cambio*
exchange rate *el tipo de cambio*

expensive *caro/a*
market *el mercado*
note/coin *le billete/la moneda*
police (policeman) *la policía (el policía)*
post office *el correo*
public telephone *el teléfono público*
supermarket *el supermercado*
ticket office *la taquilla*

**Getting around**

aeroplane *el avión*
airport *el aeropuerto*

arrival/departure *la llegada/salida*
avenue *la avenida*

block *la cuadra*
border *la frontera*
bus station *la terminal de autobuses/camiones*
bus *el bus/el autobús/el camión*
collective/fixed-route taxi *el colectivo*
corner *la esquina*
customs *la aduana*
first/second class *primera/segunda clase*
left/right *izquierda/derecha*
ticket *el boleto*
empty/full *vacío/lleno*
highway, main road *la carretera*
immigration *la inmigración*
insurance *el seguro*
insured person *el/la asegurado/a*
to insure yourself against *asegurarse contra*

luggage *el equipaje*
motorway, freeway *el autopista/la carretera*
north, south, east, west *norte, sur, este (oriente), oeste (occidente)*
oil *el aceite*
to park *estacionarse*
passport *el pasaporte*
petrol/gasoline *la gasolina*
puncture *el pinchazo/la ponchadura*
street *la calle*
that way *por allí/por allá*
this way *por aquí/por acá*
tourist card/visa *la tarjeta de turista*
tyre *la llanta*
unleaded *sin plomo*
to walk *caminar/andar*

**Accommodation**

air conditioning *el aire acondicionado*
all-inclusive *todo incluido*
bathroom, private *el baño privado*
bed, double/single *la cama matrimonial/sencilla*
blankets *las cobijas/mantas*
to clean *limpiar*
dining room *el comedor*
guesthouse *la casa de huéspedes*
hotel *el hotel*
noisy *ruidoso*
pillows *las almohadas*

power cut *el apagón/corte*
restaurant *el restaurante*
room/bedroom *el cuarto/la habitación*
sheets *las sábanas*
shower *la ducha/regadera*
soap *el jabón*
toilet *el sanitario/excusado*
toilet paper *el papel higiénico*
towels, clean/dirty *las toallas limpias/sucias*
water, hot/cold *el agua caliente/fría*

**Health**

aspirin *la aspirina*
blood *la sangre*
chemist *la farmacia*
condoms *los preservativos, los condones*
contact lenses *los lentes de contacto*
contraceptives *los anticonceptivos*
contraceptive pill *la píldora anticonceptiva*
diarrhoea *la diarrea*

doctor *el médico*
fever/sweat *la fiebre/el sudor*
pain *el dolor*
head *la cabeza*
period/sanitary towels *la regla/las toallas femeninas*
stomach *el estómago*
altitude sickness *el soroche*

## Family

| | |
|---|---|
| family | *la familia* |
| friend | *el amigo/la amiga* |
| brother/sister | *el hermano/la hermana* |
| daughter/son | *la hija/el hijo* |
| father/mother | *el padre/la madre* |
| husband/wife | *el esposo (marido)/ la esposa* |
| boyfriend/girlfriend | *el novio/la novia* |
| married | *casado/a* |
| single/unmarried | *soltero/a* |

## Months, days and time

| | |
|---|---|
| January | *enero* |
| February | *febrero* |
| March | *marzo* |
| April | *abril* |
| May | *mayo* |
| June | *junio* |
| July | *julio* |
| August | *agosto* |
| September | *septiembre* |
| October | *octubre* |
| November | *noviembre* |
| December | *diciembre* |

| | |
|---|---|
| Monday | *lunes* |
| Tuesday | *martes* |
| Wednesday | *miércoles* |
| Thursday | *jueves* |
| Friday | *viernes* |
| Saturday | *sábado* |
| Sunday | *domingo* |

| | |
|---|---|
| at one o'clock | *a la una* |
| at half past two | *a las dos y media* |
| at a quarter to three | *a cuarto para las tres/a las tres menos quince* |
| it's one o'clock | *es la una* |
| it's seven o'clock | *son las siete* |
| it's six twenty | *son las seis y veinte* |
| it's five to nine | *son las nueve menos cinco* |
| in ten minutes | *en diez minutos* |
| five hours | *cinco horas* |
| does it take long? | *¿tarda mucho?* |

## Numbers

| | |
|---|---|
| one | *uno/una* |
| two | *dos* |
| three | *tres* |
| four | *cuatro* |
| five | *cinco* |
| six | *seis* |
| seven | *siete* |
| eight | *ocho* |
| nine | *nueve* |
| ten | *diez* |
| eleven | *once* |
| twelve | *doce* |
| thirteen | *trece* |
| fourteen | *catorce* |
| fifteen | *quince* |
| sixteen | *dieciséis* |
| seventeen | *diecisiete* |
| eighteen | *dieciocho* |
| nineteen | *diecinueve* |
| twenty | *veinte* |
| twenty-one | *veintiuno* |
| thirty | *treinta* |
| forty | *cuarenta* |
| fifty | *cincuenta* |
| sixty | *sesenta* |
| seventy | *setenta* |
| eighty | *ochenta* |
| ninety | *noventa* |
| hundred | *cien/ciento* |
| thousand | *mil* |

## Menu reader

Regional specialities are described on page 27. Some of the standard items on the menu are:

| | |
|---|---|
| *Ajiaco* | a thick soup made with potatoes, chicken and cream. Especially popular in Bogotá. |
| *Almojábanas* | sour milk/cheese bread roll, great for breakfast when freshly made. |
| *Arepas* | flat maize griddle cakes found throughout the country and often served as an alternative to bread. |
| *Arequipe* | sugar-based brown syrup used for desserts and confectionary, universally loved by Colombians. |
| *Arroz con pollo* | chicken and rice, one of the standard Latin American dishes, is excellent in Colombia. |
| *Brevas* | figs. They are served with *arequipe* as a popular dessert. |
| *Buñuelos* | 4-6 cm balls of wheat flour and egg dough, deep-fried and best when still warm. |
| *Carne asada* | grilled beefsteak, usually an inexpensive cut, served with *papas fritas* (chips) or rice and a vegetable of the day. |
| *Chicha* | corn-based drink with sugar and/or *panela* added. |
| *Champús* | corn-based drink with fruit, *panela*, cloves and cinnamon. |
| *Empanadas* | maize pasties, filled with chicken, meat or vegetables and deep fried in oil. A popular snack. |
| *Huevos pericos* | eggs scrambled with onions and tomatoes. A popular, cheap and nourishing snack available almost everywhere, especially for breakfast. |
| *Pan de bono* | cheese-flavoured bread. |
| *Patacones* | cakes of mashed and baked *platano* (large green banana). |
| *Sancocho* | a meat stock (may be fish on the coast) with potato, corn (on the cob), yucca, sweet potato and plantain. |
| *Sobrebarriga* | belly of beef served with varieties of potato in a tomato and onion sauce. |
| *Tamales* | meat pies made from chopped pork, potato, rice, peas, onions and eggs in a maize dough. They are wrapped in banana leaves (which you don't eat) and steamed. Other ingredients may include olives, garlic, cloves and paprika. In certain areas Colombians eat *tamales* for breakfast with hot chocolate. |

## Food

avocado  *la palta*
baked  *al horno*
bakery  *la panadería*
banana  *la banana*
beans  *los frijoles/las habichuelas*
beef  *la carne de res*
beef steak  *el lomo*
boiled rice  *el arroz blanco*
bread  *el pan*
breakfast  *el desayuno*
butter  *la manteca*
cake  *la torta*
chewing gum  *el chicle*
chicken  *el pollo*
chilli or green pepper  *el ají/pimiento*
clear soup, stock  *el caldo*
cooked  *cocido*
dining room  *el comedor*
egg  *el huevo*
fish  *el pescado*
fork  *el tenedor*
fried  *frito*
garlic  *el ajo*
goat  *el chivo*
grapefruit  *la toronja/el pomelo*
grill  *la parrilla*
grilled/griddled  *a la plancha*
guava  *la guayaba*
ham  *el jamón*
hamburger  *la hamburguesa*
hot, spicy  *picante*
ice cream  *el helado*
jam  *la mermelada*
knife  *el cuchillo*

lemon  *el limón*
lobster  *la langosta*
lunch  *el almuerzo/la comida*
meal  *la comida*
meat  *la carne*
minced meat  *la carne picada*
onion  *la cebolla*
orange  *la naranja*
pepper  *el pimiento*
pasty, turnover  *la empanada/el pastelito*
pork  *el cerdo*
potato  *la papa*
prawns  *los camarones*
raw  *crudo*
restaurant  *el restaurante*
salad  *la ensalada*
salt  *la sal*
sandwich  *el bocadillo*
sauce  *la salsa*
sausage  *la longaniza/el chorizo*
scrambled eggs  *los huevos revueltos*
seafood  *los mariscos*
soup  *la sopa*
spoon  *la cuchara*
squash  *la calabaza*
squid  *los calamares*
supper  *la cena*
sweet  *dulce*
to eat  *comer*
toasted  *tostado*
turkey  *el pavo*
vegetables  *los legumbres/vegetales*
without meat  *sin carne*
yam  *el camote*

## Drink

beer  *la cerveza*
boiled  *hervido/a*
bottled  *en botella*
camomile tea  *la manzanilla*
canned  *en lata*
coffee  *el café*
coffee, white  *el café con leche*
cold  *frío*

cup  *la taza*
drink  *la bebida*
drunk  *borracho/a*
firewater  *el aguardiente*
fruit milkshake  *el batido/licuado*
glass  *el vaso*
hot  *caliente*
ice/without ice  *el hielo/sin hielo*

juice  *el jugo*
lemonade  *la limonada*
milk  *la leche*
mint  *la menta*
rum  *el ron*
soft drink  *el refresco*
sugar  *el azúcar*
tea  *el té*

to drink  *beber/tomar*
water  *el agua*
water, carbonated  *el agua mineral con gas*
water, still mineral  *el agua mineral sin gas*
wine, red  *el vino tinto*
wine, white  *el vino blanco*

**Key verbs**

| to go | ir | | to be | ser | estar |
|-------|-----|---|-------|-----|-------|
| I go | *voy* | | I am | *soy* | *estoy* |
| you go (familiar) | *vas* | | you are | *eres* | *estás* |
| he, she, it goes, you (formal) go | *va* | | he, she, it is, you (formal) are | *es* | *está* |
| we go | *vamos* | | we are | *somos* | *estamos* |
| they, you (plural) go | *van* | | they, you (plural) are | *son* | *están* |

(*ser* is used to denote a permanent state, whereas *estar* is used to detote a positional or temporary state.)

| to have (possess) | tener |
|-------------------|-------|
| I have | *tengo* |
| you (familiar) have | *tienes* |
| he, she, it, you (formal) have | *tiene* |
| we have | *tenemos* |
| they, you (plural) have | *tienen* |
| there is/are | *hay* |
| there isn't/aren't | *no hay* |

This section has been assembled on the basis of glossaries compiled by André de Mendonça and David Gilmour of South American Experience, London, and the Latin American Travel Advisor, No 9, March 1996.

# Index → *Entries in* **bold** *refer to maps*

## Advertisers' index

# FOOTPRINT

## Features

# Acknowledgements

My thanks to the following people, without whom this book would never have been finished: Oscar Gilède; family Cano: Verónica, Ana-María, Merly and Rogelio; Soledad and John Jiménez; Juan Pablo Echeverri; Juan Ananda; Don Jorge Díaz; Shaun Clohesy; Milo Butterick; 'Gringo' Mike Anderson; Paul Reidy; Patrick Fleming; Jean-Phillipe Gibelin; Cristina Zapata Naranjo; María Fernanda Suárez, and all the kindly folks at all the tourist offices in all the cities and towns in Colombia (except Cali). Finally, thanks to Ben Box, Anna Maria Espsäter and the team at Footprint.

# Credits

**Footprint credits**
**Editor**: Sophie Blacksell Jones
**Production and layout**: Emma Bryers
**Maps**: Kevin Feeney
**Colour section**: Angus Dawson

**Publisher**: Patrick Dawson
**Managing Editor**: Felicity Laughton
**Administration**: Elizabeth Taylor
**Advertising sales and marketing**:
John Sadler, Kirsty Holmes

**Photography credits**
**Front cover**: Toniflap/Shutterstock.com
**Back cover**: Top: javarman/Shutterstock.com. Bottom : Jess Kraft/Shutterstock.com

**Colour section**
**Inside front cover**: superstock: Axiom Photographic/Design Pics/Axiom Photographic/Design Pics; Shutterstock: Toniflap, Jess Kraft. **Page 1**: dreamstime: Efeather/Dreamstime.com. **Page 2**: Shutterstock: Jess Kraft. **Page 4**: Shutterstock: Jess Kraft; superstock: Kaehler, Wolfgang/ Kaehler, Wolfgang, Christian Kober/Robert Harding Picture Library. **Page 5**: Shutterstock: Watchtheworld, urosr, Rafal Cichawa. **Page 6**: Shutterstock: Rafal Cichawa; superstock: Visual & Written/Visual & Written, Christian Kober/Robert Harding Picture Library. **Page 7**: Shutterstock: imageBROKER/imageBROKER; nicolasdecorte; superstock: VWPics/age fotostock. **Page 10**: Shutterstock: Ksenia Ragozina. **Page 11**: superstock: Iberfoto/ Iberfoto. **Page 12**: Shutterstock: Jess Kraft. **Page 13**: superstock: Christian Kober/ Robert Harding Picture Library, VWPics/ age fotostock. **Page 14**: Shutterstock: Vilainecrevette, christian kober, Jess Kraft. **Page 15**: Shutterstock: Jess Kraft, Curioso; superstock: Jan Sochor/age fotostock. **Page 16**: superstock: Art Wolfe Stock/ Cultura Limited.

Printed in Spain by GraphyCems

**Publishing information**
Footprint Colombia
5th edition
© Footprint Handbooks Ltd
May 2015

ISBN: 978 1 910120 30 9
CIP DATA: A catalogue record for this book is available from the British Library

® Footprint Handbooks and the Footprint mark are a registered trademark of Footprint Handbooks Ltd

Published by Footprint
6 Riverside Court
Lower Bristol Road
Bath BA2 3DZ, UK
T +44 (0)1225 469141
F +44 (0)1225 469461
footprinttravelguides.com

Distributed in the USA by
National Book Network, Inc.

Every effort has been made to ensure that the facts in this guidebook are accurate. However, travellers should still obtain advice from consulates, airlines, etc about travel and visa requirements before travelling. The authors and publishers cannot accept responsibility for any loss, injury or inconvenience however caused.

DEC 08 2015

# Footprint Mini Atlas
# Colombia

*Caribbean Sea*

N

100 km
100 miles

**1 inset**
*Providencia
San Andrés*

PANAMA

**①**

**②**

**③**

**④**

Riohacha
Santa Marta
Maicao
Barranquilla
Maracaibo
Valledupar
Cartagena

Sincelejo

Montería

*Río Cauca*

Turbo

*Río Magdalena*

Cúcuta

PANAMA

VENEZUELA

Barrancabermeja

Bucaramanga

Aracua

Puerto
Carreñ

*Pacific
Ocean*

*Río Atrato*

Medellín
Bahía Solano
Quibdó

Villa de
Leiva

Tunja

Yopal

*Río Meta*

Puerto Ayacucho

Istmina

Manizales

Cartago
Pereira
Armenia
Ibagué

☐ BOGOTA

Villavicencio

Puerto
Inírida

*Río Orinoco*

Buenaventura

*Isla
Gorgona*

Cali

Neiva

San José del
Guaviare

*Río Guaviare*

*Río Guainía*

Guapi

Popayán
La Plata
Garzón

San
Agustín

Florencia

*Río Vaupés*

Mitú

Tumaco

Pasto

Mocoa

Ipiales
Puerto Asis

*Río Apaporis*

Tulcán

Leguizamo

*Río Caquetá*

ECUADOR

BRAZIL

PERU

*Río Putumayo*

Tarapacá

Altitude in metres
4000
3000
2000
1000
500
200
0
Neighbouring
country

Paved road

Unpaved all
weather road

Seasonal
unpaved road

Track

Rail

*Río Amazonas*

Leticia

Benjamín
Constant

# Map 1

## San Andrés & Providencia

Cayos de Roncador

Providencia

*Caribbean Sea*

San Andrés
Cayos de ESE
Cayos de Alburquerque

PANAMA

N

100 km
100 miles

COLOMBIA

---

*Caribbean Sea*

**A**

**B**

**C**

Parque Nacional Tayrona

Cañaveral
Calabazo
Taganga
**Santa Marta**
Rodadero
Bonda
Minca
San Lorenzo
Ciudad Perdida
Ciénaga

Las Flores
Puerto Colombia
**Barranquilla**
Soledad
Ciénaga de Sta Marta
Galerazamba
V de Totumo
Baranoa
Santo Tomás
Palmar de Varela
Pueblo Nuevo
Usiacuri
Luruaco
Sabanalarga
**ATLÁNTICO**
Pivijay
Aracataca
Fúndación

Santa Catalena
Bayunca
Pto Giraldo
Salamina
**MAGDALENA**
Santa Rosa
La Boquilla
**Cartagena**
Villanueva
Tierrabomba
Turbaco
Canal del Dique
Caracolicito
Santa Ana
Turbana
Calamar
Parque Nacional
Corales del Rosario
Barú
Cobado
Arjona
Malagana
Rocha
San Cayetano

Islas del Rosario

Nepomuceno
Tenerife
Difícil

Islas de San Bernardo
San Jacinto
Zambrano
Plato
San Onofre
El Carmen
Arjona

Tolú
Ovejas
Pinto
Santa Ana
San Bernado
del Viento
Coveñas
Toluviejo
Chimichagua
Isla Fuerte
Corozal
Mompós
El Banco
Lorica
**Sincelejo**
Magangué

Chinú
**SUCRE**

Ceretè
Sahagún

Arboletes
Mulatos
Caribia
**Monterría**
Río Cauca
**BOLÍVAR**
Necocli
Río Mulatos
Planeta Rica
fo de
abd
**CORDOBA**
Turbo
*Bahía Colombia*
Montelibano
Caucasia
Río Magdalena
Río Sinú
Apartadó

Río León
Chigorodó
Barranquillita
Parque Nacional Natural Paramillo
Tarazá

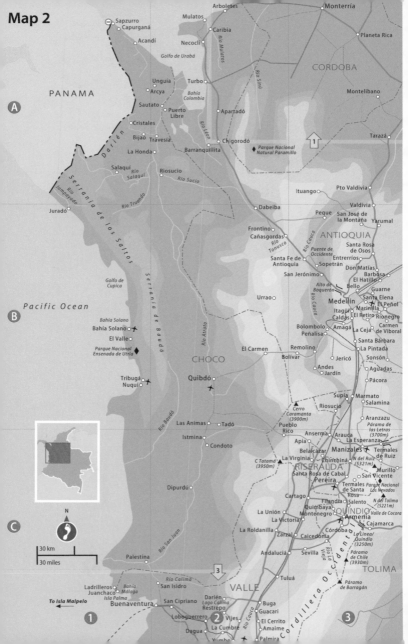

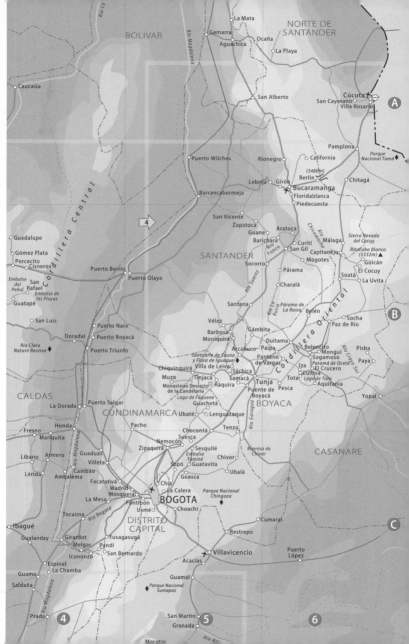

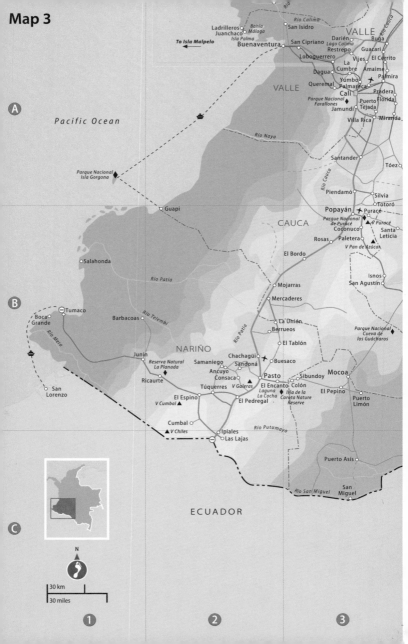

# Map 3

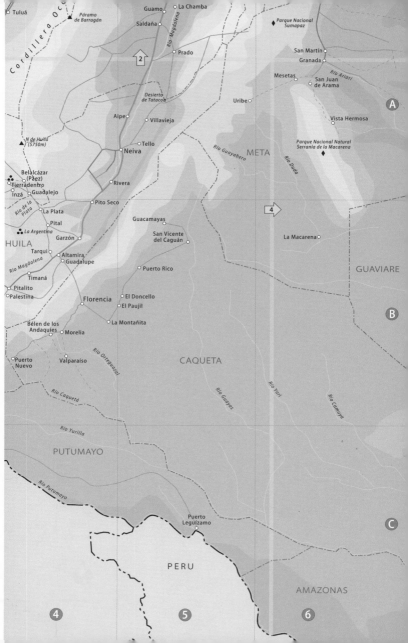

# Map 4

VENEZUELA

BRAZIL

PERU

Cúcuta
Villa Rosario
Pamplona
Puerto Wilches
Chitaga
Barráncabermeja
★Bucaramanga
Parque Nacional Tamá
SANTANDER
Sierra Nevada
del Cocuy
Tame
ARAUCA
Rio Arauca
Arauca
BOYACÁ
Puerto Olaya
San Gil
Rio Casanare
Barbosa
Duitama
Chiquinquira
Sogamoso
Pore
El Pretexto
Trinidad
Rio Meta
Rio Meta
Puerto
Carreño
Pacho
Tunja
Yopal
CASANARE
La Primavera
Casuarito
Rio Tomo
Nemocón
Oracué
Rio Tuparro
★BOGOTA
San Pedro
de Arimena
VICHADA
Santa Rita
Rio Orinoco
Parque Nacional
Chingata
Cumaral
Restrepo
San Miguel
Rio Vichada
Villavicencio
Puerto Gaitán
Acacias
Guamal
Puerto López
Parque
Nacional
Sumapaz
San Martín
META
Puerto Inírida
Granada
Mesetas
Rio Guaviare
San Juan
de Arama
Rio Infreda
Vista Hermosa
GUAINIA
Parque Nacional
Natural Serranía
de la Macarena
San José del
Guaviare
Rio Guainia
La Macarena
Bocas de
Casiquiare
Calamar
GUAVIARE
Rio Vaupes
Mitú
VAUPES
CAQUETA
Rio Mesoy
Rio Apaporis
Rio Caqueta
Araracuara
Puerto Santander
Rio Caqueta
AMAZONAS
La Chorrera
Rio Cahuinari
Bocas de
Cahuinari
Rio Igara Parana
San Rafael
El Encanto
Rio Putumayo
Tarapaca
Parque
Nacional
Amacayacú
Puerto Nariño
Rio Amazonas
Leticia
Rio Yavari

N

100 km
100 miles

1        2        3